Routledge Handbook of Identity Studies

The *Handbook of Identity Studies* offers an exceptionally clear overview of the analysis of identity in the social sciences, and in so doing seeks to develop a new agenda for identity studies in the twenty-first century.

The key theories of identity, ranging from classical accounts to postmodern, psychoanalytic and feminist approaches, are drawn together and critically appraised, and there are substantive sections looking at racial, ethnic, gendered, queer, consumerist, virtual and global identities.

The *Handbook* also makes an essential contribution to the debate now opening up over identity-politics and its cultural consequences. From anti-globalization protestors to new ecological warriors, from devotees of therapy culture to defenders of international human rights: the culture of identity-politics is fast redefining the public political sphere. What future for politics is there after the turn to identity?

Throughout there is a strong emphasis on interdisciplinarity with essays covering sociology, psychology, politics, cultural studies and history. The *Handbook*'s clear and direct style will appeal to a wide undergraduate audience in the social sciences and humanities.

Anthony Elliott is Professor of Sociology, Flinders University, Australia, Visiting Research Professor at the Open University, UK and Visiting Professor at University College Dublin, Ireland. A specialist in the field of identity studies, Professor Elliott's related books include *Subject to Ourselves, 2nd edn* (2004), *Social Theory Since Freud* (2004), *The New Individualism* (2005, with Charles Lemert), *Concepts of the Self, 2nd edn* (2007), *Making The Cut: How Cosmetic Surgery is Transforming Our Lives* (2008), *Identity in Question* (2008, with Paul du Gay) and *Mobile Lives* (2010, with John Urry).

Routledge Handbook of Identity Studies

Edited by Anthony Elliott

LONDON AND NEW YORK

First published 2011 by Routledge
2 Park Square, Milton Park, Abingdon, Oxon, OX14 4RN

Simultaneously published in the USA and Canada
by Routledge
711 Third Avenue, New York, NY 10017

Routledge is an imprint of the Taylor & Francis Group, an informa business

British Library Cataloguing in Publication Data
A catalogue record for this book is available from the British Library

Library of Congress Cataloging in Publication Data
   Routledge handbook identity studies / Edited by Anthony Elliott.
   p. cm.
   1. Identity (Psychology)—Social aspects. 2. Group identity.
   3. Identity politics. I. Elliott, Anthony.
   BF697.5.S65R68 2011
   320'.1—dc22
   2010050601

ISBN: 978–0–415–55558–6 (hbk)
ISBN: 978–0–203–86971–0 (ebk)

Typeset in Bembo
by Swales & Willis Ltd, Exeter, Devon

MIX
Paper from
responsible sources
FSC® C004839
www.fsc.org

Printed and bound in Great Britain by
CPI Antony Rowe, Chippenham, Wiltshire

Contents

Contents

Contents

Contributors

Sundas Ali is a DPhil student in Sociology at Nuffield College, University of Oxford. Her research interests cover identity, immigration, inequalities and social cohesion, particularly in relation to Muslims. Amongst her recent publications is a chapter on identity and public opinion for the book *Race and Ethnicity in the 21st Century* and a report on the economic crisis and geopolitical and migration order for Oxford's Centre on Migration Policy and Society. She has a forthcoming journal article on the reporting of Muslim public opinion polls and is currently working with Professor David Miller on a paper testing the national identity argument empirically. She has carried out policy work for the Aga Khan Foundation on minority groups in the UK.

Ann Branaman is Associate Professor of Sociology at Florida Atlantic University, USA. Publications include *The Goffman Reader* (co-edited with Charles Lemert, 1997) and *Self and Society* (2001).

Mark Casey is a Lecturer in Sociology at Newcastle University where he teaches in sexuality, gender and tourism. He is currently involved in a research project with Dr Yvette Taylor examining the everyday lives of lesbian and gay men in the north-east England. Mark is one of the guest editors of the recent publication of a special issue of *Sociology* 44: (5) focused upon sexuality.

Daniel Chaffee is a Lecturer in Sociology at Flinders University, Australia. His research interests include identity and culture, social theory, globalization, and he is co-editor of *Globalization: A Reader* (Routledge, 2010).

Anthony Elliott is Professor of Sociology at Flinders University, Australia, Visiting Research Chair of Sociology at the Open University, UK, and Visiting Professor at the Department of Sociology, UCD, Ireland. He has written extensively on the topic of identity, and several of his books in this sub-field of social theory have become academic best-sellers – including *Concepts of the Self* (2nd edn, 2007), *Psychoanalytic Theory: An Introduction* (2nd edn, 2002) and *The New Individualism* (2nd edn, 2009, with Charles Lemert). His other books on the broad theme of identity include *Social Theory Since Freud* (2004), *Subject to Ourselves* (2nd edn, 2004) and *Mobile Lives* (2010, with John Urry).

Catherine Eschle is a Senior Lecturer at Strathclyde University in Glasgow, Scotland, where she teaches classes in international relations and feminism. Her research focuses on globalisation/global governance and its contestation, and social movement theory and practice. Recent publications include *Making Feminist Sense of the Global Justice Movement*, co-authored with Bice Maiguashca (Rowman and Littlefield, 2010).

Stephen Frosh is Pro-Vice-Master, Head of the Department of Psychosocial Studies and Professor of Psychology at Birkbeck College, University of London. He is the author of many books and papers on psychosocial studies and on psychoanalysis, including *Psychoanalysis Outside the Clinic* (Palgrave, 2010), *Hate and the Jewish Science: Anti-Semitism, Nazism and Psychoanalysis* (Palgrave, 2005), *For and Against Psychoanalysis* (Routledge, 2006), *After Words* (Palgrave, 2002) and *The Politics of Psychoanalysis* (Palgrave, 1999). His most recent book is *Feelings* (Routledge, 2011).

Sam Han is Instructional Technology Fellow of the Macaulay Honors College and a doctoral candidate in Sociology at the Graduate Center of the City University of New York. He is author of *Navigating Technomedia: Caught in the Web* (2007), *Web 2.0* (Routledge, 2011) and editor (with Daniel Chaffee) of *The Race of Time: A Charles Lemert Reader* (2009). He is currently working on a dissertation entitled *Technologies of Spirit: The Digital Worlds of Contemporary Christianity*.

Mary Holmes is a sociologist at Flinders University in Adelaide. Her research interests include intimacy, emotions and bodies as well as the sociology of gender. She has published widely on these topics and is the author of *What is Gender?* and *Gender in Everyday Life*. She is also co-author of a forthcoming book with Routledge on *Heterosexuality: Theory and Practice*, which will appear as part of the series on Advances in Feminist Studies and Intersectionality.

Cosmo Howard is an Associate Professor in the Department of Political Science and the School of Public Administration at the University of Victoria, Canada. His research interests include theories of individualization, government service transformation and governance challenges for national statistical agencies. His books include *Social Policy, Public Policy* (Allen and Unwin, 2001), *Contested Individualization* (Palgrave Macmillan, 2007) and *The Service State* (University of Ottawa, 2010).

Eric L. Hsu is Associate Lecturer in Sociology at Flinders University, Australia. Publications include *Globalization: A Reader* (with Charles Lemert, Anthony Elliott and Daniel Chaffee, 2010).

Gavin Kendall is Professor of Sociology at Queensland University of Technology, Brisbane, Australia. He previously worked at Lancaster University in England. He was educated in England, at Cambridge, Manchester and London universities. He is the author of *The Sociology of Cosmopolitanism* (Palgrave, 2009), *State, Democracy and Globalization* (Palgrave, 2004), *Understanding Culture* (Sage, 2001) and *Using Foucault's Methods* (Sage, 1999).

Charles Lemert is University Professor and John E. Andrus Professor of Social Theory Emeritus at Wesleyan University and Senior Fellow, Center for Comparative Research in Sociology, at Yale University.

Eileen McGurty is the Director of the Graduate Programs in Environmental Studies at Johns Hopkins University. She is the author of *Transforming Environmentalism: PCBs, Warren County, and the Origins of Environmental Justice* (Rutgers University Press, 2007). She writes widely in the areas of environmental justice, gender and environment, and risk in waste policy.

Contributors

Daniel Mendelson is a PhD candidate at Flinders University, Australia. He was the assistant editor of the *Routledge Companion to Social Theory* (2010), and composed its glossary. Most recently, his book review of *Enough: Why the World's Poorest Starve in an Age of Plenty* (2009) was published in *Contemporary Sociology*. He is writing his dissertation on the social theory of food and hunger.

Anthony Moran is a lecturer in Social Sciences at La Trobe University, Bundoora, Australia. He is the author of *Australia: Nation, Belonging and Globalization* (Routledge, 2005), the co-author (with Judith Brett) of *Ordinary People's Politics* (Pluto Press Australia, 2006), and the co-editor (with Sean Watson) of *Trust, Risk and Uncertainty* (Palgrave Macmillan, 2005). He has published many articles in international journals on issues of race, ethnicity, multiculturalism, indigenous/settler politics and relations, cosmopolitanism and nationalism.

Roberta Sassatelli is Associate Professor of Sociology at the University of Milan (Italy). Her research focus on the historical development of consumer societies and the theory of consumer action, with a particular interest for the contested development of the notion of the consumer as against notions such as citizen or person. She has done empirical research on ethical consumption, the commercialization of sport and leisure, consumption and class boundaries, and commodities and the sexualization of the body. She also works in the sociology of the body, gender and visual representation. Among her recent books in English is *Consumer Culture: History, Theory and Politics* (Sage, 2007) and *Fitness Culture: Gyms and the Commercialisation of Discipline and Fun* (Palgrave, 2010).

Giorgio Shani is Associate Professor of Politics and International Relations at the International Christian University (ICU) in Tokyo, Japan. He is author of *Sikh Nationalism and Identity in a Global Age* (Routledge 2007) and was lead editor of *Protecting Human Security in a Post 9/11 World* (Palgrave 2007). Currently, he is serving as Chair of the Global Development Section (2010–11) of the International Studies Association.

David Stein is a PhD candidate in American Studies and Ethnicity at University of Southern California. He co-edited *Abolition Now! Ten Years of Strategy and Struggle to Abolish the Prison Industrial Complex* (AK Press, 2008), as part of the CR10 Publications Collective. His dissertation research investigates the increase in US federal governmental involvement and budgetary support for crime control from 1968 to 1996, and the form of the racial capitalist state.

Nick Stevenson is a Reader in Cultural Sociology at the University of Nottingham. He is the author of *David Bowie* (Polity, 2006), *Cultural Citizenship* (Open University Press, 2003), *Culture and Citizenship* (Sage, 2002), *Understanding Media Cultures* (Sage, 2001), *Making Sense of Men's Lifestyle Magazines* (Polity, 2001), *The Transformation of the Media* (Longman, 1999), *Culture, Ideology and Socialism* (Avebury, 1995) and *Education and Cultural Citizenship* (Sage, 2011) amongst other titles. He is currently working on a short book called *Freedom* for the Routledge 'Shortcuts' series.

Tamara Waraschinski is a PhD candidate in the Sociology Department of Flinders University. Her research interests, among other subjects, include sociology of death, theories of the self, psychoanalysis and philosophy of body and mind.

Acknowledgments

Many people have contributed, either directly or indirectly, to this book. Gerhard Boomgaarden deserves my special thanks – not only for originally suggesting the project but also for work-ing with me – patiently and calmly – throughout the long haul of its delivery. There are few in academic publishing that have such a finely honed sense of the creative possibilities of social science, and (yet again) it has been my very good fortune to work with him on the production of this *Handbook*. Jennifer Dodd at Routledge has also played a key role and I thank her for terrific support throughout. Many thanks to Janice Baiton for her remarkably helpful work in copy-editing the text.

I have discussed the topic of identity more intensively with Charles Lemert than anyone else over the last decade, in fact to such a degree that it is sometimes difficult to now see where our thinking separates. His support of this project has been invaluable, and I am deeply indebted to him for the various ways in which he has both contributed and co-created the project.

Considerable thanks are also owed to the following persons who have influenced my research on identity and thus the ultimate shape of this book: Zygmunt Bauman, Tony Giddens, Jeffrey Prager, Charles Spezzano, Anthony Moran, Nick Stevenson, Fiore Inglese, John Urry, Paul du Gay, Paul Hoggett, Bo-Magnus Salenius, Deborah Maxwell, John Cash, Conrad Meyer, Kriss McKie and Stephen Frosh. Administrative and research support was provided by Tamara Waraschinski, who diligently worked with authors to ensure a consistent approach to the book. I owe considerable thanks to colleagues and students at the institutions where I have over recent years divided my time: the Department of Sociology, Flinders University, Australia; the Department of Sociology, the Open University, UK; and the Department of Sociology, University College Dublin, Ireland.

Finally, my greatest thanks of all is to Nicola Geraghty, whose support of my intellectual projects seems to know no limit!

Anthony Elliott
Adelaide, 2010

Editor's introduction

Anthony Elliott

The notion of identity is curiously puzzling; the lived experience of identity is mysteriously contradictory. The puzzle and contradiction of identity, both as idea and as reality, is easily demonstrated with reference to current social transformations of the early twenty-first century. Today there are two striking tendencies (others abound) governing the production of identities in the expensive, polished cities of the West. On the one hand, people today lavish astonishing attention upon the presentation and appearance of their identities: some are obsessed by "celebrity identities" marked by fitness, slimness, youth and sex appeal; some are infatuated with self-help guides and do-it-yourself guidelines on how to improve and refashion identities; some are preoccupied with their emotional lives, and spend large amounts of time and money in psycho-therapies of various kinds; some are gripped by cosmetic surgery and the makeover industries, contemplating and undergoing various procedures in order to produce a "newer version" of their identity; and many are fanatical about shopping and consumer culture in the never-ending search for a quick-fix identity-transformation. On the other hand, and notwithstanding all of this attention devoted to the care of the self, identity processes are today more and more shot through with individual pathologies, compulsions and addictions. From anorexia and bulimia to Internet addiction to obsessive compulsive shopping, dysfunctional identities proliferate. It is as if the freedom to explore and experiment with identities inaugurated by our 24/7 world of intensive globalization has lead to its opposite – that is to say, a shift toward non-identity, or the attempt to close down on (and perhaps eradicate?) any existing identity.

Various writers have sought to understand these current dilemmas of identity. Zygmunt Bauman describes in detail the liquidization of contemporary identity processes, with self and society refashioned as "liquid life" and "liquid modernity" respectively. Ulrich Beck speaks of "individualization", the arrival of a post-traditional process of identity-construction in which people have no choice but to make choices about their identities. Anthony Giddens has written of the rise and rise of "reflexivity", conceived as a kind of continuous flow of incoming self-information through which identities are made, remade and transformed. Along with Charles Lemert, I have written about the emergence of a "new individualism", underwritten by a cultural obsession with self-reinvention and instant identity changes. Richard Sennett has elaborated a sociological argument concerning the "corrosion of character", in which the durability of daily personal life is rendered brittle as a result of the rise of short-term thinking. Julia Kristeva has provocatively suggested that identity in the twenty-first century is shaped to its core by "new maladies of the soul", conceptualized as a heady cocktail of depression, mourning and melancholia. And on and on runs the encounter with the complexities of identity in the social sciences and humanities.

In editing the *Routledge Handbook of Identity Studies* I have been particularly mindful of these complexities and paradoxes of identity; one aim of this handbook is, among others, to capture how the puzzles and contradictions of identity raise major consequences for most of the categories by which the social sciences and humanities critique the character of personal and social life. Throughout, the aim of the handbook is to offer a reasonably comprehensive introduction to the leading themes, traditions and territories of classical and contemporary approaches to the analysis and critique of identity. The breadth of approaches to identity outlined in this handbook is a reflection of the explosion of interest in identities over the last few decades in the social sciences and humanities. This diversification of conceptual approaches, ranging from psychoanalytical theory and post-structuralism to post-feminism and postmodernism, is equally matched by the incredible diversification of approaches to the lived realities of identity-politics – and to that end there are contributions contained within covering racial, ethnic, gendered, consumerist, cosmopolitan and global identities.

The *Routledge Handbook of Identity Studies* is thus designed as a systematic, critical and inter-disciplinary reference work for students and teachers in the social sciences and humanities. More specifically, the handbook is divided into three parts: (1) theories of identity; (2) the analysis of identity; and (3) identity-politics and its consequences. Contributions to the handbook have been written from distinct theoretical, analytical or methodological perspectives, but always with a view toward engaging the central issue of how the notion of identity can help us to analyse the world in which we live. There is also a uniformity of approach to these contributions which, hopefully, makes the handbook user-friendly. As a handbook, this is a reference work which I hope will be "handy" – in the broadest intellectual and public political sense. Accordingly, contributors set out their literatures and arguments through reference to the following structure: chapters cover (1) the historical and intellectual development of specific sub-fields of identity studies; (2) discuss the major claims of the sub-field, outlining the work of key intellectual contributors; (3) outline the main criticisms of these contributions; and (4) examine anticipated future developments in the field. Each chapter contains carefully selected core references and sources which will direct students to areas of further study.

In this brief introduction, my aim is not to analyse in any detail the framework of critical traditions and theoretical controversies which the notion of identity has spawned in the social sciences and the humanities over recent decades – that is the work of the contributors. Rather, I shall try in what follows to signal some of the salient themes and intellectual concerns arising from identity studies, stressing throughout how a critical social theory of identity can be brought to bear on some of the main issues confronting the contemporary social world.

What is identity? Contextualizing theories and concepts

Much talk these days is about identity: identity and its problems, the transformation of identity, and, perhaps most fashionably, the end of identity or "death of the subject". It is fair to say that, in recent years, identity appears in the social sciences and humanities as everything from reconstructed and reinvented to displaced and disowned to loveless and liquidized. There is indeed a huge and growing literature on identity, and the field of "identity studies" has become of key significance to the social sciences and humanities the world over. In the United Kingdom, for example, the Economic and Social Research Council funded in the early 2000s a five-year, multi-million pound programme of interdisciplinary research under the banner "Identities and Social Action". In Europe and North America, many leading social theorists and public intellectuals now write on identity – from Jurgen Habermas to Manuel Castells, from Amitai Etzioni to Robert Putnum. However, there are also significant problems in existing approaches to identity studies: (1) there is frequent confusion between the terms *identity*, *self* and *subjectivity*; (2) there is a tendency to take a sociologically shallow or reductive view of identity; (3) many new approaches to identity studies (psychoanalysis, queer theory and globalization theory, for example) have been poorly treated or conceptualized in existing literature; and (4) there is also undue optimism about the possibilities arising from the rise of identity-politics, with insufficient regard paid to the complex ways in which identity-politics and institutional politics interweave. These are all matters which are addressed in various ways by contributors to this handbook.

But this is rushing ahead. What, after all, is identity? At first sight, we might say that identity is something profoundly individual, subjective, personal and private. Even a definition as psychologically tame as this, however, soon runs into immediate problems. Is it really possible for identity to refer only to the individual Self – that is, an inward reality? Can a person really be self-identical to herself? Are not society, culture, history and politics written all across the "texts" of human identity?

Certainly the large bulk of social-scientific analysis of the topic suggests that the social is intricately interwoven with the production of identities. In our own time of accelerated globalization and rampant consumerism, the cult of identity has become increasingly central to the organization of modern societies. In contrast to traditional forms of social organization in which a person's social place was determined by a more general scheme (custom, caste, religion), the post-traditional cult of identity celebrates the idea of absolute difference, of an *irreducible personality*. What is important about identity from this vantage point is the unique inward reality of the self. It is not that social differences of class, race, gender and the like are unimportant; on the contrary, such differences are essential to grasping the social field from which the conduct of identity is built and sustained. Yet the deeper point, analytically speaking, is to penetrate beyond the realm of social affinities and differences and to enter the hidden depths of the self. From psychoanalysis to hermeneutics, the social sciences have constructed a way of seeing identity which emphasizes the need for laborious deciphering, analytical interpretation and the deconstruction of differences between outer appearance and inner reality. After all, if modernity generates a new kind of social experience based increasingly around movement, dispersal and fragmentation, then it is reasonable to assume that such a condition goes all the way down – right to the very tissue of lived experience and psychic structure. In a rapidly fragmenting society, the self or "personality" is not immune to change: it is rather the very object of social change, and this notwithstanding that various aspects of such social transformations are carried out by human agents themselves. Indeed, this is one reason why traditional classifications of character (based, say, on religion or class) begin to fall on hard times. It is also why public fascination with people's differentiations of identity rises to the fore.

The idea that there is something clandestine in the constitution of identities is especially important to various forms of late nineteenth-century and early twentieth-century social thought. It is evident, for example, in Freudian psychoanalysis with its emphasis on the hidden, repressed dimensions of the self. It is also clearly evident in the Marxist interpretation of the capitalist phase of social history, in which human subjects (and the commodification of identities) fall under the tyrannical sway of oppressive power relations. And yet there are other traditions of social thought in which the idea of a concealed depth to identity is revealed as merely illusory. This is an approach, elaborated in both classical and contemporary theories, which views identity as coterminous with how it appears. American social theorist Charles Lemert traces out these various competing versions of identity in the opening chapter of this handbook, noting the complex, contradictory political implications of theories of identity that celebrate the immediacy or appearance of identity on the one hand, and those theories which are more sceptical of identity appearances on the other. This opening chapter by Lemert offers an extended treatment of the history of theories of identity, and in various ways it forms a conceptual backcloth for the contributions contained in this handbook. It is suggested that, whilst chapters in this volume can be read in any order, the reader should begin with Lemert's contextualization of identity theories, in order to best appreciate the other contributions contained herein.

If value, meaning and signification reside at the level of both the individual self and the social network, then there is a sense in which identity is at once psychological and sociological. Social theory, as an interdisciplinary enterprise of the social sciences and humanities, has long been attuned to this *doubled* aspect of identity and has consistently sought to confront this dilemma through analysis of the dualities of action and structure, subject and system. For many social theorists, from George Simmel to Anthony Giddens, the answer to the question "What is identity?" would be something like this: "An enigmatic paradox!" The paradox concerns the complex ways in which identity wraps together subjectivity and objectivity. Let me expand on this point a little, as the tension between subjective and objective aspects of identity-processes is fundamental to social science research. On the one hand, it can be said that individuals go about the daily business of forging, reproducing and transforming their identities primarily through the deployment of subtle social skills, emotional receptions to others and interpersonal relationships, and intricate understandings of the world around them. In short, individuals are highly skilled, knowledgeable agents. On the other hand, however, individuals can only make and remake their identities by virtue of the fact that they are embedded in, and supported by, hugely complex and highly technical systems. From automobilities to aeromobilities, from digital technologies to global finance: the "identity" of any human agent acting in the world is intricately interwoven with the complex technical systems – administrative, technological, financial, governmental – of modern societies. From this angle, some versions of social theory have underscored the relatively puny powers of people in the wider social context of identity-production. Identity, in this sense, is certainly subjectively fabricated, but it is shot through and through with technologies of the social. Not all versions of social theory, however, emphasize the power of the social network over and above the skilled accomplishments of human agents. Traditions of social thought ranging from symbolic interactionism to ethnomethodology, and from phenomenology to psychoanalysis, stress the crucial significance of human subjectivity in relation to social, cultural and political processes. What almost all social theories have in common, though, is the conceptualization of the paradoxical blending of the subjective and objective in the constitution of identities – sometimes glimpsed as a kind of utopian reconciliation, though more often portrayed as dislocated and dislocating.

Arguably one of the most vital theoretical and political contributions to the critique of identity has been feminism. Particular attention is given throughout this handbook to the interlocking of identity and gender, which is explored from different conceptual and sociological angles throughout the text. But the study of gender, through either a feminist or post-feminist lens, is widely regarded as a specific field of identity studies – and accordingly the handbook contains a contribution from Ann Branaman (Chapter 2) which explores research on the complex relations between identity, gender and feminism. Inspired by the re-emergence of the women's movement in the late 1960s, feminist social theorists have developed powerful and rich accounts which view gender identity as inscribed within socio-structural relations of gender, as well as the social and political dimensions of women's oppression and the analysis of male domination (or patriarchy). While feminists stress that the social world is a gendered world, such has been the rapid proliferation and diversification of feminist theorizing that there is by no means a consensus about the sources and dynamics of how gendered identities are produced, reproduced and transformed. Indeed, the very diversity of women's personal and political positions in society and representations in culture has been increasingly explored in contemporary feminist theory, from issues of child-rearing arrangements, through the meanings and values of sexual difference, to the denial or suppression of racial and ethnic-gendered identities.

In this way, feminism has emerged as an interdisciplinary site of lively controversy in contemporary social theory. Current varieties of feminist social thought are wide ranging, and include liberal, radical, post-structuralist, postmodernist, post-Marxist, psychoanalytic and Foucauldian forms – with each carrying quite distinct implications for understandings of theory, politics and methodology.[1] Against the backdrop of this theoretical complexity, the following questions emerge as central in current feminist social thought. How are gender systems of domination and oppression constituted and reproduced across time and space? How does gender relate to sexuality and sexual practice? How does gender interconnect with other forms of social relations such as class and race? How are relations of difference and otherness established between men and women, and how might these relate to the construction of sexualities, masculinities, femininities? What are the important determinants of the widespread socio-political denigration of women and the feminine? How can previously repressed, unarticulated or denied aspects of femininity be reclaimed for creative social relationships?

Much traditional feminist talk assumed that an appeal to women in general was a sufficient foundational basis upon which to construct a radical theory of sexual politics. The distinction between sex and gender was crucial in this respect, and provided the conceptual underpinnings upon which many in the women's movement argued for new articulations of gender identities and sexual politics. Feminists such as Kate Millett and Ann Oakley challenged popular understandings of biology as fixed and immutable, and instead concentrated on the construction of biological differences in conjunction with the social environment.[2] If the cultural meanings and representations attached to biological differences of sex are changeable, then so too it is possible – and indeed urgent – to promote the reconstruction of the system of gender power which characterizes modern societies. Taken as a whole, however, this unification of women under the sign of a universal male dominance became increasingly implausible. In time, it was feminists of color, sex radicals and lesbian feminists who brought issues of their own gender-specificities and differences to the fore, while other self-styled critical and postmodern feminists attempted to rethink certain normative issues arising from the reconstruction of gendered identity for social theory.

In some contemporary (post-)feminist circles, the problem of identity has been raised to the second power. This has been so to such an extent that many feminists have suggested that appeals to the idea of identity should be set aside altogether. Indeed, for the post-structuralist feminist theorist Judith Butler the very notion of identity has served to constrain the political possibilities for transforming current gender regimes. Indeed, traditional feminist appeals to the "identity of women", in her view, have unintentionally served to reinforce a binary gender order which ruthlessly colonizes and controls dispersed identities and fractured subjectivities. Identity for Butler is thus a form of repression – it is part of a covertly paranoid system of gender roles and compulsive heterosexuality. Specifically, Butler interrogates Lacanian and post-Lacanian theoretical accounts of the binary gender order, and attempts to open up a space for seeing gender as a repetitive performance. She argues that individuals model their gender performances after fantasies, imitations and idealizations of what it means to be a man or woman within current gender regimes. In this view, our gender performances are analyzed as copies, imitations and repetitions of cultural stereotypes, linguistic conventions and symbolic forms governing the production of masculinity and femininity. Subverting the repetition of male-dominated gender regimes and the rigid identity scripts to which they give rise, says Butler, is the key task of a critical feminist genealogy.

Feminism and post-feminism, then, have promoted interesting ways of conceiving of interiority in the constitution of gendered identities. However, there have been various other attempts to capture the deeply layered, symbolic complexities of identity, and perhaps nowhere more famously in the modernist era than in Freudian psychoanalysis. Freud is essentially synonymous in popular culture with the notion of the "repressed unconscious": the idea that there is a fundamental part of our identities hidden from ourselves and others – that is to say, an aspect of identity cut-off and buried from consciousness. Freud, in particular, radicalizes the way in which we have come to think about self-identity. For in suggesting that dreams are the "royal road to the unconscious", Freud shows the ego not to be the master of its own home. The presence of unconscious desires were detected at work almost everywhere by Freud, in slips of the tongue, bungled actions, failures of memory, misinterpretations and misreadings. Unconscious desire for Freud is essentially sexual or libidinal, and it is precisely for this reason that the ego blocks off knowledge defensively, shifting the energy that subsists in repressed desire to the moral prohibitions and restrictions of the superego. Ego, id and superego are the key agencies in Freud's model of the human mind, a model designed to help practitioners assist the mentally ill or disturbed. But psychoanalysis is much more than just a therapeutical practice. It is also a radical theory about the fundamental emotional creativity of human beings, focusing as it does on the passions and prohibitions that provide civilization with its basic structure. From this angle alone, Freud's work is instructive for rethinking the emotional dimensions infusing the intricate links between identity and culture – dimensions which have been reductively and deterministically understood by traditional thought. Freud's writings have come to exert a profound influence over contemporary theories of identity, especially in social theory, philosophy, feminist theory and cultural studies.[3] In Chapter 3, Stephen Frosh examines the import of psychoanalysis – from Freud and beyond – for the critique of identity and considers a number of identity-problems anew from this perspective.

The late French historian Michel Foucault is widely considered the major social theorist on the twinning of identity and power, particularly as regards the complex disciplinary or coercive regulation of identity. For Foucault, the production of identity discourses, texts or scripts are deeply interwoven with the operation of power in society. Identity is viewed by Foucault, at least in the early phase of his career, as an upshot or product of discursive positioning and fixation; the individual is increasingly subjected to subtle forms of power, regulation and control, captured by Foucault under the banner of a "disciplinary society". At the level of identity, the notion of discipline or regulation might appear to correspond in some sense to the psychoanalytical conceptualization of unconscious repression. But this is certainly not the case from the standpoint of Foucault, who sought strenuously to distance his own approach to identity from that of Freudian theory in particular. In *The History of Sexuality*, Foucault set out to overturn what he calls "the repressive hypothesis" – as set out by Freud and elaborated by his followers. According to this hypothesis, the healthy expression of sexuality has been censured, negated or forbidden in cultural life; at any rate, this is held to be the case in the West. Sexuality as repressed: this theorem has been crucial not only to Freudian and post-Freudian theory but also to various sexual liberationists. Foucault, however, rejects the thesis of sexual repression. Sex, he says, has not been driven underground in contemporary culture. On the contrary, there has been a widening discussion of sex and sexuality. Sexuality, says Foucault, has flourished. Sexuality for Foucault is an end effect, a product, of our endless monitoring, discussion, classification, ordering, recording and regulation of sex. In Chapter 4, Gavin Kendall traces Foucault's highly distinctive approach to identity and also considers ways in which his legacy has been subsequently developed within identity studies more generally.

If Freudian psychoanalysis signals a dethroning of identity as sovereign, supreme or singular, then this is equally true of structuralist linguistics. Ferdinand de Saussure's *Course in General Linguistics* (1916) is pivotal in this connection, a posthumously published book which profoundly shaped the development of French structuralism and post-structuralism and subsequent critiques of identity.[4] In developing a critique of meaning, Saussure paid special attention to what is social, as opposed to what is individual, in the production of language. According to Saussure, there is no intrinsic connection between a word and an object, like the term "dog" and the flesh and blood animal that lies in the back garden. Instead, meaning is constituted through the unity of a sound-image (or signifier) and a concept (or signified). For Saussure, the relation between signifier and signified is *radically arbitrary*. This notion of the arbitrary character of the sign does not mean, absurdly, that individual speakers can make whatever utterances they like in day-to-day conversation and interaction. On the contrary, individual speakers are strongly bound by the conventional usage of linguistic terms in order to be understood. Rather, the principle of relative arbitrariness refers to the internal composition of language as a structure. Language, Saussure suggests, is composed of a set of binary oppositions of signifiers – "day" is only constituted as a sign in terms of its difference from "night", "black" from "white", and the like. Although in Saussure a certain indebtedness to psychology is still evident, the main focus is upon the analysis of language (*langue*) as a system of collective representations, rather than the actual substance of individual speech (*parole*). That is to say, Saussure was not so much concerned with the actual things about which people spoke, but rather with how a signifier comes to be isolated from other signifiers in the preservation of difference. "In language", as Saussure said, "there are only differences *without positive terms*. Whether we take the signified or the signifier, language has neither ideas nor sounds that existed before the linguistic system, but only conceptual and phonic differences that have issued from the system".[5] In this framework, therefore, language is considered as a system of values structured in terms of their internal and oppositional relations, and speech is the individual or subjective realization of language.

In extending the methods of analysis worked out by Saussure, social theorists influenced by structuralist linguistics seek to discern the complex, contradictory connections between language and the production of social life. This concern with signifying practices has come to be referred to as the "linguistic turn" of social theory, and anthropologist Claude Lévi-Strauss's *The Elementary Structures of Kinship* is widely considered one of the first main experiments in sociological semiotics. Linguists and social scientists, Lévi-Strauss contends, "do not merely apply the same methods, but are studying the same thing"[6] – a statement which underwrites the structure of language as of central importance to the explication of social life. This interest in and enthusiasm for linguistics can be characterized as a theoretical means for (1) the critique of a system of signs at any given point in time as an approach to the explication of meaning, and (2) the critical appraisal of objective structures which makes the speech of individual identities possible in the first place. These basic premises of structuralism remain current, albeit in a transformed fashion, in the subsequent theoretical mutations of post-structuralism, literary deconstruction and postmodernism in radical social theory from the 1970s onwards. In Chapter 5, Sam Han examines post-structuralist and postmodern critiques of identity, paying particular attention to the conceptual departures of Jacques Lacan and Jacques Derrida.

It is, it goes without saying, impossible to contextualize the terrain of identity studies – especially from the 1970s onwards in Europe, but also increasingly North America too – without making reference to Lacan's theory of the symbolic splitting of the subject and also his account of the mirror stage. Lacan, in a provocative "return to Freud", sought to rework the main concepts of psychoanalysis in line with core Saussurian concepts, such as system, difference and the arbitrary relation between signifier and signified. Now Lacan's writings are notoriously dense, complex, elusive; and yet Lacan's Freud has exercised considerable influence in contemporary identity studies, from the structuralist Marxism of Louis Althusser to the deconstructive feminism of Luce Irigaray.[7] One of the most important features of Lacan's psychoanalysis is the idea that the unconscious, just like language, is an endless process of difference, lack and absence. For Lacan, as for Saussure, the "I" is a *linguistic shifter* that marks difference and division in the social field; there is always in speech a split between the self which utters "I" and the word "I" which is spoken. The human subject is structured by and denies this splitting, shifting from one signifier to another in a potentially endless play of desires. Language and the unconscious thus thrive on difference: signs fill-in for the absence of actual objects at the level of the mind and in social exchange. This is central to Lacan's theory that social relations, or what he calls the Symbolic Order, depend on the repression of desire. "Civilization is built upon a renunciation of drives" wrote Freud, and Lacan's account of the unconscious/language relation is an impressive attempt to theorize this insight in terms of the intersubjective workings of desire and recognition.

The repression of desire is at one with the very constitution of identity, and according to Lacan this is a process which leaves the human subject forever scarred or internally divided. In setting out an arrestingly original conception of a "mirror stage" of human development, Lacan emphasized the *narcissistic positioning* of the child on an imaginary level of perception. At some point between six and eighteen months, the child identifies with itself by seeing its image reflected in a mirror. The mirror-stage, Lacan argues, founds an imaginary identity through a narcissistic relationship to images and doubles. The child reacts with a sense of jubilation in seeing itself whole and complete in the mirror, yet this self-recognition is in fact a *misrecognition* since the child is still dependent upon other people for its own physical needs. The process of self-identification, because it is occurs via a mirror which is outside and other, is actually one of alienation. In a word, the mirror *lies*. The very process of achieving self-identification, which is necessary to becoming a positioned subject in the social world, renders the child at odds with itself. Lacan's argument that the subject finds an imaginary identity through an image granted by another represents a major advance on approaches which uncritically assume that the ego or the "I" is at the center of psychological functioning. In stressing that the "I" is an alienating fiction, a misrecognition that masks the split and fractured nature of unconscious desire, social theorists influenced by Lacan locate a sense of otherness at the heart of the self – a theme which runs deep in contemporary thought. The reader of this *Handbook* will find various analyses of Lacan's approach to identity contained here – in Stephen Frosh's review of psychoanalysis (Chapter 3), Sam Han's discussion of post-structuralism (Chapter 5) and Mary Holmes's consideration of the production of gendered identities (Chapter 11).

One legacy of structuralism, still discernable in various post-structuralist and postmodern analyses, is that identity is conceived as largely an outcrop of structures. It follows from this that structuralism preserves a series of oppositions and antinomies that have plagued social theory – for example, the individual versus society, action versus structure, and subject versus object. In recent decades, a variety of social theorists have sought to overcome these divisions. Perhaps the most original formulations of this transformation in contemporary social theory is to be found in the writings of Anthony Giddens.[8] Essential to these attempts is the relating of identity and society without prioritizing one term at the expense of the other. The conceptualization of such a relation, it is argued, requires attention not to how structure fixes action or how repetitive actions constitute structures, but rather how action is *structured* and *reproduced* in contexts of daily life. Such a self-monitoring pattern as regards the constitution, reproduction and transformation of identities is carried out with reference to "reflexivity" – the ongoing, relentless work of tracking and tracing incoming information about identity in the process of staging engagements between the self and others. In Chapter 6, Daniel Chaffee guides the reader through some of the recent social-theoretical debates on reflexive identities and considers possibilities for identity transformations in this light.

When social theorists today reflect on the changing relations between the individual and society, they generally do so in ways that are profoundly shaped by methodological concerns which underscore actor and/or system-based models of analysis. Yet for many social theorists, these issues cannot be worked out at the level of methodology alone. For some theorists the transformations of modernity, such as globalization and the changing character of the public sphere, directly impact upon the nature of the self as well as the textures of day-to-day social life – reshaping the very definition of what is meant by the constitution of personal and social life. According to German sociologist Ulrich Beck, for example, the antithesis between individual and system-based social-theoretic perspectives is itself brought low by a new riskiness to risk, the consequences of which people confront everywhere around the globe. What Beck calls "risk society" – an emerging global technological world which generates a diversity of possible dangers, hazards and futures – is said to bring people into a more active engagement with aspects of their lives, aspects that were previously the terrain of tradition or taken-for-granted norms.[9] In Chapter 7, Cosmo Howard addresses directly Beck's thesis of "individualization" – the emergence of a post-traditional, DIY identity orientation. He reviews the various ways in which Beck's risk society opens out to an expansion of choice at the level of identity, or an individual engagement with the self, with the body, with relationships and marriage, with gender, and with work.

Current debates in identity studies over reflexivity and individualization emphasize the increasingly revisable nature of selfhood. But revisions to identity may not be the core-defining feature of our global age. According to the theory of "new individualism" – developed by myself and Charles Lemert and extended in some of my more recent writings – it is *reinvention* (rather than revision) of identity which emerges in our own time as a defining plank of personal and social life. The new individualism, as I define it, concerns four key transformational aspects of identity-constitution: (1) a relentless emphasis on self-reinvention; (2) an endless hunger for instant change; (3) a fascination with speed and dynamism; and (4) a preoccupation with short-term thinking. In Chapter 8, Eric Hsu reviews and examines the core claims of the thesis of new individualism, setting this account of transformations of identity in the broader context of globalization and new information technologies.

The analysis of identity

If identity is increasingly rendered fractured, dispersed, split and ambivalent in conditions of advanced globalization – as theorized in various traditions of contemporary social thought – then it is hardly surprising that the lived experience of identities is always implicated in processes of transformation. That is to say, the ways in which people live their lives today – the narration and navigation of identities – involves an ongoing stress on renewal, reinvention, reconstruction and the broader ethical search for how the self can live rewardingly with others. Recognition of the daily, transformative power of identities means that we need to be alert to the gains and losses of what Anthony Giddens has called "life-politics" in all of its various dimensions – in personal and intimate life, work and the professions, race and ethnicity, and the like. Attention to the interplay of theory and practice is thus critical to the work of identity studies. This means that while identity studies needs to be theoretically sophisticated, always keeping an eye on how the ontological register intersects with politics and society, it also needs to be grounded in the concrete analysis of the practices of identity as conducted by contemporary women and men. In Part 2, such a sociological grounding of identity is viewed through various optics – including race (Anthony Moran in Chapter 10), media (Nick Stevenson in Chapter 12), virtuality (Sam Han in Chapter 13) and mortality and death (Tamara Waraschinski and Charles Lemert in Chapter 15).

In our own age of globalization, new information technologies, the spread of a near-universal consumerism and DIY life-politics, the analysis of identity has, perhaps not surprisingly, been viewed by many commentators as deeply interwoven with the social logics of privatization. From the narcissistic lures of psychotherapy to the technocratic imaginary of cyberspace and vitural reality to the solitary addictions of compulsive consumerism, identity in the twenty-first century has been cast as essentially privatized. At a political level, this twinning of privatization and identity is evident from a range of policy changes that have brought about radical cutbacks in the Keynesian welfare state across Europe as well as the rise of neoliberalism in the United States. These changes include the neoliberal restructuring of national economies into the global electronic economy; the deregulation of financial and labour markets, currency and banking systems; and, the dismantling (read: privatization) of public institutions – such as the partial or complete sell-off of banks, gas, electricity, water, airlines, telecommunications, and the like. Privatization, however, should not only be thought of at the level of political institutions; rather, the intended or unintended consequences of the political deregulation of state and public agencies has been a thorough-going privatization of identity (or identity-strategies) in general. In privatized, postmodern society, as Bauman among others has demonstrated, the individual is recast first and foremost as a *consumer identity*. This is a consumer identity that drifts from seduction to seduction, anxious to keep disabling anxieties from breaking into consciousness. This lifting of consumer identities to the second power under social conditions of multinational capitalism is explored in Chapter 14 by Roberta Sassatelli. But it is not only consumer identities that undergo a kind of privatized version of neoliberalism in contemporary societies. Privatization sets itself against all traditional ways of living and conduct at the level of daily life. For example, jobs-for-life are replaced by individualized contracts, as the notion of "career" becomes a relic of the past. The transformation of working identities, in particular the shift from relatively stable patterns of class identities to episodic, short-term and dislocated working identities, is reviewed by Daniel Mendelson in Chapter 9. Something similar is true of gendered identities today, as till-death-us-do-part marriages are broken, restaged and broken again. This transformation of gendered, intimate ties from a kind of semi-permanence to the "until further notice" variety is appraised by Mary Holmes in Chapter 11.

Identity-politics and its consequences

Identity, as we have seen, is at once concept and reality, high theory and lived experience. For a person to have a sense of "identity" necessarily requires all sorts of thoughts, assumptions, beliefs and affects about who they are and what their relationship is to others as well as the wider world. These will not necessarily be consciously known thoughts; rather, semi-conscious thoughts about the self are likely to be key. There might be other feelings or affects too which are buried from consciousness, stored in the unconscious. But it is clear that identity, in order to be lived, requires immersion in received thought, language, family inheritance and social relationships. And yet identity is more than just ideas, as well as more than the realm of ordinary experience. Identity is also, fundamentally, political. The political currents which dominate the global agenda in the early twenty-first century – including environmental politics, sexual politics and ethnic struggle – place identity at their center. Identity, lived experience and freedom are the key terms in which life-politics is expressed and contested. Ever since the 1960s when people have forged unities and come together in search of specific forms of social and political change, the outcome has been termed *identity-politics*. Much of the core of identity-politics has focused on race and ethnicity, anchored as this brand of politics was in the civil rights movement in the United States. Yet it is no surprise to find that identity-politics has spread out to encompass an astonishing array of cultural and political interests. The deployment of "identity" within the women's movement, disability organizations and gay and lesbian politics – to name but a few – has generated a whole new sub-political axis for the conflicts of identity-politics.

It is perhaps easy to see why some political interests have been disturbed by the onset of identity-politics. If identity-politics is dispersed and plural – extending into race, ethnicity, sexual orientation, citizenship, environmentalism – traditional institutional politics is about structure and unity. Identity-politics confronts traditional institutional politics with a demand for social change that, from one angle, is excessive – jealously protective as identity-politics is of its particular claims for collective awareness and political recognition. Identity-politics is also self-organizing, bred largely as a result of the mobilization of other groups undertaking political action. Thus the desegregation victories of marginalized African-Americans prompted, in turn, other groups to develop specific political agendas. This is certainly true of the identity-politics around various sexual identities and key sexual minority movements. In Chapter 16, Mark Casey reviews these historical and intellectual developments in the gay liberation and lesbian feminist movements during the 1960s and 1970s, and considers the claims of sexual minority movements for "sexual citizenship" through to the emergence of queer activism in the 1980s and 1990s. In another sense this self-generative dynamism is also true of environmental identity-politics, which is at once about specific local groups and particular forms of protest on the one hand, and the universal sweep of environmental risks and dangers on the other. In Chapter 17, Eileen M. McGurty examines the rise of environmental identity-politics and the search for environmental justice, highlighting throughout how the impacts of global warming and climate change are experienced in specific places by specific people which, in turn, generates its own complexities for the politics of ecology.

Identity-politics is routinely dismissed, on both the political left and the political right, as culturally divisive and detrimental to democracy. The American political philosopher Amy Gutmann has powerfully argued, however, that what matters in assessing identity-politics are those demands of groups that aid or impede justice. To do justice to identity-politics, in other words, requires sorting out the gains from the losses as to the wider democratic good. One area where it is widely agreed that identity-politics has enjoyed various successes in resisting discrimination and overturning social prejudice is that of race and ethnicity. Certainly recent debates on race, ethnicity and multiculturalism have fueled discussions of social identities and values excluded or marginalized in the academic culture of the West. Issues of imperialism and decolonization, which have been substantially addressed through debates about the nation-state, nationalism and the Third World, have served to highlight the exclusions and omissions of cultural identities from many of the core institutions of liberal, representative democracies. These debates have in turn underlined the Eurocentric bias of many Western social theories of identity, and extended appreciation of the interweaving of race, ethnicity and cultural differences as sites for the production and politics of identity.

The participants in these debates are in considerable degree all struggling with a number of core questions and issues, many of which bear the strong imprint of current developments in social theory.[10] What are the connections between modernity and its racialized history of identity exclusions? How have racial exclusions and racist dominations become naturalized or normalized in the Eurocentered vision of Western traditional thought? How might racist states of mind best be understood? What are the psychic roots of racist practices? How might social theory best develop a non-reductionist and anti-essential analysis of racist ideology and racially discriminated identities? What are the chances of multicultural diversity, and what threat of new racisms, in the postmodern, postcommunist and postcolonial era of transnationalism? How might the current multiplicity of anti-racisms be linked to critical theory and specifically the social theory of identity?

The bulk of contributions in this handbook reviewing the extensive literatures on identity-politics and race, ethnicity and multiculturalism underscore the specific interconnections between particular experiences, identities, cultures and politics in the widest sense. In Chapter 18, David Stein scrutinizes the history of slavery, the resistances of African American identities and black freedom struggles. Sundas Ali examines the politics of Islamic identities in Chapter 19, drawing out key analytical and political distinctions between "Islamic" and "Islamist" identity-politics and asking whether the narrative surrounding radical Islamic identities trespasses the greater democratic good. In Chapter 20, Anthony Moran provides a scintillating account of how racial prejudices need to be understood in a broad sociological and historical context – as he reviews the literature on indigenous identities from the standpoints of Western expansionism, colonialism and post-colonialism.

The identity-politics that perhaps has attracted greatest worldwide attention in recent times is the anti-globalization movement. The anti-globalization movement has attracted global attention by taking its protest to the streets – in Seattle, Genoa, Porto Alegre and elsewhere, indeed wherever the imperial and corporate powers happen to meet. The brand of identity-politics promoted by the anti-globalization movement, in all its manifestations from anti-capitalist protesters to policy think-tanks, puts forward a list of powerful charges cataloguing the democratic deficits of globalization. Globalism has allegedly empowered multinational corporations and speculative finance, compounded inequality and eroded democracy, promoted Western imperialism and the Americanization of the world, destroyed environmental standards, as well as brutalized the public sphere and the state governmental structures through which it operates. The emergence of a planetary scale global market with ever-decreasing tariffs, ever greater international production, as well as more integrated financial markets with higher trade flows, has unleashed a turbo-charged capitalism of unprecedented intensity, the consequence of which for the anti-globalization movement has been severe economic exploitation and political oppression. The various, complex resistance identities that comprise the identity-politics of the anti-globalization movement is explored by Catherine Eschle in Chapter 21.

Finally, this brings me to a consideration of globalization as it affects cultural identities and the future prospects of identity-politics more generally. The 24/7 world of intensive globalization is clearly enough transformational of modern institutions – for example, the emergence of transnational media and global electronic money-markets are two fields that come readily to mind. And yet globalization impacts more than just institutional life, it also cuts to the core of everyday practices and lived experience, social relationships and cultural values. Globalization, it thus can be said, reshapes the contours of identity-politics to its very roots. But if this is so, it would seem that we live with a challenging paradox. The paradox is, simply, that while the insidious force of economic globalization – of, say, McDonaldization – grows unstoppably, there are few grounds for thinking that a parallel globalization of cultural identities has taken place. Certainly cultural forms such as Google, MTV and CNN may promote consumerist orientations of various kinds, but as yet they are not indicative of a fully fledged "global identity". Whether the notion of "global identity" is defensible or plausible is considered in some detail in the final contribution to this handbook, where Giorgio Shani in Chapter 22 reflects on identity-politics in the global age.

Notes

1 For critical discussions of varieties of feminist social theory see Lois McNay, *Gender and Agency: Reconfiguring the Subject in Feminist and Social Theory* (Oxford: Blackwell, 2000); Judith Butler, *Gender Trouble: Feminism and the Subversion of Identity* (10th anniversary edition) (New York: Routledge, 1999); Ann J. Cahill and Jennifer Hansen, *Continental Feminism Reader* (Lanham: Rowman and Littlefield Publishers,

Inc, 2003); Diana T. Meyers (ed.), *Feminist Social Thought: A Reader* (New York: Routledge, 1997); Barbara L. Marshall and Anne M. Witz (eds), *Engendering the Social: Feminist Encounters with Sociological Theory* (New York: Open University Press, 2004).

2 See Kate Millett, *Sexual Politics* (London: Hart-Davis, 1971) and Ann Oakley, *Sex, Gender and Society* (London: Temple-Smith, 1972).

3 For further discussion of the influence of Freud and psychoanalysis in contemporary social and political theory see Anthony Elliott, *Social Theory Since Freud* (London and New York: Routledge, 2004); Stephen Frosh, *Psychoanalysis Outside the Clinic: Interventions in Psychosocial Studies* (London: Palgrave, 2010); Jeffrey Prager, *Presenting the Past: Psychoanalysis and the Sociology of Misremembering* (Cambridge, MA: Harvard University Press, 1998); David James Fisher, *Cultural Theory and Psychoanalytic Traditions* (New Brunswick, NJ: Transaction Publishers, 2009).

4 Saussure was Professor of General Linguistics at the University of Geneva, and his *Course in General Linguistics* was posthumously reconstructed from the notes of his students. See Ferdinand de Saussure, *Course in General Linguistics* (London: Fontana, 1974). There are many criticisms made of Saussure's theories, including the important objection that the explication of meaning is isolated from the social environments of language use as well as the psychological processing of signification, representation, and affect. For useful discussions of Saussure see Simon Clarke, *The Foundations of Structuralism* (Sussex: Harvester, 1981); Anthony Giddens, *Central Problems in Social Theory* (London: Macmillan, 1979), chapter 1.

5 Saussure, *Course in General Linguistics*, p. 120.

6 Claude Lévi-Strauss, *The Elementary Structures of Kinship* (London: Eyre and Spottiswoode, 1969), p. 493.

7 For critical discussions of Lacan's work in relation to social theory see Anthony Elliott, *Social Theory and Psychoanalysis in Transition* (London: Free Association Books, 1999), chapter 4. See also Sean Homer, *Jacques Lacan* (Abingdon, Oxon: Routledge, 2005); Ian Parker, *Lacanian Psychoanalysis: Revolutions in Subjectivity* (Hove, East Sussex: Routledge, 2010); Kristin Campbell, *Jacques Lacan and Feminist Epistemology* (London: Sage, 2005).

8 For useful introductory overviews and critical appraisals of the writings of Pierre Bourdieu and Anthony Giddens see John B. Thompson, *Studies in the Theory of Ideology* (Cambridge: Polity, 1984), chapters 2 and 4; Charles Lemert, *Sociology after the Crisis* (New York: Westview Press, 1991), chapter 7.

9 See Ulrich Beck, *Risk Society: Toward a New Modernity* (London: Sage, 1992).

10 There are many fine overviews of the construction and deconstruction of race and ethnicity in social theory, in particular, see Rogers Brubaker, *Ethnicity Without Groups* (Cambridge: Harvard University Press, 2004); Stephen Cornell and Douglas Hartman, *Ethnicity and Race: Making Identities in a Changing World* (2nd edition) (Thousand Oaks, CA: Sage Publications, 2007); Les Black and John Solomos (eds), *Theories of Race and Racism: A Reader* (2nd edition) (London: Routledge, 2009); Joe R. Feagin, *The White Racial Frame: Centuries of Racial Framing and Counter-framing* (New York: Routledge, 2009); and John Stone and Rutledge Dennis (eds), *Race and Ethnicity: Comparative and Theoretical Approaches*, (Malden, MA: Blackwell Publishing, 2003).

Part 1
Theories of identity

1

A history of identity
The riddle at the heart of the mystery of life

Charles Lemert

Think of it this way: If A = B, then 0, which is to say: zero, zed, nothing. For anything to be thought, any given A, whatever its content, cannot be exactly identical to any given B. In social life, this is clearly true and practically well understood. If I am A, of whichever personal name (the name being just an arbitrary personal marker, as Erving Goffman put it), then I cannot be exactly the same in all essential aspects as any given B for if I were, then, as Mark Twain or some one like that once said, one of us would be useless.

This riddle, of sorts, is quite evident in the course of ordinary human life in, at least, the modern worlds where we like to think of ourselves as having a Self, if not a soul, that provides a degree of interior regularity which social theorists have come to call self-identity. It seems also true in virtually every field of intellectual or scientific practice. If each and every A (where for now A can stand in as a name for any given thing of potential value) were equal in value to each and every B, we would all be dead or, more elegantly put, the universe of living things such as we experience and know of them would have reached the maximum degree of entropy. All energy would have collapsed into a mass of sameness because, at the deepest analytic level, energy is information of a special kind and information systems depend entirely on differences of all kinds – electromagnetic, sexual, grammatical tables, maps, climates, digits (both anatomical and cybernetic), money systems, economic trade, and so on, and on, without seeming end.

We could consider this riddle on even more grand metaphysical and ethical terms – without death, no life; where A (death) is not B (life). Dying is much more than, as many say, an end of life, or others say, part of the life process. Being dead is something of another kind, a marker whereby, at the least, life itself (measured by both medical and religious rules) is the state that ends the complex bioenergetic information system that is life, whether the life is mine in particular, or yours, or the life of a species or an ecosystem, or at the extreme (a theoretically likely extreme) the end of all life itself.

Hence, the mystery of life, at the heart of which is the riddle of identity theories of all kinds: life, on all levels, is a vitality that for the time of its duration is, if not entirely, stable and fixed. Life (a category so general was to verge on an incoherence of its own special kind), thus, is a structure of sorts with any number of moving and functioning parts that together must work more or less well enough to keep the ship of structured life afloat. When a structure hits its fatal iceberg and sinks to the bottom, it ceases to endure because it ceases to function, which is to say it ceases to be a vital organism that is salient enough to organize its working members. There is an iceberg out there waiting for all structures. The penultimate mystery of life is: when will it strike? But the final mystery is: why it must be there?

To make the riddle personal, hence social (which is where it interests social theorists most keenly), from the point of view of life what is the purpose of death or, more broadly, and for present purposes aptly, what does it have to do with the nature and history of identities? The answer, in general: death in the sense of a pure Zero is the key to everything at least in a strong metaphorical sense. Even the fervidly religious in some faiths will grant that Death is at least a Beyond by which the value of a life lived is measured. Death could be said to be the one condition in which A = A, where for all intents and purposes life and the wide-awake living recognize what is technically called its Zero Signifier. A = A is pure identity. We know that there is no such thing. Practically speaking, we cannot be identical to ourselves, anymore that we can be precisely the same as any given B, or all of them for that matter.

Pure identity – whether as a mathematic abstraction or as the Zero Signifier of ordinary meanings – is then the utter lack of difference and if there were no differences there can be no information, no energy, no vitality, and no life; of which none more pure than the Zed of the Dead. Yet, in practical life, it is very hard, probably impossible, to grasp the meaning of A = A. We may even strive for it over the course of time or in a line of action – and when we do we are seeking the ideal of pure identity of purpose or sense of Self. But, when we are sane about the strivings, we usually pull up short when (or if) we come to see that pure identity is what Søren Kierkegaard (1941 [1962]) called the sickness unto death or, more plainly put, it is the condition of pure boredom in which one might wish to die even if he cannot (that was Kierkegaard's point).

The Zero Signifier, by several names is a common concept in many fields, having begun as a discovery of linguistics. When it comes to languages, the sounds we are able to form with vocal cords, tongue, lips, and the express of air are a closed structure, unique to a given language system. At the heart of each and every system of spoken speech there is a zero sound against which all vocalizations are articulated. I cannot tell you what it is in my languages (though I am sure that there are theories on this). It is hard, which is to say virtually impossible, to speak of in so many words because, by its nature, that zero vocal sound is inexpressible. It is silence of a distinctive kind – less a silence that interrupts the sounds of speaking (or music, writing, or much else), than a pure silence behind all locutions. We know, however, that something like this exists because when learning a foreign language there are certain sounds that require sometimes years of training and experience to vocalize. I cannot, for example, roll the Spanish "r." I can at long last pronounce the French "ieu" (as in the name Bourdieu) but only after a year-long study under French nuns in Paris. I was slow. They were patient. English simply does not have these sounds. They are part of the blank, empty, zero signifying space that allows English speakers to do what they do and accordingly others, say Mandarin speakers, to do what they do (which after some experience sounds lovely in its way but impermeably strange to me).

But it is not just language, but many (perhaps most other) systems of thought and expression that depend on a Zero Signifier. There would be no economic value, if all commodities on the market place were exactly the same. Economic exchange, as Marx taught, depends on quantitative equivalencies and qualitative differences. I do not need your pen if I have one of the same kind. I might want it, even feel I need it, if the pen I had was to me of lesser quality, in which case I might offer two or three of mine for the one you have. And so on. A = A is the zero circumstance of pure qualitative and quantitative equivalence, or identity, at which point there is no value or meaning or, at the extreme, no life. Everything begins with A being unequal to B qualitatively such that an arguable N (which is to say, number) of either one can excite an exchange, from which life goes on. But any fool on the street without a certificate of social incompetence knows enough not to trade, say, his shirt for the identical one worn by other – unless, say, his is dirty and the other's is cleaner; or the exchange of equivalents is part of a flawed potlatch or some other gift-giving ritual of a local tribe.

Thus, if we are to trace the history of the Identity concept without trying to cover the whole of life and history themselves, it will be necessary to keep the riddle provoked by the silence of A = A always in the back of our minds, while moving on to the practical considerations that since Descartes, or perhaps Augustine, have led over many centuries to the modern concept of identity as a social category – to, that is, a self-identity assumed to be somehow or another at the core of social life (which, after all, is nothing more than a series of exchanges of different values). That history, thus limited, will be further limited because in many ways the riddle of self-identification as we moderns (or, if you prefer, late or postmoderns) encounter it had to await the invention of the Self concept (in respect to which we shall hold off for now in concluding whether the Self in the locution concept self-identity is itself a kind of surd or zero sign of the problem of identity itself).

The ancient history of identity, such as it was

One of the habits of modern cultures, especially those of the Occident, is to assume that cultural innovations of modern times (say, for simplicity's sake, since the sixteenth century or so) have their analogues if not their origins in ancient times. The historical basis for this habit is twofold. First, in a sense it is true, but especially again in the West which enjoyed (or suffered if you wish) a long feudal or medieval period in which the dominant religions of the West and its peripheral regions (notably those to which Christianity, Islam, and Judaism had spread) took some of their key ideas, in part, from the Hellenic cultures that had earlier dominated the area. These borrowings may be thought by some to have been limited to later Judaism and early Christianity, but as it concerns the medieval period it was the key Greek texts – especially those that Islamic (by Avicenna of Baghdad) and Moorish schools had maintained and used in Northern Africa and Iberia (notably Averroes of Cordova) – that were introduced primarily in Paris in the twelfth and thirteenth century. Thus, Roman Christendom's Scholasticism, an invention almost exclusively of St Thomas of Aquinas (1225–1274), is through and through Aristotelian in its philosophical framework. Similarly, the Italian Renaissance in the several centuries following this Aristotelian renewal in Paris was, likewise, a fusion of Christian iconography and Greek and Roman artistic form. This is the truth of the matter.

The second point to note in respect to the idea that the modern era was born at a deferral in time in Greek and Rome is that the fully modern academic scholarship in Europe and North America in the nineteenth century were based on primary learning of the Greek and Latin languages, and also the cultures. Thus, among the educated elite, Plato and Homer, Cicero and Virgil or Ovid were the familiar authors of high culture in the era before mass public education. The persistence of classical languages and learning made it perfectly natural that so much of the modern university system insofar as it was devoted to the mastery of letters as of science was devoted to the history, language, literature, art, and above all philosophy of the classical Hellenic world.

This digression into the disputable origins of modern thought is worth the while when it comes to the history of so thoroughly, even utterly, a modern concept as the Self and its ability to identify itself, reflectively. There is on the surface very good reason to suggest that the Greeks especially never really had a clear-cut concept of what modern culture calls "the individual" which is to say the locus of a Self (as distinct from a soul) in respect to which the individual is thought to be capable of identifying itself. Thus, as Charles Taylor found in his essay on Plato in *Sources of the Self: The Making of Modern Identity* (1989), the major Greek philosophies had, at best, a feeble sense of what today we call a Self and certainly of a Self able to engaging in Self-identifications.

What the Greeks had, conceptually speaking, was the soul concept, which from the Greek term *psychos* we derive the modern ideas of psyche or, even, mind – though the latter is a stretch one encounters in translations of classic Greek texts such as Plato's *Republic* (360 BCE). But in the *Republic* (importantly not a psychology but a political theory), one searches in vain for anything like a concept of the individual. Something like what we today would call an individual (in the sense of an autonomous actor) does of course present himself in a shadowy way but always as a member of a category such as *the just man*. In Plato's famous dialogue between Socrates and Thrasymachus in the early sections of the *Republic*, one encounters the idea of a just man, but, in the latter's futile argument with Socrates, the just man is never more than a member of a stronger class. Where Thrasymachus falters is in his admission to Socrates' relentless questioning that "justice is the excellence of the soul, and injustice the defect of the soul." Thus, in passages like this one, the modern is tempted to say that there is to be found a precursor of the modern concept Self. Yet, since a Self – in the modern sense of one who is capable of recognizing herself as a distinctive A who is not B – does not appear.

Where Plato offers in the *Republic*, and elsewhere, a direct analysis of the soul is, again, interesting, when it comes to his just as famous comparison of the forms or categories of social formations to the tri-partite structure of the soul. The soul comprises knowledge or wisdom, anger among the passions (the overcoming of which is honorable), and appetites (also among the passions of which gain or greed is prominent); to these there are the corresponding "the three classes of men – lovers of wisdom, lovers of honor, and lovers of gain" (344). To the extent that Plato allows for anything like what moderns call *an* individual, it is in the ideal of wisdom as the controlling force against, even honor, but also the bodily passions in general. But, again, it is the social and political necessity that trumps the unique individual. Here, at the end of the *Republic*, Thrasymachus is again rebuked by Plato's assertion of the power of "divine wisdom dwelling within" for without this (and he grants that it is not widely achieved) it becomes necessary for an "external authority" to govern "in order that we may all be, as far as possible, under the same government, friends and equals." Hence, justice is not the will of the powerful but of the wise.

It would be extreme to say that there is nothing here to which we can trace modern ideas but, in the end, Plato's divine wisdom is an eternal form that resides in the soul which is, in effect, in constant struggle with the bodily passions. And when it came to Aristotle it was these forms that dominated the soul all the more. Though Aristotle allows for versions of Plato's aspects of the soul, what fades away is even Plato's thin commitment to the principle that wisdom is the active agent of anything like an individual. Aristotle, for one example (from end of Book I of *The Nicomachean Ethics* (W.D. Ross translation)): "In speaking abut a man's character we do not say that he is wise or has understanding but that he is good-tempered or temperate; yet we praise the wise man also with respect to his state of mind; and of states of mind we call those which praise, virtues." And, for Aristotle the wise man is the one who contemplates the eternal virtues. Even Charles Taylor, again in *Sources of the Self: The Making of Modern Identity*, who does his best to find an aspect of the modern Self in the Greeks (particularly Plato), concedes that at best they offer a moral source for the Self concept: "Just as the eye cannot exercise its function of seeing unless there is reality there and its properly illuminated, so reason cannot realize its function until we are turned toward real reason, illuminated by the Good" (Taylor 1989: 124).

It is far beyond what is possible in this essay to make the comparison of the Ancient Occident to the traditional Orient. But it is important to say, by way of that incomplete comparison, that though there are indeed elements that could be read, as we say, as concepts of a soul/self in the Greeks, in the Orient many of the dominant religions do not even go as far as Plato. Buddhists, for example, begin with three principles of life: impermanence, suffering, and *no-self* (for two of many examples from modern Buddhist teachings, see Trungpa 2009; and on no-self see Chödrön 2002). In this respect, as many have said, Buddhism is as much a psychology as a religion but in either case, the Self concept (as it is discussed by contemporary Buddhist teachers) is explicitly denied. As Buddhist teachings have come down into the West, they are usually in the form of advice given for the practice of Enlightenment. One finds instructions as to practices that lead to the avoidance of the distractions of the mind and the contemplative methods that, in focusing on the breath, bring impermanence into the practice by which, in time, and in principle, suffering is relieved by, as some put it, the in-breath of a painful experience and out-breath which allows the mind to accept the impermanence of no-self. Though Confucian, Hindu, and Taoist practices are more practical ethics than psychologies, there the practices of learning and right action are those readily assimilated into a fusion with the collective and political life. Except in certain modernized versions – and of course in the general influence of Western thought in the East – one is hard put to find in traditional Oriental cultures and practices anything like the modern idea of a Self-identifying individual.

Returning to the Occidental history, after Plato, one must wait until Augustine of Hippo (354–430 CE) before anything like a Self concept, much less a principle of identity, emerges. To be sure, Augustine drew from Plato, as he did from Christian and philosophical writings of the late Roman period. In *The Trinity* (dated between 400 and 420 CE), Augustine naturally begins with an exposition of the Christian doctrine of the Trinity – God as Father, Son, and Spirit. But, quite remarkably, a little more than halfway through he turns his attention to what can be called the first fully coherent psychology of soul that allowed for a principle of identity.

> Let the mind then not go looking for a look at itself as if it were absent, but rather take pains to tell itself apart as present. Let it not try to learn itself as if it did not know itself, but rather to discern itself from what it knows to be other. How will it see to act on the command it hears, *Know Thyself*, if it does not know what "know" is or what "thyself" is?"
>
> (Augustine (400–420 CE) 1991: 295)

There could not be a stronger rebuke of the Greek slogan to know thyself which, in effect, depended on knowledge or wisdom but seemed entirely to lack an active idea of the self one is advised to know. Also in Augustine's *The Trinity* there is a tripartite theory of mind as memory, understanding, and will. At first these may seem to bear a comparison to Plato's soul, except that memory is the element that allows for the possibility of self-knowledge which, for the Bishop of Hippo, was that which was suppressed under the conditions of sin. But as his discussion continues, Augustine more and more lets in elements of self-identification, even in the theological doctrine that we do not know that we will die, but we can think death, as one of the fundamental differences by which the self or soul or mind understands, at the least, its limits in its difference from others, thus, by implication, its self-identity. This is a very long way from modern thought. But it is an important step toward what would come to be, a good many centuries later.

It is often said that Augustine was the father both of medieval Catholicism and of early modern Protestantism. It is in the latter connection that the lineage of modern theories of an independent Self began to surface. It is said (rightly I think) that in Christianity a reformulated

Platonic idea surfaced in the early Church (notably St Paul and author of the Gospel of John), resurfaced in Augustine, then came to fruition in the Protestant reformers. The very idea of the Protestant Reformation was that it was the individual alone who acts in faith to believe and, by the time one gets to later Calvinism, the believing individual is meant to demonstrate faith by acting as if he one were among the saved – this by the hard work of building up God's world. This is a story very familiar to modern social theorists through Max Weber's *Protestant Ethic and the Spirit of Capitalism* (1904–05) which is the *locus classicus* of the historical argument that modern individualism (in the form of a secular spirit of capitalism, or this-worldly entrepreneurial disposition) arose in the Protestant and by the eighteenth and nineteenth centuries emerged as an ethic of the secular individual as the agent of future progress, including economic progress.

Needless to say the Protestant line of development was not the sole nor (some would argue) even the major source of the well-identified Self. There were, of course, many other movements that ran parallel to Protestantism of which Rene Descartes (1596–1650) is usually cast as the first to break through to a concept of self-reflection, thus of self-identification. It is always trite to mention "Cogito, ergo sum" – "I think, therefore I am." Yet, it is hard to find a more evident place to locate the beginning of systematic thought based on, and directed toward, the existence of a Self – here, the "ego" (or later the "I").

Descartes was of course very much more than the one who coined a slogan of modern thought, but that slogan was the lynch-pin of his method of systematic doubt directed, in *Discourse of Method* (1637), on himself, on which he based the pure rational method whereby his own existence could be proven and that proof was, of course, the ability to think – to doubt yes, eventually to think rationally in science, but primordially to think as the sign and assurance of the existence of the individual being.

Charles Taylor (1989: 154) sees Descartes as taking up what Augustine began and setting it in newly modern terms. To be sure, Descartes, among seventeenth-century thinkers from Bacon and Hobbes to Spinoza and Leibnitz, and others, were crucial to what we can call the founding generation of the modern thinking subject. Here began the still-enduring debate between the rationalist method (mostly Continental – notably Descartes, Spinoza and Leibnitz) and the empiricist method (mostly English and Scottish – notably Locke and Hume). This was important because it utterly smashed, in due course, the stranglehold of Aristotelian scholasticism of the later Middle Ages. In this sense, the seventeeth-century philosophers of reason in both traditions were working parallel to the new methods founded in the sixteenth century by Protestantism and before that in the Renaissance. The philosophers of the seventeeth-century Age of Reason were of course also the foundation of divisions of philosophical thinking on politics, which was the principal of sources of later social theory. The rationalists mostly in France were founders, in effect, of the tradition of the social contract which, though identified mainly with Rousseau, was a general principle found in a long lineage – awkwardly even in Hobbes, but clearly in Montesquieu as well as Rousseau, in Saint-Simon and Comte in the nineteenth century, and prominently in Durkheim on the cusp of the twentieth century wherein social order was first conceived as the original social category. By contrast, it hardly need be said, the English and Scottish lines of thought (to which Hobbes on margin also belonged) held to the primacy of the individual in ethical, political, and economic life – hence the ideas of individual rights and freedoms, of the centrality of utilitarian self-interest in economics, and also even of the much fabled free market and minimalist state – concepts that owe to Locke, Hume, Mills, Bentham, even Adam Smith, the English lineage.

Thus, very early in the modern period, was established the deep structural tension of the Enlightenment in which the opposing principles of a social contract and social justice were set against those of individual rights and freedoms. The introduction of the modern individual was a necessary move that appeared in parallel in the religious movements of the previous century where, when the Weberian formula on Protestantism is added in, were the preconditions of a Self able to reflect on himself to the end of calculating future projects whereby his interests will be advanced. The very prospect of a modern Self able to see himself, if not always clearly, for what he is in the present, as occupying a social or economic position sometime in the future is, as it turned out, absolutely crucial to disentangling the Self from the soul of the ancients and thus to setting the course for modern theories of identity that did not surface until, actually, late in the nineteenth century.

We must give ourselves permission, at least on this occasion, to skip over the crucial advances made by Kant, Hegel, and even Marx. Kant sought to free the thinking individual from analytic reason by proposing a comprehensive philosophy based on practical reason that, strictly speaking, was neither rationalist or empiricist as they were conceived in the seventeenth century. Hegel, of course, took up the idealist version of self-consciousness and projected it onto the dialectic movements of history itself. Except for glimmers here and there (and of course in *Phenomenology of the Spirit*), Hegel's grand scheme was less a psychology than a philosophy of History, with a capital "H," that was a necessary correlate of the principle of practical actions leading to historical progress. And Marx, whose philosophy of historical materialism – almost empty in respect to the historical freedoms and autonomy of the historical subject – began with a strongly Hegelian theory of reification or alienation of the universal man who was, precisely, the one requiring the working-class revolution to overcome the dominating power of the bourgeois revolution. None is an identity theorist, in our sense, but all were already, even as they differed from each other and what came before, committed to the Zero-signifying principle that A cannot purely equal itself. For them all differences were essential to practical, historical, and political action and their philosophies were, in effect, proto-philosophies of the dialectic of these differences in human history.

Identity, at long last, enters

It would not be until quite late in the nineteenth century and early in the twentieth that the Identity concept would come into the form by which we use it today. Why so late? The most succinct answer might be the one offered by Georg Simmel in the opening lines of his famous 1903 essay "The Metropolis and Mental Life": "The deepest problems of modern life flow from the attempt of the individual to maintain the independence and individuality of his existence against the sovereign powers of society, against the weight of the historical heritage and the external cultural and technique of life" (Simmel 1971 [1903]: 324). This indeed was a widely shared concern of the day, and remains so today. One finds it in Weber's famous figure of the iron cage of the "enormous cosmos" of capitalism and rationalized modern life undermining the humanity of the individual subject. It appears in Durkheim's theory that society and society alone can provide the individual with sufficient moral guidance to overcome the violence created by too extreme a commitment to individualism (or as he put it in *Suicide* in 1897, egoism). It is apparent in Marx's idea that under the capitalist mode of production the human subject is alienated from himself, hence from the social world about. And, more generally, Simmel's lament is consistent with the fact that, with rare exception, modern social thought investigated the social problems arising in the modern industrial city and state in contrast to the simpler more traditional (and in theory more "human") habits of the simpler agrarian life. As the "sovereign powers" of society, as Simmel put it, loomed all the greater, especially in urban life, so individuals (who had possessed a sense of their individual identities only vaguely since the sixteenth century or so) came, one might say, to take themselves seriously as somehow at risk in the then new world order.

One might ask, then, in what ways was the modern metropolis all that different from the sovereign powers of the polis, or of despotic regimes, or the great empires, or of the feudal lords, or of the church or the Hellenic gods, and so on? For which the simple answer would be that, without a self-conscious sense of the Self concept, however large or menacing the prevailing societal order may be, the sense of threat to the individual could only be felt if the culture allowed for a sense that one exists qua individual – as an individual meant to think, act, and be on his own terms – and to do so with some resolute sense of her subjective purpose. Hence, the irony that because of advances in philosophical theories of knowledge and ethics after Descartes and Hobbes, the general concept of the subject thinking of, and acting against, a world of objects arose long before the Identity concept. This is why I have spent so many words tracing equally the emergence (or non-emergence) of "the individual" as a condition for the Identity concept in the current sense, after Simmel's generation. It is also why, before I am done, I will expend more words on a related but quite different ethical concept – individualism – which is linked of course to a theory of the Individual, and thereby bears on identity as such, but is a distinct set of troubles for identity theory itself.

The earliest, and clearest, late modern statement of the identity problem as linked to an individual psychology of the Self owes to William James in *Principles of Psychology* (1890). Here the key essay is the chapter "The Consciousness of Self" in which James offers what is surely the clearest early definition of the social self: "Properly speaking a man has as many social selves as there are individuals who recognize him" (James 1982 [1892]: 281). In this line is everything that is at once distinctive and troubling about the Identity concept – that in complex societies individual identity owes to our being identified ("recognized") by others. It requires a modern (even as Simmel said, metropolitan) social environment in which the practice of identification is a common practical accomplishment. Reaching back many centuries to Augustine you can begin to see how hard a struggle it was for this notion to surface in a social sense because, with Augustine in the fifth century, the kernel of self-identification was stated as a recognition of differences – and, in passing, we might add, that the fall of Rome in 410 CE was likely in the background providing Augustine a sense of urgency to the question of how one survives when living in a fallen empire. Still the normal urgency of identity as the recognition of Self had to await a modern world wherein, over time, different individuals lived as individuals with each other in close quarters.

But, of course, James's social self concept has it own set of problems. If the individual has as many selves as there are those who identify him or her, who is he or she after all in the welter of recognitions? James offers a somewhat ambivalent answer. On the one hand he proposes a spiritual self that would be the Self of all of the social selves in the interior life. But this idea never achieved much attention for the simple reason that it seems to be a kind of warmed over theory of the Soul. Where the better, if still not satisfactory, answer lay was in James's idea of the pure ego from which he derives the sense of personal identity in a formula that is at once scientific and practical: how can one say that "I am the same self that I was yesterday" (316)? when there can be and are many social selves, and when the individual lacks the armament of a strong spiritual self, how indeed does one identify himself as the same from day to day? The multiplicities of the modern social order would seem to make this possibility at least very hard to explain much less to act on. Yet, the very sense of self-identity is, at least, contained in James's aphorism.

No one before James tried so clearly to set up the self-identity dilemma which became, in many ways a staple of subsequent social theories in the Pragmatist tradition he helped found. Charles Horton Cooley's famous idea of "the Looking Glass Self" (in *Human Nature and the Social Order* [1902]) follows James in the principle that the interior "I" of the Self sees itself as others see it. In an even more compelling way, James's student W.E.B. Du Bois in *Souls of Black Folk* (1903) wrote of the double consciousness of the American Negro arising from, again, the Self defined by historical circumstances. The self or soul of the American Negro, however, is differentiated from the dominant social others by the contempt with which American whites looked upon the Negro – a contempt that shaped the souls of Black folk, equally for their misery but also for their unique and individual personal strengths.

But, of course, the definitive development of a social solution to James's dilemma of social self and the need for personal identity is widely thought to have been George Herbert Mead's teachings, collected in the book *Mind, Self, and Society* (1962 [1934]). Mead's solution (1962: 195–6) lay in the proposition that the Self engages in an interior dialogue between the "I" (or, roughly, the pure ego) and the "Me" (James's social self). Mead proposes, thereby, that Self-identity is a dynamic process, never ending, in which, as new social impingements affect one's interior sense of identity – the "I" reacts and shapes what Mead supposes to be a continuous sense of self-identity or, at least, a symbolic flow of constancy. Hence one of his more charming observations that the "Me" of this second becomes the "I" of the next. Mead's ideas were of course the beginning of the line of American social theory that came to be known as Symbolic Interactionism which has spawned numerous advances in our understanding of self-identity in modern life. Whether or not, this extension of the pragmatist line of thought solves the problem is unclear. The common criticism of Symbolic Interactionism is that – even in its most advanced forms later in the twentieth century – an inner dialogue and its entailments does not go very far toward accounting for the "sovereign powers," the large social structures of modern life that clearly affect how an individual thinks and acts as an individual. But, here with James, American pragmatism and its emergent traditions at least the problem is strongly put. If pragmatism as a social theory was weak on the question of social structures, at least it put the contradiction at the heart of identity in a way in which subsequent thinkers could determine how to use it or get around its troubles.

But, and again most evidently with James, the identity problem as we stated it at the beginning remained hard to resolve. If A = A is the Zero condition of identifications of all kinds this essentially nonsensical equation serves as the silent primordial impossibility – that A = B – from which springs the prospect of meaningful identity and when it comes to social identities no prospect is more perfect. The reason James balked in his theory of personal identity is that it is fully evident than an individual cannot ever be the same A she was the day before. She might be one who is similar in some ways, but if social realities impinge on personal identifications, then to some degree self-identity must change or at least adjust. One is always more of a B (or one might say A-) over time than the original pure A. This was the issue George Herbert Mead was trying to resolve with the on-going dialogue of the "I" and the social "Me" but it is very hard to get eventually to anything like James's Self of selves if the dynamic is ever ongoing.

Clearly some more radical approach is required. One arose in Europe in the two decades following James's *Principles of Psychology* in the writings of Sigmund Freud. From his first major work, *The Interpretation of Dreams* (1900), through quite a number of changes in his thinking over a long life, the one constant in Freud's thinking about the individual's mental life is that it is always under assault on several fronts. Just the same, the mind is possessed of a crucial survival mechanism – that of putting off the emotional charges arising from within and from the external world into the Unconscious; hence the centrality of dreams as the mechanism for releasing the interior tensions when the mind is at rest. The dream is never fully accessible in the waking life but Freud's talking therapy as it has come down to us is an attempt to use what is remembered of dreams as the principal element of the wide-awake mental means by which the relaxed patient is able to bring into consciousness those disturbing emotional charges.

11

Before going any farther, it must be said that Freud's scheme, in whichever of its several variants it is read, does not *sound* like an identity theory. But it is, insofar as it radicalizes even so unruly a theme as perturbations caused by the social self. In a fashion, what Freud did (without using the language of James or others in America) was to call the social self what it was – a target of stimuli from the outer world; and those external stimuli did not serve the needs of the "ego." Freud's ego is a deep interior, but half-conscious element of the psyche. Against the ego, facing the outside world, Freud famously posed the Superego, which is the source of the moral demands of society, mediated in childhood through the parental objects. The Superego is the judge of the social world, always promising punishment for misbehavior. In this aspect of Freud's thinking he simultaneously pulls together what the pragmatists left loose and incoherent in Mead's theories of the "I" and the "Me."

Freud, in effect, endows the social factor of the individual subject with qualities that Simmel and Weber wrote of without fully appreciating their force. The "sovereign power of society" is indeed overwhelming, as Simmel taught, but in being so it is also punitive and restrictive Freud added. Weber had some sense of this in his fear that the modern world could crush the humanity of the subject (and in this sense he was closer to Marx than many suppose). But Durkheim was utterly naïve on this element of the social bond. Society, for Durkheim, guides the individual into productive social life where his only identity is assured and when society withdraws the individual withers unto death.

In his basic formula, Freud clearly was less naïve than Durkheim and more thorough as regards the true nature and status of the individual than, certainly, Weber and Marx but also the American pragmatists who followed James. Yet, and again, the question can be put: Is this really the modern Identity concept? Could it not be said to be a step backwards into earlier murky waters wherein both the Self and the individual drown? On this latter point the answers would be Yes and No, in that order. Strictly speaking, if the standard for the Self concept is anything too close to the principle that seems to haunt James that there must be a pure ego (in which A = A), then Freud clearly rejects this line. No one, to my knowledge, has put this better than Anthony Elliott: "Freud laid the foundation for an understanding of the self as radically divided, fractured and ambivalent; he detailed a concept of the individual subject as always at odds with itself" (Elliott 2001: 49). Following Elliott, we can agree that in Freud there is no Self in the pure ego sense of the concept, but there is an individual even if one is always unsettled by conflict.

But what does this mean for the Identity concept in addition to the powerful honesty Freud introduces as regards the individual in the modern world – honesty that Marx, Simmel, and Weber among others pointed to but could not explain on their own terms? Here, of course, the individual is fraught with the conflict that these other thinkers realized. The difference Freud makes is that of bringing the conflict into the open. Here, of course, we must let drop the other shoe in his famous tripartite theory of the psyche – that of the deeper recesses of the Unconscious, namely the infamous "id" that forms the interior (and more powerful) line of assault on the work of the ego. The "id" it could be said attacks the "I." The id is the source of the drives, or the oddly translated, primitive instincts – of which the two most potent are Eros and Thanatos; or the drive toward building up constructive relations and its opposite – the drive to destruction.

Taking Freud at face value, what these drives do is aggravate the already punitive and destructive work of society through the Superego by energizing deeply mysterious interior (even natural) desires that put the ego in a quandary.

> The task [of the ego] is self-preservation. As regards *external* events, it performs that task by becoming aware of stimuli, by storing up experiences about them (in memory), by

avoiding excessively strong stimuli (through flight), by dealing with moderate stimuli (through adaptation) and finally by learning to bring about expedient changes in the external world. As regards *internal* events, in relation to the id, [the ego] performs that task by gaining control over the demands of the instincts, by deciding which are to be allowed satisfaction, by postponing that satisfaction to times and circumstances favorable in the external world or by suppressing their excitations entirely.

(Freud 1949 [1940]: 14–15)

If we were to allow Freud's ego to serve as at least a homologue to the Self concept, then this passage alone indicates the extent to which, at least with respect to the forces of the external world, he had a more realistic explanation for the troubles of personal identity individuals actually encounter in real life. In a word, the battle with the world is not always won, but we do remember, flee, adapt, or change things. This is not exactly the image of a pure ego maintaining self-identity through the course of obnoxious and multiple stimuli, but, truth be told, this is what most of us go through in trying to be something like the A we imagine ourselves to be without becoming a pure B. The Ego's work in controlling the internal impulses is harder to accept for some – in part because the drives concept is so far beyond traditional methods of empirical research. But we do, again if we are honest, recognize that whatever we call it – an Ego or Self – this aspect of our Self-being is very leaky. Desires cause us (against our better judgment) to love over much (often repetitively the wrong kind of person for us) or to do and say destructive things (that often end up injuring us). That impulses sneak through, not only in dreams, which are entirely about wishes, but also in repetitive behaviors, is a fact of individual life that the idea of a pure ego reconciling differences cannot explain.

So then what becomes of identity with Freud? For one, the starkness of it all notwithstanding, identity in Freud is the first fully analytic notion that accounts for the fact that identity as lived can never be a pure A = A – that the Zero Signifier of selfhood is never pure and never present in conscious life. Or – to put it otherwise, as Freud on the Unconscious – the ego is always at work against a Dark Continent that is always mysterious and for the most part silent. In other, better, words, the ego is a working faculty, working against threatening differences that arise from the interior and come down from the outside world.

Still what in Freud is identity? "Identification is known in psycho-analysis as the earliest expression of an emotional tie with another person" (1959: 27). First, and foremost, identification is emotional and, second, just as important, it is early – very early in the preverbal state of infancy. Identity is not so much an accomplishment for Freud as, in his word, a cathexis (or powerful attraction) to another person. But, and here he turns the tables on us, the other person is never purely a real object in the emotion-laden mind. The original object (using the Oedipal example Freud often gives) of the mother as an object to the infant, she (normally) is eventually introjected (that is taken into the emotional experience) of (infamously) the boy. The object of identification thus is projected or displaced, never real and stable as such; and if this is so, then it follows that the individual's identity is constantly disrupted by the presence within of illusions of objects without. Identifications are experienced as necessary objects of one's life, when in fact they are traces seen through a glass dimly (dreams in particular).

Freud's is not exactly the kind of Identity concept that modern thought had been seeking over all those years. But, however fragmentary his theory of the individual may be (not to mention his many digressions and errors), Freud did wrench open the Identity concept in productive ways that, since, have led to more honest and many fruitful developments, as we will see. For the moment, however, let the assessment rest on the very practical question that can be derived from the working formula of this essay. If, in regards personal identity, A = A is impossible, then how much is any individual personal A identity ever and always edging toward becoming or being a B, if not a B like another other? And where is that result gained (if that is the word), if one does not account for the unruly striking differences deep in the Unconscious interior? Whatever the final answer, if indeed one can be had, Freud at least allows us to question whether the centuries-long struggle to reconcile subjects and objects, individuals and social structures, reason and empiricism, and so on and so forth, cannot be advanced by new tricks of the theoretical trade but by coming to terms with the fundamental fact of social life – that the social individual is not, and can never be, a rational miniature of the social macrocosm; nor can she be merely a source of agency and autonomous action. This is because historical structures, though themselves fragile and permeable, always hold the upper hand in the differences; and they hold that hand close to the chest – in the interior struggle of the ego to preserve individual life, a struggle it cannot win, but must not loose.

Developments in identity theory since 1920, and the social assaults on individualism

In 1930, Freud published one of his most explicit essays of social analysis, *Civilization and its Discontents*, in which, in effect, he extended his dual drive theory to society itself with special attention to the evident spread of the Death or Destructive drive that was still, a good decade after the end of the First Word War of 1914, threatening the very core of European, hence modern, values and culture. By 1930, when Freud wrote, the unimaginably worse was already in full evidence, especially in the German-speaking parts of Europe. Elsewhere, the signs of global economic collapse and the rise of Fascism were evident. These signs and their eventualities as they so bloodily came to pass would make Simmel's and Weber's dire warnings about the threats of the modern era to the human individual, even humanity itself, seem mild by the contrast.

Thus began a series of twntieth-century attempts to account for self-identity – attempts that were at once more sociological and historical than any before, but attempts that turned on a later developing practical application of the ideal of the uniquely identified individual – the Individualism concept. In the history of the Identity concept, individualism is a tricky concept – one might even call it a tangent. In one sense, it is, for the most part, a kind of practical ethic of the personal life in which to be an individual is to be what men (or *certain* men, we must say) are expected (and privileged) to be. Where individualism is symptomatic of the troubles of the Identity concept is that by the mid-twentieth century, in the period that so shocked Freud and others in Europe, the ethic was itself under assault due in part to the gradual but evident erosion of the social status of the bourgeois classes in the West, but strikingly, after the Depression of 1929, in America as well.

Nearly a century before the early terrors of the 1930s, the term "Individualism" was first used in the 1830s by Alexis de Tocqueville in *Democracy in America* (1835). "Individualism," he said "is a mature and calm feeling, which disposes each member of the community to sever himself from the mass of his fellow-creatures, and draw apart with his family and friends" (1969 [1835], 506). Tocqueville was, to be sure, referring to what then was a distinctive aspect of American social life where, as is well known, individualism (in the more technical and conceptual sense) has always been more salient than in Europe. Still, the definition foretells what would come to pass in different, but not unrelated, ways more than a century later – that the individual as a moral being is somehow meant to find himself apart from "the mass of his fellow-creature." In 1835, in small town America, Tocqueville had in mind a quality of individual life that, to be sure, was only truly available to the bourgeois gentleman. In Europe, where class standing and social hierarchy were then much more powerful than in post-revolutionary America, individualism was a much less salient idea. This surely is why Tocqueville, always a keen observer of social life, was struck by just how powerful individualism was in America. American culture, especially early in the nineteenth century, was effectively a culture of the individual. It was a political and social, not to mention economic, order in which individual freedoms prevailed over social justices and in which even the ill-formed new American bourgeoisie was then deeply suspicious of urban life with its growing masses of industrial workers. Marx, though he was thoroughly familiar with American life, could not have written at length about the primacy of *class* conflict had he been an American.

In America, individualism has always trumped class in the European sense of the world – which is one of the reasons why Marx was not read widely in the US until later on the twentieth century. Thus, also, the nascent bourgeois classes Tocqueville observed in the 1830s were transposed in the 1930s only partly into a working-class movement. After the Second World War even this oppositional class was more or less absorbed into today's middle classes (which included an upper working class or lower middle class and in time an upper middle class just shy of the lower upper class), bourgeois values and ideals (largely borrowed from Europe) began to fade away. In America, the Crash of 1929 spelt the beginning of its decline in a quarter century of economic crisis and war after which, from 1945, a time of affluence that in turn sharpened the idea not of the value of the bourgeois gentleman but of the near-sacred importance of the hard working middle classes.

In Europe the story was different. For a much longer time, the bourgeois gentleman remained the model for the good, so to speak, cultural identity. In the long run, Matthew Arnold's *Culture and Anarchy* (1869) did not win the day for his defense of what came to be called high-culture (for which in England the purported elite values of Oxbridge was a recognized instance). Arnold's most famous line is "culture . . . is the best that has been thought and said in world" (1869: x). He was, thereby, suspicious of the threat to the integrity of society not only of the uneducated masses but also perhaps even more of the new bourgeois entrepreneur, devoted to the technical life of crass profit making. Still, what endured longer in Europe than ever in the United States was, in social terms, the crucial cultural identity of the elite gentlemanly class whose vocation it was to preserve the highest values of national culture that were the only hope to prevent social anarchy. While it would be a bit too harsh to accuse, say, Durkheim of a similar idea, it does remain a fact of his life that this small-town boy made his adult life on the basis of the highest learning available in Paris, from which he taught the ideas that moral education was the necessary protection of the individual from the ravages of individualism or, again, egoism.

In *The New Individualism: The Emotional Costs of Globalization* (2009), Anthony Elliott and I offer a somewhat more detailed history of individualism (and its relations to identity theory) than is possible here. But, in brief, that story is one that began in the 1920s and 1930s with the emergence in Germany (then in exile in America) of what we now call the tradition of Critical Theory. Its key founding figures, Max Horkheimer and Theodor Adorno, lived through the Fascist terrors of the Nazis. As social theorists what struck them hard was the ease with which Hitler was able to overwhelm the masses by a pervasively effective propaganda machine. Their joint manifesto, *The Dialectic of Enlightenment* (1944), tackles the problem for which the critical theorists in this tradition are famous. The project of Enlightened modernity was put at risk by the events of the twentieth century even as it remained the chief hope for what would later be called a politics of emancipatory knowledge. But in *Dialectic of Enlightenment*, the most famous of its essays is "The Culture Industry: Enlightenment as Mass Deception" in which they declared, as in subsequent writings, their fervent criticisms of mass cultures of all kinds – from radio and film to music, even jazz: "The culture industry endlessly cheats its consumers out of what it endlessly promises" (Horkheimer and Adorno 2001: 111). This long, still vibrant, tradition was, often implicitly, founded in the concern they witnessed in the 1930s and 1940s in Europe of the vulnerability of individualism to the manipulations of mass culture. Theirs was not, by any means, a critique of the same order as Matthew Arnold's in 1869. Theirs was shaped not by general theories of the masses, but by actual historical experience of just how easily even high-culture intellectuals, the bourgeoisie, as well as the masses, could give up their individual free-doms to the worst sort of political ideologies. The problem they identified remains acute today, which is why their line of critical political and social thought remains vital to our understanding of political and cultural life and, not incidentally, to the fate of democratic individualism in post-Second World War democracies.

That post-war era was very different in America that, especially in the 1950s, enjoyed an affluence that was due to its industrial might built up in the Second World War. This led, as is well known, to a period of unrivaled prosperity that indeed filtered down to the working classes – men and women who had served the war effort, either at home in the manufacturing sector or abroad in military action. As the American economy converted to the production of con-sumption goods including many of the new gadgets and machines applicable to domestic life, there were jobs aplenty. Thus began, in the 1950s, new social and commercial innovations that had never been available before, at least not to the newly affluent working and middle classes. Automobiles and washing machines were available in local retail markets. The mall emerged in this era as the cathedral of consumption. Television entered the home as a popular and principal medium of family entertainment. And, strangest of all, the "teenager" came into existence, now as the youth whose school years were prolonged and whose purchasing power was enhanced.

By 1950, very early in these developments, social criticisms began to describe the danger of these new forms of social life. Two in particular were, and remain, important documents in the twentieth-century history of the Identity concept. One was David Riesman's *Lonely Crowd* (1950) in which he and his coauthors bemoaned the threats of consumption culture to the central character in American cultural life – what Riesman called the "inner directed" individual or (since a great deal of Riesman's thinking is owed to Max Weber) the hard-work-ing productive individual imbued with a spirit of capitalism. The figure of the inner-directed individual had become not only the dominant ideal of nineteenth- and early twentieth-century American popular culture but also, as we have seen, in many ways it was the figure behind the early twentieth-century Identity concept. The "I" of personal identity (in both James's and Mead's formulations) was in effect the sturdy disciplined individual of, first, small town bour-geois America, and then of its expanding working and middle class of the high industrial period. Still today Americans brag about the superior "productivity" of their workers. What Riesman and others argued was that the inner directed man was giving way to the other-directed indi-vidual. As the middle-level corporate workers who were forced to conform to prevailing values and to become "team players" in order to climb the ladder of success, at the same time, with money in their pockets, they also became consumers of cars, suburban houses, faddish clothes, and well-equipped leisure life styles.

The irony here is that as other-directed conformism worried the social critic (and for good reason) and their worry was based on the solid evidence that the new post-war life (at first in America, a decade plus later in Europe too) was somehow the life of a new kind of individual – one at once more isolated from the masses as she retreated into dull individualized suburbs, shopped for cars and televisions that further isolated family life, and tried to come to terms with growing teenagers who were, like their parents, bored with the suburban or corporate life. They, the youth, were the focus of a second important theory of post-war individualism – Erik

Erikson's writings of the same period on the identity crisis of youth. For him the aimless inter-regnum of the teen years, a product of economic and social changes, created an identity crisis that would, as Riesman also thought, eventually become a crisis for American national character. As life became more contradictory and fluid under the pressure of changes in personal life and individual values, so the precise status of the individual becomes troubled: "We must try to formulate the way in which self-contradictions in American history may expose her youth to an emotional and political short circuit and thus endanger her dynamic potential" (Erikson 1950: 263).

The contradictions of American life had always been there lurking behind its cultural devotion to the primacy of the individual and its freedoms. Yet, Erikson and Riesman, writing from quite different points of view, both contributed importantly to an understanding of the crisis of the individual – hence of the individual's ability to identify his unique qualities. They saw that those qualities of individualism were aggravated by sudden changes in what both of them called American national character. For the moment, however, the point is to note that, quite apart from the enormous differences between America and Europe at the time, and thus between the critical theorists of German descent and the more Native American social critics, the period from the 1930s through the 1950s gave fair warning of changes yet to come.

One of those changes in the understanding of individualism and identity was the emergence (actually a good many decades later) in the writings of European authors such as Anthony Giddens and Ulrich Beck, and others in the 1990s, of the individual (like the world itself) as necessarily, inescapably reflexive (Beck, Giddens, and Lash 1994). At the time, their prominent theory of identity as a social problem was nurtured by the dramatic changes in the speed and nature of global exchanges – travel, the Internet, migrations, multiculturalism, and related phenomena. In a certain sense this third new movement in the study of individualism can be explained by the enormous pressures associated with globalization. As individuals traveled (not always for pleasure or business, sometimes to escape starvation and civil strife), they encountered new social forms. One might even say, remembering William James's first slogan, that they encountered new worlds in which the others there encountered really could not recognize them any more than they could these others. In this period, and still today all the more acutely, an individual's identity could not be explained even by the complicated task of dealing with the social powers of one's own society. It is one thing for middle-class individuals to have a social self as well as the mannered methods by which their social inferiors or superiors recognize them. One's social status and his sense of personal worth may in principle be elevated or depressed depending who recognizes him and how. But it is quite another matter that the Korean grocer or Pakistani taxi driver is himself inscrutable (largely and often because of language problems) and, at the same time, the newly immigrated merchant or driver simply is not familiar with the local signals appropriate to the giving and receiving of identity recognitions.

All too simply put, writers such as Giddens and Beck proposed that in this sort of complex globalized circumstance the individual was forced to adopt a reflexive identity. This is an idea that goes far beyond the pragmatists theory of the "I" reflecting on and adjusting to her "Me" stimuli. Gone is the prospect that a mere inner dialogue could resolve the situation, an identity challenge that is ever present because the character of complex, multicultural, fluid, and global worlds will not let the individual rest. The new reflexive individual's sense of personal identity was (and remains) a bold, even necessary, theory of self-identity in the late modern world. There can hardly be any doubt that among the many (well-off and marginal alike), the ability to adjust one's self to the fluidity of global world – adjustments that include learning new languages, new manners, moving to different more opportune parts of the world, and much else – is a new fact of life that complicates the modern Identity concept.

At the same time, in *The New Individualism*, Elliott and I also note a trend verging at its

extremes on the pathological emotional costs of globalization – those who through body sur-
geries, sexual experimentation, various therapies, and Internet lives and relationships, and the
like – who essentially lose their sense of themselves in the self-transformations they undertake
trying to catch up with the world. This is something more and more alarming than the idea of
self-reflexivity, and it stands as a deeply disturbing trend of early twenty-first-century life.

What is the lesson of this short history of individualism and identity from the 1930s through
and after the 1990s? At many points the twists and turns of the major movements have not been
identity theories at all. Yet, from the German critical theories of the manipulated individual,
through the American social criticisms of a slippage in natural character that dissipates the notion
of identity as a forward-thinking project of an ideal self, to the theories of self reflexivity brought
on by the pressures of global process, at least two significant factors entered the discussion of
the Identity concept. One was a renewal and development of the specific and historical roles
of (again Simmel's phrase) the sovereign powers of society. Fascism and mass media, consumption culture and conformism, globalization and the reflexive imperative were all as much social
theories of larger – much larger – social forces than anything that had appeared before. One
might protest that certainly Marx, Weber, and Durkheim offered theories of the evils and/or
benefits of the new capitalist and industrial orders of their times. They did, of course, but in all
three cases (though less so with Weber) they did so at a cost to their ability to provide a sense of
the individual's ability to attain what Weber might have called subjective meaning or certainly
what the earlier classically liberal economists thought of the primacy of individual freedoms.
The twentieth century was a time of trial for many of the great nineteenth-century early modern ideas. When it came to Self theories, or theories of the individual, thinking seemed to break
down into two groups: a society-first line in which the individual is lost in the welter of social
impressions; and an individual-first line that established individual identities as a property of the
free, in principle autonomies, Self. Neither was completely satisfactory, even though both did
their best to point to the plight of the individual (as did Weber, Marx, and Durkheim) or to
the social effects on self-identification (as did James and Mead and others in the traditions they
spawned). What came to pass, by contrast, in the twentieth century after the 1920s was a series
of identity theories (whether explicit or implicit) that saw the individual as in a quandary of loss
or brave self-reflexivity.

Yet, important to say, in the same century and up through the late 1980s and early 1990s,
there was another set of developments that contribution a fresh and challenging element to the
modern history of identity studies.

Identity-politics

As the modern history of the individualism concept worked its way through the thicket of twentieth-century troubles, another movement – one arising from outside the dominant centers of
intellectual authority – was making its way into the core and its allies at the global centers. In due
course, this movement would come to be called, for a time at least, identity-politics. Before getting
into the details of what identity-politics had come to mean, we can state that, as a general rule, it
is comparable to the three stages of individualisms in the twentieth century in that identity-politics
was a debate precisely over the question of whether identity is an interior quality of the individual
or a social category individuals could enter. The major difference this alternative tradition imposed
was that, more times than not, it did not arise out of specific and detailed references to prevailing
social crises such as mass media, consumption orientation, and globalization.

At the same time, even when a good bit of identity-politics theory made little or no reference
to structural, historical transformations, the impact of global history was very often quite evident

or, at least, detectable. There could be no better illustration of this rule than the first sociologist to use the phrase "the politics of identity." In fact, one of the most thorough and explicit, if controversial, theories of the politics of identity was written by the inventor of the phrase and of a startling departure in the social theory of the Self.

Erving Goffman, in his short but pungent 1963 book, *Stigma: Notes on the Management of Spoiled Identity*, broke identity down into three analytic elements: social, personal, and ego identities. When he wrote in 1963 these categories were of course already familiar at least since William James in 1892. Yet, Goffman, a Canadian whose career was pursued in major American universities, upset the American pragmatist applecart; and this in spite of the fact that he was trained at the University of Chicago in the 1950s where George Herbert Mead earlier had held forth and where, in Goffman's student days, a good deal of modern Symbolic Interactionism was encouraged. Just the same, Goffman belonged to no school but his own. His was a line of severe skepticism (even at points dismissal) of the, by then, centuries-long history of a search for a coherent theory of the thinking subject or, as it came to be, Self theory; hence, also of identity as primarily a property of the interior Self.

By contrast to nearly everything written before him, Goffman argued, and persuasively so, that identity is a public performance with almost no interior affect. Ego identity, he argued, was not at all Mead's "I," nor even Freud's "ego," but simply an individual's *feeling* about his identity situation and not the traditional interior ego or I that possesses and gives life a self: "Self is, as must be, a resident alien, a voice of the group that speaks for and through him" (1963: 123). *Stigma*, as the key word suggests, is a book not about normal identities. It concerns individuals whose identity had been spoiled, causing such an individual to be stigmatized by others in the social around; hence, put at risk by the normals. From this perspective, for Goffman, the two primary identities were social and personal. The former is the public identity that the individual performs well enough such that others around him are brought into the drama in which he stars as a individual of his own making – a hero, a poet, and good person, so forth. Underneath, at the margins (not the deep interior) of the personal life lies a series of personal identity markers of many kinds – a police or prison record, a history of plagiarism, evidence of criminal or other kinds of deviant behavior, a hidden ethnicity or political affiliation, and so forth. Goffman went further to include bodily marks (like warts or tattoos), medical or dental histories, fingerprints, or in our time DNA – any mark, or trace, that is unique to the individual person. Thus personal identity, he said, is information and not information one would want known by others. To the point of his book's subject, some personal information, if known to others, would spoil the individual's performed social identity, thereby discrediting the individual (or, as he said in an earlier essay, causing him to lose face). The discrediting is due to the inadvertent release or discovery of a personal identity marker that spoils the act. It may be so normal a discovery as a lover smelling the scent of another lover on the body or, even, the accident of leaving out a box of not so old papers or legal documents where a friend could come across evidence of the individual's prison record or some other behaviors thought to be deviant. Goffman's *Stigma* was a completely systematic theory in that it ended up dismissing altogether the concept of ego–identity as no more than a feeling. How the individual feels about his personal identity and its deviations from the social face or the identity he has managed to put over on others. If, for example, that feeling is guilt, this could cause the individual to slip in the control of his personal information, causing him to be discredited.

Thus, and finally, for Goffman, identity was mostly a struggle for information control between the facts of an individual's biography and the social face he has managed to build up – a face, or identity, that Goffman argued was always at odds with some or another, deep or strategic, secret that must not ever, or ought not at a given moment, be revealed without disastrous results. Hence, also, Goffman's identity theory, in addition to being emphatically social, was a more or less universal theory of all identities. So-called normals are no different in the methods they use to manage their social identities. Thus when, at the end of *Stigma*, Goffman wrote of *normal deviancy* as the foremost characteristic of all social selves, he was defining his politics of identity as interactional politics of controlling one's social identity which is always at risk of being discredited, however slightly or severely. The methods used to this universal human end, Goffman said, are exactly the same for normals as for deviants – hence: normal deviancy.

It would not be too far wrong to say that Goffman's identity theory bears some parallels to Freud's in that both argued that an individual cannot avoid a struggle to maintain a sense of social and personal balance. For Freud that struggle was entirely on the interior; for Goffman it was so to speak on the skin of the self where personal secrets were at risk of destroying a well-made social identity. And both, in effect, argued that, to use our word, whatever identity amounts to, it is never simply wise, good, or true. There are always hidden, destructive forces that can ruin the whole thing. One might say therefore that the only difference between the normal individual and the mental patient or the prostitute is that the latter types do their identity work in public and thus have revealed many of the very same facts or feelings that the legendary good man or the idealized loving wife may experience in their inner most beings.

Still, though Freud, in *Civilization and Its Discontents*, among other writings made more or less overt references to the external social histories of his day (and before); Goffman never did. In fact, the absence of a politics beyond identity-politics is a common criticism of him. At the same time, there are reasons to say that Goffman (his silence on the matter notwithstanding) was a product of his times. For one, it is important to note that his first major work, *The Presentation of Self in Everyday Life* (1956), was the foundational work of a theory of self production as a social drama, thus of impression management. This book first appear in early form in 1956 in Scotland, just when Riesman, Erikson, and other more popular writers were already deeply engaged with the emergence of a conformist or other-directed individualism especially in middle-class American culture in the 1950s. It, therefore, would be hard to conclude that Goffman's thinking was out of a historical vacuum. Plato's ideas on wisdom and knowledge were shaped by the culture of Athens. Augustine's early identity theory seems to have been shaped by the fall of Rome. James and Weber, as well as Simmel, wrote in the period of the rise of the modern industrial order, and so on through the developments in the twentieth century. Goffman too was influenced by his times and, as those times came to be, it became more or more clear that in some strange way Goffman also in weird but evident ways was an original social theorist of many of the changes that took place in the 1960s. That he did not note them, does not mean he did not notice them.

Identity-politics were shaped by global forces that came to a head late in the 1960s. Of these, none was more important than a global movement that began late in the 1940s with the liberation of India from the British (1947), after which, in rapid-fire succession, once colonized peoples in Africa, Asia, the Caribbean, others in every corner of the southern tier of the world, began their own decolonization struggles. Some succeeded in due course (China, Vietnam, most of the Caribbean nations, north Africa, Cuba), others (mostly in sub-Saharan Africa, but also Haiti, Cuba in another sense, and parts of South Asia) struggled to form independent nation states relatively free of the older colonial powers. Whether they were successful or not, this global movement clearly affected the world order. In the background of a less centralized world system stood a still powerful Western dominance of global affairs. The West (notably the US in the 1950s and 1960s) remained in the core position, but (and especially due to the effects of the Cold War after 1946) its power was far less than absolute. When some, today, talk of the world as post-modern and mean by that fragmented, they are at least referring to the shattering of the

Euro-American hegemony over the cultures and affairs of the world's regions. Perhaps the most famous declaration of this connection was a statement made in 1966 by Jacques Derrida when he referred in "Structure, Sign and Play in the Discourse of the Human Sciences" to "something has occurred in the history of the concept structure that could be called an 'event'" (1978 [1966], 278). Derrida was of course referring to an event in culture but, in the late 1960s when he wrote, and in France especially, there could hardly have been any question that in the back of his mind was the decolonizing, hence fragmenting, of the world itself. Derrida surely felt this as a native of Algeria which had won its independence from France in 1962. Thus entered the language of the decentering of culture and social thought – the post-structuralist critique of overly strong structural theories – and also the emergence of the idea that thought, culture, like the world itself, were (and ought to be) increasingly decentered. The central organizing powers may remain in force even when their cultural authority is broken.

At the interior of those core or central powers, in their major cultural centers, world-wide – Paris, Berlin, Birmingham and the rest of the American South, Berkeley and Chicago, and many others – there were strikes, rebellions, resistances against the status quo, which as it turned out was a global as well as a national status quo. Hence, there were new worker movements, to be sure, but more strikingly there came into play what we now recognize as New Social Movements – Blacks in the American South and Northern cities, women world-wide, Latinos and other ethnic groups around the world, gays and lesbians, and many others among those in social groups that had been treated as "minorities" which in practical effect meant outsiders, inferiors. These were called *New* Social Movements because as Immanuel Wallerstein among many others has said (Wallerstein 2004: 83–6, et passim), until then, struggles for freedom and recognition were of two types (2004: 67–73) – national liberation movements (as in Cuba and India) or working-class revolutions or revolts of "the people", real and theoretical (as in Russia and differently China and the NLF in Vietnam). The line between the two was not always clear but they had in common the traditional assumption that freedoms were gained in and against prevailing nation-states – one's own, or the local colonial powers. Wallerstein stood virtually alone in noting that these traditional movements were harbingers of today's anti-systemic movements, that is, movements against the dominant global forces of the world-system. He thus called 1968 a world revolution. Still, however one describes the political turmoil in the centuries leading up to global 1960s, what the more traditional movements, including decolonization, led to, in due course, was a series of mixed results. The national independence movements were either slow to settle into progress (India) or vulnerable to corrupt dictators put in power by the interests of the powerful nations (Congo, Uganda). On the other hand, the worker revolutions of earlier in the twentieth century themselves were never truly international. Where they attained power, as in Russia, they failed, as again Immanuel Wallerstein in particular puts it, in state formation – in, that is, putting the revolutionary principles into workable political and social institutions. Hence, the important difference between the New Social Movements (NSM) and traditional social movements. The NSM do not primarily aim for a complete upheaval in the state or class structures of a given society. What, on the other hand, they are inclined to do is base political action not only on local or regional concerns of the group acting but also to envision in the long run globally effective new social movements. Thus, in particular the American Civil Rights Movement eventually transformed itself into a fusion of, often, Islamic ideas or, more traditionally, as a vital part of the Pan-African movement that had long been a factor in the world-wide African Diaspora; likewise, nation-based women's movements took different forms in, say, the US and France or the UK, but in time they increasingly saw themselves as part of a global movement for women's rights.

These political developments that came to the fore in the 1960s, notably in and after 1968, thus had a telling effect on the Identity concept. They were, historically, the basis for identity-politics of a kind much more overtly political than Goffman's but also, importantly, identity-politics arising from the New Social Movements were arguably more openly social and political. Within these changes rooted late in 1940s and coming to full force in the 1980s, the Identity concept thus came to a breaking point and, as we will see, a break that called into question the very nature of radical politics and, more generally, of the nation-state as the primary social location of what social identification an individual might have.

From one point of view the most terrifying evidence that the nation-states, even the strongest, after decolonizing and the world revolution of 1968 were loosing their ability to manage their national identities occurred in more recent times (especially after 1989–91) with the worldwide outbreak in ethnic hostilities in states and regions once controlled by great powers. Examples are everywhere – neither the US nor the EU know exactly what to do with ethnic worker populations (Chicanos in the US, Muslims most currently in Europe); China, even as it uses force, has long been beset by the resistance of ethnic regions (such as Tibet and the Turkic populations in West); in the former Soviet Union ethnic violence has been continuous (for example in 2010 in Kyrgyzstan between Uzbeks in the south and the Kyrgyz in the north; in the Balkans and Palestine, Rwanda and Congo, Shi'a and Sunni struggles in the Islamic Diaspora (notably in Iraq) – virtually everywhere). These conflicts within and on the margin of once-stable (if ruthlessly so) states have a long history that, it turned out, were not suppressed at all by long periods of colonial administration and ill-conceived new national forms such as the Soviet Union. Ethnic renewal and its concomitant resistance movements can clearly be said to be one of the more salient if tragic forms of identity-politics in the current period. In all of these cases, and others, national identities faded (if ever they were primary) in favor of hitherto subterranean ethnic loyalties. Here identity-politics approaches the maximum point of pure social definition. Individuals who collectively suffered the strife and slaughter of ethnic violence hardly mattered at all. Whether or not modern democratic values had made themselves felt in the regions or the revivals of ethnic pride for a strong sense of individual rights (as very few did, and nearly none in the modern sense of the ideal of individualism), the deeper story is of a tragic element in this sad story of identity-politics.

Yet, from another point of view, these events took quite a while to formulate their contributions to identity studies and theories. It was well into the late 1970s and 1980s before post-colonial studies (and ethnic studies) came to the fore in universities. Edward Said's *Orientalism* (1978) was an early contribution even though the identity question there was implicit. Some argue that Gayatri Spivak's "Can the Subaltern Speak?" (1988) is the *locus classicus* of postcolonial identity theory. From another angle (and one not always clear) there was some very good and interesting work on social and political identification in the emergence later in the 1980s and in the 1990s of multiculturalism. Multiculturalism, still a term in use, was mostly an ideal that by the second decade of the 2000s had been largely abandoned. Just the same, the enduring effect of multicultural theory was that it, as both a theory and a social movement, brought into the public and intellectual spheres the irrefutably of two fundamental historical changes: first, that identities are socially formed and, second, that social identities from one group to another are different, perhaps irreparably so.

In public politics these desiderata of multiculturalism entailed a recognition (still denied by conservative thinkers) that the liberal ideal of assimilation needed to be rethought. Assimilationist politics had its apparently most dramatic success in the American "melting pot" of immigrant workers from Europe. Many we now know had their European names arbitrarily Americanized as they disembarked at Ellis Island. Many of the European workers did in fact over many generations become "American" and give up for the most part many of their traditions that were not reinforced by strict religious affiliations. Second and third generation Latinos and Koreans often do not speak the languages of their parents and grandparents, just as Italians and Germans had given up their ancestral languages and habits in favor of American ones. But, even though America and Europe remain today important destinations for people seeking economic opportunity and Western educations, many others from South Asia, China, Haiti and others continue to live in immigrant enclaves or practice Westernized forms of the native cultures. Multiculturalism, as a theory and a practice, essentially affirmed these differences (even when the enclaves remained for economic as opposed to cultural reasons). Multiculturalism has, for the most part, become a fact of life throughout North America and the EU, if not China or Russia. That fact has obvious implications for the options available now for identity formation, options that may entail personal choices with profound implications for an individual's sense of self-identity, but options made possible by a sometimes welcome and other times begrudging recognition that multicultural reality is here to stay, which is in effect to grant that social differences among identities are real, if not immutable.

Yet, these historical events notwithstanding, identity-politics took shape largely in the more rarefied climate of academic and occasionally public intellectual debate. Though there are many instances (of which lately the importance of Queer Theory) no NSM was more important to the reshaping of identity-politics than feminism. Why this is so is a topic for another time, but at the least we can say it had a great deal to do with the fact that second-wave feminists in the 1970s, following in the tradition of women who had participated in the student and civil rights movements of the 1960s, entered public life and academic work in increasing numbers. Many of them brought with them, or looked closely at, the stories of other women's experiences in mass social movements such as Civil Rights in the US and student revolts in Germany and France. At the first, again in the 1970s, political feminism borrowed mostly from pre-existing political ideas. Of them, the most appealing (and in the US freshly understood) was a vaguely Marxist or, better, Socialist Feminism. Here, and I put this crudely, as in: if in socialism the working class is the universal revolutionary class, then a socialist women's liberation movement is a movement of the same kind – gender first, then class. If the working class suffered false consciousness that could only be relieved by political and economic crisis, so for women the crises of the 1960s were the provocations for rethinking not just women's role in relation to men and to society (often called consciousness raising) but also of the deeper nature of Woman's identity as conceived independently of the traditional sex roles theories that assigned to women the role of moral leader of the household and, among the bourgeois and white classes, keepers of the personal domestic needs of the husband.

From this arose, in an attempt to fashion a serious (my phrase) feminist Identity concept, a number of important writings in the 1970s. Many of these drew on traditional sources such as Simone de Beauvoir's *The Second Sex* (1949), but for the most part they were formulated against or drawn from classic sources familiar to academic writers. The first of these positions to emerge was feminist standpoint theory which sought to outline and detail the distinctive aspects of, as one of the standpoint theorists put it, the distinctive experience of women that could be acquired from women's practical experience for a distinctively feminist theory of knowledge and power. As Sandra Harding (1990: 99) so aptly put it, standpoint theory is directed at the "essentialism androcentrism assigns to women." In the background is Beauvoir's idea that androcentrism (a term coined by the Charlotte Perkins Gilman in the 1890s) defines Woman as the Other to man, as exactly the second sex. Thus standpoint theorists such as Dorothy Smith (1974 [1990]), borrowing from Marx and ethnomethodology, analyzed the distinctive features of the woman's standpoint as a site for the renewal of social research and knowledge

Charles Lemert

– this because the woman's experience is (for better or worse) rooted in practical interests of daily life to a far greater extent than men's experience which, in the 1970s especially, was based on their working in the relations of ruling in government and corporate life where objective, official knowledge was primary. The writings of Smith and other standpoint feminists such as Nancy Hartsock (1983) were met in the academy initially by male disdain and suspicion. But among feminists they were powerful, and no more so than in setting feminist identity in lived experience and thus as not a naturalistic sex role but a historical formed and transmutable way of identifying the feminist identity as both different and distinct from the prevailing ideas of gender assimilation and the gender caste system. As such, standpoint feminism was a basis for rethinking the nature and role of women in social life. It was not, to be sure, an explicit identity theory in the traditional sense, but it did deeply challenge the old identity theories many of which were accepted as given in nature even by women, even those earlier first- and second-wave feminists who argued for a women's equality to men, thus the right to vote, and the protection of gender-based rights. Standpoint feminism, it could be said, put the final nail in the coffin of the European gentleman – the man of learning and elite-class values who was culturally thought to represent the universal humanist identity to which all ought to aspire.

But the standpoint feminist position did not hold the ground it captured in the 1970s. It was quickly met, especially between 1980 and 1990, by a series of challenges from feminists whose experiences diverged from those the standpoint theorists *seemed* (even when they did not) to have had in mind. Early in the 1980s the standpoint position was often attacked as a strategic essentialism – that standpoint feminism was proposing the woman's standpoint as not just different but perhaps superior to that of the Universal Man of Liberal culture. Dorothy Smith protested reasonably to the criticism. Still, the claim was fair enough because any strong standpoint position sets up at least an implicit essentialism that allowed for the extension that Woman was One – that all women have the same experiences. One of the most robust criticisms of this kind cane from Audre Lorde's famous 1979 paper (first a speech to a convention of white feminists) – "The Master's Tools Will Never Dismantle the Master's House") in which she rebukes the white feminists gathered at a New York University conference for their, at the time, ignorance of the sharp differences among women, and therefore among feminisms. Lorde was a poet, but also Black and a lesbian. Her challenge, in the last lines of the paper, was telling: "I urge each one of us to reach down into that deep place of knowledge *inside herself* and touch the terror and loathing of any difference that lives there"– a foretelling of the principle that an identity-politics of sharp differences were in the outside world to be sure but also on the inside. Many others took up the same criticism of what some considered standpoint feminism's essentialism.

In effect the lesson learned from standpoint feminism and its detractors is that once identity ceases to be a universal attribute of total human experience like that of women (but in principle others as well), then the very fact of differences erodes any possibility of even an historically conditioned identity as pure and simply feminine, Black, queer, or whatever. Identity differences alter identity theory in ways that cannot be retrieved.

In the mid-1980s a quite puzzling and eventually highly influential paper began to circulate widely in the academy. Donna Haraway's "A Manifesto for Cyborgs "(1985) put forward the figure of the cyborg as a form arising from the interpenetration of natural and technological elements in the formation; in effect, of human identity in the late modern world. Today, when individuals are attached to cell phones, heart monitors, hearing aids, implanted medical devices, and the like, the idea is less shocking than it was in the mid-1980s. As confusing as this theme was, what was stunningly clear, but still upsetting to many readers, was Haraway's affirmative statement that "identities seem contradictory, partial, and strategic" (1991 [1985]: 154); hence, the expression she made famous (though she borrowed the idea from others) is that identities

24

are, at least for those in the excluded and marginal subject positions, always "fractured identities." Yet, though the term came to be used for a more general identity theory, Haraway's fractured identities referred to the necessary reality of the experience of excluded women who could be, endlessly, women, yes, but also lesbian, Latina, poor, just to name the more obvious fractures that cut through the identity experiences of many woman for whom the "consciousness of exclusion is acute" (1991 [1985]: 154). The *locus classicus* of a fully articulated fractured identity is Gloria Anzaldúa's *Borderlands/La Frontera* (1987) in which she writes poetically of her shared identities with Chicana lesbians who speak English, Mexican, and their indigenous languages and who work hard in the American southwest on the economic margins of a wealthy nation, yet are cut-off from their homelands. They cannot go home. They live on a border – both the real one between the US and Mexico (always, especially today, contested) and the interior borders within that mark the fractures she must live with (and in) these multiple identities and live always contradictorily, partially, and strategically when facing the exterior world.

The differences between standpoint and fractured identity feminisms are real, but they also, in a sense lead one to the other. Once, feminist identity is understood to be different from a universalizing cultural norm, then it is virtually impossible not to come soon enough to the final implication that if Woman (or in principle any other social category of similar social experience) is different, then her differences are exposed to obvious fractures with which, truth be told, women, more than men (as a rule), must contend – whether as the good wife who experiences the condescensions to which her status exposes her or, let us say, the Black or Latina domestic who cleans and cares for the homemaker yet who must return to her separate life where she cares for her own home, her own children, and her own racial, ethnic, and other differences.

It is impossible here to trace all the ways identity-politics in the 1980s played out in other areas besides feminisms. Postcolonial theory is one. To a lesser extent race theory has been another. And Queer theory was, by the 1990s, an especially important one that here must be discussed, however briefly.

In 1990, two modern-classic works in the identity-politics debate were published. One was Patricia Hill Collins's *Black Feminist Thought: Knowledge, Consciousness and the Politics of Empowerment* (1990). Though Collins, at several points, presented her work as an Black feminist standpoint theory, in fact the book is a wide-ranging historical and analytic presentation of the multiple identities Black women in America must contend with. Yet, like Anna Julia Cooper in the 1890s, Collins interpreted these fractured experiences as a political and moral strength, which led her to adopt a concept (originally coined by bell hooks) that lent important subtlety to the fractured identity position – the matrix of domination. In effect, she said that domination in society is never a unidirectional force from the top down on the oppressed classes. Rather power in society works as a series of vectors moving in several directions down and even in principle up to affect any given individual or group of individuals in multiple ways. The matrix thus affects Black women in their several identities by, so to speak, the privilege of their knowledge of the structure of the social array by virtue of being at or near the lower end of the field of vectors of oppression. Hence, the startling, but true statement: "No two biographies are the same" (1990: 227). She did not intend to atomize individuals from one and other, but instead to explain that the experiences of oppressions – many shared, however partially, by Black women (also Women of Color globally) – created both the knowledge and power necessary for resistance to the dominant powers. Collins was, thus, the first to offer a robust, structural theory, historically grounded, of the complexities of national (and by extension) global dominations as they affect the near universal fracturing of identities, hence the politics of identity (or we must now say identities).

Also in 1990, Judith Butler's *Gender Trouble: Feminism and the Subversion of Identity* appeared. This one book brought to the fore insights that had been implicit to the beginnings of the fractured identities tradition but also in the, by then, emerging queer theory line of thought. As the subtitle suggests here, Butler begins to call into question the very concept of identity or, at least, of identity being able to refer to an analytically stable concept such as gender in the case of feminism, or sexuality in the case of queer theory, or, by implication, race, class, postcolonial status. In Butler's words:

> The task of this work is to center on – or to decenter – such defining institutions [as] phallogocentrism and compulsory heterosexuality. . . . Precisely because "female" no longer appears to be a stable notion, its meaning is as troubled and unfixed as "woman" . . . It is no longer clear that feminist theory ought to try to settle the questions of primary identity in order to get on with the tasks of politics. Instead, we ought to ask, what political possibilities are the consequence of a radical critique of the categories of identity?
>
> *(Butler 1990: ix)*

From this programmatic statement came a book that, as its primary title suggests, served to trouble not only the Identity concept but also just as much gender itself and by implication any such unstable category. Yet, in this statement and subsequent writings, Butler is clear that in some sense gender is, if not the most troubling of concepts, at least the one that, as it had been opened up to inspection in the two preceding decades, led in due course to the questions she poses of identity. Why? Butler's answer was the answer that had been anticipated in a goodly number of queer (or if one prefers gay and lesbian) theory. Gender is a term that replaced an abstract concept sex – as in the nineteenth-century locution, the female sex. What is apparent, or was by the 1990s certainly, is that sex is not an abstract social category but a very particular, even juicy, bodily experience. Woman is not a sex, but she has sex, or desires to have it, and the sex she has or seeks may be with men or with women, or with both, or, for that matter, she may wish, or choose to become, a he, and vice versa. Butler's most pungent expression is that all sex is a kind of necessary drag. Gays and lesbians are not imitating heterosexual roles anymore than heterosexuals are enacting naturalistic categories. If, we could say, gender identity is not a category defined by natural sex roles, then certainly sex itself is not. Crudely put, Butler's book inspired a subsequent line of thought that argued that gender like sex is performed and if this is so, then all socially available categories are not so much constructed (for good or ill) but performed. Butler's idea of performativity is one with a separate and philosophically sophisticated history, so it would not be accurate, strictly speaking, to compare it to Goffman's performed self or face. Yet, we are reminded that what began in the 1960s, when Goffman however unwittingly invented the ideal of identity-politics, grew decade by decade to call into question the concept of identity.

The long history of the Identity concept from its thin intimations in Plato, through the Greeks and then Augustine, the Protestants and the early modern philosophy of self-consciousness, to Freud and Simmel, then through the 1950s in Europe and America, followed a very clear path. Identity, as we use it, required something like a modern world in which it was necessary (or at least philosophically possible) to think of a self as, in Descartes's principle, the thinking I that in reflection finds itself thinking thereby existing, then the ego of modern future oriented capitalism, to in the twentieth century after 1920 an enormous wall of social crises that led from Adorno to Riesman to Giddens on the one hand and from Beauvoir to standpoint feminists, to fractured identity theorists and to Butler and queer theorists of identity as performed on the other. Whether or not the Identity concept has out lived its usefulness, remains to be seen.

Future developments

Whether, in the twenty-first century, the Identity concept is to remake itself depends to a considerable extent on which identity theorists and more empirical students of the subject study it with respect to the dramatically altered social and historical circumstances of our time. Some would all too simply call this the post-9/11 realities. Others would call it (all too simply) the world of globalizations. Fewer perhaps, but some just the same, would call it a migratory world in which extreme poverty and social exclusions define the global realities as much as does the speed of information transfers.

Whatever, in our day, the Identity concept will become, it will have to abandon, or so I suppose, some of the tried-and-true verities of its history. If, for one example, one grants Haraway's fractured identities, then the ideal of strong interior Self is severely crippled. If, for an earlier example, one grants that, among the more affluent of the world, Riesman's inner-directed Self has become consumption- or other-directed, then, as the history has shown, it is necessary to make identity at least as much a social, as a psychological, attribute. But if, as many thoughtful conservatives argue, multiculturalism leads to the loss of individualism, then what is to become of the nation – of the social collective of whichever scale, and thus of politics in the sense of democracies of whichever kind? And if, to end a list that could go on endlessly, there is anything to the fact that the world is global in the sense that everyone, rich or poor, is exposed to necessity of travel or migration, to seeking refuge or appropriating marginal urban spaces as they gather on the edges of today's growing, southern tier mega metropolises, then what becomes of the state or the city or even the town as a territorial zone of security and citizenship, and thus of the protection of individuals from the ravages of the global fluctuations – whether economic deprivation or war and other insidious forms of violence?

At the very least, students of the Identity concept must respect the history of concept which has never for very long been a stable analytic category. Recalling William James's principle of a pure ego we must indeed have some way to know that we are the same today as we were yesterday. It is far from clear that waking up in globally standard furnished room in the local Hyatt hotel in Bishkek or the same refugee camp in Chad or on the same subway grate in any big city is a sufficient social basis for self-recognition. Never before in modern times has it been more true that $A = A$ cannot yield a singular from day to day. These, to be sure, are the absurd extremes of the social forms of identity, but they are the realities of the present situation which, by all measures, is more violent, less secure, more mobile, less human than the inventors of modern cultural values in the seventeenth and eighteenth centuries could have ever supposed. These realities are, even far worse than my parents who lived through the Depression and two world wars could have imagined. Yet, identity theory has always had to come to terms with social realities, even in the days when the bourgeois gentleman thought himself above all that. This is the actually quite sturdy historical resource upon which the study of the Identity concept can drawn for clues as to what to make of it in the future.

It is entirely possible that, beyond the troubles of fracturing identities, the ironic benefit will be a greater clarity of the elementary fact that in order to be an individual one has no choice but to act as if she were, say, not one but several beings at once. To try to be a pure ego is try to become an A that always equals itself – a true impossibility; hence, the Zero Signifier of self-identification is, for all intents and purposes, a deadly state of self affairs. Death may well be the final zero of all meanings of this kind, but in the short run to live as though one's interior and exterior circumstances are always at risk is to live life as it is. All grass withers; all life dies. But during the course of the days it may live, it must live in daytime and night, through sun and rain, and all the rest. It is not by accident that Donna Haraway's essay on fractured identities begins with a cyborg figure that affirms not just the border humans share with their own technologies but with their natural – which is to say, animal – beings. In one sense, the modern theory of identity was founded, however cryptically, on the strong theory that the human being is somehow special, superior to the rest of nature and this may be why it has been so deadly – always, as time went by, trying to cleanse the house of impure animals who are in fact our ancestors in the biological scheme of things.

If, in the course of our time we living beings may have, we let Life become the Zero Signifier instead of the death that is to come, then we, so to speak, can be One in a sense that reaches deep below the surface differences to find the common ground all creatures depend on to be, to live. That ground is not, nor could it ever have been, a pure ego or Self; but it does nurture a strong moral and practical ability to be a one among the many in the sisterhood of traveling life. Such a one – however odd it may seem to moderns who desire a pure identity – is not by any means morbid, nor is it foolish. When you stop to think of it the modern ideals of the pure ego were always, however loosely, mixed up with political programs to purify the race of lesser beings in a holocaust of vain social arrogance. We humanoids have nearly killed the air and waters. We have spoiled the good earth, as we have killed each other. War is indeed politics by another means, but we must consider what politics are if they have not been what Achille Mbembe has so aptly called necropolitics.

However you slice it, to live with a sense of ourselves comes down in the end to two possibilities. To live life as it comes to us, often dirty and always several or more; or to die prematurely. If the history of the last several centuries means anything at all, it is that as humans have sought a pure identity under the shelter of an ideology of human specialness, they (which is to say we) have lived all too violently with death in our hearts. If we slaughter the animals we eat without regard for our relation to them, then how much easier it would be to kill or maim our human neighbors. That is the truth of history. Identity theory must deal with it.

References

Anzaldúa, G. (1987) *Borderlands/La Frontera: The New Mestiza*. San Francisco: Spinsters/Aunt Lute Books.

Aristotle (n.d. [350 BCE]) *Nicomachean Ethics*. Internet Classics Archive Online: http://classics.mit.edu/Aristotle/nicomachaen.html.

Arnold, M. (1869) *Culture and Anarchy*. Project Gutenberg Original Edition. Online: www.gutenberg.org/cache/epub/4212/pg4212.html.

Augustine (1991 [400–420 CE]) *The Trinity*. Translated by Edmund Hill. Brooklyn: New City Press.

Beck, U., Giddens, A. and Lash, S. (1994) *Reflexive Modernization: Politics, Tradition and Aesthetics in the Modern Social Order*. Stanford, CA: Stanford University Press.

Beauvoir, S. de (1949) *The Second Sex*. New York: Knopf.

Butler, J. (1990) *Gender Trouble: Feminism and The Subversion of Identity*. New York: Routledge.

Chödrön, P. (2002) *The Places That Scare You: A Guide to Fearlessness in Difficult Times*. Boston: Shambhala.

Collins, P. (1990) *Black Feminist Thought: Knowledge, Consciousness, and the Politics of Empowerment*. New York: Routledge.

Cooley, C.H. (1902) *Human Nature and the Social Order*. New York: Scribner's.

Derrida, J. (1978 [1966]) "Structure, Sign and Play in the Discourse of the Human Sciences," in *Writing and Difference*. Translated by Alan Bass. Chicago: University of Chicago Press.

Du Bois, W.E.B. (1903) *The Souls of Black Folk*. Chicago: McClurg & Co.

Elliott, A. (2001) *Concepts of the Self*. Cambridge: Polity Press.

Elliott, A. and Lemert, C. (2006) *The New Individualism: The Emotional Costs of Globalization*. Revised edition. London: Routledge.

Erikson, E. (1963 [1950]) *Childhood and Society*. New York: W.W. Norton.

Freud, S. (1961 [1900]) *The Interpretation of Dreams*. Translated by James Strachey. New York: Basic Books.

Freud, S. (1959 [1921]) *Group Psychology and the Analysis of the Ego*. Translated by James Strachey. New York: W.W. Norton.

Freud, S. (1961 [1930]) *Civilization and Its Discontents*. Translated by James Strachey. New York: W.W. Norton.

Freud, S. (1949 [1940]) *An Outline of Psych-Analysis*. Translated by James Strachey. New York: W.W. Norton.

Goffman, E. (1956 [1959, revised US edition]) *Presentation of Self in Everyday Life*. New York: Anchor Books.

Goffman, E. (1963) *Stigma: Notes on the Management of Spoiled Identity*. New York: Simon and Schuster.

Haraway, D. (1991 [1985]) "A Manifesto for Cyborgs: Science, Technology, and Socialist Feminism in the 1980s", in *Simians, Cyborgs, and Women: The Reinvention of Nature*. New York: Routledge.

Harding, S. (1990) "Feminism, Science, and the Anti-enlightenment Critique", in L. Nicholson (ed.), *Feminism/Postmodernism*. New York: Routledge, 83–106.

Hartsock, N. (1983) "The Feminist Standpoint", in S. Harding and M. B. Hintikka (eds), *Discovering Reality*. Boston: D. Riedel Publishing Company, 283–310.

Horkheimer, M. and Adorno, T. (2001 [1944]) "The Culture Industry: Enlightenment as Mass Deception", in *The Dialectic of Enlightenment*. Translated by Edmund Jebhcott. Palo Alto, CA: Stanford University Press.

James, W. (1982 [1892]) *The Principles of Psychology*. Cambridge, MA: Harvard University Press.

Lorde, A. (1984 [1979]) "The Master's Tools Will Never Dismantle the Master's House", in *Sister Outside: Essays and Speeches*. Freedom, CA: Crossing Press.

Kierkegaard, S. (1941 [1848]) *Sickness Unto Death*. Princeton: Princeton University Press.

Mead, G.H. (1934 [1962]) *Mind, Self, and Society*. Edited by Charles Morris. Chicago: University of Chicago Press.

Plato (n.d. [360 BCE]) *The Republic*. Translated by B. Jowett. New York: The Modern Library.

Riesman, D. et al. (1950) *The Lonely Crowd: A Study of Changing American Character*. New Haven: Yale University Press.

Said, E. (1978) *Orientalism*. New York: Pantheon.

Simmel, G. (1971 [1903]) *Georg Simmel On Individuality and Social Forms*. Translated by Edward Shils; edited by Donald Levine. Chicago: University of Chicago Press.

Smith, D. (1974 [1990]) "Women's Experience as a Radical Critique of Sociology", in *Conceptual Practices of Power: A Feminist Sociology of Knowledge*. Boston, Northeastern University Press, 11–30.

Spivak, G.C. (1988) "Can the Subaltern Speak?" in C. Nelson and L. Grossberg (eds), *Marxism and the Interpretation of Culture*. Urbana, IL: University of Illinois Press, 271–313.

Taylor, C. (1989) *Sources of the Self: The Making of the Modern Identity*. Cambridge, MA: Harvard University Press.

Tocqueville, A. (1969 [1835]) *Democracy in America*. Translated by George Lawrence. New York: Anchor Books.

Trungpa, C. (2009) *The Truth of Suffering and the Path of Liberation*. Boston: Shambhala.

Wallerstein, I. (2004) *World-Systems Analysis: An Introduction*. Durham, NC: Duke University Press.

Weber. M. (1958 [1904–05]) *The Protestant Ethic and the Spirit of Capitalism*. Translated by Talcott Parsons. New York: Scribner's.

2

Feminism and identity

Ann Branaman

Historical and intellectual development of topic

In a basic sense, identity has always been a central issue for feminism. The nature of its significance and the degree of its centrality, however, has varied across each of the three "waves" of
feminism and among the many different feminist perspectives that have developed over the
latter part of the twentieth century. The primary, nearly exclusive, focus of first-wave feminism
in North America and Europe was equal rights for women; the identity issue at the heart of
early feminist struggle, if we could name it as such with a concept that had yet to be developed
in any of the senses commonly meant by contemporary scholars, was the matter of women's
identity as human and, therefore, their claim to human rights. Fundamental to this issue was
the question of women's sameness to or difference from men. This question entered into the
nineteenth-century struggle for equal rights, as it would again with the emergence of second-
wave feminism in the latter part of the twentieth century. Many nineteenth-century feminists focused on men's and women's common humanity and, while they advocated women's
development of virtues conventionally exclusive to men, argued that this common human
identity warranted the extension of human rights to women; other feminists of the era argued
that women were as fully human as men, although they emphasized women's distinctive (and,
in some respects, superior) traits and abilities and used these as an argument for why women
should be entrusted with responsibility equal to men's in matters of politics and property. But
while debate about human nature and natural differences between men and women surrounded
the struggle over women's rights in the nineteenth century, a self-conscious feminist interest in
"identity" would not emerge until the 1970s. At this time, the concept of "identity" emerged
as central to the social sciences and humanities; feminism was one of several social movements
that contributed to the rise of identity studies.

Second-wave feminism renewed the first-wave struggle for equal rights as well as the debate
over the extent and significance of sameness and difference between men and women: the
three major forms of second-wave feminism (liberal, Marxist/socialist, and radical) differed in
their relative emphasis on these issues. For some second-wave feminists, issues of identity were
no more important than they were for first-wave feminists. Second-wave liberal feminists, in
particular, focused on the removal of barriers to women's equality, including the division of

paid work into women's jobs and men's jobs, devaluation and low pay of women's jobs, women's primary responsibility for housework and childcare, the "glass ceiling" that limited women's advancement into top positions, limited procreative choice, and gendered socialization of children (Lorber 2010). Among these, only the liberal feminist opposition to gendered socialization of children focused on questions of identity, but it typically resolved the identity issue by making the case for the removal of normative pressure that caused most males and females to adopt narrowly "masculine" or "feminine" identities. An emerging liberal feminist psychology buttressed this argument by simultaneously exploring the ways in which gendered socialization was restrictive and sub-optimal for the psychological development of both males and females. Liberal feminists tended to be most concerned with gender *inequality* and focused on how gendered socialization limited women's opportunities for economic or political advancement; they encouraged women to resist (exclusive) self-identification with the narrow, devalued, and disempowering roles of wife, mother, and object of men's sexual desire, or, more generally, the subsuming of their own self-identities under those of their husbands and families (as was common among white middle-class heterosexual women in Europe and the United States).

Identity was not, at least at first, a central issue for Marxist and socialist feminisms. The focus of these perspectives was women's *work*: their largely invisible and unpaid work in the home, their low pay in paid work, and their role as a reserve army of industrial labor (Lorber 2010). But many Marxist and socialist feminists gradually extended Marx's analysis of class interests and class consciousness to an analysis of gender consciousness. Through this route, Marxist and socialist feminists became interested in matters of identity. Many Marxist-socialist feminists, reflecting the broader "cultural turn" in leftist thought, concluded that gendered oppression could not be eliminated by institutional change alone but additionally required transformation of identity. Their work on psychology, consciousness, and identity drew on the several of the key Frankfurt School theorists as well as the resurgence of interest in Antonio Gramsci's work and grappled with questions of consciousness and culture. Later, identity emerged as a central concept in standpoint feminism, a perspective rooted in the Marxian notion that consciousness reflects the material conditions of our lives as they exist in particular social-historical circumstances. This perspective argued that identities rooted in the experience of marginalization and subordination were potentially generative of a critical understanding of the workings of the systems of domination from which these identities emanate (Smith 1987; Hill Collins 1990).

In contrast to liberal feminism and Marxist/socialist feminisms, radical feminism began with a central focus on identity issues. Radical feminism came to be so called, in opposition to the reformism of second-wave liberal feminism, because of its position that the oppression of women by men was the most fundamental of all oppressions. Radical feminist theorists argued that this oppression was so entrenched in culture and social institutions that liberal reform could achieve nothing other than to permit some women entrance into institutions that would continue to operate according to masculine principles and values and to reinforce assumptions of masculine superiority. Whereas liberal feminists accepted the basic values of liberal, democratic societies but called for their extension to women, radical feminists called for a thorough re-evaluation of standards, values, assumptions, and identities that they argued were rooted in and supportive of masculine superiority and male domination. An influential school of radical feminism, designated by subsequent scholars as "cultural feminism" (Alcoff 1988), focused on the origins of masculine self-identity and its key role in gender inequality. They analyzed male domination as an attempt to control, exploit, devalue, and denigrate women and femininity rooted in male envy of women's vital life energies and the positive values inherent in femininity. Cultural feminism encouraged feminists to reclaim sexual difference and the feminine principles that had been culturally devalued, and to resist identification with dominant ideologies of the inferiority of women and femininity. Radical feminists believed that it was essential to challenge male domination in all its forms, within all social institutions, cultural belief systems, and particularly in sexuality, family relations, and personal identities.

The development of psychoanalytic-feminist perspectives in the 1970s and 1980s followed from and intensified feminist concern with understanding the formation of gendered identities and with how differences in men's and women's psychological development reflected and contributed to male domination and female submission. Some psychoanalytic-feminist theory, notably the work of Juliet Mitchell (Mitchell 1974), developed out of a Marxist-socialist feminist perspective following an emergent consensus that a psychologically oriented theory of gendered oppression was needed to complement the traditional Marxist-socialist emphasis on the economic arrangements of capitalism (Tong 2009). Other developments in psychoanalytic-feminist theory were more aligned with the cultural feminists' argument that male domination was rooted in male envy and possessiveness of women and femininity, and these drew upon psychoanalytic theory to understand the psychological basis for male domination. These strongly feminist psychoanalytic approaches joined existing critiques of gender analyses within psychoanalytic theory. Well prior to the emergence of second-wave feminism, Freudian psychoanalytic theory had been criticized by neo-Freudian psychoanalysts, most notably Alfred Adler, Karen Horney, and Clara Thompson, who viewed the development of distinct male and female gender identities as socially constructed rather than biologically determined. These critics argued that women's "neurosis" derived from their subordinate position within patriarchal societies; they also reinterpreted controversial Freudian ideas such as "penis envy" as symbolic of women's envy of the greater power and value that men enjoyed in patriarchal societies. While psychoanalytic theory was viewed with animosity by leading liberal and radical feminists, including especially Betty Friedan, Shulamith Firestone, and Kate Millett, because of its historical sexism and androcentric assumptions, other second-wave feminists followed the lead of Adler, Horney, and Thompson in appropriating psychoanalytic theory to develop an analysis of the socially constructed psychodynamics of the development of gendered and hierarchical identities. Psychoanalytic-feminist theories developed along at least two relatively distinct paths. One followed neo-Freudian relational theories and focused on understanding how differences in boys' and girls' early relational environments produced gendered personalities; the other borrowed heavily from Jacques Lacan and from post-structuralist thought in its focus on the ways in which language constructs sexual difference and on males' and females' different relationships to what Lacan called the "Symbolic Order."

As second-wave feminism developed in the 1960s and 1970s, tensions emerged over the question of the social identity of feminism's "woman." Despite significant diversity in the perspectives of second-wave feminists, critics alleged that they shared a common failure to speak to the experiences and interests of women who were not white, middle class, heterosexual, or citizens of countries of the global North. Multicultural, postcolonial and global feminisms emerged in the 1980s and 1990s, challenging earlier feminist assumptions that all women shared interests with other women *as women*, that gender-based oppression was the most fundamental form of oppression experienced by any women, or that feminism could be easily organized based on an assumption of a core common identity and set of interests among women. Accordingly, the initial focus of these post-second-wave feminisms centered on matters of identity, in particular the meaning of the identity "woman" and the implications of the multiple, intersecting identities based in experiences of marginalization and subordination. As these alternatives to second-wave feminism developed, though, some versions of postcolonial feminism and global feminism shifted their emphasis away from identity and to material deprivation. Although they argue that poverty matters far more than issues of identity to many women around the world, however, they continue to consider and critique the identity issue.

As the 1980s gave way to the 1990s, concurrent with the emergence of a strong critique of the premises of second-wave feminism by multicultural, postcolonial, and globally oriented feminists, new forms of feminist theory emerged that were equally critical of the second wave but from a perspective on identity shaped by post-structural and postmodern social thought. Although many feminists were suspicious initially of the potentially de-politicizing implications of the post-structural and postmodernist critique of identity, most recognized an affinity with postmodernists' critique of "essentialism," its deconstruction of the universality of the modern Western conception of "man," and its critique of the binary, hierarchical oppositions (e.g., man/woman, reason/emotion, culture/nature) that structure modern Western thought. The thought of Michel Foucault served especially as a focal point for feminist debate about subjectivity and identity, with some adopting Foucault's view of identity as social control and advocating an "anti-identity" position, while others resisted what they viewed as the politically enervating effects of the wholesale critique of the "subject" characteristic of post-structuralist and postmodern thought. Postmodern feminism extended cultural feminists' challenge to the universality of the modern, Western conception of man by additionally challenging the universality of the concept of "woman" and the feminist political projects associated with it; like multicultural, postcolonial, and global feminists, postmodern feminists emphasized differences *among* women based on race, class, ethnicity, nationality, sexuality, and differences in the intersection of these and other social and personal differences. Postmodern feminists called for the repudiation of essentialist conceptions of identity within feminism, which they argued reflected the experiences of privileged white Western women as much as the Enlightenment conception of man had reflected the ideals of privileged white Western men. In the terminology of Donna Haraway (1991), postmodern feminists called for the recognition of "fractured identities" and for political coalitions representing diverse interests rather than a singular feminist project dominated by the experiences and goals of privileged women. Postmodern feminists drew upon the postmodernist critique of identity to challenge the idea of gendered identities as being stable, inner, and core, emphasizing instead the fluid, transient, multiple, and contradictory nature of identities. Although there are many different postmodern feminist positions on the question of the sorts of identification most compatible with feminist goals of social and personal transformation, most have agreed on the importance of the challenge to the hegemony of the modern, Western, masculine ideal and the necessity of a critique of essentialist conceptions of "woman."

Analysts disagree on the meaning and/or appropriate designation for the most current wave of feminism, with some using the term "third-wave feminism" and others "post-feminism"; there is, however, general agreement that the nature of feminism has been significantly transformed in the decades following the heyday of second-wave feminism in the 1970s and early 1980s. Third-wave feminisms and post-feminisms have been heavily influenced by the postmodern critique of identity and multicultural, postcolonial, global feminist emphases on differences among women. They resist normative standards defining the meaning of the "good feminist" and of what women *should* want (Tong 2009), adopting the position that there are no inherent commonalities in the interests and experiences of women and that the "politics" of feminism should consist solely in defending individual women's rights to define themselves and their desires in any way that they see fit. This stance has been called post-feminism by some because of its refusal to define a feminist identity or, as some would argue, to draw normative distinctions between feminist and anti-feminist patterns of identification. Some view post-feminism as a non-feminism because it seems to give implicit support to the claim that gender-based domination, restrictive barriers linked to gender, and prescriptions for appropriate identities for men and women no longer exist; some critics argue that post-feminism is a profoundly neoliberal ideology, advocating individual responsibility for constructing one's own self-identity according to one's own independently defined desires and interests and in the absence of or irrespective of any structural or cultural constraints. Others, however, view post-feminism as compatible with the overall aims of feminism, insofar as it advocates increased power and self-determination for girls and women; according to this position, post-feminism does not require a naïve belief in gender's irrelevance as a basis for structuring, still to male advantage, men's and women's opportunities.

Major claims, developments, contributions

From the beginning of second-wave feminism in the early 1970s to the present, feminist claims about identity have been complex and contested. Feminist theorists have developed critiques of dominant, masculinist conceptualizations of self-identity and have proposed alternative feminist ways of thinking about the self; they have analyzed male domination and female subordination as formative of women's and men's identities and have theorized various processes by which gender identities are produced; they have theorized avenues by which women might resist subordination and transform identities that inhibit women's agency; they have analyzed how gender intersects with other sources of identity and debated how best to engage a broadly inclusive feminist politics; they have assessed the implications of changes in gender expectations and relations that have occurred in recent decades; and they have continued a long tradition of disagreeing over the appropriate goals of and strategies for feminist (or post-feminist) politics. A significant impetus for debate on some of these issues and for criticism of the conceptions of many of the prominent feminist theorists of the 1970s and 1980s was the emerging awareness of important differences between women – based on class, race, ethnicity, nationality, religion, geographic location, sexuality, (dis)-ability, or any difference that caused significant variation in life experience and interests among women. Another important source of debates in feminist theory was closely linked to debates within social and political thought, as feminist theories developed out of or in relationship to an array of competing perspectives in social theory.

Feminist perspectives on self-identity

One important contribution of feminist theory to identity studies has been the exploration of normative questions about the values inherent in dominant conceptions of masculinity, femininity, and humanity; in different ways, feminist scholars have challenged the assumed virtues of masculinity and have posed alternative visions of identity, subjectivity, or selfhood as more compatible with feminist politics and values.

As second-wave feminism developed in the 1970s and 1980s, a key point of contention was the question of what sort of identity women *should* want. Three major positions on this question emerged. The first position, adopted by earlier feminists such as Mary Wollstonecraft in the eighteenth century and Simone de Beauvoir in the middle of the twentieth century, was to advocate that women claim their autonomy and subjectivity as defined by Western Enlightenment thought. Wollstonecraft and de Beauvoir were contemptuous of femininity constructed according to the dominant standards of their day, viewing women who adhered to these ideals and norms as lacking in human virtue or, in de Beauvoir's words, "mutilated" and "immanent" (1953). Shortly after the emergence of second-wave feminism in the 1970s, though, cultural feminist theory began to move feminist theory away from its relatively uncritical adoption of these prevailing and presumably masculine ideals of self-development.

A second position on identity emerged out of the cultural feminist project of challenging the presumed superiority of masculinity over femininity; cultural feminists focused attention on the positive values and attributes associated with femininity and developed by women even in the context of their subordinate roles. Instead of encouraging women to renounce caretaking roles as wives, mothers, nurses, pre-school teachers, or in any of a number of jobs usually performed by women and involving service to the needs of others, cultural feminists called for recognition of the value of and the skill and competence inherent in the nurturance and caretaking women provide. Challenging Lawrence Kohlberg's claim that women were usually incapable of advanced moral reasoning, psychologist Carol Gilligan (1982) famously argued that women only seemed to be morally inferior to men if one assumed, as Kohlberg did, that adherence to abstract principles was the highest form of moral reasoning. Women, Gilligan argued, had a *different but equally admirable* approach, considering the particularities of actors and the circumstances they faced when making moral judgments about behavior. Kohlberg *defined* this as an inferior form of moral reasoning, but Gilligan argued that there was no defensible basis for concluding that it was a lesser moral position. Gilligan's work played a particularly significant role in the larger cultural feminist project of reclaiming the value of attributes associated with women and femininity.

A third position developed out of criticisms of the cultural feminists. Critics identified a tendency for cultural feminists to uncritically valorize stereotypical feminine attributes and behaviors and uncritically accept all women's identities as inherently worthy of positive recognition. So, rejecting both the uncritical acceptance of a masculine standard and an equally uncritical embrace of the feminine status quo, the emergent position necessarily subjected dominant conceptions of *both* masculinity and femininity to careful critique, recognizing valuable components of each but shifting attention to the ways in which the *gender system*, the binary and hierarchical opposition between masculinity and femininity and structured inequalities of power between men and women, produces contradictions and distortions in the development of gendered identities.

An early example of this third position is represented by psychologist Jean Baker Miller's *Towards a New Psychology of Women* (1976). In this work, she systematically outlined the positive worth of qualities, attributes, and behaviors associated with femininity and women's roles and challenged the dominant tendency to devalue and denigrate many of these; in addition, though, she also analyzed how many of these potentially valuable qualities could become distorted and harmful when developed from a position of subordination. Caretaking, for example, is a highly valuable and admirable skill that had been culturally devalued through its association with the feminine. While Miller argued that it should be revalued, she also argued that it could be distorted when practiced by a person whose emotional development had been stunted and damaged by subordination: under such circumstances, it could devolve into the projection of one's own denied and unrealized needs onto the object of care, resulting in a failure to respond empathically to the needs of the person to whom care is directed. Miller similarly subjected masculinity to systematic critique, showing how attributes associated with masculinity were, in some common manifestations, unworthy of the valorization they had received. She distinguished between valuable and harmful manifestations of several masculine attributes, showing how the hierarchical gender system systematically distorted potentially valuable attributes into harmful and anti-social forms. Although Miller's work was influential among feminist psychologists and broadly popular, her work was not all that influential among second-wave feminist theorists, likely because her work initially was misconstrued as aligned with the early argument that gender roles harmed both males and females. Nonetheless, her work is one of the early attempts by feminist theorists to illuminate the limitations of uncritical valorization or devaluation of masculine or feminine qualities.

This third position is manifested in contemporary feminist theorizing in which scholars pose alternative visions of identity, subjectivity, or selfhood that they measure against feminist politics and ideals. In departure from 1970s cultural feminism, these more contemporary visions do not seek to reverse the masculine–feminine hierarchy of values, but instead attempt to break out of the hierarchical gender system with a wide variety of alternative concepts of identity they provide. Although feminist theorists have hardly reached consensus on the worthiness of various alternative visions of identity, subjectivity, and selfhood, the key points of the feminist critique of dominant Western and masculinist concepts of self is a broadly shared position among feminists.

Meyers (2010) identifies the Kantian subject and *homo economicus* as the two key dimensions of Western post-Enlightenment conceptions of selfhood. Building on a large body of feminist work on this topic, Meyers argues that these models of selfhood portray *male* subjectivity as the highest form of human subjectivity. In other words, these models elevate the Kantian moral subject who exercises independent judgment through the use of abstract, rational principles and the rational economic actor, *homo economicus*, who makes rational decisions in order to maximize self-interest in the marketplace, over "lower" forms of subjectivity that lack rationality or autonomy. Meyers argues that these dominant models not only imply male superiority by defining stereotypically masculine styles of thinking as the highest form of human subjectivity, but they are also fictional in their characterization of human subjectivity. Summarizing major themes of feminist critique, Meyers (2010) argues that these dominant models of selfhood:

1   deny the rootedness of subjectivity in personal relationships and unchosen circumstances;
2   ignore the ways in which subjectivity is shaped by the intersection of multiple social identities, such as gender, race, nationality, age, or sexual orientation;
3   assume that structural domination does not penetrate the "inner citadel" of selfhood;
4   assume the transparency of the self to the gaze of its possessor, the immunity of the self to noxious influences, and the reliability of reason as a corrective to distorted moral judgments;
5   deny internal diversity and conflict within selves;
6   assume self-sufficiency and absence of responsibilities to others with emphasis on the self's capacity for independence and planning;
7   fail to take into account internalized oppression and the process of overcoming it.

One of the key contributions of feminist theory, particularly in the 1970s and early 1980s, was its critique of Western, masculinist models of self-development and the positing of alternate models that paid more attention to relational capacities, empathy, care, interdependence, emotional expressiveness, vulnerability, and other attributes associated with women's roles and cultural expectations of femininity. Irrespective of later criticism of these perspectives for uncritically valorizing women and femininity, never again would there be a credible feminist, or *any*, conceptualization of self that would deny the inherent rootedness of the self in relationships and the enormous value of relational skills long associated with women's roles and cultural standards of femininity.

But even if there was widespread agreement on these basic points, there was hardly agreement on the conceptualization of self that should replace those widely agreed to be lacking in merit. One debate among feminist scholars concerned the question of whether conceiving "self" or "identity" as an integrated and unified whole was inherently repressive, denying internal complexity and validating a form of self-policing that would make it difficult to struggle toward freedom from oppressive standards. On one side, some postmodern feminists, including feminist scholars influenced by Foucault, followed Foucault's line of argument and made the case that "self" or "identity" was inherently repressive; the quest to attain a unified sense of self only solidified the power of the dominant patriarchal discourse, so resistance could be achieved only by breaking with the idea of self or identity. Other feminist theorists, some influenced by their work as psychoanalysts or psychologists, argued that the absence of a core sense of self is an excruciatingly painful experience indicative of a severe level of psychological damage; it could not be a viable feminist strategy for resisting male domination.

Acceptance of the necessity of the self, though, opened the question of how to create a feminist self. A feminist conceptualization must, on the one hand, make sense of the myriad ways in which consciousness is distorted, selves are harmed, or domination or subordination internalized as individuals establish and maintain gendered identities but, simultaneously, make sense of the desire and ability to resist the internalization of dominant identity models, critically reflect on the internal contradictions between competing bases of identity, act as agents in choosing selves or in creatively constructing their own self-identities, and acknowledge people's ability to transform their self-identities. Yet another line of feminist theorizing, rooted in critical theory, cautioned against seemingly widespread tendencies among feminist theorists to dismiss the ideal of autonomy as an inherently masculinist concept that denied the fundamental rootedness of identity in relationships; instead, theorists such as Jessica Benjamin (1988, 1995) and Allison Weir (1996) have developed conceptualizations of "autonomy" and "intersubjectivity" as complementary rather than contradictory ideals.

Conceptualizing the formation of gendered identities

Although the claim is not unique to feminism, one of the most basic ideas of feminism is that gendered identity is not natural or inevitable but is socially constructed. As Simone de Beauvoir (1953) famously put it, "Woman is made, not born." This idea has largely been taken for granted among feminist theorists, although a few in the radical feminist tradition have embraced some biologically essentialist elements. In general, though, the key differences among feminist theorists come in the ways in which they conceptualize the processes by which gendered identities are formed.

Feminist psychology began from a liberal feminist perspective and has emphasized the role of culture, societal structures, and sex-linked behavioral and emotional norms in producing characteristic "masculine" and "feminine" identities in men and women. In the 1970s and 1980s, research focused on parental socialization of children, identifying both overt and subtle differences in how parents socialized boys and girls such that boys came to internalize a masculine identity and girls a feminine identity. A predominant theme that emerged from this research was that rigid expectations for masculinity in boys and femininity in girls limited the development of both. Rigid expectations for males to be masculine and to avoid qualities associated with femininity, it was argued, limited males' ability to express a range of emotions, to empathize with others' experience, and to develop satisfying emotional intimacy in their relationships; it also tended to result in a preoccupation with power, dominance, and superiority, which, in some cases, manifested in uncontrolled aggression resulting in self-harm and violence to others, intolerance of vulnerability, and a tendency to denigrate women and femininity. Conversely, rigid expectations for femininity were equally, if not more, limiting for girls and women, causing them to have less self-confidence, a weaker sense of independence, lack of an achievement orientation, an excessive preoccupation with meeting male-defined standards of feminine attractiveness, and an emphasis on meeting the needs of others that often resulted in subordination and self-abnegation. In the 1970s, a predominant ideal espoused by feminist psychologists was the ideal of androgyny; building on empirical research, feminist psychologists argued that both males and females were psychologically and socially better adjusted if they incorporated the positive aspects of both masculinity and femininity into their personalities.

Psychological research on the damaging developmental consequences of sex-typed socialization, and the promotion of the ideal of androgyny, quickly drew criticism from feminists who argued that the perspective minimized the relationship between gender *difference* and gender *inequality*. Many feminists thought that such perspectives downplayed the benefits that men obtain, and the disadvantages suffered by women, as a result of sex-typed socialization; males and females were not, it was argued, equal victims of rigid sex-typed socialization, with men as damaged as much by expectations of invulnerability, for example, as women were by expectations for meeting exacting standards of physical attractiveness or for putting the needs of others above their own. Masculine identity, it was argued, offered men power; feminine identity, conversely, led to the subordination and objectification of women.

Not only was psychological research criticized for its neglect of the link between gender difference and gender inequality, but it was also criticized in several other ways as well. Two of these lines of criticism led to alternative ways of thinking about the formation of gendered identities. On the one hand, psychoanalytically oriented feminist perspectives argued that psychologists' preoccupation with sex-role socialization was too superficial in its understanding of how children come to internalize gendered identities. The acquisition of gendered self-identity was not so much a matter of sex-role training, that is, teaching children to behave according to cultural expectations of sex-appropriateness, but rather involved deeper, more unconscious, differences in the ways parents related to and identified with their children depending on the child's sex. An equally damning but completely alternative line of criticism came out of post-structuralist social theory and sociological theory and research. This criticism alleged that the psychological perspective was wrong to assume that gendered identities were deeply rooted in the personality. Critics argued that gendered identity was only as stable as the power and pervasiveness of societal structures and cultural norms that dictated the continual enactment of gendered identities in everyday social life.

Psychoanalytic feminism

Arguably one of the most significant developments in feminist theorizing of identity was the development of psychoanalytic-feminist theories in the 1970s and 1980s. Following the publication of Juliet Mitchell's *Psychoanalysis and Feminism* (1974), which called upon feminists to take Freudian psychoanalytic theory seriously as a theory of the development of masculinity and femininity in modern patriarchal societies, psychoanalytic-feminist theorizing developed along two seemingly divergent paths: one, represented by Nancy Chodorow and Jessica Benjamin, explained how masculinity and femininity were deeply inscribed in persons' psyches as a consequence of the complex emotional dynamics of the relationship between parents and children during infancy and early childhood; the other, represented by Luce Irigiray and Julia Kristeva, shared the premise that masculinity and femininity were deeply inscribed in persons' psyches during infancy and early childhood but explained this instead as a consequence of the acquisition of language and culture by which all human subjectivity is formed.

Nancy Chodorow's classic *The Reproduction of Mothering: Psychoanalysis and the Sociology of Gender* (1978) was one of the most significant contributions among psychoanalytic feminist theories rooted in "object-relations" psychoanalytic theory, a perspective that built on the ideas of neo-Freudian theorists such as D.W. Winnicott, John Bowlby, and others who shifted away from the classical Freudian focus on instinctual drives to an emphasis on the early relationship between the infant/child and primary caretaker(s) as formative of identity. Chodorow's basic argument was that women's role as primary caretaker of infants and small children produces a tendency for girls to develop personalities rooted centrally in relationships to others and a tendency for boys' personalities to be marked more by an emphasis on independence, power, and success. In her view, there are a number of differences in how parents (and especially mothers) relate to girls and boys that contribute to this basic difference in personality development. First, mothers tend to identify with girls more than they do with boys, while they are more likely to experience boys as sexual others. Because of her greater identification with the girl as well as the decreased likelihood of the mother–daughter bond being perceived as incestuous or threatening to the father, the mother allows the female child to remain in the symbiotic bond of infancy longer than she does the male child. In families characterized by the mid-twentieth century's conventional middle-class male breadwinner/female homemaker family form, the development of masculine identity occurs largely in the absence of the kind of real relationship to the father that the girl has with the mother. Insofar as both boys and girls develop their primary senses of self in relationship to their usually female primary caretaker, boys learn to define masculinity as that which is "not feminine," as separation from the mother, as independence, and in terms of an often idealized image of the father's and men's attributes and roles in society. Hence, the boy moves toward the glorification of the father and of masculinity and the promise of "having" a mother/wife when he attains the independence, power, and achievement of his father or other adult men. For both boys and girls, the mother (or other primary caretaker) is the first and most powerful love object; the girl, in contrast to the boy, learns that she may never *have* (the presumed heterosexual) mother but, through her mother's identification with her, that she may *be* like her. Both men and women are motivated, usually unconsciously, throughout their lives to recreate the intensity of the symbiotic mother–child bond of early infancy. Whereas the boy struggles to gain autonomy, power, and success in an unconscious effort to live up to the masculine ideal that will allow him to "win" the mother, the girl recreates the mother–infant unity vicariously through mothering and nurturance of others, usually husband and children.

A decade later, Jessica Benjamin published other work in this line of feminist theorizing, including *The Bonds of Love: Psychoanalysis, Feminism, and the Problem of Domination* (1988) and, later, *Like Subjects, Love Objects: Essays on Recognition and Sexual Difference* (1995). Like Chodorow, Benjamin's work is heavily rooted in neo-Freudian object relations theories; Benjamin relies heavily on Chodorow's theory, in fact, to develop her own theory. In contrast to Chodorow, though, Benjamin shifts from explaining the reproduction of gendered personalities to explaining the psychodynamics of domination and subordination in relationships. *Recognition*, or intersubjectivity, is the term Benjamin uses to characterize relationships between two people in which both are able to recognize the other as an independent subject, identifying with the other while at the same time acknowledging their difference. To be able to relate to other human beings as equals, Benjamin argues, requires most importantly that the developing baby/child learns to see its mother as an independent subject with needs and desires of her own. Failure to recognize the subjectivity of the mother, in her view, impedes our ability to see others in the world as equals (Benjamin 1995).

In Benjamin's analysis, domination and submission are relational orientations that express not inequalities of positive attributes and resources but rather an obstruction of mutuality built upon denial of the subjectivity of oneself or the other. Domination and submission result, she argues, when there is a "breakdown of the necessary tension between self-assertion and mutual recognition that allows self and other to meet as sovereign equals" (1988: 12). Patterns of domination or submission are attempts to get either recognition of self or connection to the other when integration of both seems impossible. Benjamin showed that both domination and

submission ultimately fail to gain either recognition or connection. On the side of the dominant, recognition of the other is necessary to give meaning to the other's recognition of oneself;
though illusions of such can be temporarily sustained, achievement of meaningful recognition
by others is ultimately impossible without recognizing the independent subjectivity of others.
On the side of the subordinate, the subordinate who sacrifices the drive for recognition of self
in order to gain connection to the dominant other renders oneself inessential and risks loss of
the connection to the dominant other for this reason. According to Benjamin's analysis, neither
domination nor submission can achieve even their one-sided purposes of gaining recognition or
connection; mutual recognition is necessary for both but is denied in relations of dominance and
subordination. Even as Benjamin argues that domination and submission ultimately fail to produce fulfilling relationships, however, Benjamin suggests that such patterns are widely prevalent
in our culture and are fostered by heterosexual gender complementarity. Despite the illusions
upon which they rest and the dissatisfactions they may cause, both dominants and subordinates
gain some compensation through sustaining such relationships.

Given a breakdown in mutual recognition and connection in the relation between self and
other – a breakdown which Benjamin suggests happens frequently in our culture in the early
relation between parent and child – domination is a compensatory way of establishing differentiation from the other. Domination entails differentiating from the other not by recognizing the
independent subjectivity of the other but rather by denying the independent subjectivity of the
other. Masculinity, according to Benjamin's analysis, is achieved by disavowal and repudiation
of femininity (p. 164). Independence, according to the culturally dominant male model, means
establishing difference, power, and control in relation to the devalued maternal object (p. 78)
– an illusory independence that ultimately backfires or at least requires continual defensive work
to maintain. The contradiction produced by defining independence and male superiority on the
basis of disavowal of femininity is that such a disavowal mean dis-identification with that which
was satisfying and fulfilling in relation to the mother and creates a sense of helpless dependence
on the maternal object (p. 174). In reaction to this helpless dependence on the mother outside
themselves, according to Benjamin, men attempt to do without her or to dominate her (p.
174).

In addition to serving the function of establishing a defensive sense of differentiation, domination also allows the subject to maintain control over a source of drive satisfaction. Domination
makes for a sense of differentiation or independence from the devalued object, but it is only an
illusion of such (since the other is not given up as a source of drive satisfaction.) Not only does
domination entail using the other as a source of drive satisfaction, but also using the other as a
negative pole against which one's independence, superiority, and power are defined. The position of domination does produce some dissatisfaction – for example, loneliness in not having a
person recognized as an independent person with whom to relate, an underlying sense of threat
at the possibility of the emergence of the independent subjectivity of the subordinate, a diver-
sion of energy into defensive functions – and is ultimately contradictory. As long as masculinity
depends on disavowal of femininity and dis-identification with the valued maternal capacities
of tenderness and holding, the mother remains the only source of goodness. Yet, at the same
time, reduction of her to an extension of self or object of drive satisfaction risks using her up;
similarly, defensive idealization of autonomous individuality, rationality, self-sufficiency, competition negates the value of alternative orientations associated with the mother so thoroughly
that needed maternal resources are experienced as worthless (pp. 205–6).

Although ultimately less satisfying than mutual recognition might be, domination does serve
the compensatory functions of sustaining a sense of power, independence, and value as well as
maintaining a stable source of drive satisfaction. The distorted nature of domination is expressed

in this contradiction: "wanting to devalue and control the other while still drawing sustenance from her, wanting to keep mother in captivity and yet alive and strong" (p. 8). The recognition of the independent subjectivity of the other, in fact, is necessary both to give meaning to the other's recognition of oneself and to give emotional meaning to the connection with the other.

Chodorow's work had been criticized for its apparent argument that, because gendered personalities emerged from particular childrearing systems, the solution to gendered personalities – and the inequality that they reproduced – lay in a particular arrangement of mixed-sex shared parenting. In Benjamin's account, though, what are more important to destabilizing the gender system than the particular family arrangements are the patterns of love and identification that characterize early parent–child relations. Current patterns build masters and slaves, so a new pattern is needed. For Benjamin the new patterns must permit both male and female children to establish a deep sense of connection with adult caregivers, while also giving them the means to differentiate from those caregivers and develop agency as autonomous subjects. The foundation for this alternative pattern occurs in both the pre-oedipal and oedipal phases of development in relationship to mothers, fathers, or other primary caretakers. The key to subverting the system of gendered domination and subordination, or at least the avoidance of rigidity as children recognize sexual difference during the oedipal period, is for the developing child to be able to recognize mothers, fathers, and themselves as "love objects" and "like subjects."

Across the Atlantic and contemporaneously, other scholars were engaged in a seemingly very different mode of psychoanalytically oriented feminist theorizing, one rooted in the psychoanalytic theory of French psychoanalyst Jacques Lacan. Luce Irigaray and Julia Kristeva, two of the most influential contributors, differed from Chodorow and Benjamin in their emphasis, following Lacan, on the formation of subjectivity via internalization of language and culture rather than the actual relationships of a child's early life. They viewed the development of identity as a process by which children emerge from the symbiotic unity of the early relationship between mother and infant. This process was possible only by the child's entrance into the patriarchal "Symbolic Order." But because the Symbolic Order was thoroughly patriarchal, only boys and men were able to fully establish subjectivity within it. The subjectivity of girls and women could never be as fully developed and absolute, not only because patriarchal discourse constructs the woman as other to the male subject, but also because girls and women were more likely to maintain intra-psychic connection to the preverbal semiotic realm of the mother–infant symbiosis.

Irigiray argued that women in Western culture have been associated with "nature" and "matter" in contrast to men's association with "culture" and "subjectivity"; further, *all* women are defined fundamentally by the role "mother." Irigaray saw women's position in Western culture as Beauvoir had: men are subjects; women are "other." Psychoanalytic theory and Western philosophy, she argues, are two influential discourses that deny women autonomous subjectivity and portray them as lacking in mature subjectivity. The only possibility for a woman to assume a subject position, she argued, was by assimilating to male subjectivity, transcending nature and entering culture. Irigaray argued that there was no separate subject position for women; insofar as women assume masculine subject positions, however, they reinforce the hierarchical opposition between culture and nature and mind and body and, by association, between men and masculinity and women and femininity. Consistent with her rootedness in post-structural social theory, Irigiray found these oppositions untenable. She believed that both men and women would have to reconfigure their subjectivity in such a manner as to reflect their understanding of themselves as equally nature and culture (Donovan 2005). Departing from Lacan's view of the Symbolic Order as fixed, unified, and a-historical, Irigiray believed that a different Symbolic

Order could be constructed, one that allowed *real* sexual difference by allowing subject positions that women could assume without renouncing everything associated with women and femininity.

According to Kristeva, women can use their less complete entrance into the Symbolic Order as the basis for their intra-psychic resistance to the patriarchal order. So, in direct opposition to de Beauvoir, who urged women to assert their own subjectivity over and against the subjectivity of others, Irigiray and Kristeva urge women to tap the power of the semiotic, preverbal relational realm to which they have privileged access and from which they can counter the dominance of patriarchal logic and principles. In *Revolution in Poetic Language* (Kristeva 1984), Kristeva had established the ground for thinking that the patriarchal order is never as stable as a more determinist Lacanian account would have it. In this work, Kristeva rejects the structuralist view of language as fixed and homogenous, constructed on the basis of a unitary social order. For Kristeva, subjectivity is constituted on the basis of both symbolic and semiotic dimensions of experience; even as the patriarchal social order attempts to marginalize the semiotic, subjectivity cannot ever be absolutely divorced from the unconsciousness processes, heterogenous drives, and maternal power associated with semiotic experience. The Kristevan subject is inherently a "subject-in-process" – structured by the Symbolic but at the same time, by virtue of the semiotic experience from which it cannot detach itself, subversive of it. In patriarchal society, however, cultural myths and male ideals of power serve to relegate semiotic experience (and women who are associated with it) to a marginal position. Subjectivity in patriarchal society becomes a matter of striving to achieve autonomy from semiotic experience – from heterogeneous drives and from the early experience of relation to the mother. The political problem, for Kristeva, is to recover these marginalized experiences – for example, experiences of abjection, melancholy, foreignness – in such a way that they can provide a basis for creative resistance (Elliot 1991). Because the semiotic can only exert creative power through the mediation of symbolic experience, however, Kristeva suggests that it may be up to men – who have achieved a more stable position within the Symbolic Order – to experience a crisis in their own system of meaning and to then seek reinfusion of subjectivity with semiotic experience. Even so, Kristeva found a basis of resistance to the patriarchal order within women's own experience of marginality.

In *Black Sun* (Kristeva 1989), Kristeva suggests a creativity inherent in women's depression – a depression which stems not only from failure to identify with a meaning outside, but also from the failure to find sustenance in the loveless maternal bond. Kristeva suggests that depression is a powerful affect and source of integration that allows the subject to resist the emptiness of the Symbolic Order and to create outside of it. In depression, a woman experiences the meaninglessness of the order outside herself. She attempts to create in herself integrity apart from the outside world. Depression is her support – although a negative one – that makes up for her failure to be validated within the outside world (p. 19). In other words, she constantly utters "that's meaningless" when invited to take up an identification in a world she knows to exclude her most fundamental desires (p. 19). In her depression, she refuses to lose until she has been compensated for her loss (p. 5); an identification with male ideals in a patriarchal order which denies her, severs her from the maternal power with which she identifies, is no compensation. Kristeva characterizes depression as "the imprint of a humankind that is surely not triumphant but subtle, ready to fight, and creative" (p. 22).

Kristeva argues, in *Black Sun* as in other works, that creation out of depression is possible only by identification with a third party – with the father and/or with language (p. 23). The function of psychoanalysis, as she sees it, is to provide the missing identification – this time one that provides a real compensation for her early loss – that makes it possible to move out of the deadening mother–child fusion. But, does this make the psychoanalyst the new bearer of patriarchal law? Kristeva does not think so. Patriarchy maintains itself by excluding the desires which emanate from experience of primal loss, and with it women's power. Instead of being another – but more deceptive – political discourse which mobilizes our energies into exclusive identifications, psychoanalysis can work only by joining the power of our heterogeneous experience with language. Psychoanalytic interpretation points to the unpredictable elements of human existence, those which resist incorporation by a unitary system of meaning; yet it does not leave them in a politically inert state of meaninglessness but attempts to approach them and bring them into thought and language in a way that renders them meaningful and effective (Kristeva and Waller 1982).

Foucauldian feminist theories of identity

As seemingly different from one another as were the two versions of psychoanalytic-feminist theories, both shared the assumption that gendered identity was deeply rooted in the human psyche and that its explanation revolved around the development of the self in the early years of life. A very different line of feminist theorizing of identity, however, drew on the work of Michel Foucault and departed from the interior focus of psychoanalytic-feminist theory by developing a far more exterior analysis of institutionalized practices in everyday life as the basis for gendered identities. Sandra Bartky and Judith Butler are two well-known feminist theorists who have drawn on the ideas of Foucault to develop theories of gendered identity.

Bartky draws upon Foucault's analysis of the construction of self-identity through discipline and surveillance, extending Foucault's emphasis on practices more characteristic of the lives of men to an analysis of a distinct set of bodily practices central to the construction of femininity. Bartky (1990) analyzes the "techniques" or disciplinary practices that produce the feminine body, distinguishing three categories: "1) those that aim to produce a body of a certain size and general configuration; 2) those that bring forth from this body a specific repertoire of gestures, postures, and movements; and 3) those directed toward the display of this body as an ornamented surface" (p. 65). These disciplinary practices, she argues, profoundly shape female identity and subjectivity, representing a "modernization of patriarchal power." Bartky argues that patriarchal standards of bodily acceptability become "internalized" by nearly all women, causing women to see themselves as bodily beings from the perspective of a generalized male witness. But, following Foucault, Bartky argues that this internalization of patriarchal power cannot be understood simply as repressive or disempowering, but that it also "can provide the individual upon whom it is imposed with a sense of mastery as well as a secure sense of identity" (p. 77). To challenge the patriarchal construction of the female body, Bartky argues, threatens women with deskilling, denying the worth of the vast array of skills required by these bodily disciplines and with a loss of identity tied to a sense of competence in the performance of these bodily disciplines. Most crucially, the abandonment of these bodily disciplines may threaten the individual's sense of herself as a person at all, since having a "feminine" body is crucial to most women's sense of self.

Following a parallel line of Foucauldian reasoning, with the publication of *Gender Trouble* in 1990, Judith Butler established herself as one of, if not *the*, most influential contemporary feminist identity theorists. Butler's main contribution was her theorization of gender, sex and sexuality as *performative*. In her view, if masculinity or femininity appears in men and women to be natural or "core," this is only because men and women repeatedly enact masculinity or femininity in their bodily stylization. For Butler, this is anything but a voluntary choice; "regulative discourses," "frameworks of intelligibility," and "disciplinary regimes" dictate the range of acceptable stylized acts and coerce individuals to maintain the appearance of having a "core" gendered identity. Butler challenges Chodorow's theory of the development of gender identity, arguing that gendered identities are neither "internalized" nor as fixed, coherent, and uncontradictory as Chodorow's account suggests. She argues that children of both sexes identify with both men and women, not only in their early relationships to their primary parents but also to a wide array of other people and idealized images of masculinity and femininity.

Sociological perspectives on gender and identity

The idea that gender is something that a person *does* rather than something a person *is* has a somewhat longer history in sociological theory and research than in general social theory. Coming from the interactionist and ethnomethodological traditions in sociology, West and Zimmerman (1987) famously developed the concept "doing gender," a concept similar in its most basic concept to Butler's performative theory of gender. In this classic work, they argued that gender was *not* a set of internal traits but rather was something that people do in their everyday interactions and social relationships. The routine "doing" (i.e., performing) of gender in everyday life creates the appearance of essential differences between men and women. Interestingly, Erving Goffman had argued essentially the same point in *Gender Advertisements* and "The theory of the relations between the sexes." Because Goffman was an outsider to feminism, though, his work on gender identity was not widely recognized within the feminist literature. His ideas, however, greatly influenced West and Zimmerman's conceptualization of what it meant to "do" gender.

In sociology, West's and Zimmerman's concept "doing gender" has become foundational; sociologists working from other traditions of sociological theory and research have contributed in various ways to advancing the notion that gender is an enactment rather than a set of internal traits. Barbara Risman (1987), for example, employed the "microstructural" perspective in sociology to demonstrate the inaccuracy of common assumptions about differences in women's and men's abilities to care for and nurture small children. In her study of men who had become the primary caretaker of their children following desertion by or death of the mother, she found that the men often surprised themselves with the development of seemingly new, more feminine, *traits* as they took on the job of primary caretaker for the children. Risman concluded that the widespread belief in women's superior nurturing and caretaking capacities was supported by the widespread expectations that women *should* provide nurturing and caretaking. When situational expectations changed, as they did in the study for the men who had newly assumed the role of primary caretaker (a role that carries expectations of *maternal* care), men's maternal capacities turned out to have equaled those of female mothers. The "doing gender" concept has become the dominant understanding of gender among feminist sociologists; rather than conceptualizing gender as deeply rooted in individual psyche, sociologists tend to see gender as rooted in social positions and expectations.

Criticisms

Feminist theorizing of identity is anything but a "normal science." There are seemingly irreconcilable differences in certain core assumptions. Some see identity as deeply rooted in the psyche, while others view identity as an externally mandated everyday performance. Some hold the establishment of a coherent, authentic, and autonomous identity to be a desirable human outcome, while others are equally convinced that gender can only be toppled by an assault on the integrated self. Some emphasize the importance of a person's relational biography in constructing self-identity, while others place far greater emphasis on culture, language, and discourse. Although the lines of these disagreements are clearly drawn in the arena of feminist theory, one of the hallmarks of that arena is that the disagreements lack ferocity. While these may have been hotly contested issues in past decades as feminism struggled for *its* identity, they hardly seem so contentious now. The most prevalent view among the vast array of scholars in the area, however, seems to be to accept that each of the competing perspectives on these core questions provide valuable but partial insight.

Basic points of agreement have emerged out of dialogue among feminist theorists of varying perspectives; mostly, feminist theorists have come to a consensus on the validity of a set of criticisms that had been directed against earlier feminist work on identity Three major criticisms of these earlier feminist theories of identity are widely accepted by contemporary theorists:

1   The early theories are essentialist and exclusionary in their failure to carefully think through the implications of diversity among women for theorizing identity and for conceiving a non-essentialist, non-exclusionary feminist politics.
2   The early theories are misguided in their focus on identity and neglectful of structural, institutional, and material dimensions of gender inequality.
3   The early theories are overly deterministic, incapable of making sense of women's agency and resistance to dominant identity frameworks.

While there is little agreement about which earlier theorists were most misguided or which current theorists persist in these errors, there is broad agreement that the set of criticisms directed against earlier work are serious charges that future work should confront.

The charge of essentialism and failure to think through the implications of diversity among women for theorizing identity and for developing a broadly inclusive political agenda is one that nearly all Western feminists have taken very seriously. Among contemporary feminist theorists, Chodorow's work exemplifies better than any other the problem of essentialism in early second-wave feminist theory. Chodorow's work, critics contend, make a number of problematic essentialist assumptions: the universality or at least widespread prevalence of the male breadwinner/female homemaker white middle-class family form; heterosexuality; coherent, unified gendered identities; and seamless reproduction of distinct gendered identities and roles. Critics have questioned how such a theory could make sense of the formation of gendered identities in the context of an array of diverse family forms that depart from these assumptions. Chodorow and other second-wave feminists have responded to these criticisms and have attempted to move away from theorizing the formation of gendered identities as a generic process and from the view of the child's early relational context as necessarily the most important determinant of identity development. In more recent work, for example, Chodorow (1995) develops a theory of gendered identity as a cultural and personal construct. Because of Chodorow's role as exemplar of the pitfalls of essentialism, however, the prevailing tendency among contemporary feminist theorists is to dismiss this entire line of relational psychoanalytic-feminist theorizing. Even if one of the costs of the essentialism charge was to foreclose or stall some lines of feminist theorizing that had yet the opportunity to mature, the charge of essentialism has been generally productive; it has led to a broadening of feminist dialogue across class, race, nationality, culture, sexual orientation, or other social differences. And it has also led to critical reflection on the implications of multiple, intersecting social identities on an individual's sense of self-identity as well as on feminist conceptions of the shared experiences and political interests of women.

The charge that feminist theorists' focus on identity is misguided is not one feminist theorists of identity would readily accept; their continued analysis of such matters belies this point of view. Nonetheless, most feminist theorists, including those whose work has focused heavily on identity issues, take seriously what they hear as a warning to keep in focus those sorts of things that were important to both liberal and Marxist-socialist feminists in the 1970s and that are important to postcolonial and global feminists in the present: material needs, work issues, and the vast array of institutional barriers to the achievement of gender equality. Judith Butler's work, for example, has been heavily criticized by feminist theorists with a more materialist orientation for her seemingly exclusive focus on culture and discourse as constitutive of gendered identities and for her seemingly trivializing portrayal of "drag" and other forms of stylistic gender non-conformity as viable strategies for the subversion of gender. Nancy Fraser's classic essay "From redistribution to recognition?" (Fraser 1997) best summarizes what has become, arguably, the prevailing view among feminist theorists of identity: material redistribution and identity recognition are *both* important projects in the quest for social justice and are, in many instances, fundamentally related and mutually determinative.

Finally, the charge of determinism has been directed toward nearly all of the major feminist theories of the social construction of gendered identities. This is hardly surprising, since the primary aim of these theories was to explain the persistence of gendered identities and the relationship of them to gender inequality. Nonetheless, feminist theorizing of agency and resistance in the 1990s responded to this charge by shifting from explaining the structuring of identity by the male-dominant/female-subordinate gender system to theorizing women's agency and resistance. This theorizing of agency and resistance proceeded in at least a few different directions. Among psychoanalytically oriented feminist theorists, one avenue involved theorizing the internal contradictions, distortions, and intra-psychic pressure that might provide the impetus, *if* appropriately interpreted, for women to resist domination and/or for men to relinquish their dominant subject positions. In each of the theories considered here, there is variation in the relative emphasis on theorizing of resistance and agency in comparison to the emphasis on explaining how masculinity and femininity, domination and subordination, and male superiority and female inferiority become intra-psychically established. Of the four, Chodorow's theory was considered most determinist because it seemed to suggest that the construction of gendered identities was a seamless and self-perpetuating process and underplayed the ways in which these identities were fraught with contradictions and distortions, even though a thorough reading of her work reveals that she too recognized these. At least some part of the appeal of French post-structuralist psychoanalytic-feminist theories as North American and British feminists began reading translations of this work in the 1980s and 1990s was that they seemed to attribute an intra- psychic basis of resistance to and subversion of the patriarchal Symbolic Order.

Among Foucauldian/feminist theorists, debate about resistance and agency formed the basis of a division between at least a couple different varieties of Foucauldian-feminism. One version of Foucauldian feminism, exemplified by Bartky and Susan Bordo (Bordo 1993), drew upon Foucault's analyses of discipline and surveillance to develop an analysis of the disciplinary project of femininity, focusing on the techniques of bodily transformation women readily learn and perform to establish femininity. Bartky and Bordo were heavily criticized by other feminist theorists for portraying women as passive robots who willingly succumb to the forces of discipline, always striving to more closely approximate idealized images of femininity. Critics contend that women have a range of reasons and desires for dieting, exercising, or other work on their bodies and that it is simplistic to reduce it all to an imposed effect of disciplinary power (McLaughlin 2003). A very different version of Foucauldian-feminism draws upon Foucault's ideas about power and resistance to theorize possibilities for women's resistance to gendered power relations. Foucault's conceptualization of power, these theorists argue, departs from more typical understandings that define some people or groups as *having* power and others as *lacking* power; according to Foucault's conceptualization, power is inherently relational and is played out in many forms in everyday social relations (Sawicki 1991). For Foucault, power is all-pervasive, extending through what he called "capillaries" of power into all aspects of people's everyday lives; because power is relational and active, however, there are an abundance of opportunities for everyday resistance to gendered power relations.

Another line of feminist theorizing about agency stems from feminist efforts to understand gendered identities in the context of what several non-feminist social theorists have designated as the post-traditional era. Following the movements of the late 1960s and early 1970s and the rapidly increasing rate of female labor force participation that began also in the 1970s, the "traditional" (1950s–1960s) roles of men and women that formed the basis for second-wave feminist theories of male domination and female subordination had become far less pervasive than theories such as Chodorow's had suggested. Some argued that it no longer made sense to conceptualize gendered identities in terms of domination and subordination; others argued that gender had become far more fluid and flexible, with men and women far less constrained by gender norms in their development of self-identity. Some theorists of de-traditionalization, reflexive modernity, or individualization had argued that gender no longer weighed heavily at all as a determinant of a person's identity, that it had become largely irrelevant as both constraint and basis of inequality. Recent feminist work on identity (e.g., Adkins 2002) has engaged with these theories; while dismissing the notion of gender's supposed irrelevance, this work attempts to conceptualize the formation and enactment of gendered identities in ways that take into account the implications of the changes associated with the idea of post-traditionalism.

References

Adkins, L. (2002) *Revisions: gender and sexuality in late modernity*. Buckingham, UK and Philadelphia: Open University Press.

Alcoff, L. (1988) "Cultural feminism versus post-structuralism: the identity crisis in feminist theory," *Signs* 13(3): 405–36.

Bartky, S.L. (1990) *Femininity and Domination: studies in the phenomenology of oppression*. New York: Routledge.

Beauvoir, S. de (1953) *The Second Sex*. New York: Knopf.

Benjamin, J. (1988) *The Bonds of Love: psychoanalysis, feminism, and the problem of domination*. New York: Pantheon Books.

Benjamin, J. (1995) *Like Subjects, Love Objects: essays on recognition and sexual difference*. New Haven: Yale University Press.

Bordo, S. (1993) *Unbearable Weight: feminism, Western culture, and the body*. Berkeley: University of California Press.

Butler, J. (1990) *Gender Trouble: feminism and the subversion of identity*. New York: Routledge.

Chodorow, N. (1978) *The Reproduction of Mothering: psychoanalysis and the sociology of gender*. Berkeley: University of California Press.

Chodorow, N.J. (1995) "Gender as a personal and cultural construction," *Signs* 20(3): 516–44.

Donovan, S.K. (2005) "Luce Irigiray (1932–present)," *Internet Encyclopedia of Philosophy*. Online: www.iep.utm.edu/irigaray.

Elliot, P. (1991) *From Mastery to Analysis: theories of gender in psychoanalytic feminism*. Ithaca, NY: Cornell University Press.

Fraser, N. (1997) "From redistribution to recognition?" in *Justice Interruptus: critical reflections on the "postsocialist" condition*. New York: Routledge, 11–40.

Gilligan, C. (1982) *In a Different Voice: psychological theory and women's development*. Cambridge, MA: Harvard University Press.

Haraway, D. (1991) "A cyborg manifesto: science, technology, and socialist-feminism in the late twentieth century," in *Simians, Cyborgs, and Women: The Reinvention of Nature*. New York: Routledge, 149–81.

Hill Collins, P. (1990) *Black Feminist Thought: knowledge, consciousness, and the politics of empowerment*. Boston: Unwin Hyman.

Kristeva, J. (1984) *Revolution in Poetic Language*. New York: Columbia University Press.

Kristeva, J. (1989) *Black Sun: depression and melancholia*. New York: Columbia University Press.

Kristeva, J. and Waller, M. (1982) "Psychoanalysis and the Polis," *Critical Inquiry* 9(1): 77–92.

Lorber, J. (2010) *Gender Inequality: feminist theories and politics*. New York: Oxford University Press.

McLaughlin, J. (2003) *Feminist Social and Political Theory: contemporary debates and dialogues*. Basingstoke, Hampshire, and New York: Palgrave Macmillan.

Meyers, D.T. (2010) "Feminist perspectives on the self," *Stanford Encyclopedia of Philosophy*. Online: http://plato.stanford.edu/entries/feminism-self/.

Miller, J.B. (1976) *Toward a New Psychology of Women*. Boston: Beacon Press.

Mitchell, J. (1974) *Psychoanalysis and Feminism*. New York: Pantheon Books.

Risman, B.J. (1987) "Intimate relationships from a microstructural perspective: men who mother," *Gender and Society* 1(1): 6–32.

Sawicki, J. (1991) *Disciplining Foucault: feminism, power, and the body*. New York: Routledge.

Smith, D.E. (1987) *The Everyday World as Problematic: a feminist sociology*. Boston: Northeastern University Press.

Tong, R. (2009) *Feminist Thought: a more comprehensive introduction*. Boulder, CO: Westview Press.

Weir, A. (1996) *Sacrificial Logics: feminist theory and the critique of identity*. New York: Routledge.

West, C. and Zimmerman, D. (1987) "Doing gender," *Gender and Society* 1(2): 125–51.

3

Identity after psychoanalysis[1]

Stephen Frosh

Historical and intellectual development

If identity is one of the most hotly contested aspects of the post-structuralist and postmodern era, then psychoanalysis, which might be expected to have much to say about identity, is equally polymorphous and contentious. Both are clearly *constructs* – the former as a way of characterising the experience of drawing together the elements of a subject (of a life, one might say) to create an 'essence', a core of consciously recognisable selfhood that defines the situation of a subject as a certain kind of being. Psychoanalysis, too, is a construct, nowadays (actually, for a very long time) hard to consider as a 'science', but more thinkable as a narrative or discourse – a way of articulating the subject under the conditions of modernity, as a place in which the criss-crossing vectors of various forces (desire, wish, language, otherness) collide. Psychoanalysis deals with the materialisation of the subject into language, quintessentially in the consulting room where patient meets analyst, but also *theoretically*, as a structure within which the subject is interrogated and interpreted. As such, it should have much to say about identity, because in its own way it confers identity *onto* the subject. That is, people come to know themselves largely *through* psychoanalysis, which provides key notions used to make sense of the experience of being subjects. What is 'identity' here? Something that has to do with how we cope with having an unconscious life that we can be at variance with (so that disturbances of identity are possible), having a private internal arena that others do not necessarily know (hiding one's identity), having a capacity for narcissistic masquerade, lying to oneself, being mis-recognised, losing any sense of one's boundaries when, for example one is in a crowd. Without psychoanalytic concepts it would be significantly harder to think each of these things, to discuss how one's identity is under attack, or how one's sense of belonging can emerge, or what it might mean to say that one is in search of one's self, trying to find an identity that makes sense.

Yet, there is rather little, at least in classical psychoanalysis, that deals with the notion of 'identity' as commonly understood. As noted elsewhere (Frosh 2010), Freud himself seems only once to have used the term in the social psychological sense of belonging to something that gives rootedness to one's life, and this in a distinctly personal comment. In a letter written on the occasion of his seventieth birthday to the Vienna Bnai Brith, the Jewish 'lodge' which had sheltered him when he felt rejected by the medical society of Vienna in the late 1890s, Freud tries to give an account of what had drawn him to this organisation, of what it was that had made him feel at home amongst his fellow Jews. Rejecting the possibility that it might have anything to do with religious or Zionist belief, he comments:

> But plenty of other things remained over to make the attraction of Jewry and Jews irresist-ible – many obscure emotional forces, which were the more powerful the less they could be expressed in words, as well as a clear consciousness of inner identity, the safe privacy of a common mental construction.
>
> *(Freud 1926: 273–4)*

The 'safe privacy of a common mental construction' is a nice phrase when linked to the notion of 'inner' identity, because it connects this 'internal' world with the external one, with the positioning of the subject in a social nexus with others with whom he or she might identify. Freud is claiming that there is something automatic, something received, familiar and 'safe', in his contact with other Jews, and that this derives from a common 'mental construction', a way of thinking, a cognitive or unconscious framework, which allows immediate understanding of each other to come about. The bond is not that of shared belief (neither Judaism nor Zionism), but of a commonality of mental structure that allows things to be easily understood, that signi-fies familiarity and belonging. Erik Erikson, in his most important paper on identity, reads this quotation as evidence that identity is necessarily tied up with the social environment, that 'It is the identity of something in the individual's core with an essential aspect of a group's inner coherence which is under consideration here' (1956: 57). Certainly this is the gist of Freud's comment: in his 'core' he is aligned with his social group, the Jews (and misaligned with the rest of his society, it seems). But this does not seem adequately to capture the subtlety of what it might mean to have an 'inner identity', nor does it flag up its problems, so we must seek further than this.

What is distinctive about a psychoanalytic approach to identities is the main subject of this chapter, but the question of what it might mean to frame this as 'identity *after* psychoanalysis' is worth addressing at the start. 'After' suggests something has passed, as if psychoanalysis has come and gone and we are now in another of those 'post-' periods with which the contemporary social scene is saturated (post-structuralism, postcolonialism, postmodernism). In certain respects this is true. Psychoanalysis is well past its clinical heyday, suffering badly from criticisms con-cerning elitism and its failure to provide a convincing evidence base for its interventions; and if there is a continuing profligacy of psychoanalytic publications, it is not necessarily in the sphere either of the clinic or of direct studies of identity that its creativity can be observed. One could therefore say that we are 'after' psychoanalysis in the sense of a clinical discipline with recognis-able autonomy and standing. However, there is also a continuing and variegated use of psy-choanalysis, often drifting a long way from its origins into work 'outside the clinic' that makes some considerable assumptions about the transmissibility of concepts such as the unconscious, transference or repression into the social field. This work suggests psychoanalysis continues to be as source of intrigue and fertile speculation, drawn on by social scientists and others who are on the whole outsiders to the institutions of psychoanalysis, but somehow are seduced into it and see it as having something important to offer to their work. In this sense, we are 'after' psychoanalysis: psychoanalysis has happened, and whether or not it remains in force in the same way that it did half a century ago, it has changed the landscape irretrievably.

As noted above, however, the question of 'after' goes further than this acknowledgement of its effects on scholarship in the social sciences and humanities. This has to do with the issue of 'reflexivity', which emphasises the effects on, and of, knowledge arising from the meaning-making activities of human subjects. At its most mundane this produces a requirement within the social sciences that the investments and actions of the researcher are included in the scrutiny of the research process (Frosh and Baraitser 2008). However, of potentially greater significance for discussions of the legacy of psychoanalysis on identities is the way in which human subjects utilise social knowledge as part of their lived experience of accounting for themselves – something the 'discursive turn' in the social sciences has revealed very compellingly (e.g. Potter and Wetherell 1987). In the case of psychoanalysis, which has saturated Western culture to a degree matched by very few other intellectual systems, 'after' means that people make use of routine modes of broadly psychoanalytic understanding when accounting for their own and others' actions (Parker 1997). These include, notably, the motivated nature of human action, the importance of early childhood experiences and the existence of wishes and impulses of which individuals themselves may have little awareness. If one is thinking about 'identity' as a constructive process in which a sense of inner coherence is achieved through piecing together aspects of a subject's experience, then this kind of utilisation of the meaning-making resources made available in a culture will be an activity of central importance. That is, the lens on identity offered by psychoanalysis is inescapable, even if particular subjects resist it: every identity judgement is made in its wake. The main idea here is that *we cannot know ourselves*; translated into the terms of identity, this means that our identities may be striven towards, but not ever fully achieved. Even a particular subject's complacent refutation of this notion, her or his claim to fully inhabit a particular identity, has to happen in the light of what psychoanalysis suggests is the alternative. 'I am what I am' is, indeed, how the Bible conveys God's distinctiveness from His human subjects (Exodus 3, verse 14), perhaps recognising what would be required for someone to adopt a truly secure identity position. It is not only psychoanalysis that has revealed this, of course (presumably the Bible was not written by a psychoanalyst), but psychoanalysis is one 'hegemonic discourse' feeding into people's self-constructions, and even creating the identity positions that are available to them. The Romantic ideas of 'child as father to the man', of affective complexity and of motivational depth controlling the surface of behaviour, are drawn together in psychoanalysis and distributed so thoroughly within Western culture that no self-constructive process by its subjects can escape their influence.

Psychoanalysis has, as a matter of necessity as well as choice, transformed itself since its early days, in ways which again have considerable significance for identity studies. The key moves here have been from the drive model deployed by Freud to a now dominant relational model, though this move has been neither smooth nor total. As has been described in numerous writings (e.g. Frosh 1999), there are considerable variations to be found in the assumptions, emphases and formulations of differing approaches – all of which would call themselves psychoanalytic. Some of these reflect significant differences of theory and practice amongst adherents of different schools of thought. In fact, some critics of psychoanalysis have used this variability to pour scorn on psychoanalytic claims in general: 'the existence of assorted orthodox, deviant, neo-, and post-Freudian schools that all regard themselves as psychoanalytic points unmistakably to an absence, within the movement at large, of any clear path connecting facts to suppositions' (Crews 1995: 19). In itself, however, this variability is to be expected, given the accidents of choice of analysts' own analysts, of the school of thought in which they become immersed through training or reading, and perhaps particularly of the individual cultural circumstances making one or other analytic position fashionable. Putting this in a positive light, the close relationship between the specific problematic experiences with which people are engaged at any one time, the kinds of patients who come to analysis, and the development of new psychoanalytic theories, can perhaps be seen as testimony to psychoanalysis' capacity to remain open to the pressures and alterations at work in the surrounding culture. Freud was dealing with a situation primarily of repression, in which sexual and aggressive urges were constrained until they could be held in check no longer, and then burst out destructively across Europe; his 'depth model' of the psyche reflects this in a highly evocative way. Post-Second World War analysts, on the other hand, have been dealing more with a culture in which the major difficulties – which can certainly be termed difficulties of identity – lie in the formation of rewarding *relationships*, which means that interest has been focused on the necessary psychic conditions that make this possible. Thus, clinical concern has moved largely away from hysteria, obsessive-compulsive neurosis and phobias understood as failures of repression, and more towards narcissism, borderline states and melancholy, which can be seen as disorders organised around relational disturbances and loss (Frosh 1991). This leads additionally to an interest in 'otherness' (e.g. Laplanche 1999; Butler 2005), which asks what it is about the so-called psychoanalytic 'object' that infects the subject through processes of identification and internalisation, shaping and constructing personal as well as social identities.

Because of the developing interest in relationality, the clarity of differentiation between the various schools of psychoanalysis seems to have become less apparent in recent years. In fact, as I have previously noted (Frosh 2006: 18), 'To a considerable degree, all the mainstream psychoanalytic schools, including those in the U.S.A., have turned their attention to what is best termed "intersubjectivity" – the ways in which mental representations of relationships are formed and the effects these have on the development and actual social relationships of individuals.' Intersubjectivist theory builds upon object relations theory with its emphasis on the relational capacities of the human subject, but spotlights the question of *recognition*, of appreciating, accepting and relating to others as 'like subjects' (Benjamin 1995). Its language of objects, of representations, of 'inner worlds' in which relational constructs dominate, and of 'intersubjectivity' to reference particularly the interweaving of the 'subjective worlds of child and caregiver or of patient and analyst' (Stolorow 2006: 250), is now central to the vocabulary of psychoanalysts of all persuasions. Stolorow comments (ibid.: 250), 'Recognition of intersubjectivity does not entail adherence to or rejection of any specific psychodynamic theory. In fact, acceptance of the foundational significance of intersubjectivity enables therapists to employ the various psychodynamic concepts with greater discrimination and effectiveness.' This might not actually be completely true, with the Lacanians coming in as an exception to this generalisation. Nevertheless, outside Lacanian thought, it is fairly hard to find any contemporary psychoanalyst who does not accord central significance to object relationships, even if they differ on many other aspects of theory or practice. Included in this is the notion that 'bridging' difference is key; that is, that the task is to find ways to link with others, to translate their needs and one's own into something that can form the basis for relationships that can be mutually fulfilling. The self consequently can be seen to arise out of a process of recognising the intentionality and agency of the loved other and identifying with this. This idea emphasises people's active agency in their lives, as well as directing theory and research towards the infant's incipient self and in so doing communicating the significance and centrality of the appreciation of other people's minds – an issue that has been taken up in much Anglo-American developmental psychoanalysis (Fonagy and Target 1996).

As in many other things, Lacanians are an exception to the relational trend. Although this is not the place to develop the Lacanian position in any detail, it is worth holding in mind their rigorous critique of object relational ideas. This is not because they deny the importance of social relationships, but rather because they are antagonistic to the idea that mature relationships are possible in any straightforward sense – or that knowledge of another, that is, intersubjectivity, is an achievable state of human affairs. For Lacanians, all interpersonal relationships, and indeed the structure of the individual human subject as well, are penetrated by cultural and social forces with distorting and obscuring effects. It is therefore not possible to achieve unmediated knowledge of the other of a kind that could give rise to the types of resolved, reciprocal relationships postulated by object relations theorists and often taken as a loose yardstick of mental health. Moreover, Lacanians suggest that even in the intimate and intense encounter of the psychoanalyst with the patient, something interferes with the capacity of either protagonist to understand or recognise the other. Intersubjectivity even here is blocked by some other feature – the limits of language, the structure of authority, the impossibility of being fully at one with any other person.

Major claims and developments

This set of issues surrounding relationality, otherness and alienation reflect importantly on the psychoanalytic contribution to identity studies. Here, there are a number of key concepts at play. The first is simply that of the dynamic unconscious, perhaps the single idea that actually binds together psychoanalysts of all the different schools. The core notion is very well known (e.g. Frosh 2002) and probably does not require amplification here; it is hopefully sufficient to note its very radical nature. First, postulation of a dynamic unconscious that runs through the subject is also a claim about the impossibility of an identity based on an integrated self. In making behaviour comprehensible only through reference to a site other than consciousness, a site which is hidden yet still 'internal' to the person, Freud argues that behind the experience that we may have of ourselves as coherent psychological beings there exists a basic split in the psyche. We may think we choose what to say, select what to do (the 'we' here being our conscious, articulated selves), but in fact our choices are constrained and determined by forces which lie outside of conscious control or easy access. Second, Freud's description of the unconscious is an *explanatory* account, claiming to tell us what causes our behaviour and how and why these causes become hidden. Unconscious wishes are disturbing, so they are kept repressed; this means that they continue to operate, but are not controlled (or at least are not *fully* controlled) by the ego. Psychoanalysis thus challenges the view that the distinguishing mark of humanity is reason and rationality, arguing instead that the human 'essence' lies in unacceptable and hence repressed impulses towards sexuality and aggression. As Freud himself noted, this represents an attack on the narcissism of the individual because it displaces each one of us from the centre of our own agency, proving 'to the ego that it is not even master in its own house, but must content itself with scanty information of what is going on unconsciously in its mind' (Freud 1917: 285). Psychoanalysis insists on there being always something else speaking *in the place of the subject*, which means that there may be a fantasy of coherent identity, but it is undermined, dispersed, even mocked by the relentless pressure that comes from unconscious life. It is as if the human subject is plugged into something else that gives it its energy 'from outside', yet presents the fiction that this comes from within. Identity thus becomes an *artifice*, giving leverage to those who are interested in how it is developed, and what alternative truths it might hide.

Within this general framework of disruption of claims for integrated identities, psychoanalysis might crudely be thought of as offering three general strands of commentary on the construct of identity, loosely implicit in different psychoanalytic models. These are:

* ego identity as mastery (ego psychology);
* identity as relational accomplishment (object relations, Kleinian and intersubjectivist theory);
* identity deconstruction (Lacanian theory).

Each of these can only be dealt with briefly here, but it is worth teasing out some of the most significant claims that they make.

Ego identity as mastery

Ego psychology has been under strong criticism in the last twenty years or so, and has as a consequence lost its position of unquestioned dominance in the American psychoanalytic world, and has had its influence reduced elsewhere (Frosh 1999). In Britain, major adherents of Anna Freud's approach have become enamoured of attachment theory, cognitive extensions of psychoanalysis through 'mentalisation', and neuropsychology (e.g. Fonagy and Target 2007; Allen and Fonagy 2006). The classical focus on drives and the analysis of the ego can be seen at work in a diffuse way in this. For example, mentalisation, which concerns the ability to imagine others' mental and emotional states, is a concept that includes unconscious levels of functioning but focuses more strongly on capacities that can be made conscious and are more like cognitions than phantasy states. As implied above, the shift to a more relational stance in psychoanalysis has affected ego psychology very greatly in the USA, where the influence of self psychology and the growth of the relational and intersubjectivist movement has been very marked. This has also brought about a slight rapprochement between object relational and Anna Freudian analysts in the UK.

Despite this watering down of ego psychological orthodoxies, there remain some important issues in relation to identities. The first concerns the emphasis on closely observed development throughout the span of childhood, not just in early infancy. For example, Anna Freud's own tendency to think of child development in terms of 'basic interactions between id and ego' (1966: 59) produced the concept of developmental lines: sequences in which particular aspects of personality gradually unfold, always from a position of relative dominance by the id to relative control by the ego. Thus, even though numerous different developmental lines can be described (for instance, from infantile sucking to organised eating, from wetting and soiling to bladder control and bowel control, or from erotic play to work), they all follow the same path: 'In every instance they trace the child's gradual outgrowing of dependent, irrational, id- and object-determined attitudes to an increasing mastery of his internal and external world' (ibid.: 60). The notion of developmental lines has proved to be an important addition to the psychoanalytic vocabulary. Descriptively, its assumption of continuities in development moves the theory away from the traditional Freudian concentration on fixations and regressions – that is, it is not so reliant on the idea that there is an undiluted retention of the past in everything that happens throughout life. Regressions do occur; in fact, they are predictable consequences of stress. However, the thrust of development is cumulative: at every point, the child is shifting along a graduated course, each step produced by past steps and by the current state of the drives and the environment. This approach has considerable practical utility; for instance, making it possible to offer guidance on particular children's developmental problems. It also presents a fuller psychological account of development than is possible from the pathology- and drive-oriented approach of Freud himself. In relation to identity formation, it suggests the gradual coming together of cognitive and social competencies attuned to unconscious drives and their implication in networks of social relationship. It thus has something to say both to studies of personal identity and to those which focus on identity as a phenomenon of group adaptation.

It is in the ego psychological work of Erik Erikson that the most extensive psychoanalytic discussion of identity can be found. This work has been much criticised both from within psychoanalysis, where it has often been regarded as more social-psychological than properly psychoanalytic (e.g. Jacobson 1964), and as normative in its implications that somehow each subject 'must' adapt to the surrounding culture (Frosh 1999). There is something to be said for both these criticisms, which flow from the way in which the developmental history that Erikson produces is one firmly centred on the ego: how the individual struggles with the issues presented at each stage of the life cycle and makes sense out of experience. That said, however, there is much that is of interest in the Eriksonian account, and it looks as though a slight revaluation of his work has been going on in both psychoanalytic and psychosocial circles (e.g. Wallerstein 1998). As described elsewhere (Frosh 2010), Erikson's (1956) discussion of 'ego–identity' is particularly interesting as an attempt to account for identity in its various registers: as a conscious state of personal self-naming; as a relationship to the social environment; and as an unconscious process of striving. He writes: 'At one time . . . it will appear to refer to a conscious *sense of individual identity*; at another to an unconscious striving for a *continuity of personal character*; and, finally, as a maintenance of an inner *solidarity* with a group's ideals and identity' (ibid.: 57). It is also a process that is never completed, but instead comes to the fore at all those moments where the individual (developmental) needs of the subject interface with the culture in which she or he lives; at those moments, what matters is *both* that the individual is responsive to the culture *and* that the culture recognises the individual for what she or he truly can become.

> From a genetic point of view, the process of identity formation emerges as an *evolving configuration* – a configuration which is gradually established by successive ego syntheses and resyntheses throughout childhood; it is a configuration gradually integrating *constitutional givens, idiosyncratic libidinal needs, favored capacities, significant identifications, effective defences, successful sublimations, and consistent roles.*
>
> *(ibid.: 71)*

In Erikson's formulation, cultural considerations, particularly as revealed in differing child-rearing techniques, influence the manner in which common problems such as autonomy and separation or the generative demands of adulthood are coped with, with the crucial issue being the extent to which each individual can absorb the available cultural values and internalise them to produce a set of ego functions that are at one with the surrounding society. Mental health is basically a product of successful adaptation to culture or, rather, a successful use of cultural resources to enable integration of the ego as a centre of a coherent personal identity.

Erikson's focus on process across the lifespan has proved to be a productive one for social psychological researchers; and if its limitation lies with the assumption of a fundamentally benevolent environment which can make identity flower, it is not naïve. Indeed, one might suggest that implicit in it is a critique of totalitarian and other societies which are at odds with the identity needs of their subjects. That is, it poses a question about failures of identity-formation that may not be reducible to individual pathologies of adjustment. This might also connect with an element of ego psychology that is only slowly being reclaimed from the over-generalised complaint about its conformist characteristics. It is true that the focus on the ego leads to an over-reliance on rationality and hence a neglect of what might be thought of as the true core of psychoanalysis – its appreciation of the way in which irrationality operates at the heart of the human subject. However, the impulse to work in this way, to turn one's back on the irrational, arose in part from the particular conditions of post-Second World War society, with its appreciation of the enormous costs of the outburst of irrationality represented by Nazism. The aspiration to articulate a model based on the mutual support of a balanced identity with a reasonable and tolerant society was not necessarily totally misguided, even if it also produced a blindness towards ways in which such liberalism could itself be mis-used.

The point here is that the impulse to mastery to be found in ego psychology speaks quite powerfully to a familiar aspect of identity: that it is a way of drawing together heterogeneous forces and impulses in the subject and her or his environment, and making of them some kind of integrated, rational whole. This has benefits, but it also has drawbacks; specifically, it allows one to conceptualise identity as a process of overcoming of splits and deficiencies, but it also produces a model of covering-over of antagonism which may miss the more profound insight psychoanalysis offers, which is that splits and contradictions are of the very essence of subject-hood.

Identity as relational accomplishment

The second broad group of psychoanalytic positions can be gathered together in what is here termed the 'relational' school of thought. This is a very large grouping with some significant differences between sub-groups – for example, some of the American 'intersubjectivists' are highly critical of Kleinian approaches to clinical work. Thus, Benjamin (2004: 35), echoing a long tradition of British debates between Kleinians and their more environmentally oriented object relations colleagues, objects to what she sees as the Kleinian analysts' refusal to become relationally involved with the patient, and their insistence 'that the patient is ultimately helped only by understanding rather than by being understood'. What she is referencing here is a question about how 'real' the analyst can be to the patient, how active a presence in the treatment. Nevertheless, everyone in this group, from object relations theorists and Kleinians in Britain, through to the interpersonal and intersubjectivist analysts in the United States, is united by adherence to a model postulating that *relationality* is the primary concern of psychoanalysis, and also the major motivational and explanatory concept to be used both in clinical work and in broader theorising involving psychoanalysis. Psychoanalysis from this perspective involves a focus on the quality of the contact between analyst and patient as a way of addressing uncon-scious features of the patient's relational practices. How such unconscious features are theorised and exactly how psychoanalysis addresses them varies considerably. For example, Kleinians focus on 'inner world' features of the patient, understood to be built up out of a complex mix-ture of psychological drives and relationships with internal 'objects' (crudely, representations of people or parts of people). For them, the way in which unconscious phantasies attached to objects operate within the patient is demonstrated through transference-countertransference exchanges in therapy, and the analyst's task is to utilise these exchanges to help the patient recognise and work through the conflicts produced by these phantasies (Frosh 1999). In the context of identity, the Kleinian perspective is one in which the early or 'primitive' tendency towards fragmentary, split modes of relating are gradually replaced by more integrated ego-object relationships as a consequence of the internalisation of relatively benign environmental (that is, relational) experiences. So, 'paranoid-schizoid' functioning, which is characteristic both of early infancy and of regressed states of mind throughout life, has the subject unable to manage her or his destructive and loving impulses together, but rather placed in a phenomenological state in which these are felt to be bearing down on the ego from outside, as a hostile (paranoid) world that is more-or-less ameliorated by the presence of caring objects (mother or analyst). The fragmentation of identity is a way of defending it against being ruined by the envious, deathly elements in the mind's own structure; optimal development involves a gradual lessening of the force of these negative elements as they become mitigated by contrary loving impulses and gratifying experiences. In the subsequent 'depressive' position, the subject is more capable of tolerating ambivalence both in the drives and in the object. Whilst this is never a final process (the fissiparous tendency remains throughout life, activated when the subject is under stress or in boundary-disturbing situations such as masses or large groups – e.g. Frosh 2008), it means that identity is forged as a process of gradual working through of destructiveness and of splitting to produce a more integrated being, capable not only of conscious reflection on itself but also of the lived experience of being 'together', with relationships to itself and to others characterised by balance and depth.

For other analysts of the British object relations school (e.g. Casement 2002) and the American intersubjectivists (Benjamin 2004, 2009), there is relatively more interest in the 'reality' of the relationship between subjects, including patients and analysts. What is of interest here is that whereas for Kleinians paranoid-schizoid functioning is a ubiquitous and necessary state of development that is overcome only partially and at the expense of a great deal of intersubjective work, for traditional object relations theorists the early ego is a whole – at least potentially – and is brought into the disrepair of a psychic split as a result of a kind of environmental failure. The classic case here is that of Winnicott, for whom destructiveness takes the form initially of an 'aggression' that is 'almost synonymous with activity' (1960: 204). In this account, aggression and eroticism are two components of an initially unified 'life force' which splits in early development before, all being well, becoming the basis of an integrated or 'fused' self. The aggressive component has the important function of allowing the infant to establish its opposition to – or difference from – the external world, thus helping to establish the boundaries of the self. As Phillips (1988: 110) notes, Winnicott is much more interested in this differentiating facility of aggression than he is in the traditional Freudian concern of erotic life:

> There is in Winnicott's account of the early pre-fused era a distrust of the erotic and a curiously idealised nostalgia for the unfused ruthlessly aggressive component. . . . Vitality and the sense of being really alive are clearly bound up for him with the aggressive component.

Thus, aggression has in many respects lost its destructive elements in Winnicott's account, reflecting the object relations tendency to see the developmental process as one of active striving with external objects in the service of an integrating relational urge. There is also a very strong presentation here of the central role of the subject's surrounding environment in recognising her or his psychic needs. This is achieved through a peculiar process of 'mirroring', in which the subject's uncertain and seemingly fragmentary experiences become bound together in the gaze of the other, who lends it the meaning that it actually has – in other words, who translates it from something pressing and potentially disturbing to something that has integrity and makes psychic sense. This idea permeates much of Winnicott's thought, and in different ways is central to his continuing influence. For example, Winnicott (1960) presents a notion of a 'true self' as a subject's in-built *potential* for growth that will naturally unfold under the right circumstances, and that can be damaged or hidden in a hostile environment. The mother's capacity to recognise and reflect the infant's needs allows them to be translated into something safe and comprehensible, and provides the necessary scaffolding for the self to develop as secure, integrated and creative. Spontaneity, the capacity to be alone or to be in states of 'disunity' out of which new modes of experience can emerge, follows from this. Denial of this recognition, however, means that the infant is unable to organise her or his experience and leads to anxiety about total disintegration. This results in a defensive hiding away of the child's spontaneous desires in the form of a secret true self, which avoids expression because of the danger that it will be destroyed by the inadequate environment. To enable transactions with reality, a conformist and inauthentic 'false self' is formed, split off from the true self and protecting its integrity by adapting itself to the demands of the other (the depressed mother, for example) and consequently lacking in depth and autonomy.

The structure of this argument is one in which a naturally developing process – the emergence of a true self and an integrated identity – is watered by the careful, synchronising care of another who can recognise the subject's implicitly expressed essence, and accept it. Identity-formation thus becomes the realisation of an authentic state of being, founded in a secure self that has the capacity to recognise its own needs and the confidence to express them with an assurance that they will be met. Interruptions to this process result in distortions of selfhood characterised particularly by a thinness of identity in which the subject is always trying to second-guess what is required of it, to adapt to a world that never seems quite right. This is a powerful portrayal of a certain kind of identity crisis symptomatic of an alienating society, in which the needs of the subject are systematically distorted and left unmet, and it also offers a seductive set of images to describe the needs of the healthy, autonomous subject. However, it also perhaps warrants criticism as an idealisation, implying that each subject has an inbuilt tendency towards wholeness and integrity, and that it is possible for this to be recognised under conditions of perfect care. What this might miss is the extent to which all 'translations' are provisional and approximate, that is, in naming others' needs to them, one might be providing them with a code which makes those needs manageable and meaningful; but the 'name' is still coming from without, from the place of the other, and not from the subjects themselves. This basic point, which argues that mirroring is not a matter of reflecting what is 'really there' more or less accurately, but instead is a process of *colonisation*, in which the subject becomes infiltrated, or structured, by and through something that lies outside it, is a powerful insight of several other psychoanalytic theorists, including (in different ways) Jean Laplanche (1999), who emphasises the 'untranslatability' of many of the messages received from the mother in early life, their 'enigmatic' nature, and Jacques Lacan. In relation to identity, this raises the question of whether the Winnicottian idealisation may be a smokescreen obscuring a darker realisation – that the subject can never be known – and that identity is consequently an attempt to pull together things using the 'bric-à-brac of its props department' (Lacan 1954–5: 155) as a defence against falling apart.

Jessica Benjamin's take on intersubjectivity is an especially significant contemporary variant of the general approach described here. For Benjamin, the intersubjective stance is a specific move within the general domain of relational theorising, one which holds onto a position in which the other is related *to* but is not *appropriated*. It is a stance that understands the appeal of omnipotence (in knowing the other we come to colonise her or him) but works against it. The manner in which omnipotence is contested is through a process of recognition that acknowledges the other as a source of subjectivity and gives rise to what Benjamin (1998) calls a 'subject–subject' psychology. This stance echoes the 'I–thou' relationship described by Martin Buber (1959), a mode of reciprocity in which there is engagement with the other as a full being, in contrast to the more instrumental 'I–it' relationship in which the other is a means to an end. It is also closely connected to the kind of Winnicottian mirroring described above, but with the difference that 'subject–subject' recognition is built out of an understanding of the other's continuing *otherness*, maintaining the subjecthood of both participants in the exchange who are thus autonomous and yet also exist in relation to one another. In 'the intersubjective conception of recognition', writes Benjamin (1998: 29), 'two active subjects may exchange, may alternate in expressing and receiving, cocreating a mutuality that allows for and presumes separateness'. Benjamin's approach seeks a balance between theories that emphasise difference and those visions of subjectivity that implicitly require disappearance in or of the other, either through self-effacement (as in many theories of mothering), or through instrumental use of the other (the main thrust of rationality). Recognition staves off the absorption of self into the other just as it prevents the other being colonised by the self; it is, in this sense, a process in which what is found in the other is also cherished specifically for its capacity to be different, and its otherness.

In her analysis of the implications of Benjamin's theory for mothering, Baraitser (2009) describes how Benjamin's account draws on Winnicott's (1969) ideas about a developmental phase that involves 'object use'. Winnicott's argument is that what he calls the use of an object is made possible through seeing that the (paradigmatically, maternal) object survives unconscious destruction. Assuming that the infant, through frustration and also the expression of 'natural' aggression, attacks the object, Winnicott claims that the infant's perception of the existence of a real external other is enhanced so long as the mother survives and is non-retaliatory in her response. That is, what the infant is supposed to discover is that the mother is not subject to the infant's 'internal' experience of having destroyed her, and hence is an object with more than merely imaginary existence. Benjamin builds on this idea by suggesting that recognition depends on processes of destruction in the form of 'negation' which test the reality of the other by establishing the degree to which it is resilient and hence has a subjective trajectory of its own. Baraitser (2009: 30) comments: 'In Benjamin's view there is an ongoing and endless cycle of the establishment of mutual recognition followed by its negation, constituting a never-ending tension between complementarity and mutuality, between relating to the other as object or like subject.' This might mark up one of the deficiencies of relational theory in the context of the revelations of psychoanalysis about the passionate feelings so often associated which destructive urges. It sometimes seems as if the humanistic component of relational work trumps its analytic rigour; even the notion of 'destruction' lacks the passion of, for example, the Kleinian concept of envy, with its connotations of greed and murderous violence. Judith Butler comments on this:

> Although Benjamin clearly makes the point that recognition risks falling into destruction, it seems to me that she still holds out for an ideal of recognition in which destruction is an occasional and lamentable occurrence, one that is reversed and overcome in the therapeutic situation and that does not turn out to constitute recognition essentially.
>
> *(2000: 273)*

This translation of destruction as a fall from grace that can be overcome by a reparative relation- ship is perhaps part of the legacy of an object relations position which assumes the existence of an integrated psyche at birth that then becomes split because of frustration and loss (Frosh 1999). In contrast, the Kleinian view is that destructiveness is a basic force that always has to be contended with and can never be fully resolved. Without being a Kleinian, Butler picks up this issue to wonder about the authenticity of an approach that assumes destructiveness can be overcome. Addressing Benjamin's use of negation, she asks:

> And if negation is destruction that is survived, of what does survival consist? Certainly, the formulation implies that destruction is somehow overcome, even overcome once and for all. But is this ever really possible – for humans, that is? And would we trust those who claim to have overcome destructiveness for the harmonious dyad once and for all? I, for one, would be wary.
>
> *(Butler 2000: 285)*

This criticism, which in effect charges Benjamin with idealising human relationships, is akin to the one outlined above. It suggests that in their keenness to instate the intense, authentic encounter at the core of psychoanalysis, relational theorists might be missing the, at times, dispiriting way in which relationships are *mediated* experiences, refracted through a lens that always 'distorts' them, that always blocks absolute recognition. If this is so, then identity too is constructed from reflections in a dim glass, not quite true, not quite in tune, disturbed by something enigmatic that can never fully be translated.

Identity deconstruction

The criticism developed above of the relational strand in psychoanalysis is closely linked with thinking produced outside psychoanalysis in post-structuralism and postmodernism, and within it in the wake of the Lacanian school. The complex and evocative stance of Lacan on the ego and what he terms the 'Imaginary' has been described in detail elsewhere (Frosh 2006, 2010), where what is drawn out is the difference between the Lacanian theorisation of 'mirroring' and the Winnicottian and intersubjectivist versions. In brief, whereas Winnicott proposes that the infantile self is secured through experiencing accurate mirroring of its true needs, in a kind of affective 'naming' of its inner reality that recognises it and allows it to self-organise and grow, Lacanians dispute the authenticity of this process. 'In' the mirror, the subject sees not its 'real' self, but an image of what it would wish to be. This comes *from outside*; the mirror/other/mother cannot know the 'reality' of the subject because that reality does not exist in a knowable form; moreover, all knowledge is in any case mediated by the materiality of both language and the unconscious. Recognition is always 'mis-recognition'. In the famous 'mirror stage' paper, Lacan writes:

> The fact is that the total form of the body by which the subject anticipates in a mirage the maturation of his power is given to him only as a *Gestalt*, that is to say, in an exteriority in which this form is certainly more constituent than constituted, but in which it appears to him above all in a contrasting size that fixes it and in a symmetry that inverts it, in contrast with the turbulent movements that the subject feels are animating him.
>
> *(1949: 2)*

Unpacking this, what is being described is a process whereby the subject 'anticipates' something that does not yet exist, seeing it in a 'mirage' – that is, formulating a fantasy of future deliverance. It is a 'Gestalt', a whole, but it is 'exterior' rather than interior, something which delivers identity as 'constituent', as ready-made. Most importantly, it is 'fixed', obviously distorted (contrasting size and inverted symmetry), but relieving the subject of the stress that is placed upon it by its own 'turbulent' movement. Perhaps here can be seen not only how the Lacanians draw attention to the exteriority of identity, but also to the stasis it produces: the subject is always in motion, riven by drives that do not organise themselves into a satisfying whole; identity, in this model, is one way of alleviating this, but it does not speak its truth.

The emphasis on *division* produced by the mediation or insertion of 'external' structures is a major thrust of Lacanian thought. As discussed in the other sources referenced above, this appears both in the notion of the Imaginary and in that of the Symbolic, the Lacanian reworking of the Oedipus complex as a principle in which the unconscious is formed out of the split induced by confrontation with the law of culture. In relation to identity, the Imaginary is a stage or way of relating that is dominated by narcissism, the fantasy being that completeness is possible and that the other can become absorbed into the ego to make a whole. The search for a totally satisfying identity, just like the search for any other full 'answer' to the questions of existence, is an Imaginary search, constituted through a wish that the internal and external blocks and splits would go away. The theory of the Symbolic emphasises that the positioning of the subject with respect to language requires an encounter with otherness in a way that fractures the omnipotence of this mirrored 'I' in the Imaginary, just as the father blocks the incestuous relation of mother and son in classical theory. Once the 'accession' to the Symbolic occurs, there is no way back: the division it produces, coded most notably in sexuality, results in a region of the left-out and unsymbolisable (the Real, in Lacanian terminology) that is always present just out of sight, disrupting the hope of a settled existence in which everything is static, integrated and known – but also keeping alive the hope that something might *happen*.

If the emphasis on 'structuration' in Lacanian theory is highly distinctive and also damaging for representations of identity as indicating some kind of personal truth, it also blocks the adaptational attitude that sees identity as social belonging. Or, rather, it makes problematic the assumption that an alignment of the subject with 'society' is possible in ways that are not intrinsically alienating – whatever the nature of that society might be. The Symbolic *always* interferes with integrity and autonomy; it cannot be otherwise. Some of the force of this can be seen in the Lacanian emphasis on *lack*, which has been taken up not only in clinical work, but also in the application of psychoanalysis to politics. As noted already, the division between the registers of Imaginary, Symbolic and Real classifies a discrepancy between what is imagined to be true (the holistic fantasy of an ego that can function autonomously and with integrity, of a subject that can fully know the truth); what can be symbolised and consequently manipulated, investigated and analysed (so psychoanalysis itself operates in the domain of the Symbolic); and what can never be known, or can be known only at the edges or by its sudden appearance in moments of breakthrough, never fully symbolisable, always at work but never quite there. These elements of the Lacanian scheme frame a set of 'lacks' contributing in different ways to the subject as a social and political entity. One is the theorisation of the subject as riven with splits; a second portrays the subject as intrinsically lacking in the sense of being cut off from the source of power, which always lies outside it as an Other that gives form and force to the subject's being. Both these types of lack are central to the Lacanian account of how the human subject is constituted. Indeed, the second type, which is essentially a description of how the Symbolic works, is vital to Lacanian ideas on sexual difference and on the construction of the subject in language. It stresses that the subject is not *a centre to itself*, but rather, in line with Freudian theory, is displaced and inhabited by something outside it. The subject is always constructed according to the desire of the Other, always answerable to a 'big Other' that is over and beyond itself and can perhaps be thought of as 'society' (amongst other things).

> A lack is encountered by the subject in the Other, in the very intimation that the Other makes to him by his discourse. In the intervals of the discourse of the Other, there emerges in the experience of the child something . . . namely, *He is saying this to me, but what does he want?* The desire of the Other is apprehended by the subject . . . in the lacks of the discourse of the Other, and all the child's *whys* reveal not so much an avidity for the reason of things, as a testing of the adult, a *Why are you telling me this?* ever-resuscitated from its base, which is the enigma of the adult's desire.
>
> *(Lacan 1973: 214)*

Hook draws out the political implications of this position, commenting that:

> Once we realise that the linked questions of desire (*'What do I want?'*) and social location (*'What makes sense of the position I occupy in society?'*) are really unanswerable – because they always rebound in the form of another question – then we start to understand the futility of such recourse to the Other, at least within the realm of the signifier, and the alienation of the subject that inevitably results.
>
> *(2008: 279)*

The interesting point here is that the Other is conceptualised not as a solid structure of power that acts over and against the subject, but as lacking, as having a desire of its own, which the subject is also immersed in. If the Other is lacking (if 'it needs me'), then the subject is faced with the question of what it is in the subject that is desired, and hence of what kind of lack in the Other can be filled by the (also lacking) subject. This is linked to the Lacanian notion of the *object a* as the object cause of desire – the thing in the other that provokes the desire of the subject, that moves it into action.

Identity then arises in this complex array of interlinked abstractions surrounding lack: the mutual construction of lacking subjectivities produces a play of investments that circulate between subject and Other and operate in the social field. This perspective is not confined to the Lacanians. For example, the theory of otherness propounded by Jean Laplanche (1999) has become increasingly significant in contemporary psychoanalytic and social thought; one indication of this is that it forms a core thread in Butler's (2005) examination of ethical relationality. Laplanche's ideas here are posited as an alternative basis for an understanding of identity-politics that conceptualises the subject as split and socially riven from the start. The extrinsic formulation of the subject is expressed in the theory of enigmatic signifiers, untranslatable messages from the adult which become the foundation for the infant's unconscious life and which are the residue of the process of unconscious seduction passed on through generations from parent to child. This adds a strand of 'alienness' at the core of subjecthood: central to each subject is an unconscious dimension, as psychoanalysis always asserts, but this unconscious does not 'belong' to the 'person', but rather arises from an act of mis-communication, a mode of unwitting seduction, in which the parental desire excites the child, without being understood.

> So we have the reality of the message and the irreducibility of the fact of communication. What psychoanalysis adds is a fact of its experience, namely that this message is frequently compromised, that it both fails and succeeds at one and the same time. It is opaque to its recipient and its transmitter alike.
>
> *(Laplanche 1999: 169)*

It is no longer a matter of intention; what comes from the other to the subject is something unknown to both, yet is intense in its effect (and affect). The infant is invaded by an unconscious message, its private spaces inflicted with the sense of 'something else', something excessive and too strong, always hinting at its presence without ever letting itself be fully known. The adult, too, holds an alien message inside: there is something no one can ever properly know. If this model has force, it is very difficult to imagine what a personal, authentic presocial space can be; however 'deep' we go, we find the other already there. In contrast to the object relational stance, the split human subject 'hidden' behind the ego (which is really a Lacanian formulation, but has influenced a generation of French analysts), is brought into being by the other. It is not excisable from the other and hence is 'always-already' social. Identity struggle is consequently never going to be a matter of striving for recognition of what one authentically 'is'; it is rather a matter of *producing* a subject in line with certain aspired-for values, creating a subject with force in the world. Specifically, recognition of the subject as a being with rights, for instance as 'black' or 'gay', is not a matter of putting a name to a mode of authenticity that is pre-given, but rather of creating the conditions under which discursively constructed possibilities are given shape and allotted agentic power. Psychoanalysis of this kind would not by any means preclude identity struggle; but it also places under scrutiny the notion of 'identity' itself as something constructed rather than basic, something importantly flawed rather than assumed to be ideally whole.

Challenges and future developments

This chapter has emphasised the fecundity of psychoanalysis in disturbing the parameters of identity studies, in particular querying assumptions of psychic and hence identity integrity. There are many remaining issues, which concern not only differences within the psychoanalytic field over questions of agency, subjecthood, structuration and otherness, but also whether psychoanalysis can ever speak convincingly of the inter-relation between identity as 'social belonging' and as 'personal being' – a particular case of the general problem of whether psychoanalysis is always psychologically reductionist. In this regard, by way of a kind of evaluative conclusion, it is perhaps interesting to see how some psychoanalytic thinking has come to permeate theoretical work on identities even when the position taken up by the theorist is not initially rooted in psychoanalysis. For example, Judith Butler's (1990) relatively early work on gendered and sexed identities had an enormous impact because of its vivacious presentation of the performativity of gendered identity, an approach which on the face of it was not well attuned to psychoanalysis. In later work, however, she has consistently drawn on different modes of psychoanalysis to elaborate an account of the 'melancholy' aspects of gender (Butler 1997), culminating in her masterly application of Laplanchian theory to present the thinking on ethical relationality mentioned earlier (Butler 2005). In another major area of identity studies, that of *diasporic* identities, some similar features can be observed. For many of the most important scholars on diaspora (e.g. Hall 1990), much of the analytic thrust of diaspora studies is given by explorations of art works of various kinds, including music, writing, performance and installations as well as visual arts. The reason for this is that for many such writers, the 'voice' of diaspora has often struggled to be heard in academic work, and instead is expressed through modes of representation that trigger affective rather than 'intellectual' responses. Despite harbouring doubts about the applicability of psychoanalysis to this area, Couze Venn nevertheless develops a productive account of the relationship between psychoanalytic thinking and the social discourses more characteristic of diaspora studies, as follows:

> [E]xpressive or creative media such as novels, painting, film and so on are themselves the means or vehicles whereby what cannot be presented in the form of critiques or sociological data can be intimated or presented at the affective and emotional levels. The importance from the point of view of transformation in subjectivity and identity is in emphasising the aesthetic-affective labour which is necessary for this to happen, in the form of an anamnesis, that is, a process of working through that produces a rememorisation . . . and in the form of self-reflection working at the thresholds between unconscious psychic economy and conscious activity, individual identity and collective identity, the process of individualisation and the trans-subjective domain.
>
> *(2009: 15)*

What might be meant by this kind of 'aesthetic-affective labour' and how can psychoanalysis contribute to its promotion as well as its comprehension? Venn himself draws on the work of a psychoanalyst who is also an artist, Bracha Ettinger (2006), whose theory of the 'matrixial' as a kind of intrauterine-originated connective network offers a way of thinking about subjectivity and identity that immerses them in a pattern of connectivity and encounter. The emphasis here is on what is *shared*, what links across subjects, and it is characteristic of a mode of psychoanalytic reasoning that has moved away from the classical 'closed' system of mainstream Freudianism and also from its focus on 'depth', and towards issues of relationality and intersubjectivity. What is additionally specific to psychoanalysis is the constitution of affectivity as that which 'fuels'

63

subjectivity, that is, in this context, as a mode of *investment* which promotes the materialisation of identity as linked to specific practices of belonging and becoming. 'Affective labour' does not have to be theorised psychoanalytically: the Deleuzian turn is a major example of an alternative tendency in the social sciences. However, the psychoanalytic apparatus allows it to be conceptualised as a process in which the different specific forces acting in and on the subject – drives, bodily experiences, social positions, ideologies, practices of oppression and emancipation, phantasies and fears – can be brought into contact with one another as the framework for an understanding that is genuinely 'dynamic', in the sense of being 'on the move'. Venn refers to 'a process of working through that produces a rememorisation'; these terms ('working through', 'rememorisation') are saturated with psychoanalytic resonances. Indeed, one might argue that psychoanalysis makes such ideas thinkable.

In relation to the impact of this work on psychoanalysis itself, it is clear that the emergence of theories stressing migrancy, unsettledness, fluidity and networks shifts attention away from drive models and towards relational approaches. However, there is nothing cosy in this. If psychoanalysis allows space for such moves, through its object relations and more recent inter-subjectivist traditions, it also maintains an investment in fields of force that interrogate and disrupt, that puncture even the most carefully maintained relational networks. Many theorists emphasise the reimagining of identity that is constantly demanded in the light of contemporary subjectivities. In so doing they advance a critique of theories – including psychoanalysis – that seem to neglect the social and historical forces operating on the subject, and also to focus only on loss and lack rather than on the transformative fullness of subjecthood. Psychoanalysis has to respond to this if it is to continue to contribute to identity studies, but it also has something additional in its armoury. This is linked to its understanding of what Lacan (1959–60: 139) calls 'extimacy', which refers to the problematisation of the distinction between 'inside' and 'out' and the way the 'centre of the subject is outside; the subject is ex-centric' (Evans 1996: 59). But more than this, it also resides in psychoanalysis' fascination with what is disruptive and uncertain, so that disturbance in the stability of what is taken to be identity is at the core of its concerns. Psychoanalysis certainly must develop its awareness of how the positioning of the subject in historical and contingent networks of relations produces identities of various kinds, fluid and partial in their nature. If it can do this, it can then offer back to the field its own peculiar expertise: that of a discipline that knows about unsettledness, that has marginality and diaspora as part of its own source (in the historical development of psychoanalysis out of certain Jewish diasporic experiences – see Frosh 2005), and that is always reminding its acolytes that nothing can be taken for granted, that no self-definition or affective state is ever quite what it seems.

Note

1 Some material in this chapter comes from Stephen Frosh, *Psychoanalysis outside the Clinic*. London: Palgrave, 2010.

References

Allen, J. and Fonagy, P. (eds) (2006) *Handbook of Mentalisation-Based Treatment*. Chichester: Wiley.

Baraitser, L. (2009) *Maternal Encounters: The Ethics of Interruption*. London: Routledge.

Benjamin, J. (1995) *Like Subjects, Love Objects: Essays on Recognition and Sexual Difference*. London: Yale University Press.

Benjamin, J. (1998) *Shadow of the Other: Intersubjectivity and Gender in Psychoanalysis*. New York: Routledge.

Benjamin, J. (2004) 'Beyond doer and done to: an intersubjective view of thirdness', *Psychoanalytic Quarterly*, 73: 5–46.

Benjamin, J. (2009) 'A relational psychoanalysis perspective on the necessity of acknowledging failure in order to restore the facilitating and containing features of the intersubjective relationship (the shared third)', *International Journal of Psychoanalysis*, 90: 441–50.

Buber, M. (1923/2004) *I and Thou*. London: Continuum.

Butler, J. (1990) *Gender Trouble: Feminism and the Subversion of Identity*. London: Routledge.

Butler, J. (1997) *The Psychic life of Power*. Stanford: Stanford University Press.

Butler, J. (2000) 'Longing for recognition', *Studies in Gender and Sexuality*, 1: 271–90.

Butler, J. (2005) *Giving an Account of Oneself*. New York: Fordham University Press.

Casement, P. (2002) *Learning from our Mistakes: Beyond Dogma in Psychoanalysis and Psychotherapy*. Hove: Brunner-Routledge.

Crews, F. (1995) *The Memory Wars: Freud's Legacy in Dispute*. London: Granta.

Erikson, E. (1956) 'The problem of ego identity', *Journal of the American Psychoanalytic Association*, 4: 56–121.

Ettinger, B. (2006) *The Matrixial Borderspace*. Minneapolis: University of Minnesota Press.

Evans, D. (1996) *An Introductory Dictionary of Lacanian Psychoanalysis*. London: Routledge.

Fonagy, P. and Target, M. (1996) 'Playing with reality: 1. Theory of mind and the normal development of psychic reality', *International Journal of Psycho-Analysis*, 77: 217–33.

Fonagy, P. and Target, M. (2007) 'The rooting of the mind in the body: new links between attachment theory and psychoanalytic thought', *Journal of the American Psychoanalytic Association*, 55: 411–56.

Freud, A. (1966/1973) *Normality and Pathology in Childhood*. Harmondsworth: Penguin.

Freud, S. (1917) 'Introductory lectures on psycho-analysis', *The Standard Edition of the Complete Psychological Works of Sigmund Freud, Volume XVI (1916–1917): Introductory Lectures on Psycho-Analysis (Part III)*, 241–463.

Freud, S. (1926) 'Address to the Society of B'Nai B'Rith', *The Standard Edition of the Complete Psychological Works of Sigmund Freud, Volume XX (1925–1926): An Autobiographical Study, Inhibitions, Symptoms and Anxiety, The Question of Lay Analysis and Other Works*, 271–4.

Frosh, S. (1991) *Identity Crisis: Modernity, Psychoanalysis and the Self*. London: Macmillan.

Frosh, S. (1999) *The Politics of Psychoanalysis: An Introduction to Freudian and Post-Freudian Theory*. London: Palgrave.

Frosh, S. (2002) *Key Concepts in Psychoanalysis*. London: The British Library.

Frosh, S. (2005) *Hate and the 'Jewish Science': Anti-Semitism, Nazism and Psychoanalysis*. London: Palgrave.

Frosh, S. (2006) *For and Against Psychoanalysis*. London: Routledge.

Frosh, S. (2008) 'Desire, demand and psychotherapy: on large groups and neighbours', *Psychotherapy and Politics International*, 6: 185–97.

Frosh, S. (2010) 'Psychoanalytic perspectives on identity: from ego to ethics', in M. Wetherell and C. Mohanty (eds) *The Sage Handbook of Identities*. London: Sage.

Frosh, S. and Baraitser, L. (2008) 'Psychoanalysis and psychosocial studies', *Psychoanalysis, Culture and Society*, 13: 346–65.

Hall, S. (1990) 'Cultural identity and diaspora', in J. Rutherford (ed.) *Identity: Community, Culture, Difference*. London: Lawrence and Wisehart.

Hook, D. (2008) 'Fantasmatic transactions: on the persistence of apartheid ideology', *Subjectivity*, 24: 275–97.

Jacobson, E. (1964) *The Self and the Object World*. London: Hogarth Press.

Lacan, J. (1949/1977) 'The mirror stage as formative of the function on the I as revealed in the psychoanalytic experience', in J. Lacan, *Écrits: A Selection*. London: Tavistock.

Lacan, J. (1954–5) *The Seminars of Jacques Lacan, Book II: The Ego in Freud's Theory and in the Technique of Psychoanalysis*. Cambridge: Cambridge University Press.

Lacan, J. (1959–60/1992) *The Ethics of Psychoanalysis. The Seminar of Jacques Lacan Book VII*. London: Routledge.

Lacan, J. (1973/1979). *The Four Fundamental Concepts of Psychoanalysis*. Harmondsworth: Penguin.

Laplanche, J. (1999) 'The unfinished Copernican revolution', in J. Laplanche, *Essays on Otherness*. London: Routledge.

Parker, I. (1997) *Psychoanalytic Culture: Psychoanalytic Discourse in Western Society*. London: Sage.

Phillips, A. (1989) *Winnicott*. Cambridge, MA: Harvard University Press.

Potter, J. and Wetherell, M. (1987) *Discourse and Social Psychology: Beyond Attitudes and Behaviour*. London: Sage.

Stolorow, R. (2006) 'Intersubjectivity theory and intersubjective systems theory', in R. Skelton (ed.) *The Edinburgh International Encyclopaedia of Psychoanalysis*. Edinburgh: Edinburgh University Press.

Stephen Frosh

Venn, C. (2009) 'Identity, diasporas and subjective change: the role of affect, the relation to the other, and the aesthetic', *Subjectivity*, 26: 3–28.

Wallerstein, R. (1998) 'Erikson's concept of ego identity reconsidered', *Journal of the American Psychoanalytic Association*, 46: 229–47.

Winnicott, D. (1960/1965) 'Ego distortion in terms of true and false self', in D.W. Winnicott, *The Maturational Process and the Facilitating Environment*. London: Hogarth Press.

Winnicott, D. (1969) 'The use of an object', *International Journal of Psychoanalysis*, 50: 711–16.

4

Foucauldian approaches to the self

Gavin Kendall

Introduction

Michel Foucault, when he is read in the company of the many other significant thinkers on the self and on identity gathered in this collection, may well – and, indeed, should – be perceived as an 'outsider'. The reason for this is that Foucault is not, in any meaningful sense, a theorist of self or identity. Rather, his major contribution to this field is the contrary of a theoretical one: he gives us a series of empirical studies, using the standard historical approach of documentary analysis, of how the self has, at various important junctures, been problematised in terms of the relation it has to itself. Yet Foucault's interest was not so much in a kind of relativised, historically changing self, but in the differing types of relations the self has established with itself; and, moreover, in the differing types of relations the self has established with others, especially to the extent that these self–other relationships are typically relations of power or government. Additionally, we can say that, for Foucault, the self is simply *one of any number of ways* in which human beings have given meaning to their experiences of themselves. It just so happens to be our current mode of experience, and for that reason alone, is of special interest to us. Still further, we can state that the focus of Foucault's enquiries was more upon the systems which have been invented to problematise the self, rather than upon the self which is the result of those very systems.

It is vital to grasp this distinction between what Foucault tried to do and what most thinkers on the self and on identity have tried to do, or else we are doomed to misunderstand and misappropriate Foucault. So we need to emphasise the difference. For most who theorise the self, the exercise is about the generation of a (more or less) universally applicable account of the self. There are two ways of being this type of 'grand theorist of the self': one can either assume a certain universality in the self, a certain historical continuity, and aim to isolate and describe these transcendent characteristics, taking it for granted that the social contexts within which the self finds itself are of little relevance; or, one can assume a series of historical shifts which cause the emergence of new types of self (a third possibility is an offshoot of the second: the assumption of a series of historical shifts in the form of the self which cause the emergence of new types of society). In the first camp, one can place thinkers such as Kant or Freud, for whom the self has a transhistorical durability, and is characterised by reason, the ego, the unconscious, the personality, or whatever; in the second camp, one can place most sociologists, who tend to theorise the self as causally emergent from, or, in rare cases (in the 'offshoot' manifestation), causative of, great social and cultural shifts, and for whom, then, changed forms of self map neatly (and causally) onto changing forms of social organisation. This second group end up with both a relativistic and a deterministic notion of self, as transformations from, for example, the pre-modern to the modern world, or from *Gemeinschaft* to *Gesellschaft*, force the self to transform; perhaps to become the blasé self, for example, to use a characterisation from Georg Simmel, or to become the alienated self, to take Marx's hypothesis. Interestingly enough, both these approaches – the self-as-universal and the self-as-constructed – tend to give the self a certain historical consistency: in the first case, of course, the self is unchanging, and has a universal, timeless essence; in the second case, it must have enough of a universal essence to respond with a certain regularity and consistency to social change. Further, to examine those 'offshoot' thinkers in the second camp who posit a changing form of self which *leads* to a series of new social arrangements – and here we might think of Max Weber's work on the role of the puritan personality in the emergence of capitalism, or Norbert Elias's work on the causative role a new 'courteous' self played in the emergence of the European state – again, the self needs to be understood as having a certain consistency which enables it to react to and connect with changing social conditions; historical differences in forms of self, then, are superficial, because we can see that the self always reacts predictably to external stimuli. Elias, to follow our last example, uses psychoanalytical concepts to theorise the 'inner core' of the historically variable self.

Foucault is sometimes thought to belong to the second camp, to be some sort of constructivist. In his earliest writings, as he sought to derive a form of analysis that avoided what he saw as the weaknesses of existentialism and phenomenology, there are hints that such a characterisation might have been accurate. However, by the time of his last writings, on governmentality and on the care and technologies of the self, it is clear that Foucault was in neither camp. We must start with these earlier writings, and analyse Foucault's conceptual work on self and identity.

Historical and intellectual development

Experience books, 1954–69: leaving the past behind

The context in which Foucault began his career – the context against which he felt he must write – were the linked traditions of existentialism and phenomenology. For Foucault, both these approaches erred in their emphasis on personal experience, whether the stress was on a deformed type of self denied its authentic destiny, or on the examination of natural forms of experience. Sartre was the person who dominated French intellectual life when Foucault emerged as a key thinker, and in response to Sartre, Foucault produced a form of historical work which, while still analysing types of experience, nonetheless assumed the self to be a historical rather than a natural kind, and which aimed to avoid any sort of psychological essentialism. So, for example, in *Madness and Civilization*, Foucault refused the concept of madness as a universal experience. He historicised madness, focusing not so much on the experience of being mad itself, but on the ways in which the experience of madness has been given meaning. These latter ways of 'being given meaning' were understood as historically located. Here, we can see Foucault using historical techniques to generate not so much a general theory of the experience of madness but an empirical study of how the experience of madness was thinkable at certain key moments. His anti-humanistic antipathy to a general theory of the self was clear at this time, and he was so far from considering the self as a valid object of a theory that, understandably, he became linked in popular consciousness with the structuralist thinkers of the time, many of whom eschewed the self other than as a kind of terminal point of deep structural rules. So, famously, in the structural linguistics of Saussure or the structural Freudianism of Jacques Lacan, the self is a constructed mechanism, ultimately dependent on social structures, such as language or the 'unconscious structured as a language'; and in Louis Althusser's work, the self is, in the last instance, a weak entity, emerging deterministically ('interpellated', as Althusser puts it) from the great social forces that surround it. While Foucault's work in the first phase of his career has some resonance with this deterministic, structuralist way of thinking about the self, once again Foucault is somewhat of an outsider, since he was never especially interested in the self as a theoretical problem; for him, the point of analysis was to generate empirical, historical accounts of the conditions within which forms of experience have meaning, and 'the self' is just one of those ways in which we can experience ourselves. The difference in approach is subtle, and led to a number of charged debates, especially a tetchy and drawn out argument between Foucault and Jacques Derrida about what exactly the object of Foucault's analysis might be (madness itself? the experience of madness? the historical conditions which allowed madness to be silenced?). During this period in his work (roughly from 1954 to the late 1960s), and continuing on through the second phase of his work (roughly through the 1970s), Foucault demonstrated his aversion towards the active, authentic and authorial self, sometimes aligning himself with a Barthesian view which seeks to decentre authorial power, and expressed his boredom and unease with the simple correspondence lazily made between the author's history and the meaning of a new work. On the other hand, this anti-biographical stance was somewhat softened from time to time, as for example when he suggested (1991a: 25ff.) that his books be understood as 'experience books': that the idea of them is to change the self and to allow it to think in a different way, to escape what is known and comfortable, rather than be 'books of truth'. Foucault was also fascinated by the power of the thought from outside, the irruption of the thought of the outcast (the madman, the artist) as a way of derailing the truisms of our times: here, he envisaged a Nietzsche, an Artaud, a Van Gogh shaking up the settled truths of a culture, and in this way Foucault seemed to allow the existence of a particularly powerful form of subjectivity that comes from nowhere (Foucault and Blanchot 1989).

Nonetheless, in this phase of his career, the self was not an especially important problem, and he tended to assign it a rather low level of attention. The key problem Foucault sought to address is the problem of knowledge, and later, from the early 1970s, the problem of the relation between knowledge and power. Crudely, we can say that *Madness and Civilization* is a book about the knowledge systems which target madness; *The Birth of the Clinic* is a book about the knowledge systems of clinical medicine; *The Order of Things* is a book about three knowledge systems, those which concern themselves with life, labour and language; and *The Archaeology of Knowledge* is a theoretical and methodological account of and companion piece to those three earlier books.

Major claims and developments

Games of power, 1970–76: the subject as a doubling upon itself

By the time he came to write *Discipline and Punish* and *The History of Sexuality Vol. I*, Foucault had added the analysis of power to his famed 'archaeological' method, which he renamed 'genealogy'. Thus, *Discipline and Punish* focused on the power-knowledge arrangements found in forms of punishment and incarceration, while *The History of Sexuality Vol. I* analysed the systems of control that connected up to anxiety about sexuality. When we consider this oeuvre, we see that Foucault develops a complex understanding of knowledge, discourse and power, and, consequently, the role of the subject in this system. For Foucault, knowledge has two poles or forms: the discursive and the non-discursive. Roughly, this is a division between the ways of speaking, thinking and talking about objects ('the sayable'), and the objects themselves ('the visible'). Foucault grants the discursive pole of knowledge primacy; in his analyses of madness, clinical medicine, life, labour and language, the emphasis was squarely on the discursive – the ways of understanding, of speaking, of practising – that came to form the objects, the bodies and the practical systems that were implanted in our societies.

It is especially in the books on the prison and on sexuality that Foucault addresses the problem of power, and to an extent this is done to remedy a problem of determinism in the relationship between the discursive and the non-discursive poles of knowledge. For Foucault, power is the vector that helps maintain an agonism between the discursive and the non-discursive, and ensures that the latter is not consumed by the former. Power is a *strategy* which maintains a relation between the sayable (the discursive) and the visible (the non-discursive). The visible is in danger of exhaustion because it is potentially completely determined by the sayable: the problem for Foucault is one of how the visible, being completely receptive, is inexhaustible. The solution begins in regarding the two poles of knowledge as always in conflict, and he often describes their interrelation by martial metaphors. The sayable and the visible are divided from each other, yet insinuate themselves inside the relation between the other and its conditions. The sayable offers the visible in a 'space of dissemination', while offering itself up as a 'form of exteriority' (Deleuze 1986: 66, 73).

Foucault liked to say that he was interested in games of truth, games of power, and games around the self. We can understand the earliest phase of his work (1954–69) as being especially about games of truth: the point of his analysis of knowledge is to understand what counts as true at a given time, and what are the conditions that allow the formation of a 'regime of truth'. The next phase of his work (1970–76) is especially about the games of power: in *Discipline and Punish* and *The History of Sexuality Vol. I,* he sought to understand the power relations that infested societies such as ours. Although power is now placed in the foreground, it is clear in these two books that the effects of power are co-dependent with the games of truth around punishment and sexuality. The self, or the subject, makes a restricted, if clearly more central, appearance in this phase of Foucault's work, but not enough to satisfy his critics. Duccio Trombadori, for example, is worried about the disappearance of 'real' subjects in Foucault, and the lack of any account of who struggles against whom: 'One profound criticism [of Foucault] remains that of the lack of individuating real *subjects* who are capable of determining a relation of power . . . *who* struggles against *whom?*' (Foucault 1991a: 112–13, emphasis in original). The games of self are not yet central to Foucault's thought, but it is in his analysis of the relationship between knowledge and power that a key role emerges for the subject. We can begin to notice the shift in Foucault's writing: as power becomes more central, the self or the subject begins to feature more heavily. For example, he writes: 'My objective . . . has been to create a history of the different modes by which, in our culture, human beings are made subjects' (1982: 208), and: 'One has to dispense with the constituent subject, to get rid of the subject itself, that's to say, to arrive at an analysis which can account for the constitution of the subject within a historical framework' (1980: 117).

Again, we must remind ourselves that Foucault does not think of the self, or the subject, as anything more than a historically specific mode within which human beings can experience themselves; the subject, though real enough (a 'truth effect'), is not *necessary*. That being said, Foucault insists upon an active role for subjects in societies such as ours; subjects are active in producing themselves in the sense of being *subjected* to power, so Foucault's goal is to describe the 'immense labor to which the West has submitted generations in order to produce . . . men's subjection: their constitution as subjects in both senses of the word' (1978: 60).

The notions of discourse, the non-discursive and power are all involved here. Subjects' actions take place in discourse, and subjects themselves are produced through discourse. Subjects are the punctuation of discourse, and provide the bodies on and through which discourse may act. In line with this, we may say that subjects form some of the conditions for knowledge. Human action within discourse is positional: it occurs through a subject position inhabiting a space between the two poles of knowledge, the discursive and the non-discursive. But subjective action also takes place at the moment at which power doubles over upon itself. Just as knowledge is the agonism between the two forms – those of the discursive and the non-discursive – so power is the agonism between or action of a force upon another force.

For Foucault, then, power is a series of relations between forces, and knowledge is a series of relations between forms. But what are the relations between these relations, between power and knowledge? The two are completely heterogeneous, but engage in a process of contest. However, power passes through forces not forms; it is *diagrammatic* (Foucault discusses the Panopticon as diagram in *Discipline and Punish* (1977: 205) in the following terms: the presentation of the relations between forces unique to a particular formation; the distribution of the power to affect and be affected; the mixing of non-formalised pure functions and unformed pure matter; a transmission or distribution of particular features). In being diagrammatic in this way, power mobilises non-stratified matter and functions, it is local and unstable, and it is flexible. Knowledge is stratified, archivised, and rigidly segmented; power is strategic, but it is anonymous. The strategies of power are mute and blind, precisely because they avoid the forms of knowledge, the sayable and the visible. This production of subjectivity occurs within this system, as a doubling of self upon self in every realm, in the realm of the body, the realm of force (power), and the realm of forms (knowledge).

It might be thought that such an account of the subject raises the problems of discourse determinism and the essentialisation of power: the subject seems at times to be moved mechanically through discourse by the workings of power relations which themselves only seem to be exercised through what we might term a 'will to power'. However, to the contrary, the complex intertwining of power, knowledge and the subject precludes the questions of origin and of determination. The triad power, knowledge and the subject is so systematic that it makes little sense to consider each component separately – they all condition, and form the conditions for, each other. The circularity of interdependence precludes questions of primacy, since none of the components of the triad would exist (except in a virtual form) without the others.

By the middle of the 1970s (certainly by the time of the publication of *The History of Sexuality Vol. I* in France in 1976), Foucault had developed his own unique approach to the empirical investigation of the working of knowledge, power and the subject – probably in that order – and was now paying increased attention to the subject in his writing. So, for example, in *Discipline and Punish,* the emphasis is simultaneously on forms of knowledge such as penology, the relations of power that connect to those knowledges, and the subject positions that are the third term in the equation: the disciplined individual as an exemplary form of modern subjectivity is very much a key aspect of the book. Similarly, in *The History of Sexuality Vol. I,* while much of the book is about power and knowledge, the types of self specific to these power-knowledge arrangements – such as the self who is enjoined to find freedom, forgiveness or truth through confessing – have been moved to centre stage.

Foucault was famous for his constant reinterpretation of what his books were about – sometimes he claims they are books about truth, sometimes books about experience, sometimes books about power, and sometimes books about the self. What makes this series of books so valuable is that they have a number of interlocking themes, and the reading of later volumes often draws one's attention to previously unnoticed lines in the earlier books. For example, once one has read *Discipline and Punish,* if one returns to *Madness and Civilization,* it becomes much clearer how the latter book was simultaneously a book about the forms of knowledge that gave meaning to a human experience, a book about the power relations that played between those knowledges, and a book about the forms of self-experience (madman, psychiatrist) that emerged from these systems. While power and the subject are not to the fore in *Madness and Civilization,* the careful reader can discern a consistency between the approach of the early work and the later.

Techniques of the self, 1977–84: the relation of self to self, and self to other

As we have already seen, the interest in power led Foucault to pay more sustained attention to the problem of the subject. The issue of the subject and the forms of power over it (anatomo-politics – power over the body; and biopolitics – power over life itself) drew Foucault's focus not just to the relationships between the self and the other who sought to govern it, but also to the relationship the self had to itself. Foucault had originally planned to extend the *History of Sexuality* series into six (and then later into four) volumes, but his developing interest in these two key types of relationships with the self caused him to reformulate this plan, and to delay for some time as he battled with a series of new literatures which were not just about sexuality, but also about the ethics of the self.

Foucault was about to join a group of thinkers who argue that the self is contingent, transitory, piecemeal, and, above all, *technical*: that the self is an agglomeration of 'techniques' for doing things. This perspective has perhaps been most famously suggested by Marcel Mauss (see, for example, 1973); Mauss described various 'techniques of the body' that are used in different societies at different historical conjunctures, stressing their contingent form. For Mauss, there is no truly or simply human way of walking, eating or swimming, for example. In similar vein, Norbert Elias dealt with the formation of the person of the Renaissance courtier: the courtier does not build up a coherent form of selfhood based on some *telos,* but merely takes elements from here and there, as they are pleasing and useful. The self is an aggregation of these 'pleasing ways', but not especially systematic or coherent: rather it is emergent and contingent. In the later Foucault (especially 1986), we see an analysis of the antique self as 'technical', and the emergence of a new vocabulary which stresses 'techniques of the self' and 'technologies of the self'. Foucault (unlike most post-Foucauldians) does discriminate carefully between these two terms, using the French *technique* to refer to a practical *instance,* while the term *technologie* refers to a practical *system.* Techniques are singular and elemental, while technologies are accretions of techniques formed into a logical and systematic whole. When we think of this vocabulary as applied to the object 'the self', a technique of the self is a skill or procedure, possibly isolated or possibly integrated with other techniques; a technology of the self, by contrast, is something much more systematic.

The Greeks did not use a word equivalent to 'technology' to describe forms of activity or creation. The Greek term *techne* (plural *technai*) is closer to our term 'technique', but should be carefully discriminated from it. A *techne* refers to any skill or ability. Etymologically it is connected to the word for 'weaving' and, further down the road of derivation, to the word for a 'text', a thing that has been woven together out of words. The Greeks, then, have a very hands-on and, one may say, organic view of the *technai.* They are understood as practical, rather than mental, applications. A technique of the self (or *techne heautou*) is not simply a reflective sense of self but a lived and practical experience. We must bear this in mind when we read Foucault: the antique sense of self he analyses is nothing like a contemporary Western idea of a reflective, intellectual self divorced from the realm of the body, but it is a self formed from the playing out of ways of comporting oneself in the *bios politikos,* public life.

In the later Foucault, we hear a lot about the self (*soi*), but Foucault also likes to make use of a variety of terms that are cognate with 'subjectivity', such as *sujet*, *assujettir* and *assujettissement*. For example, in *The Use of Pleasure*, Foucault speaks of a 'mode of subjection' or 'mode of subjectification' (*mode d'assujettissement*) (1984: 27). The self is understood as the subject in a linguistic sense – that is to say, as notionally (grammatically) the one who speaks, but at the same time a function of a social system (language). The subject can simultaneously be the source of action (or the agent), without necessarily being the conscious originator of that action. On the other hand, one can be a subject while simultaneously being 'subjected' – governed by a series of external rules and conventions. Here we also get a hint of the omnipresence of power, in that the subject is both governor and governed, subjecting others while simultaneously subject to others, and subject to the self.

Foucault does not favour what he regards as a prosaic and fixed term: *identité*. Rather, he prefers *sujet* to refer to the various manifestations of self, always-already located within discourses. Just as discourses are plural, so manifestations of subjectivity are plural. Subjectivity is nomadic, temporary, contradictory, and heterogeneous, while identity is stable, permanent, coherent and homogeneous. For Foucault, the character of discourse, which he regards as in flux and characterised by martial relationships, does not support something like 'identity'. The subject, the fragile result of specific discursive combinations, is what interests Foucault, and moreover we can immediately see that this subject represents a kind of 'disempowering' of identity-politics: if identity is an illusion, a straitjacket description of something far more tenuous and subtle, if 'the sides' one takes are constantly reformulating and dissolving, then where is the authoritative place from which one can locate the self and be located in order to speak for or against a political position? It is for this reason that one sees in the later Foucault a description of forms of self that seem to be impossible to link to 'politics' in a straightforward sense. However, Foucault does allow the contradictory *sujet* to act consistently: he likes to use the term *multiplicité* as a way of conveying the idea that a subject, though multiple and fractured, can still act in 'singular' fashion.

At this point, we need to summarise Foucault's last major research project, his work on the self. Again, it is important to remember that this is in no way a general theory of self, but is rather a series of empirical enquiries into the ways in which the possibility of experiencing the self were systematised – how those systems worked, what their logic was, and whence they arose. We must also remember that Foucault was writing about antique forms of self – those of Classical Greece and the Hellenistic Age, and those of the early Christian West – and offered no more than a few passing remarks on the character of more recent forms of self. With these caveats in place, we can begin. First of all, Foucault found the ancients interesting because they appeared, like us, to assign a major role to what Foucault called 'ethics'. Foucault liked to make a distinction between morals and ethics, and suggested that in the ancient world it is possible to identify a shift from an emphasis on the former to an emphasis on the latter – from a simple, externally imposed system of rules for conduct, to an internal reflection on how to constitute oneself as a subject of one's own actions. The ethical dimension is about the construction of a relationship with oneself (the *rapport à soi*); the moral dimension concerns how the human being simply obeys a code which is external to it and with which it does not engage in any dynamic and mutually transformatory relationship. Foucault thought he could discern some similarities between our own age and that of the Greeks; for us, as for them, the question of our relation to ourselves has slowly shifted from the moral to the ethical, especially as our society has become more secular:

> I wonder if our problem nowadays is not, in a way, similar to this one [sc. the Greeks' concern with the ethics of the self], since most of us no longer believe that ethics is founded in

religion, nor do we want a legal system to intervene in our moral, personal, private life . . .
I am struck by the similarity of problems.

(Foucault 1997: 255–6)

And so he announced his intention to write a 'genealogy of ethics' (Foucault 1997: 266). In this seminal paper, 'On the genealogy of ethics', Foucault gives an extremely clear summary of the approach given a longer treatment in *The Use of Pleasure* (1984) and *The Care of the Self* (1986). He argues that the Greeks had a 'four-fold' schema which allowed them to make sense of their 'ethic of self': the four elements are ontology, deontology, ascetics and teleology. Ontology, or what Foucault sometimes calls the 'ethical substance', concerns the material that needs to be worked over by ethics, the element that is of ethical concern and needs to be made part of a system that can manage it. For the Greeks of the Classical Age, the pleasures, or the *aphrodisia*, are the ethical substance. Pleasures themselves have no ethical charge – they are in themselves neither good nor bad – but as Foucault shows, they are problematic, and must be subjected to some regime of management, whether through acts of moderation or acts of renunciation. The second element – the deontological element – concerns how one is invited to recognise one's ethical/moral obligation, and is also labelled by Foucault, as we discussed earlier, the 'mode of subjectification'. Again, for the Classical Athenians, this element concerns attempts to fashion a particular type of beautiful or noble life, and so is an aesthetic choice. The third element, termed the ascetics, concerns the sorts of trainings and other activities that one must undergo in relation to these ethical problems. This element is the core of the 'techniques of the self', and can be seen in the variety of techniques the Greeks used to enable them to have an appropriate relationship to the pleasures, or the *aphrodisia*. The techniques of *askesis* are outlined in Foucault (1984, 1986), but there are important clarifications in three papers from the 1997 collection *Ethics: Subjectivity and Truth* ('The ethics of the concern of the self as a practice of freedom', 'Self writing' and 'Technologies of the self'), and in the 1981–82 lecture series at the Collège de France (2005). In these six sources, we can see a range of trainings that were employed by the Classical Athenians, including the sorts of erotic techniques that could be used to manage the problematic relationship between men and boys, or between the husband and the wife. The final element, concerning the teleology, is the ultimate goal of all of this ethical work. For the Athenians, this goal was mastery of the self.

We can go through an example of how all this worked in practice so we can be absolutely clear about the four elements and their interconnection. The Athenians, as has already been mentioned, did not regard the *aphrodisia* or pleasures (the ontological element, or the ethical substance) as having any particular ethical or moral charge. Pleasures are dangerous, and need to be used and enjoyed appropriately, but the pleasures themselves are not regarded as dishonourable. The point is to ensure the correct use of these pleasures, and the Athenians developed a complex economy of pleasure which suggested the times when it might best be taken, the direction in which it should travel, its intensity, and so forth. To take an example of one pleasure – that of sex with boys – there is no law or custom which prohibits this, but it is important that it be done suitably. One engages in sexual acts in the approved manner and shows that one is living the noble and beautiful life: one behaves honourably, one acts according to one's status as a citizen, and one plays an important part in the young boy's life as his noble companion and guide. Here, then, we can see two elements – the access to pleasure (the ethical substance) and the living of the beautiful life (the mode of subjectification) – as interconnected. There are also a series of erotic techniques which are the ascetic element of this use of pleasures. In our example of sex with young boys, there are some difficulties to be managed. First, the older man must always be active, never passive. Yet he must respect the younger boy and act in his interests. As for the boy, he must not be active in sex (this would be seen as abhorrent and contrary to nature); yet he cannot be passive either, since one day, in the near future, he will be a full citizen, and to be passive is unworthy of the citizen. The young boy must not give in to the demands of the older man for sex too easily, of course, because this would be shameful, but should only relent as a sign of the great friendship the two have. All of this is managed through the erotic technique of intercrural sex, where the man ejaculates between the legs of the boy, but without penetration. A number of other techniques, including ideas about when sex should take place (some seasons are better than others, for example) also feed into this complex economy of the use of pleasures (*chresis aphrodision*). Finally, for the Athenian, the point of all this – its *telos* – is self-mastery. The problem with the pleasures is that they can become the master rather than the slave, but the honourable citizen who lives the beautiful and noble life does not let this happen. In being the master of the pleasures – including the pleasure of sex with boys, but also including many other pleasures such as eating, drinking, sleeping, and so forth – and not their slave, the Athenian adult male citizen shows how the practical aim of self-mastery connects up to his social status. So we can see in this example how the four elements interlink in an everyday ethic of self – how an Athenian is enjoined to think about how he understands and experiences himself, and how he relates to himself and others.

Foucault suggests that these four elements shift somewhat over time. By the time of the Hellenistic Age, for example, Foucault suggests that not least because of social and political shifts (changes in the domestic sphere, particularly in relation to the wife, and the decline in the classical city state), the Hellenistic Stoics reconfigure the four-fold. The ontological element does not change, however, and the pleasures are still the ethical substance. The mode of subjectification does alter: the Stoics come to emphasise themselves as rational beings, and invoke a type of universalism which is different from the beautiful life of the Classical Age, as the human being is understood as subjected to universal laws. The Hellenistic ascetics are also somewhat refined and developed, and include a variety of newly invented techniques of self-examination, including the use of diaries, letter-writing and the *hupomnemata*, the note books which were used as guides for life conduct. We also see the implantation of a series of techniques of the self which emphasise austerity and self-renunciation; Epictetus and Seneca, for example, speak of exercises such as depriving oneself of food for a few days. The Hellenistic *telos* changes too: the Athenians had a strong sense of self-mastery which had little concern for the other, but was very much inwardly focused. The Stoics change that, introducing a greater degree of reciprocity between self and other. The goal is still self-mastery, but it is in a rational world in which a series of self-mastering selves interact with each other:

> in the classical perspective, to be master of oneself meant, first, taking into account oneself and not the other, because to be master of oneself meant that you were able to rule others. So the mastery of oneself was directly related to a dissymmetrical relation to others. You should be master of yourself in a sense of activity, dissymmetry, and nonreciprocity. Later on . . . mastery of oneself is not something that is primarily related to power over others: you have to be master of yourself not only in order to rule others, as it was in the case of Alcibiades or Nicocles, but you have to be master of yourself because you are a rational being. And in this mastery of yourself, you are related to other people, who are also masters of themselves. And this new kind of relation to the other is much less nonreciprocal than before.
>
> *(Foucault 1997: 267)*

Foucault notices that in the movement from the Classical Athenians to the Hellenistic Stoics, we see a growing austerity, an austerity which would be intensified by the early Christians.

The four-fold now starts to look very different. First of all, the ethical substance is quite altered: rather than the pleasures, the Christians are concerned with desire and the flesh. The mode of subjectification is no longer a personal-aesthetic choice, but divine law as set out by God. The techniques of the self that are the types of *askesis* develop the Stoic austerity themes, and centre on a variety of techniques of self-examination and self-mortification. The Christian techniques of mortification – fasting, penance, and so forth – are well known, but Foucault has a special interest in confession as a technique for self-examination. The development of the confessional is seen by Foucault as a fundamental feature of Christian culture, and is one which is never erased, even as our society becomes more secular: the spirit of the confession lives on in psychoanalysis, but also in the general sense of achieving freedom through unburdening oneself of one's inner thoughts, through such practices as counselling, psychotherapy, friendship, or even the problem pages of magazines and the lurid revelations of 'trash TV' talk shows. The history of the confession strengthening its grip on our society and our ways of experiencing our selves is a long one: Foucault stresses the importance of the Fourth Lateran Council of 1215 and the Council of Trent (1545–63) both for making confession a much more regular event in the lives of the faithful and for shifting the confessional material from deeds alone to deeds and thoughts. Finally, for the early Christians, the *telos* no longer revolves around self-mastery, but has shifted to purity (in this life) and immortality (for the next).

The modern four-fold?

Foucault has little to say about how this four-fold is adapted by us moderns – and, indeed, we must be sceptical about whether it can be adapted, since Foucault has not given us a grid which can be laid across all times to interpret them; once again, his work is empirical rather than a work of general theory. Nonetheless, there is a sense that we have yet to fully escape our Christian (and thus Hellenistic Stoic, and thus Classical Greek) set of problematisations of the self. It is because of the *rarity* of historical innovation, because of the fact that we are dealing from a very limited set of cards, that the history of the four-fold seems in many ways rather uninventive (Foucault (1984: 250) refers to the 'poverty and monotony of interdictions' that successive societies work with). So, we can piece together a modern four-fold, especially by remembering some of the lessons from Foucault's (1978) *History of Sexuality Vol. I*, that might look as follows: first, the modern form of ethical substance is sexuality; the mode of subjectification is through psychological understandings of self knowledge, especially to the extent that these are vectors for a Kantian sense of universal rationality; the techniques of self remain practices of self-examination and self-decipherment, especially as these emerge out of the 'psy sciences' (psychology, psychiatry, psychoanalysis, psychotherapy, and all the other modern scientific analyses of the self that begin with 'psy'); finally, the modern *telos* is the desire for the emancipation of the self, especially through sexual and other forms of personal liberation. We can represent these various incarnations of the four-fold in Table 4.1.

Main criticisms and developments of Foucault on the self

We can quickly canvass, and summarily dismiss, most criticisms of Foucault's work on the self. This is because virtually all these criticisms wrongly assume Foucault's point was to develop a generalised theory of the self, rather than to provide empirical studies of various historically located systems which have as their goal the giving of meaning to the experience of being human. Consequently, when critics suggest Foucault has not given enough weight to gender, class, race or resistance, we can usually see behind that criticism an expectation that Foucault's

Table 4.1

	Ethical Substance	Mode of Subjectification	Askesis	Telos
Classical Athenians	Pleasures	Politico-aesthetic choice	Techniques of self	Self-mastery (non-reciprocal)
Stoics	Pleasures	Universal law	Techniques of self, increased self-examination	Self-mastery (reciprocal)
Early Christians	Flesh, desire	Divine law	Self-examination	Immortality, purity
We Moderns	Sexuality	Psy sciences	Psy techniques for self-decipherment	Sexual/personal liberation

work should have had a level of generality to encompass these concerns – to have been a 'grand theory' of the self. The only response to these criticisms is to assert firmly that anyone interested in extending Foucault's thoughts on the self to the realm of those systems which allow the experience of the gendered subject, or any other type of subject, is welcome to do so; but Foucault should not be castigated for failing to do others' work for them. A second type of critique suggests that Foucault's work on the self is too deterministic – that the self is seen as a rather mechanical result of the power-knowledge system, or of the four-fold system, that produces it. By this account, the active nature of the self, and its capacity to resist and reinvent, is underestimated in Foucault. This second critique, however, is virtually identical to the first: such a critique can only be mounted from the assumption that the self has a series of pre-existing capacities that must be respected by a comprehensive social theory: that the self can somehow stand outside the systems and resist them. Foucault is not interested in this approach, other than in relation to the exceptional 'thought from outside': his point is rather to show the conditions which allow a certain restricted form of self to be *one possible result*. It is quite possible, although difficult, for human beings to refuse to see themselves in the ways given to them, but again this is rather tangential to the main thrust of Foucault's analytical work. On the other hand, Foucault is very interested in the idea that one of the results of his analytical work might be that one is enabled to take a 'transcendent' view, and refuse to be who we currently are. We should, in passing, also make it clear that it may well be the case that a general theory of self is possible, and that there is evidence of so little variability in the way humans experience themselves that pronouncements on the character of a universal self are possible; however, we should leave this question to one side, because Foucault is not much help in this regard.

The critic of Foucault is on surer ground when arguing about the correctness of the empirical studies themselves. We need to ascertain whether Foucault's accounts of the techniques of self are accurate. One criticism is that Foucault was over-reliant on Kenneth Dover's groundbreaking work on Greek homosexuality, which allowed him to develop an account of the neutrality of the *aphrodisia* (contrary to the concern with the flesh and with sexuality that characterise later ages) and of the Classical emphasis on activity and mastery (as opposed to the more passive *telos* of purity and immortality that succeeded it). In this way, Foucault is able to argue for a line of development from moderation to austerity, and to suggest that the austerity themes which can be seen in Christian interdictions are still at work in our society. Recent scholarship is giving us a more nuanced picture of this moderation/austerity divide (for a useful review, although clearly pushing a strong agenda, see Davidson 2007). Nonetheless, other scholars of the ancient world, such as Peter Brown, Geoffrey Lloyd and Pierre Hadot, tend to give (qualified, but strong) support to the analysis Foucault draws. While it is a useful and important continuing endeavour to finesse Foucault's account, and to provide the occasional correctives, we can be confident in accepting its general thrust.

Much of the value of Foucault's work can be found in the developments in thinking about the self and subjectification to which it has directly led. It is in these fields that Foucault's work is most alive, and it is here that we can see the enduring power and value of Foucault's pioneering work. It is difficult to survey these fields briefly, because of the enormously wide impact his work has had across the humanities and social sciences. However, to return to the point made earlier in our discussion, much post-Foucault analysis makes the mistake of thinking of Foucault's work on the self as grand-theoretical, at which point the task is seen as applying that grand-theoretical grid to a new series of problems. This approach is likely to find exactly what it is looking for: the self described by Foucault present in a range of other settings. But we might be justly worried here that the tail is wagging the dog, because the task is not a deductive one; the point is not to use a general grid to enable us to specify a growing range of examples, but to engage in fresh empirical work which enables us to chart the various ways in which human beings are able to experience themselves.

Perhaps the most interesting and fertile development of Foucault's approach is that which has investigated those practices of government of self and others which can be discerned in liberalism and neo-liberalism. Foucault himself made relatively few remarks (brilliantly insightful though they were) about these modern forms of understanding the activity of government, but it is clear he regarded neo-liberalism as a fascinating and intellectually complex system of thought. His lectures feature a number of interesting treatments of the problem of liberalism and neo-liberalism, but no book-length treatment of these topics was ever produced. His sketchy but provocative essay on 'Governmentality' (1991b) was the impetus for much work on this intellectual problem after his death, but the best of that work makes the connection between the 'history of political thought' angle, which is represented in the 'Governmentality' essay, and the work on the self, which dominated the last phase of Foucault's writing. Nikolas Rose's work (see, for example, 1996) is an excellent illustration of this tradition. Rose understands well that Foucault's work on the self is not an analysis in the sphere of culture (the typical concern of the grand theorist of self), but in the sphere of government. Consequently, he sets out to show the interconnection between modern forms of self–self/self–other relations and modern forms of government, all the time understanding the self as a kind of 'irreal projection' of systems of thought and systems of social regulation. What Rose does so well is take the *spirit* of Foucault's line of enquiry, and use it to develop his own empirical analysis of the major role played by the psy sciences in our society. Rose argues that the type of self these psy sciences implant and then assume to be foundational is a recent phenomenon, a fresh example of a way in which human beings have been asked to establish a relationship with themselves and with other human beings. This understanding of the self has been translated from the psy sciences into many other realms of life (politics, business, economics, private life, and so forth), and this 'generosity', as Rose puts it, has allowed the power of, and range of application of, concepts such as self-fulfilment, freedom and autonomy to increase until they have become unquestioned cultural imperatives.

This research tradition has drawn our attention to the way that a mutuality between governing others and governing our selves became intensified, especially with nineteenth-century liberalism, at a moment when the conduct of rule became a matter of passionate concern and reflection: this was not only a reflection on the techniques and forms of rule, it was also an inquisition into the ethical justification for rule. Foucault suggests that the West has a long tradition of assuming a set of connections between forms of government and mastery at a variety of levels, usually the self, the family and others. It has been a repeated theme in Western culture, as Foucault shows, for an intimate relationship between self-mastery and the mastery of others to be assumed and insisted upon: if you want to govern other people you must first learn to govern yourself. This theme of the relationship between the government of self and of others is very noticeable in the nineteenth-century liberal tradition, and continues to this day. Liberalism (and neo-liberalism) is insistent upon the notion that government of others requires self-mastery. It is perhaps useful here to think of liberalism, not especially in terms of political philosophy or practice, but as the constant problematisation of government: liberalism contains within it the fear of over-governing and so is prone constantly to review and renew the activities of governing. The liberal *rapport à soi*, then, is a means of establishing something like an ethical authority to govern. The monotonous repetition of this historical imperative connecting the government of self and the government of others can be seen in empirical analyses of many periods of our culture; for example in Peter Brown's work on the ancients, Gerhard Oestreich's account of the development of the early modern state, or in Stefan Collini's analysis of nineteenth-century political authority. The neoliberalism/governmentality research tradition shows us exactly how these recurrent themes have been adjusted, reconceptualised and intensified.

A second interesting development of Foucault's work on the self pushes the notion of the technical nature of subjectification still further. There are two limits to Foucault's analysis that we may try to move beyond. The first is the point that Foucault's analysis is limited to the realm of the *self*, in particular the realm of the *conduct* of the self. However, as Osborne (1994) points out, there are a range of other concerns that scholars have busied themselves with: we might think of the history of systems for experiencing consciousness sketched out by Paul Hirst, or Peter Brown's work on the history of systems for experiencing conscience. This emphasises once again the point that the self, and the problematisation of its conduct, is not the only way in which humans have experiences of themselves. Further, we could add new possibilities for 'techniques of the mind' – including analyses of the roles of numeracy and literacy (using the work of Patricia Cline-Cohen and Elizabeth Eisenstein respectively) in reshaping human beings (Rose 1996: 31) – and techniques of the body (in addition to the work of Elias and Mauss already mentioned, we can mention here the work of Judith Butler). The second limit we may move beyond is that while Foucault's account is concerned with techniques of a restricted sort, in our society we have seen a sudden growth in the sorts of technical means by which human beings come to experience themselves. Again, Nikolas Rose is at the forefront of this development, with his more recent work on the targeting of the human being by the bio-sciences. It is also worth briefly mentioning the influence of Bruno Latour and actor-network theory. Latour has developed a series of analyses of socio-technical systems which, while not being especially concerned with the problem of subject-formation, nonetheless show us the power of an analysis of the *socio-technical* shaping of conduct (see, for example, Latour 1992); so, for example, automatic door-closers and seat belts play a role in the formation of human subjectivity and come to shape human action, even though they are nonhuman 'actants'. The most mature uses of this thoroughly technological way of thinking about self and identity can be found in Donna Haraway (e.g. 1991) and Mike Michael (e.g. 2006). This work on the routinised generation of forms of subjectivity in networks dovetails nicely with the Foucauldian approach, and represents an interesting future trajectory; many scholars, including Andrew Barry, John Law and John Urry, have pursued this 'technologised' theme, in which the process of subjectification is understood as much more contingent, partial, contradictory, and above all *technological,* than has been common in the social sciences. In some of these scholars, the connection to Foucault is to the fore, in others he is more to the background, but his work still sets much of the agenda.

Another new direction or development of Foucault's work that we should consider is the gradually increasingly recourse to Gilles Deleuze's (1986, 1992) work on 'the fold' as a useful addendum to and clarification of Foucault's approach. Deleuze introduces the concept of the fold as a way of expressing Foucault's anti-phenomenology, and especially to show how Foucault can be distinguished from Heidegger; the details of this do not concern us here, but Deleuze's goal is to show the possibility of avoiding psychologism (the assumption of the existence of a separate sphere of the psychological). As we have already hinted at in our earlier discussion, for Foucault, the concept of the fold – the doubling over of knowledge upon itself, or power upon itself – allows the formation of a pocket within the smooth line of the exterior; this pocket of 'interiority' is the zone of the self, simultaneously 'inside' and 'outside'. A technical term in embryology which captures this movement is 'invagination', the process whereby in the developing cell, the cell wall folds back on itself to form an 'interior' pocket; this is the process by which internal organs are formed in developing organisms. We are used to this idea in fully developed biological entities, where we are aware, for example, of the lungs, throat, rectum or vagina as being internal organs or parts that are 'folds' in the line of the exterior: always simultaneously inside and outside. A metaphor that may help here is to think of a sheet of material which is occasionally pleated; the pleats are the zone of subjectification – both inside and outside, and rather temporary and reformable (as the sheet is stretched out and then folded upon itself again).

The reason this metaphor may be useful is that it enables us to investigate the history of subjectification without having to start from the perspective of an essentialised psychological subject, which our empirical enquiries suggest to be a fairly recent historical arrival; it gives us 'a way we might think of an internality being brought into existence without postulating any prior interiority, and thus without binding ourselves to . . . the law of this interiority whose history we are seeking to diagnose and disturb' (Rose 1996: 37). The fold is an encapsulation of all sorts of techniques, habits, moments of authority, which may, occasionally, become stabilised through routine and through human memory. Crucially, however, it is not simply the human body that is the site of this folding:

> the lines of these folds do not run through a domain coterminous with the [flesh] . . . Human being is emplaced, enacted through a regime of devices, gazes, techniques that extend beyond the limits of the flesh. Memory . . . is not a simple psychological capacity, but is organised through rituals of storytelling, supported through artifacts such as photograph albums . . . The regimes of bureaucracy are not merely ethical procedures infolded into the soul, but occupy a matrix of offices, files . . . Folding being is not a matter of bodies, but of assembled locales.
>
> *(Rose 1996: 38)*

Here we can see the connection to the Latourian injunction to consider non-human actors as crucial 'actants'; we can begin to unpack the array of techniques that localise a form of experience of self *across a network* which is hybrid. As we give proper weight to the hybrid nature of these processes, we see that they are not simply 'human' or 'psychological', but extend out into what we once could only see as inhuman wastelands.

Without wishing to labour the point: while to some eyes this Deleuzian move may seem like a shift to a theory of self, the point of it is quite the reverse. If we wish to follow Foucault, to continue to write genealogies of the self, and genealogies of other ways in which human beings relate to themselves and to others, we cannot start from the ground of a psychology of the self. The aim here is to start with scepticism about the self, and allow the genealogy of the various guises of subjectification to break out of the psychologism of our culture.

Conclusion

In 'The subject and power', Foucault (1982: 208) usefully summarises 'three modes of objectification which transform human beings into subjects'. The first mode concerns those sciences which objectivise, for example, the speaking subject (linguistics) or the labouring subject (economics); the second mode concerns the 'dividing practices' which either split a subject internally, or split certain subjects from others (for example, the mad from the sane, the criminal from the good, or the sick from the healthy); and the third mode refers to 'the way a human being turns him- or herself into a subject'. In all three of these types of analysis, one can sense the pessimism of Foucault; he shows us the genealogy of these various modes of subjectification, and as we better understand the long history they have, how thoroughly burnt into our souls are the rituals of mortification, for example, or the malign problem of pleasure, we might wonder whether there is any escape, whether any other forms of experience of ourselves are possible. On the other hand, we can also see the recent lineage of certain shifts, such as the liberal moment, which, while clearly an intensification of earlier themes to which it bears a family resemblance, nonetheless always has a fragile hold on the reality it seeks to programme. Foucault's final works on the self demonstrate to us the role particular forms of self are asked to play in the maintenance of the social; and his work has inspired vigorous new traditions which analyse the interconnection between the subject and government. Yet there is no theory here to be applied; no simple correspondence between the problems of one age, and the problems of our own, which would enable us to read off similarities and diagnose our contemporary problems. Just as for the Greeks, for whom the flexibility of their ethical code meant that the construction of a beautiful life has its elective moments; just as for the liberals, for whom the problematisation of government meant there were no simple answers to questions of ethical rule; so for us, the question of self is perhaps more about diagnosis and the raising of new questions than it is about giving the self a cosy pigeonhole to occupy.

Acknowledgements

Thanks go to the following for discussions and comments on earlier drafts: Matt Ball, Christian Callisen, Clare O'Farrell, Nick Osbaldiston, Theresa Sauter and Gary Wickham.

References

Davidson, J. (2007) *The Greeks and Greek Love: A Radical Reappraisal of Homosexuality in Ancient Greece*. London: Weidenfeld and Nicolson.

Deleuze, G. (1986) *Foucault*. London: Athlone.

Deleuze, G. (1992) *The Fold: Leibniz and the Baroque*. Minneapolis: University of Minnesota Press.

Foucault, M. (1977) *Discipline and Punish: The Birth of the Prison*. London: Allen Lane.

Foucault, M. (1978) *The History of Sexuality Volume I: An Introduction*. New York: Pantheon.

Foucault, M. (1980) 'Truth and power'. In C. Gordon (ed.) *Michel Foucault. Power/Knowledge: Selected Interviews and Other Writings 1972–1977)* Brighton: Harvester.

Foucault, M. (1982) 'The Subject and power', in H. Dreyfus and P. Rabinow (eds) *Michel Foucault: Beyond Structuralism and Hermeneutics*. Chicago: University of Chicago Press.

Foucault, M. (1984) *The Use of Pleasure*. New York: Pantheon.

Foucault, M. (1986) *The Care of the Self*. New York: Pantheon.

Foucault, M. (1991a) *Remarks on Marx: Conversations with Duccio Trombadori*. New York: Semiotext(e).

Foucault, M. (1991b) 'Governmentality', in G. Burchell, C. Gordon and P. Miller (eds) *The Foucault Effect: Studies in Governmentality*. Brighton: Harvester Wheatsheaf.

Foucault, M. (1997) 'On the genealogy of ethics: an overview of work in progress', in *Ethics: Subjectivity and Truth*. New York: New Press.

Foucault, M. (2005) *The Hermeneutics of the Subject: Lectures at the Collège de France 1981–1982*. New York: Picador.

Foucault, M. and Blanchot, M. (1989) *Maurice Blanchot: The Thought from Outside and Michel Foucault as I Imagine Him*. New York: Zone.

Haraway, D. (1991) *Simians, Cyborgs and Women*. London: Routledge.

Latour, B. (1992) 'Where are the missing masses?' in W.E. Bijker and J. Law (eds) *Shaping Technology/Building Society*. Cambridge, MA: MIT Press.

Mauss, M. (1973) 'Techniques of the body', *Economy and Society* 2(1): 70–88.

Michael, M. (2006) *Technoscience and Everyday Life: The Complex Simplicities of the Mundane*. Maidenhead, Berks: Open University Press/McGraw-Hill.

Osborne, T. (1994) 'Sociology, liberalism and the historicity of conduct', *Economy and Society* 23(4): 484–501.

Rose, N. (1996) *Inventing Ourselves: Psychology, Power and Personhood*. Cambridge: Cambridge University Press.

5

The fragmentation of identity

Post-structuralist and postmodern theories

Sam Han

Introduction

Unfortunately, the terms "post-structuralism" and "postmodernism" are sources of confusion too often within and outside the halls of the academy. At times collapsed into each other, and also given the jingoistic moniker of "French theory" (Cusset 2008), post-structuralism and post-modernism, though perhaps already passé, are still terms that are worth clarifying. If anything, though they are rarely understood (well at least), post-structuralist and postmodern thought, at this point, are too widely influential in a variety of disciplines not to be taken seriously. And it is precisely because post-structuralist and postmodern thought have gained some kind of "legitimacy" in Western academic discourse that I believe it is high time to revisit it.

Broadly speaking, post-structuralism is an intellectual trend (as distinct from an intellectual movement) that began sometime in the 1960s in France. As inspiration, it drew from structuralism, an approach to the study of social phenomena that was rooted in the structural linguistics of Ferdinand de Saussure. Post-structuralism, simultaneously an immanent critique and logical extension of structuralism, also drew from the work of the Swiss linguist but with a critical difference on key issues. Associated with it is an entire generation of French thinkers including Roland Barthes, Jacques Derrida, Julia Kristeva, Luce Irigaray, Michel Foucault, Gilles Deleuze, and Jean Baudrillard among others.

Postmodernism, which, of the two, has gained far more traction in non-academic contexts, in an ironic twist of fate, has become the most floating of signifiers, used now to describe everything from the American comedy series *The Simpsons* to contemporary capitalism. Many view the term to have emerged, not in the social sciences or philosophy, as did "structuralism" and "post-structuralism," but in architecture in the works of figures such as Robert Venturi, which later on led to its use in various contexts (Venturi, Scott Brown, and Izenour 1972).

In the context of this collection, it is important to revisit post-structuralism and postmodernism with specific attention paid to the concept of identity, since it was the particular implications for prior theories of identity that post-structuralist and postmodern critique challenged, that sounded the alarm for a sustained backlash in the academy. One of the major discourses that stemmed from post-structuralist and postmodern thought has been what has been called "death of the Subject." By this, many of post-structuralism and postmodernism's critics were trying to point out that the logical extension of the critique of the Enlightenment and its modern categories of knowledge that characterized much of post-structuralist and postmodern theory would mean that human subjectivity itself was at stake.

Surprisingly enough, they were *not* wrong.

Post-structuralist and postmodern thought, if it is to be categorized at all, can be described in the words of the philosopher Jean-François Lyotard, who was one of the first to use the term "postmodern" – "incredulity to metanarratives" (Lyotard 1984). Of the several metanarratives he lists, along with Hegel's teleological dialectics of Spirit and the hermeneutics of meaning, is what he refers to as the "emancipation" of the rational subject. The rational subject is the *cogito ego* of Descartes, a founding principle upon which all of modern thought is based. The Cartesian *cogito* privileges the individual subject as the bearer of Reason, and separates her from objects. The subject, in short, is the observer; the object is observed. Indeed, even Kant's Three Critiques, which were to have been a "Copernican revolution" in the realm of the subject–object problem, owed much intellectual debt to Descartes. By expressing skepticism toward the narrative of the self, Lyotard was up-ending the entire Western epistemological tradition that was based on the mutual exclusivity of subject and object.

Fredric Jameson, perhaps the most well-known theorist of the postmodern in North America, argues along these lines that the "death of the subject" can be viewed in relation to the changes in cultural production and capitalism (Jameson 1998). According to Jameson, the discourse surrounding the death of the subject is speaking directly about a particular *kind* of subject – the bourgeois individual subject. If one chooses to look in the history of aesthetic modernism, the idea that one's art is "in some way organically linked to the conception of a unique self and private identity, a unique personality and individuality, which can be expected to generate its own unique vision of the world and to forge its own unique unmistakable style" has withered away due, in part, to the type of ideological shift correlative to the changes in the capitalist mode of production (ibid.: 115). Hence, the classic age of "competitive capitalism" wrought the nuclear family, social class and individualism in the arts. In contemporary corporate capitalism, this no longer exists. Yet, Jameson also notes that there can be another way of looking at the "death of the subject," which he describes as the "post-structuralist position." This position maintains that not only is the bourgeois, individual subject passé but it may have never existed. It is, according to this position, a myth, "merely a philosophical and cultural mystification which sought to persuade people that they 'had' individual subjects and possessed this unique personal identity" (ibid.: 115).

This chapter will provide an overview of key developments in post-structuralism and postmodernism that bear most heavily on identity studies. It will begin with a brief account of structuralism, focusing on the use of Saussurian linguistics by Claude Lévi-Strauss, Jacques Derrida, and Jacques Lacan. The importance of the linguistics of Ferdinand de Saussure cannot be overemphasized in the trajectory of post-structuralist and postmodern theory. Then, it will proceed to looking at key figures in post-structuralism and postmodernism, including Judith Butler, Donna Haraway, and Jean Baudrillard, as well as some of their key interlocutors including Nancy Fraser and Anthony Giddens, teasing out key arguments that resonate most strongly to theories of identity. The chapter concludes with a look at the future directions of post-structuralist and postmodern identity studies.

Historical and intellectual development of structuralist and post-structuralist critiques of identity

In the lore surrounding post-structuralism, a paper by philosopher Jacques Derrida called "Structure, sign and play in the human sciences," presented at the Johns Hopkins University in 1966 for a conference entitled "The Languages of Criticism and the Sciences of Man," is viewed to have signaled the beginning of post-structuralism (though the irony seems lost to many who hold this position since it would be quite un-Derridean to posit an "origin" of post-structuralism, as will be made clear below). Whether one chooses to invest in the aura of this event or not, it is indeed the case that post-structuralism, though perhaps yet unnamed and unknown as such at the time, began to gel around a group of concepts and positions that would eventually be coherent enough for scholars to then proceed to draw from it, resulting in its influence in a variety of academic fields, including art history, psychoanalysis, anthropology, sociology and literature.

As the "post-" makes clear, post-structuralism was as much a radical break from structuralism as it was a logical outgrowth of it. It is, if anything, a critique of structuralism from within. Hence, "Structure, sign and play" is at once a pointed critique of Claude Lévi-Strauss's structural anthropology, as it is an appreciation. Lévi-Strauss, in 1966, was still at the height of his intellectual powers. By then, not only had he occupied the chair once held by anthropologist Marcel Mauss at the College de France, one of the most distinguished academic posts any French intellectual could attain, but also his book *Savage Mind* had been published to critical success. At the time, Lévi-Strauss was *the* doyen of Parisian intellectual life, due in part to his devastating critique of Sartre, which, in effect, put the last nail in the coffin of existentialism's dominance at the hands of structuralism. Hence, to offer a critical reading of Lévi-Strauss, as Derrida did, was to attack the leading intellectual in France.

Structuralism differed from existentialism in key ways. While existentialism drew from phenomenology and thus inherited the latter's main analytic tool – consciousness – structuralism drew from the linguistics of Ferdinand de Saussure, effectively jettisoning the individual as the starting-point of analysis for something Lévi-Strauss believed to be "above" (or "below") the individual – structure, as exemplified by language. It could be said that structuralism and post-structuralism are explicitly philosophies of language that extend far beyond the eponymous philosophical subfield, which in the analytic tradition goes back to Wittgenstein. They are intellectual moves that can be called what Richard Rorty, in another context, called "the linguistic turn."

Saussure's key insights in *Course in General Linguistics* (1966), collected and published posthumously by his students, consisted of two radical separations: (1) between *la langue* (language-itself) and *parole* (speech), (2) between words ("the signifier") and the things to which they referred ("signified"). The first separation was between *parole* and *langue*. *Parole*, for him, consists of individual production of meaningful statements; in other words, the way in which language is put into practice as what are called "speech acts." *La langue*, however, is the system of language itself – its grammar, syntax, and other rules – that individuals, when speaking or writing, draw upon passively, if one wishes to think of it that way, but do not engage in the rule-making process themselves. *Parole*, therefore, can be thought of as heterogeneous, subject to individual interpretation, as is made clear by the varieties of patois and slang that are produced in nearly all languages. *Langue*, on the other hand, is homogeneous, systematic and rigid; in other words, *structured* and thus more open to study in a scientific manner.

Additionally, against the understanding of language as derivative of an innate relationship between word and object, Saussure suggests that the relationship between the signifier and signified was arbitrary. To put a twist to his famous example, the word "tree" made up of the letters "t," "r," and "e" have no relationship to the object in the world. However, for those of us who are English-speaking, "tree" nonetheless will create an image in our minds of that brown, usually vertical object with green leaves hanging from its limbs called branches. Hence, the relation of "tree" (signifier) and a tree as existing in the world (signified) is constituted, reinforced and maintained *socially*. That is to say, this relation must be confirmed over and again in use with others. When they come together, they form a sign. Language, the system of signs, is then a rooted in a system of differences held tenuously together under the sign. Therefore it comes as no surprise that Saussure called his version of linguistics "semiology" – the study of signs as they are used socially.

Saussure's ideas became popular in the post-war intellectual life of Paris, especially among literary scholars, who saw semiology as the basis of a new way of thinking about literature beyond the individual work itself as part of a great web of texts. Among them was literary critic Roland Barthes, who was one of the first to adopt Saussure's ideas in the analysis of culture and literature. In anthropology, Claude Lévi-Strauss became the torchbearer of structuralism, beginning with his *Elementary Structures of Kinship* and reaching a boiling point with the publication of *The Savage Mind*.

Lévi-Strauss's structural anthropology incorporated aspects of Saussure's semiology to analyze collective phenomena such as what was then called "primitive religion," in particular the study of myth (Lévi-Strauss 1955). Myths, according to Lévi-Strass, can be thought of as language. They are both made up of structural elements. While language contains morphemes, phonemes and sememes, myths contain what he dubs "mythemes." These units form relations with each other, to form binaries.

Myths are not cosmological explanations of universal, existential questions such as the nature of the universe, life, death and the after-life, but something else. They exhibit, he argues, a structure much like that of language since myths must be uttered and spoken. Like Saussure before him, Lévi-Strauss suggests two levels of myth: (1) as they are uttered and spoken; and (2) as they are structured. In studying the structured, more rigid aspect of myth, *la langue* of myth if you will, he argues that myths contain a similar structure across cultures though varying in content, even modern ones. In widely read essay "The structural study of myth," Lévi-Strauss analyzes the myth of Oedipus, which of course holds a prominent place in Western culture, not only as it is written by one of the most revered ancient dramatists, Sophocles, but also because it plays such a prominent role in Freudian psychoanalysis. Knowingly, Lévi-Strauss argues that the structural units of myth present in the Oedipal myth exist in myths of North American Indians, illustrating the presence of the family drama of Oedipus, more specifically the theme of parental attachment, in Zuni and Pueblo mythology. Thus, he argues, that the structure of myths are universal, a markedly different position from those of anthropologists who had treated so-called primitive societies' systems of cultural symbols as chaotic and unorganized.

In turn, Derrida's "Structure, sign and play" (1978) critiqued the "structurality" of structuralism, using the very linguistic theory of Saussure, from which Lévi-Strauss drew. The basis of Derrida's critique of Lévi-Strauss is on his concept of the "Center," one of the most oft-used phrases of Derrida's philosophy. In spite of the aura surrounding the word "deconstruction," which was, at first, Derrida's invocation of Heidegger's *destruktion*, and would later became a part of popular lexicon, as some commentators have already suggested, Derrida's philosophy could be better described as "de-centering." "Center" is how Derrida explains the aspect of "structure" that holds, in his estimation, metaphysical tendencies of totality, presence and origin. "The function of this center," he writes, "was not only to orient, balance, and organize the structure . . . but above all to make sure that the organizing principle of the structure would limit what we might call the *freeplay* of the structure" (Derrida 1978: 352). This center that exists in all forms of thought in the Western tradition, not just in structuralism, he goes on to argue, is disturbed by the introduction of linguistic analysis. Building on Saussure's insistence of the arbitrariness of the sign, Derrida writes:

> This moment was that in which language invaded the universal problematic; that in which, in the absence of a center or origin, everything became discourse – provided we can agree on this word – that is to say, when everything became a system where the central signified, the original or transcendental signified, is never absolutely present outside a system of difference.
>
> *(1978: 358)*

In both statements, Derrida is taking from Saussure's earlier pronouncement of the arbitrariness of sign and radicalizing it to the point where he argues that reality itself must be scrutinized as part of language. By arguing that language allowed viewing "everything" as "discourse," he is prefiguring a later statement that he became quite famous for: "There is no outside-text" (Derrida 1998: 158). (As we shall see below, it is this statement above others, which caused most trouble for skeptics of Derrida and post-structuralism.)

Consequently, it is no surprise that his critique of Lévi-Strauss begins from, what he views to be the "center" of structure of myths – its supposed "origin." But as Derrida points out, even Lévi-Strauss acknowledges that myths do not have an absolute origin. They are passed down from generation to generation; there is no way to know who it was that started it. Hence, myths, for Derrida, are rather "acentric" structures. In addition, Derrida also points out the rather totalizing nature of Lévi-Strauss structuralist reading of myth. For Lévi-Strauss, mythical structures are ahistorical and universal. Though varying in content, the structure remains the same across cultures and linguistics groups, not to mention historical periods. For Derrida, this is a *misreading* of Saussurian linguistics for, in effect, as the tenuous and rather arbitrary relation of the signifier and signified hints at, language "excludes totalization," as it is a system of an infinite potential connections. Derrida calls this element of language "free play."

> If totalization no longer has any meaning, it is not because the infinity of a field cannot be covered by a finite glance or a finite discourse, but because the nature of the field – that is, language and a finite language – excludes totalization. This field is in fact that of *freeplay*, that is to say, a field of infinite substitutions in the closure of a finite ensemble.
>
> *(Derrida 1978: 289)*

"Freeplay" is in opposition to what Derrida refers to throughout his corpus as the "philosophy of presence," which he considers to be a metaphysical remnant of Platonism. Presence, for Derrida, was an ideal in Western philosophy that was at the root of the concept of Being. To "be" was to be "here." But Derrida views this to be disingenuous as no entity can ever be fully "present" especially in a system of representative differences such as that of *la langue*. A signifier such as the word "cow" does not conjure an actual beast when used by a speaker nor when written on a page. In every instance of signification, for Derrida, exists a contingent agreement of meaning that allows for communication built on a foundation of sand. The accomplishment of meaning is never a *fait accompli* but one that is reached tentatively, if looked at from the perspective of the numerous (or infinite) possibilities of the signifier.

> Freeplay is the disruption of presence. The presence of an element is always a signifying and substitutive reference inscribed in a system of differences and the movement of a chain.

Freeplay is always an interplay of absence and presence, but if it is to be radically conceived, freeplay must be conceived of before the alternative of presence and absence; being must be conceived of as presence or absence beginning with the possibility of freeplay and not the other way around.

(Derrida 1978: 292)

In this way, Derrida juxtaposes his reading of Saussure to Lévi-Strauss, thus concluding that there are two approaches to structure – one based on the sign, the other based on freeplay. The former emphasizes "the sign" as the Center, the privileged element of language. The latter, which he associates with his own approach, focuses less on the accomplishment of the positive identification of the signifier and signified in the sign, but wades in the tenuousness and arbitrariness of the system itself. Thus, Derrida's subsequent writings are full of double-entendre, which was in no small part, one of the major reasons why so many American scholars had such difficulty with his work.

Major claims and developments, and key contributions of post-structuralist perspectives of identity

In this brief engagement with the work of Saussure, Lévi-Strauss and Derrida, I have attempted to draw out the principle themes of post-structuralism – center, origin and totality. These three themes, though they are particular to Derrida's lexicon, do indeed point us toward some of the key concepts utilized by post-structuralist thinkers who have contributed to new understandings of identity. Although Derrida does not explicitly address issues of identity, one can find in the work of psychoanalyst Jacques Lacan similar themes that are more explicitly oriented toward the study of identity, or in this case, the Freudian "ego" or more properly "the I."

In his "Mirror Stage" essay of 1949, Lacan offers a unique and radical theory of the infant development of the ego, arguing that the infant does not fully realize her body to be a unitary totality until she is able to see herself in a reflection of a mirror, or some other kind of reflective surface. It is only after this stage, he argues, that the child understands herself to be a total unit, an effect of identification with her *imago*, and thus attaining the proper coordination of her limbs. "It suffices," he writes, "to understand the mirror stage in this context *as an identification*, in the full sense analysis gives to the term: namely, the transformation that takes place in the subject when he assumes [*assume*] an image" (Lacan 2006: 76). Prior to this stage, the infant experiences her body as fragmented, as different pieces – an arm here, arm there. But when she views, what he calls, her "specular image," she begins to identify with it in all of its totality.

The specular image, which Lacan refers to as the *imago*, is an ideal-I, a *representation* of the ego, not the ego itself. In fact, one of the major critiques that Lacan launches is of the "I's mental permanence," so as to say that the I does not exist prior to this encounter with its *imago*. This then assumes not only the *social* nature of the formation of the ego, but also that the I's primordial nature is necessarily fragmentary.

[T]he mirror stage is a drama whose internal pressure pushes precipitously from insufficiency to anticipation – and, for the subject caught up in the lure of spatial identification, turns out fantasies that proceed from a *fragmented* image of the body to what I will call an "orthopedic" form of its *totality* – to the finally donned armor of an alienating identity that will mark his entire mental development with its rigid structure.

(Lacan 2006: 78; emphasis added)

Further, Lacan insists that the fragmentary primordial nature of the ego actualizes symptomatically in the appearance of disconnected limbs and exoscopical organs in dreams later in life. Indeed, what he is proposing is no less than a full reconsideration of the way in which identity is viewed, beginning with the Platonic equation of the psyche with the soul through Descartes's "cogito," as beginning with the self, the I, the internal. But as he says, if he were to build strictly from subjective data to build his theory of the ego, then he would be "lapsing into the unthinkable, that of an absolute subject" of the Platonic/Aristotelian tradition (ibid.: 79). The moment of the encounter with the mirror, for the infant,

> decisively tips the whole of human knowledge into being mediated by the other's desire, constitutes its objects in an abstract equivalence due to competition from other people, and turns the *I* into an apparatus to which every instinctual pressure constitutes a danger, even if it corresponds to a natural maturation process. The very normalization of this maturation is henceforth dependent in man on *cultural* intervention.
>
> *(ibid.: 79; emphasis added)*

Lacan's dual emphasis on fragmentation and recuperation of alienation resonates with Derrida's, albeit chronologically later, skepticism toward notions of the Center, origin and totality. By suggesting that the infant's experiences her own body as initially fragmented, Lacan is engaged in a de-centering project himself. Whereas Derrida's decentering involved moving away from the characterization of the relation of the signifier and signified under "the regime of the sign" as he called it, Lacan's, however, is from the definition of identity as unitary and total, which judging from the term's current popular usage remains. Indeed even today, some North American recent college graduates go off on road trips seeking their "true" identities, as if it were a tangible thing that one could seek and adopt. Therefore, Lacan concludes, the formation of the ego or the "I" is a result of a "misunderstanding" [méconnaissance]. At the very moment when humans are forming their "sense of self" or identity, he suggests, it is, in fact, with an image and a "function of misrecognition" (ibid.: 80). At the heart of identity is, therefore, a void, a lack.

Thus, we can view Derrida and Lacan as prototypes for subsequent post-structuralist thought on identity. The themes explored above – decentering, freeplay, (anti-) origin, and (anti-) totality – become articulated as a move away from the self-sameness of the fixed notion of modern identity through a critique of categorizations. If modern identities are based on a logic of accumulation, in which one's identity can be attributed to her membership into a variety of categories such as race, gender, class, religion, ethnicity, etc., then postmodern identities reject categories in favor of fluidity.

Main criticisms of post-structuralist perspectives of identity

To a large extent, the criticisms of post-structuralist and postmodern theories of identity have been launched within the realm of politics. In particular, critics have charged theorists in this tradition of being apolitical. In other words, they claim that a post-structuralist and postmodern view of identity would only lead to political fragmentation and, potentially, complacency. This tension played itself out most demonstrably in the debates of the 1980s and 1990s. In order to review some of the main criticisms of post-strucuralist and postmodern theories of identity, let us look with some level of detail at a very specific debate about identity-politics within feminist theory. We can treat it as a microcosm of the core issues that lay underneath the detractions of post-structuralist and postmodern theories of identity.

Sam Han

One of the major intellectual inheritors of post-structuralist identity theory in America has been Judith Butler, whose early work *Gender Trouble: Feminism and the Subversion of Identity* is a contemporary classic. Drawing from Derrida, Butler's work on gender argues against an essentialist, biological notion of gender and sexual identity in favor of a performative one. In her much anthologized essay "Imitation and gender insubordination" (1991), Butler begins by rejecting identity categories, *including* "lesbian" and "gay," as they "tend to be instruments of regulatory regimes, whether as the normalizing categories of oppressive structures or as the rallying points of a liberatory contestation of that very oppression" (p. 558). Butler's resistance to fixed categories of "gay" or "lesbian" is indicative of the intellectual movement of which she is arguably the chief theorist – queer theory. Once a common homophobic slur in the Anglophone world, "queer" was reinterpreted by the gay liberation movements of the 1960s and 1970s as a label of self-identification to remove the stigma of the term. Additionally, "queer" also has the added bonus of not reproducing the binary logic of "heterosexual/homosexual" and "male/female," which, as we shall see, is something that Butler attempts to move away from in her analysis of gay/lesbian identity.

Drawing from Esther Newton's work on drag, Butler asserts that gender identity is always an imitation of a set of behavioral practices that are not biologically innate but a result of the social process of imitation much like drag. While "drag" is commonly understood as a member of one gender imitating (usually comically) the normative behaviors of another, Butler widens this meaning to encompass all gender practices, thus claiming that "drag enacts the very structure of impersonation by which *any gender* is assumed" (p. 563; emphasis added). She, however, radicalizes the notion of drag by delinking it from being a "copy" of an "originary" gendered behavior:

> Drag is not the putting on of a gender that belongs properly to some other group, i.e. an act of *ex*propriation or *ap*propriation that assumes that gender is the rightful property of sex, that "masculine" belongs to "male" and "feminine" belongs to "female." There is no "proper" gender, a gender proper to one sex rather than another, which is in some sense that sex's cultural property . . . Drag constitutes the mundane way in which genders are appropriated, theatricalized, worn and, done; it implies that all gendering is a kind of impersonation and approximation . . . [G]ender is a kind of imitation for which there is no original.
>
> (p. 563)

In arguing that gender identity is not only delinked from sex but, more importantly, that no set of behaviors are exclusively a property of one sex or another, Butler is effectively evoking the key themes of post-structuralism as represented by Derrida and Lacan. On the one hand, by suggesting that all identity is performed, Butler is evoking the Derridean notion of "freeplay," by removing the centrality of the sex-gender correlation that is so naturalized in contemporary society. Further, the idea of gender as a copy or "imitation without an original," her critique of an "originary" masculine or feminine behavior, recalls Derrida's critique of the "origin" of myths or what he calls "the Center."

According to Butler, what is constructed, as "the Center" or the "origin," is heterosexuality. All others are seen as copies, imitations or fakes. However, she contends that the logic of homophobia is not simply rooted seeing homosexual identity as a copy of straight identity but, moreover, an investment in a system of knowledge that privileges the "originary" or the real. Within this framework, all imitations are delegitimized. Thus, in reference to the heterosexist charge that queens and butches and femmes are "copies" of a heterosexual original, Butler retorts:

90

Logically, this notion of an "origin" is suspect, for how can something operate as an origin if there are no secondary consequences which retrospectively confirm the originality of that origin? The origin requires its derivatives in order to affirm itself as an origin, for origins only make sense to the extent that they are differentiated from that which they produce as derivatives. Hence, if it were not for the notion of the homosexual *as copy*, there would be no construct of heterosexuality *as* origin.

(p. 563)

In other words, heterosexuality, the purported "original" sexuality, requires its "fakes" to maintain its originary status. Heterosexuality and homosexuality, then, are locked into a definitional relationship in which each term comes to be and attains its meaning through the differentiation of the other, without a stable ground. "The parodic or imitative effect of gay identities [as queens, butches or femmes]," Butler concludes, "works neither to copy nor to emulate heterosexuality, but rather, to expose heterosexuality as an incessant and *panicked* imitation of its own naturalized idealization" (p. 564). For Butler, identity, more broadly, is not so much rooted in "ontological security" as sociologist Anthony Giddens has argued (Giddens 1991), but is an unstable process, inverting the unease that instability usually connotes. Instability, that is, the uncategorizability of identity, in Butler's view, does not cause existential anxiety but rather provides a certain kind of "pleasure" (Butler 1991: 558).

The emergence and widespread influence of Butler's and sympathetic approaches to identity in addition to the fall of socialism as well as the surfacing of what were called "new social movements" created in the 1980s and 1990s a rather lively debate around the politics of identity. Social theorists of various disciplinary backgrounds weighed in on the merits of social movements rooted in newly visible and politicized identities such as LGBT identities in lieu of older, more traditional identitarian positions such as "working class." One of the major criticisms of the identity theory proposed by Butler has come from socialist-feminist social theorist Nancy Fraser, who has had several exchanges in books and journals with Butler regarding the politics of identity.

Fraser's critique of Butler begins from an analytic separation between a politics of recognition and a politics of redistribution. The former, encompassing Butler and likeminded post-structuralist theories of identity, work to destabilize traditional identity categories so as to effect a multitude of identities. This, in Fraser's estimation, comes precisely at the wrong time in the history of capitalism. On the one hand, the call to recognize various identities are coming when issues of economic justice are much more pertinent, or so Fraser claims, in an era of unfettered global capitalism, and serves to merely complicate the issue of economic justice. This, she argues, is indicative of a "culturalist" bias in Butler and others. On the other hand, Fraser argues, Butler's position also promotes a particularism in left politics, leaving little to no room for coalition building based on commonalities. Further, this position *reifies* identities, she contends:

In this way, culturalist proponents of identity-politics simply reverse the claims of an earlier form of vulgar Marxist economism: they allow the politics of recognition to displace the politics of redistribution, just as vulgar Marxism once allowed the politics of redistribution to displace the politics of recognition. In fact, vulgar culturalism is no more adequate for understanding contemporary society than vulgar economism was.

(Fraser 2000: 111)

Judging from this line of argument, it is unsurprising that a repeated theme in the various critiques of Butler has been on the issue of what Fraser perceives to be a lack of attention paid to social structure and too much attention paid to language. This, Fraser goes on to argue, is a symptom of post-structuralism's larger problem of ahistoricism as it relies on linguistic analysis, which Fraser accuses of being transhistorical. Thus, in lieu of Butler's approach, Fraser opts for what she calls the "status model" as opposed to the "identity model" that "can remedy misrecognition without encouraging displacement and reification," since it understands recognition as a proxy of economic class (Fraser 2000: 120).

The key differences between Fraser and Butler, and in turn those between socialist-feminism and post-structuralism, are thus made clear in viewing the identity model in opposition to the status model. Fraser's concern is with what she calls the politics of redistribution, which have to do with issues of economic justice in the face of structured inequality in capitalist society. Butler's, however, is a social theory of differences that does not separate issues of economic redistribution from issues that are "merely cultural," as Butler notes in tongue-in-cheek fashion. In her estimation, Fraser's argument is too subservient to the idea of a unified left, which, as far as Butler is concerned, overlooks the differences *within* identity movements and deems the issues of recognition as secondary. For her, fragmentation within "the Left" shows the shaky ground upon which the idea of a unified Left stood upon:

> Factionalization, understood as the process whereby one identity excludes another in order to fortify its own unity and coherence, makes the mistake of locating the problem of difference as that which emerges *between* one identity and another; but difference is the condition of possibility of identity or, rather, its constitutive limit: what makes its articulation possible at the same time what makes any final or closed articulation possible.
>
> *(Butler 1998: 37)*

In sum, there is no essential or universal Left experience for Left identity to appeal to.

Major claims and developments, and key contributions of postmodern perspectives of identity

In 1980, another conference occurred, though in France this time, presented by Jean-Luc Nancy and Phillip Lacoue-Labarthe, on the work of Jacques Derrida and the political, entitled "Les Fins de l'homme" ("The ends of man"). If we are to call "Structure, sign and play" as the "beginning" of post-structuralism, then we can tentatively call "The ends of man" conference the beginning of post-post-structuralism, which is how one could view "postmodernism." As the name of the conference would suggest, a major tenet of *post*-post-structuralism, which we can cautiously call "postmodern," is a critique of *humanism* in particular.

For post-structuralists such as Derrida and even more so Michel Foucault, who referred to the "Figure of Man," in hopes of labeling it as a *discursive* formation, against the normative claim of the "givenness" of human nature. Humanism was a remnant of metaphysics, a leftover of the Enlightenment, which while it tooted its own secularist horn, functionally replaced "God" for "the human" as its holy category. Hence, the critique of identity put forth by post-structuralist theories was pushed to the limit in postmodern theories of identity, to the point of challenging human ontology itself.

This is made no clearer than in the contemporary discourse around the post-human and the cyborg, of which Donna Haraway made the first call in her "A manifesto for cyborgs: science, technology and socialist feminism in the 1980s" (Haraway 1990). The image of the cyborg is a rhetorical and political strategy that Haraway deploys in order to accomplish one of the major themes of her essay – hybridity. "A cyborg," she writes, "is a cybernetic organism, a hybrid of machine and organism, a creature of social reality as well as a creature of fiction" (ibid.: 191). As Haraway argues, what a post-modernist theory of identity demands is a reconsideration of the boundaries of what any identity is. In her case, she is most concerned with feminism, and thus what counts as "women's experience." According to her, "women's experience," the collective object of feminism, is built upon a totalized, and abstracted, view of what binds women together and is political fiction, albeit useful at times. Cyborg, she contends, could serve a similar function though without an appeal to an originary or natural unity.

Like Butler, Haraway suggests that there is a "pleasure in the confusion of boundaries and for responsibility in their construction" (ibid.). The last portion, about responsibility of the construction of categories, is perhaps the key phrase in the entirety of the "Cyborg Manifesto," as it has been subsequently called. Haraway's use of the image of the cyborg is not so much a rejection of the existence of categories, but a call to try to acknowledge the social, historical and political *construction* of them, though they take on such magnitude in everyday life that they take on a "givenness" or (second-) natural state. Therefore, one can view the overall project of the cyborg manifesto as the de-naturalization of categories of thought, especially one in particular – the human.

Though according to Genesis the human emerged as *imago Dei* from dust, it has always been defined in relation to beings considered non-human – one being animal, the other being machine. But, according to Haraway, the distinctions between animal/human/machine have become "leaky" thanks to advances in biology, evolutionary theory, cybernetics, and microelectronic technologies, which are indicative of a greater diminishing boundary – between physical and nonphysical. Thus, the cyborg is representative of a kind of identity that takes into account these various diminishing distinctions that, for Haraway, signal a new way of thinking about identities and standpoints as always partial and contradictory, or, as she is noted for putting it, *fractured*:

> Identities seem contradictory, partial, and strategic. With the hard-won recognition of their social and historical constitution, gender, race, and class cannot provide the basis for belief in "essential" unity. There is nothing about being "female" that naturally binds women. There is not even such a state as "being" female, itself a highly other social practices . . . Which identities are available to ground such a potent political myth called "us," and what could motivate enlistment in this collectivity?
>
> *(Haraway 1990: 197)*

Though it is clear that Haraway displays the anti-essentialism of Butler, and shares the suspicion of the politics grounded in a concept of "us," what distinguishes her is the historical nature of her argument for cyborg imagery. The cyborg, she argues, is necessitated by an intensification of the relationship between capitalism and technoscience, whereby a major shift in social, economic, and political relations – the changes in domesticity, economic neoliberalization, the decline of the American welfare state, among other things – have caused a related shift in the epistemological assumptions of modernity, the most crucial of which in her estimation is dualism:

> Cyborg imagery can suggest a way out of the maze of dualisms in which we have explained our bodies and our tools to ourselves. This is a dream not of a common language but of a powerful infidel heteroglossia.
>
> *(ibid.: 223)*

Thus, to appeal to the category of "woman" based on something such as "women's experience" is to deny not only the multitude of different experiences but to orient a politics that is unreflective of the types (or informatics, as Haraway refers to them) of domination that exist in late twentieth-century capitalist societies.

It should be noted here that Haraway's arguments can be read as having parallels to Fraser's, especially in either theorist's resistance to the reification of identity. They, however, come to this end from very different routes. Fraser's argument against the reification of identity stems from the privileging of labor and class in the articulation of left politics. Hence, "new" identities, such as those based on race, gender, and sexuality, that ask for recognition become distractions to the goals of economic redistributive justice. Haraway, on the other hand, resists the reification of identity based on a suspicion of any unitary thinking, a trait she shares with Butler. Thus, to form a politics based on a rigid categories is, for her, a failure of epistemology to get beyond humanism.

We can, at this point, say that Haraway's cyborg brings into relief the vast *epistemological suspicion* characteristic of postmodern thought. Indeed, this stems from the reading of Saussure that highlights the arbitrariness of the signifier. The signifier does not have a natural relation to that which is being signified. Let us explore these themes in greater detail. For the epistemological suspicion, we will look at the work of Jean Baudrillard, whose early work consisted of attempts to synthesize Marx and Saussure and who was unquestionably one of the leading voices of the postmodern epistemological challenge. As brilliant an analyst of contemporary culture as he was an intellectual provocateur (he once expressed his desire to be known as the "[Salman] Rushdie of the Left"), Baudrillard looks at the role of media technologies that function to represent reality and, more scandalously, the separation of reality from its representation, in many of his key works. Like other post-structuralists and postmodernists, Baudrillard frequently uses Saussurian linguistics in his writings. But to say that Baudrillard "uses" anything is a bit of a misnomer as he turns "Saussure against Saussure." For instance, he rejects Saussure's attempt to neatly systematize the process of signification. Indeed like subsequent commentators on Saussure such as Lévi-Strauss and Derrida, Baudrillard pulls from structural linguistics the potentiality of its theory of language as a system of differences and applies it to, most fruitfully, two aspects of Western epistemology – interpretation and Truth, which do not exactly bear on the issue of identity directly; but, there is, in his work, a rich conceptualization of the process of identification, which he argues has undergone massive changes due to the development of media technologies and consumer capitalism.

One of the recurrent themes in Baudrillard's work is the radical separation between images and appearances from meaning – an effect, he argues, of the increasing mediatized representation of reality today. New media, particularly television and the World Wide Web, he suggests give the effect of a being "realer than real," what he calls the "hyperreal." Hence, he calls the represented reality of television news, for instance, "disenchanted simulation," akin to "porn, more real than the real" (Baudrillard 1988: 154). This is a phenomenon that subsequent critics have referred to as the "crisis of representation." For Baudrillard, the mediatization of reality is not so much a crisis but the upending of the representational hierarchy, upon which our concept of reality is rooted. An instance of such a case is in the way wars are reported by 24-hour cable news networks. In the recent American invasion in Iraq, networks such as CNN utilized "embedded reporters," fitted with night-vision cameras, so as to give the audience the effect of "taking part" in a firefight with the enemy. This experience allows the viewer, according to Baudrillard, to be "seized" by the images:

> As a result, this seizure rebounds on the surrounding world we call "real," revealing to us that "reality" is nothing but a staged world, objectified according to rules of depth, that is to say, the *principle* upon which paintings, sculptures and the architecture of a period are

defined, but only a principle; a simulacrum which the experimental hypersimulation of the trompe-l'oeil undermines.

(p. 156)

Thus, Baudrillard argues that in today's mediatized world, "interpretation" is no longer an appropriate term to describe the process of identification, or more generally the knowing subject in relation to her object of knowledge.

In his view, "meaning has been abducted," effectively delinking appearance from meaning, which of course the exercise of interpretation assumes. Contemporary media achieves what the Surrealists attempted as a rupture, an intervention, into modern consciousness. Though he may not have put it this way, the triumph of the image or appearance has had the same effect in the realm of "reality" as what Derrida claimed the arbitrary signifier had on language, but on reality itself, undermining, as Baudrillard put it, "the world's certainty" (p. 157).

It should be clear, at this point, that Baudrillard is reinterpreting the "arbitrary signifier" of Saussure and applying it to not only language but also to reality itself. Representations of reality are so far removed from "truth" that Baudrillard sees them as simulation. The logic of correlation exemplified, for instance between signifier and signified, is broken to the point where there is no signified due to the "substituting [of] signs of the real for the real itself" (p. 167). The certainty of Truth, Baudrillard contends, no longer holds. We can think of this difference as between the regime of representation and the regime of simulation. The regime of representation is founded upon a logic of equivalence between "the sign and the real," which Baudrillard parenthetically notes is "utopian." This, of course, is the basis of successful communication, of symbolic exchange. On the contrary, the regime of simulation rips open the boundary between true/false and real/imaginary. "Whereas representation tries to absorb simulation by interpreting it as false representation," Baudrillard writes, "simulation envelops the whole edifice of representation as itself a simulacrum" (p. 170).

Baudrillard has made several public pronouncements based on his theory of simulation and hyperreality. Perhaps one of the most well known of them was in regards to Disneyland in Southern California, which he argues is a miniaturized simulation of America itself. Its main thematic elements – pirates, the frontier, future world – are all at the root of what sociologist of religion Robert Bellah, in another context, called American "civil religion." Baudrillard offers this phenomenological account:

> [W]hat draws the crowds is undoubtedly much more the social microcosm, the miniaturized and *religious* reveling in real America, in its delights and drawbacks. You park outside, queue up inside, and are totally abandoned at the exit. In this imaginary world the only phantasmagoria is in the inherent warmth and affection of the crowd, and in that sufficiently excessive number of gadgets used there to specifically maintain the multitudinous affect.
>
> *(p. 171)*

The function of Disneyland, then, is to maintain the status quo in the certainty of reality as such. Disneyland is there, and assumed to be imaginary and "not real," to make us think that the rest of the world, outside of Disneyland, is somehow real. However, Baudrillard argues, Disneyland operates much like how the prisons work in modern societies, to mask the carceral nature of society itself, an argument that has parallels with Durkheimian and Foucauldian perspectives on this issue. It is, as Baudrillard calls it, a deterrence machine, attempting to withhold from us the receding horizon of the reality principle.

Main criticisms of post-modern perspectives of identity

If there is no certainty in ontological reality, how can there be ontological security of the self to ward off existential anxiety? This is precisely how sociologist Anthony Giddens frames the questions that arise from the questions asked by Baudrillard's analysis. Whereas Baudrillard's position on the hyperreal is fatalistic, Giddens holds a normative component, with clear tendencies toward the necessity of stability in self-identity. Before moving onto the work of Giddens, it must be noted that he is not in any way a part of what can be described as the postmodern backlash, which is full of critics who do not take any serious consideration of postmodern theories. A self-described "radical modern," Giddens is quite sympathetic to many postmodern theories. Thus, the difference between Giddens and Baudrillard is one of degree not of kind.

According to Giddens, self-identity is based on reflexivity, knowing, either cognitively or subconsciously, what one is doing and why (Giddens 1991). He goes on to argue that the most important element in modern identity is "ontological security," which refers "to the confidence that most human beings have in the continuity of their self-identity and in the constancy of the surrounding social and material environments of action" (p. 92). Thus, ontological security is not only the ability for the individual to construct a narrative of the self, but also ensure that the uncertainties of the world do not negatively affect her to the point where she develops existential anxiety, a concept, which of course Giddens takes from Kierkegaard and subsequent existential thinkers.

Why Giddens places such emphasis on security is revealed by another category that is crucial to his social theory – trust. According to him, because one's self-identity is always a product of the social process, *trust*, in Giddens's estimation, is paramount. But Giddens defines the term in a very particular way; it is a trust in a collective *reality*. This provides the existential anchorings of identity, allowing for the individual to rely confidently on other persons. Drawing on the British psychoanalyst D.W. Winnicott, who famously endowed the world with the concept of the "transitional object," Giddens suggests that "reality" is not a given object-world but constructed through mutuality, such as the one between the infant and the caretaker. Because of this mutual experience of trust, one is able to develop confidence in the reliability of other persons. A threat to the reality of things, such as the one that Baudrillard signals, is, for Giddens, a threat to ontological security, and cause for potential chaos, which he describes as "the loss of a sense of the very reality of things and of other persons" (p. 36).

> The chaos that threatens on the otherside of the ordinariness of everyday conventions can be seen psychologically as *dread* in Kierkegaard's sense: the prospect of being overwhelmed by anxieties that reach to the very roots of our coherent sense of "being in the world."
>
> *(p. 37)*

We can clearly see a few thematic differences between Giddens and Baudrillard here. Whereas Giddens understands the coherence of reality to be an absolutely essential part of self-identity, Baudrillard views reality to have "imploded." This difference in coherence of reality leads us to another point of disagreement between Giddens and Baudrillard, that of the stakes of reality. As mentioned above, there is a strong normative strain in the former's social theory of identity. The latter, however, does not. The normative feature of Giddens's formulation of self-identity and reality makes for a particular adherence and investment in the faith, or correlation, between, in post-structuralist terms, the signifier and the real. As he puts it:

> It is "faith" in the reliability and integrity of others which is at stake here. Trust in others begins in the context of individual confidence – confidence in the caretaking figures . . .

Trust, interpersonal relations and a conviction of "reality" of things go hand in hand in the social settings of adult life.

(pp. 51–2)

Hence, for Giddens, to see the self as fragmented would then be to concede the possibility of epistemology and individual agency, upon which his reputed concept of "reflexivity" rests. If the individual is simply seen as powerless, simply riding the wave of meaningless signifiers, there could be no possibility of the process of the dialectical process of reflexive self-identity. (See Chapter 7 on this topic in this volume.) If reality were not stable and constant, there would be, in turn, no trust and therefore no ontological security. Baudrillard's simulacrum is, quite simply, Giddens's nightmare.

The continuing importance of post-structuralist and postmodern theories of identity, and future prospects

Today, post-structuralist and postmodern theory has made its way into a variety of disciplines, some of which are the former hotbeds of earlier backlash against post-structuralism. Yet, its influence cannot be said to exist in a singular discipline more than any other. Its impact cannot, however, be seen in the adoption of various principles of post-structuralist and postmodern thought. But rather it can be found in the continually widespread skepticism toward foundationalism and anti-essentialism, in theory and research on identity.

One of the places in which it is occurring most visibly is at the intersection of media/technology and science studies. It is in this nether region in which the epistemological and ontological suspicions of post-structuralism and postmodernism come together. A good example of such is Bruno Latour's actor-network theory (ANT). As its name suggest, actor-network theory is a radical departure from the dominant social-science framework that views social identity as the interplay of social structure and agency. Moreover, ANT views non-human entities as agentive forces along with humans. It is this radical de-privileging of the human subject in the research process that one can view ANT as having incorporated both the epistemological critique of "reality" in Baudrillard, for instance, and the ontological critique of "the human" in Haraway.

The incorporation of anti-foundationalist tenets of post-structuralist and postmodern thought are not, however, strictly limited to actor-network theory. Along similar lines, sociologists Karen Knorr-Cetina and Sherry Turkle have created fruitful research programs that view "objects" (again, non-human entities) with a level of sociality. In the case of Knorr-Cetina, she presents "objectualization" as an alternative to "individualization," a term that "ignores the degree to which the modern untying of identities has been accompanied by the expansion of object-centered environments which situate and stabilize selves, define individual identity just as much as communities or families used to do, and which promote forms of sociality . . . that feed on and supplement the human forms of sociality" (Knorr-Cetina 1997: 1). Thus, "objectualization" takes into consideration the very techniques by which the modern self has been, as she put it, untied. This has led her to claim that we no longer exist within the same social structures as we did in the past.

Similarly, Sherry Turkle (2007) has used the term "evocative objects" to develop a research paradigm that views sociality and identity beyond the subject by beginning with "objects," things that she argues express identities. Hence, to study identity, in fact, may fruitfully begin with not the "bearer" of the identity itself but that which reflects it. As she writes:

> The notion of evocative objects brings together these two less familiar ideas, underscoring the inseparability of thought and feeling in our relationship to things. We think with the objects we love; we love the objects we think with.
>
> *(2007: 5)*

Thus, we see in Turkle the thread of post-structuralist and postmodern thought that shirks the research on identity that starts from "within" human consciousness. Scott Lash has recently even called for studying "technological forms of life" (Lash 2001).

In our increasingly technological world, post-structuralist and postmodern theories of identity remain most significant for new research on science, technologies and media, areas of research that broaden the notion of identity to non-human entities. Judging by the use of the World Wide Web, mobile smart phones and other new media in the realm of not only "social networking," as has been greatly publicized in news media, but also for full-scale political movements such as that of what is called the Green Movement in Iran, which emerged after the contested presidential elections of 2009, it seems that media and technology studies will undoubtedly be where greater research takes place across disciplines and across particular academic interests as the world itself becomes more aware of its technicity.

> When we live with implanted chips, we will be on a different footing in our relationships with computers. When we share other people's tissue and genetic material, we will be on a different footing with the bodies of others. Our theories tell us stories about the objects of our lives. As we begin to live with objects that challenge the boundaries between the born and created and between humans and everything else, we will need to tell ourselves different stories.
>
> *(Turkle 2007: 326)*

If we are to believe Turkle's portrayal of our technological future (and there is much evidence that supports it), the ghost of post-structuralist and postmodernist thought will haunt the future of identity studies for some time to come.

References

Baudrillard, Jean (1988) *Jean Baudrillard: Selected Writings*. Standford, CA: Stanford University Press.

Butler, Judith (1991) "Imitation and gender insubordination," in D. Fuss (ed.) *Inside/out: Lesbian Theories, Gay Theories*. New York: Routledge, vi, 426.

Cusset, François (2008) *French Theory: How Foucault, Derrida, Deleuze, & Co. Transformed the Intellectual Life of the United States*. Minneapolis: University of Minnesota Press.

Derrida, Jacques (1978) *Writing and Difference*. Chicago: University of Chicago Press.

Fraser, Nancy (2000) "Rethinking recognition," *New Left Review* 3: 107–20.

Giddens, Anthony (1991) *Modernity and Self-Identity: Self and Society in the Late Modern Age*. Stanford, CA: Stanford University Press.

Haraway, Donna (1990) "A manifesto for cyborgs: science, technology, and socialist feminism in the 1980s," in L. Nicholson (ed.) *Feminism/Postmodernism*. New York and London: Routledge.

Jameson, Frederic (1998) "Postmodernism and consumer society," in H. Foster (ed.) *The Anti-aesthetic: Essays on Postmodern Culture*. New York: New Press, distributed by W.W. Norton, xvi, 159.

Knorr-Cetina, K. (1997) "Sociality with objects: Social relations in postsocial knowledge societies," *Theory, Culture & Society*, 14(4): 1–30.

Lacan, Jacques and Fink, Bruce (2006) *Écrits: The First Complete Edition in English*. New York: W. W. Norton & Company.

Lash, S. (2001) "Technological forms of life," *Theory, Culture & Society* 18: 105.

Lévi-Strauss, Claude (1955) "The structural study of myth," *The Journal of American Folklore*, 68: 428–44.

Lyotard, Jean-François (1984) *The Postmodern Condition: A Report on Knowledge*. Minneapolis: University of Minnesota Press.

Saussure, Ferdinand de (1966) *Course in General Linguistics*. New York: McGraw-Hill Book Co.

Turkle, Sherry (2007) *Evocative Objects: Things We Think With*. Cambridge, MA: MIT Press.

Venturi, Robert, Denise Scott Brown, and Steven Izenour (1972) *Learning from Las Vegas*. Cambridge, MA: MIT Press.

6

Reflexive identities

Daniel Chaffee

Introduction

Reflexivity, in its various forms, is a core concept of personal and social identity. In the broadest of definitions, reflexivity means that which takes account of itself. Individuals monitor the world around them, and change their behavior in light of incoming information. Reflexivity is not so much a component of identity, but a process that is a driver in its formation and maintenance on a very basic level. Since the unsettling forces of globalization, increased information, and thus increased mediation, reflexivity has come to play a heightened or radicalized role in identity construction, specifically as a renegotiation of the interrelationship of individuals to broader social institutions and structures.

In this chapter, I trace the historical and intellectual development of reflexive identity. In the second section, I focus on the work of Anthony Giddens and Ulrich Beck, who have both argued that identity in the contemporary world is individualized and reflexive.

Historical and intellectual development

The reflexive process in social theory can, and often is, split into several different types (May 2000; Pollner 1991). The historical development of reflexivity has focused on reflexivity on a more constitutive level: that of a cognitive process involving self and others that is an essential part of identity. Identity, who we are and who we think ourselves to be, is not innate, but is something that is constructed as part of a dialogue with ourselves, others, and social institutions and structures. Peter Caws frames the stance succinctly: "Identity, psychologically as well as logically, is a *reflexive* relation, a relation of myself to myself, but it can be a mediated relation: I relate to myself through my interaction with others *and with the world*" (1994: 378). Identity is not something that we simply have, but rather, identity is something that is created. Timothy May calls this type of reflexivity, endogenous: "Endogenous reflexivity refers to an awareness of the knowledge that is born in and through the actions of members of a given community in terms of their contribution to social reality. This includes an understanding not only of 'who' someone is, but also 'how' others view them" (May 1999).

In social theory, one prominent trend is to argue that identity is not something that can be determined, or studied by an investigation of individuals alone. Reflexivity is integral to the process by which identity is social, as it involves the back and forth nature of the constructing of identity. Anthony Elliott (2007: 10) writes, "The self is recursive or reflexive to the degree that people constantly monitor, or watch, their own activities, thoughts or emotions as a means of *generating* these aspects of their identity." For Elliott, to study identity means to study the various kinds of interpretations that individuals make. In this sense, however, interpretation, and the process of reflecting information back to the self, is a mediated process. To reflect on others, social institutions, and even the self, involves representations, and signs, and most frequently, language. One of the leading promoters of the dialogical theory of the self is the philosopher Charles Taylor.

> This crucial feature of human life is its fundamentally *dialogical* character. We become full human agents, capable of understanding ourselves, and hence of defining our identity, through our acquisition of rich human languages of expression . . . I want to take *language* in a broad sense, covering not only the words we speak, but also other modes of expression whereby we define ourselves, including the "languages" of art, of gesture, of love, and the like. But we learn these modes of expression through exchanges with others.
>
> *(Taylor 1994: 79)*

Identity relies on definitions of the self, definitions that we acquire through reflexive exchange with other people, various cultures, and ourselves. This process happens through "articulating" versions of self-identity; these views of ourselves come to actually constitute identity when they are filtered back to us through the outside world (ibid.: 78).

In part, Taylor draws this view of the self from the history of philosophy, where a version of this idea of a reflexive self has been stated in various forms, perhaps the first clear version of it coming from René Descartes. In thinking about himself and his position in the world, he overcame his doubt about the existence of the outside world, with the realization that there is an "I" doing the thinking (*cogito ergo sum*). For both Kant, and Hegel, reflexivity is important for self-consciousness and ultimately for consciousness to be able to apprehend the outside world.

One of the most significant figures in the development of understanding reflexive identity is George Herbert Mead. As Taylor points out, Mead was one of the first to realize that the acquisition of language happens through the interaction with others. For Mead (1962: 140), "the self, as that which can be an object to itself, is essentially a social structure." The possibility of coming to know one's self is based on the reflexive capacity to monitor the self from another's assumed position. Taylor comments, "People do not acquire the languages needed for self-definition on their own" (1994: 79). He draws on Mead's idea of "significant others," who introduce us to important aspects of selfhood. Thus, identity, for Mead and Taylor, is always reflexively produced. Taylor writes, "We define our identity always in dialogue with, sometimes in struggle against, the things our significant others want to see in us" (1994: 79). Identity rests upon the ability to monitor our actions with reference to others.

For Mead, not all of our identity is social. We have desires and impulses that arise purely within us, and not in dialogue with others. Thus Mead distinguished the social self, what he termed "me," from the unsocialized self, the "I." The social self is reflexively organized, but the relationship between I and me is also reflexively organized. The ability of individuals to distinguish between these aspects of themselves leads to self-awareness.

Another major figure in the development of concepts of reflexivity in identity is Erving Goffman. For Goffman, the strange thing about social identity is that individuals rarely are aware that they are deciding to be a part of social structures. However, the decision is not the most important aspect, but rather that, as individuals, we are constantly making analyses of social situations and adapting our behavior to them. In his book *Presentation of the Self in Everyday Life* (1959), Goffman likens social life to a drama. Identity for Goffman is something that is performed by individuals within various interactive frameworks. Social actors have to work with the environment, to work with others, and, most importantly of all, to continually monitor how the performance is functioning. Goffman puts a high degree of emphasis on the necessity of continually monitoring and displaying social competence as elements of the successful production of identity.

There is a way in which reflexive identity can be considered a distinctly modern phenomenon. Not only because philosophy turned to thinking about rational agents in modern times, but because there seems to be something different about the modern era which means that the task of maintaining an identity falls on the individual. Lash and Friedman write, "pre-modern identity can be very generally understood as externally (or in Kant's sense 'heteronomously') determined. In 'tribal' societies it is kinship-ordered cosmologies that define identity in terms of deciding *who* someone is" (1992: 4). Taylor (1994: 80) argues that people in pre-modern times did not lack the concept of identity, but rather structures were such that identity, and its recognition by others, was not a problem as such.

In many contemporary social theoretical accounts of the contemporary world, the modern way of life is under pressure from globalization. While it is beyond this chapter to engage the debates in social theory about the nature of globalization, there is a general consensus that globalization in general means that life, at least for many in the expensive West, has become faster and more complex. Zygmunt Bauman sums up well the feeling of globalization:

> To put it in a nutshell: no one seems to be now in control. Worse still, it is not clear what "being in control" could, under the circumstances, be like. As before, all ordering is local and issue-oriented, but there is no locality that could pronounce for humankind as a whole, or an issue that could stand up for the totality of global affairs. It is this novel and uncomfortable perception which has been articulated (with little benefit to intellectual clarity) in the currently fashionable concept of globalization.
>
> *(1998: 38)*

With regards to identity, without putting any specificity on it, modern sources of identity have come under increasing pressure. Things such as the nation-state have been pressured by immigration, stable lifetime jobs are now seemingly gone, on average nearly 50 percent of marriages end in divorce. From national belonging to the most intimate sphere, there has been a shakedown.

Globalization and its unsettling force on the stable institutions of modernity has come from technological innovation both through the ability of people to physically move around the globe and through being exposed to new information. John Urry (2007) pointed out that in 2010 there would be an estimated one billion international arrivals. Perhaps more significantly there has been a rise of new communication technologies including the internet and mobile phones. As of 2010, there was an estimated 1.9 billion internet users (out of a world population of 6.8 billion). People can connect in new and diverse ways to other people and to other cultures that are not necessary physically proximate.

These distinct changes, brought on by globalization have distinct impacts for reflexive identity. The modern identity had reflexivity as a core component of social identity, and in a globalizing world, it is suggested, reflexivity has become radicalized. Bauman sums up the new era of reflexive identity quite well: "Needing to become what one is is the hallmark of modern living" (Bauman in Beck and Beck-Gernsheim 2001: xv). Identity, in this conception is an individualized project. It is not something external, determined by language, but something that is continually worked on.

The major claims and contributions of the theory of reflexive identity

Reflexivity has always played a constitutive role in modern understandings of social identity; in the global era, reflexivity, argue Anthony Giddens and Ulrich Beck, has taken a radicalized turn. Through conditions of heightened reflexivity, the twining of global structures and personal identity has taken place. No longer, they argue is reflexivity just an incidental part of the construction of social identity, but it has taken on a constitutive role in the renegotiation of self and society. Thus they argue that the contemporary era could be labeled "Reflexive Modernity." This turn of phrase makes reference to the postmodernism debate, suggesting that the project of identity has not been entirely displaced but that the role of identity in the contemporary world has changed. Anthony Elliott writes, "observation of, and reflection upon, the social world by human agents comes to reshape the very forms of life instituted by society" (Elliott 2009: 287). For theories of reflexive individualization, not only does our self-knowledge matter to us and to the creation of identity but also it actually constitutes social structures.

The extreme shifts of the global (and modern) world are the starting point of British sociologist Anthony Giddens's theory of reflexivity. He has developed one of the most powerful and influential accounts of the effects of reflexivity on identity. In his books *The Consequences of Modernity* (1990), *Modernity and Self-Identity* (1991), and *The Transformation of Intimacy* (1992), Giddens provides a compelling account of shifts to the experience of everyday life, and the fundamental role that reflexivity has come to play in the formation of identity. His theory of reflexivity brings together two major strands of this thinking and theory: his arguments about the recursive nature of social life, and the experience of living in the modern world. For Giddens the deep structural and institutional changes of globalization impact upon the self, and that "for the first time in human history, 'self' and 'society' are interrelated" (1991: 32). He argues that human societies should be viewed as constantly under construction, always being reconstructed.

Giddens's account of the rise of reflexivity as a driving force of self-identity in the contemporary era begins with an account of the dislocating nature of modernity and globalization. Through the use of terms such as "runaway world" and "juggernaut," Giddens calls attention to the way in which the experience of daily life is turbulent. He defines the juggernaut as "a runaway engine of enormous power which, collectively as human beings, we can drive to some extent but which also threatens to rush out of control" (1990: 139). This is not to say that changes to social life are anything new, but for Giddens, the experience of change itself is constitutively different. What is new is that "change does not consistently conform either to human expectation or to human control" (1991: 28).

This contemporary world of unpredictable change is marked by a process of detraditionalization, or traditions that have been unseated. The complexity of the modern world, both in the explosion of information and in the movements of people around the globe, have changed the nature of community. Traditions were embedded in communities marked by physical co-presence. Giddens writes, "tradition always discriminates between 'insider' and 'other', because participation in ritual and acceptance of formulaic truth is the condition for its existence" (1994: 79). While traditions are certainly not disappearing, they are being eclipsed and renegotiated and their ability to determine status in the community is disappearing. Habermas writes of multicultural societies:

when a culture has become reflexive, the only traditions and forms of life that can sustain themselves are those that bind their members while at the same time subjecting themselves to critical examination and leaving later generations the option of learning from other traditions or converting and setting out for other shores.

(1994: 130–1)

This points to detraditionalization as a reflexive process of determination of group status, something that is reflexively negotiated.

In addition to detraditionalization, Giddens identifies a general process of what he calls "disembedding" (1990, 1991). By disembedding he means that social processes are pulled, or lifted out of a particular locality and become stretched over time and space. Giddens argues that as social actors we always to some extent have knowledge of what we are doing. This involves he argues, both practical knowledge of how to get by and discursive knowledge. However, our ability to get by in the modern world is challenged by feelings of uncertainty, anxiety and risk, which Giddens lumps under the category "ontological security." The need and mode of monitoring of social action has been stretched beyond the confines of trust as we knew it. Without being able to have knowledge over local community and area, and with social interaction stretched over long distances, and including people and symbols that are not physically co-present, this alters the nature of trust. Trust is different when you cannot monitor the actions of others face to face, and when there are too many things to monitor. Similarly, risk is not equivalent to danger, but rather it is a danger over which you do not have knowledge, and so you have to trust in expert systems to keep going. Part of the heightening of reflexivity is that physical co-presence is not necessary to undertaking social interaction, including the building of identity. In short, individuals must create new modes of behavior, and new identities to cope with the uncertainties of a runaway world. While this all sounds very dire for individuals, Giddens has a positive spin on it. Previous societies that were more locked into tradition were fundamentally not open to self-awareness. Reflexivity exists more in the realm of re-embedding social practices.

In the post-traditional order, self and self-identity are negotiated with a plurality of choice (Giddens 1991: 82). While traditions have not necessarily disappeared, they have lost the social weight that gave them the ability to organize social identities. This means that our everyday experience at one and the same time is more diverse and more segmented. One example of this is that people tend to live geographically separated from work and family, which is a sense of isolation, but we are now confronted with many other people's workplaces and experiences which run through our own. It is nearly impossible to walk down a street in a global city and not see many different cultural ways of living and have some experience of it. Even the ability of religion to provide cogent narratives of self has become contextualized. This is integrally linked to the change of religion, but people tend less and less to believe in absolutes, and to qualify beliefs within certain contexts.

Additionally, Giddens does not see reflexivity as a coping strategy, but actually a repositioning of the importance of reflexive self-identity as a means of negotiating the connection between self and social structure. On one level, Giddens maintains a concept of reflexivity as that of being a human with social knowledge and ability. On another, more serious level, the incorporation of new knowledges and information alter the very fabric of social life. In Giddens's formulation of reflexivity, there is not simply a "bending back upon" or a reflection, but individuals through their reflexive action change social institutions and structures themselves. Giddens writes, "The reflexivity of modern social life consists in the fact that social practices are constantly examined and reformed in the light of incoming information about those very practices, thus constitutively altering their character" (1990: 38). Thus, reflexivity is not just reflection, or the reflective agent, but one who constitutively and actively alters the social landscape. Not only do we monitor social actions, but we also monitor the monitoring of social action.

The consequence of a shift to reflexive identity is of a switch from self as complete and internally constituted to a self, which is constantly being remade. Giddens calls this state a "plastic" state. The way in which we are able to maintain an identity is through the maintenance of a particular narrative of the self. Giddens writes:

> A person's identity is not to be found in behaviour, nor – important though this is – in the reactions of others, but in the capacity to keep a particular narrative going. The individual's biography, if she is to maintain regular interaction with others in the day-to-day world, cannot be wholly fictive. It must continually integrate events which occur in the external world, and sort them into the ongoing 'story' about the self.
>
> *(1991: 54)*

In creating a revisable identity, there is something about a reflexive identity that is more unifying than the postmodern one. Reflexive identity reinscribes people into new narratives and global structures.

Giddens argues that there are two sides to the increasing connectedness of globalization. Most often people focus on the way in which globalization is a top-down process, something like the spread of a homogenous (and often Americanized) culture. In contrast to that, reflexive identity highlights the way in which globalization moves bottom up. Giddens (1994: 58) points out that when you purchase an item of clothing, or particular kind of food, you are part of an extensive global web. The shirt might be made in Thailand, shipped by a Dutch company, on a ship based in Singapore. The simple act of deciding what suit to buy, actually comes to constitute trade patterns. Our actions come to be linked through risk, as there are ecological and ethical consequences to the decisions we make that link us all together.

For Giddens, reflexivity has come to affect self-identity all the way down through intimate relationships. In his book *The Transformation of Intimacy* (1992), Giddens provides a study in the transformative power of reflexivity on self-identity. With the slackening of tradition, people now have greater choice over who they get into relationships with, and what kind of relationship they have. The basis for this increased choice is social reflexivity, that people choose what kind of self they want to be, and come to choose what kind of relationship they want. So while many social critics decry the high rate of divorce in Western societies, Giddens argues that there is something reflexive and positive here. Couples are now engaging in what he terms "pure relationships," that is, they are engaging in and staying in relationships to the extent that they desire to. The bonds of love are not anchored by societal demands, but by reflexive choice. Reflexivity is integral to the creation of the pure relationship in that these changes do not happen in a vacuum. When a couple walks down the aisle, they know that they have only about a 50 percent chance of staying married. The arrangement of marriage is undertaken with an awareness of what is happening socially.

Social science is affected by the reflexive state of affairs as well. Sociology, for Giddens, will always be reflexively a part of the world that it attempts to study; subject and object are intimately and reflexively linked. Natural scientists, Giddens argues, try to understand the world from a single point of interpretation, that is, the "world" which they are studying has clear parameters. Social scientists on the other hand are studying a world which they have influence over, and at the same time a world which influences them. Giddens writes:

The social sciences operate within a double hermeneutic, involving two-way ties with the actions and institutions of those they study. Sociological observers depend upon lay concepts to generate accurate descriptions of social processes; and agents regularly appropriate theories and concepts of social science within their behaviour, thus potentially changing its character.

(1987: 30)

The double hermeneutic relates back to Giddens's view about the constitution of society as built upon the practical consciousness of social actors. The double hermeneutic affects the social scientist as much as the "contents of the research" for the social scientist is changing from the attitude and responses of the "subject" as quickly as the subject is changing in response to the social scientist. The findings of social science have the possibility of altering social life far beyond the immediate context of the research.

Ulrich Beck has developed an account of reflexive modernization and the effect on individual identity that is similar in many ways to Anthony Giddens, yet critically different. Much like Giddens, Beck argues that there is a major structural shift in society that pushes individuals into a position where identity is their task. Not simply any more do individuals rely on old social categories to provide meaning, but individuals need to become who they are. As Beck and Beck-Gernsheim put it, "Life loses its self-evident quality; the social 'instinct substitute' which supports and guides it is caught up in the grinding mills of what needs to be thought out and decided" (2001: 7). Thus, Beck and Beck-Gernsheim argue that reflexive modernization is driving reflexive individualism, that individuals are becoming pushed to negotiate their place and identity.

The central claim, for Beck of reflexive modernization lies in the development of "risk society" which he outlines in his book *Risk Society* (1992). In a risk society, individuals become freed from structural forms of social life. Initially, the shift from traditional societies to industrial societies was the paradigm of industrialization. For Beck, the key characteristic of reflexive modernization is that modernity "modernized" itself. He makes a distinction between first modernity and second, or reflexive modernity. The first modernity was characterized by heavy, stable industrial capitalism, marked by the presence of the welfare nation-state. Personal life and identity were created through well-structured and bounded forms of collective life.

The second modernity has disembedded these ways of life. Primarily the side-effects, or unintended consequences of first modernity have lead to an unsettled and highly reflexive second modernity marked by risk. This second modernity is marked by a criticism of science for the ill effects of technology such as atomic disasters (in particular Chernobyl), polluted environment, a nation-state that has lost the ability to ensure welfare, and a working life that is marked by flexibility. Above all, society is marked by a new problem of risk. While risk is seemingly nothing new, Beck argues that in first modernity, there were dangers, but they were readily apparent. You worry about the danger of getting hit by a car crossing the road for example. A risk, by comparison, is the danger of chemicals leaching into your bottled water. There is less transparency, the problems are part and parcel with scientific knowledge, and distinctly out of the control of the individual.

For Beck, reflexive individualism does not mean more reflection. He argues that this shift to risk society is out of control of individuals. He writes of how reflexive modernization comes to exist in the shift from first to second modernity:

In view of these two stages and their sequence, the concept of "reflexive modernization" may be introduced. This precisely does not mean reflection (as the adjective "'reflexive" seems to suggest), but above all self-confrontation. The transition from the industrial to the risk epoch of modernity occurs unintentionally, unseen, compulsively, in the course of a dynamic of modernization which has made itself autonomous, on the pattern of latent side-effects. One can almost say that the constellations of risk society are created because the self-evident truths of industrial society (the consensus on progress, the abstraction from economic consequences and hazards) dominate the thinking and behaviour of human beings and institutions. Risk society is not an option which could be chosen or rejected in the course of political debate. It arises through the automatic operation of autonomous modernization processes which are blind and deaf to consequences and dangers. In total, and latently, these produce hazards which call into question – indeed abolish – the basis of industrial society.

(Beck 1996: 28)

Beck is not arguing that industrial society has necessarily disappeared, but rather that the dynamic of industrial society undercut itself. Reflexive modernization means self-transformation more than self-reflection.

One the side of reflexive individualism, Beck makes a similar argument. For Giddens, reflexive self-identity, as a response to ontological security, means a renegotiation. While there are many out of control parts, this seems to be a way in which people successfully renegotiate their identity. Hence relationships detraditionalized through reflexive awareness have led to "pure relationships," ones that are marked by people actively engaged in relationships that matter to them. Reflexive individualism does not mean that people are more conscious, but rather they are more aware that control is impossible (Beck et al. 2003: 3).

For Beck, there has been a complete erosion of stable collective identity. The old social categories of life in industrial modernity were, as Bauman puts it, simply facts of life. However, Beck argues that in second modernity, the individual becomes the central point of organization for his life. He writes, "This 'self' (the contour) of industrial modernity gets lost in the modernization process, which shifts its own foundation and coordinates; it is replaced by another self which must be reconstructed, theoretically and politically" (Beck 1997: 25). No longer does one simply fit into the old categories, but the self is different, one that is negotiated. This process is one that is forced, and conflicted, for the old categories such as nation-state, family, class, Beck calls "zombie categories" (Beck and Beck-Gernsheim 2001). They are still around, but they have lost the definition that they once had. "You may and you must lead your own independent life, outside the old bonds of family, tribe, religion, origin and class; and you must do this within the new guidelines and rules which the state, the job market, the bureaucracy etc. lay down" (ibid.: 11).

Main criticisms of reflexive identities

One of the general charges against reflexivity is that it encourages narcissism. Excessive individualism, and focus on the self, is generally seen as a negative moral quality. In the context of the global world, Richard Sennett has argued that the qualities that make individual strong performers in a culture of new capitalism, which includes above all flexibility, is leading to a decline of moral values. The reflexive capacities of effective functioning in the global economic marketplace are not the values that make for good character. In his book *The Corrosion of Character* (1998), he details ways in which the ability of individuals to reflexively form identity does nothing to help them weather the effects of short-termism. For Sennett, reflexivity is an inherent part of maintaining an identity, but that there are transcendal values that remain fixed and outside of the capacity of reflexivity to change. He writes, "The maintenance of oneself is a shifting activity, as one's circumstances change and one's experience accumulates; fidelity to oneself, as in being honest about one's faults, out to be constant, no matter where or what age one is" (Sennett 1998: 145). People, in modern capitalism, are treated as disposable, and they are fundamentally individualized, pushed to become flexible, but are cut off from meaningful shared narratives.

Scott Lash (Lash and Urry 1994) asks why it seems that reflexive individualization seems to be happening in London, but not in the relatively less wealthy north of England. There is an implicit class divide in the possibility of increased reflexive identity, those with access to new communication technologies, and those that are already in a socio-economic position to renegotiate identity. Anthony Elliott expands this point to encompass the globe. He points out that in the contemporary era of radical and global instability, there is a rise of social behavior that is distinctly not reflexive:

> Much of Beck's work has been concerned to emphasize the degree of reflexive institutional dynamism involved in the restructuring of personal, social and political life, from the reforging of intimate relationships to the reinvention of politics. But there are disturbing dimensions here as well, which the spread of cultural, ethnic, racial and gendered conflict has shown only too well, and often in ways in which one would be hard pressed to find forms of personal or social reflexive activity.
>
> *(Elliott 2002: 301)*

Elliott's point is a sharp one for the concept of reflexive identity in both personal and social dimensions. In Sennett's account, individuals are isolated from shared narratives, but in various ethnic or cultural conflicts, there is a sense in which individual identity is dominated by the cultural and material circumstances of birth.

With regards to the theory of reflexive individualization, one of the major points of contention is the relationship of the reflexive individual to broader social structures. Zygmunt Bauman points out that there is not enough in the concept of reflection to explain how self-mastery leads to change:.

> We are all engaged in "life politics" – we are "reflexive beings'" who look closely at every move we take and are seldom satisfied with its results. Somehow, however, that reflexion does not reach far enough to embrace the conditions which connect our moves with the results and decide their outcomes.
>
> *(2001: 19)*

How is it that radicalized self-identity actually comes to alter social institutions? In a similar vein to Bauman, Jeffrey Alexander (1996) asserts that contemporary society is marked by a greater separation of the individual from cultural forms. Alexander argues that reflexivity is inherent in social action, but cannot be separated from it: "Typification, invention and strategization are simultaneous moment of every social action; they cannot be separated and compartmentalized in a historicist way" (1996: 136).

All accounts of reflexive identity, from Mead and Goffman through to Giddens and Beck, seem to present an individual that is able to effectively monitor social behavior and then to change their own behavior accordingly. In the accounts by Giddens and Beck, social actors have the capacity to make transformative choices. But if we take seriously psychoanalytic theories of the self, the reflexive individual might not be fully conscious of all the factors in play. Certainly

Anthony Giddens does include some aspects of the work of Erik Ericson on trust, but Beck makes no allowance at all for the fact that as social agents, individuals are not able to access their own feelings and information reliably. Beck and Giddens certainly do allow that there is much beyond the control of the individual, but they have no allowance for the idea that the individual herself might not be accessible to herself. Thus, Anthony Elliott (2007) argues that there is little room for psychoanalytic concepts of the self with regard to reflexive individualism.

Furthering this line of critique against the component of cognitive self-mastery in theories of reflexive individualism, it could be added that reflexivity only seems to be seen in times of crisis. As already noted, for Goffman, individuals show great practical competence in the reflexive production of the self, but they do not seem to show much discursive awareness of reflexive self-identity. What is the role of the cognitive capacity of self-reflection? Beck argues that reflexivity is about reflex. It is not that there is more individual reflexivity, but that there is systemic reflexivity. The capable acting agent really only seems to be reflexive because of globalization and increasing structural connectivity. Which is a structural connection, not one that has anything to do with cognitive capacity of self-reflection. There are in essence, no changes that the acting agent makes that are themselves reflexive. Alexander takes the line of critique one step further by arguing that this type of structural embeddedness is distinctly non-reflexive. He writes, "Rather than reflexivity being understood in term of scientific, rational mastery of spatially separated environment, social self-control can successfully emerge only when modernist actors and institutions are embedded in relations of non-reflexive trust and commitments of a decidedly traditional kind" (Alexander 1996: 136).

Manuel Castells tends to agree with Giddens that contemporary identity is marked by a new emphasis on identity-building. However, he argues, "the network society is built on the systemic disjunction between the local and the global for most individuals and social groups" (Castells 1997: 11). He goes on to say that most new identities are actually structured in *opposition* to the networked and global changes. Because of increasing amounts of information, the control of meaningful representations critical to Giddens's idea of self-identity is beyond individual and local actors, and thus the possibility of reflexive self-masterly remains beyond the reach of individuals. Additionally, he argues that it was a robust civil society that provided the basis for individuals to engage in the kind of reflexive politics that Giddens forsees, and thus the possibility of increased self-reflexivity is decreased here too.

One of the more serious charges against the theories of reflexive individualism is that they elide the true workings of power. Beck argues that the traditional catagories have lost their power. But take a look at the earning power of men and women in Western society, and there is a pretty clear picture that there is not equality between the genders. Habermas argues this point saying that there is even a "reflexively produced discrimination" of women. Policies meant to move women toward freedom have actually produced and normalized a more covert system of discrimination. Thus reflexivity actually aids in eliding the working of power.

In contrast to the theories of reflexive individualism presented by Giddens and Beck, Margaret Archer (2007: 4) argues that reflexivity is an "unacknowledged aspect" of social life. She argues that the reflexive individual portrayed by Giddens and Beck is too free floating. Identity for Archer is not so free floating. She defines reflexivity as "the regular exercise of the mental ability, shared by all normal people, to consider themselves in relations to their (social) contexts and vice versa." In Archer's version, reflexivity is part of an internal dialogue held by people in the construction of identity. Her argument is that reflexivity can be seen in the myriad ways that people negotiate the social world. In this way, we are not wholly determined by outside forces, but can have causal power as agents in a relatively structural world, but constructing ourselves as projects.

Daniel Chaffee

Scott Lash and John Urry (1994) argue that the theory of reflexive individualization of Beck and Giddens is overly cognitive, and that reflexivity actually lies in processes of production and accumulation. They argue that individuals are not always empowered to take control of self-identity and of life narrative (p. 314). They argue "that reflexivity is not merely a matter of cognition or of ethics, but also for aesthetics" (p. 322). Individuals are increasingly reflexive, but they are also embedding in systems, which are themselves reflexive.

The future of reflexive identities

Reflexivity is a critical concept in theorizing social identity, and thus will not be dislodged from its role. However, Archer (2007) might be right that not enough has been done to understand how reflexivity functions in the creation of self-narratives. Mary Holmes (2010) argues that the debate over reflexive identity has left out emotions. Not only do people draw on rational, or information accounts of the social world, but they also draw on emotional resources. She writes, "more work is needed in order to understand how emotions are involved in reflexivity" (Holmes 2010: 148). Social identity cannot just be defined through the reflexive monitoring of social action, and the requisite adjustment to the self without making reference to how it feels. Additionally, there is very little reference to the body in the literature on reflexive identity.

In this author's mind, the most interesting direction for reflexivity is suggested by Anthony Elliott and Charles Lemert (2005) with their concept of the new individualism. They are at pains to distance the new individualism from reflexive individualism precisely because reflexive individualism does not take into account the unconscious. Life in the fast paced global world does indeed lead to higher reflexivity, and there is more attention to the self, and self-mastery, but for Elliott and Lemert, self-identity has turned to self-reinvention. Giddens argued that reflexive self-identity was partially a response to feelings of ontological insecurity, the failure of social structures to sufficiently anchor our identities. But in the theory of the new individualism, as opposed to theories of reflexive individualism, processes of reinvention, which are certainly driven in part by reflexivity, foster only more fear and anxiety. More can be theorized and researched in this vein, trying to fuse together reflexivity with some robust account of the unconscious.

Large global questions, such as climate change, are forcing individuals to renegotiate identity in a social and ethical sense. In the absence of grand societal narratives, this process of finding new identities for a new world order can only be a reflexive one.

References

Alexander, Jeffrey (1996) "Critical Reflections on 'Reflexive Modernization,'", *Theory, Culture & Society*, 13(4):133–8.
Archer, Margaret (2007) *Making our Way through the World: Human Reflexivity and Social Mobility*. New York: Cambridge University Press.
Bauman, Zygmunt (1998) "On glocalization: or globalization for some, localization for others", *Thesis Eleven* 54: 37–49.
Bauman, Zygmunt (2001) *The Individualized Society*. Cambridge: Polity Press.
Beck, Ulrich (1992) *Risk Society*. London: Sage.
Beck, Ulrich (1996) "Risk society and the provident state", in Scott Lash et al. (eds) *Risk, Environment and Modernity: Towards a New Ecology*. London: Sage.
Beck, Ulrich (1997) *The Reinvention of Politics*. Cambridge: Polity Press.
Beck, Ulrich and Elisabeth Beck-Gernsheim (2001) *Individualization: Institutionalized Individualism and Its Social and Political Consequences*. London and Thousand Oaks: Sage.

Beck, Ulrich, Giddens, A., and Lash, S. (1994) *Reflexive Modernization: Politics, Tradition and Aesthetics in the Modern Social Order*, Stanford, CA: Stanford University Press.

Castells, Manuel (1997) *The Power of Identity, The Information Age Volume II*. Oxford: Blackwell.

Caws, Peter (1994) "Identity: cultural, transcultural, and multicultural", in Goldberg, David Theo (ed.) *Multiculturalism: A Critical Reader*. Oxford: Blackwell, pp. 371–87.

Elliott, Anthony (2002) "Beck's sociology of risk: a critical assessment", *Sociology* 36(2): 293–315.

Elliott, Anthony (2007) *Concepts of the Self*. 2nd edn. Cambridge: Polity Press.

Elliott, Anthony (2009) *Contemporary Social Theory*. London: Routledge.

Giddens, A. (1987) *Social Theory and Modern Sociology*. Cambridge: Polity Press.

Giddens, A. (1990) *The Consequences of Modernity*. Cambridge: Polity Press.

Giddens, A. (1991) *Modernity and Self-Identity: Self and Society in the Late Modern Age*, Cambridge: Polity Press.

Giddens, A. (1992) *The Transformation of Intimacy: Sexuality, Love and Eroticism in Modern Society*. Cambridge: Polity Press.

Giddens, A. (1994) "Living in a post-traditional society", in Beck et al. (eds) *Reflexive Modernization: Politics, Tradition and Aesthetics in the Modern Social Order*, Stanford, CA: Stanford University Press, pp. 110–73.

Goffman, Erving (1959) *The Presentation of the Self in Everyday Life*. New York: Doubleday.

Habermas, Jurgen (1994) "Struggles for recognition in the democratic constitutional state", in Gutmann, Amy (ed.) *Multiculturalism: Examining the Politics of Recognition*. Princeton: Princeton University Press, pp. 107–48.

Holmes, Mary (2010) "The emotionalization of reflexivity", *Sociology* 44(1): 139–54.

Lash, Scott (1994) "Reflexivity and its doubles: structure, aesthetics, community," in Beck, Ulrich, Giddens, Anthony, and Lash, Scott (eds) *Reflexive Modernization*. Cambridge: Polity Press, pp. 174–215.

Lash, Scott and John Urry (1994) *Economies of Signs and Space*. London: Sage.

Lash, Scott and Jonathan Friedman (eds) (1994) *Modernity and Identity*. Oxford: Wiley-Blackwell.

Lemert, Charles and Anthony Elliott (2006) *The New Individualism: The Emotional Costs of Globalization*. London: Routledge.

May, Tim (1999) "Reflexivity in social life and sociological practice: a rejoinder to Roger Slack", *Sociological Research Online* 5(1). Online: www.socresonline.org.uk/5/1/may.html.

Mead, George Herbert (1962) *Mind, Self and Society*. Chicago: University of Chicago Press.

Pollner, M. (1991) "Left of ethnomethodology: the rise and decline of radical reflexivity", *American Sociological Review* 56(3): 370–80.

Sennett, Richard (1998) *The Corrosion of Character: The Personal Consequences of Work in the New Capitalism*. New York: W.W. Norton and Company.

Taylor, Charles (1994) "The politics of recognition", in Goldberg, David Theo (ed.) *Multiculturalism: A Critical Reader*. Oxford: Blackwell, pp. 75–106.

Urry, John (2007) *Mobilities*. Cambridge: Polity Press.

7

Individualization

Cosmo Howard

Introduction

Few recent developments in the cultural and political life of the West have received as much intellectual interest as the alleged "rise of the individual" and obverse "death of the social" (Rose 1996). Contemporary processes of "individualization" have attracted the attention of scholars in many disciplines, each with their own interpretations of the phenomenon and its consequences. Arguably the most prominent and influential perspective has emerged from political sociology, in the works of authors who have come to be known as the "individualization theorists": Anthony Giddens, Ulrich Beck, Elizabeth Beck-Gernsheim, and Zygmunt Bauman. Taken together, their analyses are often grouped and understood as a coherent "individualization thesis." The ideas of these individualization theorists were developed as contributions to debates in the last decades of the twentieth century about the changing nature of modernity, including the impacts of globalization, cultural pluralism, post-materialism, individualism, and ethical permissivism. In addition, this work directly engages the governmental politics of "late modernity," in particular the ascendency of neoconservative and neoliberal valorizations of self-reliance, as well as backlashes against individualistic modernity found in new forms of communitarianism, fundamentalism, and terrorism. This work on individualization is part of a larger narrative that integrates influential concepts such as "risk society" and "reflexive modernity." In true sociological fashion, these analyses connect personal experiences of individualization with economic, social and political developments that transcend the individual.

The individualization theorists draw extensively from the works of classical sociologists, but they also attempt to reinterpret and renew these intellectual legacies. At the core is an attempt to give an account of the rise of the individual not in terms of the decline of the social, but as a social phenomenon. In this respect, they engage with many of the same puzzles as the classical sociologists, such as how it is that individuality and self-identity become more important in epochs dominated by impersonal and increasingly global institutions. They claim that individual freedom and authentic self-identity are not only compatible with contemporary institutions, but also heavily dependent on them.

While the individualization theorists share crucial assumptions, commentators and critics have often overlooked their differences (Howard 2007). The theorists use divergent theoretical bases and methodologies, focus on different empirical data, and produce different, at times even contradictory, portraits of the contemporary individual. Taken individually and together, their works highlight the diverse elements of contemporary processes of individualization, the tensions and dilemmas forced on individuals, and the risks and anxieties that currently confront people in their daily lives.

This chapter provides a summary of work on the individualization thesis and its implications for identity. It starts by locating the thesis in its historical context. The chapter then addresses the key contributions of the theorists, with particular attention to the disagreements and contradictions within and between their works. The following section addresses the most common and most important critiques of the individualization thesis. Finally, I end with a discussion of the significance of the individualization thesis for studies of identity.

Historical evolution of the concept

The individualization theorists draw primarily from the sociological tradition and engage questions that have vexed sociologists for over a century. How can individuals exist and coexist within large societies? How should we understand the simultaneous rise of emphasis on individual freedom in modernity, along with the growth in mass organizations, technologies of impersonal exchange and instruments of destruction and violence that are too large and complex to be controlled by individuals? How does the modern individual maintain an authentic and coherent sense of self – an identity – if they are cajoled and coerced into adopting ascribed identities embedded in ethnic, racial, industrial, national, and supra-national groupings? In short, how does the individual survive and thrive given the social encroachments modernity has built?

The founders of sociology addressed these puzzles by showing how the individual and the social are interdependent in modernity. In *The Protestant Ethic and the Spirit of Capitalism* (1905), Max Weber posited that individuality was encouraged by protestant sects which stressed that God gave each individual a "calling," that only individuals themselves could discover their calling, and which proposed individual material success as a way of assuring oneself of spiritual salvation. Weber's work on bureaucracy showed how rationalistic impersonal social organization actually facilitated individual difference by sequestering personal and professional lives, thereby allowing people private space to develop their identities (cf. du Gay 2000). In *The Division of Labor in Society* (1893) Emile Durkheim argued loyalty in modern societies was no longer achieved through sameness, but through specialization and interdependence within a complex division of labour, since the division of social roles produced spaces for individual difference. In his 1903 essay "Metropolis and mental life," Georg Simmel claimed modern cities, in which interactions take place between strangers and anonymity is ensured by the crowd, permitted a greater degree of individuality than small, tightly knit communities.

The individualization theorists also engage with more recent sociology, as well as work from other disciplines. One important influence is Norbert Elias, who addresses the ways in which children are encouraged to develop a coherent sense of themselves and their needs, wants, and desires through the recognition and coercion of others in *The Society of Individuals* (1939). In the absence of these external recognitions, the will of the individual does not develop coherence and persistence. For Elias, individuality reflects the differences in how each individual internalizes and embodies "psychic self controls." Michel Foucault has also influenced the work of the individualization theorists. Foucault's arguments in *Discipline and Punish: the birth of the prison* (1977), about how "disciplinary" institutions such as schools, prisons, and military barracks can be simultaneously totalitarian and individualizing, show that individuality can go hand in hand with mass society and "total institutions." Furthermore, his focus on the politics of the body, and how individuals are encouraged to reflexively work upon themselves, is taken up extensively by Giddens in *Modernity and Self-Identity: self and society in the late modern age* (1991).

At minimum, we can say that the individualization theorists are updating the sociological contribution to reflect the social changes of the last half century. To this end, the individualization theorists divide modernity into "early" and "late" phases. These authors associate a number of critical developments with the late modernity that distinguish it from the early phase, including the rise of administrative and welfare states, changes in the nature of the family including increased divorce, the emergence of new technologies such as the contraceptive pill, an increasingly "global" outlook driven by new communication technologies, accelerated movements of trade and people, the demise of the Eastern Bloc, and greater awareness of the transnational nature of threats such as nuclear proliferation and environmental damage. In terms of scholarship, the theorists consciously engage arguments that Western societies have given up core elements of modernity and are now "post modern," "post-Fordist," "post-industrial," "post-material," and so on. As we shall see, the theorists agree with aspects of these claims, yet they are unwilling to accept the implication that we have left the essential components of modernity behind. Their discussion is focused on how modernity has evolved and adapted.

Major claims and developments in the field

The individualization theorists draw from a shared intellectual heritage, respond to similar concerns, and make many similar observations. In the first part of this section I address the common points of Giddens, Bauman, and Beck and Beck-Gernsheim. Next I deal with the distinctive points presented by each author. I will suggest that even though the individualization theorists all regard self-identity as a key concern of late modernity, they disagree about the extent to which individuals can create and maintain authentic, unified senses of self.

Bauman, Beck and Beck-Gernsheim, and Giddens all start with the observation that modernity has corroded social structures that once compelled people to live according to historically predetermined and externally imposed rules and norms. Like their forebears in classical sociology, these authors highlight the declining importance of tradition (the notion that actions and structures can be justified by the fact that people have always acted the same way, and the same structures have always existed) in determining the direction and content of people's lives. Whereas the early sociologists focused on the historical period in which the authority of tradition was confronted and overcome by the disruptive forces of rationalist modernity, the individualization theorists concentrate on the experience of living after traditions have been dismantled – in a "post-traditional" society (see Beck et al. 1994). They point to the fact that certain traditions such as patriarchal authority lingered in and were to some extent reinforced by elements of early modernity; for example, Fordist modes of governance relied upon patriarchal traditions to legitimize full-time male employment and the relegation of women to the private sphere of social reproduction. Their arguments are consistent with Weber's observation that early modernity benefited from the inheritance of pre-modern status traditions because these eased social acceptance of new forms of stratification and submission such as bureaucratic hierarchy.

According to the individualization theorists, modernity has also undermined important social groupings that in the past prescribed behaviors, supplied identities, and offered material and emotional support to members. The family no longer provides set roles and reliable supports: the high rate of divorce in late modernity makes financial reliance on spouses problematic, while women's increased participation in the labour market and social expectations of gender equality throw open the question of how partnered women (and men) will allocate their time and define their roles (Beck and Beck-Gernsheim 2001). Labour unions, which formed stable collectives and supplied material supports and shared identities to the working class in the early modernity, have been sidelined by economic and political transformations to the point where workers in most industries can no longer rely on them for career security. Conventional churches have also experienced marked declines in participation and membership, and with this a loss in their capacity to engage in behavioral regulation. With growing geographical mobility, increased urbanization and new communication technologies, local communities have lost their powers to monitor, control and sanction behavior. The result, according to the individualization theorists, is that individuals have been liberated to take greater control over their lives, but at the same time, they also face greater responsibility for meeting their own needs, and they have lost the certainty that came with tradition and collective responsibility for individual circumstances. In this sense, the rise of the individual is both a cause and a consequence of the shift toward "risk society" (Beck 1992).

It is tempting to conclude that these observations are a variation on the familiar story of individual emancipation from social constraints (Howard 2007). Yet the individualization theorists reject the idea that social factors and forces are less significant in late modernity than in earlier periods. Instead they argue that the nature of social structure has changed, so as to encourage and ultimately compel people to become individuals. As Beck puts it, "individualization *is* the social structure of the second modernity" (in Beck and Willms 2004: 63, emphasis original). Our lives are no less dominated by social structure than in previous times; it is simply that social structure compels us to be individuals. Hence individuality is not a matter of individual choice – it is a social obligation (see Bauman 2000).

It is also a mistake to interpret the individualization theorists as arguing that individualization means the wholesale removal of external supports, forcing people to fend for themselves and become completely independent. To be sure, individualization does suggest the withdrawal of certain supports, but Giddens, Beck and Beck-Gernsheim, and Bauman do not argue that individualization unambiguously represents greater independence and self-sufficiency. Instead, they show how individualization involves a *shift* in dependency, away from traditions and collectives, and toward modern *institutions*. The theorists point to several critical institutions on which modern individuals depend: the labour market, education systems, welfare states, the discipline of psychology, the mass media, and consumer capitalism. These institutions are different from the old objects of dependency for several reasons. First, they do not supply coherent ready-made identities, or "default options," that people can select and thereby avoid the effort and uncertainty of self-definition. Second, they usually provide supports that enable individuals to shape their own identities and differentiate themselves from others. Third, they almost always demand those who participate in them share responsibility for decisions and outcomes.

None of the individualization theorists believe contemporary processes of individualization are completely linear and straightforward, for individuals or societies. All acknowledge that there are great tensions in the process – for instance, between the demands of different individuals for their own spaces for personal growth and freedom, and between individual priorities and institutional pressures. For Beck and Beck-Gernsheim (2001), women especially experience individualization as a series of tensions, since they are caught between continuing to bear a disproportionate share of caring and household work, and the expectations and in some cases necessity that they actively take part in paid work. Yet these contradictions – between career and family, for instance – which reflect structural problems, are not met with comprehensive structural or systemic solutions. Rather, individuals are compelled to "seek biographical solutions to systemic contradictions" (Beck and Beck-Gernsheim 2001: xxii), meaning they must individually work out how to survive and live meaningful lives in the context of economic, political, and social forces beyond their control.

Finally, while processes of individualization are ultimately non-negotiable, some segments of society put up considerable resistance to the personal responsibility and uncertainty associated with individual self-definition. The individualization theorists suggest new movements have emerged to cater these needs, including ideological and religious fundamentalisms, as well as new philosophies of and experiments in communitarianism. Bauman, Giddens and Beck are consistently hostile toward contemporary efforts to reassert community and tradition – they see in them evidence of and potential for authoritarianism, violence, and denial of personal growth. These agendas pose particular dangers for traditionally depersonalized subjects, including women, migrants, and persons with disabilities, because of the risk of a re-emergence of the violence that was systematically visited upon such people within traditional communities. Thus the authors place themselves in disagreement with scholars who condemn the late modern erosion of community and the rise of individualism, such as Etzioni in *The Spirit of the Community: rights, responsibilities, and the communitarian agenda* (1993) and Putnam in *Bowling Alone: the collapse and revival of American community* (2000).

The above outline of shared themes in the works of Bauman, Beck and Beck-Gernsheim, and Giddens glossed over important differences. The theorists employ different methods: Giddens uses ideal types to characterize contemporary individualization processes, and as such it is not always clear that he intends to provide an accurate description of late modern self-identity. Bauman's work, which draws heavily on cultural material such as literary fiction, news and entertainment media, does not give explicit consideration to epistemology. The Becks are the most clearly empirical, using case studies, statistical data, interpretive interviews, and comparative analyses to support their arguments about the complexities and contradictions of late modern individuality. As a result, these authors produce divergent portraits of individual self-identity.

In Giddens's account, late modernity encourages a particular kind of reflexive individuality, tied to a coherent self-directed path or "trajectory." Although Giddens shares with his contemporaries the notion that late modern life contains contradictory pressures and fragmenting discontinuities, his work on identity stresses the ways in which individuals can surmount these conditions to develop a coherent sense of self-identity. To do this they rely on institutions, in two ways. First, late modern institutions "sequester" our experiences, meaning they shut out difficult existential and moral issues, as well as troubling phenomena such as madness and death, which might produce contradictory and emotionally overwhelming psychic states. Although some see specialization and the division of labour as alienating and depersonalizing, Giddens (1991) suggests these technologies actually enhance choice and self-determination, by carving out spaces in which individuals can control their lives without taking into consideration deeper existential questions.

Second, late modern institutions provide tools for individuals to make rational choices about and thus take deliberate control of their lives. Giddens sees institutions as stores of specialist expertise that can help people to better understand their circumstances and the constraints they face, enabling them to more systematically make life choices. Here Giddens challenges the conventional critique of professional expertise as a source of power that allows experts to unilaterally dominate lay people. For example, Giddens addresses psychological therapy, which for him is not only a profession characterized by asymmetries of expertise between therapist and patient, but also a set of tools and practices for self-discovery and self-healing. Therapy typically encourages individuals to work on themselves and to implement practices such as journaling and "autobiography." Giddens regards autobiography as a crucial self-practice of late modernity that allows individuals to stitch together diverse experiences from the past, present, and future into a coherent self-narrative.

Other late modern social institutions also promote self-trajectories. For instance, whereas intimate relationships were once formed and structured according to external commands and conditions, such as the economic necessity to find a spouse or to marry in the case of pregnancy, as well as the patriarchal traditions that governed gender roles in marriage, in *The Transformation of Intimacy* (1992) Giddens suggests relationships are now more likely to be governed by the internal desires and aspirations of the parties involved. The contraceptive pill and social acceptability of divorce have turned intimate relationships into pure expressions of the personalities, interactions, and wills of partners, who are free to "exit" whenever they choose. Although these "pure relationships" create stress and insecurity for partners, they also open up space for individuality. Importantly, Giddens suggests that these kinds of pure relationships, in which partners seek each other for their individual characteristics, do not just tolerate but actually affirm and reinforce self-identity. In this way, we see how Giddens's work interprets late modern individuality as socially rooted. Formal and informal institutions of late modernity compel and support the formation and maintenance of a coherent self-identity.

Giddens is vague about how much reality matches these ideal types, though he strongly implies that the coherent self-trajectory is the norm in late modernity. He does this in part by exploring exceptions that prove the rule, or examples of self-identities he regards as "pathological." Giddens draws upon R.D. Laing's concept of the "ontologically insecure individual" in *The Divided Self: an existential study in sanity and madness* (1964) to describe those cases where sense of self and of continuity is "fractured" (Giddens 1991: 53). According to Giddens's account of Laing, the ontologically insecure individual sees life in terms of "[d]iscontinuity in temporal experience" and interprets time "as a series of discrete moments, each of which severs prior experiences from subsequent ones in such a way that no continuous 'narrative' can be sustained" (ibid.: 53; see also Yeatman 2007). Such persons are "obsessively preoccupied with apprehension of possible risks to [their] existence" and, as such, are "paralysed in terms of practical action" (Giddens 1991: 53).

Other deviations from the norm occur when the reflexive planning and self-control implied in the trajectoral biography become excessive and dysfunctional, as is the case, according to Giddens, in sufferers of anorexia nervosa. This disorder reflects a "pathology of reflexive self-control" in which some women try to reconcile the prevailing social discourses of individualism and gender inequality with their continued oppression by exercising an extreme form of reflexivity over their bodies (ibid.: 105). In anorexia, the attempt to exercise control over one's future, to set a trajectory of change and improvement, becomes compulsive and self-destructive. Furthermore, while Giddens recognizes that modern life creates several "dilemmas," he argues that these lead to disjointed biographies only in exceptional cases (ibid.). Hence, in Giddens's analysis, the normality of reflexive biography is reinforced by casting as pathological and dysfunctional those individuals whose subjective experiences do not conform to his linear model of self-development. In this way, Giddens implies that a coherent self-identity is both possible and normal.

Whereas Giddens's model of contemporary identity strongly emphasizes the continuity of the self, Zygmunt Bauman's approach to understanding personal identity stresses fluidity. Bauman suggests that late modern life has no certainties and that individuals are compelled to face and embrace biographical discontinuity. He argues it is increasingly difficult to settle one's self-identity because the accelerating pace and widening scope of cultural, economic, political, and social change forces individuals continuously to dispose of existing identities and replace them with fresh biographical narratives. In this context, all arrangements and relationships become fluid, impermanent, and unpredictable, such that, even at the level of intimate and personal associations, continuity cannot be taken for granted, and commitments are only sustained "until further notice" (see Bauman 2003: 10). The changing nature of personal life, and the new demands of governance and political economy, favor those who can move quickly and are able to adapt to changes and exploit emerging opportunities, unencumbered by commitments to particular identities, others, and places. According to Bauman (2000), inhabiting a liquid-modern world is like living in a labyrinth, with no clear paths or directions, many options, and little ability to look forward or backward in time and space, since one's footprints are always disappearing.

While Bauman's late modern individuals need to move and change, all do not have equal facilities and resources at their disposal for undertaking biographical reinvention (Bauman 2000; see also Bauman 2004). His analysis suggests that those with the power and resources to regularly adapt their identities will do so. He gives the example of Bill Gates, who, at first glance, might be said to embody and express a trajectoral biography comprising a spectacular accumulation of accomplishments and attainments. Yet, in spite of all that Gates has achieved, he allegedly dis-likes "permanence," is not emotionally committed to or invested in his past accomplishments, and prefers a "network of opportunities" from which he can choose to develop new affiliations and experiences (Sennett in Bauman 2000: 124). In late modernity, the nomad, once regarded as primitive, becomes the coveted model of individuality, while those tied to time and place are disadvantaged by their biographical fixity. For Bauman (2000), the key mechanism of power in liquid modernity is the ability to "escape" from bonds and commitments to one's self and oth-ers, and for this reason individuals, institutions, and organizations increasingly avoid long-term involvements and set out to keep their options open.

Bauman's model of disposable biography is closely related to his observation that the transi-tion from "solid" to "liquid" modernity involves a shift from production to consumption as the primary source of individual identity (Bauman 2000). In a society of producers, as existed in the "heavy" or "solid" modernity (Bauman's preferred terms for early modernity), individu-als see their primary roles and tasks in terms of the production of valuable things. Individual actions are necessarily regulated through the imposition of discipline and routine, while personal advancement depends upon the acquisition, mastery, and augmentation of specialist skills over time. Self-development in the context of production and work follows the logics of career and promotion, a sense of *accumulation* of achievements, advancing toward a goal or position. However, in the consumer society of liquid modernity, these producer-oriented values are increasingly irrelevant and counterproductive. Instead of building their biographies, individu-als now purchase ready-made components of self-identity, choosing from a range of options. Not surprisingly, industries have sprung up to commodify and profit from the distribution of biographical components; chat shows on commercial television networks, such as *Oprah*, which supply viewers with examples of biographies, are an excellent example (ibid.). Critically, unlike producers, consuming individuals do not attempt to invest in and work on what already exists, but rather continuously refresh their stock of identity goods. Biographical improvement in liquid modernity thus occurs through *updating*, a central component of which is the disposal of existing self-narratives, or the willingness to discard old self-identities (Bauman 2003: 21, 49).

Bauman claims that there has been a general deterioration in the quality and quantity of collective dialogue about public issues in recent decades, and he attributes this in part to the rise of identity-politics (Bauman 2000, 2004). Whereas some commentators interpret the emer-gence of identity-politics in the 1960s and 1970s in terms of the opening up of personal life to public scrutiny and political contestation, Bauman suggests that such movements encouraged individuals to turn away from the public sphere and to focus inwardly on their private tribula-tions. He argues that contemporary identity movements on the "cultural left" tend to be preoc-cupied with issues of personal identity at the expense of pressing public concerns such as job insecurity, poverty, and social inequality (Bauman 2004: 36). Thus, Bauman suggests that we are witnessing

> the renunciation of the duty which intellectuals who were social critics once believed they owed to the rest of their contemporaries, particularly those who were less privileged and happy than themselves. With that duty no longer acknowledged, their descendents may now focus on their own tender, touchy and sore spots, struggling to raise the respect and adulation they enjoy to the level of the economic heights they have already gained. They are, stubbornly, self-concerned and self-referential. . . . The war for social justice has therefore been shortchanged for a plethora of battles for recognition.
>
> *(ibid.: 37)*

As a result of these and other recent developments, Bauman suggests it is increasingly difficult to mobilize individuals around collective causes, and that the public sphere has gradually been colonized by individuals who feel compelled to divulge personal experiences and private issues, to the extent that discussion of public concerns has been crowded out by self-stories (Bauman 2000).

Whereas Giddens portrays contemporary self-identity as a coherent trajectory, and Bauman tells a story of biographical fluidity and uncertainty, Beck and Beck Gernsheim (2001) focus on individuals' creative efforts to build identities for themselves in the face of structural contradictions. The institutions of late modernity force people to take responsibility for their own lives, compelling them to make themselves the focus of their efforts. However, many of life's problems remain structural, or beyond the immediate control of individuals, such as the continuing disconnect between women's career expectations and the reality of unequally distributed household work. Formal institutions reinforce these contradictions: while some, like schools and universities, actively encourage and support women to pursue careers in the paid workforce, others, such as social insurance and welfare systems, fail to provide supports for women's independence, including adequate organized child care and income support for single parents. Beck and Beck-Gernsheim claim that it is not possible for individuals to find complete biographical solutions to structural problems, and in the absence of collective or public efforts to overcome these difficulties, individuals are forced to search for the best means of creatively coping with the contradictions and tensions they encounter in their own lives.

Beck and Beck-Gernsheim argue that this context demands that individuals adopt an experimental attitude toward their lives, that they create and test a range of biographical prototypes in order to find models that will offer comfort and meaning in a world of contradiction and uncertainty. Importantly, individuals cannot devise biographical responses on their own, but rather depend fundamentally on institutions for support and guidance. In this account, the welfare state plays a critical role in facilitating experimentation.

Like Giddens, Beck (Beck and Willms 2004: 82–3) regards "basic security" as a fundamental prerequisite of modern individualization, and he sees the welfare state as a key component in this framework of ontological certainty. Yet Beck and Beck-Gernsheim's notion of the experimental biography differs from Giddens's linear model of self-identity because it assumes a degree of contradiction and risk that precludes neat trajectories. While institutions offer a mixture of supports that individuals can take up in their search for individualized coping strategies, these supports do not overcome the dilemmas and uncertainties of late modern life. Thus, individual biographical experiments are always at risk of failing, and self-identities face the constant threat of "breakdown" (Beck and Beck-Gernsheim 2001: 3). Furthermore, in contrast to Giddens's arguments about the sequestration of experience, Beck and Beck-Gernsheim suggest that late-modern institutions do not shut out or overcome difficult moral questions, but rather introduce new dilemmas and compel individuals to deal with paradoxes on a continuing basis (Beck and Beck-Gernsheim 2001). For example, pre-natal screening technologies force expectant parents who interact with modern medical institutions to confront profound ethical and decisional dilemmas that did not exist in earlier eras. Beck and Beck-Gernsheim's approach also diverges from Bauman's in their focus on the need for individuals to invest time and energy in creating and maintaining viable biographical coping strategies, implying that people do not simply consume and discard pre-made identity components.

Beck (Beck and Willms 2004: 83) argues that in order to facilitate biographical experimentation, it is necessary to institute a system of guaranteed basic incomes for all citizens. Although Beck believes that the post-war welfare state enabled new levels of independence for many individuals, he also argues that this system reinforced a number of important traditional dependencies and inequalities. Social supports in many countries were (and in many cases are still) tied to participation in the labor market, and recent welfare reforms have tightened the nexus between paid work and support, removing assistance from those who seek alternative lifestyles or who undertake activities, such as caring, that do not involve direct engagement in the labor market. By contrast, the model proposed by Beck would do away with these employment conditions by extending a minimum income or "basic wage" to all citizens. Such a system would ameliorate many of the pressures and tensions of late-modern life, and should allow individuals the freedom to test biographical alternatives without the fear of falling into poverty if their experiments fail.

To summarize, the individualization theorists all document the demise of tradition and community in determining and supporting behaviours, the rising dependency of individuals on institutions, and the risks and dilemmas associated with individualized biographies. Their accounts differ on the possibility of maintaining a coherent self-identity in late modernity.

Criticisms

While influential, the individualization thesis has also been subject to vigorous criticism. Here I address five objections:

1   The individualization thesis is largely a restatement of existing social theories, since these ideas were previously addressed in classical sociology and other disciplines.
2   The individualization thesis erroneously suggests inequality is no longer structural, because it rejects the explanatory validity of class and other structured forms of stratification.
3   Individualization is inappropriately presented as a universal experience, whereas individualized identity is properly understood as only experienced by a privileged few.
4   Individualization is better understood as a governance strategy, rather than a social structure.
5   The normative aspects of the individualization thesis are problematic.

The first criticism of the individualization thesis suggests that it is not as novel as its proponents suggest. Instead, it essentially represents the continuation of a tradition of work in sociology and related disciplines (see above) into the late modernity. Even if it incorporates contemporary observations, the underlying theoretical frameworks and epistemologies are not new (Schroer 2000; Mills 2007; Nollman and Strasser 2007). The same fundamental insights into de-traditionalization and the structural rise of the individual were captured by Tonnies in *Community and Civil Society* (1887), Weber (1905) and Durkheim (1893); similar connections were made between personal relationships and individualized identity by Freud in *Civilization and Its*

Discontents (1930), Elias (1939), and Laing (1964); the thesis resonates with work on reflexivity and the body by Foucault (1977, 1978); and arguments about the carving up of public spaces into individualized realms are found in earlier work by Foucault (1977) and Sennett in *The Fall of Public Man* (1977).

The individualization authors do acknowledge and engage with earlier contributors. They also explicitly differentiate themselves. Beck and Beck-Gernsheim (2001) argue that Weber's portrait of a modernity haunted by pre-modern traditions and statues is not relevant in the second half of the twentieth century. Similarly, Bauman (2000) suggests Weber's idea of modernity as increasingly instrumentally rational, and dominated by a small number of institutions which dictate morality, has been replaced by a society in which there are no centralized value-defining institutions, leaving individuals preoccupied with what ends they should seek given a plethora of means. Giddens (1991) argues that his work on self-identity suggests a need rethink the historical emphasis on internalization of social norms, since late modernity encourages individuals to regulate themselves according to their own desires, not prohibitions. The point, as Giddens stresses, is not to reject these earlier theorists, but to provide a more nuanced account that considers complex, non-linear developments and trends within modernity and in the formation, compilation, and negotiation identities. In this way, the individualization theorists move away from the early modern story of progressive social evolution toward individualism and rationalism.

The second body of criticism suggests the individualization theorists overestimate the decline of structures of inequality such as class and gender. Beck has written extensively about the "death of class," much to the chagrin of scholars who see class continuing to profoundly affect identity and material circumstances (Goldthorpe 2000; Savage 2000; Coté 2003). Beck stresses that late modernity has transformed the relatively rigid hierarchies of industrialism into much less stable patterns of inequality, where no one is completely insulated from the threat of poverty and social alienation, and where individual decisions now carry greater risks because there are no traditional supports such as the family, community, corporation, and union to fall back on (Beck 1992; Beck et al. 1994). Significant empirical evidence has been assembled suggesting that class continues to have an important impact on both identification and life chances (see Mills 2007). In light of this, some critics read Beck's arguments as suggesting that everyone faces the same risks of hardship, the same opportunities for success, and that individualization means individuals are now solely responsible for their material fates (Brannen and Nilsen 2005; Gillies 2005; Mythen 2005). Beck does indeed suggest that late modernity, individualization, and risk society create new insecurities for the privileged, but he does not see the death of class as the death of structures of inequality. Rather, new forms and axes of inequality have emerged to replace industrial modes of stratification, based around intra- and international disparities in access to institutional resources (Beck and Willms 2004). Furthermore, Beck suggests experiences of inequality become sharper and more painful when juxtaposed against late modern discourses of individual opportunity and self-reliance. As Bauman (2000) stresses, inequality has not diminished, but the disappearance of class from public discourse leaves individuals without vocabularies to publicly convey their "private" struggles. Recent interpretive research on class and self-identity suggests a complex mixture of individual and structural stories and identifications (Mills 2007; Nollmann and Strasser 2007).

The third criticism suggests the individualization theorists tend to universalize the social processes they describe, implying that all people, irrespective of class, gender and race, feel compelled to develop distinct self-identities (Roseneil 2007). Critics note access to the spaces and supports that allow for identity building is not evenly distributed, so that individualized identity itself can become a key dimension of inequality (Elliott 2002). Others argue individualized identity is a luxury that one can only turn one's attention to once basic needs are met, equivalent to the role of self-actualization in Malsow's hierarchy of needs (Mills 2007). In *Class, Self and Culture* (2003) Skeggs claims the individualization theorists mistakenly apply their own middle-class experience and interest in reflexivity to the population as a whole. Coté (2003) observes that youth who are unable or unwilling to invest the effort, resources, and time necessary to individualize their identities end up falling back on "default biographies" in which they adopt an orientation of conformity with fads and fashions.

The individualization thesis is also criticized for failing to take gender into account. Hey (2005) uses interview research to argue that working-class women do not identify with reflex-ive self-hood as suggested by the individualization theorists. Furthermore, numerous observers have expressed opposition to Giddens's account of the "pure relationship," and in particular the implication that women now generally experience intimate relationships as empowering and liberating. They note the ongoing presence of gendered disparities in paid work and care, the continuing dominance of "heteronormative" relationship models, and the compounding effects of intersections between gender, class and race (Duncan and Edwards 1999; Jamieson 1999; Ribbens McCarthy and Edwards 2002; Skeggs 2003). Bauman rarely mentions gender (Howard 2007). One worry is that the individualization theorists tell the story of men's experiences of individualization as if they apply equally to women as well. For instance, Giddens's notion of self-identity as a trajectory fits better with men's uninterrupted career paths than women's discontinuous and shifting engagements with paid work and household labor (Howard 2007).

Considerable empirical evidence has been assembled to show that individualization is not a universal experience. Yet, as Roseneil (2007) suggests, it is a mistake to see these observa-tions as "fatally undermining" the concept of individualization. Those who argue individualiza-tion is only for the privileged tend to ignore the ways in which life for the disadvantaged has become highly individualized. To be sure, these subjects do not experience individualization straightforwardly as a process of liberation, self-expression, and personal fulfillment, yet their lack of resources means they frequently confront situations in which they are forced to rely on themselves, make choices and take responsibility for their situations. In this sense, the poor may experience individualization more intensely and consistently than the wealthy (Giddens 1991).

Furthermore, as Ferguson (2007) and James (2006) have argued, the idea that we can neatly separate out questions of material survival and identity is highly problematic. Ferguson (2007) shows how situations of deprivation, abuse, and violence usually go hand in hand with denial of the victim's autonomy and refusal to acknowledge their distinct identity. This interpretation of the individualization problematizes the binary opposition between "recognition" and "redistribu-tion" (cf. James 2006), along with Bauman's dismissive characterization of identity-politics as a bourgeois, narcissistic preoccupation. It suggests individual control over biography and identity are not luxuries, but basic prerequisites for the alleviation of social disadvantage in late modernity. For these reasons, the idea that individualization is something that just matters to the powerful and wealthy, who have secured themselves physically and financially, is not tenable. Nevertheless, it seems clear that the content and implications of individualization vary considerably across numer-ous dimensions, including gender, race, sexuality, and socio-economic position.

Fourth, some argue that individualization is better understood as a governance paradigm rather than a social structure. Comparisons are sometimes made between the individualization thesis and the neo-Foucauldian governmentality literature (see Budgeon 2003; Henman 2007; Johansson 2007). Although Beck and Giddens explicitly reject many of Foucault's theories of individual-ity, there are very important similarities between their work and the Foucauldian concept of governmentality (Dean 1999; Rose 1999; Brady 2007; Henman 2007). Governmentality suggests a shift away from "total institutions," in which individuals are subjected to direct and severe forms of control (Foucault 1977), toward new kinds of regulation and manipulation that work indirectly on individuals "at a distance" (Rose 1999). Foucault and his followers are especially interested in how (neo)liberal societies manage to function in a productive and orderly manner, in spite of the fact that they grant considerable freedom to individuals. Techniques of discipline are still involved, but activities of social governance are increasingly conducted by individual subjects themselves. Institutions do not operate by dominating their subjects, but are rather engaged in a subtle process of instructing individuals in the use of particular "techniques of the self," which build individuals' capacities to govern themselves and to assess and correct their own physical, intellectual, and emotional deficits (Dean 1998, 1999). Importantly, these "microphysics of power" are linked to broader neoliberal governance agendas (Dean 1999; Rose 1996; Brady 2007; Henman 2007).

Whereas the individualization theorists are primarily concerned with broad shifts in social structure, governmentality authors tend to analyze specific attempts to govern people as individuals, usually through detailed examinations of particular public programs or policy initiatives. They rely mostly on official texts, documents and administrative manuals, and seek to describe the specifics of how individuals are supervised, constituted as particular kinds of subjects, and encouraged systematically to regulate their own conduct. In this way, they provide a more grounded and contextual understanding of individualization. On the other hand, the governmentality approach tends to overemphasize the coherence of policies and programs, in part because it seeks to establish connections between micro-practices and macro-agendas, but also because most empirical governmentality research addresses official documents, not the subjects being governed (Li 2007; Mitchell 2006). As a result, the approach downplays the contradictions and fissures in contemporary individualization that might form possibilities for individuals to resist and escape neoliberal governance. Rather than regarding the individualization and governmentality theses as rival approaches, this discussion suggests they potentially complement each other by illuminating different aspects of contemporary identity formation.

Finally, the individualization thesis has stirred up a lively debate about whether these developments in late modernity should be seen as positive or negative. Giddens has been criticized for stressing the emancipatory potential of individualization, for suggesting that it makes almost everyone happier (Ribbens McCarthy et al. 2003), and for failing to seriously consider the anxiety and pain associated with increased insecurity in intimate relationships (Roseneil 2007). Bauman, on the other hand, is associated with a negative focus on the uncertainties and stresses associated with increased freedom, to the point that Roseneil (2007) calls him a "patriarchal pessimist," suggesting his distaste for liquid modernity reflects nostalgia for the comfort and certainty of the patriarchal family. Nevertheless, none of these theorists see the most commonly invoked alternatives to individualization as desirable or sustainable. Current efforts to counter late modern "individualism" and to build "community" and "social capital" are greeted by these authors with great skepticism and trepidation. They say critics who stress the negatives of individualization have yet to clearly articulate how alternative social structures premised on community will not discriminate, dominate, exclude, and normalize.

The individualization theorists are also normative in the sense that they present prescriptions for policy reform to facilitate individualized identities in late modernity. Two key examples are Giddens's "third way" and Beck's "basic security." Both proposals build logically from the authors' analyses of social trends in late modernity. As we shall see, both proposals are subject to important critiques.

Giddens claims that his interpretation of contemporary self-identity provides an alternative to dominant neoliberal discourses and governing programmes (Giddens 1998, 2000). His "third way" explicitly rejects the suggestion that governments must withdraw from individuals' lives in order to expand personal freedom. Giddens observes considerable differences in the abilities of individuals to act positively in shaping their own biographies and managing risks. He is particularly concerned about the "socially excluded" (Giddens 1998: 102–11): such individuals fail to conform to the dominant model of biography because their lives do not assume a positive trajectory. Instead, their biographies are circular and repetitive, since they are stuck in cycles of poverty (ibid.: 109). In Giddens's vision, the state should intervene and provide support for those excluded from social networks and lacking the skills of biographical self-management, by providing them with skills to help them manage risks in their own lives. This support differs from that provided by post-war welfare state, since it demands that individuals become active in shaping their own lives.

Critics note that in practice there are important affinities between Giddens's third way and neoliberal governance (Bourdieu and Wacquant 2001; Hall 2003). Giddens's prescriptions have been adopted and adapted to suit neoliberal agendas. For example, third way-style capacity building and life-planning programs have been used in several jurisdictions to compel recipients of state assistance to improve their own labor-market prospects in the name of reducing welfare dependency and improving economic competitiveness (Clarke 2004; Rose 1999; Brady 2007; Brodie 2007; Henman 2007). These programs often fail to open up space for authentic biographical exploration, but instead force individuals to adopt particular identities and make specific lifestyle choices (Brady 2007; Henman 2007).

Whereas Giddens's third way has been associated with restricting entitlements to income supports, Beck argues that in order to facilitate individualized identities, it is necessary to institute a system of guaranteed basic incomes for all citizens (Beck and Willms 2004: 83). Such a system would ameliorate many of the pressures and tensions of late modern life, and should allow individuals the freedom to test biographical alternatives without the fear of falling into poverty if their experiments fail (ibid.). Unfortunately, Beck has not articulated how a guaranteed minimum income could be reconciled with the contemporary social policy context that features cuts to entitlements and new "workfare" interventions that compel recipients of state support to seek and undertake activation as a condition of receiving assistance (Peck 2006; Brady 2007; Brodie 2007; Henman 2007; van Berkel and Valkenburg 2007).

Beck and Beck-Gernsheim (2001: 24) and Beck (in Beck and Willms 2004: 78) insist that their preferred model of "social-experimental" individualization is deliberately antithetical to neoliberal "atomization." While Beck's advocacy of a basic income system is inconsistent with neoliberal emphases on self-sufficiency and welfare retrenchment, in other respects, the model is decidedly "liberal" in its assumptions and implications. Beck's basic wage rests on the liberal premise that individuals are inherently capable of acting as autonomous and creative agents so long as external constraints do not impede their freedom. This implies that individualization is primarily a process of emancipation of inherently capable individuals from bonds of familial and material dependency. Yet this emancipatory model does not address social contexts in which individual "exit" is impossible, such as parent–child relationships. Individualization as emancipation from material dependency is also problematic in situations where institutions are called upon to facilitate the individuality of those who lack certain important capacities, such as persons with intellectual or psychiatric disabilities (cf. Yeatman 1997). This issue connects to the more general question about how late modern institutions should intervene in individuals' lives to promote and support the development of distinctive self-identities and unique biographies. While Beck and Beck-Gernsheim admit that such interventions are inevitable and necessary, they do not elaborate on the specific principles that should guide the design of policies and programs in the context of "institutionalized individualism" (Beck and Beck-Gernsheim 2001).

Beck and Beck-Gernsheim's public support for social experimentation is presented as being substantially at odds with neoliberal atomism. Yet neoliberals have also embraced the language of state-sponsored experimentation and modified it to fit their own agendas. Brodie (2007) explores how neoliberal policy initiatives appeal to the logic of experimentation in place of notions of linear and universal development and progressive expansion found in earlier social programs (see also Howard 2006; Larner and Walters 2000). In this respect, the governmentality approach, which reminds us that individualization is not just a form of social structure but also a series of governmental projects tied to particular interests and objectives, helps keep the focus on how discourses of individualization are constructed and appropriated by political actors for strategic ends.

This review of key criticisms of the individualization thesis highlighted some important problems with the theories of Bauman, Beck, Beck-Gernsheim, and Giddens. Individualization is clearly a contested and contentious approach within contemporary studies of identity. Yet we have also seen that some criticisms are misplaced, especially those that fail to appreciate the nuance and complexity of the individualization thesis, or which selectively focus on empirical evidence that contravenes the individualization story.

Conclusion: the contribution of individualization theories

The individualization theories discussed in this chapter have had a substantial impact on contemporary studies of identity. They combine theoretical and methodological flexibility with compelling empirical insights into what it means to be an individual and to develop and maintain a sense of self in late modernity. The individualization theorists deliberately carry forward the sociological tradition of understanding individuality in the context and as a product of social forces. They update classical approaches to reflect current conditions. Their work is not principally focused on processes of de-traditionalization and linear modernization, but on the progressions and inversions of modernity after the imprint of tradition has faded. The individualization theorists convincingly show that important elements of modernity remain, that the "social" is still central to self-formation, and that we should not discount the significance of structures in the formation of personality and identity. They have spurred debates about the extent to which they really are different from earlier scholars, and arguably contributed to a resurgence of interest in classical sociology. They also challenge us to reconsider the stability and relevance of taken-for-granted concepts, such as class, family, and community.

A great strength of recent work on individualization is its interdisciplinary character. Though rooted in the sociological tradition, these authors promiscuously engage with political science, political philosophy, critical and cultural studies, psychology, and psychoanalysis to make their cases. As a result, they attract the attention of scholars working in many fields, and their ideas have been taken up across the social sciences. Furthermore, the individualization thesis encourages empirical exploration using all manner of methods and methodologies. Some scholars have employed sophisticated quantitative techniques to test the predictions of the individualization theorists in a positivistic fashion; some use state-of-the-art ethnographic approaches to interpret the meaning of individualized self identity; still others eschew empirical methods and focus on textual and discursive analyses of social and governmental practices of individual freedom. This unwillingness to preclude particular ways of knowing makes the body of work complex and powerful.

Finally, the individualization thesis is important because it explicitly confronts currently dominant political discourses of self-reliance and individualism (Howard 2007). It shows that late modern individuals are not independent or self-sufficient; they depend on institutions in order to build a sense of self and to achieve their life goals. It dismisses the myth that individuals can triumph over social challenges, by pointing out the non-negotiable aspects of social life and the structural contradictions of late modern identity. It suggests the public sphere has not been eradicated, but instead colonized by private interests and turned over to promoters of "identity goods." Yet it disturbs the faith some have placed in reactions to individualization, on both the left and the right. Political projects based on localism, communitarianism, anti-rationalism, traditionalism, and fundamentalism are all challenged on the grounds that they sacrifice individual freedom in return for a false sense of certainty and security. By recognizing that late modernity requires us to reconcile self-determination with institutional dependence, Bauman, Beck, Beck-Gernsheim, and Giddens offer a compelling starting point for reframing the politics of our age.

References

Bauman, Z. (2000) *Liquid Modernity*. Cambridge: Polity Press.

Bauman, Z. (2003) *Liquid Love: on the frailty of human bonds*. Cambridge: Polity Press.

Bauman, Z. (2004) *Identity: conversations with Benedetto Vecchi*. Cambridge: Polity Press.

Beck, U. (1992) *Risk Society: toward a new modernity*. London: Sage.

Beck, U. and Beck-Gernsheim, E. (2001) *Individualization: institutionalized individualism and its social and political consequences*. London: Sage.

Beck, U. and Willms, J. (2004) *Conversations with Ulrich Beck*. Cambridge: Polity Press.

Beck, U., Giddens, A. and Lash, S. (1994) *Reflexive Modernization: Politics, Tradition and Aesthetics in the Modern Social Order*. Stanford, CA: Stanford University Press.

Bourdieu, P. and Wacquant, L. (2001) "NewLiberalSpeak: notes on the new planetary vulgate", *Radical Philosophy*, 105: 2–5.

Brady, M. (2007) "Institutionalized individualism and the care of the self: single mothers and the state", in C. Howard (ed.) *Contested Individualization: debates about contemporary personhood*. New York: Palgrave Macmillan.

Brannen, J. and Nilsen. A. (2005) "Individualisation, choice and structure: a discussion of current trends in sociological analysis", *Sociological Review*, 53(3): 412–28.

Brodie, J. (2007) "The new social 'isms': individualization and the social policy reform in Canada", in C. Howard (ed.) *Contested Individualization: debates about contemporary personhood*. New York: Palgrave Macmillan.

Budgeon, S. (2003) *Choosing a Self: young women and the individualization of identity*. Westport, CT: Praeger.

Clarke, J. (2004) "Dissolving the public realm? The logics and limits of neo-liberalism", *Journal of Social Policy*, 33(1): 27–48.

Coté, J. (2003) *Arrested Adulthood: the changing nature of maturity and identity*. New York: New York University Press.

Dean, M. (1998) "Administering asceticism: reworking the ethical life of the unemployed citizen", in M. Dean and B. Hindess (eds) *Governing Australia: studies in contemporary rationalities of government*. Melbourne, Australia: Cambridge University Press.

Dean, M. (1999) *Governmentality: power and rule in modern society*. London: Sage.

du Gay, P. (2000) *In Praise of Bureaucracy: Weber, organization, ethics*. London: Sage.

Duncan, S. and Edwards, R. (1999) *Lone Mothers, Paid Work and Gendered Moral Rationalities*. London: Macmillan.

Durkheim, E (1893/1964) *The Division of Labor in Society*, trans. G. Simpson. Glencoe, IL: The Free Press.

Elias, N. (1939) *The Society of Individuals*. London: Continuum.

Elliott, A. (2002) "Beck's sociology of risk: a critical assessment", *Sociology*, 36(2): 293–315.

Etzioni, A. (1993) *The Spirit of the Community: rights, responsibilities, and the communitarian agenda*. New York: Crown.

Ferguson, H. (2007) "'Lives of their own' free from violence: individualization and child-welfare interventions", in C. Howard (ed.) *Contested Individualization: debates about contemporary personhood*. New York: Palgrave Macmillan.

Foucault, M. (1977) *Discipline and Punish: the birth of the prison*. London: Allen Lane.

Foucault, M. (1978) *The History of Sexuality Volume I: an introduction*. New York: Pantheon.

Giddens, A. (1991) *Modernity and Self-Identity: self and society in the late modern age.* Cambridge: Polity Press.

Giddens, A. (1992) *The Transformation of Intimacy: sexuality, love and eroticism in modern societies.* Cambridge: Polity Press.

Giddens, A. (1998) *The Third Way: the renewal of social democracy.* Cambridge: Polity Press.

Giddens, A. (2000) *The Third Way and Its Critics.* Cambridge: Polity Press.

Gillies, V. (2005) "Raising the 'meritocracy': parenting and the individualization of social class", *Sociology – The Journal of the British Sociological Association*, 39(5): 835–53.

Goldthorpe, J.H. (2000) "Rent, class conflict and class structure: a commentary on Sorensen", *American Journal of Sociology*, 105: 1572–82.

Hall, S. (2003) "The great going nowhere show", in A. Chadwick and R. Heffernan (eds) *The New Labour Reader.* Cambridge: Polity, 82–7.

Henman, P. (2007) "Governing individuality", in C. Howard (ed.) *Contested Individualization: debates about contemporary personhood.* New York: Palgrave Macmillan.

Hey, V. (2005) "The constricting social logics of sociality and survival: cultures of classed be/longing in late modernity", *Sociology*, 39(5): 855–72.

Howard, C. (2006) "The new governance of Australian welfare: street-level contingencies", in P. Henman and M. Fenger (eds) *Administering Welfare Reform: international transformations in welfare governance.* Bristol: Policy Press, 137–59.

James, M. (2006) *Misrecognized Materialists: social movements in Canadian constitutional politics.* Vancouver: University of British Columbia Press.

Jamieson, L. (1999) "Intimacy transformed? a critical look at the 'pure relationship'", *Sociology*, 33(3): 477–94.

Johansson, H. (2007) "Placing the individual 'at the forefront': Beck and individual approaches in activation", in R. van Berkel and B. Valkenburg (eds) *Making it Personal.* Bristol: Policy Press.

Laing, R.D. (1964) *The Divided Self: an existential study in sanity and madness.* Harmondsworth: Penguin.

Larner, W. and Walters, W. (2000) "Privatisation, governance and identity: the United Kingdom and New Zealand compared", *Policy & Politics*, 28(3): 361–77.

Li, T. (2007) "Practices of assemblage and community forest management", *Economy and Society*, 36(2): 263–93.

Li, T.M. (2007) *Will to Improve: governmentality, development, and the practice of politics.* Durham, NC: Duke University Press.

Mills, M. (2007) "Individualization and the life course: toward a theoretical model and empirical evidence", in C. Howard (ed.) *Contested Individualization: debates about contemporary personhood.* New York: Palgrave Macmillan.

Mitchell, K. (2006) "Neoliberal governmentality in the European Union: education, training, and technologies of citizenship", *Environment and Planning D: Society and Space*, 24: 389–407.

Mythen, G. (2005) "Employment, individualization and insecurity: rethinking the risk society perspective", *The Sociological Review*, 53(1): 129–49.

Nollmann, G. and Strasser, H. (2007) "The twofold class concept: traditional limitations and new perspectives of class research", *Canadian Journal of Sociology*, 32(3): 371–96.

Peck, J. (2006) *Workfare States.* New York: Guilford Press.

Putnam, R.D. (2000) *Bowling Alone: the collapse and revival of American community.* New York: Simon & Schuster.

Ribbens McCarthy, J. and Edwards, R. (2002) "The individual in public and private life: the significance of mothers and children", in S. Carling, S. Duncan and R. Edwards (eds) *Analysing Families: morality and rationality in policy and practice.* London: Routledge.

Ribbens McCarthy, J., Edwards, R. and Gillies, V. (2003) *Making Families: moral tales of parenting and step-parenting.* York: Sociology Press.

Rose, N. (1996) "The death of the social? Re-figuring the territory of government", *Economy and Society*, 25(3): 327–56.

Rose, N. (1999) *Powers of Freedom: reframing political thought* Cambridge: Cambridge University Press.

Roseneil, S. (2007) "Sutured selves, queer connections: rethinking intimacy and individualization", in C. Howard (ed.) *Contested Individualization: debates about contemporary personhood.* New York: Palgrave Macmillan.

Savage, M. (2000) *Class Analysis and Social Transformation.* Milton Keynes: Open University Press.

Sennett, R. (1977) *The Fall of Public Man.* New York: Knopf.

Skeggs, B. (2003) *Class, Self and Culture*. London: Routledge.

van Berkel, R. and Valkenburg, B. (eds) *Making it Personal*. Bristol: Policy Press.

Weber. M (1905) *The Protestant Ethic and the Spirit of Capitalism*, translated by Talcott Parsons. New York: Scribner's.

Schroer, M. (2000) *Das Individuum der Gesellschaft: synchrone und diachrone theorieperspektiven*. Germany: Suhrkamp Verlag.

Yeatman, A. (1997) "Contract, status and personhood", in G. Davis, B. Sullivan and A. Yeatman (eds) *The New Contractualism*. Melbourne, Australia: Macmillan.

Yeatman, A. (2007) "Varieties of individualism", in C. Howard (ed.) *Contested Individualization: debates about contemporary personhood*. New York: Palgrave Macmillan.

8

New identities, new individualism

Eric L. Hsu

Introduction: historical and intellectual development of individualism

At least since the early modern era, the concept of individualism has been extolled within social theory as contributing new and significant understandings of identity. This is especially the case in recent times. Here, research on individualism has been used to track broader social developments and changes. But what exactly does individualism connote and why has it received so much attention? Why have authors as far ranging as Alexis de Tocqueville, Anthony Giddens, Stephen Lukes, Anthony Elliott and Charles Lemert devoted so much time to its study and what do they each have to tell us? This chapter seeks to address such questions by offering a broad overview of how individualism has been explored in both classical and contemporary social theory through an investigation of its historical and varied meanings. In doing so, it ultimately argues that the recent introduction of a temporal dimension has been a major breakthrough in how individualism has come to be understood.

To date with a few notable exceptions, the core concern of most research on individualism has been to highlight its contrast to a more collectivist disposition within society. Absent, however, in this account is a consideration of how quickly or slowly that individualism now occurs in the Western world. Correspondingly, the work of some contemporary social theorists – of which Anthony Elliott and Charles Lemert come foremost to mind – has been concerned about addressing this particular deficiency. Here what is fundamentally at issue is the claim that speed matters when it comes to understanding individualism. Likewise to such an end, this chapter seeks to extend this line of thought by exploring what new insights are gained when the speed of individualism is taken into account. Further, it looks at aspects of speed that have not yet been explored with regards to the individualist mindset. In turn, it advocates for a temporal conceptualization of individualism that not only considers how it has been accelerated but also how social deceleration plays a factor as well.

The etymological origins of individualism

Before it is possible to grasp why some contemporary social theorists have found individualism to be a concept of great utility, it is first necessary to trace its origins to the early modernist period. That is when individualism first began to develop as a more well-defined idea which arguably changed the course of many Western societies.

One of the places where the term "individualism" first entered popular intellectual circulation was in early nineteenth-century France. Initially, it was employed to criticize what some saw were the dangers of the French Revolution (1798–99) and, in turn, the Enlightenment. As Stephen Lukes writes, "[t]he Revolution was proof [for some conservative thinkers] that ideas exalting the individual imperiled the stability of the commonwealth, dissolving it into 'an unsocial, uncivil, unconnected chaos of elementary principles'" (1973: 3). "*Individualisme*," the French variant of individualism, thus came to stand for the belief that the individual is more ultimately important than the collective social order. As such, those Enlightenment philosophes who were seen to be supportive of *individualisme* such as John Locke and Immanuel Kant were depicted as dangerous figures because they pushed for a society which appeared to be lawless and unruly.

Of those who wrote in this vein, it was decidedly the disciples of the influential French thinker Claude Henri de Saint-Simon who brought "*individualisme*" into common usage in the broader European intellectual landscape. They did so by contrasting the term with "organic" periods of history which represented a more harmonious and collectivist-centered society (Lukes 1973: 6–7). For them, "*individualisme*" represented a time when society was thrown into chaos – this is because it conjured up a time when individuals thought exclusively for themselves and not for the good of the larger public.

Of course, individualism still today carries this pejorative connotation of selfishness within much of Western contemporary social thought as it still does presently in the French language. However, this by no means is the whole story; for as is commonly known, other interpretations of individualism exist today as well.

These other takes on individualism also find their roots around the same period as when the term first came to connote an egoistic mindset. One of the other ways that individualism was viewed was through a more positive lens. This occurred – although perhaps unintentionally – in Alexis de Tocqueville's 1835 text, *Democracy in America*. As a French writer sent by his government to better comprehend the New World, Tocqueville sought to understand in this work just how different the United States of America was to Old World Europe.

Out of his many observations, a more notable conclusion of his was that individualism played a significant role in allowing the US to have a democratic form of government. However, Tocqueville, like the followers of Saint Simon, saw this rise of individualism to be a rather negative consequence; for like them, he linked individualism to selfishness. What Tocqueville identified as being principally troublesome about individualism was its isolating quality. Because it encouraged the common man to "withdraw to one side with his family and friends," this meant that eventually, society at large would eventually be forsaken – something that Tocqueville wrote with great lament (Tocqueville 2000: 482).

Of course, to be sure, Tocqueville did not just have negative things to say about the American enterprise. For, at the same time, what he considered to be most impressive about the American spirit was that Americans could overcome their selfish tendencies. They did so by addressing the pitfalls of their individualisms by setting up what he called "free institutions." In more direct terms, this meant that American society did not dissolve into anarchic self-interest because they had political and social structures in place which would temper any such transgressions. Nevertheless though, Tocqueville still saw individualism as an obstacle to be dealt with. If not for other mitigating factors, individualism he believed would thwart the establishment of an orderly society in America.

Despite this initial negative understanding of individualism, however, Americans themselves would come to see things differently. In fact, the term in the US would become less of an insult as it did a point of celebration. Much of this change had to do with the American tendency at the time to celebrate free-market capitalist principles and liberal democracy (Lukes 1973: 26). Thus, Tocqueville's usage of individualism became less a denigration of American culture as it did a rallying cry for the American way of life. Stephen Lukes in his study of American individualism identifies this shift in thinking by tracing the work of a Transcendentalist writer a few years after Tocqueville's work was published. Here, Lukes quotes the author as having:

> inaccurately but significantly expounding Tocqueville's concept of individualism as expressing "that strong confidence in self, or reliance upon one's own exertion and resources" and as "the strife of all our citizens for wealth and distinctions of *their own* and their contempt of reflected honours."
>
> *(ibid.: 27)*

As Lukes and others have pointed out, this revision in thinking about individualism was repeated many times elsewhere in the American popular press. So much so that individualism became one of the core foundational values of the American spirit. This, for instance, was quite notably reflected in E.L. Godkin's 1896 essay "Aristocratic opinions of a democracy." Here, Godkin criticized Tocqueville for misunderstanding the nature of individualism. Rather than being the quality which would bring down the crucial structures of society, Godkin believed individualism was what gave Americans their strength to carry on as a free and democratic society and not the other way around (Arieli 1964: 200).

Of course, it almost goes without saying that much more can be said about individualism's long and storied history, as witnessed by Lukes's other investigations of individualism in the British or German context. But what hopefully appears apparent in all of this is that individualism did not simply emerge in a vacuum. Alongside it also were a whole host of other social developments, such as the Enlightenment, Capitalism, Liberalism, Modernity, etc. To speak of individualism then is also to have bearing on these other issues and vice versa.

Major claims and developments of the field, and key contributions

As varied as the early history of individualism has been, the same can be said about its meaning in the present day. Max Weber perhaps summed it up best in 1930 when he made the observation that "the expression 'individualism' includes the most heterogeneous things imaginable."

However, this is not to say that individualism is an empty term. For example, much has been done in recent times to distinguish the expression from other concepts such as individualization. Whilst the two terms are somewhat related, it is nonetheless said that individualization still means something different because it connotes a type of process whereas individualism more strongly entails a type of belief or attitude.

Yet how can this sort of work be possible given that individualism holds so many different meanings? What does individualism actually mean and can it even be properly defined given its multi-dimensional character?

To begin to answer such questions, an appeal to the Merriam Webster English dictionary might be helpful. There it defines individualism as "a doctrine that the interests of the individual are or ought to be ethically paramount." This, however, is just one part of the story. In the eyes of one pre-eminent scholar of individualism, Stephen Lukes, the term has also come to encapsulate four other key characteristics: (1) the inherent dignity of the individual, (2) autonomy, (3) privacy, and (4) self-development. In his view, only when we begin to understand these different elements can we begin to gain a truer picture of what individualism actually entails.

When it comes to the first key characteristic of individualism – the inherent dignity of the individual – Lukes points out that this quality can be historically traced back to certain religious movements which occurred many years prior to the modern industrial period. This is a thread also taken up by the twentieth-century French anthropologist, Louis Dumont. In a work entitled, "Essays on individualism," Dumont sets out his thesis that the notion of the individual as such could be detected in early European Christian history (1986: 24). Here, what he first identifies is the fact that the individual was a construct that did not always exist in the Western world. That people can be considered individually separate from one another was something that had to come about. Beforehand (and to some extent still today), the prevailing view was that people did not have their own individual existence. This he identified in the concept of "*universitas*" which posited the "social body as a whole of which living men are merely the parts" (ibid.: 63). After certain "revolutions" of thought, however (of which a great number of them are listed in Dumont's scholarship), Dumont contends that this way of thinking about individuals eventually gave way to the individualist mode of thinking that most of us in the West are more presently familiar with: the view that each of us is a distinct entity which is in some way irreducible to a larger whole.

One such revolution that led to this type of thinking was the one advanced by the work of certain Enlightenment thinkers – particularly those who advocated for Democratic Liberal ideals – occurring around the seventeenth to nineteenth centuries. At the center of this revolution was the shared idea that people should not be thought of as mere parts of a puzzle. Politically and morally speaking, this translated to the belief that "Man is too noble a being to serve simply as an instrument for others" which was how one particularly influential thinker, Jean Jacques Rousseau, described it (quoted in Lukes 1973: 49). Accompanying this view were a whole host of other like-minded expressions that came from other philosophes, which included such notable names as Immanuel Kant and John Locke. Of course, while there was certainly some variation as to how each thinker articulated their particular sentiments, nevertheless, a unifying theme for these philosophes was that individuality was of paramount importance. And in turn, this is what eventually filtered into the language of individualism.

Another characteristic of individualism that Lukes identifies is autonomy (ibid.: 52). By this, Lukes means to say that individualism also encapsulates the idea that individuals by their own accord can change their respective destinies. Principally, this is accomplished by appealing to one's own faculties and resources. Such a view can be contrasted to the notion that it is the larger whole of society which determines *in toto* the course of life that each of us will live. To be individualist then is to reject such deterministic ways of thinking.

While Lukes draws out a number of lines of thought which contributed to this connotation of individualism, one in particular deserves special mention. This is the thought of the seventeeth-century Dutch philosopher Benedict de Spinoza. Although Spinoza's views were sometimes inconsistent, as the Spinozan scholar Robert McShea tells us, nonetheless "there is enough evidence to establish Spinoza as an unmitigated individualist" (1975: 108). How Spinoza expressed his individualist view was by linking the usage of one's individual ability to reason with the idea of freedom. As he writes,

> I call a man completely free in so far as he is guided by reason, for then he is determined to action by causes which can be adequately understood through his own nature alone.
>
> *(quoted in McShea 1975: 109)*

This amounts to saying that, for Spinoza, freedom is attached to the condition of thinking rationally for oneself. It is by not accepting what has been already decided that captures the autonomous quality of individualism.

In the present day, individualism still retains this connotation in a number of arenas, although to be sure not just in the way Spinoza articulated. A good example of this can be found in David Reisman's work *The Lonely Crowd*. There, he is famously noted for postulating that "the 'autonomous' are those who on the whole are capable of conforming to the behavioral norms of their society . . . but who are free to choose whether to conform or not" (Reisman 1961: 241). It is this quality of choosing which individualism still to this day connotes.

Besides the inherent dignity of the individual and autonomy, individualism also encapsulates the characteristic of privacy in Lukes's account. What this refers to is the articulation of a "private existence within a public world, an area within which the individual is or should be left alone by others and able to do and think whatever he chooses" (ibid.: 59).

As a number of scholars of individualism have noted, a major strand of thought which has made the case for this conceptualization is historically that of Political Liberalism – which Lukes goes most in-depth with through the writings of John Stuart Mill, the nineteenth-century English political theorist. One of Mill's arguments that features prominently in this discussion is his claim that individuals should be left alone by the sovereign of a society if his or her "conduct affects the interests of no persons besides himself" (2008 [1859]: 84). Mill reasons this should be the case because allowing people to decide what is best for their own lives is what enables any happiness to be experienced in the greater society. This stands in stark contrast to a social environment which does not allow individuality to flourish (ibid.: 63).

In turn, Mill is keen to mark out a personal sphere of existence then that cannot be breached except in extreme instances. This is a thread in his work which emphasizes the importance of preserving minority thoughts and opinions. Why the minority must be preserved, according to Mill, is because the majority is not always correct, which he puts down to the fact that no one person is ever completely privy to the experience of others (ibid.: 93).

Correspondingly, Lukes is convinced that because of ideas such as these from Mill, individualism has come also to be connected to the notion of privacy. However, as he also notes, this has given grounds for some other social thinkers to criticize individualism, a theme that is explored later in this chapter.

Finally, in addition to the three other features of individualism which Lukes attributes, the last characteristic Lukes explores is the feature of self-development (ibid.: 67). What self-development partly refers to is the idea that the self is both mysterious and to an extent always unfolding.

Of those who brought about this connection between individualism and self-development, one strand of thought which Lukes considers to be extremely influential is that of Marxism (ibid.: 70). And according to Lukes, this connection is quite obvious. One way this is made so is by looking at Karl Marx's conceptualization of human nature as being about the actualization of its creative potentialities. Marx partly dwells on this topic in his famous essay "Estranged labor." Here, one of the claims he makes is that what makes humans unique in comparison to the inorganic and animal world is by virtue that humans produce even "when [they] are free from physical need" (1969: 113). This is so because for Marx, humans can relate to that which they produce through the process of reflection which in turn allows them to "form things in accordance with the laws of beauty" (ibid.: 114).

These points are made all the more salient by Marx's analysis of how the capitalist system has in some ways stunted the human propensity to be creative. Marx refers to this stunting as an *estrangement* or in other translations, alienation. Why estrangement is an essential feature of capitalism for Marx belongs in large part to how products are produced in its system. This is a process whereby workers by and large do not control what they are actually creating. In fact, Marx prefers to think of labor in a capitalist system as not so much being voluntary as much as being *forced* (ibid.: 110–11). Workers in this climate, in his view, are for the most part told what to do, without immediately the power to change why they are told to do so.

Against this backdrop, one of Marx's projects then is to overturn this way of producing things by way of a Communist revolution. One of the consequences he believes will come about when capitalism is overturned for communism is that people will finally be free to explore their individual possibilities. To illustrate, what Marx cites in his co-authored work with Friedrich Engels, *The German Ideology*, is the example of artistic painting. Whereas now in a capitalist system, "the exclusive concentration of artistic talent" is bound up in particular individuals because of the division of labor, "in a communist society there are no painters but at most people who engage in painting among other activities." In other words, Marx believes that communism allows people to *experiment* with their identities and in doing so, allows their distinctly human capabilities to develop.

Of course, as Lukes notes, there have been other ways in which self-development has been linked to individualism – ones that have been perhaps less communally focused than the approach Marx employed. Nonetheless, Marxism still plays a role in perpetuating this association.

Taken in sum, individualism then can be said to entail at least four different characteristics: the inherent dignity of the individual, autonomy, privacy, and self-development. However, there are other ways of covering how individualism can be thought about. Another way to define individualism, as a number of social thinkers tell us, is to look at the different ways in which it can be applied: these include political individualism, economic individualism, moral individualism, and methodological individualism.

While the ultimate goal of this chapter is not to explore in any substantial depth each of these applications, nevertheless, what is important about these different meanings and usages is that they encapsulate a great number of dimensions of social life. Individualism thus is not just an economic matter nor is it just a cultural one. The same can be said about its varied meanings and connotations. Neither is it just about autonomy nor just about privacy.

Contemporary usages and applications

That individualism has so many meanings and connotations is also in some measure why it has occupied so much public debate in recent times. This has been made manifest in the sheer number of recent academic and popular texts that have been devoted to its study. Because of its multi-faceted nature, politicians, social commentators, and academics alike have all engaged with the issue in whole host of different ways – some of which have been in dialogue with one another and some of which have been irreconcilable.

One of the key themes that have emerged out of this varied discussion has been whether or not individualism still even exists in contemporary Western society – specifically if it does so in the USA. For some, this question is rightfully answered in the affirmative. This is a thread picked up by Paul Leinberger and Bruce Tucker, who in their work *The New Individualists* (1991) contend that the moral and economic individualist mindset in America has over the last few decades become significantly heightened. They make such a claim by comparing the actions and attitudes of those individuals in America who were studied in William Whyte's work *The Organization Man* (1960) in the 1950s with the actions and attitudes of their children just a couple of decades later. One of the key differences that Leinberger and Tucker find between the two groups is just how dependent each are to their respective social structures – of which the workplace is given particular emphasis. Whereas those in the "organization" man generation expressed more loyalty to their places of employment (which in turn was also reciprocated vice versa), Leinberger and Tucker believe that such a world no longer exists for the organization man's offspring.

This view is guided by a number of recent developments in both the American and the global workplace. First and foremost of these is the fact that nowadays "job security" is increasingly considered to be a sort of oxymoron. To work is to be in a sense insecure since the prospect of unemployment constantly lurks at every corner. For Leinberger and Tucker, that companies no longer necessarily keep salaried employees on the payroll through difficult times speaks to the force of this point. At any moment, companies can make massive cuts to their resources and downsize their staff, depending on market conditions.

In turn, Leinberger and Tucker write that principles such as loyalty are no longer so well prized in this new economic climate. This applies not only for those on the top but also those on the bottom of the organizational structure: managers and workers alike face a world where "at any time they can wake up and discover that their job – or company – no longer exists" (1991: 210). Further, Leinberger and Tucker point to the fact that little opportunity remains for young workers to "rise steadily through the ranks." Instead, they believe that these days, "jobs mobility must often be sought outside one's company in a constant game of musical chairs throughout entire industries and professions" (ibid.).

As result, Leinberger and Tucker believe a new ethos of identity has arisen because of these new workplace conditions. This ethos is one which celebrates flexibility and provisional arrangements, a stark contrast to earlier times which had placed a higher premium on values such as trustworthiness and reliability. To drive home this point, Leinberger and Tucker make a distinction between the practice of "*choosing*" and "*having chosen correctly*." Whereas the organizational man was more focused on doing the latter, Leinberger and Tucker suggest that the former is nowadays considered to be the more important virtue (ibid.: 260). Why this is the case is because the status of conformity has changed in recent decades. No longer, they write, is it ultimately something which individuals concern themselves with. Instead, the focus has shifted onto wanting to be unique and creatively self-actualizing. In turn, the act of *choosing* has taken on a desirable quality because it indicates that one is always on the move. By contrast, "*having chosen correctly*" is denigrated because it suggests one's immobility.

If Leinberger and Tucker are to be believed, then individualism thus thrives in today's social climate because of this new restless spirit. Concepts such as community are in urgent need of re-description because the social bonds which have traditionally held us together have changed considerably. And this, they say, is due mainly to the new individualism which is now upon us.

Affirming Leinberger and Tucker's thesis that individualism has taken hold in contemporary American society is also the work of the American scholar Robert Putnam. This link is most clearly established in Putnam's most widely known text, *Bowling Alone* (2000). There Putnam paints a picture of American society which highlights its ever-increasing lack of civic engagement. Gone are the times when people more fully interacted with one another. This for Putnam can be clearly seen in the ways in which Americans nowadays take a less active role in the social and political life of their own communities, especially when compared to the first two-thirds of the twentieth century.

A metaphor that Putnam deploys to illuminate his arguments involves the practice of ten-pin bowling. This activity, he argues, was once considered to be a more collective pastime. As evidence, Putnam cites statistics which showcase the popularity of bowling leagues from the 1950s to the 1970s. During this period, bowling membership in America hit such a high note that at one point, 8 percent of *all* American men and nearly 5 percent of *all* American women considered themselves members. But this participation, as Putnam notes, was not to last, for just a few years later, bowling league membership would see a significant drop in numbers – a trend which continues to the present day.

Eric L. Hsu

Curiously though, as Putnam notes, bowling as a recreational sport has not lost its popularity. In fact there are figures which suggest that in the present day it is as prevalent as ever, which Putnam buttresses by quoting the eye-opening statistic that 25 percent more Americans bowled at some point in 1996 than voted in the 1998 congressional elections (2000: 113).

What then is to explain this particular phenomenon? Why has membership in bowling leagues decreased so dramatically even though bowling itself has become more popular? For Putnam the answer to this riddle can be found in the decline of what he calls "social capital," which he defines as the "features of social organization such as networks, norms, and social trust that facilitate coordination and cooperation for mutual benefit" (1995: 67).

One possible explanation that Putnam offers for why social capital has declined in recent times is that there are many aspects of contemporary life which no longer require the presence of others. This, in Putnam's account, has much to do with the rise of certain technologies such as the television and telephone. The path they have led us down is one where we can witness (and even in some cases interact with) a great number of events that might not have happened in previous times. However, Putnam focuses on the fact that this has come at the expense of our no longer having to be actually be there to witness a person accomplish some landmark feat (ibid.: 75). We can simply do so through the "miracles" of the television. Consequently, Putnam contends that this is why many of us lead such isolated lives.

Another explanation that Putnam offers for the recent decline in social capital rests on the issue of suburbanization. Here, what Putnam contends is that the founding of suburbs has created a great number of places in the US where individuals no longer necessarily have to form strong bonds with their neighbors, which in turn has made life for many suburbanites a very privatized experience (2000: 210).

Taken in sum, a consequence of Putnam's thinking then is that contemporary American society appears to us as being extremely individualistic, especially in its connotations of privacy and atomization. In this new age, values such as community and organization are no longer so well prized, which Putnam generally believes that the American people are worse off for.

A third voice which echoes the view that individualism has taken hold in Western society belongs to the noted British sociologist Anthony Giddens. However, unlike the first two approaches, Giddens is decidedly more optimistic (or at the very least more nuanced) about the onset of an individualist mindset.

One particular way in which Giddens expresses this optimism is through his discussion of what many have termed the rise of a "me-first" generation. This discussion typically proceeds from the claim that individualism is to blame for destroying common values and shirking public responsibilities. Giddens, however, believes this not to be the case. What Giddens finds to be particularly problematic about the "me generation" thesis is that it too readily posits that we are currently in an age of moral decay – which is another way of saying that people are fast becoming amoral. Giddens prefers to see things in a different light; in his view, ours is not so much an age of moral decay as much as it is an age of moral transition. The reasoning behind this lies in Giddens's attention to detail as to what the new individualism actually entails. *Pace* many contemporary thinkers, Giddens tells us that individualism is not just about "economic selfishness" or coterminous with a hyper-consumer culture. In his view, what we must also consider about individualism is that it "is a structural phenomenon in societies breaking free from the hold of tradition and custom" (2001: 4). This is another way of saying that individualism is not just about thinking for one's own well-being alone as much as it is also about the de-legitimization of tradition as bearer of absolute authority.

Consequently, Giddens contends that this is why we should think of individualism more positively. Dismissing it altogether neglects the fact that individualism has in some cases made

136

advances on a number of social problems, of which changing gender relations are a particularly salient instance. Owing in part to individualism, Giddens writes that "women no longer are inevitably 'fated' to lives of domesticity and the rearing of children"; additionally, Giddens cites the fact that women have also "entered the labour force in large numbers and have acquired many of the freedoms that were long mainly the freedoms of men – including the right to divorce" (ibid.). Those who would criticize individualism *in toto* then ignore such positive outcomes – however incomplete as they may be.

Giddens though is still aware of the reality that the new individualism continues to possess its own shortcomings. It may be the case that individualism does indeed share overlap with the selfish ideology of egoism. It may also be the case that individualism does in some important measure lead to a decline in social solidarity. However, Giddens is not convinced that this is all that there is. In an age where individualism takes hold, "new worries and anxieties come to the fore" but as he writes, so too do "many more positive possibilities" (1998: 37).

Main criticisms

While the notion that individualism has more or less run rampant among the West has been an influential one, there are still those, however, who present a countering view. Their version of contemporary society is one which portrays individualism not on the increase but on the decline. One such voice who expresses this sort of sentiment is the American thinker Richard Botelho. For Botelho, there is cause to believe that individualism no longer holds sway in the Western world – specifically in the US – because people no longer feel like they can be *autonomous*. This has a lot to do with, in his mind, the fact that we are now "conditioned to believe in the superiority of others, presumably those in power positions" (1996: 6). Why we do owes in some part to the dependent relationship that many of us now hold to our social institutions, for it is they we now trust over our own "abilities, judgments, characters and intellects" (ibid.: 14). Botelho evidences this claim by looking at the lack of "self-correcting" mechanisms in a whole host of social arenas of which the US political system serves as an exemplary case. Why the US political system is proof that individualism has been in decline is because "after virtually every election, the electorate is left with the feeling that nothing will ultimately change" (ibid.: 7). Botelho puts such a situation ultimately down to the fact that individuals no longer trust themselves to address large social problems. After all as this line of thinking goes, what can one person do in the face of a broken but overwhelming system?

Accordingly, this is what fuels Botelho's argument that there needs to be a revival of individualism amongst the general populace (ibid.: 12). If individualism is not more embraced, Botelho fears that many social ills and problems such as widespread poverty will become exacerbated.

Botelho, however, is not alone in his belief that individualism needs to be reinvigorated. A similar thread can also be detected in the famous American sociologist C. Wright Mills's work *The Sane Society*. Mills, who was writing in the 1950s, likewise echoes that individualism is no longer the popular sentiment that it once was. In his view, this can be attributed to the shift away from a public to a mass society. Whereas before a healthier public sphere encouraged people of all kinds to publicize their own opinions, nowadays Mills believes that such a world is no longer with us. In its place, Mills writes, is a mass society which discourages people from making their views known to others. This is a society in which people "have no autonomy from institutions." In fact, according to Mills, just the opposite appears to be happening. Institutions themselves appear to have control over the people they were originally meant to serve and this is in large part due to the fact that people no longer feel welcome or even able to change the social world around them.

Hints of Mills's claims about mass society can also be detected in the research of more recent authors. This is particularly the case if we examine, for example, Jaron Lanier's noted work *You Are Not a Gadget*. Here, Lanier paints a picture of the world which at first appears to be in stark contrast to the world of which Mills wrote. With the advent of the Internet and many new tele-visual/communication devices, gone are the days when the media had a monolithic hold over a captive audience. This is particularly true of what many have termed to be the Web 2.0 revolution. What Web 2.0 commonly refers to is that Internet content these days is not something exclusively determined by experts. This is because Internet users themselves are nowadays expected to play a hand in the process, whereas before they were largely absent.

Lanier, however, is not convinced that this Web 2.0 revolution has allowed us to become more individualist. Lanier reasons this is so because the Web 2.0 paradigm increasingly treats people not as individuals as such but more as parts of a larger aggregate, which he refers to as the "hive-mind." Worst yet, Lanier believes that we have forfeited our individualist sensibility to the "hive mind" of Web 2.0 without many of us actually realizing it. Lanier evidences his claims by looking at new Web programs such as Facebook and Wikipedia. While he grants that programs like these do give people the opportunity to express themselves as individuals in some small fashion, Lanier focuses on the *standardized* and *automated* ways in which such exchanges occur. What is particularly troubling about these exchanges for Lanier is that the onus is placed on computerized systems and not the humans who operate them as drivers of knowledge. Case in point, recent versions of Microsoft Word; whereas before it more akin to a typewriter, nowadays, with built in functions such as spelling check and predictive text, Microsoft Word has evolved to the point where it appears to "know" what you would like to do. Wrongly indent a paragraph? A pop-up appears. Want to write a letter? The program will automatically fill in the typical pleasantries. A similar phenomenon can also be detected in search engine programs such as Google whereby people are more prone to trust computer-generated results than their own judgment.

Correspondingly, from Lanier's viewpoint, what this all spells is a world that greatly devalues individual voices. He thinks this way because he believes that more of our confidence is being put into computer systems than in personal ingenuity (2010: 27). Correspondingly this leads Lanier, like Botelho, to believe that individualism therefore needs to be reinvigorated. If we do not, he fears that the innovative and pioneering quality which once characterized the Internet will gradually fade into oblivion (ibid.: 4).

Taken as a whole, what thus emerges is a snapshot of individualism which underlines its highly contested status within contemporary social thought. For some, it indeed exists in the Western world, whereas for others it is in dire need of a revival. Which camp is ultimately correct is not something that can be so easily decided. For indeed it may even be the case that both are somewhat correct.

The point of this chapter therefore is not to decide once and for all which view holds the most water but rather to identify how the debate over individualism has thus far been couched. And in this respect, hopefully at least one thing has become apparent: with a few noticeable exceptions, individualism has for the most part been cast in terms of its opposition to a more collectivist sentiment. Yet, as this chapter argues, other considerations about individualism remain which have up until this point been rather understudied. It is these aspects that this chapter now turns to.

The continuing importance of perspectives on individualism, and anticipated future developments

Speed and individualism

Whilst it is clear that much ink has been spilled over the issue of individualism in recent times, what has been conspicuously absent from these discussions has been how the issue of speed might factor in. This is a thread that has been recently taken up by Anthony Elliott and Charles Lemert in their seminal work *The New Individualism* (2009b). In this particular text, what Elliott and Lemert highlight is how our understanding of individualism has recently experienced a considerable amount of revision. Whereas before, the discussion of individualism mainly dwelt on whether or not it still existed in Western societies – which was discussed in length in the last section – today, a new concern has come to the fore: to what extent our conceptualization of individualism has been altered by the issue of speed.

When it comes to individualism, there are least two reasons why the topic of speed has come to occupy more attention. The first is related to the fact that in general speed is no longer such a widely ignored concept within contemporary social theory. This stands in stark contrast to earlier times when speed hardly made much of an impact on social thought. Even when it was mentioned, especially in the writings of some classical social scientists, it cropped up at best as a mere "adjunct to other debates and issues" (Tomlinson 2007: 5).

Partly, as some have noted, this had much to do with the absence of a sophisticated understanding of the temporal matters in social research. Why speed did not factor into people's social theories was because time was such a taken for granted experience. Not so though in this day and age. In more recent times, contemporary sociology has been more attuned to the significance of time and, in turn, the matter of speed. This can be seen in the number of key texts which have outlined speed as a watershed concept for a whole plethora of social phenomena. These have included such seminal ideas as modernity (Tomlinson 2007), globalization (Scholte 2005), and liberal democracy (Scheuerman 2004).

A second reason why speed has become a more prominent issue in discussions about individualism is because the stakes regarding speed have arguably been raised in comparison to earlier times. This view is grounded in the fact that the world we now live in is arguably faster than ever before. Of course, this is not to say that there were not momentous events in earlier times which significantly altered people's pace of life. To do so would be foolish given the amount of historical record which suggests otherwise. Yet, as many social thinkers have argued, ours is the age where decidedly speed has been taken to heights that it has never been before. John Tomlinson's work *The Culture of Speed* (2007) adroitly addresses this very issue. There he makes the claim that what distinguishes speed in the present day from earlier times has to do with how significant the concept of *immediacy* has recently become.

Previously, talk of speed in the West mainly centered on its machinist manifestations. That is to say, speed was dealt in terms of how quickly something could be sped up – often under the banner of progress (i.e., railway travel). Tomlinson, however, believes that in the present day, a new cultural understanding of speed has arisen – one which has supplanted the notion of machine speed as the dominant discourse. This new understanding he believes can be encapsulated by the term, "immediacy." For Tomlinson, what is distinctive about the condition of immediacy is that it suggests that speed in some regards has been pressed to its limits. So much so that it has forced us to re-think basic truths about human life. To illustrate, Tomlinson examines the "gap" we normally assume to exist between the desire for some object and its attainment (2007: 90). As this line of thinking goes, some period of delay always exists in the act of wishing.

So in previous times, if I had wanted to listen to a newly released single, I would have had to wait a certain amount of time to do so because a number of intermediary steps exist along the way (e.g., having to locate and then purchase the single from an outlet).

By contrast, the condition of immediacy dictates that such a gap no longer exists (ibid.: 91). This occurs by virtue that immediacy culture tries to leave us with the impression, often successfully, that waiting is no longer necessary. Thus nowadays if one desires to hear a particular song, one can simply download it at near-instantaneous speeds from a mobile hand-held phone.

The same phenomenon has also been detected in a number of different social practices, including warfare and political polling, to name just a couple. Correspondingly this has led some social thinkers to proclaim that ours is the age where speed, for better or worse, demands our full attention since it is getting more difficult to ignore the impacts of social acceleration.

Taken as a whole it is against this backdrop that talk of speed has also entered into the discourse surrounding individualism. As previously mentioned, the work of Anthony Elliott and Charles Lemert has played an extremely influential role in this endeavor. What they reveal in their numerous texts on the matter is a view of individualism which appreciates its temporal dynamism. However, the speed they most pay attention to is the type of individualism which they believe to be most currently endemic: hyper-individualism, a term which they do not actually utilize, but which conveys much of what they seem to argue.

One of the ways in which Elliott and Lemert suggest that individualism must be rethought is by breaking down the components of what the new individualism involves as a result of its acceleration. Among other things, this encapsulates "a relentless emphasis on *self-reinvention*; an endless hunger for *instance change*; a pre-occupation with *short-termism* and episodicity; and a fascination with *speed* and *dynamism*" (Elliott and Lemert 2009b: xi). By all of this, the key point Elliott and Lemert wish to make is just how much individualism has been transformed by the onset of a high speed society.

A key feature of this transformation is what the two authors identify as a "*disappearance of context*" (ibid.: 13). This is their argument that the erstwhile ways in which people used to make sense of their lives has gradually been made outmoded – to the point where traditional customs no longer hold sway. Instead, Elliott and Lemert write that "individuals are increasingly expected to produce context for themselves" – an imperative which has become "deeply rooted as both social norm and cultural obligation" (ibid.).

Yet in this respect, what deserves particular mention in the author's view is just how quickly the "designing of life, of a self-project" is expected to occur. Elliott, in his monograph *Making the Cut* (2008), is particularly interested in exploring this issue. Such is evident in his discussion of "the new paradigm of self-making." The backdrop he sets the new "reinvention craze" against is the onset of the "fast-paced, techy culture of globalization" (2008: 45). What the new global economy has wrought, he contends, is a world where people are now placed "under intense pressure to keep pace with the sheer speed of change" (p. 46).

Elliott is able to make such a claim because of his sophisticated understanding of what outcomes the new global economy has brought about. For him, profit margins, hiring practices, and capital exchanges are not the only things that have been impacted by recent globalizing forces. Instead, what Elliott seeks to underscore is just how "transformations in the new economy and in self-identity . . . are increasingly becoming intermeshed" (p. 45). This is another way of saying that globalization is not just an "out there" phenomenon as it is something that has in some senses intruded into people's emotional lives (p. 9).

As such, business practices such as "short-term contracts, endless downsizings, just-in-time deliveries and multiple careers" – which many social thinkers have identified as being largely peculiar to the current time period – have also had great bearing to how individuals nowadays are able to constitute themselves (p. 122). Elliott identifies one of these personal changes to be a new found "faith in flexibility, plasticity, and incessant reinvention"; qualities which suggest that "we are no longer judged on what we have done and achieved; we're now judged on our flexibility, on our readiness for personal makeover" (p. 122).

However, what Elliott and Lemert wish to stress is that these "makeovers" and "reinventions" are not merely figurative. The new individualism, as they posit it, has real effects on our conceptions of identity which has also greatly transformed our bodies (p. 46).

For Elliott, this latter point also doubles as a site for empirical study, in that the acceleration of individualism can also be tracked through the rise of cosmetic surgical culture. Here, Elliott's thesis is that the increase in popularity of cosmetic surgery can in some large measure be attributed to the mounting pressures that individuals feel to be "more efficient, faster, leaner, inventive and self-actualizing than they were previously" (p. 126).

Elliott underscores this point by noting that cosmetic surgery is increasingly seen in this day and age as a measure of one's plasticity. As this line of thinking dictates, to prove that one can keep up with rough and tumble of today's changing economic climate, one must be willing to go under the surgeon's knife. As an illustrative example, Elliott cites a growing trend of highly skilled global professionals willing to get plastic surgery for a leg up on the competition. Says one of Elliott's interviewees,

> I don't think you understand the reasons these people have for wanting surgery – it's not vanity or celebrity-inspired. They just don't want to look fazed at work, or appear too hassled by the demands of the job.
>
> *(p. 111)*

Elliott is especially keen to pick up on this latter point about plastic surgery and the workplace. In his view, what is most telling is just how much more of an accepted practice plastic surgery has become in the business community. As he writes,

> Not all that long time ago, anyone who wanted cosmetic surgery would have been recommended therapy in the first instance. Today, by contrast, there is a widespread acceptance that cosmetic surgical culture is beneficial and even desirable. Especially for tough-minded, highly motivated professionals, to be surgically "freshened up" provides an edge in the marketplace.
>
> *(p. 145)*

Further, Elliott notes that there is mounting statistical evidence to suggest that this is indeed occurring, not just in the polished cities of the West but in the wider world. Thus, we find studies which report that cosmetic plastic surgery has now grown into an estimated $15 to $20 billion dollars a year industry in the US alone, as well as other studies which report similar findings in the rate of growth in East Asian countries such as Taiwan, South Korea, and Thailand. The message here is thus that not only is cosmetic surgery becoming more widespread, but also that this process is somehow becoming more frequent – in other words, faster.

Yet in the midst of all this, Elliott and Lemert are decidedly ambivalent about these changes to identity brought about by the new individualism. This largely owes to the fact that they read the new individualism "as a doubled edged phenomenon – one that promotes the realization of self-fulfillment as well as the cultivation of self-limitation" (2009b: 12).

On the one hand, the latter is the case because the imperative to constantly be on the move is an endeavor that invariably produces new anxieties and dangers. They identify a few of these in those who have been on the losing end of the new individualist paradigm. One term which might capture the plight of these individuals is that of "waste." Drawing upon the work of Zygmunt Bauman, Elliott and Lemert identify a main motor which drives people to perpetuate the new individualist mindset: the "ambient fear . . . of being dumped, on becoming waste, of exclusion" (ibid.: 102). Unfortunately however, this fear is not just a possibility but a reality for a good number of individuals. Played out in cosmetic surgical culture, this is made manifest in the number of high-profile cases of plastic surgery "addicts"; those people who in the process of trying find the right identity, seemingly lose their bearings. Elliott attributes this occurrence to the twisted logics cosmetic surgical cultures can sometimes unleash – namely, that one rarely feels completely satisfied in the long term after they get plastic surgery. This latter point owes to the fact that cosmetic surgical products do not always have the longest shelf life, which Elliott believes to be intentionally so (Elliott 2008: 90). For what drives contemporary consumerist culture is not just the satisfaction of needs as much as it is the creation of them – a reality which is reflected in recent figures which reveal that a high percentage of plastic surgery is done on repeat customers.

Another reason why Elliott and Lemert believe we should express concern over the new individualism is because they fear that the promises of a living in a high-speed society can mask the continued growth of "privatized worlds" (Elliott and Lemert 2009a: 61). This concern is not too dissimilar from some of the authors that were discussed earlier, namely Robert Putnam. Like them, Elliott and Lemert too are concerned about the ways in which "people, increasingly are seeking personal solutions to social problems" (ibid.: 62). And in the process, they highlight the lamentable decline of individuals opening themselves to others (2009b: xxi).

At the same time however, Elliott and Lemert also do not wish to discount the favorable aspects of the new individualism as well. This owes in part to the creative possibilities the two authors believe the new individualism has opened up. In particular, they reference the wider avenues in which people now can draw from to construct their sense of self (ibid.: 120). Among other things, these avenues take the form of new tele-communication technologies, such as the advent of the Internet and mobile phone. One particular consequence of this new digital world is that situations are created when people can try out new identities. For instance, Elliott and Lemert find that one of their interviewees, Ruth, is someone who has used the Internet to feel more confident about knowing what her "real" life should be like (ibid.: 125). She was able to be so because online chatting communities opened her life "to others beyond the local determinations of everyday life" (ibid.: 123), which they in some regards identify as being associated with the new individualism. Concomitantly, people such as Ruth are also able to experiment with their identities because there is now a greater culture acceptance of such behaviors. In fact, acceptance is perhaps not the most apt word in this instance as much as is the term "dictum."

Curiously on this point, however, one of the things explicitly missing from Elliott and Lemert's analysis is the mention of speed and its positive aspects. That is to say, nowhere in their texts do they directly connect acceleration with issues to do with social justice and/or autonomy, as is the case in other authors (e.g., Scheuerman 2004). Yet, if one reads this point in the context of their wider argument, it becomes extremely evident that speed at the very least lurks in the background. It is because individuals such as Ruth do not need to physically traverse such distances to interact with distant others, which "costs" time, that the new individualism can offer creative possibilities.

In sum, what Elliott and Lemert thus contribute is a view of individualism which appreciates its recent *temporal* transformation. In doing so, they focus on the way in which the *hyper* form of individualism radically changes how we might think of the concept more generally. Elliott and Lemert are also attuned to the new dangers and possibilities created by this transformation of individualism, which they believe have something to do with the issue of speed.

Toward a theory of decelerated individualism

If there is criticism to be made about Elliott and Lemert's work, however, it is that in some respects their scholarship into speed does not extend far enough. Specifically, what seems particularly underdeveloped is a conceptualization of speed and time which looks at not only social acceleration but also at deceleration. That is to say, whilst they deftly identify how differently we might think of individualism in an age of acceleration, what Elliott and Lemert do not attend as well to is the varied temporality in which individualism currently exists. This amounts to saying then that the trends to slow down individualism is not something that is explicitly acknowledged in their work. And consequently, this gives us a less than complete picture about the different temporal-scapes in which individualism currently operates under.

To better illuminate the reasoning behind these critiques, it is useful to appeal to the work of the German social theorist Hartmut Rosa, who has become a leading contemporary voice on social acceleration. One of the main arguments he has put forth in recent times is that social acceleration cannot be properly understood if we do not also consider the phenomenon of deceleration. Rosa rests this claim on his observation that most, if not all, types of acceleration invariably encounter resistances and/or countertrends (Rosa 2003: 15). These slowdowns can either be intentional, unintentional or, as is often the case, a mixture of both. Further, these slowdowns in some cases can also be enabling of later acceleration as they can also be possibly genuine contraventions.

One particular example that can be used to illustrate these claims is that of the automobile. *Prima facie*, its invention is supposed to have allowed individuals to get to different places at a faster speed when compared to earlier technologies (i.e., horse-drawn carriage). Yet, as the top speeds of automobiles have gotten faster, a good deal of people, especially those living in urban centers, have not benefited from these technological advances. Much of this, of course, has to do with the phenomenon of the traffic jam where in the pursuit of rapidity, individuals find themselves experiencing delay. Through the lens of Rosa, what this speaks to thus is that the move to accelerate social processes does not always lead to desired outcomes (ibid.: 15). Things may go unintentionally awry.

At the same time, Rosa believes that social deceleration can also occur intentionally as well. This, he argues, is evidenced in part by the integral role decelerations can play in helping later accelerations along. These often times are deceleration which "preserve the capacity to function" so as to make advances in the future. On the individual level, Rosa believes these manifest themselves as "time-outs" which allow people to catch their breaths from accelerating forces, only of course to be confronted with more acceleration down the road (ibid.: 16).

By contrast though, Rosa also wishes to acknowledge the presence of another type of deceleration which actually tries to avoid being enlisted in the service of the broader desire to accelerate. While Rosa believes that historically each of these type of decelerating movements have failed in the long run, nevertheless, they are still important for us to keep in mind for they offer the possibility that at some point acceleration will turn in on itself.

Given then that acceleration is never a smooth or straightforward process, Rosa thus concludes that we should be cautious "about the dangers of an overly general diagnosis concerning social acceleration." In order to understand the complex nature of social acceleration, we must also be prepared to look at its various disjunctures and paradoxes.

While Elliott and Lemert do not necessarily overtly speak about social deceleration and its relation to individualism, this does not mean, however, that their work has not in some ways had bearing on the issue. Indeed, as it is my claim, even though the two authors have not yet overtly taken up the subject matter, there nevertheless exists in their texts tactful hints on how to proceed with developing an understanding of a *decelerated* form of individualism.

One place to begin is by exploring their inquiry on how people "survive" the new individualism in the present day. Here, an interesting observation that they make is that keeping up with ceaseless self-reinvention craze is not necessarily the only way to live one's life in the present moment. Such an approach, they contend, sometimes leads to the recipe of a burnout, as perhaps might have been the case with C. Wright Mills. As an alternative, they point to valuable words of wisdom left by the American psychoanalytic thinker Phyllis Meadow. Her answer on to how "to survive full of creative energy to live a long life" was simply put, "aggression!" (Elliott and Lemert 2009b: 190). Though the authors are quite nebulous at times about what makes aggression a viable life strategy, nonetheless they put much weight into its counteracting potential. In particular, they are keen to note that aggression is linked to a form of persistence (ibid.: 194). Though not explicitly defined as being so, if one interprets closely, then herein rests one of Elliott and Lemert's thoughts about a decelerated individualism. For them, a temporal dynamism *does* exist with regards to individualism if one considers that change and liquidity are not the only qualities which occupy the current social landscape.

How this link can be made between deceleration and aggression owes in great deal to Freudian psychoanalytic notions of the latter term. Sigmund Freud, especially in his later writings, goes to great lengths to emphasize the centrality of aggression in our everyday lives. For him, it is a drama which we must always continually contend with. Yet why this is so belongs to the occurrence of one of Freud's more contentious but nevertheless seminal theories: the death drive (*Todestrieb*).

What the theory of the death drive entails is that human beings are impelled on the one hand by the desire for deadness. One particular reason why Freud was compelled to take on such a belief came curiously enough from observing a young child repeat what seemed like a displeasing event: the habitual departure of his mother from the young child's side. This repetition was played out not through the actual disappearance of the mother per se as much as it was displaced onto a game the child would play. Freud famously notes that this game involved the child "taking any small objects he could get hold of and throwing them away from him into a corner . . . so that hunting for his toys and picking them up was often quite a business" (Freud [1920] 1961: 13). As he did this, he would make an utterance which closely resembled "fort" (the German word for "gone") whenever he threw something and then as he recovered an object he would utter the German phrase for "there" ("da!").

For Freud what was particularly perplexing about this practice was that it went against a core belief of his at the time, which was that the attainment of pleasure was the ultimate goal of human beings. Why then would a child continually play out a scenario which would have him experience the pain of losing a cherished figure? The answer to this question as Freud wrote was not to be found in his theory of the pleasure principle but instead in his concept of the death drive. Freud grounded this claim in his theory that human life was not just about making things anew. For him, this was a truth which could be evidenced by one of the most obvious certainties about the nature of life – namely that eventually it invariably ends (ibid.: 43). In turn, Freud took this fact also to mean that there is an inherent urge in all life to return to a previous state, which to Freud's mind would also then explain why individuals are prone to repeat painful events. Freud linked the will to master something – of which repetition is one viable path – to the drive to the restore things as they once were.

Accordingly, aggression would factor into this equation because for Freud it was a natural consequence for the death drive to be deflected from the self onto the external world. This process, for Freud, was termed aggression and it led him to postulate in numerous instances that its existence was the greatest obstacle for social individuals to attain some palpable level of happiness.

Freud considered the human propensity to be aggressive as an ever-ongoing obstacle to be dealt with because it did not mesh particularly well with the requirements of living with others. This latter point was famously elaborated in Freud's most well-known text, *Civilization and Its Discontents*. Here, Freud put forth his thesis that a key condition of living with others dictates that aggression must not be allowed to run unabated. This meant that individuals are not allowed to completely give in to their inclination to destroy some other thing or person, if they are to live cooperatively with others. And yet, for Freud, this did not mean that aggression could ever be overcome. If it was not directed toward others, then its energies would be directed toward one's self – a point captured in his discussion of his concept of the super-ego.

For our purposes though, what is of particular importance here is how Freud conceptualized the aim of aggression. The point is not just that aggression holds the potential of destroying social bonds but that in large measure it is in the service of a drive which utilizes the practice of *repetition* and *mastery*. To be aggressive then is in a sense also to be able to actualize these latter features.

When we return to the work of Elliott and Lemert on this issue, it becomes difficult at first to see how their understanding of aggression meshes with Freud's conceptualization. This is especially so if we consider that Freud's idea of aggression is seemingly linked to the destruction of others if not also one's own self. How then does this allow individuals to "survive" the new individualism as the two authors so boldly claim?

Fortunately, this paradox becomes resolved once we consider the temporal context in which Elliott and Lemert are writing. Read in a different light, aggression in some respects can actually allow a greater amount of sociality to occur because of its *persistent* quality. This is another way of saying that the drive for repetition – which can also be interpreted as the drive for wanting normalcy – is what can allow people to occupy different temporal frameworks than what is currently configured in the new individualism. By being aggressive, one is opting out of a time which some authors have described as being "timeless," "accelerated" or "instantaneous."

This notion becomes particularly clear if we consider that aggression can be in some respects contrasted with the notion of reflexivity. To be reflexive, especially as Elliott and Lemert refer to it, is to be open and responsive to change (2009b: 174). However, aggressiveness clashes with this particular outlook because the former involves the strong tendency to engage in repetition. This occurs at the expense of choosing to have new experiences and lifestyles and is correspondingly why aggression then can stem the tide of the societal pressures for ceaseless change. In the example of Phyllis Meadow, this can be said to be played out in how she sometimes spoke to others. As Elliott and Lemert identify this: "[w]hen people tried to tell her she could not do what she set about doing," she would often reply, "Of course not. Life is impossible. Don't try to change me" (2009b: 189).

It is this unwillingness to change which offers the potential of living in a different temporal form of individualism. And in turn, this is why Elliott and Lemert leave the readers of their work *The New Individualism* with a discussion of aggression as a way forward. One of their concerns is that because aggression has become a less well-cultivated capacity, individuals will feel like they have no other option but to submit to the pressures of social acceleration.

Yet there is also a danger here which Elliott and Lemert only off-handedly acknowledge. And that is that aggressiveness taken to its destructive extremes can also potentially close down on the possibility of social acceleration and, in so doing, the benefits which might have resulted. This potential becomes all the more real if aggression is more greatly in the service of the death drive. In this case, aggression can develop into a form of self-destructive psychosis – one which attempts to prevent change at all costs.

To avoid going down this path, it is therefore necessary to consider forces which might counteract the mastering tendencies of aggression. In Freud's account, one possibility lay in the expression of what he termed "the life drive" (Eros). For Freud, what is significant about this drive is that it points to the fact that death and its corollaries are not the only forces that impel us. This is the case because if that were so, human beings would not continue to endure as a species. If there were only the drive toward death, nothing new would ever develop, which as history suggests is certainly not the case. To account for the fact that human beings do undergo transformations and (sexually) reproduce themselves then, Freud famously posited the existence of a drive which could counteract the effects of the death drive. This drive, in contrast to the focus of restoring things to a previous state, primarily seeks to make new connections – which in turn can also be interpreted as complicating life.

Correspondingly, this complicating tendency can also be linked to the move to social acceleration for in both cases the aim is to create novel experiences. Elliott and Lemert, who are privy to this idea, thus point to the fact that in the case of Meadow, she would not have been able to accomplish the things she did "*just* by being aggressive"; "The aggression was always balanced," they say, "against the love of others and the constructive desire to join them working to build a better world" (2009b: 193).

Derivatively, this balance is also true of how we might understand the varied temporal dimensions in which individualism now currently exists. Just as there have been moves to live in a world of hyper-individualism, counter-trends can be identified as well. And if the latter do exist, then aggression is a useful concept to identify its manifestations.

On a greater level, if this latter thesis of the chapter holds, then one of the consequences is that both speed and individualism are issues which need to be understood as psychical and bodily matters. In the case of individualism, this means it is not just a detached philosophical inquiry as much it also is a *lived* experience with psychical implications. According to Daniel Shanahan, this has been a consideration that some scholars of individualism have not paid enough attention to, for they have largely set it in rationalist terms alone at the cost of psychological naiveté (1992: 3).

In the work of Elliott and Lemert, however, a more psychical approach to individualism is indeed employed. And accordingly, it has been the contention of this chapter that such a tactic has proved to be extremely insightful. In particular, it has given us new bearings on how deceleration might play a more significant role in understanding individualism for the future – and in so doing a more balanced and robust understanding of individualism's temporality.

References

Arieli, Y. (1964) *Individualism and Nationalism in American Ideology*. Cambridge, MA: Harvard University Press.

Botelho, R. (1996) *The New Individualism*. Danville, CA: Windstream Publishing Company.

Dumont, L. (1986) *Essays on Individualism*. Chicago: University of Chicago Press.

Elliott, A. (2008) *Making the Cut*. London: Reaktion.

Elliott, A. and Lemert, C. (2009a) "The Global New Individualist Debate," in A. Elliott and P. du Gay (eds) *Identity in Question*. London: Sage Publications, 37–64.

Elliott, A. and Lemert, C. (2009b) *The New Individualism: The Emotional Costs of Globalization* (revised edition). New York: Routledge.

Freud, S. [1920] (1961) *Beyond the Pleasure Principle*. New York: W. W. Norton and Company.

Giddens, A. (1998) *The Third Way*. Cambridge: Polity Press.

Giddens, A. (2001) "Introduction", in A. Giddens (ed.) *The Global Third Way Debate*. Cambridge: Polity Press, 1–21.

Lanier, J. (2010) *You Are Not a Gadget: A Manifesto*. New York: Knopf.

Leinberger, P. and Tucker, B. (1991) *The New Individualists*. New York: Harper Collins.

Lukes, S. (1973) *Individualism*. Oxford: Basil Blackwell.

Marx, K. (1969) *Economic and Philosophic Manuscripts of 1844*. New York: International Publishers.

McShea, R. (1975) "Spinoza: Human Nature and History", in E. Freeman and M. Mandelbaum (ed.) *Spinoza: Essays in Interpretation*. LaSalle: Open Court, 101–15.

Mill, J. [1859] (2008) *On Liberty and Other Essays*. Oxford: Oxford University Press.

Putnam, R. (1995) "Bowling Alone: America's Declining Social Capital," *Journal of Democracy*, 6(1): 65–78.

Putnam, R. (2000) *Bowling Alone: The Collapse and Revival of American Community*. New York and London: Simon & Schuster.

Riesman, D. (1961) *The Lonely Crowd*. New Haven, CT: Yale University Press.

Rosa, H. (2003) "Social acceleration: ethical and political consequences of a desynchronized high speed society," *Constellations*, 10(1): 3–33.

Scheuerman, W. (2004) *Liberal Democracy and the Social Acceleration of Time*. Baltimore: Johns Hopkins University Press.

Scholte, J. (2005) *Globalization: A Critical Introduction*. New York: Palgrave Macmillan.

Shanahan, D. (1992) *Toward a Genealogy of Individualism*. Amherst: University of Massachusetts Press.

Tocqueville, A. (2000) *Democracy in America*. Chicago: University of Chicago Press.

Tomlinson, J. (2007) *The Culture of Speed*. London: Sage Publications.

Part 2
The analysis of identity

9

Transformations of working identities

Labour and the self

Daniel Mendelson

Introduction

To speak of a single work or labour identity would be as grievous an error as the essentializing universalisms espoused by early theorists of gender and race. Just as W.E.B. Du Bois's notion of the veil and Simone de Beauvoir's (1949) maxim 'one is not born a woman but becomes one' overlooked the diversity of experience of their respective Othered peoples, forcing a false amalgamation of experience, so too should we be careful to not speak of any universal experience of work. Theorists of labour have increasingly identified that one individual's work is another's leisure, and vice versa; lines in contemporary times have blurred further, as especially noteworthy with reference to professional athletes (though arguably debates surrounding pleasure and work have been intimately intertwined since the beginning of 'professions' in the case of sex workers). This chapter will attempt to defend a multifaceted approach to work identities, as the mechanisms of certain trends such as globalization are reasonably identifiable, but vitally, their phenomenological impacts are quite diverse. The variegated social, aesthetic and even physiological experiences of work will be a primary overarching theme of the following exposition. Of course, this is significantly due to the preliminary problem of describing exactly what 'work' is; as André Gorz (1999: 3) notes, '[w]hy do we say that a woman "works" when she takes care of children in a nursery school and "does not work" when she stays at home to take care or her own children?' For many thinkers, the inherently subjective and socially constructed nature of the topic is what makes the study of work so intriguing.

A second initial consideration, interrelated to the sundry perceptions of work that will be explored in the following piece, will be that of social-historical change. All too often, social-historical change is portrayed as a positivist occurrence, leading in a sole direction: improvement, growth, progress, and among some theorists, perfection. But the reality of contemporary work identities contrasts any such notion. As will be explored in the final section of this chapter, millions of workers inhabit torturous identities, living what Giorgio Agamben (1998) has termed 'bare life', in which one is biologically alive but politically dead; following Zygmunt

Bauman's (1989) thesis of the Holocaust being decidedly at home in modernity, perhaps the same is true of such debased labour, as barbaric treatment reaches its pinnacle with technological rationalization and innovation.

This is not to say that social-historical change is unapparent or, when apparent, always negative. Analysis of the Industrial Revolution reveals the interrelation of benefits (technological innovations, immense wealth) and costs (awful working conditions, immense poverty). In the tradition of Anthony Giddens (1984), it will not be argued that such impacts can be reduced to simplistic zero-sum pathways of gain and loss. Rather, the contention will be made that only through a multifarious perspective of historical narratives, one that resists posing simplistic, exponential, single-directional movement, can the globalized nature of work identity be understood.

Given how momentous labour has been to human history and sociality, it would be impossible to cover the entire topic in a book-length piece, let alone a single chapter. The rationale behind the specific theorists explicated below is based on the notion that a critical analysis of an issue is best accomplished through exploration of debates. Chronologically organized, the preliminary section provides an in-depth analysis, defence and critique of classical social theorists Émile Durkehim and Karl Marx, situating their contrasting views of modernized labour. Following this exposition, contemporary theorists of labour will be explicated, beginning with the cautionary tales of short-termism and uncertainty in Ulrich Beck, Richard Sennett and Bauman. A manifold section of critique will initiate with the tempering optimism of Giddensian-influenced theorists of reflexive work; yet the counterpoint of reflexivity will itself be critically evaluated using Arlie Hochschild's (2003/1983) powerful account of 'emotional labor'. Finally, two brief case studies will illuminate the darker side of labour identities, simultaneously reinforcing much of the previous theory, while further exploring the deficiencies of any approach that fails to consider the most debased of labourers.

Historical and intellectual development of labour identity

Classical social theory is in a precarious position; written between a century and a century and a half ago, it is argued that such analyses cannot help but be outdated. Truly, this is the case in some regards, as especially evident regarding women's work identities. Yet for all the social-historical change that has occurred since Durkheim's theories on division of labour and Marx's writing on alienating work, there are significant continuities. Additionally, the framing of contemporary issues surrounding labour is provided with an essential background by such previous thinkers.

Astute readers will note that Max Weber, author of *The Protestant Ethic and Spirit of Capitalism* (1905), has been omitted from this section. Truly Weber contributed a vital perspective to early theories of work identity, especially his thought on bureaucracy, rationality, and work ethic. These terms' prevalence in contemporary society is a testament to his insights. Yet as the purpose of this section is to illustrate the differing views on work as modernity took hold in factories under the first century of the Industrial Revolution, Marx was chosen as the more telling counterpoint to Durkheim.

Durkheim, labour's division and solidarity

Durkheim's contributions to the early sociological inquiry of labour are best situated within the backdrop of his life's mission: to affirm sociology, then a suspiciously novel discipline, as an appropriate (or perhaps, the only) method of solving the predicaments of a changing sociality. Like many of his contemporaries, he sought to address the, at times, uneasy progression from traditional to modern civilization. When he presented his dissertation in 1893, the later canonized *Division of Labour in Society*, it was by no means a foregone conclusion that sociology would survive the turbulent atmosphere of exclusionary academia. Yet Durkheim seemingly relished the challenge. Indeed, as Steven Lukes notes in *Emile Durkheim: his life and work*, the fierce defence of his first major work won sociology 'the right to be mentioned at the Sorbonne' (1973: 299). He would go on to refine his position for the prodigious quarter of a century that remained of his life, which was unfortunately cut short in part, some suppose, by the grief of the loss of his son in the Serbian campaign of the First World War. However, this chapter's focus will be on that seminal early work, elaborating specifically on the interaction between the then modern labour identity and social collectivity.

The transition of solidarity types

Essential to understanding *The Division of Labour in Society* is the distinction Durkheim made between mechanical and organic solidarity. Intriguingly, the former is associated with pre-modern societies, while the latter is attributed to a developing modernity (the idea of a not fully developed organic solidarity is an important caveat, and will soon be explicated). These classifications seem illogical at first glance: was not the Industrial Revolution the age of mechanics? Was not the nostalgia for a less-developed past often coupled with an 'organic' societal essence? Yet, in considering more deeply Durkheim's functionalist brand of sociology, complete with his ardent biological metaphors, the terminology is quite coherent.

Starting with the former, Durkheim intended mechanical solidarity as a reference to the lack of structural division, and hence a 'mechanical' simplicity that characterized an organism without a complex organization. Regarding work, this referred to the lack of differentiation among most labourers, as they spanned very few specializations (religion, war and agriculture being dominant), and hence a lesser level of interdependence was exhibited. Indeed, as he stated quite plainly without any of the wistfulness of those who lamented the trajectory of modernity:

> If we try to construct intellectually the ideal type of a society whose cohesion was exclusively the result of resemblances, we should have to conceive it as an absolutely homogeneous mass whose parts were not distinguished . . . they would have no arrangement; in short, it would be devoid of all definite form and all organization. It would be the veritable social protoplasm, the germ whence would arise all social types.
>
> *(1964/1933: 174)*

Restricted levels of individuation, bonded mostly through a strong religiously based collective consciousness and a repressive, universally held penal law, summed, for Durkheim, to a mechanical identity.

On the other hand, modern society was likened to an evolved biological cell with diverse division in function and high levels of organization and interdependence; hence, he attributed the notion of an 'organic' solidarity (Durkheim 1964/1933: 111–33). Mutual interdependence is essential, both for ribosomes, mitochondria and the nucleus, and likewise for the individual labourers in society. The chef can hardly be expected to conjure her magic without the farmers and butchers, let alone the maker of her pan, knife, stove and refrigerator. To some extent differing from Weber and Marx, one can see his perspective of organic solidarity as being quite positive: people are different in their abilities and interests, and ideally develop mutual respect through such co-beneficial arrangements. One can take pride in the utilization of their talents and abilities to contribute to the greater function of the grand social cell, society.

153

Not quite fully organic

However, what are vitally significant, and perhaps quell some of the critics that fail to make it to the third section of *The Division of Labour in Society*, 'Abnormal Forms', were the clauses Durkheim supposed that tempered his optimism. Key to these was the notion of anomie, and the incomplete transition within modern civilization to an organic solidarity.

Anomie, quite simplified, refers to an absence of norms; for Durkheim, this often had a wearisome effect on individuals, and troubling consequences for society. Mechanical solidarity was almost completely absent of anomic states, as evidenced by two universally held norms (which obviously differed in kind between clans and cultures): religious belief and penal punishment (Durkheim 1964/1933: 70–110). One might say there was little grey area in these primitive civilizations, as the laws and rules were quite simply constructed and nearly unanimously understood. Yet the absence of anomie is not always positive. Breaching norms had brutal consequences, as violence was essential to their upholding (Giddens 1972: 10).

A fairly apparent observation, but unfair critique of Durkheim, is that for all the supposed benefits of organic solidarity, anomic labour identities were rampant. More recently, the economic downturn, which gained traction on the amorally greedy and risky actions of extremely wealthy individuals, signified a social cell that is not quite in tune with the metaphorical biological ideal. Many workers lost significant portions of their hard-earned savings, while bonuses larger than a lifetime of the median salary continued to be paid out to the executives at fault. Yet crucially, Durkheim believed that organic solidarity was still in its infant stages, and that modern civilization still had progress to make, as 'at certain points in the organism certain social functions are not adjusted to each other' (Durkheim 1964/1933: 354).

Essential to his view of labour identity, and perhaps most insightful, was that mutual respect among workers of different kinds was encouraged under a division of labour, but additionally required strong moral norms and equal opportunity for the pursuit of one's talents and specific abilities. It was not enough to simply have differentiation, as Durkheim critiqued Hebert Spencer's position; division of labour must involve a fair diffusion of specialization, and in doing so, it moderated competition instead of fruitlessly attempting to suppress it (Durkheim 1964/1933: 354, 365). Across his corpus, there are not recommendations akin to Marx's abolition of private property, as Durkheim supposed that there was an intrinsic hierarchy among individuals. Yet he also believed that through the obliteration of anomie and increased organic solidarity, instead of material superiority determining ability, superior ability would determine material rewards. With the former in place, organic solidarity would never be fully realized.

Inequality could not (and should not) be eliminated, but rather would be rational; indeed, the cell only functions effectively in response to the diversity of tasks and stimuli it encounters because there is difference among the parts. However, that difference could not be fraudulently surmised, as such an arrangement would deteriorate any sense of solidarity. Durkheim would certainly be disappointed by the lack of advance towards clear moral imperatives among contemporary labourers, but the ill outcomes would not be wholly surprising.

Dividing labour and contentious identity formation

This is not to say that Durkheim's view on working identities avoids stinging critique. A 'spontaneous' division of labour in which 'intrinsic' abilities allowed individuals to pursue their 'natural' talents has much potential, optimistically; organic solidarity could certainly follow if all believed to be playing their working part in the grander structure of society, and that their counterparts were similarly involved in the social cell. Many take pride in their labours, and the resulting contributions to the progress of modern civilization. Yet Durkheim's prudent caution, noted earlier, that 'certain social functions are not adjusted to each other' is a significant predicament.

Perhaps the most problematic aspect of the thesis surrounds the crux of the work, namely the definition one attributes to 'spontaneity' in the division of labour. As Durkheim states, this element of the arrangement is essential; forced division of labour creates tension that unsettles organic solidarity and encourages anomic behaviour (1964/1933: 383–5). Even if granted the ideal set of individuals whose differences would harmoniously comprise the necessary labours for society's functioning, Durkheim's thesis is based on the (now) politically incorrect notion that some individuals are simply suited to lesser work. As he states, 'labour is divided spontaneously only if society is constituted in such a way that social inequalities exactly express natural inequalities' (cited in Giddens 1972: 12). Feminists have rightly lambasted this aspect of his theory, as one could easily deduce from his perspective that women were 'naturally' matched with domestic labour. Though such work involves a diversity of difficult tasks and requires a nurturing patience that should be coveted among human characteristics, the darker and deeply troubling implication of this statement is that women are therefore unsuitable for 'professional' endeavours. For a theorist that stressed the wrongful direction of cause and effect in social situations, it is either a glaring omission, or extremely wishful thinking, to suppose that our 'natural inequalities' are not, to a large extent, socially determined.

Marx, alienated labour and spirit life

Though Marx primarily addressed the issue of work through the demonizing lens of labour's alienating, estranging and deteriorating features, it is essential to regard his philosophical orientation as anything but anti-work. Indeed, these aforementioned virulent declarations may give, at initial glance, an impression that he despised the idea of labour, and considered work to be a nuisance at best, and a plague on humanity at worst. From this standpoint, it is tempting to conclude that Marx's views on work do not speak to identity to the extent of categorical division in Durkheim or Weber's take on work ethic and rationality, given his undeniably critical spirit. This position is incredulously misplaced, and misunderstands the fundamental position Marx attributed to labour in the composition of society.

Rather, his social theory makes a strong proclamation (at least in the earlier writings) concerning the inherently intertwined nature of one's labour and identity. The power that lies in work was, for Marx, its candid and usually cruel route of self-formation. Truly, his primary focus was on its ability to effect self-*deformation*, perhaps best exemplified in the work of his friend and contemporary Friedrich Engels in the influential *Condition of the Working Class in England in 1844* (1950/1887). One should not be surprised by their depressed impressions given the awful circumstances of nineteenth-century factory work. Yet, if labour is so significant as to enable horrible distortions of human life and activity, Marx's critique of capitalism also simultaneously affirmed labour's primary role in the making of one's identity. If work can separate 'species from man' (cited in Tucker 1978: 75), it necessarily is also involved, provided optimal circumstances, in the positioning of oneself in organic relation to their species being.

Without a proper background, the arguments surrounding 'species being' and 'inorganic nature' seem fanciful and lacking in objectivity. Even supporters of Marx, usually proponents of his later work *Capital* (1906/1867), dismiss the radical humanism of the famed *Economic and Philosophic Manuscripts of 1844* (Marx 1964/1844; for critique, see Althusser 1971). Yet for the purposes of a classical exploration into work identity, arguably no better engagement exists. As will be briefly explicated in the conclusion of this subsection, his view went beyond the

Durkheimian functionalism concerned with collectivity and sociality of categories of work; debatably, Marx provided a deeper analysis of the secular spirituality of labour in reaction to two of his primary influences, Georg Hegel and Ludwig Feuerbach. To fully understand and situate this philosophical position, it is necessary to first explore what Marx meant by estranged labour and alienation.

Estranged labour and the four aspects of alienation

David B. Riazanov, the director of the Marx–Engels Institute in the 1920s, is said to have remarked that Marx was translated twice: first from his difficult handwriting to legible German, and then from German into (in Riazanov's case) Russian. The implications surrounding the translation of Marx's famed section *Die entfremdete Arbeit* (here, 'Estranged Labour') are significant, as is the case with deciphering many philosophical works for an audience not versed in the native language of the text. Following Martin Milligan's (cited in Tucker 1978) interpretation, the recurrent term in Marx's work *Entfremdung* is translated as 'estrangement'. The creation of this sense of estrangement is referred to through the term *Entäusserung*, or alienation (though, as Tucker insightfully notes, a more literal translation would be objectification). The interaction of the process of alienation and its resulting estrangement from one's fruits of labour is key to an understanding of identity formation in Marx's thinking.

Alienation begins with the uniquely externalized nature of labour under capitalism. From the infamous proclamation, '[w]e proceed from an *actual* economic fact', Marx (ibid.: 71) makes the claim that an inverse relationship exists between the wealth produced by one's labour and the individual's personal financial situation. While this 'fact' is clearly an absurd generalization in contemporary society (though the final section of this chapter will support its continuing relevance concerning largely invisible labourers, as witnessed through brief case studies of immigrant meat workers in the USA and global sex workers), in the mid-nineteenth century, it was a remarkable observation. City life provided images of wealth never before observed by rural migrants, but the harsh reality was that their share would not increase, obfuscated and pilfered through structural objectification of their labour power.

Indeed, while Marx at times nostalgically portrayed a romanticized version of pre-modern labour, it was certainly the case that a tradesperson even in feudal times was more directly linked to the products of their labour than the factory worker of early capitalism. He did not deceive himself into thinking a labourer had more wealth in centuries past, or had life any easier; but Marx's Unthinkable, as Charles Lemert (2007) has termed it, was that modernity should have provided a better life. As Marx (cited in Tucker 1978: 71) succinctly stated, contradictorily, '[w]ith the increasing value of the world of things proceeds in direct proportion the devaluation of the world of men'. Noteworthy from this analysis was the congealing, as Marx had it, of labour in a product, one that was foreign to the interests of its producer. Of course, work often results in external products; this was not novel. Yet Marx argued, beyond this given, that the process of alienating objectification constructed a newly felt estrangement, one in which the labourer was physically and mentally separated from his toils: 'the more values he creates, the more valueless . . . the better formed his product, the more deformed becomes the worker . . . the more ingenious labour becomes, the duller becomes the worker' (ibid.: 73). The labourer, in effect, was reduced in factory work to an exploited commodity making machine, producing products for 'an alien world antagonistically opposed to him' (ibid.: 74).

This estrangement through one's labour product was only one of four dimensions of alienation proposed by Marx; the others follow a similar logic. Workers were also estranged from themselves. In devoting physical and mental energy to the creation of the alien product described above, the process itself contorted the life of the labourer, wherein one 'no longer feels himself to be freely active in any but his animal functions – eating, drinking, procreating . . . in his human functions he no longer feels himself to be anything but an animal' (ibid.: 74). Once again, some may challenge such a statement in contemporary society, but the less fortunate labourers among us are undoubtedly far more constricted; those confined to sweatshops have been noted to be denied even the most basic 'animal' functions. Indeed, as stated at the outset of this chapter, work identities are not definable in singularities, or even dualities. A continuum is the only possible framework to make sense of the modern phenomenology of labour. But even within democratic nations with labour laws, as Barbara Ehrenreich's (2001) brief colleagues at Wal-Mart could attest to, there is the sting of Marx's proclamation: our activity turned against us, our self-estrangement.

Most abstract and theoretical was the third level of estrangement, namely the separation from one's species being. By species being, Marx meant, quite simplified, what makes us human. Instantly a paradox seemingly arises: how is it that one could be other than what one is? Many consider freedom to be paramount to the human experience; the language surrounding prison 'taking away inmates' freedom' is a testament to this. Marx believed alienating labour to be near to imprisonment, in that it did not serve beyond a 'means of satisfying a need – the need to maintain the physical existence' (cited in Tucker 1978: 75–6). Answering only to this need was part of the third process of alienation. The fourth and final stage of estrangement is simply a cumulative deduction; after alienation from one's product, oneself, and one's species being, it is not a large leap to suppose that workers are estranged from each other. Yet it is perhaps the deeper philosophical point on estranged species being that is most pertinent to modern discussions of labour.

Species being and work identity

Evaluated through a contemporary lens, Marx's writings on estrangement and alienation are argued to be cursory generalizations. Movements of workers are seemingly more connected to their labour than ever before, as a significant and growing group have attained the status as 'new independent workers', as Daniel Pink (2001) contends in *Free Agent Nation*. Forcefully, Pink and those of a similar standpoint challenge the relevance of bourgeois versus proletariat, factory owners versus workers, property owners versus the property-less in an age of blurred categories of employment and class. What these analysts fail to register are the massive groups of workers who embody anything but independence, as outlined in the case studies of the third section of this chapter. Yet beyond these ideal alienated types (ideal in the Weberian sense; they are very sad cases), the lasting resonance for society at large, even those most affluent among us, is the loss of 'live-activity', as estranged labour is capable of tearing from us our 'species life, [our] real species objectivity' (Marx, cited in Tucker 1978: 76), a claim which necessitates further explication.

'The animal is immediately identical with its life-activity. It does not distinguish itself from it. It is *its life-activity*' (ibid.: 76). What distinguished humans and animals, for Marx, was that our life-activity is conscious, and this fundamental difference is what makes us species beings. Our freedom derives from producing beyond immediate needs. As he brilliantly deduced, '[o]r it is only because he is a species being that he is a Conscious Being, i.e. that his own life is an object for him' (ibid.: 76). Estranged labour, however, had the effect of reversing this connection between life and object, as commodities preceded workers' identities.

Herein the muddled connections of estrangement versus organic life-activity come to light, especially considering Marx's critique, influenced partly by Feuerbach, of Hegel's philosophical religiosity. Marx was building a secular notion of what it is to be human, and based it on the free fulfilment of one's intellectual and physical powers. Harnessed away from one's self, life's purpose was necessarily limited. As he lamented, 'estranged labour . . . transforms his advantage over animals into the disadvantage that his inorganic body, nature, is taken from him . . . in degrading spontaneous activity, free activity, to a means, estranged labour makes man's species life a means to his physical existence' (ibid.: 77). Marx did not feel it necessary to utilize a framework of the dualistic religious soul to feel estranged. For all the proper critiques of Marx, including his neglect of the specifically feminine perspective, and the universalist nature of his claims, the inversion of life's relation to objects, and the resulting detriment to species life, is quite truly a widely held predicament to this day.

To finish on this note, however, would only do justice to half of Marx's conception of labour identity. The reversal just explicated does have severely menacing consequences, but there also is an inherent optimism to his critique. The inverse of this reversal clues into the importance he attributed to labour identity; species being, intimately linked with free, organic work, is a wonderfully unique possibility of humanness. Indeed, labour beyond coerced tasks is, for Marx, a fundamental aspect of humanity, intertwined with the 'laws of beauty' (ibid.: 76).

Contemporary labour identities

'The "jobs for life" has disappeared', commences Ulrich Beck's (2000: 2) influential book, *The Brave New World of Work*. Translated from German, it is quite possible that Beck did not mean jobs, but rather meant careers; for as Richard Sennett (1998: 9) notes in the preface of his work, *The Corrosion of Character*,

> The emphasis is on flexibility . . . this emphasis . . . is changing the very meaning of work, and so the words we use for it. 'Career,' for instance, in its English origins meant a road for carriages, and as eventually applied to [labour] meant a lifelong channel for one's economic pursuits . . . The word 'job' in English of the fourteenth century meant a lump or piece of something which could be carted around. Flexibility today brings back this arcane sense of the job, as people do lumps of [labour], pieces of work, over the course of a lifetime.

This passage has been reproduced at length for the simple reason that Sennett here acutely encapsulates the position of many social theorists concerning contemporary working identities. Beck and Sennett share two readily identifiable commonalities: each uses the word 'new' in the title of their works, and, additionally, the allusion to Aldous Huxley's *Brave New World* by Beck (or his English translator) and the diction of 'corrosion' throughout Sennett's writing clearly indicate, at the very least, an apprehensive position to labour in the late twentieth century. Though occasionally theory is unfortunately aloof, there is substantial objective evidence that grounds these claims: Sennett (1998: 22) cites Manpower Inc., a temporary job agency, as the largest employer in the United States; Beck (2000: 2) cites the decrease in German full-time job holders from nine in ten in the 1960s to only two-thirds in the 1990s. Along with Bauman (2004), the trio cover a diverse set of theoretical stances, but all three argue persuasively regarding the precarious situation of temporary work.

As will be explicated below, the terminology differs: appropriating their thematic arguments, Beck refers to risky work, Sennett to corrosive work and short-termism, and Bauman to liquid work and redundant labour. Their foci are significant, but so too are the works of feminist theorists of labour; later, Hochschild's pioneering concept of 'emotional labor' (2003/1983) will also be engaged. What might be said of this section is that just as Durkheim and Marx were both intrigued and afraid of the shift from labour identities in traditional civilizations to those in modern societies, so too are many theorists today concerned and frequently ominous (thereby less Durkheimian) in their assessments of contemporary work and predictions for the trajectory into the future. New paradigms necessitate novel philosophies and critiques, yet classical theory continues to be significant.

But as was stated at the outset of this chapter, it would be quite mistaken to appropriate an essentialized view of labour in which a universal phenomenological work identity attempts to encapsulate all working individuals. The pernicious atmosphere portrayed by Beck, Sennett and Bauman will necessarily be counterpoised against and critiqued by those who relish the new world of work, as embodied by Pink in his 'manifesto', *Free Agent Nation* (2001), and parts of Anthony Elliott and John Urry's forthcoming *Mobile Lives* (2010). These thinkers will be situated within Anthony Giddens' notion of reflexivity (1984), illustrating that a deterministic approach to working identities removes, to an unreasonable extent, the agency of individuals in forming their future trajectories. To assist the comprehension of the diverse array of literature covered in the subsequent sections, the following broad categorical divisions will be made: concerns surrounding new work (Beck, Sennett and Bauman), a critique of the aforementioned concerns (Giddens, Pink, Elliott and Urry), followed by a special consideration of the authentic (especially feminine) self under new labour (Hochschild and Goffman).

Precarious labour

Beck, Sennett and Bauman have all made distinct contributions to the analysis of the new structure (or lack thereof) of work, yet for all their differences, much is similar as well. Each sees an era, typically referred to as Fordism, as having ended, replaced by a neoteric arrangement that bears little in resemblance to previous conceptions. Fordism takes as an archetypal example its namesake, Henry Ford and his motor company, in illuminating the practice of labour in the early twentieth century. Ford's workers were among the first to experience a production line, in which each individual was responsible for a single task as the product moved from its bare essentials to a finished, sellable commodity. However, more importantly, this standardized atmosphere extended well beyond the physical process of production: their lives too ran in a similar fashion. An individual would often perform the same task from entering the workforce as a young adult until retirement. Consistency was expected at the job, but was likewise provided for the labourer. It was a cyclical union between the labour process, the labourer's product and the labourer's identity – a steadiness that kept all boats from rocking too much. Sennett refers to an 'era of relative stability' (1998: 23). As Daniel Cohen notes, Ford claimed to double the wages of his workforce so that they would be able to afford to buy their wares, but this was a farce; rather, the point was 'to fix them to the chain' (cited in Bauman 2000: 58). All three theorists in this subsection convincingly demonstrate the demise of such a labour system, a contention with which even Pink would agree.

What they each contend in a different flavour of caution, a supposition decidedly opposed to Pink's perspective, is that the calming foreknowledge of what was to come for one's working lifetime has been replaced by a troubling and frequently incapacitating dread: the dread that accompanies not knowing when one will be in or out of the labour force. Even when working with the same employer, location and tasks can change instantaneously and drastically. The standardization of production has not changed; Eric Schlosser's *Fast Food Nation* (2002) and George Ritzer's McDonaldization theses (1993) explicate quite clearly that fast-food companies have taken Taylorization, or the scientific management of labour, to a consistency-driven extreme. Yet what has eroded is the need for multinational companies, as Ford tried, to still steady their workers. Stability is now one-sided. Sennett's quote at the outset of this section stressed flexibility as a key theme of labour today. For Bauman (2000: 2), it is fluidity, as his 'liquid' metaphor so elegantly encapsulates,

> these features of fluids . . . unlike solids, cannot easily hold their shape . . . While solids have clear spatial dimensions but neutralize the impact, and thus downgrade the significance of time (effectively resist its flow or render it irrelevant), fluids do not keep to any shape for long and are constantly ready (and prone) to change it; and so for them it is the flow of time that counts, more than the space they happen to occupy: that space, after all, they fill but 'for a moment' . . . these are the reasons to consider 'fluidity' or 'liquidity' as fitting metaphors when we wish to grasp the nature of the present, in many ways *novel*, phase in the history of modernity.

Many observers may consider these trends obvious. After all, the news is constantly filled with technology stories and CEO profiles that clearly illustrate themes of speed. Stringendo refers to a quickening of tempo, but literally means a tightening, and its aptness of metaphorical application in contemporary society is no secret.

Yet the particularly significant contribution of each theorist is to elaborate on the disconcerting effects of going from moderato/allegretto to presto. Beck speaks of the risk inherent to a 'second modernity', wherein 'securities, certainties and clearly defined boundaries of the first modernity' lose ground to 'insecurities, uncertainties and loss of boundaries in the second modernity' (2000: 70). Vitally, he explains, risk as a concept may vacillate between 'an activation principle that is the glory of human civilization', or on the other end of the spectrum 'a creeping or galloping threat to human civilization and civil spirit, a catastrophic possibility that progress will swing round into barbarism' (ibid.: 71). Which occurs cannot be known, and Beck has recommendations for avoiding the latter (which will addressed in the conclusion of the chapter), but the 'blurring or fuzziness which marks the picture of work' (ibid.: 70) does not exactly elicit substantiated optimism. Sennett, in several personal case studies, documents the difficulties encountered by workers trying to keep up with the times: one apt archetype is Rose, whose desire to be perceived as youthful (in order to compete in the labour market) led her to using 'soft contacts, which were horrible', and as he deftly notes, '[they] irritated her eyes; at the office she looked like a woman constantly on the verge of tears' (Sennett 1998: 92).

Perhaps the most insightful admonitory theorist of contemporary work identity is Bauman, whose acute eloquence has an unfortunate outcome in that some readers misconstrue his project. Indeed, even Sennett misreads the prescriptions of *Liquid Modernity*, claiming that it 'adds up to more freedom in modern society, a fluid freedom', and even going so far as to associate Bauman with the 'apostles of the new capitalism' (2006: 12–13). This is an erroneous statement and could not be further from his perspective. Rather, Bauman (2000: 150) writes of a 'docile population, unable and unwilling to put up an organized resistance to whatever decision the capital might yet take'. Our supposed freedom is increasingly tempered since even when we might try to make plans, 'our earnest efforts to "put things in order" often result in more chaos, formlessness and confusion . . . our labour to eliminate contingency and accident is little more than a game of chance' (ibid.: 136). As far as our identities fare in such a game, there is no sense of brightness in a 'resemblance to the famed cyber-mole who knew how to move around seeking an electrical socket to plug into in order to replenish the energy used up in moving around in search of an electrical socket to plug into in order to replenish the energy' (ibid.: 139), continuing until one cannot find the next socket in time, or decides (perhaps is forced) to end the search prematurely. Conceivably Bauman's vision is a kind of freedom, but one accompanied by a stinging paralysis of life *only* on the move, as he quotes Emerson, 'in skating over thin ice, our safety is in our speed' (ibid.: 209); this is not a desirable safety, nor is the 'freedom' under liquid modernity covetable either.

Another distinct contribution that Bauman makes to the discourse and semantics of contemporary labour identities is the transition from 'unemployed' to 'redundant'. The prefix 'un', as he suggests, implies an 'anomaly . . . a manifestly temporary and abnormal condition . . . patently transient and curable' (Bauman 2004: 10). Unemployment was a phase; the unemployed individual would necessarily seek to remedy the juncture by finding employment, just as the unhealthy take measures to lead themselves to recovery. Further, such a linguistic framework also indicated a society whose concern for labour was paramount to identity, a perspective illustrated above through Durkheim and Marx. But not so for redundancy, whose semantic implications are of 'permanence and hints at the ordinariness of the condition', and as Bauman deftly adds, '[i]t names a condition without offering a ready-to-use antonym' (ibid.: 11). Not only are those that are redundant dispensable and disposable (quite literally, as will be shockingly elaborated on in the final section), the most unfortunate part for such individuals is the feeling that '[t]he others do not need you; they can do as well, and better, without you' (ibid.: 12). Durkheim's organic solidarity and the elimination of anomie seems a distant goal.

Criticism of contemporary labour identities: reflexive labour

One could deceptively quote Marx as having written, 'Men make their own history', though clearly the philosophically poignant and precarious qualifier that directly followed, 'but they do not make it just as they please' (cited in Lemert 2004: 42), expressed the heart of his sentiment. The role of the social actor in the making of societies has since been fiercely debated in social theory. This is not to say that Marx was the first to struggle with issues of free will and determinism, or that social theory is the only discipline concerned with its implications: from the Ancient Greeks through to the Renaissance, and still today with the advents of quantum physics, a diverse set of thinkers, from philosophical and scientific backgrounds, have contributed to our acceptance or refusal of freely, self-directed action. Literary figures have also weighed in, as two-thirds of a century before Marx wrote *The Eighteenth Brumaire of Louis Bonaparte*, the Scottish poet Robert Burns (1785) memorably opined,

> *The best laid schemes of mice and men*
> *Go often askew,*
> *And leave us nothing but grief and pain,*
> *For promised joy!*

How often our plans go askew maps the spectrum of what is known commonly in sociology as the structure-agency debate. For those in the former category, at the extreme, social structures such as schools, government, law, religion and family determine our everyday actions and future trajectories. One such social theorist was Claude Lévi-Strauss, who wrote of life as a card game, the shuffling done before we are born, with our only choice involving how to play the predetermined cards in a given rule system (1966/1962: 95). This is reminiscent of Bauman's more sobering passages. Since very few sociologists are at the other extreme end of the spectrum (as social structures are integral to the discipline), one such polemical figure was the former British prime minister Margaret Thatcher, who declared that there was no such thing as society; rather, there were only individuals, whose independently performed actions constituted all of humankind. In presenting the views of Beck, Sennett and Bauman thus far, hardly any attention has been paid to less structural views of labour identity. The latter's encapsulation of the modern worker as a cyber-mole especially ran against the notion of a freely operating labourer.

Most stinging to deterministic perspectives are those theorists who have transcended the structure–agency dichotomy, of which Anthony Giddens's theories of reflexivity and structuration are paramount. In some ways, Durkheim's functionalism was an early attempt at such a feat. As was previously discussed, the contentious idea of 'spontaneous division of labour' implied certain levels of constriction via social structures. But the organic solidarity felt thereafter in the glow of each member spontaneously coming to contribute their functional role to the operation of a grander society would provide a healthy sense of individuality. Still, Durkheim's outlook tended to stress the difficulties of a self-aware agency within modern arrangements. Many divergent contentions surrounding the theory of manipulated individualism, wherein varied structures loom large over dopey individuals, were claimed by members of the Frankfurt School; one such dope was Marcuse's (1964) one-dimensional man, unable to see the contradictions in society well enough to critique it. Giddens challenged these notions of the ignorant, puppet-like actor. Unlike those explored above who see the individual as a paralyzed robotic 'agent' in the face of a second, late or liquid modernity, the theory of reflexivity defends a decidedly more aware actor, one who can potentially thrive on the monitoring, adjusting and changing of the self in relation to others and societal structures. By no means casting away structures as did Thatcher, Giddens rather stresses that 'actors not only monitor continuously the flow of their activities and expect others to do the same for their own; they also routinely monitor aspects, social and physical of the contexts in which they move' (1984: 5). Structures still matter, but their role in the formation of identity is as part of a cyclical directing of the self. In a critique of the famed neo-Marxist Louis Althusser's argument that individuals imbued with ideology are only provided identity via an interpellated 'hailing' by the state (the 'hey you, stop!' of a police officer is the example he gives), Giddens notes that such a perspective fails to incorporate 'a theory of action which recognizes human beings as knowledgeable agents, reflexively monitoring the flow of interactions with one another' (ibid.: 30).

While contained in the theory of reflexivity are some hurdles, including the inherent uncertainty of changing selves in need of consistent monitoring and modernized addictions (beyond traditional substance abuse), within the refashioning and acclimation to modernity are significant benefits. A topical example provided by Giddens is the initial pain framed around intimacy and relationships in 'disrepair', with divorce rates constituting half of all marriages in many nations. Bauman in *Liquid Love* (2003) laments such 'top-pocket' relationships, accessible and disposable, hence consumable and commodified. But it is essential to acknowledge that the "til death do us part' of marriage was as much a prison to some as paradise for others. Giddens's interviews in *The Transformation of Intimacy* (1992) explicated the not widely enough held suspicion that women often felt locked into relationships, trapped by traditional formations of marriage. With regard to work identities, so too were many of the more reliable labour situations: the deadening of skilled work and injunction of thoughtless, menial labour documented by Harry Braverman in *Labor and Monopoly Capital: the degradation of work in the twentieth century* (1974) could provide certainty for the worker's identity, but little else of benefit. What good is attempting to prevent the corrosion of character as caused by short-termism if it only solidifies an alienated, uninspired identity? Modernity requires that actors change over the courses of their lives as the social structures around change in tandem. Elliott aptly summarizes Giddens's view, '[t]he relationship between self, society and reflexivity is a dynamic one, involving the continual overturning of traditional ways of doing things' (2007: 48–9). The contemporary world is one in which reflexivity has only recently been fully realized, but already is quite essential to a more complete satisfaction with one's trajectory of identity. In embracing such an arrangement, there is a significant chance to be dynamically engaged with one's self in a positive manner.

Though Giddens's structuration theory is not concentrated on labour as much as the previous theorists, numerous other authors have made loosely Giddensian claims regarding contemporary labour. Daniel Pink, the populist author of the work *Free Agent Nation* (2001), wrote of the release from the shackles of lifetime obedience and devotion to a company unaware of individual workers' presence. At least some of today's ultra flexible individuals thrive in their open environment, more attentive to their desires and needs from working life, and the subsequent balance with private life. Anthony Elliott and John Urry's work *Mobile Lives* (2010) further documents the advent of such trends, presenting the stories of established, yet pressured professionals whose varied (geographically, mentally and emotionally) working lives would probably be described by Bauman as a paralyzing chaos; but Elliott and Urry, while acknowledging such risks (especially over the long term with regard to dwindling resources), also illuminate the potentialities of reflexively oriented lives.

Though the socioeconomic statuses of individuals in *Mobile Lives* are quite high even for industrialized nations, and Pink's free agents are only slightly lower by global percentile of earnings and wealth, reflexivity is not simply a bourgeois-only club. A widely blogged *New York Times Magazine* article by Sara Corbett (2008) entitled 'Can the cellphone help end global poverty?' defended the idea, through a profile of Nokia's 'human behavior researcher' and 'user anthropologist' Jan Chipchase, that the poorest workers in the world also benefit from reflexive awareness, utilizing a significant 'knowledge multiplier' (Elliott and Lemert 2006) of modernity, namely the mobile phone. From farmers in Nepal getting the best prices for their produce to a 'live-in housekeeper in China who was more or less an indentured servant until she got a cellphone so that new customers could call and book her services': these 'just-in-time' moments, or what Giddens might consider rapid cycles of reflexivity (evaluating a constantly changing situation and monitoring when best to make one's move), are arguably more beneficial than for Pink's or Elliott and Urry's individuals. As Corbett (2008) deftly notes, most Blackberries and iPhones are for convenience, rather than the life and death type of reflexivity employed by 'a mother in Uganda who needs to carry a child with malaria three hours to visit the nearest doctor but who would like to know first whether that doctor is even in town'. Beyond the passive, confused ignoramuses that are portrayed in the darker portions of Beck, Sennett and Bauman, Giddens's notion of reflexivity as applied to labour illustrates the need to see a grander spectrum of involvement with identity.

Emotional labour, hidden labour and the privilege of reflexivity

The term 'emotional labor' was introduced by Arlie Hochschild, popularized through her major work *The Managed Heart: commercialization of human feeling* (2003/1983), and though published before Giddens's *Constitution of Society*, it provides the grounds for a partial critique of reflexivity in the realm of work. Both Hochschild and Giddens emphasize the importance of Erving Goffman's seminal *The Presentation of the Self in Everyday Life* (1959). Goffman's influence for these divergent theorists is contained in his dramaturgical metaphor: even in some of the most banal face-to-face interactions between individuals, highly managed attempts at specifically desired self-portrayals occur, such that each person becomes like an actor. Of great importance for Goffman was the situational effect on acting; expanding on the dramaturgy, one's front stage is the self we desire (or need) others to see, as might occur at a job interview, a first date, or even a passport interview. As intriguing, however, is the backstage, where the actor decides that acting is simply not necessary or as vital as in front stage situations, as might occur in the privacy of one's home or vehicle. This is not to say that the backstage is unable to find its way into situations normally only considered to be front stage. The maintenance of front stage composure is by no means easily accomplished. The backstage therefore may also be thought of as a break; keeping the show on at all waking hours, with all our expected conscious and unconscious manipulations, contortions and adjustments, is physically and emotionally draining. Partly for this reason, Giddens stresses from Goffman's work the immense accomplishments of everyday life, often taken for granted, that are possible solely through such reflexive directing of interactions.

While Hochschild would certainly agree with Giddens on this point in Goffman, she posits an exception to reflexivity by bringing attention to those who do emotional labour, which 'requires one to induce or suppress feeling in order to sustain the outward countenance that produces the proper state of mind in others – in this case, the sense of being cared for in a convivial and safe place' (2003/1983: 7). At first glance, this sounds fairly analogous to Goffman's focus on bodily tact and Giddens's monitoring of the self. However, her distinguishing observation follows from the potentially forced nature of the actor, as one who is caught between inner feelings and outward projections. For all the controversy over the 'authentic' self within the dramaturgical perspective, at least there is a sense of self-directedness; yet many contemporary working identities, especially in the growing service sectors, are denied this tempered autonomy. What happens when our front-stage performance is directed by our employer? For instance, the focus of much of Hochschild's analysis surrounds flight attendants, whose ability to smile no matter what emotion a difficult passenger may make them feel is paramount to the job, as she summarizes, 'in the flight attendant's work, smiling is separated from its usual function, which is to express a personal feeling, and attached to another one – expressing a company feeling' (ibid.: 127). Indeed, this is by no means limited to one occupation: a manual for legal secretaries advised, '[y]ou are pleasant under strain . . . executives hire secretaries for pleasant dispositions . . . [as one executive commented]: 'I need a secretary who can stay cheerful even when I get grouchy, work piles up, and everything else goes wrong' (cited in Hochschild, 2003/1983: 148).

It may be tempting to write off Hochschild's thesis as insignificant to working identities, but there is a decidedly ominous trajectory to the commercialization of a false emotional labour self, especially for women. Much of emotional labour is done in the service economy, which Sennett and Jonathan Cobb point out in *The Hidden Injuries of Class* (1972) is perceived by the public as among the lowest categories of work in Western society. It is also done by a ratio of nearly five women for every two men (Hochschild 2003/1983: 171). Of course, emotional labour is not limited simply to females, as by Hochschild's estimation, one in six men are expected to do some degree of feeling management. Yet at a three to one ratio of women to men across all realms of emotional labour (ibid.: 11), and significantly worse forms of emotional contortion for the former (ibid.: 162–71), there is an undeniable patriarchal legacy. An interview (cited in Hochschild 2003/1983: 183) with a sex therapist who treated approximately fifty flight attendants for 'loss of sexual interest' and 'preorgasmic problems' is especially revealing:

> These women don't ever get the chance to decide who they are, and this shows up in their sexual life . . . they don't get the chance to explore the other sides of their character and to discover their own needs, sexual or otherwise. Some of them have been so fixed on pleasing others that while they don't dislike men, they don't actively like them either . . . They hold onto their orgasmic potential as one of the few parts of themselves that someone else doesn't possess.

To stress again, Hochschild is anything but a disbeliever in reflexivity, or its potential benefits in certain situations. The same could probably be said, to a lesser degree, for Beck, Sennett and Bauman. Yet as Hochschild encapsulates, contemporary work is infused with contradictions and impediments to reflexivity, such that our self-monitoring may even be a more painful option than complete disconnection and disassociation from one's labour, in which case Bauman's cyber-mole becomes a (slightly) less insidious metaphor.

Hidden labour: case studies

Reflexivity is a grand concept, to which a diversity of successful labour identity strategies and innumerable technological benefits are attributable (the history of the personal computer is a prime example of reflexive innovation); yet its contemporary arrangement is inextricably inter-twined with those for whom reflexivity is impossible. Many of the conveniences that allow for a fuller evaluation of our lives are produced via hidden labour. The following case studies of immigrant meat workers in the USA and global sex slaves will be quite brief: entire book-length works often fail to fully cover the enormity of information that slowly pilfers through censored mediums (for a solid introduction to slavery, see Kevin Bales (1999) *Disposable People*, for sex slaves in particular see Julia O'Connell Davidson (2005) *Children in the Global Sex Trade*, and for immigrant meat workers, see the movie *Food Inc.* (2008), chapter 8 of Schlosser's *Fast Food Nation* (2002) and Phillip Martin (2009) *Importing Poverty?*). The point of this section, therefore, is not to cover an immense amount of detailed material in less space than would be possible, but rather to critique perspectives of labour identity that solely consider privileged workers, additionally grounding the theory in tangible contemporary challenges. These hidden labourers show the importance of certain theorists explored thus far, especially surrounding Marx, mate-riality and exploitation, Bauman, short-termism and disposability, and an extreme version of Hochschild's emotional labour thesis. On a broader level, surreptitious forms of labour illumi-nate further themes of great importance for social theory: first, as already discussed, the breaking of positivist and essentialist perspectives of work identities, and additionally labour's relation to colonialism, cosmopolitanism and globalization. Though these individuals experience 'bare life' in Giorgio Agamben's (1998) sense (biologically alive, dead in almost every other respect), their labour identities are of vital importance for achieving a fuller picture of work.

Before embarking on this short but difficult section, a brief clarification of terminology regarding 'slaves' is required. Pink unashamedly abuses the term without any context, referring to exploited temporary workers as 'tempslaves' (2001: 214–19). Surely the exploitation of these relatively privileged (from a global perspective) individuals is a worthwhile site of critique, but their classification as slaves prevents a rigorous academic inquiry into forced labour. Slavery is, by Bales's definition, 'the total control of one person by another for the purpose of economic exploitation' (1999: 6). The meaning of 'total control' is not exact, but it often involves encoun-ters with foreign languages and laws, and frequently mired in intimidation, both physical and mental; it is not applicable to doing safe, but boring work for low, but liveable wages. For the purposes of this chapter, Bales's categorical separation will be used, and those that cheapen the identities of forced labourers like Pink should be considered irresponsibly misleading.

The story so far (as told through hidden labourers)

It was argued above that Marx's notions of alienation and estrangement were more relevant today than the inverse relationships he proposed between labourer and capital; this is certainly the case with the types of work performed by Giddens's reflexive agents and even Sennett's corroded professionals, but immigrant meat workers in the USA (among others) tread disturbingly close to Marx's ominous predictions. Surely, these latter individuals would feel alienated and estranged if they had any idea of another possibility. Yet what becomes most significant is the unthinkable contradiction between effort and remuneration, both purely monetary and surrounding identity. As Marx (cited in Tucker 1978: 73) stated over a century and a half ago,

> The laws of political economy express the estrangement of the worker in his object thus: the more the worker produces, the less he has to consume; the more value he creates, the more valueless, the more unworthy he becomes; the better formed his product, the more deformed becomes the worker . . . the more ingenious labour becomes, the duller becomes the worker.

While not true of Pink's free agents, these 'laws' describe exactly the aforementioned meat workers. Tyson Foods, the second largest food producer in the world, slaughters, processes and packages 2.2 billion chickens per year. Though acquitted in 2003 of knowingly hiring illegal immigrants, it is widely argued that not only do upper-level management know of such hiring, but in fact arrange directly for smugglers to deliver new 'employees' (Martin 2009: 94). By virtue of both advanced machinery and absurd Taylorization of the chicken 'assembly line', each individual is equivalent to hundreds of traditional butchers in terms of productivity. Schlosser (2002: 173) notes that each worker can make upwards of 2.5 million incisions per year, and yet, they are among the most debased of all. *Food Inc.* (2008) describes the precariousness of their status, intimidated into working one hundred hour weeks, sleeping in factories, rarely if ever being paid: 'the more value he creates, the more valueless, the more unworthy he becomes'. Also, Schlosser (2002: 169–92) focuses on the scandalous percentage of life-altering injuries, titling his chapter on meat workers 'The most dangerous job' (though official statistics would be even higher if illegal immigrants received 'official' medical attention): 'the better formed his product, the more deformed becomes the worker'. Clearly, Marx's proclamations cannot be claimed to be absent in contemporary society, and need only be adjusted to include the exploited female meat workers as well.

Shifting to more recent analyses of labour identity, despite the debate over the implications of contemporary trends in work, all would agree that labour has been affected by the increasing speed of modernity; once again, hidden labourers shed much light on these insights. Bales describes how slaves were once a significant investment, often costing multiple years' salary for slave owners in nineteenth-century America. Due to these high costs and the constraints of distance under old forms of transport, they were relatively sparse and spent a long period of time with the individual who purchased them (often through multiple generations). Today, a slave can be purchased for as low as $15 USD and distance does little to hinder the practice, resulting in 'short-term relationships' in which slaves are 'disposable' (Bales 1999: 14–15). It is often cheaper to let a slave die than treat them for medical ailments. In Thailand, Bales notes, '[g]irls are so cheap that there is little reason to take care of them over the long term' (1999: 59); a positive HIV test is a death sentence, usually by starvation (Thailand now has the highest rate of HIV infection in the world). Short-termism takes on a decidedly revolting direction within modern forms of slavery, as Bauman's warning of 'wasted lives' (2004) is tragically enacted. The contemporary analysis of working identities is embodied in the lives of the most depraved workers, albeit under a significantly more sinister trajectory.

Additionally, Hochschild's emotional labour reaches its utmost stage for sex slaves, forced to put on front-stage sexual performances for upwards of twenty clients per evening despite the physical and emotional scarring of a sexualized netherworld. If their front-stage act is not convincing, sex workers are beaten. Unlike the flight attendants of *The Managed Heart*, who held onto their orgasmic potential as a last vestige, there is no such opportunity for these hidden labourers.

Grand themes, future sites of analysis

The tendency to both universalize work identities and suppose positivist eventualities of progress have both been critiqued throughout this chapter; even the most maligned individuals provide substantial evidence against such approaches. It is tempting to see all sex workers as the most dominated and exploited of labourers. Yet this has been shown to be untrue through ethnographic work by multiple theorists. O'Connell Davidson stresses that prostitution 'does not refer to a uniform experience', as there is a 'continuum in terms of earnings, working conditions and the degree of control that individuals exercise . . . the experience of those at the top of the hierarchy is vastly different from, some would say incomparable to, that of individuals on the lowest rungs of the sex trade' (2005: 34). Indeed, prostitution (in a slight number of cases) is a freeing experience, given the accounts of homosexuals oppressed in their home countries, who describe their new-found sexual freedom as sex workers (ibid.: 50–1). Just as individuals differ in their phenomenological experience of professional work in the West, so too do the (mostly) marginalized labourers.

The erratic path of meat workers in the USA over the twentieth century illustrates the difficulty in speaking of stable trajectories of working identities. Though technocrats of a positivist persuasion frame modernity as a constant process towards a better world, it is decidedly untrue of those who carry out Schlosser's most dangerous job. While it is correct that the horrifying contemporary working conditions are not that different from those described a century ago by Upton Sinclair in *The Jungle* (1906), there was a period in the middle of the century in which meat work was among the most respected and safest of blue-collar jobs in America (*Food Inc.*, 2008). It has indeed been a roller coaster for the industry, but unfortunately the highs have been abolished, and not only for illegal immigrants: a recent study found that pig-brain mist, only possible due to the practice of using high-pressure compressed air in the processing of the animals, was being inhaled by workers, causing rare immune disorders (Keim 2009). It is clearly the case that work identities change over time, but to posit any sort of linear progression would ignore the multitude of decidedly less certain routes.

Finally, labour speaks to broader themes of globalization and cosmopolitanism, and perhaps no better exemplars exist than the case studies of this section. While Elliott and Urry's (2010) globetrotting professionals embody the more glamorous side of these issues, it is the teenage girls who travel across many nations against their will that represent the dark side of globalization; they are brief globetrotters before being imprisoned in a single room for the rest of their lives. The ills of globalization continue with the illegal immigrant meat workers who are 'fired at will' (Schlosser 2002: 176) after years of debilitating labour to provide a cheaper meal to the marketplace at one of the most American of institutions, fast food. There is mounting evidence that several of the largest food companies have unofficial deals with the Department of Homeland Security to give up a few of their illegal workers per day for deportation; this satisfies the government, while not affecting the production line too greatly (*Food Inc.*, 2008). Labour identities are increasingly affected and affecting processes of globalization and cosmopolitanism, but it is extremely important to remember legacies of colonialism to temper the optimism of the more romanticized global workers. As David Held (1999) astutely notes,

> the notion of globalization as the precursor to a single world society or community is deeply flawed . . . global interconnectedness is not experience by all peoples or communities

167

Daniel Mendelson

to the same extent or even in the same way . . . On the contrary, as both Bull and Buzan
have argued, growing interconnectedness may be both a source of intense conflict (rather
than cooperation) as well as a product of shared fears and deeply held animosities (Bull
1977; Buzan 1991).

Conclusion: the continued significance of labour identity?

The theorists explored thus far have been chosen among the multitude of thinkers on labour
identities in an effort to present the significant debates surrounding work. Marx's scathing
critique of the Industrial Revolution's estranged workers was counterpoised with Durkheim's
hopeful approval of modernizing divisions of labour; Beck, Sennett and Bauman's cautionary
gloominess of short-term work was tempered by the mostly auspicious thesis of reflexive labour
via Giddens, Pink, Elliott and Urry; reflexivity was then critically assessed concerning agency
under Hochschild's emotional labourers. Because the analysis focused on the more privileged
workers, brief case studies of the most deprived labourers were presented, reinforcing many
of the themes of the chapter, and simultaneously critiquing a perspective that fails to take into
account hidden labour.

   Yet for all the proclamations against universalizing statements of labour identities and valuing
of critical analysis through debate, one glaring omission remains: every theorist was seen to posit
work as vital to identity. The vast majority of thought on labour follows this supposition. Orwell,
in his early work *Down and Out in Paris and London* (1933), concludes with a passionate plea for
ridding the dehumanizing idleness of the tramp's life. In a related way, William Julius Wilson persuasively reinforces the importance of work to identity in *When Work Disappears* (1996). Brilliantly
combining theory and data, he illustrates that for those robbed of legitimate employment opportunities, there is a grave danger of feelings of inadequacy and helplessness, usually leading such
individuals to pursue illegal means of hoisting themselves to the level of the gainfully employed.

   However, provocative and convincing arguments have been made to the contrary; one of
the most notable was ironically Marx's son-in-law, Paul Lafargue (however, it should be noted
Marx notoriously claimed if Lafargue represented 'Marxism', he himself was not a 'Marxist'). In
his most well-known piece, *The Right to be Lazy and Other Studies*, Lafargue (1883) attempted to
dismantle the discourse that supposed labour as essential to one's life spirit, stating:

> And meanwhile the proletariat, the great class embracing all the producers of civilized
> nations, the class which in freeing itself will free humanity from servile toil and will make of
> the human animal a free being, – the proletariat, betraying its instincts, despising its historic
> mission, has let itself be perverted by the dogma of work. Rude and terrible has been its
> punishment. All its individual and social woes are born of its passion for work.

Though slightly cursory theoretically, Lafargue had cued into a key idea. Arguably, the work of
Beck and Gorz has refined this position. Both theorists, by different approaches, address what
they see as the inevitability of less available labour hours (Beck 2000; Gorz 1999). Both also
argue for the potentialities of such an arrangement, with Beck calling for increased engagement
in civil society and Gorz encouraging a more voluntary approach to accomplishing society's
tasks. Even Pink (2001: 183–95) can be credited for insights on this issue, as he argued that with
flexible labour comes more time for family, friends and one's own creative projects.

   Is the future of work then one where employment, as traditionally defined, will be insignificant? Unlike Beck, I hesitate positing a 'vision of the future' (2000: 121–79). As was already
elaborated at length, pathways of labour identities are precarious and eccentric. While trends point

towards such transformations, there are no analogous laws of work in a Newtonian tradition; labour takes on a decidedly more quantum framework, based on probabilities rather than certainties. Yet for those who desire guiding proclamations through the blizzard of identities and the constantly morphing world of labour, one assured fact is that impoverished individuals will continue to be forced into exploited work (to varying degrees) without extreme intervention. Until such hidden labourers are made visible, their conditions of 'bare life' exposed and battled with the utmost vigour, work will surely continue to be relevant for the most nefarious of reasons.

References

Agamben, G. (1998) *Homo Sacer: sovereign power and bare life*, trans. D. Heller-Roazen, Stanford University Press, Stanford.

Althusser, L. (1971) *Lenin and Philosophy, and Other Essays*, trans. B. Brewster, New Left Books, London.

Bales, K. (1999) *Disposable People: new slavery in the global economy*, University of California Press, Berkley.

Bauman, Z. (2000) *Liquid Modernity*, Polity Press, Cambridge.

Bauman, Z. (2004) *Wasted Lives: modernity and its outcasts*, 2nd edition, Polity Press, Cambridge.

Beck, U. (2000) *The Brave New World of Work*, trans. P. Camiller, Polity Press, Cambridge.

Braverman, H. (1974) *Labor and Monopoly Capital: the degradation of work in the twentieth century*, Monthly Review Press, New York.

Corbett, S. (2008) 'Can the cellphone end global poverty?', *New York Times Magazine* 13 April. Online: www.nytimes.com/(2008)/04/13/magazine/13anthropology-t.html (accessed 11 November 2009).

Durkheim, E. (1964/1933) *The Division of Labor in Society*, trans. G. Simpson, The Free Press, Glencoe.

Ehrenreich, B. (2001) *Nickel and Dimed: on (not) getting by in America*, Henry Holt, New York.

Elliott, A. (2007) *Concepts of the Self*, 2nd edition, Polity Press, Cambridge.

Elliott, A. and Lemert, C. (2006) *The New Individualism: the emotional costs of globalization*, Routledge, London.

Elliott, A. and Urry, J. (2010) *Mobile Lives*, Routledge, New York.

Food Inc. (2008) R. Kenner director.

Giddens, A. (ed.) (1972) *Emile Durkheim: selected writings*, Cambridge University Press, Cambridge.

Giddens, A. (1984) *The Constitution of Society: outline of the theory of structuration*, Polity Press, Cambridge.

Gorz, A. (1999) *Reclaiming Work: beyond the wage-based society*, trans. C. Turner, Polity Press, Cambridge.

Held, D. (1999) *Global Transformations: politics, economics and culture*, Stanford University Press, Stanford.

Hochschild, A. (2003/1983) *The Managed Heart: commercialization of human feeling*, 2nd edition, University of California Press, Berkley.

Keim, B. (2009) 'Pig brain mist disease mystery concludes', *Wired Magazine* , 24 February. Online: www.wired.com/wiredscience/(2009)/02/pigbrainmystery/(accessed 12 December 2009).

Lafargue, P. (2000/1883) *The Right to be Lazy and Other Studies*, Lafargue Internet Archive. Online: www.marxists.org/archive/lafargue/(1883)/lazy/(accessed 15 December 2009).

Lemert, C. (ed.) (2004) *Social Theory: the multicultural and classic readings*, 3rd edition, Westview Press, Boulder, CO.

Lemert, C. (2007) *Thinking the Unthinkable: the riddles of classical social theories*, Paradigm Publishers, Boulder, CO.

Lévi-Strauss, C. (1966/1962) *The Savage Mind*, Weidenfeld and Nicolson, London.

Lukes, S. (1985) *Emile Durkheim: his life and work, a historical and critical study*, Stanford University Press, Stanford.

Martin, P. (2009) *Importing Poverty? Immigration and the changing face of rural America*, Yale University Press, New Haven.

O'Connell Davidson, J. (2005) *Children in the Global Sex Trade*, Polity Press, Cambridge.

Pink, D. (2001) *Free Agent Nation: how America's new independent workers are transforming the way we live*, Warner Books, New York.

Schlosser, E. (2002) *Fast Food Nation: what the all-American meal is doing to the world*, Penguin Books, London.

Sennett, R. (1998) *The Corrosion of Character: the personal consequences of work in the new capitalism*, W.W. Norton & Company, New York.

Sennett, R. (2006) *The Culture of the New Capitalism*, Yale University Press, New Haven.

Tucker, R. (ed.) (1978) *Marx-Engels Reader*, Norton, New York.

Wilson, W. (1996) *When Work Disappears*, Alfred A. Knopf Inc., New York.

10

Identity, race and ethnicity

Anthony Moran

Introduction: historical and intellectual development of race, racism and ethnicity

Race and ethnicity have been at the centre of the major cleavages of the modern world, supporting, organising, explaining and frequently justifying the claims of identity (including national identity). Many argue that race is still central to identity and social organisation, even if its manoeuvrings are hidden or obfuscated in an era that has seen the concept of biological race intellectually challenged and overturned, and racism and discrimination discredited in favour of non-discrimination and human equality. While race has been dismantled as a scientific concept, authors frequently assert its continued importance in social life as a marker of identity. People experience their physical differences as significant, in terms of how they identify themselves, the groups to which they belong, and the experiences of privilege, dis-privilege and discrimination in any given 'racialised' society. Ethnicity is seen by some to be equally as, or even more important than, race in understanding the sources for group identity in the contemporary world. As biological racism has been discredited, ethnicity has also returned to prominence as a major justification for discrimination and exclusion (Fredrickson 2002: 144–5). An influential branch of recent theory sees 'dominant ethnicity' as more important and pervasive than race in the contemporary world, and especially important for understanding the nature of identity conflicts. From this perspective, 'white racism' or 'white supremacism' are seen as more historically and specifically related to certain periods and regions of the world than ethnicity (Kaufmann 2006).

Race and identity

Central to the politics of imperialism, used as a justification for slavery, racial classification of identity held sway for large parts of the nineteenth and twentieth centuries in the Western world and its colonies and possessions. Race as an explanation for human groupings (typically four or five racial types) consolidated in the eighteenth and nineteenth centuries, though notions of race existed long before then. The modern idea of race involves belief in the permanency of the relationships between biology, culture and type. In the nineteenth century, 'racial science' (for example, eugenics) brought a new form of legitimacy to the association between race, character, superiority and inferiority. Race was also an everyday understanding of the nature of the world and its peoples, their achievements and level of civilisation, of the unequal access of some races to the world's spoils, justifying the rule of some over others. Though race thinking became an important way of explaining the world in the nineteenth century, 'racism' as a term only really came into common usage as late as the 1930s, to describe the theories and practices of the Nazis in Germany (Fredrickson 2002: 5).

In the first phase of thinking about race, the scene was dominated by white European thinkers including Robert Knox (1791–1862), Arthur de Gobineau (1816–82), and Houston Stewart Chamberlain (1855–1927) and white Jamaican planter, historian and defender of the slave trade Edward Long (1734–1813) who argued that 'blacks' were a separate, inferior, bestial and servile species fit for slavery and domination by the white race (Jordan 1969: 491–4). In the main (with exceptions) these writers viewed the races as arranged in a hierarchy of superiority and inferiority, with the white race sitting at the top and the black races at the bottom. Swedish naturalist Carl Linnaeus (1707–78), for example, while he avoided a strict hierarchical arrangement, noted that while Europeans were 'acute', 'inventive' and 'governed by laws', blacks were 'crafty, indolent, negligent . . . Governed by caprice'. The father of physical anthropology, Johann Friedrich Blumenbach (1752–1840), who was the first writer to trace the origins of the white race to the Caucasus, while regarding race in terms of biological characteristics and not attaching moral or intellectual qualities to these differences, displayed his own ethnocentric bias when he described the ideal type of the 'Caucasian' as the most beautiful of the races and the original form from which the other races diverged or degenerated (Fredrickson 2002: 56–7). It is well known among historians of race thinking that such images of beauty were of major importance to the development of notions of superior and inferior races.

This phase of 'white supremacism' involved, as noted, whites writing and theorising about other 'races', but a major development occurred in the latter half of the nineteenth century as writers from the other side of the colour line began to produce their own thoughts on race, most importantly, arguing about the specific character and experience of the races deemed inferior by whites. In the US, black writers, leaders and activists such as former slave Frederick Douglass (1818–95), Booker T. Washington (1856–1915), W.E.B. Du Bois (1868–1963), Marcus Garvey (1887–1940), and pioneering black feminist Anna Julia Cooper (1858–1964) wrote against slavery and racism, and critiqued continued white discrimination in the post-slavery period. Some, such as Garvey, wanted to 'purify and standardize' the black race (Gilroy 2000: 231–4) and advocated black separatism and a return to an African homeland, while Du Bois and Washington, also pan-Africanists, sought forms of black accommodation and prosperity in America. At the same time, these writers articulated the uniqueness of black identities, including specific African American identities. They were precursors to later black men and women who made significant contributions to critiques of racism and discrimination, often in the process articulating the nature of black identities and experiences, and highlighting the white fantasies of blackness and race.

Before, during and after the Second World War, there were also important, detailed social scientific examinations of the relationships between racism, white race consciousness, caste, class and economic and social discrimination in the US. Pioneering works included John Dollard's *Caste and Class in a Southern Town* (1937), Gunnar Myrdal's hugely influential survey *An American Dilemma* (1944), and Oliver C. Cox's *Caste, Class and Race* (1948).

In the 1930s, social anthropologists such as Franz Boas seriously challenged the concept of biological race, arguing that social differences were the result of environment and culture. Biologist Julian Huxley and anthropologist Alfred Haddon, in their famous and influential 1935 book *We Europeans: A Survey of 'Racial' Problems,* challenged the use of the race concept, which they found hopelessly confused and scientifically wrong, and argued for its replacement by 'ethnic group', better suited to signalling the cultural and social explanation for group sentiment and differences (Fenton 2003: 54–7). Nazi atrocities before and during the Second World War, justified by a virulent racist ideology and racial laws and practices, including the extermination of Jews and others deemed unworthy of life and racially dangerous or inferior, led to the further discrediting of racial classification and scientific racism after the Nazi defeat. Race as a scientific category was largely dismantled in the second half of the twentieth century. Racial science, including eugenics, collapsed as a discipline.

Nevertheless, while racism officially collapsed, the effects of race and racism continue to be felt in many countries. The violent racist regime of Apartheid in South Africa, in fact, only consolidated after 1948, and survived until the collapse of the Soviet Union and the ending of the Cold War (Fredrickson 2002: 109–10). Despite the proven emptiness of the concept of biological race, racial conflict and racialised communities have not disappeared. At the level of popular understanding and everyday life, race remains meaningful and socially significant. In the US and in many European countries, white racist nationalism remains on slow burn, flaring up in acts of terrorism and violence. The 1990s saw a rejuvenation of white racist and/or neofascist politics and explosive acts of racist violence in several countries. This was especially notable in the former communist countries of Eastern Europe, and in the former Soviet Union, but was not exclusive to them. From the late 1990s far-right political parties, riding a wave of anti-immigration and anti-asylum seeker sentiment, had considerable electoral success in countries including Austria, Italy, the Netherlands, Denmark, Norway, Belgium and France. Britain saw a noticeable increase in reported acts of racial violence and abuse from the early 1990s.

The global division of the world and of its privileges, it is arguable, is still based on the cleavages of race, with people of 'colour' disproportionately relegated to the ranks of the dispossessed or, in Frantz Fanon's famous phrase, of the 'wretched of the earth'. While many countries officially moved away from explicit forms of racial discrimination, it is far from clear that racism has been defeated, or that race is no longer part of the common-sense repertoire of many of the world's people.

Ethnicity and identity

While race refers to physical differences and their consequences (i.e. for character, temperament, culture, intelligence, ability, etc.), ethnicity has been viewed as a more culturally based phenomenon. But the distinction between race and ethnicity has never been clear or absolute. Nevertheless, from the 1950s onward 'ethnic' and 'ethnicity' became increasingly popular terms in the social sciences used to define and characterise large groups previously designated by the term 'race' (Fenton 2003). In the US, 'race' and 'racial problems' continued to be the terms used to describe the African, Hispanic and Asian American experiences, while ethnicity was used to define and explain the communities and experiences of European immigrants. In many other countries 'ethnicity' is the term used to describe what is called 'race' elsewhere.

In his essay 'What is an ethnic group?' (in Guibernau and Rex 1997: 15–26), Max Weber famously defined 'ethnic groups' as:

> those human groups that entertain a subjective belief in their common descent because of similarities of physical type or of customs or both, or because of memories of colonization and migration; this belief must be important for the propagation of group formation; conversely, it does not matter whether or not an objective blood relationship exists.
>
> *(Guibernau and Rex 1997: 18–19)*

In understanding group life, Weber placed the phenomenon of *ethnie* alongside other important forces such as class, status and party. Each of these different categories could be a basis for group formation.

Fundamentally for Weber, common ethnicity relied upon subjective consciousness of differences as the basis of group formation and closure against others. Ethnicity was not based upon biological characteristics or actual blood relations, as race was believed to be at the time Weber was writing. Ethnic groups were formed through historical and social circumstances. The differences (i.e. in language, appearance, dress, mores, customs, beliefs and ways of life) that emerged from these circumstances gradually took on a life of their own and achieved a level of importance in the lives of ethnic group members, and for others who perceived them as different.

Politics was important for Weber in turning the perception of those so-called 'ethnic differences' into a self-conscious group thinking of itself as ethnic. Members had to be politically organised and mobilised around their ethnic identity for it to be designated an ethnic group. Once ethnic groups had been constituted in this way, even if the political organisation faded away, or was crushed by some other power, the sense of ethnic belonging tended to live on as powerful memories and desires. Ethnic groups were historical, and developed a historical consciousness of a common past, an attachment to a particular territory, and certain traditions or a way of life. Through the use of symbols and myths, ethnic groups came to think of themselves as related by blood, as if they were small kinship groups where intermarriage related every person to every other person in the group. This belief in 'blood' relationship was simply a belief and not physically true, as all large groups involved physical mixing beyond kin relations. But it was nevertheless a powerfully held belief.

This Weberian concept of ethnicity has been adopted by more recent writers, such as Anthony D. Smith, who has written extensively on ethnicity and nationalism, and who defined ethnic communities as 'named human populations with shared ancestry myths, histories and cultures, having an association with a specific territory and a sense of solidarity' (Smith 1986: 243). Guibernau and Rex (1997: 8) point to the dual nature of ethnicity. On the one hand, there are the internally held meanings of ethnicity for its members: what the ethnic community means to its members and how they describe and understand the character of their own community, usually in the context of a larger society and in relation to other ethnic communities. On the other hand, there is the external meaning of ethnicity: the conception of its characteristics, and arguments and views about who belongs to a particular ethnicity, as applied to an ethnic group by others, especially by the state or a dominant society. Importantly, they argue, an ethnic community can incorporate into its own self-understandings as a culture and community, some of those meanings imposed from the outside.

The concern with ethnic groups and ethnic conflict became more important for scholars after the Second World War when it became apparent that earlier assumptions of modernisation theory – that modernity involved the dismantling of ethnic communities and traditions and the production of a more homogenous, individualist and rationalistic culture – broke down in the face of reality. Most people did not simply give up their sense of ethnic identity and belonging when they migrated to new societies, or even when they stayed put as their own societies were transformed by industrialisation, urbanisation and mass education. Even where they relinquished traditions and languages, people maintained a sense of identification with an ethnic group, a phenomenon Gans (1979) termed 'symbolic ethnicity'. Fredrik Barth (1969) had also redirected attention away from the cultural contents of ethnic groups and towards a consideration of the centrality of boundary maintenance and identification with 'in-groups' and controlled relationship with 'out-groups'. Ethnic groups might be in many respects culturally similar to other ethnic groups, but distinguish themselves by selectively emphasising and highlighting small cultural features as 'symbols and emblems of difference' (Barth 1969: 14). Ethnicity, then, is centrally organised by relationships between groups and the processes of differentiation that arise through these relationships. Ethnicity also became an important term for social scientists in the 1960s in the context of decolonisation and national liberation, used to explain the more positive senses of cultural attachment (Guibernau and Rex 1997: 1).

Major claims and developments of the field, and key contributions

Race

W.E.B. Du Bois was a towering intellectual figure from the late nineteenth century through to the time of his death in the mid-twentieth century. He made a major contribution to our understanding of the relationship between race and identity, and the course of his long career is suggestive of the ways in which race thinking changed across time. Du Bois wrote in the late nineteenth century under the assumption that there were different races, with a sort of resignation that some racial antagonism was inevitable, and set about finding ways for the 'black race' to find its true spiritual centre and reach its true possibility of 'racial' achievement. 'We believe', he wrote in his 1897 essay 'The conservation of races', 'that the Negro people, as a race, have a contribution to make to civilisation and humanity, which no other race can make' (Du Bois 1986: 825). For this reason, he did not see the solution to the Negroes' problems in America as dissolution and absorption into the white race, or that they should simply become Americans. Importantly, however, he did not arrange these 'races' into a hierarchy, and concluded that, as white and black Americans shared certain fundamental religious and legal ideals, as well as language and economic arrangements, there was no reason why they could not develop side by side in the one territory, even striving together for their independent racial excellence. His advocacy of university education, aimed at the spiritual and educational support of the elite 'Talented Tenth' of the African American population, pitted him against that other major African American intellectual and leader, Booker T. Washington, who advocated the alternative approach of establishing an African American foothold in the American economy through vocational training, moral self-improvement and accommodation with white America (Du Bois 1986: 842–61). Du Bois accepted the need for somewhat separate lines of development for the 'black' and 'white' races, and in his reflections on his own life he explained, with great poignancy, the reasons why he appeared diffident to whites and had never developed truly deep friendships with white Americans (ibid.: 1117–27). He was always acutely aware of the way in which the colour line marked all interactions between black and white in the US, and it was only in his travels in Europe that he perceived the possibility of more easeful relations between the races.

Later black writers and activists have also exhibited both inclusivist and exclusivist positions on race and identity. Malcolm X (1925–65) initially argued for the superiority of black racial identity, and advocated for the exclusivist black Nation of Islam and for separate group and institutional life for blacks. In the last phase of his life, as he travelled abroad to Cairo and Mecca where he confronted different cultural environments and people, including white Muslims, he began to move beyond race. He was still a black man, but he felt himself becoming de-racialised, no longer locked into the American prison of race that pitted superior against inferior, black against 'white devil'. Martiniquean psychiatrist, revolutionary and theorist of decolonisation Frantz Fanon (1925–61) first experienced the full brunt of racism when he moved from Martinique to France, but argued against exclusivist understandings of race and identity. He wrote of the need to move beyond 'Negritude' – a major movement of black identity at the time he was writing his masterful *Black Skin, White Masks* (1968) in the 1950s. In the 1980s, 'Black Atlantic' scholar Paul Gilroy wrote about and argued for forms of black identity and consciousness in the context of British politics, but has more recently called for a post-race understanding of 'planetary humanism' and questioned the continuing relevance of any monolithic notion of black identity (Gilroy 2000).

Du Bois's most famous contribution to the understanding of black identity came with his notion of 'double consciousness'. In *The Souls of Black Folk* he outlined the peculiar fate of African Americans who felt the contradictory pull of their Americanness and their blackness (or Africanness), evident in the much-quoted passage:

> After the Egyptian and Indian, the Greek and the Roman, the Teuton and Mongolian, the Negro is a sort of seventh son, born with a veil, and gifted with second-sight in this American world, – a world which yields him no true self-consciousness, but only lets him see himself through the revelation of the other world. It is a peculiar sensation, this double-consciousness, this sense of always looking at one's self through the eyes of others, of measuring one's soul by the tape of a world that looks on in amused contempt and pity. One ever feels his two-ness, – an American, a Negro; two souls, two thoughts, two unreconciled strivings; two warring ideals in one dark body, whose dogged strength alone keeps it from being torn asunder.
>
> *(Du Bois 1986: 364–5)*

Double-consciousness also meant that black Americans were gifted with particular insights into race relations, and also into the hidden aspects of white consciousness, including the 'public and psychological wage' of whiteness explored by Du Bois in *Black Reconstruction* (especially for poor white labourers), and in essays such as 'The souls of white folk'.

A second major figure in the understanding of racial identities was the aforementioned Frantz Fanon. In his seminal work *Black Skin, White Masks* (1968), Fanon made a significant contribution to our understanding of the injuries of race with his deft blend of phenomenology, psychoanalysis, culture and history. Locked into a vicious racist social and economic system, he argued, white and black misrecognised each other, assigning potencies drawn from images in the long history of thought about colour and race: 'the real Other for the white man is and will continue to be the Black man. And conversely' (1968: 161, footnote). For each the other became a strange and hallucinatory object that was at once desired, hated and feared. Notably, the white person saw the Black other in biological terms, at the level of repressed, wild sexuality, which he or she secretly desired – themes later explored extensively by the psychoanalyst Joel Kovel in his classic text *White Racism: A Psychohistory* (1970). But Fanon's most original contribution was to the understanding of the trials of black identity within imperialist racist social systems, including the way in which 'whiteness' also became the ideal for black people, an ideal impossible to achieve because of their blackness. This was the ultimate degradation, the way in which black people, torn from their own cultures and social systems by imperialism and colonisation, came to view themselves through white eyes, and through the social imaginary of the white world. Fanon gave this a deeply personal inflection, vividly explaining his own immersion in white ideologies of blackness. In his chapter 'The fact of blackness' he depicts how his own self-perception, including his bodily perception, under the all pervasive eyes of white people, came to be dominated by white perceptions of the black man, how his own bodily self-image underwent a seismic shift as he moved from the colonies to the white world of France where he felt the full brunt of white scrutiny. He knew what they were thinking and was swept up in their view of his body's negativity:

> I move slowly in the world, accustomed now to seek no longer for upheaval. I progress by crawling. And already I am being dissected under white eyes, the only real eyes. I am *fixed*. Having adjusted their microtomes, they objectively cut away slices of my reality. I am laid bare. I feel, I see in the white faces that it is not a new man who has come in, but a new kind of man, a new genus. Why, it's a Negro.
>
> *(Fanon 1968: 116)*

Caught within the white racist ideological fabric, while a powerful sense of alienation and dehumanisation was felt, resistance was blunted by the existence of a vacuum into which to plunge should one forsake the white world. For, through colonisation, the past to which one might have had recourse had been destroyed forever: 'However painful it may be for me to accept this conclusion, I am obliged to state it: For the Blackman there is only one destiny. And it is white' (ibid.: 12). Nevertheless, in later work, including *The Wretched of the Earth* (1967), Fanon was to articulate a form of national cultural resistance that did involve a recapturing, reinvention or reassertion of older cultural elements as colonised people sought to free themselves of the colonial yoke.

The work of writers in the UK grouped around Stuart Hall and the Contemporary Centre for Cultural Studies in Birmingham (CCCS) was influential in the 1970s and 1980s in revisiting issues of race from an innovative Marxist and cultural studies perspective. One of Hall's chief insights was to see that 'race' was the 'modality' in which class was lived and experienced in modern, capitalist societies, including contemporary Britain, a point he had made in the collaborative work *Policing the Crisis* (1978). Hall and other CCCS writers argued their way beyond the Marxist economic reductionism that reduced 'race' to issues of 'class', and instead gave full weight to the importance of race as an ideological and cultural phenomenon that was relatively autonomous from the capitalist economic base, but which was also always interrelated with class. This position was explored at great length in *Policing the Crisis* and in the CCCS book *The Empire Strikes Back* (1982). In later work, influenced by arguments about the 'decentering of identity' within psychoanalytic, post-structuralist and postmodern thought, and also by the transformations of the world brought about by the fluidity and movement of intensifying globalisation, and the cultural hybridity it stimulated, Hall (1992) also suggested the break-down of relatively fixed racial identities (or any categorical identities for that matter), emphasising the play of difference in identity – never fixed, always in formation, oriented by historical and contemporary experiences. He questioned the negative aspects of and silencing (of other, including Asian, histories, gender oppression etc.) involved in the construction of a collective, all-encompassing black identity in the political struggles of the 1970s, and suggested that this was no longer tenable as a stance, as it involved its own oppressions. Young third-generation Caribbean blacks in Britain wanted to recognise the differences concealed by a monolithic black identity, and to hold together British, black and Caribbean identities, without necessarily privileging or denying the relevance of any of them (Hall 1991).

Since the 1980s, there have been three major developments in thinking around race. The first is the idea of the 'new racism'; the second concerns the elaboration of black feminist arguments about racism and racial identities; and the third is the introduction to the scene of 'whiteness studies'.

First, since the early 1980s, sociologists of racism have made a distinction between an older biological and a newer differentialist or cultural racism (Barker 1981; Taguieff 1993–4). Barker (1981) used the term 'new racism' to explain the new forms of racism that, responding to the success of anti-racism struggles and the intellectual undermining of the concept of biological race, asserted that different cultures were incommensurable and that, therefore, some cultures could not assimilate into, for example, British culture. This, he argued, was a form of cultural racism. He saw the phenomenon as especially relevant to the right wing of the British Conservative party which articulated grievances against the large Afro-Caribbean and Indian subcontinent immigrant communities in Britain, whose presences were seen to threaten the British national way of life. This form of racism was especially concerned with issues of national identity, conceived as strong cultural affiliation. Barker argued that the new racism was distinguished from the old racism in that it did not need to adopt notions of racial inferiority and superiority, it did not need negative stereotyping of groups, and it did not need to blame the country's economic and social problems on ethnic minorities. However, the new racism was concerned with the impact of rising cultural diversity within Britain, largely brought about by post-Second World War immigration from the Caribbean and Indian subcontinent, seen to threaten Britain's capacity to preserve itself as a distinct nation with a bounded cultural identity. The new racism tended to essentialise cultural differences, so that cultures became reified rather than historical, changing phenomena.

Against later critics who argued that 'new racism' was a misnomer, Tariq Modood has made a strong case for 'cultural racism' as a new and important form of racism in modern Britain. Its meaning, he argues, is only obscured by writers or anti-racist activists who see it only as a cover for biological assumptions about culture and society. The new 'cultural racism' builds onto the antipathy, exclusivity and unequal treatment of people involved in biological racism a 'further discourse which evokes cultural differences from an alleged British or "civilised" norm to vilify, marginalise or demand cultural assimilation from groups who also suffer from biological racism' (Modood 1997: 155). While post-war British racism is simultaneously built on biological and cultural ideas, it is the latter which in fact predominate, with the former acting as a superficial marker which allows the more important and influential ideas about cultural clash to be set in motion. Anti-racists are wrong to underestimate this transformation, since they 'misread' the concerns of the 'New Right's "new racism"' of Enoch Powell and the *Salisbury Review*' as biological concerns without giving full allowance to more salient arguments about cultural distinctiveness and the inability of some cultures to assimilate into British culture (ibid.: 169). One must, as Modood correctly asserts, take seriously the beliefs that animate 'cultural racism'. Included within this category would be much of the phenomena referred to as 'Islamophobia'.

Taguieff, who coined the term 'differentialism' when explaining the rise of 'new racism' in France, saw the French new right's 'praise of difference' as its most effective ideological ploy, largely replacing the former reliance upon 'inegalitarian racism'. He argued that through it the new right had outflanked left criticism by seemingly taking up one of its most cherished ideals from the 1980s. This new differentialist racism was *heterophile* rather than *heterophobic*, emphasising the distance between cultural communities, even their incommensurability. This new racism was *mixophobic*, 'haunted by the threat of the destruction of identities through inter-breeding – physical and cultural cross-breeding' (Taguieff 1993–4: 101 for quote).

The second major development has been the emergence of non-white feminism, including more generally the confrontation of non-Western women with what was seen to be a white dominated, middle-class feminist movement that did not represent the experiences and striving of women of colour, and the emergence of black feminist thought in the US, centred upon figures including Toni Morrison, bell hooks and Patricia Hill Collins. This has involved the elaboration of a strong identity-politics around the specific racial experiences of black women that has meant that in certain situations the black experience and identity take precedence over the gender experiences that second-wave feminism had characterised as universal.

Patricia Hill Collins (1990) argues for a black feminism that is Afrocentric, and for claims to truth that are contingent, but based in particularistic experiences of black women. The argument is that only through the development of such a discourse and practice can the stand-point of black African American women be heard and validated, against the white male validation procedures that oppress black women and silence them. White, patriarchal, male Eurocentric cultures dominate academic debates and, like broader white-dominated society, have embedded within them taken-for-granted negative stereotypes of black American women. Black women's culture, and black culture more generally, carries traces of African culture: particular forms of family, particular values, particular ways of thinking and acting, and particular conceptions of religion and religious practices. Black Americans, she argues, have a distinctive way of using concrete experiences, including everyday experiences, as criteria of meaning and for establishing truth (Collins 1990: ch. 10).

Bell hooks has written of the continuing 'terrorism' inflicted by white supremacism: 'All black people in the United States, irrespective of their class status or politics, live with the possibility that they will be terrorized by whiteness' (hooks 1992: 175). She has also been a strong critic of white women and white feminists, highlighting that, historically and contemporaneously, white women have also oppressed black women, as employers (in homes and elsewhere), as co-workers, as fellow feminists and in everyday life (hooks 1981: ch. 4).

Because of the way they highlight racial differences and articulate the specificity of black identities that are often antagonistic to white society and culture, these writers have been troubling for white males and females, including liberal whites who strive to see the different peoples of the world as simply humans who should be treated as the same. They challenge the assumption that we live in a post-race world. But they have also been troubling to black people, especially males, for the ways in which they highlight not only white, but also black male misogyny. They have often occupied difficult political positions as they are faced with and challenged by other blacks for revealing unpleasant facts of contemporary black communal life, in particular black on black male oppression of women, including physical and sexual violence.

Third, from the late 1980s a new phase of race studies emerged around the concept of 'whiteness'. Characterised as 'whiteness studies' or 'critical whiteness studies' and building on the insights of black writers such as Du Bois and James Baldwin, this area sought to examine and reveal the previously hidden operation of whiteness as a 'social construction' organising the perception of other races and the operations of racism or racialisation. This was a turning of the spotlight away from the 'races' thought of as others, to the 'race' doing most of the 'othering'. Pioneering works in this field were by American historians and sociologists such as bell hooks, David Roedeger, Ruth Frankenberg, Michael Omi, Howard Winant and Theodore Allen, and also the novelist Toni Morrison who, in *Playing in the Dark*, asserted that 'until very recently, and regardless of the race of the author, the readers of virtually all American fiction have been positioned as white' (Morrison 1992: xii). The achievement of this essay was to read closely the play of images of blackness, and of black people, operating in fictional texts, as revealing of the work of whiteness. Morrison asked the crucial question of the role that this 'whiteness' played, not only in literature, 'but in the construction of what is loosely described as "American"' (ibid.: 9). This Morrison characterised as a turning of the critical gaze away from the 'racial object to the racial subject; from the described and imagined to the describers and imaginers; from the serving to the served' (ibid.: 90).

Whiteness studies as an emergent field has attempted to articulate what it means to occupy the position of whiteness. One of the central claims is that whiteness operated as a hidden universalist position from which other races were scanned and characterised, while the contours of whiteness were kept from view, almost as if there was no such thing. Societies dominated by whiteness were institutionally organised around white understandings, norms and practices. Whiteness studies aims to reveal the specifically 'white' nature of these understandings, norms and practices that parade as universal and unexamined, and the hidden privileges that this societal structure affords whites. As Ashley Doane points out, because whites are a majority, hegemonic racial group in countries such as the US, they often experience their privileges not as privileges at all, feel that they are simply part of the norm, and do not experience themselves as race subjects: 'Given that what passes as the normative center is often unnoticed or taken for granted, whites often feel a sense of culturelessness and racelessness' (Doane 2003: 7). The relativising of the white position is seen as one of the major purposes of this whole approach. It is also seen as a movement revealing and challenging the working of white hegemony.

Whiteness studies has a historical focus, but is also focused on the post–Civil Rights era (in the US) and on the supposedly post-racial world, seeking to show that race still operates as a pervasive organiser of privilege in societies. It questions the extent of the shift in racial consciousness understood to have come about through the political achievements of anti-racist struggles to remove the vestiges of institutional racism and discrimination in many Western societies since the 1960s. In fact, it is the politics of this era that leads many whites to now see race as a nonissue, and to imagine that they now live in colour-blind societies. Colour-blind ideology itself acts to maintain and reproduce white racial privilege because it continues to hide the extent of racist discrimination. It shapes policies that appear race-neutral (in areas such as housing, employment and social welfare policy, etc.) but which in reality operate as forms of ongoing discrimination, because they do not recognise the impacts of institutional racism. It also results in a situation where it is seen by many whites as illegitimate to raise the issue of 'race' in discussions about culture, economy and society – as if to do so was in itself racist (Doane 2003).

Ethnicity

As noted earlier, social scientists came to argue in the 1950s and 1960s that 'ethnicity' had to be taken seriously as a major form of group identity in the modern world. One response to the continuing ethnic reality was to account for it by asserting that ethnicity was *primordial*: that it is so deeply rooted in individuals and cultures that it was almost like a biological essence. Ethnic roots extended back through time immemorial, and formed a kind of *mythos* involving memory and legend that stood at the heart of any large, unified group. Some theorists of nationalism, most notably Anthony D. Smith, argued that while nations were relatively modern, they relied for their coherence and the strength of attachment of their members on something much older, which he called the *ethnic core*, that stretched far back through history, tying identity to mythic places and sites.

Others responded by seeing the continuing assertion of ethnic identity and community as an example of *social closure*: an instrumental way for groups to commandeer resources. Here ethnic identity became a political resource, as argued most cogently by Nathan Glazer and Daniel Moynihan in the 'Introduction' to their edited book *Ethnicity: Theory and Experience* (1975). They noted that 'ethnicity' (as opposed to ethnic group) was a recent term, missing from standard dictionaries, for example, until the 1960s. They cited the first social science use of the term by the American sociologist David Riesman (author of *The Lonely Crowd*), in 1953. And they also argued that the use of this term – including their own – signalled that we were dealing with a relatively new phenomenon, a particular form of group expression tied to new social and political conditions: 'there has been a pronounced and sudden increase in tendencies by people in many countries and in many circumstances to insist on the significance of their group distinctiveness and identity and on new rights that derive from this group character' (Glazer and Moynihan 1975: 3), a claim supported by several authors (including Daniel Bell) in their book. Glazer and Moynihan argued that, despite earlier expectations, ethnicities were not necessarily

bound to disappear through processes of assimilation; instead, modern social forces and processes actually contributed to the ongoing reproduction of ethnic identities, as major sources
of identity for people, with strong forms of emotion and identification involved. In trying to
explain why this occurred, they provided two important answers: the first an instrumentalist
understanding of ethnicity as a resource in the context of the changing role and approach of
government, and the second seeing the assertion of ethnic identity as stimulated by inequality.

The first argument tied the prevalence of ethnicity to new government practices, in particular to the way in which governments, and especially the welfare state after the Second World
War, began to organise policies in ways that recognised ethnic identities; so, for example, in the
spirit of equality, demanding of various employers and institutions that they show statistics of
the ethnic background of members, to see whether there were entrenched imbalances between
ethnic groups. This meant that ethnicity became a focal point for thinking about government
resources, and an avenue through which people could engage with government in pursuit of
their ends. Governments, for example, would design their welfare policies in areas such as health
to make provision in some circumstances for professionals of a similar ethnic background to be
available to treat people of their ethnic background, and other forms of attention to ethnicity.

The second explanation was about inequality: that in any given society, mainstream cultural
norms had been set up in such a way that it benefited certain cultures and went against certain
other cultures; success in any given society depended upon access to and attainment of certain
norms, and not all ethnic groups had an equal standing in this respect. Movements of people
around the world through migration, mainly for economic reasons, exacerbated this situation by
throwing together people from vastly different cultural backgrounds into very unequal cultural
situations. This resulted in a battle over societal norms, often between ethnic groups operating
from different, historically shaped, social norms. People from a disadvantaged group have the
best chance of achieving their aims if they organise themselves as a group claiming general group
rights, rather than as separate individuals trying to achieve change; having an ethnic identity
becomes a 'highly effective way to either defend the advantage or to overcome the disadvantage' (Glazer and Moynihan 1975: 15).

Glazer and Moynihan conclude that forms of identification as diverse as religion, language
and national origin all have something in common that means that we could use the term 'ethnicity' to explain all of them: 'What they have in common is that they have all become effective
foci for group mobilisation for concrete political ends challenging the primacy for such mobilisation of *class* on the one hand and *nation* on the other' (ibid.: 18). Thus, despite the expectation
among sociologists that class would become the main basis for group formation in the modern
world, this had not happened. Nor had 'nation' simply subdued other group identities. While
class and nation were still clearly important in explaining modern societies, and in explaining the
mobilisation of group interests, we now had to add the dimension of ethnicity.

The late twentieth century, contrary to the predictions of many, produced an ethnic resurgence that has carried through into the twenty-first century. This had complex causes. In some
circumstances, the assertion of ethnic identity and claims has been a defensive gesture in relation
to the fragmentation, fracturing, disorientation and upheaval of globalisation. Ethnic mobilisation has emerged in response to geo-political shifts, such as the collapse of communism and the
reordering of states, nations and societies that this unleashed in the former Soviet Union and
Eastern Europe. It was evident during the terrible ethno-national wars in the former Yugoslavia
in the 1990s, and also in the ethnic, tribal and religious conflicts in Africa since the 1990s. More
generally and globally, the politics of ethnic identity has also been stimulated by the spread of
racialised and ethnicised social structures resulting from the long history of colonialism and the
uneven and traumatic movement to a post-colonial global reality (Fenton 1999: 234–8).

In terms of the study of ethnicity, important theoretical developments have included the arguments pioneered by Anthony D. Smith concerning the ethnic core of nations (mentioned earlier), and the work by authors including Walker Connor and Thomas Hylland Eriksen on ethnonationalism as an important source of political and social struggle and conflict in the contemporary world. There has been a recent turn towards theorising 'dominant ethnicity'. Eric Kaufmann, among a group of like-minded writers, sees 'dominant ethnicity' as the main focus of group conflict in the world today, more important than racism (especially of the colour-coded variety). So many conflicts today, Kaufmann argues, can be understood as competition between dominant ethnicities (rather than races) in the same territories as non-dominant ethnicities. Dominant ethnic groups can be minorities or majorities in their territories, as can non-dominant ethnic groups. Though in some cases 'race' underpins perception of ethnic differences, in many cases (especially outside the West) differences are based less on visible physical differences (often these are absent) than upon religious, cultural and language differences supporting ethnic formations that assert, through memories and myths of origin, special and frequently spiritual relations with particular territories. The relationship between dominant ethnic group and nation is a major source of conflict around immigration in Europe; for example, where the argument is less concerned with protecting whiteness than it is about protecting the alignment of dominant ethnic group with territory, nation and control of the state (Kaufmann 2006: 14–15). Kaufmann has explicitly challenged 'whiteness studies' as a flawed approach that should be replaced with an emphasis on dominant ethnicity. Here, the argument should be less about the marking of boundaries than about the influence of major ethnic 'collective narratives and iconography' (ibid.: 7).

According to Kaufmann, concern with dominant ethnicity becomes more pressing in the contemporary world for two main reasons. First, under conditions of global migration and cultural exchange, coupled with the spread of cosmopolitan norms among the university educated elites of the West, many Western nations adopt a civic nationalism that threatens the alignment between dominant *ethnie* and nation, and thus the corporate identity of dominant *ethnie*, so that many dominant *ethnies* experience existential crises and push for immigration restriction and against multicultural policies (Kaufmann 2006). Second, outside the West, because of the end of the Cold War, there is increased instability in post-colonial nations, as the unity of states is exposed, and dominant ethnicities, sometimes having been created by colonial rule, are threatened.

Another important development has been in the burgeoning area of multiculturalism and multicultural studies focused upon the organised interactions between different ethnic groups within multi-ethnic societies. Influential writers such as Charles Taylor stimulated debates around multiculturalism by arguing in his essay 'The politics of recognition', about the importance of culture and ethnicity for group and individual identities, that all cultures should be accorded equal dignity and respect, and that failure to recognise the claims of culture can be one important form of oppression (Taylor 1994). Other writers in the field, such as Will Kymlicka, Bhikhu Parekh and Tariq Modood, from positions within or associated closely with liberalism, have argued for the need for various forms of recognition and accommodation of ethnicity, cultural difference and rights, in recognition of the significance and meaning of different ethnic identities. These forms of recognition call for state policies and laws concerning discrimination, and religious and racial vilification, other legal protections and exemptions, political representation and expression, education, housing, employment and social welfare more generally.

There have also been related developments in theories of transnational, hybrid and diaspora identities, reflecting on the impact of global migration. The British social scientist of race and ethnicity, Pnina Werbner (2005), argues that, at least initially, one of the appeals of a sense of ethnic community for migrants is that it provides them with a way to gradually familiarise themselves to new conditions in a new and often fundamentally different society. Focusing on the experiences of Pakistani migration and settlement in the UK, she argues that a contradictory cultural process occurs. First, that in order to sink roots into the new society the immigrants begin by setting themselves culturally and socially apart from the host society, forming what she calls 'encapsulated communities'. But those encapsulated communities, that develop a sense of boundary between themselves and the broader society, are not static, traditional, homogenous cultures. Rather, they represent fluid and dynamic cultural processes that involve important elements of adaptation to the new society. There is also much debate and conflict within these encapsulated communities, with the debate over culture and cultural expression experienced as a 'powerful imperative'. In these situations, we might say, culture is not simply the taken-for-granted background of everyday life, but becomes something fought over out in the open, especially where there is a sense of conflict between cultural norms within the encapsulated community, and within the broader society outside; or, for example, there is discrimination experienced in relation to cultural norms and practices, including language and dress, and rituals.

Werbner's argument is a direct challenge to those critics of multiculturalism who argue that, under its influence as an ideology and set of public policies, society is becoming a society of potentially or actually warring tribes. Her concept of 'encapsulation' suggests not simply separation, but also forms of engagement with and adaptation to mainstream society. Her account also suggests that ethnic identity is dynamic and changing; migrant culture becomes a hybrid mix of influences in Britain, and in terms of understanding such cultural practices and forms of community, one cannot simply seek explanation in cultures and places of origin. Instead, one must be aware of the new context in which culture and community is interacting; this includes class, intergenerational and gender struggles, the issues of power relations more generally, and the nature of transnational connections.

Main criticisms

The critiques of racial and ethnic understandings of society are quite similar, as the phenomena (including identities) addressed under the concepts of ethnicity and race have often been the same. The main critiques have been from those who argue that discrimination and prejudice based on race or ethnicity have largely been overcome in Western, democratic nations in the post-Civil Rights era, and that we now live in a post-race world. Complaints based on ethnicity or race are therefore seen as forms of special pleading, and criticised as such. Those who draw attention to ethnic or racial factors are criticised for 'playing the race card' in order to elicit sympathy for situations and actions that might otherwise result in condemnation of individual, group or communal failings. These criticisms are predominantly voiced by conservatives, who also articulated the critique of so-called political correctness in the 1980s and 1990s, as a reaction against what were seen as proscriptions on language and expression, and forms of policy that took into account issues of race, racism and ideas of recognition and preservation of cultural, ethnic and racial difference. Critics of political correctness argued that racial and ethnic minorities, and their white liberal supporters, had been successful in countries such as the US in preventing the public discussion and rigorous debate of racially and ethnically sensitive matters (in relation to crime, welfare dependency, immigration, etc.) by inducing the fear of being accused of racism in societies and cultures where racism was publicly abhorred. This also involved the critique of 'identity-politics', by which was meant the pushing of political agendas based on racial, ethnic, gender and sexual identities. Conservatives assert that the state should ignore such differences, and that policies should be universalistic rather than take into consideration specific claims based upon race, ethnic, gender or sexual identities and differences. Thus, anti-racist flag-bearer policies such as affirmative action or positive discrimination are deemed inappropriate in open, universalistic societies supposedly free of the discriminations of the past, where anyone can succeed based on merit, effort and talent. Similarly, multiculturalism came under heavy criticism for undermining social and national cohesion, for funding and creating cultural enclaves of backwardness and ethnic oppression, and for a dangerous cultural relativism.

The critique of identity-politics (and sometimes of multiculturalism) has also emanated from the social democratic left, though the reasons for the critique are different to those of the conservatives. Here the argument has been that too much emphasis on race, ethnicity or other forms of differential identity has led to more fractured social movements that are thus less committed to fighting common battles against societal inequalities, especially those based on class and economic deprivation.

There have also been critiques of developments in theorising race such as understandings of 'new racism' as cultural racism, or theorising 'whiteness'. The criticism of theories of 'new racism' is either that it is not really new – that while it seems to be based on culture, in fact culture is merely a stand-in for biological essence – or that, if it really is about culture or religion, then it is not racism at all, but better understood as a form of cultural discrimination related to ethnocentrism and sometimes xenophobia (Fredrickson 2002). Criticism of whiteness studies includes claims that whiteness is not a predominant form of identity even in societies dominated by white populations, and certainly not relevant to studying inequality and identity dynamics in most other societies in the world.

Finally, it has been argued that use of the concept of race itself reinforces a racial understanding of the world, and leads to a false, reifying of identity as racially bound and organised. Similarly, arguments about ethnic identity, especially when they are linked to advocacy of multiculturalism and preservation of cultural diversity, are criticised by some as presenting a false picture of culture as a static, traditional phenomenon, when in reality we should think of culture and identity as dynamic and changing.

The continuing importance of perspectives on race and ethnicity, and anticipated future developments in identity studies

The, by now, long tradition of studying race and racism has clearly been important in shedding light on the dynamics of a fundamental historical cleavage and major source of violence, subjugation and exclusion in modernity. The question is whether we have moved to a situation where we are now living in a post-race world, where the concept of race has become redundant and unable to shed much further light on the major dilemmas and conflicts of the contemporary world. As suggested in this chapter, there are many contemporary thinkers who dispute the claim that we have moved beyond race, and in fact see in such a claim an ideological obfuscation of continuing race privilege, and thus a contributor to racist reproduction. Through arguments about 'cultural racism' and 'whiteness', these theorists and critics have argued for the continuing importance of race, and have emphasised the need to develop more sophisticated understandings of the often hidden workings of race and discrimination in many societies. One recent perspective here is the concern with examining the workings of 'everyday racism', in particular focusing on the perceptions and insights of people who experience directly the brunt of racist exclusion and discrimination in their everyday lives, perceptions and insights unavailable to the more racially privileged, many of whom continue to act in racist ways of which they are unaware (Essed 1991). Everyday racism is non-ideological, mundane but brutalising in its effects.

The understanding of ethnic dynamics is also still valuable, and indeed may be essential to understanding important forms of identity in the contemporary world. Arguably, it is better equipped than 'racism', or more specifically whiteness studies, to explain contemporary forms of resistance to asylum seekers, refugees and immigration of culturally, religiously and ethnically different others into nations still considered by populations as ethnic homelands (Kaufmann 2006). In an era of intensifying globalisation, the understanding of ethnic processes of identification, struggle and interaction will become increasingly important as societies become ever more plural.

However, in understanding the influence of ethnicity, and ethnic forms of identity, it remains the case that it must be understood as a dimension of complex social relations, and not necessarily always the dominant element of such relations. We must continue to ask important questions about the social, cultural, ideological and economic conditions under which ethnic identities and groups are formed, and are transformed across time, and the conditions under which they become important for social structure and action. Social scientists need to be alert to the dynamics of ethnic formation. Rather than assume that ethnicities represent the continuation of pre-modern phenomena, we must continue to investigate the ways in which they respond to and are shaped by late modern trends, including ongoing tensions between individual and communal/cultural life, private and public, universalism and particularism, emotion and rationality, and class-based and other forms of inequality (Fenton 2003: ch. 9).

References

Barker, M. (1981) *The New Racism*. London: Junction Books.

Barth, F. (1969) 'Introduction', in F. Barth (ed.) *Ethnic Groups and Boundaries: The Social Organisation of Culture Difference*. London: Allen & Unwin.

Collins, P.H. (1990) *Black Feminist Thought: Knowledge, Consciousness, and the Politics of Empowerment*. New York and London: Routledge.

Doane, A.W. (2003) 'Rethinking whiteness studies', in A.W. Doane and E. Bonilla-Silva (eds) *White Out: The Continuing Significance of Race*. New York and London: Routledge, Ch. 1.

Du Bois, W.E.B. (1986) *Writings, W.E.B. Du Bois*. New York, NY: Library Classics of the United States, Viking Press.

Essed, P. (1991) *Understanding Everyday Racism: An Interdisciplinary Theory*. Newbury Park, CA: Sage.

Fanon, F. (1968) *Black Skin, White Masks*. London: MacGibbon and Kee.

Fenton, S. (1999) *Ethnicity: Racism, Class and Culture*. Basingstoke: Palgrave Macmillan.

Fenton, S. (2003) *Ethnicity*. Cambridge: Polity Press.

Fredrickson, G.M. (2002) *Racism: A Short History*. Melbourne: Scribe Publications.

Gans, H. (1979) 'Symbolic ethnicity: the future of ethnic groups in America', *Ethnic and Racial Studies*, 2(1): 1–20.

Gilroy, P. (2000) *Against Race: Imagining Political Culture Beyond the Colour Line*. Cambridge, MA: The Belknap Press of Harvard University Press.

Glazer, N. and Moynihan, D. (eds) (1975) *Ethnicity: Theory and Experience*. Cambridge, MA: Harvard University Press.

Guibernau, M. and Rex, J. (1997) (eds) *The Ethnicity Reader: Nationalism, Multiculturalism and Migration*. Cambridge: Polity Press.

Hall, S. (1991) 'Old and new identities, old and new ethnicities', in A.D. King (ed.) *Culture, Globalisation and the World-System: Contemporary Conditions for the Representation of Identity*. Minneapolis: University of Minnesota Press.

Hall, S. (1992) 'The question of cultural identity', in S. Hall, D. Held and T. McGrew (eds) *Modernity and its Futures*. Cambridge: Polity Press, in association with the Open University, Ch. 6, pp. 273–316.

hooks, b. (1981) *Ain't I A Woman: Black Women and Feminism*. London: Pluto Press.

hooks, b. (1992) *Black Looks: Race and Representation*. Boston, MA: South End Press.

Jordan, W.D. (1969) *White Over Black: American Attitudes Towards the Negro, 1550–1812*. Baltimore: Penguin Books.

Kaufmann, E.P. (2006) 'The dominant ethnic moment: towards the abolition of "whiteness"?', *Ethnicities*, 6(2): 231–66.

Modood, T. (1997) 'Difference, cultural racism and anti-racism', in P. Werbner and T. Modood (eds), *Debating Cultural Hybridity: Multi-Cultural Identities and the Politics of Anti-Racism*. London and New Jersey: Zed Books, 154–72.

Morrison, T. (1992) *Playing in the Dark: Whiteness and the Literary Imagination*. Cambridge, MA: Harvard University Press.

Smith, A.D. (1986) 'State-making and nation-building', in J.A. Hall (ed.) *States in History*. Oxford: Basil Blackwell, 228–63.

Taguieff, P.-A. (1993–4) 'From race to culture: the new right's view of European identity', *Telos*, 98–99 (Winter/Fall): 99–125.

Taylor, C. (1994) *Multiculturalism: Examining the Politics of Recognition* (edited and introduced by A. Gutmann). Princeton, NJ: Princeton University Press.

Werbner, P. (2005) 'The translocation of culture: "community cohesion" and the force of multiculturalism in history', *The Sociological Review*, 53(4): 745–68.

11

Gendered identities

Mary Holmes

Introduction

By 13, [Dave's] confusion about his gender seemed inescapable. At the same time he was playing football and hockey and building World War II airplanes, Dave began waking up in the middle of the night and tiptoeing into the bathroom to put on his mother's makeup.

(Dani's T-Room.Com 2009)

Caster Semenya's victory in the women's world championship 800 metres has been over-shadowed by a 'gender verification' test ordered by athletics officials amid claims that she is actually a man.

(The Guardian, Saturday 22 August 2009: 16)

Sex and gender identity are generally expected to match, so that females are feminine and men masculine, but this is not always the case. The young South African athlete Caster Semenya is flat chested, deep voiced, quite muscular and square jawed, attributes we associate more with the male sex, yet she has lived her life as a girl. Dave had a penis but felt he was a woman and eventually had surgery and became Donna. There are many people in everyday life who have a gender identity that does not fit with their sex.

Distinguishing sex (male/female) from gender (masculine/feminine) is analytically helpful, although later that distinction will be questioned. Genitals are the main criteria for deciding a baby's sex. However, in everyday life when genitals are not visible, we can still tell women from men by their hair, their clothes, by a curve or straightness to their bodies, by the way they walk and talk. These differences in appearance and behaviour are very much influenced by the social world in which we live. Gender refers to the social and cultural expectations and practices involved in acting as feminine or masculine. You recognise gender differences almost without thinking and expect that others will recognise your gender. Yet this is not left to nature and people spend time on their hair, their body, their clothes, their hobbies, in order to look and be more masculine or feminine. This is all part of the creation of gendered identities in which bodies meet social practices, but identity creation is not always straightforward.

Establishing a gender identity can be difficult; for example, for intersex people who cannot be clearly categorised as male or female. The statistics are unreliable, but it is possible that as many as 17 in 1000 people are intersex. Caster Semanya may be one. Intersex people are born with ambiguous genitalia and/or their sex determining chromosomes differ from the usual XX and XY pattern. Some intersex people may have both a vagina and a penis, others may have genitals that are hard to classify, being somewhere between a large clitoris and a small penis (Fausto-Sterling 2000). These conditions are relatively rare compared to those who are clearly sexed, but they exist 'naturally'. Nevertheless, the social confusion they cause is so acute that most intersex individuals are subjected to medically unnecessary, and often unsuccessful, surgery to make them fit into either the male or female category. Most people find it impossible to know how to deal with others without knowing whether they are girls or boys, men or women. In everyday life, some deviance is tolerated – for example, girls can be tomboys or men can be a little effeminate – but the general expectation is that females will behave in feminine ways and males in masculine ways. Intersex people and others whose gender identity does not match their body, indicate that it is not bodies alone that determine identity.

There is a range of ideas about how we learn gendered identities. This chapter begins by sketching an outline of the history and development of ideas about gendered identities. It then turns to setting out the major claims and key contributors to this field. These are grouped under the main schools of thought. Psychoanalysis is discussed first, as an influential, yet controversial account of gender identity. Its basic tenet is that gender identity is about making sense of our anatomy. Following discussion of various versions of psychoanalysis, we turn to social constructionism. This considers how gender identities are imposed on individuals by social forces and how individuals perform gender identities in accordance with social scripts. Post-structuralism, especially following Michel Foucault, offers accounts of gender identity, not as done by individiduals, but as produced by the internalising of gender norms. These ideas are extended in Judith Butler's work on the performativity of gender and related recognition of gendered identities as more fluid, such as in queer theory. Also important in destabilising rigid gender categorisations are ideas about the intersection of gender with other forms of identity. In addition there are approaches that see gendered identities as reflexively created. Having discussed these different approaches, their contribution is evaluated and criticisms are outlined. The chapter finishes with an account of why some of these perspectives are still important and deals briefly with the problems attached to the concept of identity, and the challenges this poses for future understandings of gender.

The historical and intellectual development of perspectives on gendered identities

The concept of gender identity refers to how we use ideas about femininity and masculinity to answer the question: who am I? Gender identity is one of the 'claims made by individuals about who or what they are in terms of *difference* from other people' (Connell 2009: 107). Up until the nineteenth century, identity referred to sameness, and we still see this in our reference to identical twins. By the late nineteenth century dominant Western ideas on identity emphasised innate differences between people, especially in terms of race, class and sex. Ideas about sex and identity were most influentially challenged by Freud, as discussed below. Then, in the 1960s, American psychiatrist Robert Stoller introduced gender identity as a term, to study people who felt their anatomical sex conflicted with their sense of self. Via his work, the concept of gender filtered into sociology, especially through Ann Oakley (1972), who used it to separate out sexed biological bodies from the social aspects of femininity and masculinity.

Sociological accounts of gender identity initially focused on how gender is socially acquired, especially through socialisation, or the process of learning to be a socially acceptable human. However, considerable early attention to gendered identities appeared within Symbolic Interactionism (SI), which understood them as formed through social interaction. American social psychologist George Herbert Mead was the main founder of this tradition, from which emerged 1960s and 1970s ethnomethodological examinations of gender identity as a managed achievement, most famously by Harold Garfinkel and by Suzanne Kessler and Wendy McKenna (see Plummer 1991).

Post-structuralism, is a more European-centred intellectual shift from the mid-twentieth century that shares SI's interest in examining how social norms are central in making (gendered) selves. Most prominent in this tradition is the work of French historian Michel Foucault. He examines how particular kinds of individuals are produced by the workings of power and knowledge. Discourses, or ways of speaking and thinking, backed up by institutional practices, are viewed as central in shaping individuals. Judith Butler published the most influential application of these ideas to gender in 1990. She draws on the work of the linguist J.L. Austin, and especially on his conceptualisation of performatives to explain how gendered individuals are brought into being by discourses. Butler's ideas about gender identities as fluid rather than fixed also fed into the development of queer theory. This was one response to questions about how different identities around gender, sexuality and other social categories are intertwined.

Efforts to consider how different (marginalised) identities intersect with gender emerged primarily out of second-wave feminist movement. Throughout that movement there were ongoing debates about the necessity of women being unified in their struggles versus the importance of recognising differences between women. One intellectual product of this was feminist standpoint theory, which argued that having a particular identity produces particular knowledges. From the 1980s this perspective was especially strong in examining how black women's experiences 'were shaped not just by race, but by gender, social class, and sexuality ... [and] interconnections among systems of oppression'. By the 1990s the term 'intersectionality' had become common to describe this (Collins 2009: 21).

There are many continuing attempts to understand intersectionality within processes of globalisation and individualisation. Some deal with the particular complexities of gender identities within postcolonial societies such as India, Australia and New Zealand (for example, Linda Tuhiwai Smith's book, *Decolonizing Methodologies*). However, the post-9/11 world has been particularly concerned with relationships between gender and Islamic identity (see below). Generally, it is argued, by theorists such as Ulrich Beck and Anthony Giddens, that globalisation and individualisation processes characterise the current age as reflexive modernity. Theories of reflexivity suggest that identity development no longer follows tradition but is a project of self-creation which involves people thinking about the kind of person they want to be and trying to be that person. The details of these broad intellectual currents will now be examined, starting with psychoanalysis.

Major claims and key contributors

Psychoanalysis

Psychoanalysis has been central in elaborating how gendered identities are formed (see also Chapter 3 in this volume). The founder of psychoanalysis, Sigmund Freud, argued that identities emerged as a result of our early experiences of relating to our parents (or parent figures). He thought that these relations were shaped by the social taboo on incest, which was fundamental in creating an ordered, civilised society and directing the sexual drive into 'normal' femininity and masculinity.

Freud proposed that there were a series of stages involved in achieving a masculine identity which culminated in the Oedipus complex. Growing children learn that the difference between girls and boys is having or not having a penis. Still attached to their mothers, boys begin to fear that their fathers may castrate them (and they will thus lose the centre of their pleasure) as punishment if they continue to try to compete for their mother's love, which the incest taboo forbids them to enjoy sexually. The Oedipus complex sees them realise that they must transfer their love for their mother to other members of the opposite sex, and learn to identify with their father and thus become masculine.

Freud tells a less complete story about the Electra complex through which feminine identity is acquired. For girls, the realisation that they do not have a penis is thought not to precipitate a clear break. Noticing their lack of a penis is said to make them envious of boys and angry with their mother, who they realise has not provided them with a penis and cannot. Girls continue to struggle over their attachment to their father, on which the incest taboo places limits. They come to identify with their mother in the hopes that by learning to be feminine like her, they will attract a man who will provide them with a penis substitute – a baby. As part of accepting their femininity they supposedly move from a clitoral-centred sexuality to a vaginal one.

French psychoanalyst Jaques Lacan has more recently reinterpreted Freud's account of gender identities to explain the ongoing difficulty women supposedly have with their sense of sexuality. Lacan argues that gender identity is achieved by the child entering society through the acquisition of language. Masculinity and femininity are subject positions integral to language and therefore acquired with it through splitting. For girls the process of splitting, of disconnecting from the mother and separating conscious from unconscious thought, is supposedly more precarious because they realise that they are already castrated.

A key variation to psychoanalytic accounts of acquiring gender identity is Nancy Chodorow's (1978) *The Reproduction of Mothering*, which argues that women learn femininity from their mothers and therefore learn that being feminine means mothering. The 'reproduction of mothering [is] a central and constituting element in the social organisation of the reproduction of gender. ... Women as mothers, produce daughters with mothering capacities and the desire to mother' (Chodorow 1978: 7). Girls can retain their pre-Oedipal attachment to their mother, they can be like their mothers and learn how to be feminine from them. According to Chodorow, the result of these differences is that girls have less of a separate sense of self and focus on relations to others. In contrast, boys develop gendered identities and resolve the Oedipus complex by detaching from their mother in order to be able to reattach to other women when they grow up. Boys have to learn to not be like their mothers in order to be masculine. They form a masculine identity principally through separation and therefore through a 'denial of relation and connection' (ibid.: 169). Thus independence from others is central to men, whereas relations with others are central to a woman's sense of self. Other psychoanalysts are more pessimistic about feminine identity.

For French scholar, Julia Kristeva, feminine identity is impossible because the symbolic ordering of meaning is patriarchal and the 'feminine' is an otherness that cannot be named. Kristeva sees femininity as closely linked to the maternal, but as existing within what she calls the semiotic (Kristeva 1982). Kristeva uses the term 'symbolic' to refer to formally organised systems of language, whilst by the semiotic she refers to extra-linguistic bodily rhythms which express drives: instinctual impulses that push us towards satisfying our desires for sex, death and so on. The symbolic and the semiotic are inseparable parts of the signifying process through which meaning is made.

Kristeva conceptualises femininity not as an essence but as constructed by processes beyond language, which devalue it. She speaks about this devaluing in terms of abjection, a psycho-analytic concept defined as 'the subject's reaction to the failure of the subject/object opposi-tion to express adequately the subject's corporeality and its tenuous bodily boundaries' (Grosz 1989: 70). Abjection is a fear of becoming an object of disgust by breaking bodily boundaries. Someone can thus become a non-person, as Kristeva explains with the help of anthropologist Mary Douglas's ideas about pollution as crucial to maintaining social divides. Bodies that lack firm boundaries tend to be thought filthy, as are fluids such as sweat and milk that leak out beyond bodies and become 'matter out of place'. Menstrual blood is particularly problematic, according to Kristeva, because it represents women's otherness and danger. Faeces is also polluting because it is a reminder of potty training as key to the exercise of maternal author-ity. This authority acts upon the body through prohibition, rather than paternal or symbolic law which operates partly via separation from the maternal and the bodily. In Freudian (and Lacanian) terms, identity is about separating oneself from the bodily and the motherly. Ideas about pollution accentuate the divisions made between bodies (as feminine disorder) and language (as masculine order). Excluding the maternal and the bodily is thus core to systems of meaning.

In contrast to Kristeva, French psychoanalyst Luce Irigaray questions Freud's understanding of women's identity and sexuality as defined around lacking a penis. Irigaray recognises wom-en's autonomy and sexual specificity (Grosz 1989: 100–1). She argues that Freud's phallocen-trism tries to capture women within a logic of sameness, rendering them as not like men, and as inferior to them. She proposes the possibility of thinking about bodies differently, so that the feminine is no longer divided from, but instead related to, the masculine (Irigaray 1985). Her view is that women's sexuality, and therefore subjectivity, is plural. The two lips of women's genitalia constantly touch and thus pleasure is always available to them. This multiple and active sexuality does not fit the dominant phallocentric model of sexuality based on men. Therefore women's subjectivity is presently inexpressible and/or excessive in relation to patriarchal ways of thinking. Women remain outside discourse, but their excess can be a basis for agency, for making active choices. For example, more women are taking on paid work and thus enter-ing 'the circuits of production'. At the same time, contraception and abortion allows potential freedom from constant motherhood. These possibilities emerge because of changes in women's social position that mean they have begun to take on 'that impossible role: being a woman' (Irigaray 1985: 83).

The social construction of gendered identities

Social forces play a key role in shaping gender identities. Although bodies and biology are important, sociologists argue that gender identities cannot be reduced to some biological essence such as having a womb, vagina, or a penis. Essentialist ideas still have a lot of currency and many people still believe that gender identities are naturally formed, being based on physical and genetic differences between the sexes. For example, men are thought to be 'naturally' stronger, more aggressive and have stronger sex drives. However, an overview of the science tends to indicate that in fact the sexes are overwhelmingly similar, with few physical and psychological differences and these minor (Connell 2009). Thus the social basis of gendered identities requires explanation.

One explanation of gendered identities is that boys and girls are socialised differently from birth (Oakley 1972; see also American sociologist Jessie Bernard's book, *The Female World*). People have different expectations of girls and boys and these expectations are reinforced by social institutions such as the family, the school and the workplace. The most crucial gender socialisation takes place within the family, according to Oakley (1972). Parents, particularly mothers, fuss over girls and treat boys as though they are more robust and independent. Whether children recognise and conform to a gender identity by about four years old, or whether they learn it each time they are rewarded for 'appropriate' behaviour, their family will have a profound affect on how gender identity develops. However, Oakley also notes that children compare their parents to others around them, so they quickly learn how men and women are expected to behave in their society, even if their parents do things differently.

School is also a key agent of gender socialisation. Prior to the 1980s there was considerable concern over girls underperforming at school because readers, textbooks and teachers tended to reinforce gender stereotypes of boys as active, competent leaders and girls as passive followers. However, changes were made on the basis of this kind of research and girls began to outperform boys, so concern shifted to why boys were not doing as well at school. Now, there are efforts to focus more on the similarities between girls and boys (see Skelton 2006).

The ongoing construction of gender identity continues in the workplace. For example, employers and managers often reinforce common notions of gender by choosing men to do jobs supposedly requiring strength and women to do jobs involving serving or nurturing others. This wrongly assumes that women are always physically weaker and that men are not good at nurturing. It also puts women into jobs where they are especially prone to pressure to be (sexually) appealing (Adkins 1995). Despite the many political and social gains that women have made there are social constraints as well as personal choices.

Symbolic interactionism understands self and identity as formed through interaction with others. A major figure in Symbolic Interactionism, Chicago sociologist Erving Goffman (1979), argues that gender is an illusion maintained by its performance in relation to others. He notes the importance of gender displays: events indicating the identity, mood, intent, expectations, and relative relations of actors. Goffman (1979: 1) is suggesting that gender as 'the culturally established correlates of sex' is not natural but merely something considered socially relevant in interactions and therefore signalled to others at the start (and end) of those interactions. If we meet someone of ambiguous gender, we find it almost impossible to know how to interact with them and will look for clues to help us. Displays are these cues, including things such as men standing when women enter a room or opening doors for them. Displays also involve certain styles which identify gender, so that women and men have different hairstyles, different gestures and wear their clothing differently. Goffman is critical of how most gender displays signal and reinforce the idea that women are socially inferior and make that inequality seem 'natural'. He analysed advertisements in magazines to illustrate this idea, showing how they portrayed larger men in protective poses looking down on smaller women, who were represented as passive and childlike. So prevalent are these displays that we come to mistake these socially created scripts for gender for something natural. To Goffman and other Symbolic Interactionists, gender is merely a role that we perform in conjunction with others, following social expectations. Like actors we add our own interpretation of the role.

Candace West and Don Zimmerman (1987) are also part of the Symbolic Interactionist tradition, but understand gender not as play but as something we must continually work at as we interact. People will 'do' their gender differently when with their grandmother than with their sexual partner, for example. We have to manage our presentation of femininity and masculinity according to the social expectations of different audiences and this may involve considerable work, such as lifting weights to build 'manly' muscles or spending time carefully applying make-up to look more feminine. Similar ideas are evident in post-structuralism.

Post-structuralism

Post-structuralist approaches to gender identity focus on regulation, disciplining and performativity. Michel Foucault argues that dominant forms of knowledge (medicine and science in the Western world) provide powerful ideas about what 'normal' healthy women and men should be like and people are encouraged to work on themselves in order to conform.

Judith Butler (1990) uses Foucauldian principles in her explanation of gender as brought into being by discourses, which are sets of ideas and practices. Butler is critical of conventional understandings of identity as formed by excluding otherness from one's sense of self. She argues that the gendering process begins with a newly born child being announced: 'it's a girl'. From that point the girling of the girl starts (and the boying of the boy) by selecting from available meanings about gender. She describes this citation of gender norms as central to gender practices. Butler also draws on the work of the linguist J.L. Austin, and especially on his conceptualisation of performatives. Performatives are words or phrases that bring into being the thing of which they speak. For example, the utterance 'it's a girl' brings feminine girls into being.

In contrast to common-sense ideas that gender is core to our identity, Butler proposes a view of gender as something that is fluid and a set of meanings that can be played around with. She suggests 'troubling' (Butler 1990) gender by questioning the opposition of the categories feminine and masculine. The most often-repeated example she uses is that of drag, which she claims upsets the idea that maleness must be expressed as masculinity because it shows men can dress and act in 'feminine' ways. This questions the idea of gender as fixed.

Queer theorists, including Butler as well as Annamarie Jagose or Steven Seidman, see identities as multiple, fragmented and constantly shifting. Sexual desires are thought to be fluid, and people as capable of resisting norms which present heterosexuality as normal and other sexualities as deviant. People can get into gender bending, be transvestites, transsexuals, or indeed refuse to take on any particular label for who they are sexually, perhaps enjoying sex with both men and women, or at least remaining open to the potential of doing so. For desire to be freely exercised, queer theorists argue that heterosexist stories about identity must be challenged. These stories distinguish girls from boys and women from men, because of beliefs that the 'natural' order is one in which men and women are attracted to each other so that they can get together and reproduce (Butler 1990). Change requires deconstructing, or taking apart, notions of gender and sexual identity as a core part of a unified individual self.

Intersectionality of identities

Intersectionality is an attempt to deconstruct ideas of a unified self and consider how gender is related to other forms of identity. Originally feminist standpoint theorists, such as Dorothy Smith and Patricia Hill Collins (see below), talked about women's standpoint, or black women's standpoint. Now they consider the nature of relations between diverse groups of women and the formation of particular identities and knowledges. As work on masculinities developed, that too sought to address the variety of ways of being a man and the difference in privilege attached to different groups (e.g. Connell 1995). Lack of space prevents discussion of all these strands. For example, there is interesting work on understanding identity as relationally constituted through narratives. However, I will focus on highly influential ideas around black women and identity.

Key writers exploring intersections between gender, race and class were African American feminists including bell hooks, Angela Davis and Patricia Hill Collins. I here refer mostly to Patricia Hill Collins, as a gateway for learning more about black feminist thought. For Collins (2009), it is the experience of intersecting oppressions, accompanied in the United States by a history of racial segregation, which stimulates a collective black women's identity. Not all black women have the same experiences, but all must 'struggle to replace controlling images with self-defined knowledge deemed personally important, usually knowledge essential to black women's survival' (Collins 2009: 110–11). As bell hooks (1989: 9) puts it:

> Moving from silence into speech is for the oppressed, the colonized, the exploited, and those who stand and struggle side by side, as gesture of defiance that heals, that makes new life and new growth possible. It is that art of speech, of 'talking back', that is no mere gesture of empty words, that is the expression of our movement from object to subject – the liberated voice.

Most feminist scholars of race/ethnicity have noted the importance of relation to others in constructing gendered identities. A key essay, especially in its connection to feminist politics, was Chandra Talpade Mohanty's 1986 piece 'Under Western eyes: feminist scholarships and colonial discourses'. In it Mohanty (2003: 17) argues that the feminist movement and Western feminists had forged a sense of identity partly through a 'production of the "Third World" woman as a singular, monolithic subject'. Certain analytic principles underlie these ethnocentric discourses. First, Third World women are seen as a coherent group with identical interests, instead of as diverse in their economic and cultural contexts. Second, uncritical use is made of empirical data supposedly demonstrating 'the universal cross-cultural operation of male dominance and female exploitation' (ibid.: 33). For example, Moslem women wearing the veil does not always signify the sexual control of women by men, but in some specific historical contexts has been used by women as a sign of revolution or resistance. Third, and implied by the other points, Third World women are represented as eternal victims, living highly constrained lives in contrast to the self-representation of Western women as modern and in control. This 'othering' of Third World women has to be challenged and Third World women, in all their diversity, need to represent themselves in order for this to change. Meanwhile, Gayatri Spivak challenges Western women to unlearn their privilege as loss. It is intellectually and politically productive for white women to rethink their identity in terms of their minority position in the world and how their privilege divides them from the majority of women globally.

There are now scholars in the 'majority world', meaning non-Western nations where most of the world's population live, working on how gender identity relates to ethnic identity. Raewyn Connell (2009) is one of the few minority world intellectuals to attend to their work. Connell notes debates, including those around whether the concept of gender identity applies in other cultures. Oyeronke Oyéwùmí, from Benin, for example, has argued that gender was not relevant in pre-colonial Oyo-Yoruba society, where seniority was at the centre of social organisation. Others such as Bibi Bakare-Yusuf disagree claiming that there is evidence of gender as a key aspect of social distinctions via which Yoruba identified themselves prior to colonisation, even if gender patterns were different. She reminds us that cultures and identities are never static and always open to change. This theme is also evident in Latin American and Arab thinkers' concerns with gender identities, which have especially adhered around machismo and how masculine identities have been disturbed by processes of globalisation (Connell 2009: 47–8) and increased reflexivity.

Gendered identities in reflexive modernity

Theories of reflexivity try to understand how people have to form their own sense of identity and make their own lives given that traditional ways of doing things have supposedly lost their hold.

Reflexivity has been a way to understand the diminished impact of structure in organising people's lives and the increased importance of agency. Ulrich Beck and Elisabeth Beck-Gernsheim (2002) argue that women are becoming drawn into processes of individualisation that compel people to take responsibility for themselves, and weaken their connections to others. In their version of the individualisation thesis, women are increasingly looking out for themselves, as they gain the independence arising from having jobs that make it possible to survive without a man.

Pierre Bourdieu's notion of habitus provides some counterpoint by examining how (gendered) reflexivity is still a relational production. Habitus refers to ingrained collective practices that produce and are produced by individuals as they operate within a particular field; for example, politics, law, or academia. People 'play the game' required in a field, but their feel for the game is not consciously practised, nor thought through. The practices involved are learnt and done in a habitual way: they are taken for granted. Even if people no longer rely on tradition, that does not necessarily mean a reflexive reworking of gender, and possibly 'reflexivity is better conceived as habits of gender in later modernity' (Adkins 2003: 22).

There remain constraints on how gender is done, and critical reflexivity is not separate from habit so that people weave structural aspects such as class and gender into their identities, often in ways that retraditionalise gender. For example, the kind of reflexive performativity of gender that is encouraged in the workplace, say through training, often reaffirms traditional notions of femininity and women's abilities (Adkins 2003). Going beyond these problems means recognising that subjects never quite fit the norm and that practices shift little by little through time.

The principal contributions of perspectives on gendered identities

Freud's psychoanalytic approach is important because he was one of the first to think about the role that bodies and the social meanings attached to them play in developing masculine and feminine identities. Lacan and other less literal interpretations furthered this by suggesting that women are not envious of penises per se but realise that having one means being able to enjoy social privileges and power. Lacan views the development of gendered identity as relying not on the actual penis, but the symbolic representation of the penis: the phallus. The phallus represents difference, it stands for the social and cultural value given to masculinity. Taking on masculine and feminine identities is about learning that the masculine will be privileged, and that femininity will be devalued. But there are related accounts of the acquisition of gender identity that try to get away from conceiving of femininity as lack.

For Chodorow, the social structure is crucial in reproducing gendered identities and this makes her work an interesting blend of sociology and psychoanalysis. She is adamant that women's nurturing capacities are an outcome of the 'sexual and familial division of labor' which makes women responsible for caring and nurturing others (Chodorow 1978: 7). Her emphasis on the way in which families are socially organised makes change easier to explain. For example, since the 1970s many more mothers have entered paid work and some fathers are more involved in parenting. This may enable children to see their mothers in other roles and to experience fathers as nurturing and thus to acquire broader and more flexible gender identities.

Nevertheless, feminine identity remains devalued and Kristeva's and Irigaray's work has value in explaining this by linking biological bodies with socially organised language. Irigaray is especially admirable in her endeavours to think about woman's identity as 'a woman, a subject with a life, sex and desires of her own' (Grosz 1989: 179). These perspectives can also offer an alternative to voluntaristic ideas which assume that actors consciously or rationally control their actions.

For Rosi Braidotti (2003: 52), Irigaray is important because she gives strategic attention to femininity not as something stable and essential but as part of 'the transformative flows that destabilise all identities'. This balances the asymmetry that has existed in sexual difference (man as the one to whom woman is compared and found lacking) and gets away from the categories of minority and majority that structure how we think about and do identities. Braidotti instead proposes that people are nomadic, travelling through changes in the self, largely because of their desires to interconnect with other people. However, she is clear that society would have to undergo major changes for new possibilities for desire to emerge and to allow for radically new subjectivities. Such attention to the social is rare in much psychoanalysis.

Social constructionist approaches have attended to how society genders individuals. Initially focus was on learning gender through socialisation processes. Ann Oakley (1972) was one of the first sociologists to explain how socialisation was fundamentally gendered and provided important social analysis of how gender was learned, especially within the family. The struggles accompanying gender socialisation are somewhat clearer in key literature on education. Views of gender identity formation at school tend currently to be based on ideas about how girls and boys 'play' at gender, meaning that they construct a sense of gender identity in relation to others and in ongoing and active ways (see Skelton 2006).

Symbolic Interactionism examines gendered identities as formed through interaction and is highly useful as a basis for more relational understandings of gender. It was one of the first areas of sociology to pay attention to gender. Symbolic Interactionist approaches offered a challenge to usual conceptions of gender identity as a core part of someone's self, residing somehow within them.

Judith Butler's work has been crucial in further building a non-essentialist way of understanding gender, with radical implications. Butler focuses on gender as a set of ideas and practices which constitute the subjectivity of individuals. Her work is subtly different from Symbolic Interactionist claims that gender is a managed achievement, or something that is done in interaction with others (e.g. West and Zimmerman 1987). For Butler, individuals do not 'do' gender: there is no '"doer" behind the deed' (Butler 1990: 25). Butler is trying to avoid voluntarism – the suggestion that people choose how to act – whilst still recognising agency and not assuming that discourses totally determine gendered individuals. She does this via a view of the self and subjectivity which rejects any 'real' basis to gender identity. Gender is a masquerade with no substance behind it and is only evident in terms of ever-shifting discourses which set out what it means to be feminine (or masculine) in a particular time and place. Femininity and masculinity are not derived from bodies or experiences, but a set of made-up ideas about how to act feminine or masculine. However, this illusion of gender is powerful because it includes the idea that gender is at the core of our identity. Butler can help us think about how gender shapes us, but not in entirely pre-determined ways. Queer theories add to this literature by radically challenging binary ways of thinking about gender identity as either feminine or masculine and the related distinction between heterosexual and homosexual. This is part of the wider tendencies to understand gender in relation to other forms of identity.

Standpoint theory and intersectionality may be accused of essentialism but are in fact trying to understand gendered identities as complex social constructions. They are not simply an individualised project of self, but about seeking for 'the connected self and the individual empowerment that comes from change in the context of community' (Collins 2009: 129). Pierre Bourdieu's notion of habitus brings together structure and action, in an arguably similar way to the notion of standpoint as a knowledge or point of view determined by social position. Both sets of ideas have potential for providing ways to consider reflexivity that are less cognitive, more relational and more practice oriented. To further establish the value of these various contributions we need to turn to criticisms of the perspectives covered.

Criticisms

Although psychoanalysis has made a huge contribution to understanding gender, and allowed for unconscious influences on identity, Freud's story has been widely criticised (for example Barrett 1980) because it assumes that women form a gender identity based on lacking a penis and not being like men. He unconvincingly posits that girls abandon an active clitorial sexuality for a passive vaginal one because they recognise their sexual organs as inferior, which assumes that penises are somehow naturally and inevitably better (Barrett 1980: 56–7). It also understands 'active' sexuality in relentlessly masculine terms, and indeed the whole psychoanalytic model of gender identity struggles to escape from the dichotomy: man as active subject, woman as passive lack.

Even less literal interpretations are limited because remaining within the logic of Freudian accounts often means that women who are not nurturing and men who are caring are often stigmatised as having abnormal or 'unsuccessful' acquisitions of gender identity. Feminist psychoanalysts have struggled with similar problems.

There are serious limitations to Kristeva's vision of (feminine) identity, despite the welcome effort to theorise women's embodiment. She sets up a restrictive view of women as a semiotic, rather than symbolic, presence within systems of meaning. This leaves a portrait of woman passively waiting for a masculine imprint to give her meaning. It does not explain how women have managed to say anything about themselves that might resist patriarchal views of them as inferior beings. Yet feminism has managed to do this, and by using rational arguments. Kristeva (1982) is, however, critical of feminism for being negative. She instead advocates breaking down binary identities (e.g. feminine/masculine), but her vision of women places them in a position 'outside' the symbolic order which means they cannot achieve such a change. This insufficiently reworked version of psychoanalysis leaves her trapped within the assumptions that femininity is an inferior, castrated subjectivity (Grosz 1989: 63–7).

Irigaray's work also has problems with the focus on women's bodies as specifically sexualised. It is arguably a form of essentialism, in danger of reducing 'women' to their biology and assuming that actions and agency come from those particular bodies. This is limiting for considering how femininity changes across history and cultures and for challenging essentialist and sexist views of gendered identities.

Although Freudian psychoanalysis tries to avoid biological determinism, it can reduce issues of identity to the biological level. It is criticised for rendering identity as solely a product of how children come to understand what it means to have a female or male body. Freud's analysis of how girls become women tends to reinscribe notions of women as 'inferior'. Lacan's re-readings of Freud are not taken to really improve on this, nor to overcome the sexism. Other psychoanalytic accounts, such as Chodorow's, make attempts to forge more positive ways of understanding femininity, but struggle to do so because they are still based on most of Freud's assumptions (Barrett 1980). Despite the problems noted, psychoanalysis has gained some currency within sociology (see Elliott 2007). However, most sociological accounts of gender identity are based on different assumptions.

Sociological stories of gender as socially produced also have faults. For example, the early sociological focus on socialisation gave too much attention to the early years of life, to mothers, and not enough to how children might be active in forming their own and each other's gender identities around a set of often contradictory social expectations. Symbolic Interactionism provides more complex accounts of social scripts for gender identities, but can get lost at the micro-level. For instance, Goffman concentrates too much on gender as displayed at the beginning and end of social interactions, rather than as central throughout interactions (West and Zimmerman 1987).

Overall, constructionist views of identity tend to portray the individual as engaged in continual refashioning of the self. This implies that people can choose how to do their gender. The more sophisticated versions of Symbolic Interactionism recognise that people perform, or do, gender according to existing social scripts. However, such approaches suggest that individuals perform their gender identities in a knowing way, trying to present the best version of themselves. There remain questions about whether people are always aware of what different audiences expect in terms of doing gender, how much control they have over their performance, and whether the performance is ever sincere. In the late twentieth century, thinkers tried to address some of these questions by understanding how gender norms are internalised though discourse.

Judith Butler sometime slips from her radical decentring of the individual in thinking about gendered identities as produced by discourse. Troubling gender does not seem to involve imagining its disappearance. She notes that gendering brings into being the kind of individuals that make sense in our culture. Butler also says that gender is a matter of copying, with slight variations, existing ways of doing gender. Individuals are doing the copying, but this conflicts with her saying that individuals do not do gender, they are produced by gender discourses.

A more sociological model might focus less on discourse and more on the relational construction of gender identity. Ian Burkitt (1998) proposes that Butler's discursive reading of Foucault is limiting, especially as it relates to power. Butler argues that the view of gender identities as organised around oppositions (man/woman, heterosexual/homosexual) is a fantasy, produced and regulated via laws and taboos. The performance of gender makes them look real. Butler's analysis is relational only insofar as categories (e.g. female, woman) are related discursively, and Burkitt (1998: 490) maintains that it ignores Foucault's attempt to place discourses, of sex especially, 'in the context of a history of power relations'. He argues that 'individuals are interrelated through emotional and physical dependencies as well as through discursive orientations' (ibid.: 491). Identities are not simply constructed by disciplinary and regulatory practices, but travel between people's everyday practices and official pronouncements. Burkitt points out that it is not only the law that regulates gender relations, but other institutions such as medicine and education. Therefore:

> the relations that produce gendered identities and sexual variation are not just those between signifiers in a linguistic system: they are relations between the players in a political process – for example, between classes, sexes and races, and on a more micro-level between doctors and patients, educators and pupils, and parents and children.
>
> *(ibid.: 501)*

Nevertheless, there are aspects of Butler's work that remain extremely useful and in particular the part this work played in establishing queer theory.

Criticisms of queer theory centre around how it can underestimate 'sedimented' gendered inequalities in their approaches to gender identity. Deconstructing identities is not thought helpful for sexual minorities struggling for social acceptance. As Chris Beasley suggests in her work, queer theory could also be more radical if it focused not just on non-heterosexuals, but also on the subversive possibilities of heterosexuality. This would require some care, because of the political need to avoid re-centring heterosexuality. However, just being gay or lesbian does not automatically mean resisting the current gender order, and gay and lesbian individuals can sometimes 'do' identities that reinforce conventional forms of gender. For example, there are very macho gay men, there are lesbians who take butch or femme roles, and there are drag queens who perform rather stereotypical versions of ultra-femininity. Queer theory demands more complex explanations of how gender relates to sexuality and there are similar demands to consider the relationships between gender and other forms of identity.

Intersectionality has struggled to shake off accusations of essentialism and inflexibility associated with early versions of feminist standpoint theory, but still forms an important part of debates about the complexity of identities within reflexive modernity. In order to produce some consideration of how reflexivity is gendered in slowly shifting ways, it should be understood as fundamentally part of the embodied and unconscious habits that mould action. However, these ideas have limitations in recognising gendered subjects. Changes are slow and for most women, they and those around them continue to construct caring for others as central to women's identity. Attention to habitus and entrenched routine actions makes it hard to imagine how 'sedimented' inequalities around gender and other aspects of identity can shift.

It is difficult to rely on habit, within a world that is rapidly changing. Some thinkers such as Margaret Archer, return to the concept of the 'internal conversation' (an idea key to George Herbert Mead in developing Symbolic Interactionism). We 'talk' to ourselves and imagined others in our heads and this is crucial in ongoing and reflexive constructions of identity. While promising, many of these theories have the same problems already mentioned with assuming that identity is self-consciously, and cognitively, created. And indeed the gendered nature of this forging of lives is often insufficiently explored. There is much to do to understand the combination of the mental, embodied, habitual and emotional in how gender identity is formed and lived. This suggests it is time to assess the usefulness of the concept of identity in thinking about gender.

Understanding gendered indentities continues to be important: future developments

Questions about gendered identities are still important within and beyond the academy. For example, feminist philosopher, Rosi Braidotti (2003) has developed Luce Irigaray's ideas about how sexual difference may shape gendered identities. Braidotti is sympathetic to Irigaray's early ideas about the subject as multiple rather than unified, but as nevertheless sexed. She acknowledges that feminists needed to argue against common ideas about sexual difference as naturally fixed by bodies and as justifying women's inequality. However, Braidotti suggests that thinking about people as having bodies has been key to feminist struggles for equality and for better knowledge about women's lives. She wants to put back together the separation of sex and gender to understand subjectivity in terms of the overlap between physical bodies, the material world and symbolic systems by which we represent images and ideas. For this, Irigaray is useful because she enables the body to be thought about as shifting differences including race, ethnicity and religion as well as sex/gender. Irigaray thinks women need to represent the feminine in their own terms by a kind of creative imitation which will reinvent feminine identities. Braidotti calls this the 'virtual feminine', which is a 'definition of the feminist subject as a multiple, complex process'. She sees gender as an ongoing process of becoming.

Gender identity is socially scripted, but something that we work at continuously, as the Symbolic Interactionist tradition has explored. This work is evident in our everyday lives. For example, many employers, exercise considerable control over an employee's appearance, requiring them to do very gendered 'aesthetic labour'. In one hotel:

> extensive grooming and deportment training was given to the staff by external consultants. New employees were trained *how* to wear the uniform. Such sessions also encompassed haircuts and styling, 'acceptable' make-up, individual makeovers, how men should shave and the standards expected in relation to appearance.

(Witz et al. 2003: 48)

Post-structuralist ideas are still useful in examining such examples of how social norms are central in making selves. There are a host of television programmes, books and films about dressing, eating, cleaning, decorating, and looking 'better'. Cosmetic surgery and other less dramatic makeovers are big business. All these are part of regulatory regimes that are highly gendered. Dominant forms of knowledge (medicine and science in the Western world) provide powerful ideas about what 'normal' healthy women and men should be like and people are encouraged to work on themselves in order to conform. However, there are opportunities for resistance and for challenging gender systems, as suggested by Judith Butler (1990).

Butler has been one voice critical of identity-politics as essentialist and anti-democratic, but Patricia Hill Collins (2009) asserts its continued importance in crafting political agendas to overcome oppression. These include fashioning self-respect for black women and demanding the respect of others as a step towards solidarity and political change. Chandra Mohanty believes strongly that solidarity is possible and feminists can work together. At the beginning of the twenty-first century she argues that capitalism, rather than Eurocentrism is the key focus for struggles. In these struggles feminists need to rethink how the all-encompassing presence of a global capitalist system, and increased conflicts around religion and race/ethnicity 'recolonise the cultures and identities of people across the globe' (Mohanty 2003: 229).

Identities continue to be formed especially around major sites of inequality: gender, class, ethnicity, sexuality, age, and disability, to name the most obvious ones. Judith Butler (2008) has recently considered how Western portrayals of Islamic women, highlight some of the problems of thinking about gender equality in conjunction with cultural and religious identity. For example, the French have for some time been debating whether to ban young women from wearing Islamic head coverings to school on the grounds that France is a secular nation and that its public institutions should not tolerate a practice read in 'ignorant and hateful' (Butler 2008: 13) terms as denoting women's inferiority to men or acceptance of fundamentalism. This is just one example from a set of discourses in which sexual freedom is seen as a hallmark of rational secular modernity against which Islam is portrayed as 'backward'. This dehumanises Moslem peoples and makes seem permissible such things as the sexually humiliating torture of Iraqi prisoners by American soldiers at the Abu Ghraib jail and the wider destruction of many Moslem populations and their ways of life. Such discourses also divide struggles for sexual freedom from the struggles of religious minorities against discrimination. Butler wishes to challenge these associations and to think about how those struggles can be reconnected around a critique of state violence. As she notes: '[w]hatever the relations between Islam and the status of women, let's begin with the proposition that it is complex, historically changing and not available to a quick reduction' (Butler 2008: 19). In order to reconnect the struggles for sexual and religious freedom there needs to be criticism of ideas of progress towards a secular modernity as the ideal path for all and a thorough indictment of the brutality of powerful states in restricting both sexual and religious expression.

Choices do play a part, but people are not entirely free to reflexively make their identity. Multiple options are available, and as Anthony Giddens has noted this includes choosing to change sex. People can also fashion gender identities in a world where sexuality has supposedly become separated from reproduction, due to improved contraception and to fertility technologies such as in-vitro fertilisation. Giddens perhaps over-estimates the impact of these changes beyond a fairly small minority and tends to ignore the kind of reproductive issues crucial in shaping gender identities and relations in the majority world. These issues include AIDS, high maternal mortality, and policies aimed at limiting women's fertility such as China's one-child policy. Such policies point to the continued need for critical examinations of ideas and practices relating to gendered identities.

It remains to be seen whether gender and identity is the best partnership for examining some of the thorny issues facing women in the twenty-first century. Iris Young has suggested gender may not be a useful term for thinking about subjectivity and identity. In this she follows Toril Moi, who instead proposes the notion of the 'lived body'. Young thinks that gender is still needed as a concept to illuminate structural inequalities as they affect women and 'people who transgress heterosexual norms' (Young 2005: 13). She notes the initial importance of gender as a concept to help feminists in 'challenging the conviction that "biology is destiny"'. These challenges were then followed by attempts to understand the specificity of gendered identities (for example, standpoint theorists such as Carol Gilligan and Nancy Hartsock), which were criticised for being essentialist. Enter Judith Butler, who questioned why feminists sought a theory of gender identity. This was done because feminism was based on having a subject 'woman', but Butler wanted to disrupt any idea of a stable subject to which gender was core. Butler has been adamant that bodies are not simply a product of discourse but materially constituted by the social. Yet her theorising remains tied to the sex-gender distinction rather than going beyond it (ibid.: 15).

The lived body has the potential to reinvent debates about gender because it is about the body-in-situation. It is a concept drawn from phenomenology, which sees the mind as embodied. The concrete material situation, including relations to others, constitutes bodies but people are actors who can construct themselves in and around this situation This concept can refuse the nature/culture binary and as Linda Nicholson has proposed, can allow that gender is not just social/cultural but has embodied aspects (ibid.: 15–17). This highlights how much recent thinking has sought to breakdown the binary categories informing the defining of identities.

One major binary around which identities are formed is nature/culture, but this has been subject to major shifts as technology has developed. Donna Haraway, biologist turned philosopher, has arguably been the most prominent voice in elaborating how the boundaries between human (nature) and machine (culture) have broken down to the extent that most of us are part-human, part-machine. We are cyborgs. Many people have technological devices in their bodies, everything from pacemakers to breast implants to plastic hip joints. Our bodies are daily shaped by technology, including bras, shoes and highly chemically engineered shampoos. We also form our identities not just by using machines such as computers as mediators, but by developing relationships with those machines. Sherry Turkle (1985) provided one of the early accounts of how our relationship with computers, especially in the age of the Internet, allowed for new ways of experimenting with identity. She also thinks that use of the Internet makes real to people how 'identity can be fluid and multiple' (Turkle, 1995: 49). By playing online games, current versions of which include *Warcraft*, and by interacting in virtual worlds such as *Second Life*, people can try out being different kinds of people. Virtual spaces can be used to experiment with gender. Men can create avatars, or online personalities, that are women. Women can pretend to be men. However, although people may 'switch sides' the basic structure of gender relations is not really altered. There were some options to be gender neutral, but still human, in the text-based multi-user 'games' of the 1990s (ibid.), but these seem to have disappeared in the increasingly sophisticated graphics-driven virtual worlds of today. Turkle is also writing before the emergence of social networking sites such as Facebook and My Space. These probably account for most of the online activity of the millions of people with sufficient Internet access to utilise them. Such sites are less about pretending to be someone else and more about trying to portray a 'brand': a coherent, recognisable and likable self, often across different networking sites (Hardey 2008). This may involve some experimentation, but is as likely to reinforce as to challenge conventional gender identities.

Gender identities are not fixed and stable. Individuals do not always fit the boxes male/masculine, female/feminine. Most social scientists emphasise the learned nature of gender identities. Psychoanalysis proposes that learning to direct sex drives into socially acceptable channels is crucial to how masculinity and femininity are formed. There are various stories of how this happens. Some argue that the emphasis on anatomy in psychoanalysis reduces gender identity to biological difference. Sociological accounts of gender identity as both learned and socially constructed by forces outside the individual can overcome these problems. They can highlight how social norms about gender are crucial to the construction of gendered identities. However, either individuals end up seen as determined by social structures, or there is too much emphasis on individual agency in doing gender. More recent work such as Butler's tries to think beyond this by seeing gender as a discourse that produces gendered individuals, through regulation and through individuals internalising social norms. Current thinking also focuses on how relations to others shape and reshape identity in complex ways. This may require seeing identity as fluid. Such a vision would collapse binary classifications of identity which suggest it is an either/or choice: feminine or masculine, heterosexual or homosexual, natural or cultural, self or other. Some theorists conclude that we must reflexively make our (gender) identity. Questions then arise about what role traditional and conventional ways of doing gender play in these ongoing fashionings and whether more relational ways of identifying are still necessary or even indispensible, especially for groups who have been categorised as the inferior 'other'.

The problem with gender identities as a concept may lie not with gender, but with the concept of identity itself. How identities are connected to social structures is often insufficiently considered, as is how identities might be better understood as structured relations to others. From a sociological viewpoint, identities are always structurally informed, if not entirely structurally determined. Identity could be thought as a continuum of connection and disconnection from others within the social world. Gender is done (to us and by us), undone and redone and every now and then momentarily forgotten. It is thought about, but sometimes unconscious or done habitually, in some circumstances it is practised with great care. It is felt, through bodies and emotions. Most of all gendering is an ongoing process, situated firmly within the social interactions that constitute our lives. Relationality is not about how a self/other distinction defines identity, but about how gendered interactions with fellow embodied humans determine our every day answers to the question: who am I?

References

Adkins, L. (1995) *Gendered Work: Sexuality, Family and the Labour Market*. Buckingham: Open University Press.

Adkins, L. (2003) 'Reflexivity: freedom or habit of gender?', *Theory, Culture & Society*, 20(6): 21–42.

Barrett, M. (1980) *Women's Oppression Today*. London: Verso Books.

Beck, U. and Beck-Gernsheim, E. (2002) *Individualization: Institutionalized Individualism and its Social and Political Consequences*. London: Sage.

Bernard, J. (1981) *The Female World*. New York: Free Press.

Braidotti, R. (2003) 'Becoming woman: or sexual difference revisited', *Theory, Culture & Society*, 20(3): 43–64.

Burkitt, I. (1998) 'Sexuality and gender identity: from a discursive to a relational analysis', *Sociological Review*, 46(3): 483–504.

Butler, J. (2008) 'Sexual politics, torture and secular time', *The British Journal of Sociology*, 59(1): 1–22.

Butler, J. (1990) *Gender Trouble: Feminism and the Subversion of Identity*. London: Routledge.

Chodorow, N. (1978) *The Reproduction of Mothering*. Berkeley: University of California Press.

Collins, P.H. (2009) *Black Feminist Thought*. London and New York: Routledge.

Connell, R.W. (1995) *Masculinities*. Cambridge: Polity Press.

Connell, R. (2009) *Gender: In World Perspective*. Cambridge: Polity.

Elliott, A. (2007) *Concepts of the Self.* Cambridge: Polity.

Fausto-Sterling, A. (2000) *Sexing the Body: Gender Politics and the Construction of Sexuality.* New York: Basic Books.

Goffman, E. (1979) *Gender Advertisements.* Basingstoke: Macmillan.

Grosz, E. (1989) *Sexual Subversions: Three French Feminists.* Sydney: Allen and Unwin.

Hardey, M. (2008) 'Seriously social: making connections in the information age', unpublished PhD thesis, University of York.

hooks, b. (1989) *Talking Back: Thinking Feminist, Thinking Black.* Boston, MA: South End Press.

Irigaray, L. (1985) *This Sex Which is Not One.* Ithaca, NY: Cornell University Press.

Kristeva, J. (1982) *Powers of Horror,* trans. L. Roudiez. New York: Columbia University Press.

Mohanty, C.H. (2003) *Feminism without Borders: Decolonizing Theory, Practicing Solidarity.* Durham and London: Duke University Press.

Oakley, A. (1972) *Sex, Gender and Society.* London: Temple Smith.

Plummer, K. (ed.) (1991) *Symblic Interactionism.* Aldershot: Edward Elgar.

Skelton, C. (2006) 'Boys and girls in the elementary school', in C. Skelton, B. Francis and L. Smulyan (eds) *The Sage Handbook of Gender and Education.* London: Sage, 139–51.

Tuhiwai-Smith, L. (1998) *Decolonizing Methodologies: Research and Indigenous Peoples.* London: Zed Books.

Turkle, S. (1995) *Life on the Screen: Identity in the Age of the Internet.* New York: Touchstone.

West, C. and Zimmerman, D. (1987) 'Doing gender', *Gender and Society,* 1(2): 125–51.

Witz, A. Warhurst, C. and Nickson, D. (2003) 'The labour of aesthetics and the aesthetics of organization', *Organization* 10(1): 33–54.

Young, I.M. (2005) 'Lived body vs. gender: reflections on social structure and subjectivity' in I.M. Young, *On Female Body Experience: 'Throwing Like a Girl' and other Essays.* Oxford: Oxford University Press.

12
Media and identity

Nick Stevenson

A Brechtian maxim: 'Don't start from the good old things but the bad new ones'.
(Benjamin 1998: 121)

Historical and intellectual development

The technological innovation of contemporary forms of communication has been one of the most startling developments of modern times. In living memory for many contemporary citizens is a world before the Internet, DVD players, downloading music, blog sites, multi-channel television, real-time global communication and digital cameras. Perhaps more so than any other area of our shared cultural life communications technology has changed so quickly. This then is the first media saturated society. Yet, as we shall see, it is very easy to get carried away with a sense of change and transformation. Here I shall argue that if the media landscape has indeed changed and is continuing to change, there is no need to assume that the underlining critical project in respect of the media of mass communication has entirely altered. Previous generations of critics from Walter Benjamin to Raymond Williams and from Jurgen Habermas to Bertold Brecht have sought to press for an agenda of a radically democratised communications system. The terms of this debate may have radically altered but its essential features have arguably remained the same. Here I shall argue for the critical recovery of a diverse tradition of thinking that spans both critical theory and cultural studies which remains central to the future of a more emancipated system of media power. This agenda has radical implications for the ways in which we understand our shared identities as democratic citizens and consumers of media culture more generally. In terms of the relationship between media and identity the important question remains the extent to which we are able to perceive ourselves as civic actors in an increasingly complex mediascape. To what extent then does the media of mass communications aim to foster democratic and critical identities amongst its citizens? This raises a number of inter-related questions which are crucial to the formation of contemporary identities. That is, despite the recent pluralisation of the media of mass communication, the crucial questions in respect of media remain related to questions of voice, autonomy and empowerment. Here I shall seek to investigate the extent to which questions of ownership and control, the techonological development of modern media, the mix between public and private media, the commodification of the media and the development of a genuinely citizens' media might all be said to impact upon questions of media and identity. Here we need to ask to what extent citizens are encouraged to view the media as a means of democratic communication, and alternatively to what extent are they positioned as passive consumers of information within a centrally controlled communication system whose priorities are largely determined by the respective roles of the economic system and the state. Here we might wonder to what extent media can become a voice for civic protest, alternative perspectives and projects other than those sanctioned by the powerful and influential. In this respect then I shall investigate the role that the media of mass communication plays in respect of the development of social and cultural identities.

Major claims and development

Benjamin, Brecht and Adorno

Writing in the context of the 1930s, both Walter Benjamin and Bertold Brecht made seminal contributions to questions of media, identity and democracy. Arguably Benjamin's great critical insight was that new mediums of communication could actually enhance the development of democratic sensibilities. The model of dialectic thinking that is offered here suggests that if capitalism sought to colonise the media to its own ends, then a more democratic system of media making should seek to release the emancipatory potential latent within new forms of communication. When Benjamin and Brecht were writing in the 1930s, the arrival of the radio, cinema and the camera seemed as pregnant with possibility as new media does today. In particular, both Benjamin and Brecht argued that it was the institution of the division of labour between the producers and the consumers of media that undermined its democratic potential. Media needs to be emancipated from a world where citizens are reduced to being passive listeners and consumers of mass-mediated messages. This they argued can only be achieved if they are able to realise their identities as cultural producers of meaning rather than being merely consumers. If much critical thought during this period could only see the media's role in manipulation, both Brecht and Benjamin pointed towards a more democratic arrangement. The problem with fellow critical Marxist thinkers was that they overwhelmingly saw the media as the site of manipulation and control thereby unable to adequately account for how more critical forms of understanding might emerge from within the masses themselves. Crudely put, this view tended to suggest that just as the capitalist class owns and controls the large conglomerates that control the economy, then the same could also be said of the media. Hence just as capitalism seeks to run the economy according to the interests of the rich and powerful, then its media are unlikely to carry critical or alternative perspectives preferring instead to propagate views sympathetic with the status quo. However, what Benjamin and Brecht perceived was that if media technology was intrinsically authoritarian and served the interests of capitalism, how could a more democratic system emerge at some point in the future? If capitalism simply imposed a commodified, homogeneous mass culture upon the masses, then it was difficult to perceive how an alternative system of communication might emerge. Indeed, if the fear was that the 'new consciousness industry' had entirely saturated the critical potential of modern society, both Benjamin and Brecht suggested that this was far from the case. In criticising an increasingly capitalist-dominated and authoritarian media system, many critical thinkers had overstated the closed nature of the media and failed to acknowledge its potential for transformation.

Brecht and Benjamin perceived critical potential within the development of a genuinely mass popular culture made up of new technologies. Indeed, unlike more artistic endeavours such as painting and writing, the new media of the 1930s were not restricted to the educationally privileged classes. Both Benjamin and Brecht were excited by the prospect of simple and seemingly easy-to-use technological forms that could potentially enable ordinary citizens to become writers as well as readers. The key to producing more democratic identities lay less in the actual media content, but more in the social relations entered into in shaping, producing and receiving media content.

For Benjamin (1973) the development of new media had shattered the hold of more traditional artistic forms. The transportability of images through time and space, the decline in 'aura' of high art, the endless possibilities involved in the reproduction of images and the possibilities hearalded by the rise of the popular culture meant that 'at any moment the reader is ready to turn into a writer' (Benjamin 1973: 225). In particular, Benjamin offers a key comparison between the cameraman and the painter. For Benjamin, whereas the painter offers a contemplative view of reality, the cameraman seeks (like a surgeon) to cut into it. New media forms should not be dismissed as simply imposing false consciousness, or indeed as forms of manipulation, but carry within them the seeds of a more emancipated and participatory society. This does not (as many have sought to claim) convert Benjamin into being a technological optimist. Instead, Benjamin was interested in the technological developments of the 1930s as it potentially enabled ordinary people to become authors, thereby democratising the production of culture. Here Benjamin (1978) argues that the politics of a work of art or cultural artefact is less about the ideological position of the text, but more whether it enables the oppressed to become their own authors. Benjamin was rightly suspicious of those who sought to exchange the rule of capital for the rule of well-intentioned intellectuals whatever their political sympathies. A more democratic system of communication requires new institutional arrangements and a deep questioning of processes of professionalisation and specialisation in the production of culture. In the process of converting readers into authors and consumers into citizens, Benjamin drew directly from a number of features that are evident in Brecht's epic theatre. Cultural producers are urged to use a number of techniques to shock members of the audience into thinking for themselves. The idea of Brechtian theatre through certain 'alienation' effects was to stir the audience into assuming a critical, active and reflective disposition. Brechtian theatre classically did this by seeking to remind the audience that they were watching a play (thereby pointing to the artificiality of the setting), by punctuating the flow of the performance through the use of songs and other features, by making the 'ordinary' seem strange and by locating the 'action' in a field of social relationships. All these features Brecht hoped would prevent the audience from viewing works of art as mind numbing forms of mass entertainment. For Brecht and Benjamin, much bourgeois talk about art in the context of the rise of facism had a self-indulgent tone. The critical task of the present was not to worry about the preservation of 'aura' of the artist but to politicise and democratise art to build a more democratic society. Particularly important at this juncture is the celebrated dispute between Benjamin and Adorno on the nature of art in the context of a capitalist society.

Adorno's (1991) writing on the culture industry sought to outline the impact of capitalism on the production of culture. As Adorno explained through a number of critical modes and essays, the effects of the capitalist mode of production upon culture were almost entirely negative. Adrono's (1991) notion of the culture industry argued that processes of mass production were coming to dominate the cultural sphere. This lead to the dominance of instrumental forms of reason coming to administer, control and produce a superficial consumer culture. The dominant culture of capitalism of the 1930s and 1940s sought to repress all forms of conflict, heterogeneity and particularity from the cultural sphere. Here what becomes valued is the exchange of culture over the quality of culture. Mass produced culture is commodified and produces a regressive desire on the part of the audience for the same over and over again. However, despite the critical importance of these arguments, they can seem problematic in more democratic contexts and settings. For example, Adorno's remarks on the jazz of the 1930s describe it as trading upon easily learnt formulas and standarised procedures. If jazz might be viewed positively as erasing the boundary between high and low culure, Adorno argues that such features replace the prospect of autonomous art with the lowbrow. While Adorno's writing is meant to provoke the reader into critical forms of reflection by pointing to the effects of the progressive commodification of culture, many have been critical of its high cultural tone and lack of democratic resonance. Often missing from these formulations, arguably evident in Benjamin, is a more ambivalent understanding of contemporary cultural technologies.

Habermas and Williams

The debate between Adorno and Benjamin was to play a part in shaping the political writing of a later generation of critical theorists and cultural thinkers, namely Jurgen Habermas and Raymond Williams. Habermas's (1989) idea of the public sphere is a central concept in the development of social and cultural theory and media studies. Habermas's work on the public sphere provides a historical account of the development of the crucial role played by civic spaces such as coffee houses and salons in the eighteenth century in helping to provide the context for the development of democratic ways of life. The purpose of the public sphere was to allow citizens to critically reflect upon themselves, civil society and the practices of the state. It allowed the bourgeoise, nobles and intellectuals to meet to discuss works of literature, and then later more overtly political affairs. While recognising that questions of public discourse were restricted to an elite, Habermas argued that they had a historic critical potential. This was mainly through the establishment of the idea of justification through the use of public reason. The public sphere helped solidify the notion necessary for democracy of the importance of critical forms of engagement on public questions by citizens. It is this that helps establish the foundation of modern democratic societies. Yet the public sphere was a fragile construction, and after the rise of conglomerate capitalism, it was replaced by more overt forms of manipulation. After the 1870s, the democratic potential of the public sphere became progressively undermined as the press were run on more overtly commercial lines. The rise of the mass media in the early part of the twentieth century not only eliminated more public forms of discussion but also produced cultural texts where there was little possibility of the audience answering back. Yet contrary to Benjamin, Habermas claims that notions of 'aura' have not been defeated by the invention of new technological forms. The new stars of the media age are well-known personalities, celebrities and charismatic politicians. Indeed, we shall see in the next sections in respect of the debates on the society of the spectacle just how far these processes seem to have gone. Here the importance of rational dialogue had been marginalised by the dominance of mediated mass entertainment. If then Habermas builds upon Adorno's critique of Benjamin, he also criticises Adorno for ignoring the critical potential of ordinary speech and language that could be developed in democratic contexts.

Habermas (1996) was to revise these arguments by moving away from the idea that the public use of reason had been effectively colonised by the operation of money and power. In his later work, Habermas recognises there are actually a number of competing public spheres operating on different levels. These could be global, national or local in orientation and included a number of cultural practices from the theatre, television, the press and popular music, amongst others. However, Habermas continued to argue that the possibility of getting your voice heard and participating in the public sphere were unequally distributed within society. Public opinion is predominantly shaped by powerful vested interests such as spin doctors, pollsters, media mogels and media-trained politicians. However, many of these voices were contested by civil actors from the non-governmental sector capable depending upon the context of getting different views and perspectives onto the agenda. The public sphere is an endlessly contested domain where democratic politics is a matter of ongoing controversy. The public sphere in any democratic society needs to be able to focus on a wide range of public arenas on specific questions. Only then through energetic public discourses and civic engagement can democracy be said to become realised as a practice.

Despite Habermas's concern to rethink his earlier work, many have noted its overly rationalistic orientation. The point of engaging in the public sphere is sometimes reduced to the cold exchange of reasons and the need to find agreement amongst a diversity of opinion. What is missing here is a critical politics of voice and learning. If we view the idea of the public sphere through a more pedagogic frame of reference, we need to consider who is empowered to speak, who is silenced and whose voices are rendered Other. Further, what does it mean to produce an 'opinion' and what are the limits of what can be said in public? What role do different artistic forms of expression play in this process and how does this relate to the more formal public sphere? Also how might more marginal voices and communities become empowered within media debates and on-going forms of controversy? Notably these questions never become centre stage in Habermas's thinking. Elsewhere these concerns have been called cultural citizenship (Stevenson 2003). Here a number of scholars have begun to explore a critical politics of respect. What becomes significant at this juncture is a critical politics of voice, listening and democratic engagement. None of these concerns are adequately dealt with through a paradigm that is overly driven by the ability to reason and argue. Indeed, as we shall see, these features are more closely associated historically with the work of Raymond Williams.

Raymond Williams (1962) coined the idea of the 'long revolution' in the early 1960s. For Williams, liberal democratic national societies were unable to fully incorporate the creative and dialogic potential of all of its citizens. For Williams, the dominant capitalist system had sought to progressively introduce a system of communication and learning where the interests of markets and commerce were predominant. Williams (1980) witnessed first hand the rapid development of a modern consumer society built upon fantasy and magic seeking to induce citizens to construct their imaginary lives around the need to consume. The capitalist-driven societies of the 1960s witnessed the rapid development of commercial television, magazines, suburban living, privately owned motor vehicles and the logic of consumption spreading into other domains such as the political system. While this period also saw the rise of a number of more sub-cultural developments that became associated with music and new forms of radical identity-politics such as the politicisation of race and gender relations these were subordinate to new accumulation strategies introduce by the dominant capitalist system. Further this period also witnessed the partial erosion of earlier distinctions between a literary culture and a mass-produced consumer culture. In this respect, Williams was a distinctive voice given that his analysis is critical of a cultural conservatism evident on the Left and the Right that either sought to either take refuge in the superiority of literature or simply to celebrate the development of new means of communication as opening out a more liberated society. It was not that Williams was unaware of the critical potential of literature, but that, like Benjamin and Brecht before him, the rise of new media (this time television) offered new opportunities for the development of democratic criticism. Avoiding the twin logics of cultural elitism and technological optimism, Williams was mainly concerned with the development of a society based upon the principles of equality, solidarity and a shared democratic civic status. The progressive intrusion of the power of certain commercial images and brands all selling the consuming life sought to persuade ordinary people that their primary identities were those of consumers rather than citizens. It was here that Williams began to perceive the different interests that prevail within private as opposed to genuinely public systems of communication.

Williams's writing is also attentive to the need to produce a society based upon the 'common good' where all individual citizens have the possibility of developing their own voices and critical perspectives within a shared democratic context. This could not be a society that was overly driven by the logic of capitalism, given its need for consumers, hierarchy and tendency to restrict education to training for the labour market. A genuinely democratic society required a media and education system that helped sustain a politics of voice, critique and dialogue. Such features evidently could not be solely delivered by a democratic communicaton system, but would require the idea of democracy to find expression within the work place, the home, the education system and within other dominant social and cultural institutions.

Further, Williams recognised that the media of mass communication was technologically organised in such a way that meant that most of the information that people received flowed from the centre to the periphery. This one-way flow of information was objectionable as it left many citizens passive in the construction of the central meanings of the media. The commercial as well as the public broadcasters had all helped construct a system of communication where the many attended to the voices, opinions and images of the few. Williams perceived this to be a form of social and political control that a more emancipated society would need to over come. Williams (1980: 62–3), pre-empting much current debate on alternative media, argued that a more democratic and inclusive society required 'not only the general "recovery" of specifically alienated human capacities' but also 'the necessary institution of new and very complex communicative capacities and relationships'. This was a critical politics that insisted that a democratic society would require citizens who were not only following public debates, but had also taken the extra step to become cultural producers and participants in their own right. A democratised society required a politics of voice and the provision of complex public spaces where citizens could potentially share their experiences, critically interrogate the status quo and of course listen to a complex republic of voices and critical perspectives. The media should be a place where we learn to listen, criticise and produce our own views and perspectives. It was for these reasons that Williams (1980:62) thought that a democratised society would require more complex forms of communication than existed under capitalism. If the long revolution could be defined as the progressive development of 'an educated culture'. then Williams (1962: 176) rightly stressed the importance of mediated forms of communication. As Williams recognised, the media of mass communication were important not only because of the impact they could be said to have on our collective and personal identity, but also because they could highlight latent critical possibilities and alternative ways of living. The media in terms of its wider role within society was the most powerful 'educator' of our shared sense of self and common culture that had yet been produced by modern society. Williams analysed modern media cultures in terms of their ability to communicate a sense of our shared identities as consumers or citizens and its capacity to construct pedagogic and communicative relationships.

Main criticisms

The main argument thus far has been about how to link a critical understanding of the media of mass communication to the formation of identity in a way that is in keeping with the critical spirit of democratic societies. These concerns then arguably go far deeper than the consideration of how identity might be mobilised by particular television programmes or by the ownership of new media-related technology. Notably questions of commodification, ownership and control, technology and the wider purpose of the media are all at stake here. Here I wish to more critically evaluate some of these arguments.

Adorno does make some important criticisms of the work of Benjamin and Brecht. As Richard Wolin (1994) notes, Adorno was worried that the implications of the position outlined by Benjamin and Brecht is that art and culture are potentially reduced to a form of propaganda. Whereas for Adorno, art has a potentially utopian role to play the extent to which it can resist dominant forms of instrumental reason. Further, Adorno was concerned about what happens in Benjamin's and Brecht's analysis to works of art that are labelled politically unprogressive. Adorno then is clearly worried about the political effect of arguments such as those of Benjamin and Brecht for autonomous art. Indeed, if Benjamin's and Brecht's arguments are pushed to their logical conclusion, we may end up with a cultural sphere where citizens are active producers but mainly see themselves as consumers producing commodified products. This is perhaps to push the argument further than Adorno intended, but is certainly in keeping with the spirit of his criticism. Benjamin in particular overestimates the power of technology to empower a new generation of cultural producers, perhaps underestimating its potential to act as a form of manipulation. In this respect, Adorno points to the ways in which new technologies such as film are connected to the power of the culture industry that reduces art to the narrow margins of profit and loss. Yet in retrospect, while these are important correctives to the argumentative flow of Brecht and Benjamin, it is the seeds of their criticism we can see coming to fruition in later democratically orientated theorists. Undoubtedly Benjamin and Brecht invested too much in the deomocratic possibilities of media technology, and yet the link that is made here between identity and alternative forms of media production are crucial. As Enzensberger (1970) argues, Adorno's position could well persuade critical thinkers to take refuge in an arts and crafts style movement rather than seeking to democratise the flow of communication. Adorno's argument is criticised for inadequately appreciating the complexity of technological forms and simply viewing them as commodities. Further, becoming overly concerned with an 'art for art's sake' disposition would fail to politicise the production of art and culture more generally. For Enzensberger, radical attempts to democratise the production of media and culture requires civic activists to get their hands dirty and produce alternative cultural forms rather than simply becoming resentful of the ways in which new technological forms are undermining older media. A democratic and indeed socialist strategy in respect of the media is not simply emancipation by technology, but would require the construction of new learning possibilities. This can only be utilised by ordinary members of the public turning new media to civic purposes. This would require a media that did not so much flow from centre to periphery but empowered citizens to produce less authoritarian media structures that developed new networks of communication.

Further, Williams (1989) remains connected to the critical project formulated by Benjamin and Brecht focusing upon both how the critical potential of new media had yet to be realised in the present and how a new generation of radical dramatists (such as Ken Loach and Dennis Potter) were seeking to radicalise telelvision through what he called a 'realist' structure of feeling. Williams argued that, like Brecht, this is less naivity about dramatic modes of representation but more an attitude towards the world that promotes a political viewpoint, and offers the possibility of agency and civic momentum. Like Benjamin and Brecht, Williams was concerned to promote a democratic politics of voice that lapsed neither into cultural pessimism nor technological optimism. An active and vibrant public sphere depends upon a civic realm built less upon indifference, but upon the creation of an active and participatory citizenship.

Williams's politics then were shaped by a broader Left project to democratise systems of public service broadcasting and of course develop a strong civic sphere where the state might be expected to fund alternative artistic and creative ventures without necessarily making a profit.

In this respect, Williams was never dismissive of new technological inventions, always seeing within them possibilities for more complex communicative relations and for democratic criticism. In particular, Williams like many on the New Left was particularly keen to democratise the idea of public service broadcasting. Notably the idea of a public service broadcaster was not exclusive to the British with many other democratically inclined citizens seeking to make similar cultural provision within their own societies. What Williams and others liked about the BBC (and later Channel 4) was that it was not dominated by commercial concerns and had historically sought to promote an agenda that was dedicated to 'serious' culture and quality forms of information while encouraging citizens to participate within democratic debates and national forms of identification.

However, since the 1960s there had been a number of key cultural transformations that might be said to have changed the dimensions of the long revolution. If the good society is a society built upon the development of critical and educated perspectives by its citizens, then such features have been overtaken by a number of developments. On the one hand, the development of the Internet and associated media technologies have helped foster a communicative society unlike any seen before. The prospect of masses of people producing their own critical perspectives and engagements is a real possibility in a mass computer society. This, as much democratic criticism has recognised, offers real critical potential for the culture and society of our own times. Also Williams's dream of the educated and participatory society was an overwhelmingly national political vision and would need to be reconstituted in a more global age. The development of global forms of communication increasingly enhance the recognition of a diversity of ways in which national publics are connected to an emergent planetary society. As we shall see, this shared sense of global interconnection has arguably reconfigured the domain of radical politics. Further, the increasing penetration of the market into everyday life, class polarisation, the increasing commercialisation of broadcasting and the development of a conservative agenda within education has served to push more critical and democratic questions off the agenda. While these are all key transformations, I shall argue that Williams's central argument that sought to connect the development of communications with the potential development of an educated democracy are still valid. However, while Williams more keenly recognises the threat of commercial media than Habermas (this is certainly true of his more recent writing), neither perhaps give enough recognition to the powerful interconnections between media, technology and the power of capital to commodify communications.

Notably, relative decline of public forms of media and the rapid development of new media technologies that are mostly commercially driven has lead many to return to the writing of Guy Debord. In Debord's original formation, just as workers are separated from the products of their labour through capitalist social relations, so images take upon an autonomous appearance that have little connection with everyday life. The masses consume dramatic images of human misery and suffering that increasingly take on the appearance of unreality. In this respect, the spectacle is not the effect of technology but is the product of a centralised capitalist society that institutes an 'essentially one-way flow of information' (Debord 1994: 19). Capitalist domination is built upon alienation as people learn to recognise their needs and desires through the images and commodities offered by the dominant system. Needs and desires then are not arrived at autonomously but through a society of affluence where people are driven to consume images and commodities built upon 'the ceaseless manufacture of pseudo-needs' (ibid.: 33). The society of the spectacle has its roots in the economy and represents the further penetration of capitalism into the psyche of modern citizens. This is not the society of being but of endless cycles of having. Notably, however, some forms of critical theory and Marxism have been complicit with the dominance of the spectacle through the imposition of similarly authoritarian modes of struggle and rule. For Debord, if the alienation effect of the spectacle is to be defeated, then the subjugated would need to revolt against their imposed passivity and 'purely contemplative role' (ibid.: 87). Alienation can only be countered by entering into social and political struggle that has rejected alienated forms of life. This demands a 'theory of praxis entering into two-way communication with practical struggles' (ibid.: 89).

The other way in which the spectacle dominates the lives of modern citizens is through the elimination of historical knowledge. If the rise of capitalism eclipsed the dominance of cyclical time of the medieval world, then it did so by instituting irreversible time. For Debord, this involves ideas of progress that not only came along with capitalist modernity and calculable time necessary for the disciplining of labour and the production of commodities, but also spectacular time. Spectacular time prevents the development of historical knowledge as it organises information as dramatic events through the media that are then quickly displaced and forgotten. Similarly, Fredrick Jameson (1991) has argued that commodity capitalism has instituted a society of the timeless present. The emergence of the consumer society has fostered a culture of pastiche, nostalgia and schizophrenia. The mimicry of other styles and the endless recycling of cultural commodities ends with the blurring of distinct cultural periods and the production of cultural material that seems to float free of specific contexts. Here Jameson notes, for example, that cult films such as *Star Wars* are actually nostalgia films given that they unconsciously recycle the science fiction films of the 1930s. For Jameson, however, it is not clear that radical art and social movements can resist the schizophrenia of the present and produce a sense of historical narrative and perspective required for a more emancipated society. Indeed, what has become problematic of the high modernism represented by artists such as Brecht is that they have become canonised by the mainstream. Brecht and other modernist artists are no longer radical, given their status as classics or as part of university curriculums. Further, other radical artistic forms which have arisen as sub-cultural forms have quickly become commodified and incorporated into the cycles of fashion and consumerism. However, arguably Jameson (1991: 97) too quickly dismisses the culturally contested and fractured nature of civil society and the role of social movements and new artistic forms in recovering a more ethical and political agenda. As Williams (1962: 10) suggested in the 1960s 'the democratic revolution is still at a very early stage'. Indeed, Debord himself argued that such features could only be resisted once 'dialogue has taken up arms to impose its own conditions upon the world' (1994: 154).

However, the development of spectacular capitalism has major implication for any attempt to rethink ideas of the public sphere, and in turn the relationship between media and the formation of democratic identities. For Douglas Kellner (2003), updating Debord's original reflections, in the society of the spectacle fashion, glamour models, celebrities and icons become increasingly important. Culture becomes dominated by the power of certain images and brands. Society's central feature is the dominance of a new form of technocapitalism whereby capital accumulation, the knowledge revolution and new technology have combined to produce a new kind of society. The culture of the spectacle instigates a new form of domination of mass distraction, profit and the continuing expansion of social and cultural domains that fall under its sway from politics to sport and from music to the news media. However, Kellner seeks to expand Debord's original ideas by distinguishing between different kinds of media spectacle. These would include the megaspectacle (large-scale media events attracting mass audiences such as the war on terror or the funeral of Princess Diana), interactive spectacles (this involves different levels of audience participation such as eviction night on Big Brother) and more overtly political spectacles such as elections that are increasingly run as sensational media events only serving to drain them of any more substantial ethical criteria.

Henry Giroux (2006) has argued that while these features offer a more detailed analysis than Debord's own, these reflections need to be extended even further in the context of the war on terror. Here the attack on the Twin Towers was explicitly designed to shock. The events of 9/11 impress a new relationship between the power of the image and global politics. This new form of spectacle is quite different to the spectacles of fascism and consumerism that Debord (1988: 8) had previously labelled the concentrated and integrated spectacle. For Giroux, fear and terror have become the central components of the spectacle in a post-9/11 world. The war on terror politics explicitly adopts the language and metaphors of war. The society of the spectacle now involves not only the economy and the state but also the considerable power of the media and the rise of political fundamentalism. For Giroux, where Debord was mainly concerned with the dominance of consumer capitalism, in the context of the war on terror: 'the spectacle of terrorism affirms politics (of war, life, sacrifice, and death) over the aesthetics of commodification through an appeal to the real over the simulacrum' (Giroux 2006: 49). Giroux's central point is that control is less exercised through the promise of 'the good life' through consumption than it is through fear. It is then through fear of terrorism, the Other, Muslims, asylum seekers, the urban poor and others who would seemingly threaten our way of life that the erosion of the civic domain is legitimated. Nation-states have been able to exploit the spectacle of terrorism through new legislation that curtails the rights of citizens while subjecting them to increasing amounts of surveillance and control. The spectacle of terror reproduces a war against an ill-defined enemy and perhaps just as importantly against democracy and civic freedoms. Further, fundamentalist groups have exploited the politics of the spectacle using images and video technology to promote representations of suicide bombers, violent deaths and representations of abuse and torture. Just as the media utilises the spectacle in the search for higher ratings, so terrorist organisations use similar devices to attract potential supporters.

Similarly, Jean Baudrillard (2002) argues that the idea of the spectacle in the context of 9/11 evokes the memory of many disaster films and symbolises the fragility of the American empire. The so-called network society has actually managed to impose 'a single world order' and yet this has created its own forms of resistance and seeds of its own destruction (Baudrillard 2002: 12). However, the politics of war and fear are more part of Debord's original reflections than many seem to be aware. For Debord, the society of the spectacle is likely to produce terrorism as an alternative form of spectacular domination. Terrorism was likely to flourish as the dominant could be judged 'by its enemies rather than by its results' (Debord 1998: 24). Nevertheless both Giroux and Debord are in agreement that the spectacle can only be substantially challenged through the recovery of more democratic modes of dialogue. As we shall see, it has been new media's capacity to potentially encourage more democratic and dialogic forms of communication that has so excited media scholars. As Giroux notes, the idea of a homogeneous mass audience of the spectacle (which is also reminiscent of Adorno's writing) gives a false impression of the diverse forms of popular culture and resistance available within a global media age. If the politics of the spectacle has indeed enabled authoritiarian states to attempt to gain control over public life while continuing to induce citizens to desire a commodified life of ease and consumption, more democratic possibilities are also available. The combination of the seduction of glittering commodities and a fear of the Other may have provided new ways of undermining democratic forms of life, but there continue to exist other radical democratic possibilities. However, an open question at this point would need to explore the extent to which new forms of media promote the commodified life and associated cultures of fear, and to what extent modern electronic cultures give expression to more dissenting and overtly critical ways of life. To what extent can new forms of radical art and democratic practice be said to provide an alternative to the dominant culture of the capitalist spectacle?

Future developments: democracy, media and civic identity

When Williams formulated the idea of the long revolution in the 1960s, he was convinced that the learning and critical society could only emerge out of the agency of the labour move- ment. However, the 1980s was to see the arrival of a revived aggressive form of capitalism (or neoliberalism) that was hostile to organised labour and sought to remake society in more market-friendly terms including the lowering of taxes, the shrinking of the social state, priva- tisation and the increasing global mobility of capital. It was the labour movement in alliance with other creative social movements including environmentalism, feminism and the peace movement that Williams had hoped would radically democratise the rule of capital. However, if some of these movements have made real gains, there is little point denying that since the 1980s that society has become increasingly competitive, unequal and consumerist in orienta- tion. Neoliberalism has waged a war on democracy by eroding civil rights and yet more cru- cially shut down alternative democratic spaces that might have previously existed within the national media or within education. Both the media and education to this end have become increasingly integrated into the economy, progressively surrendering their independence while being subjected to political forms of control driven by privatisation, commercial forms of pro- gramming and, as we have seen, the politics of fear.

However, there have been a number of other perhaps more hopeful cultural transforma- tions that alter this pessimistic picture. The sociologist Manuel Castells (2009) has argued at some length that modern information societies are driven by cosmopolitan elites and computer- generated networks. Yet if computer networks and capital are global, then people are local. Castells argues that one of the fastest growing forms of popular resistance in the information age is the defence of the local against more global flows. Here Castells argues in this respect that one of the major contradictions of the network society is between the 'space of flows' (the control of space organised at a distance) and the attempt to recover the 'space of places' (the attempt to defend the integrity of place). The contrast between these two different spatial logics represents a fundamental fault line in the new information driven societies where knowledge is increas- ingly central to the circuits of capital. In new knowledge-driven societies, universities, levels of education, the customisation of products, market segmentation and levels of technology amongst other features have become increasingly central to the organisation of the economy. The knowledge society is driven by the need of the economy for 'useful' knowledge. The state in the informational world has lost much of its power, increasingly putting pressure on the provision of welfare while becoming the active manager of global processes it cannot control. If democratic forms of politics face a challenge in respect of the triumph of neoliberalism and the decreasing power of the state, it is also threatened by the rise of fundamentalism. In this context, Castells suggests that new democratic pressures are likely to emerge from below as locals seek to regain control over space. Of course there are dangers that the return to the local could become a form of local retrenchment and enhance an increasing fear of outsiders. Yet an important fea- ture of the new politics of social movements is the attempt to reconnect the local to more global concerns. Hence the new emphasis upon the local is not necessarily a form of retrenchment but actually an attempt to reconnect local spaces to more critical and global understandings.

The attempt to defend the local in the context of increasing levels of global awareness char- acterises a number of campaigns from the arms trade to environmentalism and from fair trade to the development of organic food provision. As Alberto Melucci (1996) argues, the ability of social movements to open new public spaces, re-interpret dominant discourses and suggest alternative frameworks are the central features determining their success or failure. The devel- opment of new forms of interconnection through the Internet, argues Melucci, has radically multiplied the number of communities and networks to which we can belong. This potentially weakens the grip of an older set of coordinates in respect of the construction of identity allowing for the development of new possibilities. As Kahn and Kellner (2004) argue, the emergence of Internet subcultures has significantly redefined social networking, blogs and other new media forums as places of learning, democracy and struggle. This has given rise to a new politics that can be less accurately described as localisation but as a form of globalisation from below that crucially links the local and the global. It is then the ability to act locally while maintaining a link to global concerns and developments that best describe the new politics of social movements. The interconnection of locally based social movements and global communications networks has allowed for the emergence of globally orientated local identities and agencies. Through developments in new media and social movements, what emerges are new possibilities for democratised social and cultural relationships. Crucially important in this context has been the rise of what has been called the blogosphere, where literally millions of people across the world are taking the opportunity to become cultural producers. Obviously only a small proportion of these pages will be connected to social movements and yet they potentially radically alter the possibilities for critical politics.

The development of the blogosphere is significant given its potential to allow for public forms of communication, the content of which is not directly controlled by powerful media organisations. If old media was centralised and hierarchical in the way that they organised the production of meaning, then new media forms such as blog sites offer the possibility of more horizontal structures that allow for two-way forms of communication. Blog sites make space not only for the development of the voice of particular cultural producers, but also for the posting of alternative opinions and perspectives. If more traditional media disallow the communicative practice of answering back (other than through carefully managed letters pages or other means), then new media forms suggest the emergence of more dialogic and democratic relationships. However, we need to be careful in steering clear of the argument that new technology simply makes the media more democratic. The argument that democratic engagement is the effect of certain technologies is obviously deeply misleading. It is equally troublesome to assume that technologies themselves do not have certain properties that more easily lend themselves to certain political positions rather than others. It is this aspect of the argument taken up by Brecht and Benjamin that I wish to argue has radical implications for the development of more democratic and engaged subjectivities. Indeed, if some of Brecht's and Benjamin's critics were worried that they simply assumed that new media technologies were of themselves democratising, then there is no need to reproduce these arguments now.

Further, if we consider the history of social movements, we discover a long history that sought to develop 'alternative' forms of communication. Perhaps not surprisingly, emancipatory movements in the past have tried to blur the boundaries between professional journalism and the audience. Many radical publications have sought to encourage participants within particular social movements not only to develop a more civic sense of self, but also to become actively involved through the publication of an alternative press in shaping the aims, objectives and horizons of social movements. While of course many alternative movements have remained connected to more authoritarian modes of politics and communication, others have sought to link communicative and aesthetic questions to the construction of a more active public sphere. As John H. Downing (2001) argues, in this respect there are historically two different models of alternative media. This would include a Marxist–Leninist model that seeks to transmit the views of an alternative social elite and a self-management tradition mainly concerned with a more democratic future built upon popular forms of communication and political participation. There is a recognition evident within all of the writers under review that radical politics itself can easily become trapped within new forms of manipulation and authoritarianism. Notably it was the self-management tradition that Raymond Williams sought to defend within his writing on media and communications and wider social movements. It is also the self-management tradition that sits most comfortably with the idea of an active and participatory public sphere. Here the radical democratic demand is not merely to imagine a different future, but also to begin, where possible, to practise the future more emancipated society in the present. Further, as Downing recognises, communication cannot be limited to 'rational' speech but would need to include a wide number of aesthetic practices including dance, theatre, music, performance art and other features. Even before the rise of the Internet, radical social movements had a long history of experimenting with alternative forms of communication. However, many of these publications and aesthetic experiences were unlikely to attract very large audiences. Many radical publications simply failed due to poor circulation and high start-up costs to find large audiences outside of a small circle of committed activists. What then is exciting about the Internet and blogging is that potentially the audiences are greater as distribution is now not necessarily restricted to a few outlets. The starting of a radical newspaper or television network is mostly restricted to the networks of the rich and powerful and yet anyone with access to the Internet can set up a blog site.

This has caused a considerable amount of debate amongst media scholars discussing the potential rise of the citizen journalist. Here the argument is that mobile phones, digital cameras and access to the Internet potentially allows ordinary citizens to become campaigners writing their own material and discussing their own views. Yet many have argued that despite the more accessible nature of the Internet, most of these sites are read by relatively few people (although we cannot always be sure about this) and that most of the communication that goes on within social movements is in maintaining their own in-group solidarity rather than in conversing with a wide range of citizens. In other words, media as Castells (2009) recognises, continues to be dominated by television and not interactive forms. Despite the explosion of new media it is still mainstream television networks that have the most influence in shaping the opinions, perspectives and understandings of the majority and this is likely to remain the case for the foreseeable future. In addition, Castells (2009: 51) adds that timeless time continues to dominate the consciousness of most citizens despite the new possibilities for resistant identities in the network age. Timeless time is the time of the now and the immediate (and I would add 'the spectacle') that seems to be dominant. Contemporary televisual global culture is constructed through the dominance of 24-hour news, the culture of celebrity, advertisements and quickly forgotten fashions. The challenge for radical movements is not only to connect with local identities and spaces that are under threat from global corporations but also to recover historical memory. In the media-dominated society, many citizens have become disconnected from a complex understanding of their own histories and radical traditions and it is these understandings that radical movements arguably need to reinvent and rediscover.

What is perhaps missing from the analysis of those such as Castells and Melucci who have sought to outline the radical possibilities of new forms of communication is an emphasis upon commodification. As Adorno (1991), Debord (1994) and Jameson (1998) might recognise, technologies of communication are not only pieces of technology but are themselves commodities. The culture of computers, iPods, flat-screen televisions and, of course, mobile phones are themselves marketed, branded and advertised commodities. If technologies are far from netural in terms of the effect that they have in shaping certain kinds of conversations we might have, they have also been converted into 'must have' commodities. Further, it is a matter of exploration as to whether these new forms of communication actually enhance the capacity of the civil sphere for dialogue and learning or whether they simply commodify the realm of everyday life. The complexity of these problems can be seen if we look at two recent social movements.

Nick Stevenson

The Make Poverty History campaign came to the fore in 2005 and was utilised by a number of development charities such as Oxfam to promote ideas of global solidarity and press the governing structures of global finance into action to reduce global poverty. In order to mobilise support amongst a wider public, Make Poverty History tried to create a visible form of politics by gaining the support of well-known campaigning celebrities such as Bob Geldoff and rock band U2's lead singer Bono. The campaign actively encouraged ordinary people to buy fashionable white bands and to text or email the government to end global poverty. In the UK, the BBC ran a series of programmes on global poverty under the strap line 'Africa Lives on the BBC' and during the summer broadcast the high-profile *Live 8* concert that included Pink Floyd, Madonna and Coldplay. The use of new media and music was deliberately utilised in order to gain support amongst young people. In terms of wider questions of pedagogy, the campaign failed to raise critical awareness about a number of questions in respect of global poverty. There was little historical context or indeed any mention of colonial histories or more exploitative social conditions that have played a role in creating the conditions of global poverty. Further, social movements were not offered media space to develop alternative perspectives and more critical understandings of 'development'. Instead, much of the media focused upon Western forms of generosity and a number of dominant images that gave the impression that the ending of global poverty was a matter of lifestyle choice rather than political contestation. Despite the role of new media and some leading development organisations, the Make Poverty History campaign (with some notable exceptions) was more about the politics of the spectacle than it was of developing a critical and a radical politics. The media content of the campaign in this respect failed to develop a critical cultural politics only further impressing dominant ideas about Western superiority and African underdevelopment. This example should serve as a warning that the presence of new media does not necessarily develop more civic and democratic identities, but can actually lead to their cancellation.

Alternatively, we might consider the case of the Transition Movement. The Transition Movement is a complex network organisation whose primary aim might be described as the development of a web-like structure seeking to prepare localities for a post-oil world. In pursuing these ends, the Transition Movement has a relatively flat organisational structural that is mainly driven by the enthusiasm of local members. It is different from other prominent environmental groups such as Friends of the Earth and Greenpeace as it is less centrally organised and is not as concerned to attract the attention of the media through symbolic protest. However, the Transition Movement is distinctive in that it has the aim of becoming a mass movement of ordinary citizens – the central aim being to promote local forms of resilience in terms of the local growing of food and promotion of low carbon lifestyles. The Transition Movement like other so-called 'new' social movements is less motivated by the distribution of wealth than a politics orientated around questions such as the quality of life, participation and life style. Further, the Transition Movement is extremely web-literate, making use of new media such as web and blog sites, discussion boards and of course YouTube. Much of this material is for the dissemination of information both internal and external to local groups. However, the example of the Transition Movement also points to the use of other media. Local groups regularly organise film nights to get local people interested in their activities and target local media such as radio, television and the press. In this respect, much media criticism could be said to be overstating the role of new media in the formation of oppositional and critical identities. However, it is true to say the Transition Movement is heavily reliant upon easily accessible new media. The use of blog sites and other forms of new media do indeed point to a more dialogic structure than might be said to be available to more traditional movements. The Transition Movement is a good example of a movement that is both global and local at the same time. Perhaps these brief examples should caution those who seek to make sweeping assumptions about the role of new media in the formation of resistant identities, and yet it is clear that new communicative forms cannot simply be dismissed as commodified forms but carry with them a set of democratic possibilities.

As we have seen, the relationship between the media and formation of collective cultural and personal identity is complex. Here I have sought to demonstrate the historically shifting nature of these arguments, and maintain that the media theory produced during different periods (albeit in a modified form) continues to be important to the ways in which we understand these relationships today. Undoubtedly, contemporary media has become increasingly driven by commercial imperatives seeking to promote the dominant culture of the spectacle and thereby commodifying increasing areas of social and cultural life. As I have argued, this overwhelmingly serves to drive out more democratic spaces as large media conglomerates and corporations increasingly serve to dominate socially organised communicative relations. Further, in the context of the 'war on terror', media is actively involved in the promotion of fear and the undermining of a shared civic culture based upon liberal freedoms. Yet before this analysis is pushed too far, more democratic and resistant identities through the development of the Internet have been handed new possibilities to develop alternative meanings and critical perspectives. More careful and detailed work needs to be done in this area so that we are able to carefully trace through the kind of complex pedagogic relations that are emerging in this area. Social movements through the use of new media (and other forms of communication) have a potentially transformative role to play in remaking more critical identities in the context of a modern culture that is increasingly being shaped by modern capitalism. Finally, I would argue that the new work on the Internet and social movements should seek to become connected to an earlier radical agenda that sought to argue for a democratised public sphere. Cultural institutions such as the BBC are far from being relics of the past but still, even in the age of the Internet, provide a widely trusted and still mostly (although this is changing) uncommodified zone that is accountable to members of the public and democratically elected politicians. In this respect, Williams's idea of the long revolution is far from over but needs to be expanded to include the radical possibilities of the present.

Given the impact of neoliberalism in creating increasingly unequal, competitive and commodified societies, public broadcasters have a special responsibility to give opportunities to give voice to marginalised members of the public. That this is not happening to the degree that it might suggests that public service media is less concerned with serving the public than it is with competing with its commercial rivals, satisfying the rituals of parliamentary democracy and of following established rules of professional conduct. If in the 1960s Williams perceived a new generation of working-class voices making themselves heard through new forms of cultural production, today such optimism would be misplaced. Indeed, the bodies of working-class people are often featured on reality telelvision exhibiting criminal behaviour, excessive consumption and 'vulgar' forms of popular taste. These normalising images are less based upon the politics of voice and complexity than the politics of class distinction and spectacle. A popular politics of voice and democracy in relation to mediated forms is dependent upon wider social and cultural structures and can never be considered simply to be the effect of new media forms. Yet I have also cautioned against simply dismissing new media as being just another commodity as it is still capable of radically democratising (often in surprising ways) our shared public spheres. The open question here is: how is the struggle for a more democratic media system likely to be effected by the arrival of new Internet and other technologies? This is not only a matter for theoretical debate, but also for careful analysis and empirical research in the future. While the dominant media system is likely to remain in tension for a number of years to come, what remains to be seen is whether the identity frames it seeks to foster are democratically oriented based upon a culture of voice and critical engagement or will the politics of the spectacle become even further entrenched within the media system. These crucial questions will keep alive a discussion which we have seen has a long, contested and complex history.

References

Adorno, T. (1991) *The Culture Industry*. London: Routledge.
Baudrillard, J. (2002) *The Spirit of Terrorism and Other Essays*. London: Verso.
Benjamin, W. (1973) *Illuminations*. London: Fontana.
Benjamin, W. (1978) *Reflections*. New York: A Helen and Kurt Wolf Book.
Benjamin, W. (1998) *Understanding Brecht*. London: Verso.
Castells, M. (2009) *Communication Power*. Oxford: Oxford University Press.
Debord, G. (1988) *Comments on the Society of the Spectacle*. London: Verso.
Debord, G. (1994) *The Society of the Spectacle*. New York: Zone Books.
Downing, J. (2001) *Radical Media: Rebellious Communication and Social Movements*. London: Sage.
Enzensberger, H.M. (1970) 'Constituents of a theory of the media', *New Left Review* 64: 13–36.
Giroux, H. (2006) *Beyond the Spectacle of Terrorism*. London: Paradigm Publishers.
Habermas, J. (1989) *The Structural Transformation of the Public Sphere*. Cambridge: Polity Press.
Habermas, J. (1996) *Between Facts and Norms*. Cambridge: Polity Press.
Jameson, F. (1991) *The Cultural Turn*. London: Verso.
Kellner, D. (2003) *Media Spectacle*. London: Routledge
Kahn, R. and Kellner, D. (2004) 'New media and internet activism: from the 'Battle of Seattle' to blog-ging', *New Media and Society* 6(1): 87–95.
Melucci, A. (1996) *The Playing Self: Person and Meaning in the Planetary Society*. Cambridge: Cambridge University Press.
Stevenson, N. (2003) *Cultural Citizenship*. Basingstoke: Open University Press.
Williams, R. (1962) *The Long Revolution*. London: Pelican.
Williams, R. (1980) *Culture and Materialism*. London: Verso.
Williams, R. (1989) *What I Came to Say*. London: Hutchinson Radius.
Wolin, R. (1994) *Walter Benjamin: An Aesthetic of Redemption*. Berkeley: University of California Press.

13

Virtual identities

From decentered to distributed selves

Sam Han

Introduction

In 2009 November, the *New Oxford American Dictionary* announced that the Word of the Year is "unfriend," solidifying the arrival of the Web into the lexicological mainstream (Gross 2009). The entry reads:

> unfriend – verb – To remove someone as a "friend" on a social networking site such as Facebook.
>
> As in, "I decided to *unfriend* my roommate on Facebook after we had a fight."
>
> *(Ford 2009)*

This announcement is further supported by findings of a Harris Interactive Poll that puts average Internet usage per capita at thirteen hours a week, which is almost twice as much as that of 2000 (Malik 2009).

For an increasing number of people around the globe, the Web as a major social force is not news. Thus, statistics about growing Internet use as well as the selection of "unfriend" as Word of the Year is, at best, notable and, at worst, unremarkable. The kind of unspectacular nature of the Web in many parts of the globe signals a major shift in the study of new media technologies, and in turn identity. We have perhaps reached a threshold of integration, a kind of point of no return, where the future of the world will undoubtedly be affected by new technologies.

The "what if . . .?" tone of media criticism and scholarship in the first wave of the widespread use of the Internet characteristic of the 1990s has been replaced in the new century with a "what will . . .?" This is reflective of the changing nature of the Web itself (note the recent discourse of "Web 2.0" initiated by technologist Tim O'Reilly). Indeed, the significant rise in time spent online means that many people, especially youth, have incorporated technologies into their daily lives. Everything from banking to grocery shopping can be done via the World Wide Web, not to mention the more "usual" practices of music procurement and socializing.

For identity studies, the status of "normal" that these technologies have achieved should come as a warning: to study identity without any consideration of media technologies would be to completely ignore the ways in which they have affected old forms of identity-construction and created new ones. This will inevitably be the case for the youth of today, who, unlike their older siblings, parents and grandparents, grew up with these technologies, if not readily at hand, in the culture in a significant manner.

Some scholars have argued that media and technology, in the broadest sense, have always aided the process of creating identity, and even to the "humanness" of humanity. Philosopher Bernard Stiegler has suggested that technological evolution is at the heart of "the invention of the human," drawing from the work of paleoanthropologist Andre Leroi-Gourhan, who argued that tools are at the core of the process of "hominization." It is this "technicity" that makes humans human, not an essential "humanity." Technics, or tools such as the flint, are means by which the "human invents himself in the technical by inventing the tool – by being exterior-ized techno-logically" (Stiegler 1998: 140). Thus, Stiegler concludes that there is an originary link between the human and the technical, and therefore the "history of technics . . . is also the history of humanity" (ibid.: 135).

So today, in a world where the World Wide Web is nearly second nature for the youth, we can say perhaps that the future direction of media and technology studies rests not on the valid-ity of the arguments of Stiegler and Leroi-Gourhan but is a matter of understanding their many vicissitudes, one of which is increasingly in the realm of identity, due to the current dominant regime of social media. Contemporary media scholars and media commentators suggest that new media technologies have reconstituted forms of subjectivity and identity, pointing not only to the ways in which identity on the Web is open to play and manipulability such as in the profiles of social networking sites but also to the ways in which computers and other tech-nologies have become smart (the newest generation of mobile phones are appropriately called "smartphones" in North America) and have perhaps gained a level of intelligence to merit a psychology. This is of course the much talked about discourse of "artificial intelligence."

The work of sociologist Manuel Castells, whose three-volume *The Information Age* is a mon-umental contribution to the sociological study of the Internet, brings some of these issues into relief. In the second volume of this trilogy, Castells deals specifically with issues of identity in a "network society," a society in which new media technologies play such a significant part. He defines identity as the source of meaning and experience for people. Unlike the sociological idea of roles, which are defined by institutional norms of a given society, identities are stronger sources of meaning than roles: it involves self-construction. Roles, however, are easily put on and taken off by individuals depending on institutional context. As Castells contends, "identi-ties organize the meaning, while roles organize the functions" (Castells 1996: 7). Identity, for Castells, implies something more meaningful than roles. Further, he suggests that meaning is usually organized around a *primary* identity, stating that a plurality of identities, though pos-sible for a given individual is possible, is unwanted and ultimately infrequent. "[A] plurality," he writes, "is a source of stress and contradiction in both self-representation and social action" (ibid.: 6).

Identities in the networked society no longer draw from what they used to in modernity, such as institutions that made up what was called civil society, which is "withering" as Michael Hardt has written (Hardt 1995). Although he asserts that he is by no means a "postmodern" theorist, Castells nevertheless argues that the modern understanding of identity no longer holds when looking at the impact of the Internet. In contrasting identity in network society to the "reflexivity" thesis of Anthony Giddens (see Chapter 5 this volume), Castells states that "because the network society is based on the systemic disjunction of the local and the global for most individuals," reflexive life-planning, one of Giddens's chief theoretical concepts, becomes nearly impossible (Castells 1996: 12).

This chapter will probe some of the issues raised by Castells in order to provide a critical overview of the major theories of identity as they relate to new media technologies, especially the World Wide Web, and give an account of the change in the approaches to identity by tracing the waning of one regime of new media to another. Though "virtual identity" may not be the best term, it will function provisionally to describe identities constituted through new media technologies. It will begin with an assessment of what can be called the first wave of virtual identity studies, with the work of Sherry Turkle and Howard Rheingold, two of the earliest writers that dealt with the implications of computing and the Internet on identity. Their work focuses mainly on some of the earliest virtual "communities" called MUDs (Multi-User Dungeon) and WELLs (Whole Earth 'Lectronic Link). It will also go over some of the critical engagements with these scholars, in particular that of Slavoj Žižek. Then it will proceed to "the second wave" of virtual identity studies, summarizing the work of danah boyd, Michele White and Lisa Nakamura. Unlike the work of Turkle and Rheingold, these authors focus on more contemporary uses of media technologies, in particular social networking. The chapter will finally conclude with mention of some perspectives critical of the continuing virtualization of identity that accuse virtual identities of threatening the individuality of the users of technology.

The historical and intellectual development of virtual identity studies

With the publication of *The Second Self: Computers and the Human Spirit* (1984) and later *Life on the Screen: Identity in the Age of the Internet* (1995), Sherry Turkle quickly became established as *the* social scientist working in the field of human–computer relations. Some have described her research as "subjectivist" or "psychological," which comes as no surprise since Turkle is a trained clinical psychologist and deeply engaged with psychoanalysis. And perhaps it is due to this psychoanalytic background (her first book being on Lacan), that she so ably discusses issues of subjectivity and identity in relation to technology.

For the purposes of this chapter, Turkle's work is representative of the "first wave" of virtual identity studies, which focused mostly on the study of what Howard Rheingold called "virtual communities." Rheingold defined it thus:

> Imaginary worlds in computer databases where people use words and programming languages to improvise melodramas, build worlds and all the objects in them, solve puzzles, invent amusements and tools, compete for prestige and power, gain wisdom seek revenge, indulge greed and lust and violent impulses.
>
> *(Rheingold 1993: 145)*

The work of Turkle and Rheingold and others of this wave centered on the ways in which members of such communities reinvented themselves to form "second selves," identities that were removed from their "real" (or non-virtual) lives. Members of communities were using these technologies to gender-swap, create multiple personas, etc.; thus, multiple and decentered identities became a meme of sorts that defined this wave. As this was the early years of virtual communities, the scholarship of this wave was focused also on the legitimacy of online social interactions. The connections forged in MUDs and WELLs were indeed very real, they argued.

This tendency of what I am calling the first wave of virtual identity studies is nowhere more apparent than in Turkle's *The Second Self*. In it, she presents the dynamic of identities in virtual communities as comprising construction and projection. This, she argues, is especially the case among adolescent computer users. As a constructive medium, computer programming becomes a means by which to construct what she calls a "microworld" (Turkle 1984). A microworld is "a world apart in which to build a new set of distinctions" for oneself and others. Deborah, a thirteen-year-old interview subject, utilizes computer programming to create a world that was tightly regimented by rules. According to Turkle, Deborah views the computer program as a "microworld" of control in order to explain her own issues of cutting class or eating too much candy.

> The computer provided this world. It gave her categories more useful than good or bad: things could be in or out of control. With the new distinction came a new way to think about her problems: I am in trouble because I have no rules. I am not in control. And I should be. I can be.
>
> *(ibid.: 145)*

The program thus becomes a means by which Deborah can interpret problems of control in her own life. The regimented nature of the computer program she uses, a drawing program Logo, in which she must dictate specific commands to draw pictures, becomes a world into which she is able to inject herself as in-control. The computer program, the microworld, becomes a reflection of her (albeit idealized) self.

Turkle argues that these kinds of interactions demonstrate a kind of mirror-tendency, whereby the computer "allow[s] us to see ourselves from the outside, and to objectify aspects of ourselves we had perceived only from within" (ibid.: 155), a clear nod to the theory of the mirror-stage of psychoanalyst Jacques Lacan. The computer functions as the mirror in Lacan's original formulation. It necessitates an objectification of the self in the identity-construction process.

Though some may argue that this an illusion, akin to a kind of hypnotherapy, Turkle would argue that this is not the case. She maintains that the computer, in Deborah's case, is a cyber-companion, a machine to think with, not simply "use." This brings us to an important tenet of Turkle's approach to identity studies. She rejects what philosopher Martin Heidegger once called the "anthropological view of technology" that sees machines as mere instruments for human use. Thus, the machine, without the human user, is undynamic and meaningless. This could not be further from the case for Turkle. She views the machine as a coexisting entity that helps articulate the identity of its user. It is, in some way, that which facilitates the formation of identity.

This brings us to another aspect of Turkle's work on identity, which has to do with ideas around Artificial Intelligence (AI) and the machinic metaphor of the self and human conscious-ness. Turkle's rejection of the anthropological or instrumental view of technology extends to the consideration of the machine having a "mind" or even that human minds function like "machines." The ease with which people metaphorize the human mind as a machine, Turkle suggests, is an indication of its irreducibility.

She goes even further and suggests that there is a specific aspect of the computer that makes it so close to the human mind – emergence. Emergence, according to Turkle, is similar to learning or feedback as Norbert Wiener, the father of cybernetics, the science to which much of computing is indebted. The idea that computers are unlike humans because computers do what they are "programmed" to do whereas humans do not, she writes, does not capture how computers work in the least. In fact, one does not tell computers what to do. "You don't have to tell the computer everything it needs to know; you have to arrange for it to obtain – by being told or by learning – the elements out of which something nonprogrammed can 'emerge'" (Turkle 1984: 277–8). Therefore, the relationship between computer and human cannot be described as cause and effect; it is more complicated as is the relationship between the human mind and body. Instead, she suggests that a more apt metaphor would be that of a multiprocessor. Multiprocessing entails a production system, akin to a "little society inhabited by agents each of which can recognize a specific condition and, when it arises, carry out a specific job . . . [T]he order in which the agents do their jobs is not determined by the program but by the environment in which the system finds itself" (ibid.: 282).

To think of the self in this way flies in the face of the modern, unitary self. It challenges the idea of a unitary self, which is deeply embedded into the culture of the modern West. As Turkle writes,

> The assumption that there is an "I" is solidly built into ordinary language, so much so that it is almost impossible to express "anti-ego" theory in language. From the moment that we begin to write or speak, we are trapped in formulations such as "I want," "I do," "I think."
>
> *(ibid.: 291)*

Thus, to think that the mind as a machine, no less a multiprocessing computer, according to Turkle, is to entertain the possibility of the "decentralized" self, where "there is no 'me,' no 'I,' no unitary actor" (ibid.: 290). Further, it is to call into question the machine/human distinction as Donna Haraway's work pointed toward (see Chapter 5 this volume).

It should come as no surprise that Turkle's analysis has been labeled "postmodern," in both complimentary and derogatory ways. The discourse of the "death of the subject" and "decentering" found in post-structuralism and postmodernism, she readily admits, has been presented as actualized in the practices of computer users.

This is nowhere more evident in virtual communities such as MUDs.

It is in these virtual environments, Turkle argues, that participants become authors of themselves, constructing new selves through social interaction. Users of virtual communities exercise the flexibility of virtual identity in various ways. Most users, such as Rheingold, have multiple accounts in various communities that do not necessarily correlate. Rheingold even admits, "I have three or four personae myself, in different virtual communities around the Net" (1993).

For Turkle, this multiplicity is a symptom of a deeper structural aspect of MUDS – anonymity.

> The anonymity of MUDs gives people the chance to express multiple and often unexplored aspects of the self, to play with their identity and to try out new ones. MUDs make possible the creation of an identity so fluid and multiple that it strains the limits of the notion. Identity, after all, refers to the sameness of two qualities, in this case between a person and his or her persona. But in MUDs, one can be many.
>
> *(Turkle 1996)*

As many researchers of the Internet during the 1980s and 1990s noted, much of the fluidity of online identities was actualized in "virtual gender-swapping," and indeed it is not a small part. As Turkle notes, on Habitat, a Japanese MUD, the ratio of "real-life men" to "real-life women" is 4:1 but the ratio of virtual men to women is 3:1. Additionally, some MUDders engage in virtual sex, as characters of their own gender or another. A yet smaller group engages in sex as not even humans but as animals in FurryMUDs. Gender swapping and virtual sex point toward the intellectual shift necessitated by virtual communities such as MUDs. It forces us to rethink the singularity of identity. In sum, Turkle proposes to view the effect of virtual communities as having achieved a vision of identity as multiple but also integrated, "whose flexibility, resilience and capacity for joy comes from having access to many selves" (ibid.).

Major claims and developments, and key contributions of recent virtual identity studies

Though the early wave of virtual identity studies made "disembodiment" a meme, it seems that more recent scholars of virtual identity studies have "rediscovered" the body, particularly it relates to the study of race and gender in various Web spaces. As media scholar of race and ethnicity Lisa Nakamura notes,

> In the days before widely supported graphic images generated on the fly using Web browsers became a common aspect of Internet use, the Internet was effectively a text-only space, and conversation by e-mail, chat, bulletin board, or MUD . . . was the most popular way to communicate. Users' racial [or gender] identities could not be seen as they interacted with others.
>
> *(Nakamura 2008: 1673–4)*

New media scholar Mark Hansen voices similar disdain for the rather limited study of the body in the first-wave of Internet studies and the study of technoculture more broadly. Although he acknowledges the work of the first wave of virtual identity scholars to articulate a non-identitarian relationship between the body and identity, Hansen believes that it ultimately underemphasized the "primordial tactility" of the body. He suggests that one can fruitfully look at technology's impact on experience through the lens of "disembodied embodiment" or "embodied disembodiment." It retains the indubitable effect on the traditional "body" that new media technologies facilitate while not completely jettisoning materiality. Earlier studies of virtual identity, he asserts, fell prey to the tendency to remove the brain from the body, which he rightly notes defies science and everyday bodily experience; hence, his call for studying technology *beyond* writing (Hansen 2000).

Therefore, a major consequence of this shift in virtual identity studies has been the recent reconsideration of the human body in relation to virtual communities. The first wave of virtual identity studies looked mainly at MUDs and WELLs, which exhibited a fundamental disembodying effect for its users, producing a wholly "textual identity." For these scholars, these virtual communities symbolized a delinking of identity with the physical body, which Žižek, as noted above, associated with postmodern theory. But with the emergence of a new kind of Web, and new types of virtual community, more greatly reliant upon graphics, the body, and identity more generally, cannot be said to be merely textual. Today, digital bodies are visualized and represented in cyberspace through "a series of hierarchical choices, mimicking the menu structure of modern operating systems interfaces" (Nakamura 2008: 203). What Nakamura is referring to is the way in which, for instance, avatars and profiles are constructed through the formal structures of drop-down menus. So while there is an unprecedented level of self-representability and customizability of the digital body, there are, as Nakamura notes, severe restrictions, as these customization options are given by certain webspaces.

The work of Michele White will help us elucidate this. White argues that online identities in fact stabilize identities in ways unremarked upon by the early wave of virtual identity studies. For instance, she looks at the forms which individuals must use to create accounts in portals such as Google and Yahoo!. As she notes, many of these forms ask for traditional identifiers such as gender and age. In the case of Yahoo!, the only options for gender are "Male" and "Female," and does not have the option not to respond or write one in. Furthermore, Yahoo!'s legal notice states that one must provide "true and accurate" information when creating accounts, and failure to do so could result in the termination of the account. Though clearly users of Yahoo! and other, similar portals have figured out ways around such formal rigidity, as White notes, Yahoo! and other portals "underscore traditional forms of identity and indicate that there are risks and limits to anonymity for their spectators [users]" (White 2006: 26). She, therefore, concludes that virtual identities for the most part utilize social categories that exist offline and thus mirror traditional categories of identification.

This kind of formal rigidity in the account creation process has significant effect on conceptions of identity. Highlighting the use of binary gender categories, White evokes film theorist Teresa de Lauretis's claim that checking boxes in forms, thought it seems like a banal act, categorizes, orders and shapes the individual's self-conception, for the individual begins to identify with and self-represents that gender. Thus, White reminds us that despite the early cheers of the possibilities of anonymity in MUDs and WELLs, traditional categories of identity remain online.

Along these lines, in recent virtual identity studies, privacy and anonymity have been a major concern. Writings in this realm have been centered on questions of authentication, especially since identity theft has become a pervasive scare for many as more and more activities such as banking and grocery shopping are done online. Lawrence Lessig, probably the most well-known American scholar of all matters cyberspace, defines identity as "your name, your sex, where you live, what your education is, your driver's license number, your social security number, your purchases on Amazon.com, whether you're a lawyer – and so on" (Lessig 2000: 30–1).

Authentication is how your identity becomes known. This occurs in different ways. You can choose to divulge some aspects; others are known without much choice. This is usually the case offline. As Lessig notes, "much about your identity is revealed whether you want it revealed or not. Many of the facts about you, that is, are *automatically asserted* and *self-authenticating*" (ibid.: 31). These aspects are usually phenotypical; they are physical characteristics of the person. Lessig describes this particularly well:

> If I walk into a bank, the teller will know a lot about me even if I don't say a thing: he will know I'm a puffy, middle-aged white guy with glasses and blondish hair; he will know I'm not big and not strong, though I am somewhat tall. He will know all this whether I want to tell him or not.
>
> *(ibid.: 31)*

However, as he notes, there are other things about him that the teller could not possibly know, such as one's favorite flavor of ice cream or favorite book. There are other aspects of one's identity that can only be authenticated through *credentials*. Indeed, credentials are what we usually think of when we think of authentication. Credentials usually come in the form of a document, such as government-issued ID, which still in some instances is required when making purchases with a credit card in the US. In turn, the legitimacy of the document is dependent upon the issuing institution. Social interaction offline is then highly reliant upon authentication.

Lessig suggests that as social life continues to become ever more complex and anonymous, a process most aptly captured in Baudelaire's figure of the "flaneur," which served as inspiration to both Georg Simmel (1972) and Walter Benjamin (2006). "As life becomes more anonymous," writes Lessig, "social institutions must construct credentials to authenticate facts about you that in an earlier time, or in a smaller social world, would have been authenticated by the knowledge of the community about who you are" (Lessig 2000: 31). However, anonymity,

Sam Han

not authentication, is the default of social relations online. In the TCP/IP suite, the protocols upon which the Internet exists, "reveal nothing about the user of the Internet, and very little about the data being exchanged" (ibid.: 32). Though there are still forms of identification on the Internet, such as IP (Internet Protocol) addresses, these do not authenticate. That is to say, there is no way to ensure one's identity. "Whereas in real space . . . anonymity has to be created, in cyberspace anonymity is the given" (ibid.: 33). The absence of self-authenticating mechanisms that exist in "real space" decreases the potential for regulation. Cyberspace becomes a haven for what sociologist Erving Goffman called "impression management" (Goffman 1959).

Therefore certain "architectures of identification" have been developed in order for individuals to be not only identified but also authenticated. These include cookies – small file placed onto your hard disk that lets sites know who you are, passwords in account creation, and digital certificates, which utilize cryptographic technologies. In Lessig's estimation, cryptographic technologies are the most significant technologies on the Internet as it relates to identity. For him, cryptography circumvents the key problem of entrusting identification and confidentiality.

> In its "confidentiality" function it can be "used to keep communications secret." In its identification function it can be "used to provide forgery-proof digital identities." It thus enables from regulation (as it enhances confidentiality), but it can also enable regulation (as it enhances identification).
>
> *(Baker and Hurst 1998: xv; Lessig 2000: 36)*

What we have then, in Lessig's discussion of identity, regulation, and confidentiality, is support to White's point about the extant nature of the traditional categories of identification, that what constitutes identity offline – the physical body – have, quite simply, moved online. The issue, some would say, is about how to encode one's already-existing (real space) identity into the virtual.

In addition to the issue of confidentiality and anonymity, there is another way in which offline identity is reconstituted in virtual identities – avatars. Avatars are the "visual representations that are employed in . . . graphical communications settings" (White 2006: 120). One can think of them as analogous to profiles in social networking sites. As Nakamura notes, it is in the creation of avatars that race becomes interestingly reintroduced in a space that was said to have removed traditional forms of identification.

> Digital avatars, or renditions of self, provide pipelines into the phantasmatic world of identities, those conscious or not-so-conscious racial desires and narratives that users construct and inhabit during their interactions in cyberspace.
>
> *(Nakamura 2002: 32)*

Nakamura makes an important observation when discussing the place of race in avatar-construction: the shift from mostly text-based virtual communities to graphic-based ones has had a tremendous effect on how identity is performed and constructed. This, in turn, makes the study of racial identity on the Internet all the more prescient, since the kind of anonymity heralded by early web critics was based on textual virtual communities. While she acknowledges that the Internet allows for performed identities, the kind of racial "passing" that occurs on the Web still overlooks structural cultural inequities that exist in real life, that are translated into social spaces on the Internet. Thus, Nakamura, in her work questions the celebration of the Internet as "democratic, 'race-less' place" (Nakamura 2001: 10).

The case that Nakamura studies closely is the avatar-customization in a chat space called Club Connect at NetNoir, a website for mostly African American issues. In this space, she tells us, there are vending machines where one could replace various features of one's avatar, such as hair color, skin color and hair texture. One time, she received a gift of a new "head" from a fellow user on Club Connect. The head was blonde and white-skinned, while Nakamura's avatar had been dark-haired and black. While attempting to rectify the problem of having arms of one complexion and the head of another, Nakamura found that there were vending machines that offer virtual tanning sprays. All of this happened, she indicates, without a single mention of race.

This fact points not merely "to the extent to which race has become elective in cyberspace" but to how it

> is constructed as a matter of aesthetics, or finding the color that you "like," rather than as a matter of ethnic identity or shared cultural referents. This fantasy of "color" divorced from politics, oppression, or racism seems to also celebrate color, as infinitely changeable and customizable, as entirely elective as well as non-political.
>
> *(ibid.: 10)*

Race exists in this particular chat space as a commodity, a decoration, to add to your avatar. It is for this reason that Nakamura gives the experience of avatar-construction and customization the name "identity tourism." Graphic-based virtual communities such as chat spaces that require avatars and allow for avatar-customization do not eliminate race in the least bit, but reconstitutes it as a commodity, a product for sale. Hence, anyone can "pass" on the Internet. Nakamura goes on to argue that this is reflective of the dominant, neoliberal ideology of multiculturalism that proclaims a post-racial world in which one, in the words of American satirist and television personality Stephen Colbert, "does not see race."

Media researcher danah boyd gives us another perspective regarding embodiment and the Web. From her more sociological stance, she argues that the social function of the body as a chief source for identity in real life becomes replaced by "the profile" on the Web, especially among youth. The body, in the case of boyd, is not a marker of race and gender but of cultural taste.

Boyd begins by offering a theory of social networks such as MySpace and Facebook as "networked publics." Networked publics are distinct from unmediated publics because of four properties: (1) persistence, (2) searchability, (3) replicability, and (4) invisible audiences. By persistence, she is pointing to the fact that networked communications usually are stored online somewhere. This allows for "event-ual," asynchronous communication. By searchability, boyd refers to the online communication that is done through text (even photographs are "tagged" on Facebook and Flickr and other photo-sharing websites). Replicability refers to the fact that text can easily be copied and pasted. Lastly, by invisible audiences, she is talking about the inability for one to see who exactly has seen the various self-expressions on social networks.

But before moving on to the dynamics of identity formation on social networks, one must ask why people join in the first place. According to boyd's ethnographic work, many young people who join MySpace, one of the more popular social networks, do so to "maintain connections with their friends" (boyd 2007). But as boyd suggests, part of the appeal has to do with not only social voyeurism, getting to see what others are doing without recourse (indeed "Facebook Stalking" has become a term that frequently used), but also personal representation, the ability to present one's self usually through profile creation, which is requisite for most social networks.

Profiles, then, are the chief means by which members of a social network interact with each other and thus construct their online identities. Though with significant variation between certain social networks, profiles always involve certain aspects, including forms that allow the user to write in what her favorite books, movies and music are, as well as other personal information usually skewed toward cultural taste. There is also usually a section to upload and share photos. With a social network such as MySpace, there is a further method by which users can personalize their profiles, which is through HTML and CSS modification, so as to "pimp out" their profiles.

Just as the body is the critical site for identity performance offline, boyd argues that the profile is the critical site for identity performance online. It is one's "digital body." Just as we would use gestures, clothing, and speech in order to project information about ourselves, the profile in social networking sites does the same. For boyd, "performance" is the key word here due in large part to the intellectual debt she owes to sociologist Erving Goffman, especially his concept of "impression management." To manage the impression that one gives to others is, at root, to consider identity a performance, a modular thing. With social interactions online, since the body is not immediately visible, there seems to be more control.

> They are able to carefully choose what information to put forward, thereby eliminating visceral reactions that might have seeped out in everyday communication. At the same time, these digital bodies are fundamentally coarser, making it far easier to misinterpret what someone is expressing.
>
> *(boyd 2007)*

Hence, as boyd suggests, users of social networks can "write themselves into being" through profiles.

This phenomenon of impression management of virtual identities is what boyd refers to as "faceted":

> Based on the situation, people only present a particular facet of their internal identity into a social identity for others to perceive. Based on the situation, people only present a particular facet of their internal identity for consideration. Depending on their own need to self-monitor, an individual manages what is to be seen dependent on the environment, thereby creating a social performance where they offer different faces to convey different facets of their identity.
>
> *(boyd 2002: 11)*

One thing to note is that boyd sees herself as arguing against the fragmentation or multiplicity thesis, of which Turkle is an exemplar. The notion of "facet" retains the figure of "the agent," an irreducible core of the individual who negotiates the various aspects or facets of her identity online. It does not, for boyd, signal the collapse or "end" of the individual as found in postmodern discourses of identity but rather an increase in control over one's social identity. Thus, it is the emergence of a "flexible" self, not the dissolution of the self entirely.

Boyd argues this through the lens of what she calls "context" and at times "architecture." One of the infrastructural features of the Web is its spatiality. This results in a practice common to many such as creating multiple email accounts, and using certain accounts to associate with particular contexts. According to boyd, the practice of creating multiple accounts is demonstrative of the localization of identity:

In doing so, people have started a new paradigm of social interaction online. Although this may initially appear peculiar, multiple email addresses/handles fill a desired void of the digital realm – the ability to manage the contexts locally; thus, what is aggregated is done so across a particular facet instead of a particular individual.

(ibid.: 42)

Hence, the practice of multiple accounts for multiple contexts for boyd demonstrates the increase in impression management that is available in molding virtual identities.

A key difference between the virtual communities of yesteryear, such as those analyzed by Turkle and Rheingold, and these new communities, social networking sites, are far less prone to the multiple identities of MUDs and WELLs, in large part, according to boyd, due to the fact that the primary audience of social networking profiles consist of peers that they know offline. In the case of Facebook, which was at first open to students of certain American colleges, the primary audience is usually those with whom you attend school. Nevertheless, there is, as boyd notes, a way in which certain practices reflect the MUDs' and WELLs' element of multiplicity and fantasy. Many users give false information regarding their age, sex and/or location. Many young people do this in order to hide their profiles from their parents, guardians and other adult figures in their life, to whom they do not wish to divulge the details of their online interactions. In most social networking sites today, there are privacy settings that may be adjusted by the user in order to control what certain people can see.

All of this is an indication of a new default in online communities. The individual and her interactions are no longer by default private. It is assumed that individuals are public first, and that the private individual is something that no longer exists (if it ever did). To use a much-talked-about example, it is common practice now for employers to check the Facebook profiles of potential hires. Thus, the idea of the solitary individual becomes far less tenable to most users of social media.

Main criticisms of virtual identity studies

There have been many who are critical of virtual identity studies, especially the work of what I earlier called the "first wave," which consists of Turkle and Rheingold, suggesting that the idea of a move from "the modernist culture of calculation to the postmodern culture of simulation," a phrase of Turkle's, is at best a myth, a kind of seductive charm of the postmodern idea of multiple, constructed selves. Perhaps the most exciting of critics who are skeptical is the Slovenian philosopher Slavoj Žižek. Though his work mostly comprises Lacanian psychoanalytic theory, Hegelian philosophy and Marx, Žižek's critique of Turkle in particular will provide a good counterpoint to the rather hopeful tone that exists in her work.

Instead of this hard break between modern and postmodern, Žižek poses looking at the changes implicated in new media technologies as the "threatening of boundaries" (Žižek 1997). As a matter of fact, it seems that he overstates the difference between his own position and that of Turkle and Rheingold. They often use the language of boundary crossing in their work. At any rate, Žižek proposes three boundaries in particular that are threatened by the new technological forms of sociality: (1) between "true life" and its mechanical simulation; (2) between objective reality and our false (illusory) perception of it; and (3) between fleeting affects, feelings and attitudes and the remaining core of the Self (Žižek 1997: 133). The third boundary, for our purposes, is of greatest interest.

As he describes it, MUDs have been misguidedly heralded as the culmination of postmodern discourses of the "decentered subject" and the "dissemination" of the self. The chief implication for this kind of argument is the prospect of both "total subjectivization," that "the human being will gradually lose its grounding in the concrete life-world – that is to say, the basic set of coordinates which determine its (self-)experience (the surface separating inside from outside, a direct relationship to one's own body, etc.)" and "total objectivization" where the body's internal rhythms are subordinated to external apparatuses (ibid.: 135). In the perverse fashion for which is he known, Žižek claims that subjectivity today can thus be summarized in the figure of Stephen Hawking, who is "reduced to a mass of flesh, kept functioning by mechanical prostheses and contacting the world through clicking a computer mouse, tells us something about the general state of subjectivity today" (ibid.).

Žižek characterizes virtual identification, the process by which one identifies with a screen persona, as ambiguously vacillating between fantasy and "the realer than real," constructing a self that one would not admit to in real life. These two are interconnected, since knowing one's virtual self-image is subject to manipulation allows the user to activate the fantasy, for instance, of wanting to explore gender swapping and cybersex. While this may seem like the embodiment of what Judith Butler, in another context, called "necessary drag," alluding to the performative aspect of all gender identity, Žižek takes a far more skeptical or a self-admittedly "conservative" position. Harkening back to the "repressive desublimation" argument made by Frankfurt school theorist Herbert Marcuse in the 1960s, Žižek posits that that this kind of "play" of identity may simply be a cop-out, a cheap means to unleash the "electronic id" without the anxiety; in other words, "I can do it, and since I know I'm not really doing it, the inhibition or shame is suspended" (ibid.: 138). Thus, it is important to note that Žižek's skeptical position does not come from a Luddic, culturally reactionary place, in which all technologies are painted with a broad brush as inherently alienating. That is far from the case. Žižek's critique is, to the contrary, based in a politics of fantasy, of achieving the very kinds of experiences of subjectivity that Turkle argues happen on the computer and in cyberspace. Žižek, however, just does not agree that it does.

To refute Turkle, he presents a Lacanian distinction between symbolic identification and imaginary projection-identification:

> The VR persona thus offers a case of *imaginary* deception in so far as it externalizes-displays a false of myself (a timid man playing a hero in MUD . . .) and a *symbolic* deception in so far as it expresses the truth about myself in the guise of a game (by playfully adopting an aggressive person, I disclose my true aggressivity).
>
> *(ibid.: 139, emphasis added)*

Virtual identity, Žižek goes on to argue, oscillates between these two forms. The ability to shift between different selves is not predicated upon a technological facility but reflects what Žižek calls "the empty medium of identification" itself. In other words, "the very process of shifting among multiple identifications presupposes a kind of empty band which makes the leap from one identity to another possible, and this empty band is the subject itself" (ibid.: 141). Hence, we can see the difference between Turkle and Žižek in relief. Whereas Turkle believes computer programming and virtual communities such as MUDs facilitate these changes in identification, Žižek believes that these technologies put into relief the inherent "decenterment" at the core of self-identification, online and otherwise, itself.

More recent critiques of virtual identity studies have taken aim at what is perceived to be the negative effect of social media on individualisty. For instance, in a January 2009 article in *The Chronicle Review*, the magazine of the Chronicle of Higher Education, a publication that deals with issues in American higher education, William Deresiewicz penned an article entitled

"The end of solitude," in which he opined a devastating critique of technology's effect on "the contemporary self." Mentioning in particular the convergence of the camera and the computer, he declares:

> Celebrity and connectivity are both ways of becoming known. This is what the contemporary self wants. It wants to be recognized, wants to be connected: It wants to be visible. If not to the millions, on Survivor or Oprah, then to the hundreds, on Twitter or Facebook. This is the quality that validates us, this is how we become real to ourselves – by being seen by others. The great contemporary terror is anonymity . . . [I]f the property that grounded the self, in Romanticism, was sincerity, and in modernism it was authenticity, then in postmodernism it is visibility.
>
> *(Deresiewicz 2009)*

Though from these words the reader cannot be sure whether the author is happy or upset about it, he quickly goes on to reveal his true colors: "So we live exclusively in relation to others, and what disappears from our lives is *solitude*. Technology is taking away our *privacy* and our concentration, but it is also taking away our ability to be *alone*" (ibid.).

Deresiewicz is not so much upset at new media technologies per se, but at the lack of solitude that contemporary social media has created. For him, being alone is essential to the development of modern culture. It is an occasion to remove oneself from the "jostle of quotidian interests" and access the divine, reminiscent of the Whitman, Emerson and Thoreau. While acknowledging the "good" things that the Internet has provided, Deresiewicz believes it to be too much of a good thing. The intensification of connectivity has created not a problem of loneliness, as some critics of the Internet had feared, but one of oversaturation of saccharine sociality. "Visibility secures our self-esteem," he writes, "becoming a substitute, twice removed, for genuine connection" (ibid.).

The author, however, acknowledges that the Internet is not necessarily exceptional in the effect it has on identity. In fact, he argues the "end of solitude" in a narrative history of modernity. The Romantic self, "validated by a congruity of public appearance and private essence" (ibid.) he rightly notes, was a response to the increased urbanization. The city became a labyrinth, full of the masses. In this case, solitude becomes an escape from the Hell of the Crowd. Solitude becomes a stoic act, an austere resistance toward massification, of what Marcuse referred to as "one-dimensionality" (Marcuse 1964). It is this "self" that Deresiewicz longs for and believes to be threatened by new social media:

> The MySpace page, with its shrieking typography and clamorous imagery, has replaced the journal and the letter as a way of creating and communicating one's sense of self. The suggestion is not only that such communication is to be made to the world at large rather than to oneself or one's intimates, or graphically rather than verbally, or performatively rather than narratively or analytically.
>
> *(Deresiewicz 2009)*

This kind of skeptical position regarding identity and social media can be viewed within a larger context of media studies. Neil Postman, for instance, was a chief articulator of this position in works such as *Amusing Ourselves to Death*, where he maintains a strongly humanist position, suggesting that television, among other things, was cause for concern, as it debilitated the propensity for human rationality. For Deresiewicz, the contemporary use of technology is an effort to "stave off any possibility of solitude . . . as we sit at our computer, to maintain the imaginative presence of others" (ibid.). Clearly, the social connections made on the Web via social networking are, for him, at the level of simulation. The twin evils of celebrity and connectivity facilitated by contemporary media have eaten away at not only the integrity of the self but also intimacy, or "genuine connectivity."

So why is the solitude, being alone, so valuable in the eyes of Deresiewicz?

As he argues, solitude maintains the integrity of the self. It provides the opportunity for introspection, a feature of religious life found in the tradition of the Puritanism as well as others:

> You cannot hear God when people are chattering at you, and the divine word, their pretensions notwithstanding, demurs at descending on the monarch and the priest. Communal experience is the human norm, but the solitary encounter with God is the egregious act that refreshes that norm . . . Religious solitude is a kind of self-correcting social mechanism, a way of burning out the underbrush of moral habit and spiritual custom. The seer returns with new tablets or new dances, his face bright with old truth.
>
> *(ibid.)*

Weaving between motifs of a variety of religious traditions, Deresiewicz here clearly presents a divine quality to the ability to remove oneself from the collective.

Though he does not say so explicitly, his valuation of solitude harkens to debates in philosophy and sociology of the mid-twentieth century around the issue of "massification," as I briefly alluded to above with the mention of Herbert Marcuse's one-dimensionality. The growing concern over unchecked "technological progress" began to crop up in various intellectual discussions around this time. Spanish philosopher Ortega y Gasset had already in his 1929 work *The Revolt of the Masses* hinted at the crises brought on to Western "civilization" (his words) by the appearance of "mass-man" (Ortega y Gasset 1957). The mass-man is he who is at ease or even content with being part of the crowd, a member of the masses; in short, the mass-man is one who values conformity. "Mass society," then, is the diagnosis that Ortega y Gasset offers as the "greatest crisis that can afflict peoples, nations and civilization," rooted in the belief that the effects of industrial capitalism, especially the rise of a middle-class (and the associated shrinkage of class difference in liberal democracies of the West), has severely hurt civilizational progress by targeting elites, whom he calls "select minorities," by undermining their special status. "Mass society" has allowed for the sacred functions of civilizational progress to be accessible to too many.

The advent of suburbanization and the emergence of a white middle class brought with it the widespread adoption of consumer technologies in everyday life ranging from the automobile to the toaster oven. This signaled a "new" kind of society. For Ortega y Gasset, the problem of mass society was indeed a problem of "technicism," a term he adopts from Spengler, which he equates to "primitivism." By equating technicism to primitivism, he means to suggest that technology has aided the debasement of culture by the "revolt of the masses." With the social power of qualified elites being distributed and made available to the masses by technologies, Western culture itself, he thought, was on the decline.

By the 1950s, the intellectual response to this crisis resulted in a variety of works across the human sciences. In American sociology, two works, David Riesman et al.'s *The Lonely Crowd* and C. Wright Mills's *White Collar*, demonstrated this. In Europe, Frankfurt School authors such as Theodor Adorno, Max Horkheimer and Herbert Marcuse began to wage critique on what they viewed to be the increasing "singularity of culture." German philosopher Karl Jaspers similarly voiced concern for "advanced technique," viewing it as responsible for the uprooting of man characteristic of what he called the Modern Age. Whereas traditional times allowed for an individual to have a stable knowledge of himself in relation to the world, modernity has ripped the rug from underneath him and placed him into a seemingly never-ending Heraclitean flux of movement, which Jaspers aptly calls "despiritualization," which resonates with the religious thematic underlying Deresiewicz's argument. Gabriel Marcel, who we can tentatively call Jaspers's French counterpart, also expresses similar concern about the place of technology in the production of "mass society." As he writes in *Man Against Mass Society*:

> [T]he very essence of those modern techniques of degradation . . . consists precisely in putting the individual into a situation in which he loses touch with himself, in which he is literally beside himself, even to the point of being able sincerely to disavow acts into which nevertheless he had put sincerely his whole heart, or on the other hand of being able to confess to acts which he had not committed.
>
> *(Marcel 1952/2008: 17–18)*

Thus, for thinkers of the mid-twentieth century, technologies were nothing less than a *threat* to the individual, and more so the ability to be critical.

If, as many scholars suggest, the driving force behind the work of this cadre of scholars was the not-so-distant memory of the extensive use of technology and mass psychology of Fascist societies, the worries of Deresiewicz and others are similar, though far less grave. For them, it is the impending amoebic swallowing up of the individual by the collective; it is the "hive mind."

> But we no longer believe in the solitary mind. If the Romantics had Hume and the modernists had Freud, the current psychological model – and this should come as no surprise – is that of the networked or social mind . . . The ultimate implication is that there is no mental space that is not social.
>
> *(Deresiewicz 2009)*

Despite the seemingly extreme nature of his pessimism of the prospects of the self in increasingly technologized social relations, what is striking is that Deresiewicz's alarmed position toward new media technologies is not in fact surprising. Indeed, there is a veritable cottage industry of books and articles that signal the alarm for the end of humanity that is wrought by the onset of social media. Books with titles such as *The Tyranny of Email* or *You Are Not a Gadget* regularly hit the shelves of bookstores every other week. This indicates a widespread desire for reckoning with the changes wrought by new media technologies. It is no question then that conceptions of identity will come into the conversation today more than ever. This will continue to be the case as technologies continue to play a dominant role in how human beings relate to one another and themselves.

The continuing importance of virtual identity studies, and future prospects

In this chapter, we have briefly gone over some of the major contributions to the study of what I proposed we cautiously call virtual identities, but perhaps here, in its conclusion, we challenge that modifier. Though the perspectives assessed here vary widely in enthusiasm regarding the role of technology in the reconstitution of contemporary identity and sociality, they all agree that new media technologies such as the World Wide Web are slowly becoming the major site of identity-construction and maintenance. It is where youth will socialize, interact and work. This much is agreed upon by reactionary alarmists and the most vehement of technophiles alike. Thus, it is not a stretch to suggest that future researchers of identity will be compelled to look at new media technologies.

As the work of danah boyd in particular makes clear, it is a rather odd thing to study identity strictly as it presents itself in virtual communities since many contemporary virtual communities are wholly integrated into the flesh-and-skin lives of its users. The dualistic nature of the term "virtual identity" gives a false impression of people having separate, online existences, though this may be the case for some. Most users of social networking sites such as MySpace and Facebook do not see a drastic break between their online personas and their personals IRL (In Real Life). Nevertheless, as boyd's work makes clear, there is some form of performance involved in their online social interactions. But as she points out, identity always involves the management of impressions on others, a performance as well. What I am driving at is that the study of virtual identity must move away from the ontological dualism that views one's virtual identity as somehow a fake, a copy of the real thing. As Žižek reminds us in this chapter, the process of identity-construction is a tenuous one, with or without virtual communities.

These two ideas – anti-dualism and the tenuousness of identity – continues to define and drive virtual identity studies in the future, especially as social media will longer be confined to users' interaction with computers but with mobile devices such as smartphones, a phenomenon which Henry Jenkins has deemed "convergence" (Jenkins 2006). When one is walking down the street, while maintaining dialogues on instant messenger, text, Twitter and Facebook, how can the analyst determine the true identity of this person? The ever-growing landscape of social media, as well as their interoperability across various technologies, will not only further confront scholars of identity but also analysts of social life in general to rethink their assumptions.

References

Baker, S.A. and Hurst, P.R. (1998) *Limits of Trust: Cryptography, Governments and Electronic Commerce*, 1st edition. New York: Springer.

Benjamin, W. (2006) *The Writer of Modern Life: Essays on Charles Baudelaire*. Cambridge, MA: Belknap Press of Harvard University Press.

boyd, d. (2002) *Faceted Id/entity: Managing representation in a digital world*. Cambridge, MA: Massachussetts Institute of Technology, Program in Media Arts and Sciences.

boyd, d. (2007) "Why youth (heart) social network sites: the role of networked publics in teenage social life," *MacArthur Foundation Series on Digital Learning – Youth, Identity, and Digital Media Volume* (ed. David Buckingham). Cambridge, MA: MIT Press, pp. 119–42. Online: www.danah.org/papers/WhyYouthHeart.pdf/

Castells, M. (1996) *The Rise of the Network Society*. Cambridge, MA: Blackwell Publishers.

Deresiewicz, W. (2009) "The end of solitude," *The Chronicle Review*. Online: http://chronicle.com/article/The-End-of-Solitude/3708.

Ford, R. (2009) "Oxford word of the year 2009: Unfriend," *OUPblog*. Online: http://blog.oup.com/(2009)/11/unfriend/ (accessed May 9, 2010).

Goffman, E. (1959) *The Presentation of Self in Everyday Life*. New York: Doubleday.

Gross, D. (2009) "Dictionary word of the year: 'Unfriend'," *CNN*. Online: www.cnn.com/(2009)/TECH/11/17/unfriend.word/index.html (accessed May 9, 2010).

Hansen, M. (2000) *Embodying Technesis: Technology Beyond Writing*. Ann Arbor: University of Michigan Press.

Hardt, M. (1995) "The withering of civil society," *Social Text*, 27–44.

Jenkins, H. (2006) *Convergence Culture: Where Old and New Media Collide*, illustrated edition. New York: NYU Press.

Lessig, L. (2000) *Code and Other Laws of Cyberspace*. New York: Basic Books.

Malik, O. (2009) "In 10 years, hours spent on internet almost doubled", *GigaOm*. Online: http://gigaom. com/(2009)/12/24/(1999)-(2009)-hours-spent-on-internet-nearly-doubled/ (accessed May 9, 2010).

Marcel, G. (2008) *Man against Mass Society*. South Bend, IN: St. Augustine's Press.

Marcuse, H. (1964) *One Dimensional Man: Studies in the Ideology of Advanced Industrial Society*. Boston: Beacon Press.

Mills, C.W. (2002) *White Collar*. New York: Oxford University Press.

Nakamura, L. (2001) "Head hunting in cyberspace: identity tourism, Asian avatars and racial passing on the Web," *The Women's Review of Books*, 18(5): 10–11.

Nakamura, L. (2002) *Cybertypes: Race, Ethnicity, and Identity on the Internet*. New York: Routledge.

Nakamura, L. (2008) *Digitizing Race: Visual Cultures of the Internet*. Minneapolis: University of Minnesota Press.

Ortega y Gasset, J. (1957) *The Revolt of the Masses*, authorized translation from the Spanish. New York: W.W. Norton. Originally published in Spanish, 1929; translated to English, 1932.

Rheingold, H. (1993) *The Virtual Community: Homesteading on the Electronic Frontier*. Reading, MA: Addison-Wesley.

Riesman, D., Glazer, N. and Denney, R. (2001) *The Lonely Crowd*. New Haven: Yale University Press.

Simmel, G. (1972) *On Individuality and Social Forms*, edited by Donald Levine. Chicago: University of Chicago Press.

Stiegler, B. (1998) *Technics and Time: The Fault of Epimetheus*. Stanford: Stanford University Press.

Turkle, S. (1984) *The Second Self: Computers and the Human Spirit*. New York: Simon and Schuster.

Turkle, S. (1996) "Who am we?" *Wired*, 4(01). Online: www.wired.com/wired/archive/4.01/turkle. html.

White, M. (2006) *The Body and the Screen: Theories of Internet Spectatorship*. Cambridge, MA: MIT Press.

Žižek, S. (1997) *The Plague of Fantasies*. London and New York: Verso.

14

Consumer identities

Roberta Sassatelli

Introduction

Consumption is best considered as a complex economic, social and cultural set of practices, interconnected with all of the most important phenomena which have come to make up contemporary Western society: the spread of the market economy, a developing globalisation, the creation and recreation of national traditions, a succession of technological and media innovations, etc. If it is true that in today's 'consumer society' we are born to consume, it is also true that consumption has cultural and practical implications that go way beyond satisfying our daily needs through commodities, or even symbolically play with them in variously elaborated manners. To consume is also to act as 'consumers', that is, to put on a particular kind of identity and to deal with its contradictions. In this light, consumer culture is more than commoditisation and affluence, more than conspicuous consumption and the democratisation of luxuries. Consumer culture is deeply implicated in the fabrication of identities: it produces consumers, and does so in a variety of ways. For a growing variety of activities growing numbers of people now speak of themselves as consumers, and they are being addressed as consumers by a host of institutions, within and without the market. The centrality of the 'consumer', the lengthy and contested historical processes which led to its formation, the many theoretical portrayals of consumer agency which have followed each other in a succession of criticism and cross-reference, the political implications of conceiving contemporary culture as made of consumers are addressed in this chapter. Placing emphasis on the social, cultural and institutional processes which have made consumption into a contested field of social action and public debate, I shall consider how consumer identities have been constructed and promoted as major social identities in contemporary societies.

Historical and intellectual development

In the rendering the historical development of consumer capitalism, sociology and history traditionally followed a productivist position giving production the role of the engine of history. This view, which typically presented consumer society as emerging at the beginning of the twentieth century as a reaction to the industrial revolution penetrating all social classes through the consumption of mass-produced goods, has been discredited by studies of early modern and modern material culture which have documented its growth and differentiation both before and during the industrial revolution. Attention has been given to the role of structural changes within the consumption sphere (from the diffusion of colonial goods and luxuries to housing changes, from the reverberation of a fashion system through emerging media to new ways of shopping, from increased social mobility to new gender arrangements) and to the emergence of a new social identity: the consumer (Sassatelli 2007). The latter has meant to consider the intellectual development of the notion of the consumer together with the social practices that sustained and were marshalled through it.

Asceticism, hedonism, materialism

An important step into this direction has been Colin Campbell's (1987) work on the 'Romantic ethic' and the 'spirit of consumerism'. Inspired by Weber's celebrated essay on the protestant ethic and capitalism, Campbell maintains that, from its start, capitalism needed cultural and subjective changes on the demand side as well as the production side, and concentrates on the motivational set-up which grounds modern consumption as well as production. A particular ethical and aesthetical attachment to novelty and originality drawing heavily from Romanticism is indicated as crucial. Romanticism provided people with a repertoire of justifications for their consumer desires: not some idea of otherworldly salvation, nor the ostentation of status and social climbing, but self-realisation and aesthetic enjoyment. The Romantics maintained that the goal of human beings was to make oneself in opposition to society: rather than bettering oneself through work, discipline and sacrifice, one should throw oneself into self-expression in a search for a variety of different and meaningful experiences. The constant search for new forms of gratification is not only anti-traditionalist behaviour, but also the opposite of traditional forms of hedonism. If the hedonism of the ancients was linked to certain specific sensorial practices (eating, drinking, and so on), modern hedonism is defined by the pleasures of imagination and linked to the capacity to control emotions. The modern consumer is a 'hedonist' who, Campbell (1987: 86–7) writes, continually 'withdraw[s] from reality as fast as he encounters it, ever-casting his day-dreams forward in time, attaching them to objects of desire, and then subsequently "unhooking" them from these objects as and when they are attained and experienced'. In other words, in living above the level of subsistence, modern consumers have developed a form of modern hedonism which sees objects as ripe for personal creative fantasy. Their interests are concentrated in the meanings and images which can be attributed to a product, something which requires the presence of 'novelty'. Thanks to 'private and imaginary' modern hedonism, consumption becomes not so much the ability to bargain a price, or to use products, but 'the imaginative pleasure-seeking to which the product image lends itself, "real" consumption being largely a resultant of this "mentalistic" hedonism. Viewed in this way, the emphasis upon novelty as well as that upon insatiability both become comprehensible' (ibid.: 89). While we can imagine that certain sectors of the population in the West – for example, bourgeois inhabitants of Renaissance Italian cities – might have been exposed to similar cultural tendencies of refined materialism and hedonism early on, we come across the incarnation of such consumer subjectivity when moving a little forwards in history and meet the nineteenth-century 'dandy'. In fact, the image of the dandy was linked to a particular conception of pleasure: a general disposition to new and exotic experiences rather than the enjoyment of this or that particular object. Oscar Wilde's *The Portrait of Dorian Gray* may be seen as a way of reflecting on the pleasures of consumption and their price: the possibility of exchanging one's own moral self and sense of security for the exploration, via fashion and commodities, of new experiences and new selves.

Along with the historical emergence of modern economic forms, a mix of hedonism and asceticism have come together in the fashioning of identity for ever larger sectors of the population. As Mukerji (1983: 4) nicely puts it '[h]edonism and asceticism seem, on the surface, contradictory, but they share one feature an interest in material accumulation'; both ascetics and hedonists put accumulation (of capital or consumer goods) to profit for self-enhancement (either through economic power or prestige), '[they] acted as economic innovators in the early modern period replacing a traditional pattern of hoarding wealth with new ways to use it, to make it a more active part of social and economic life'. The consolidation of the market was accompanied by shifts in economic culture with both the development of a new rationalist orientation to production and the appearance of a more reflexive and self-sustained culture of consumption. In his *An Enquiry into the Nature and Causes of the Wealth of Nations* published in the last quarter of the eighteenth century, Adam Smith, the founder of economic liberalism, sees even excessive and luxurious consumption through mercantile lenses as a factor in economic development: in his view, the expenditure of the 'great' aided the birth of a class of merchants and bourgeois who drove society towards modern capitalism and who, freed from all personal dependence, guided the entire population to civil liberty. Smith does, however, emphasise production, and it is by modelling consumption onto production that he defines correct and incorrect forms of consumption. Merchants, as we all become under market conditions, are not pictured as ascetic monks, they do not disdain the decencies of life, they are indeed good, well-behaved, rational consumers as opposed to the immoral, irrational, whimsical wasters impersonated by the old, declining nobility. To discriminate among goods, Smith thus uses the notions of convenience and decency. Decencies indicate those goods which can be used for non–ostentatious comfort. They are neither needs nor luxuries and incarnate a type of consumption which brings both order and rationality: they are bourgeois comforts, responding to the 'calm and dispassionate desire' of bettering one's own condition, while diverting from 'profusion' or the 'passion for present enjoyment'. Smith's thinking naturalises a particular way of conducting oneself as a consumer which still acts as a normative background for the legitimation of contemporary consumer culture, placing value onto the search for personal gratification whilst emphasising self-control and individual autonomy.

Flows of commodities, flows of knowledge

The growing thematisation of consumption and the consumer are crucial elements of the rise and dominance of consumer culture, which itself cannot be reduced to increased consumer spending. In all cultures and societies we may find a variety of discourses and practices through which objects and our modalities of relation to them are classified. Nevertheless, these classificatory processes were becoming markedly visible as a contested terrain from the early modern period, when the need to take account of new forms of consumption based on the growth and diversity of objects on sale, the predominance of monetary exchange and competitive display, became strongly felt (Sassatelli 2007). Consumption started to be identified as a meaningful category, standing side by side and eventually supplanting the notion of luxury in moral discourse. 'Luxury' had been the classic category used to distinguish between 'good' and 'bad' uses of objects in Western thinking. But, already half a century before Smith, with Bernard Mandeville's *Fable of the Bees*, luxury became de-moralised: it became relative (to taste, life changes, etc.) and legitimate if favouring the prosperity of the Nation. This placed emphasis on consumption as something which may simply spur commerce and which cannot be easily judged on transcendental grounds, something private and disentangled from the kind of legal–political regime provided by sumptuary laws which had regulated the acquisition of goods differently for different people in pre-modern societies. Consumption instead became caught up in the cultural–economic regime found in the dynamics of fashion. In the fashion regime, aesthetic judgements such as 'tasteful' and 'tasteless' may work as political and moral tools, to justify social inclusion or exclusion (see Bourdieu 1984).

This needs to be placed in a broader cultural geo-politics: Westerners as a whole were becoming 'consumers' and as such they had to be capable, beyond their specific social position, to procure their own satisfaction using the inflow of colonial goods. A kind of individualist materialism of the masses developed, with its roots in international commodity flows and in the idea that the satisfaction of individual desires of consumption is the principle source of the social order and a vital characteristic of any life worth living. The individual desires of Western consumers – constructed through an international division of labour that made the colonies distant reservoirs of new exotic and mysterious commodities – are described as inexhaustible and come to appear as the origin of the social world and as the source of the value of things. Thus, it is through the consumption of goods which today appear as banal – sugar, tea, coffee, etc. – that the fervent debate around the role of the consumer was born, a figure who soldered together the links between identity and consumption characterising Western contemporary culture (Sassatelli 2007).

As suggested by Appadurai (1986), material objects always implicate forms of social knowledge: as the flows of commodities became more complex, global and above all long distance, they brought with them flows of more articulate yet unequal knowledge which provided new arenas for the construction of value that engaged producers, traders and consumers. In increasingly long distance flows 'the negotiation of the tension between knowledge and ignorance becomes itself a critical determinant of the flow of commodities' (ibid.: 44): the emphasis is thus put on the ability of the consumer to recognise the value of things and it is by instructing them on the value of things through discourses of taste that consumption can be governed. In this new situation what prospective consumers are after is less exclusivity than authenticity and they have to measure themselves through narratives connecting their identities with their desires of consumption.

Consumption as a meaningful social activity

All in all, the legitimating rhetoric which emerged in the eighteenth century to justify market societies and modern cultures of consumption epitomised the entrenchment of a new sphere of action and new modalities of justification for the enjoyment of goods. Consumption was defined as a private matter, constructed as opportunely opposed to production, and envisaged as the pursuit of private happiness indirectly but firmly linked to virtuous mechanisms in the public sphere. Within this framework consumers were thus constructed as private economic hedonists, preoccupied with individual pleasures and doing all right – for the common good and themselves – provided they behaved in disciplined ways within the rules of the market. Still, as suggested, market rules themselves contained a vision of moral order and the purification of consumer identity from political and moral repertoires was never fully accomplished. As a contested identity, the consumer became an important device for political, social and cultural change.

It is especially from the late nineteenth century that a number of economic, cultural and political agencies increasingly claimed for themselves the right and duty to address consumers and to speak for them. Shopping has been recognised in a number of historical studies as crucial to this (see Sassatelli 2007). For example, studies on the development of the department stores in France, the US and the UK provide a good demonstration of how they marked the way we consume. It was thanks to the development of places which made a large quantity of goods visible to the whole population that the connection between personal identity, commerce and objects became central to a growing number of people, and it was thanks to a thematisation of consumption as a meaningful social activity that the changing patterns of consumption gave way to a consumer society as such. This was accompanied by the rise of the 'consumer' as a powerful social identity, called into life and engaged by a host of discourses and situated strategies of enticement which both democratised desires and standardised them. Market actors, and in particular retail entrepreneurs, were pivotal in such development; still, commercial processes were embedded in a conducive social environment, which, in many cases, amounted to the urban circuits of power, including universities and art museums. This should not surprise us, as shopping in the department store was indeed often portrayed as the quintessentially urban and civilised leisure activity. If the invention of leisure time for the masses can be traced to the end of the nineteenth century, mass leisure was immediately and strongly connected to commercialisation and shopping. From the nineteenth century, someone walking the streets of the first metropolises could be considered, and consider themselves, a 'consumer', an actor who could buy objects for sale in the department stores and who gained part of the meaning and significance of their walks from the display of commodities. Presenting themselves as potential buyers, everyone could enter and leave the shopping place when they desired, looking at commodities, imagining using or purchasing them, mixing the new and the old: shopping became a typically bourgeois leisure activity, a socially approved way of spending time, equal to going to the theatre or visiting a museum. In the same way the discourse surrounding commerce stopped insisting on the immediate acquisition of particular goods, and attempted to provoke a state of constant desire.

Social actors were in fact increasingly referred to as 'consumers'. This came about thanks to, among other things, market actors such as the advertising and marketing agencies which, especially in the United States, developed significantly between the nineteenth and twentieth centuries. Such development was accompanied, particularly between the two world wars, by the consolidation of new professional forms of knowledge and the institutionalisation of various professional figures: advertising executives, marketing experts, shop-assistants, etc. On the whole, especially from the beginning of the twentieth century, advertising contains an increasing emphasis on self-realisation, self-presentation and impression management, stressing the self-creating potentialities of the choosing self. Marketing and advertising were complemented by a number of other increasingly professionalised figures such as designers or fashion journalists. These different figures, the so-called 'cultural intermediaries' (Bourdieu 1984), partook to a broad process of institutionalisation, which gave way to a variety of diverse collective actors (professional organisations, market watchdogs, consumer movements, etc.) that were all busily engaged in providing their portray of consumers, of their wants and capacities.

Recent scholarship has shown that political actors were also involved in providing an image of the consumer and in designing a more explicitly public role for consumption (see Sassatelli 2007). Political ideologies and movements which dealt with consumption range from the late eighteenth-century movements against the trade slave, to nineteenth-century movements concerned with the welfare and moralisation of the lower orders, to consumer cooperatives and consumerist movements underscoring the agency and rationality of consumers in the early twentieth century. They not only responded to changes brought about by the consolidation of modern consumer society, they also imagined, theorised and mobilised people as consumers – and did so in a variety of distinctive ways according to different national traditions.

Getting personal: the consumer in society

Whenever new consumer goods have become available to upward mobile social groups or to women, strong hostile sentiments towards material riches have emerged. These sentiments may well have a disciplining function if it is true, as Veblen (1994: 53) insisted, that 'consumption of luxuries in the true sense is a consumption directed to the comfort of the consumer itself and it is therefore a mark of the master' which elicits social control. It is not surprising thus that consumption has often been seen as a negative expression of the triumph of the modern market which weakens men, turning them into useless citizens incapable of defending their own country or participating in politics, whilst making women superficial and idle, unfit as wives and mothers. Critical commentaries on the decline of 'culture' in contemporary Western societies have often featured consumer culture as the main culprit, and consumers as gullible accomplices. Voices from a range of quarters have rallied to stigmatise consumption, casting it as a source of moral disorder, a soul-corrupting mirage: 'consumerism' or 'consumer culture' gave birth to spiritual impoverishment for which people sought comfort in material goods, a surrogate for traditional forms of satisfaction, self-realisation and identification through work and political participation. Authors such as Jean Baudrillard (1998) and Christopher Lasch (1979) offered polemic views of consumer identities, considering that consumer culture had given way to unhealthy cultural contradictions which may ultimately lead to pathological subjectivity traits. If Baudrillard ultimately maintains that the possibility of subjectivity constitution through consumption is in fact removed by the incessant juxtapositions of signs produced by commercial images, Lasch maintains that the collapse of the public sphere and the bureaucratisation of work combine with a 'consumer culture' that promotes a 'narcissist personality type'. The narcissist is so obsessed by his own needs that he only sees others in relation to himself. In consumer culture, identity formation is no longer based on stable ideals maintained by the traditional family, but by the possibility of 'presenting' a convincing 'saleable' image of the self. In this perspective, where the ascetic culture of production favours the development of strong personalities attached to duties and to the family, consumer culture favours the development of weak and isolated personalities, who continually search for gratification in objects and who are fated to be continually deluded: the pleasures which they are desperately seeking out to fill their 'empty interior' is in fact a form of 'aggression' which knows nothing as sacred but reduces all to a commodity, an object interchangeable with other objects. The culture of commodities that enters the home and transforms everyone into isolated consumers is a constant source of dissatisfaction. In Lasch's view, '[t]he best defences against the terrors of existence are the homely comforts of love, work, and family life, which connect us to a world that is independent of our wishes yet responsive to our needs' (Lasch 1979: 248). Thus, consumption is positive only if it is functional to production, instead it becomes a threat where it turns in on itself and away from the rules of the traditional family.

The identification of a pathological splitting of culture within modern capitalism is a recurrent theme in academic literature and public discourse at least since Daniel Bell's works on the cultural contradictions of capitalism, and it has been taken up again by the American feminist Susan Bordo (1993). She maintains that the contemporary self is constructed around contradictory demands: to incorporate the discipline of the work ethic and to consume as many goods as possible surrendering oneself to immediate enjoyment. According to Bordo (ibid.: 199) the regulation of desire becomes a constant problem because subjects find themselves besieged by temptation and condemned if they indulge: '[o]n the one hand, as producers of goods and services we must sublimate, delay, repress desires for immediate gratification; we must cultivate the work ethic. On the other hand, as consumers we must display a boundless capacity to capitulate to desire and indulge in impulse; we must hunger for constant and immediate satisfaction'.

Eating disorders are examples of the chaos in the regulation of desires caused by consumption, something which is much harder on young women pressured to demonstrate their independence and power. Anorexia and obesity figure as opposed attempts to solve the contradictions induced by consumer culture: anorexia being 'an extreme development of the capacity for self-denial and repression of desire (the work ethic in absolute control)', and obesity 'an extreme capacity to capitulate to desire (consumerism in control)'. As such they 'can never be tolerated by a consumer system' which is, however, intimately connected to pathology. Postulating a radical split between production and consumption, Bordo (ibid.: 201–2, 187) in fact ends up maintaining that 'the "correct" management of desire' requires 'a contradictory double-bind construction of personality' and produces 'an unstable bulimic personality type as its norm'.

Analyses such as these take seriously the idea that consumer culture or society produces consumers, but offer a polemic view of consumer identities, which does not account for the plurality of ways in which consumption and identity are intertwined. They tend to consider consumer culture as producing pathological identities, and consumer agency as ultimately dominated by the commercial and promotional systems rather than embedded in meaningful social relations. In the next section, I shall consider the main contemporary theory of consumer action, departing from economics emphasis on rationality and moving towards sociology and anthropology emphasis on ritual action, showing that they stress the consumers' activities as related to their communicative and relational functions.

Main claims and contributors

A number of perspectives within sociology and anthropology specifically addressed to consumption have tried to stress the activity of the consumer, engaging with empirical studies rather than abstract theorising. They have often taken off from a criticism of neoclassical economics – its instrumentally rational, highly individualist view of the consumer. In neoclassical economics, consumption is, broadly speaking, very much emphasised, and in fact rendered through the notion of individual rational choice. Consumption is not a cultural domain but a myriad of individual, instrumental cost-benefit calculations: it is 'demand', the sum of individual purchase decisions aimed at utility maximisation predicated on consumer sovereignty. This characterisation poses a number of problems that have partly been addressed by injecting some social characterisation in an otherwise too abstract and individualistic portrayal of the consumer (Sassatelli 2007). To figure out consumers as active *and* social agents, to conceive of consumption not as instrumental, autonomous calculation but as a practical accomplishment and a ritual activity, a clearly social view of rationality has been adopted in anthropology and sociology. Consumers in current sociological and anthropological perspectives are active, but neither free nor so self-sufficient, being embedded from the start in social relations.

Sociological classics

Such a ritual, fully social perspective featured in the classic sociological works of Veblen and Simmel who considered consumption as a ceremonial process whereby social position is demonstrated and pursued. In his *The Theory of the Leisure Class* (1994/1899), Thorstein Veblen proposed the concept of 'conspicuous consumption' to indicate those phenomena of consumption which escape the logic of utility maximisation at minimal cost. He observed that, alongside necessity and calculating acts of consumption explainable by the use-value of commodities, there also operated ceremonial forms of consumption linked to status and honour; in his view, the value of some goods was exclusively determined by their capacity to make a given social position visible. Conspicuous consumption and waste thus served as demonstration/recognition of elevated social position, founded on the knowledge that 'wealth or power must be put in evidence, for esteem is granted only in evidence' (ibid.: 30). Indeed, as we can still witness on a daily basis, a costly object may be sought out precisely because of its high cost, because through displaying it social actors can visibly demonstrate what Veblen called 'pecuniary strength', thus obtaining 'good repute' and showing their good chances of controlling the future course of the social and symbolic processes.

Georg Simmel provides a similar, but more refined, perspective. In his *Philosophy of Money*, the German sociologist (Simmel 1990/1907) maintains that the value of things depends on the value they are given by the subject, rather than being founded on absolutes such as the intrinsic value of their material properties, or the amount of work necessary to produce them such as in Marxian theory and critical theory more generally. However, this subjective valuation is itself conditioned by the historical and cultural context in which it takes place. To be sure, the inhabitants of modern large cities are increasingly able to translate the value of things in monetary terms, to consider lengthy chains of cause and effect and to perform some kind of cost-benefit calculation, but they do not ever reach the calculative instrumentality which neoclassical economics holds to be the basis of action. On the contrary, it is the possibility of self-recognition within a group and distinction from others which is of utmost importance in large urban environments where one is all too easily lost in the anonymous crowd.

Consumption thus appears to Simmel as a culturally ordered field of action, rather than a threat to social order, as his French contemporary Emile Durkheim would have it. For example, it is precisely in the chaotic and over-crowded metropolis that more and more people need to dress themselves in clothes that signal their identity to others, both as a members of a group and as an individual. Fashion is indeed an excellent means of achieving both these effects, responding to both the need for cohesion or union and the need for differentiation or isolation (Simmel 1971/1904). In following fashion we align ourselves with some people and differentiate ourselves from others, but at the same time we enjoy expressing ourselves in a common language that is widely understood. For Simmel fashion is also a metaphor for the allure that 'newness' exerts on the modern subject in general, and on the bourgeoisie and the middle classes in particular. Indeed, the social position of the middle classes predisposes them to fashion; in contrast to the nobility, the bourgeoisie cannot rely on tradition and established styles and, unlike less well-to-do classes, they hope to better their social position and to find their own style.

Communication and distinction

The social and cultural embeddedness of consumer actions and identities is central to the work of both Mary Douglas and Pierre Bourdieu, both having set the standard for contemporary studies on consumption in sociology and anthropology. For these authors consumption functions as relational work, not only being embedded in social relations but also being used to maintain, negotiate and modify interpersonal connections, especially those related to family and household life, their hierarchies and power structure. Consumption may be seen as expression of kinship and other social and personal relationships, and the density of a consumer's purchases may reflect the density of his social networks.

In particular, Douglas underlines the communicative function of goods and the communicative rationality of consumers. In *The World of Goods*, a seminal work by Douglas and Isherwood (1979), we are invited to consider that objects serve as a material support for interaction as well as symbolic indicators in making the world intelligible. Goods function as sorting devices:

they 'can be used as fences or bridges' to regulate social access and belonging (ibid.: 12). Her emphasis is on identity and classification. Following Lévi-Strauss, she considers that goods 'are good to think': they can be treated as symbolic means of classifying the world, as the tools of a particular form of non-verbal communication. The social actor requires an intelligible reality of visible signs to orientate in the world, and goods serve this function through providing the material basis for stabilising cultural categories. The acquisition and use of objects is therefore a way of 'mak[ing] firm and visible a particular set of judgements in the fluid processes of classifying persons and events' (ibid.: 65, 67). Douglas conceives of consumption as a cultural battlefield, reflecting the fundamental choices on the type of society which we want to live in and on the type of person we wish to be. Interestingly, wishes are often predicated on opposition: we choose these goods over others precisely because they are culturally incompatible and even opposed to those perspectives on the organisation of society and identity which we want to refute. While the adoption of a new commodity, or the innovative use of an existing one is seen as a way of controlling precious bits of information, consumption permits a continual marking and re-marking of the surrounding world and a constant confrontation with others, and thus a control of respective identities.

While Douglas's emphasis is on cognition, Bourdieu's is on embodiment. Consumers operate though a sense of distinction which they have incorporated through taste. Consumers not only distinguish between goods in order to distinguish themselves, they also cannot do anything but distinguish goods and themselves; that is, they are placed in different categories, included or excluded, according to their capacity for distinction. Although it is expressed in the apparently neutral and innocuous language of individual preference, taste 'marries colours and also people, who make "well-matched couples", initially in regard to taste' (Bourdieu 1984: 243). Thus it is a generative and classificatory mechanism which, at the same time, classifies the classifier and contributes to stabilising his or her social position. Bourdieu proposes a theory of practice in which human action is constructed as something material and concrete and human experience understood in terms of mimesis: to this end he elaborates the notion of 'habitus', a system of durable and transposable dispositions, 'structured structures predisposed to function as structuring structures', which is written in the body through past experiences, it is established in the first years of life and works as an unconscious but extremely adaptable mechanism orientating actors towards objects, themselves and others. Tastes are conceptualised as subjective realisations of the mechanism of habitus which organise consumption.

To this complex and finely calibrated description of habitus, Bourdieu juxtaposes a hierarchical and linear vision of the social structure and of its relationship with the structuring of taste. In fact, the individual habitus stands in a relationship of homology – that is, of 'diversity within homogeneity' – with respect to the class habitus defined by structural forms of capital derived from one's own professional position, education and social networking. Tastes are thereby implicated in 'classificatory systems' which freeze 'a state of social struggle', or rather 'a given state of the distribution of advantages and obligations', and are 'not so much means of knowledge as means of power' (ibid.: 471). For example, if we consider the health market, we can clearly see that there are very different attitudes to the body and its state of health which correspond to different forms of health service consumption. The middle classes tend to operate around the idea that they can and must control themselves, their body and their state of health, and thus they generally have more medical check-ups with the result that they effectively have a longer life-span. Instead, the working classes tend to adopt a fatalist attitude, not worrying about small illnesses or discomforts, and they only reluctantly visit the doctor in cases of emergency, with the result that their life-span is less, and they are more prone to invalidating disease, therefore almost enacting their fatalistic prophecy at its worst.

Appropriating goods

Contemporary research on consumption tries to render the complexity of contemporary consumer practices in relation to ever more complex social structure while emphasising the relative autonomy of consumer practices from the broader social structure, and their role in the structuring of identity and habitus. Therefore, not only tastes and consumer practices are internally complex, but also the different contexts and cultures of consumption are key mediators in the formation of taste. As a relatively autonomous sphere of action, consumption has come to be defined as a practice of 'appropriation' which occurs in a variety of socially organised occasions, from shopping, to servicing in the home, to display in various public places, etc. (Appadurai 1986; Miller 1987; McCracken 1988). Each of these occasions is relatively self-governing, it is constituted in terms of its own symbols and rituals, and translates in these terms what has been inscribed in commodities by the circuits of production and distribution. In particular, in contemporary societies consumption engages with the nature of objects as commodities. The moment of purchase is clearly only the beginning of a complex process in which the consumer works on a commodity to re-contextualise it, so that it can eventually end up no longer having any recognisable relation with the world of monetary exchange. In fact, even the most simple article of trade does not inevitably and constantly have the character of a commodity: it may start off as such, but it often ends up being something different, at least for those who consume or possess it.

One of the key objectives of the sociology of consumption today is to focus on the concrete, active, fluid and different ways in which people transform and make their own those resources which they have acquired on the market. A similar position is held by the British anthropologist Daniel Miller. Considering consumption as a 'relatively autonomous and plural process of cultural self-construction', Miller suggests that the imperatives of consumption may be as varied as the cultural contexts from which consumers act. Consumption represents the variety of local relational networks that maintain their specificity in the face of the homogenisation of the mechanisms of production and distribution. Miller (1987: 17) maintains that, from the point of view of the subject, consumption can be considered as a form of 're-appropriation' or 'assimilation' – that is, 'the way in which a subject assimilates its own culture and uses it to develop itself as a social subject'. Thus, consumption too contains the potential to realise the human being which Marx tended to attribute only to work. The term 're-appropriation' is eloquent: obviously it implies the capacity to make an object properly *for* and *of* oneself. Commodities that are anonymous, identical or fungible at the moment of purchase can be re-contextualised in numerous different ways by consumers, so that practices of consumption tend to generate diversity rather than homogenisation. However, in Miller's view appropriation also implies feedback effects on identity, thus by appropriating, the subject expands and modifies him or herself. It is in this process of renegotiation of one's identity that a space opens up in which the advertising industry intervenes trying to manage and modify our needs. But it is thanks to this process that consumption can also be a creative act and produce something truly 'authentic' – that is, something which actors not only may use in a personal way, but which can also become part of them.

Similar views have been put forward by French theorist Michel De Certeau (1984). He sees consumption as a form of bricolage production, an 'ordinary poaching' which may be subtly subversive as it 'does not manifest itself through its own products, but rather through its ways of using the products imposed by a dominant economic order' (ibid.: xii). They also resonate in British cultural studies, and in particular in the works of Dick Hedbige and Paul Willis, and their emphasis on the creativity of sub-cultural appropriation. Youth subcultures in particular, as Hebdige (1979: 103) puts it, have been addressed as 'cultures of conspicuous consumption – even when, as with the skinheads and the punks, certain types of consumption are conspicuously refused – and it is through the distinctive rituals of consumption, through style, that the subculture at once reveals its "secret" identity and communicates its forbidden meanings'. Also in the hippy and bikers cultures studied by Willis (1978: 166), goods were attributed distinctive meanings through which the group constituted itself: the styles of consumption demonstrates the 'profane' power of subordinate and marginal groups 'to select, develop and creatively make some objects their own, to express their own meanings'. As we have learned, and these very authors acknowledged, sub-cultural appropriation may be quickly subsumed: private rebels may not become public revolutionaries and, if they do, the meanings originally associated with rebellion may be altered and subversive results are by no means guaranteed. This portrays an active but far from sovereign consumer, and a continuous dialectical constitution of consumers' identities facing the world of commodities.

The contemporary sociology of consumption is aware of the ambivalence of consumption and of the normative character of its link to the pursuit of identity. Looking at consumption and identity from the perspective of an active but socially bounded and culturally normalised identity, we may certainly appreciate that consumers are not always able to complete their rituals of consumption, appropriating commodities successfully. As Simmel (1990; see also McCraken 1988) anticipated, 'sterile ownership' is a typical disease of modern society, fuelled by the growth in material culture, the diversity of objects and their continual innovation. Thus, consumers may find themselves with objects which are useless and meaningless or even alienating, and they may be upset by having discarded an object which still represented something for them. Paradoxically enough, as consumption requires time, some forms of sterile ownership may be a feature of economies where leisure time is the shortest for the moneyed elite. Luxury requires time, thus expensive leisure goods (sophisticated cameras, camping equipment, sport accessories, etc.) may be purchased by time-pressured high-income earners to be left unused, remaining in storage at home as symbols of a potential future and a wished-for self-identity. While these luxuries are only virtually consumed, being as much bearers of frustration as they offer symbolic support in daily life, they do contribute to consumption expenditure at the macro-economic level. The idea of sterile ownership thus adumbrates the gap between consumer practices as the use of goods and demand as the purchase of commodities. It also hints at the lack of reciprocity between consumption as subjective culture and consumer culture as objective or material culture. This lack of reciprocity means that even successful appropriation in ordinary life may have perverse effects on identity and creativity. Indeed, following Simmel, Miller (2004) himself suggests that the increased pressure on individual consumer choice may have unintended cultural effects. In a recent paper he illustrates this by setting a puzzle: why do Western women dream of colourful dresses and increasingly buy black, grey and plainly unadorned clothing? His reply points to the fact that choice has become be so overwhelming that it might be given up altogether or indeed strictly regimented by resorting to hegemonic codifications: the 'little black dress' is seen as an anxiety-reducing response to the variety of clothing available and the de-classificatory trends in the fashion system.

Routine and reflexivity

While habitus, in Bourdieu's theory, is a deep-seated often unconscious mechanism for the matching of taste and goods, the normative and strategic dimensions of identity constitution through goods have been foregrounded in theories of late modernity. Participation to the market as consumers features as crucial for the accomplishment of individual identity in the age of what authors such as Beck (1992), Giddens (1991) or Baumann (1992) have called 'reflexive individualization'. Much emphasis has thus been placed on purposive individual stylisation of oneself through consumer choices. In this perspective in a situation of cultural de-classification and increasing emphasis on individuality, the self becomes a reflexive and secular project which works on ever refined levels of body presentation (Giddens 1991). This involves unremitting self-monitoring, self-scrutiny, planning and ordering of elements and choices into a coherent narrative of identity.

If, for liberalism, choice is just freedom, for these theories choice is somehow compulsory: we are forced into it not so much by the drive of the capitalist economy, but by the absence of a stable social and cultural order in a post-traditional society. Consumer choice is not only central, it is obligatory. We have 'no choice, but to choose' – writes Anthony Giddens (1991: 81). For Beck (1932: 131) '[l]iberalism presupposed a coherent identity, yet identity seems to be precisely the main problem of modern existence and is itself something to be chosen'; the self is thus 'a project which is directed to us by a pluralized world and must be pursued within that pluralized world'. Of course, together with choice comes self-responsibility for the chosen self, and risk-perception changes accordingly: now risks are in the region of anomy, linked to the incapacity to perform convincingly a positively valued self through one's own choices. As Giddens observes (1991: 80), late modernity confronts the individual with a complex diversity of choices which is 'non-foundational', produces anxiety and offers 'little help as to which options should be selected'. The solution to such risk and anxiety to be found in consumer culture is, for Baumann (1990: 200), 'technical': it solves the problem of the durable and coherent self in the face of incessant non-foundational complexity by treating all problems as solvable through specific commodities. Each of them may be highly functional to a precise task, but they still have to be arranged in a coherent, credible whole. Lifestyle, as a reflexive attempt at consumer coherence, can be seen as a way in which the pluralism of post-traditional identity is managed by individuals and organised (or exploited) by commerce.

Giddens stresses that in the context of post-traditional societies 'the cumulative choices that combine to form a lifestyle define the nucleus of a person's identity': 'the very core of self-identity' is 'mobile' and 'reflexive', made of 'routinized practices . . . reflexively open to change', with consumer choices, the 'small decisions a person makes every day', being 'not only about how to act but who to be' (1991: 81). Lifestyle orders things into a certain unity, reducing the plurality of choice and affording a sense of 'ontological security'. Social reproduction is thus transferred from traditional culture to the market for goods (and labour). The notion of individual wants becomes central to economic growth and standardised consumption patterns become central to economic stability, reducing risks not only for individuals but also for corporations. This may bring us to conceive of the self as a commodity itself, and indeed Giddens seems to adumbrate a process of self-commodification with 'self-actualisation [being] packaged and distributed according to market criteria' (ibid.: 198). While similar approaches may run the risk of over-emphasising reflexivity and its burden on identity constitution – thus echoing the works of authors such as Lasch or Baudrillard – they have recently been very important for the establishment of a reflection on consumer identities, and we shall critically elaborate on their suggestions in the last section.

Main criticisms

Polemic views on consumer identities inspired by the different works of Lasch, Baudrillard or Bordo, and often drawing on critical theories – from Adorno to Marcuse – have been as influential as they have been criticised. Not only do they rest on a value-laden opposition between the sphere of consumption and that of work which is being increasingly contradicted in the lives of especially the new middle-classes engaged in creative professions, but also they do not consider that rather than producing a pathological consumer as its norm, consumer culture offers visions of normality which people are asked to engage with. Furthermore, polemic views are often characterised by a textualist bias which derive consumers' meanings from analyses of objectified promotional texts such as advertising messages and images. Despite their popularity, such views have thus been strongly criticised as being unable to grasp the lived social experiences of consumption: consumers are not simply bombarded by advertising images, they have to decode such images and will do so in different ways according to locally situated contexts of consumption. To identify consumer culture with its most visible surface, advertising culture, draws a biased picture. How we experience ourselves, manage embodied identities, participate in social rituals and relations is, to a great extent, mediated by consumer culture. But consumer culture cannot be reduced to a collection of signs in advertising images; rather, it should be understood as lived culture made by embodied agents situated in specific institutional contexts and embedded in social relations.

As suggested, the main contemporary theories which have addressed consumer agency and identity have brought consumption back into everyday social relations, opening the way for an embedded understanding of this relevant aspect of modern subjectivity constitution. Once we move away from theories that consider consumption in late modern society as either purely instrumentally rational (such as crude versions of neoclassical economics) or purely irrational, induced or determined (a few variants of critical theory), theories of consumer agency can be placed on a fairly simple review synopsis. They may largely be divided into theories that focus on what consumers *do* and theories that focus on what they *are*, on the one hand; theories which focus on relations of power and meanings *among* consumers, and theories which focus on relations of power and meanings *of* consumers with other institutions or phenomena of modernity, on the other.

Theories of anthropological background – such as the seminal works of Bourdieu or Douglas – tend to focus on what consumers do among themselves: communication, distinction, appropriation for ritual purposes, symbolic power relations featuring consumption as a communicative or embodied practice which stabilises social relations. As such they tend to lose sight of what consumers are, or better of how they are constituted in particular vis-à-vis powerful collective actors such as the commercialisation system. That is, they tend to discount the normative aspect of consumption, and the cultural working of the circuit of the commodity. Extremely influential, the works of both Douglas and Bourdieu have also been positively criticised (Sassatelli 2007 for a detailed review). Douglas has been criticised for her cognitivist approach to identity and the possibility of re-introducing a maximising rationality connected to the reflexive pursuit of identity rather than utility. Bourdieu, on his part, has been accused of providing a fairly hierarchical and determinist picture of social stratification and of running the risk of falling into dualistic reasoning (with a structuralist explanation regarding homology and the standardisation of taste coupled with a voluntarist one at the level of individual action).

Bourdieu's work in particular has been a major source of inspiration not only for a vast amount of empirical research, but also a number of fruitful theoretical reaction and refinement. Bourdieu's thesis that differences in wants and styles are always representative of, and reducible to, intimate dispositions of taste has, for example, been considered a sort of 'material ideology' (Miller 1987: 161), a situation whereby the representations of a particular group deny alternative perspectives access to a given aspect of culture and portray the forced preferences so constructed as belonging exclusively to those excluded – such as when dominant classes attribute degrading hygienic preferences to subordinate classes, which are in fact the result of a state of necessity.

More broadly, scholars of consumer practices have focused on their internal complexity, on their creativity and on their capacity to generate classifications, styles and ultimately 'capital' in their own right (Sassatelli 2007). Whilst they are far from being the direct expression of a natural individuality or of self-interested calculation, the cultures of consumption may consolidate identities and dispositions which are relatively disarticulated from structural division (class, profession, gender). In particular, at least in some cases – for example, sub-cultures or amateur practices – it is the practices of consumption themselves which create a structure for the standardisation of taste. Bourdieu's habitus helps us consider that it is not enough to postulate a relationship between taste and the world of things, since the second does not generate the first, or vice versa. Still, to approach consumption and identity, we need to consider that their encounter is indeed creative: understanding how tastes and material culture find correspondences and are mutually shaped requires more attention to the local contexts of consumption, and in particular to the institutions which mediate acquisition and use, organising identities, interaction and manners in ways which consumers consider appropriate.

More recent works such as those of Miller, De Certeau and the British cultural studies tradition have coupled an emphasis on everyday practice with attention to the circuit of the commodity, emphasising the active role of consumers in finishing and, in fact, transforming commodities. This new wave of studies also focuses on what consumers do. Yet their attention to power relations is addressed as relations both among consumers (rituals, sub-cultures) and between consumers and other social actors (the promotional system, for example), which may illuminate the dialectical processes of commoditisation and de-commoditisation. Still, they have also been criticised. Miller's works can be read as running the risk of placing a disproportionate emphasis on a defiant consumer, emphasising the subjective consolation offered by consumption and discounting the systemic differences in power between producers and consumers. Similar criticism have also been addressed at De Certeau's discussion of consumption as a form of production, against Hedbige's treatment of sub-cultural consumption and, to a lesser extent, Willis's notion of symbolic creativity. Despite their emphasis on symbolic processes surrounding commoditisation and de-commoditisation, these approaches also largely eschew questions as to how consumers are constituted as such, in particular questions as to the normative power of the notion of the consumer as a social category.

It is precisely in addressing what consumers are that authors such as Giddens, Baumann or Beck have looked at consumer identities. This has been done largely in the framework of a theory reflexive individualisation which tends to stress reflexivity, either in a triumphant or in a worried voice, as paramount characterisation of the consumer. As suggested, identity, consumption, choice and projectuality are indeed strongly related in contemporary culture, and yet we should be wary of considering consumption as a purely reflexive activity as it may appear in theories of reflexive individualisation. Indeed, in many domains of action mediated by commercial relations we are not asked to rely only on our freedom of choice to account for participation, preference and taste. Reference to an ultimate 'authentic', 'original' and 'natural' self are becoming strong cultural options, often related to the advice of experts and supported by the norms of consumers institution, as much as other cultural options such as snobbism, imitation, distinction or fashion have come to be looked at with some suspicion (Sassatelli 2007). More broadly, routines have been shown to be important in understanding ordinary consumer practices – from eating to supermarket shopping, from going to a gym to using a car. When we consume, precisely because we act in practical ways, we do not reflect on everything; to the contrary, the meanings we attribute to our practices and the narratives with which we reflexively create our trajectory of consumption at least partly reflect (that is, blindly construct upon) the conditions in which we find ourselves and act. The bounded reflexivity of consumption corresponds to the fact that people not only express but also constitute themselves through what they get and use. Consumption not only expresses but also performs identity: through making objects their own, social actors make themselves, both as consumers and as selves with specific and different roles linked to different identity markers such as ethnicity, gender sexuality, gender, social status, etc., which are loosely coupled with specific styles of consumption. There is a tendency in the reflexive individualisation thesis to provide fairly abstract theories of consumer identity to the effect of overlooking everyday consumer practices (what people do with goods) and how they engage with a variety of social identities not reducible to consumption. This tendency corresponds to a conflation of the normative aspect of identity building (what consumers are as normative social persona) and the practical aspect of agency constitution, which is much more embedded, varied, conflicting and contested, and which provides feedback on the consumer as a normative social identity.

Future developments are anticipated

A number of issues have become central in the current scholarship on consumer agency and identity: choice, reflexivity and normativity. Developing some of the arguments sketched in the previous section, I shall consider the theory of reflexive individualisation on the backdrop of these main issues offering a few suggestions about future developments. Such developments are very likely to be crucial for contemporary culture, politics and society given the centrality that the 'consumer' as a social persona has gained in contemporary societies.

Admittedly, in post-traditional societies defined by consumer culture, the relation of the self to commodities is crucial and subjectively elaborated (via personal style, self-narration, and so forth). But just like it is wrong to conceive of it as crystalline, all-powerful reflexivity, it would be a mistake to consider that reflexive individualisation preludes to the death of the subject, as if what is expected of the consumer-self at the end of their projects is meaningless subjugation. To explore this, let us consider what Simmel, an acknowledged source of inspiration for the theories of reflexive individualisation, suggested. According to Simmel (1990), as modernity progresses social actors move from a situation in which their identity is, as it were, imposed by the things which they happen to possess (i.e. their actions are determined by bundles of objects corresponding to a traditional and rigid distribution of roles and resources), to a situation of 'absolute potentiality'. With the triumph of commercial culture individuals are freed from the structural links with goods that 'enslave' them: objects have become commodities, they can be bought and exchanged by subjects. The most immediate consequence of this is the neutralisation of the power of things to determine people's identity. However, the freedom that money confers paves the way to indeterminacy, it is a freedom 'without any directive, without any definite and determining content. Such freedom favours that emptiness and instability that allows one to give full rein to every accidental, whimsical and tempting impulse' (ibid.: 402). In this situation thus we have greater 'negative freedom' – that is, freedom *from* external bonds, including restrictions as linked to tradition, religion and magic, etc. – on what to consume and how, but 'positive freedom' – that is, freedom *to* do things – may be in jeopardy. In fact, negative freedom does not afford indications for the constitution of individual identities consistent through time; thus people's lives may be dominated by a nostalgic desire to confer new meanings to things and a constant uneasiness with respect to the rationale of their consumption.

As suggested elsewhere (Sassatelli 2007), this perspective is resolutely opposed to the idea that commoditisation, and with it the multiplications of images and objects, accompanies the dissolution of the subject and the collapse of available space for appropriating, decoding and de-commoditising objects and images. Instead, the space available for the subject increases, but paradoxically it is precisely for this reason that one can find oneself paralysed, incapable of giving personal value to things. In other words, the constitution of the subject through goods is an active but inconclusive process, a never-ending endeavour which cannot provide once and for all a stable identity. Still, it is precisely because of this inconclusiveness that consumption is a creative and dynamic process, an ongoing emancipation from the constraints implicit in the possession of any particular good or goods combination. As a corollary to this we shall consider playfulness and aestheticisation, the logic of self-experimentation, of imaginary or tamed hedonism (see Campbell 1987; Featherstone 1991; Sassatelli 2000) associated with the modern consumer as the result of a cultural obligation to produce oneself as the original source of value of commodities. Expressed in wider social–theoretical terms, we may say that contemporary consumer practices allows for a maximum of individual specificity, but pass onto the subject the onus of justification, the possibility that such specificity finds its place in the social order. This may well correspond to what Erving Goffman famously branded as 'bureaucratization of the spirit': the fragmentary condition of the modern subject who has to manage a highly specific set of different roles while projecting a unitary and coherent self. Clearly in many ways this is broader than consumption. The experimental, experiential investment of the self, for example, extends into the corporate world whereby creative workers are expected to be good at selling themselves; adopting an entrepreneurial, promotional outlook as to themselves, needing a projectual, flexible, creative self who is always pursuing some sort of activity, never to be without a project always to be looking forward to, and preparing for, something.

On these premises we should avoid considering that reflexive individualisation simply couples with an unremitting process of commoditisation which extends entirely to the self. Surely commercial relations extend today in private domains which were often encoded through what was construed as opposed to the market and coded as interpersonal, affective relations. But we have come to appreciate the extent to which market and emotions are and have always been intertwined, sustaining each other in a continuous dialectic made of conflicts and accommodations. Furthermore, if we focus on consumption and identity, we should appreciate that modern consumers are first and above all asked to be active, to produce themselves as the source of value, participating in the process of de-commoditisation and indeed constituting themselves as agents of such process. Put differently, consumption is a sphere of action regulated according to the cultural principle of individual expression. Obviously, this is not to say that the actor is absolutely free. To the contrary, the subjectivity required by consumption is, in some ways, a binding individuality. In order to adequately perform their social roles as consumers, actors must thus find a point of balance between the bored indifference of the blasé, the pursuit of difference as an end in itself of the eccentric, and indeed the other-directed strive for distinction of the snob. They must express their deepest and most peculiar subjectivities.

As a normative cultural identity, the 'consumer' appears in striking continuity with hegemonic modern views of subjectivity. As Sennett and Taylor have famously shown, the development of capitalist society has consolidated and popularised a particular notion of the subject: the autonomous actor in a growing distance from objects. As commodities, objects are increasingly seen as radically different from humans, and this growing distance between the nature of people on one side, and that of objects on the other accompanies the idea that objects can compromise people's humanity rather than complete it. Still, from Locke onward, modern identity also relies on material objects and property for grounding. There is thus a fundamental contradiction in the way in which we conceive modern identity: a paradox between idealism and materialism which clearly defines our relation with consumption. Briefly, such paradox entails that subjects perform their identity through commodities as difference from commodities. Idealism thus stimulates materialism: in fact, in contrast to many tribal societies where people become the objects through which the values of a culture are fixed, in our culture things have been given the fundamental role of objectifying cultural categories, of tangibly fixing meanings and values (Miller 1987).

In such circumstances, the notion of individual choice acquires momentum as a hegemonic normative frame which has been both sustained by expert knowledge and deployed through a myriad of local norms and particularities to evaluate consumer practices, their worth, moral adequacy and normality (Sassatelli 2007). Choosing things just for a try or just for fun, for present physical enjoyment or for sophisticated aesthetic pleasure is fine so long as it is the self who is playing the game. As such, choice relies on specific anthropological presuppositions: invited to think of themselves as choosers, individuals are asked to promote their desires and pleasures as the ultimate source of value while keeping mastery over them. To consume properly, people must be masters of their will. In other terms, consumers are sovereigns of the market in so far as they are sovereigns of themselves. The consumer's sovereignty is a double-edged sovereignty: hedonism, the search for pleasure, must be tempered by various forms of detachment which stress the subject's capacity to guide that search, to dose pleasures, to avoid addiction, to be, in a word, recognisable as someone who autonomously chooses. If renouncing the material world has been one way that many cultures have used to signal a spiritual calling (early Christian anchorites, Buddhist monks, medieval saints refusing food, etc.), our world, both idealist and materialist, calls on us all to positively demonstrate our capacity to choose. In this situation, even the fact that our desires may discover different objects, and that our chosen objects are continuously changing may help in sustaining the game of having a self-possessed self. The development of the so-called post-Fordist economy may be seen in this light: the ceaseless innovation of consumer goods, the continuously superseded adoption of different fashions, the endless combination of styles appears to grant consumers a continuous liberation from the specific objects which they have chosen, allowing for the renewed exercise of choice. Paradoxically enough, the possibility to 'exit' (i.e. choose not to choose, to discard or change) a particular good remains a powerful means to guarantee that what links us to it is indeed our choice. This obviously does not imply a return to asceticism, but rather a quest for novelty and authenticity, in the view that the emphasis must remain on the subject and his or her right to satisfy desires with objects, and not on the objects and their pleasures. Individuals who are sovereigns of themselves and of their will have not only the capacity to continue willing what they once chose as it corresponded to their desires, but they can also exit that choice should the conditions of choice be altered, the initial wants remain unsatisfied or shift in accountable ways matching market novelties and individual authenticity, or indeed their capacity for autonomous choice be put into question as happens when the specter of 'addiction' is evoked.

Today, consumption increasingly appears as a terrain of ambivalence for the development of human identities. By this I am referring to its dual character, whereby it may be able to emancipate people from some power relations, while binding them to other specific conditions; offer significant capacities which may become heavy burdens; and solve certain problems but create others. Consumption is a disputed terrain which not always heralds freedom, but nonetheless potentially carries social change, creativity and satisfaction – depending on its organisation. As suggested, in (late) modernity it has largely been organised around the expression of individual identity, with a far too autonomous, self-contained, self-possessed vision of the self as its reference point. Consumption is instead a symbolic and practical affair of a deeply social nature: it can only partly be reflexive as it is grounded in institutionally enforced rituals and interactions; it can only partly reflect the wishes of an autonomous self as this very self partly constitutes itself through practices of consumption. While not simply absorbing and dissolving the subject into the process of commoditisation which largely defines its horizon in late modern societies, consumption does not overturn commoditisation: it re-frames it, re-works on it, often at its margins, with limited consequences, and in subterraneous, rather than triumphant, ways. Sure, the same fear of consumerism and materialism which is often found in sociological reflection on consumption can also be found in many consumers all over the world, precisely when they buy, use and organise goods in everyday life. Likewise, the consumption of commodities can be one way in which global brands may be successfully confronted – that is, it is through certain kinds of consumption (green, alternative, local, traditional, etc.) that people can oppose the homogenisation promoted by capitalist production and global business. Still, the power of consumption as a practical everyday activity is also its weakness: informal, local, relatively autonomous, relatively inconsequential as such, it needs structural valorisation through the mediation of intermediaries (cultural, political, economic and the like) to acquire the normative force of a path to socially recognised and normatively approved consumer identities.

References

Appadurai, A. (ed.) (1986) *The Social Life of Things: Commodities in Cultural Perspectives*. Cambridge: Cambridge University Press.

Baudrillard, J. (1998) *The Consumer Society: Myths and Structures*. London: Sage [1970].

Bauman, Z. (1992) *Intimations of Post-Modernity*. London: Routledge.

Beck, U. (1992) *Risk Society: Towards a New Modernity*. London: Sage [1986].

Bordo, S. (1993) *Unbearable Weight: Feminism, Western Culture and the Body*. Berkeley: University of California Press.

Bourdieu, P. (1984) *Distinction: A Social Critique of the Judgement of Taste*. London: Routledge [1979].

Campbell, C. (1987) *The Romantic Ethic and the Spirit of Modern Consumerism*. Oxford: Basil Blackwell.

De Certeau, M. (1984) *The Practice of Everyday Life*. Berkeley: University of California Press [1979].

Douglas, M. and Isherwood, B. (1979) *The World of Goods: Towards and Anthropology of Consumption*. New York: Basic Books.

Featherstone, M. (1991) *Consumer Culture and Postmodernism*. London: Sage.

Giddens, A. (1991) *Modernity and Self-Identity*. Cambridge: Polity.

Hebdige, D. (1979) *Subculture: The Meaning of Style*. London: Methuen.

Lasch, C. (1991) *The Culture of Narcissism*. New York: Norton [1979].

McCracken, G. (1988) *Culture and Consumption: New Approaches to the Symbolic Character of Consumer Goods and Activities*. Bloomington: Indiana University Press.

Miller, D. (1987) *Material Culture and Mass Consumption*. Oxford: Basil Blackwell.

Miller, D. (2004) 'The little black dress is the solution, but what is the problem?', in K.M. Ekström, and H. Brembeck (eds) *Elusive Consumption*. Oxford: Berg.

Mukerji, C. (1983) *From Graven Images: Patterns of Modern Materialism*. New York: Columbia University Press.

Sassatelli, R. (2000) 'Tamed hedonism: choice, desire and deviant pleasure', in A. Warde and Y. Gronow, eds, *Ordinary Consumption*. London: Harwood, 93–106.

Sassatelli, R. (2007) *Consumer Culture: History, Theory, Politics*. London: Sage.

Simmel, G. (1971) 'Fashion', in G. Simmel, *On Individuality and Social Forms*. Chicago: Chicago University Press, 294–323, [1904].

Simmel, G. (1990) *Philosophy of Money*, 2nd edition. London: Routledge [orig. second ed. 1907].

Veblen, T. (1994) *The Theory of the Leisure Class*. London: Macmillan [1899].

Willis, P. (1978) *Profane Culture*. London: Routledge.

15

Identity, mortality and death

Tamara Waraschinski and Charles Lemert

Introduction

Through the ages death, mortality, and dying have been the official subjects of religions great and small. Almost by definition, death was then a blank spot on the map of human identities.

In ancient and traditional times, the good death, usually in battle, was a semiotic limit on mortality as the eraser of individual human worth. Heroes, knights, and a few heroines might die, such as Beowulf or Gilgamesh, in a cosmic struggle with the evil ones, thus to be remembered forever in an accretion of fictions that over centuries would attach to whatever kernel of fact remained in the cumulated legends that in time became the truth of the matter. A myth exceeds a legend, as a symbol outruns a sign, by virtue of being elevated to a transcendental status beyond the logic and proofs and that came to certify alleged facts as true accounts of some reality. Yet, even with all the powers of myth and legend, we know from the close historical record that from prehistorical times down to the modern death and dying, as deep considerations of the meaning of human life, have undergone a good number of transformations. Perhaps none were more perplexing that those that arose, roughly in the middle centuries of the modern age, from Hobbes and Descartes through Kant and Hegel; then William James and Freud brought down to the present time, nearly simultaneously, and anti–religious skepticism that has waxed and waned, nearly along the same aberrant curve as the concept of self-identity has slowly, but incompletely, wrenched itself away from the religious and cultural myths of the eternal soul.

Historical and intellectual development

History of changes in attitudes toward death in the absence of an identity concept

Attitudes toward death changed, quite naturally with changes in human interactions with their surrounds – both natural and social. This almost obvious fact is striking in inverse proportion to the small number of comprehensive histories of the death and dying. One important exception is Allan Kellehear's *A Social History of Dying* (2007) with its focus on historical and archeological material and sources that provide a reliable road through the quite different and changing stages of human experience. In Kellehear's first stage in the social history of death and dying – the Stone Age – he speculates that death must have been an "otherworldly journey." Archaeological findings indicate that the burial practices in the early prehistory of human society were based on religious beliefs about the afterlife (Kellehear 2007: 35). Dying was a displaced experience, shifted into an afterlife and out of the individual's control. This of course is a bit unremarkable when considering, as Kellehear does, that the earliest human communities were organized in the unpredictable world of the hunter and gatherer for whom death came suddenly and unexpectedly. Under these severe nomadic conditions, with all of the risks attended to changing sources of food not to mention predators, there was little opportunity, or even one might say "reason," to reflect on mortality. Death was common – so common that it would have been uncommon for social groups at this stage to engage in anything like a systematic or even narrative preparation for death. Dealing with death was not, therefore, part of the interior aspects of individuals (if we can even speak of the human "individual" at this early evolutionary stage). Instead, death, dealing with death, was the work of the group and thus a dispersed element in the cultural background of group identity (if again, we can speak of "identity" at this stage). Collectively, death was a recognizable even familiar aspect of social life and one that in a sense was accounted for in a group's understanding of itself but not an experience that could be anticipated (ibid.: 25ff.).

Kellehear's second stage in the social history of death and dying is, quite naturally, the period of settlement and early agricultural economies – which he labels the Pastoral Age. In part due to the somewhat great density of the settled populations as well as their sharper demarcations from one another, the experience of death increasingly came in the form of infectious diseases, famines, and warfare. Death became more predictable and, in this sense, Kellehear suggests one finds the traces of what he calls a "participating self" in respect to human mortality. Then emerged the outlines of the social concept of a *Good Death* whereby the dying could engage in ritualized and narratives preparations for death in cooperation with the family and community. The otherworldly journey starts in *this* life or this world and dying became "a *living* thing in this *world*" (ibid.: 86). With the *Good Death*, Kellehear defines a further development of a new awareness of dying which gave the dying person some control but also involved the entire community. Of course the flipside of this development is the *Bad Death*, which hits unawares and leaves no change to make any preparation.

Another important resource for the social history of the social understanding of death is Philippe Ariès's now classic works *Western Attitudes Toward Death* (1974) and *The Hour of Our Death* (1983). In the latter, he examines the history of burial practices and identifies among settled cultures the first signs of a shift from the anonymity of a person to, in his words, a "desire to be oneself" or "the discovery of the individual, the discovery, at the hour of our death, of one's own identity, one's personal biography, in this world as in the next" (Aries 1983: 293). In these times, roughly from Kellehear's Pastoral Age (in the West the Middle Ages) down to the earlier formations of the premodern village (again predominantly in the West), the immortal soul came to be the centre of what in latter times came to be known as the personality or the individuality itself. The soul was understood to be safe from harm after the demise of the mortal body – and this as the faculty wherein is located the capacity for a self-conscious notion of the moral worth of the mortal individual. Here, as Aries put it, death was tamed and it became normal to speak of the anticipation of mortality. The tame death was, in effect, an accompaniment to a religious belief in a peaceful and subdued afterlife – still, to be sure, a deeply religious notion, but (and especially in the West where the major religions were monotheistic) a notion that contained already the kernels of the soul as the essential interior feature of the individual;

hence, centuries later, as we will see, from the taming of the dead soul would come the modern idea of self-identity.

Through discovery of the own death, a tame death, there arose the elemental secrets of individuality (Aries 1974: 51). Beginning with the eighteenth century, death had a new emphasis – the death of the other fused with Romantic melancholy to make death admirable in its beauty (ibid.: 68). Mourning, thus, became an act of exaggeration and the death of the other was more feared than one's own death (ibid.: 68). This reluctance to accept the death of a loved one formed the basis of a cultic veneration of the dead. Criticism toward the churches, which seem to fail in caring for the souls of those who have died, arose and this in turn slowly gave way to a new belief system and a merely private handling of death. By cultivating the memory of a loved one, a new form of immortality strategy emerged that was no longer anchored in religious belief in some sort of afterlife. Due to the intolerance of another's death, friends and relatives had no longer the courage to tell the truth to a terminally ill person. This new attitude soon led to another development, a major characteristic of modernity. In Aries words:

> One must avoid – no longer for the sake of the dying person, but for society's sake, for the sake of those close to the dying person – the disturbance and the overly strong and unbearable emotion caused by the ugliness of dying and by the very presence of death in the midst of a happy life, for it is henceforth given that life is always happy or should always seem to be so.
>
> *(ibid.: 87)*

Hence, the tensions between medieval and early modern attitudes toward death clashed. In this fray the hidden seeds of the modern idea of the individual could be found – thus, in turn, of identity as related simultaneously to self-understanding and, in effect, the death of the self. Of course, it would be some time before the modern idea of self-identity would surface. These advances were, to be sure, accompaniments of the social changes of the later medieval period.

Early forms of urban development in the Late Middle Ages when the beginnings of global and region trade required larger economic conglomerations and destinations – roughly, the beginnings of the Age of the City – gave rise to the middle classes. The mercantile classes were, in effect, the occasion of the gentrification of the Good Death. The attitude toward death as a natural event in life was replaced with more anxiety and fear of death. The loss of one's dignity in a slow process of painful dying was at the center of the urban middle-class anxiety. In Kellehear's words:

> Dying, from the perspective of the anxious middle classes, could no longer be viewed as "good" if the severity of suffering took every dignity from one before the end, if one lost some of the most important values integral to one's identity: personal control, the ability to think and choose, even to arrange one's affairs with a clear mind.
>
> *(Kellehear 2007: 145)*

The Good Death was replaced with a "Well-managed Death" in which professions such as official authorities and lawyers, as well as clergy, played a major role. As the city grew into its more complex modern forms, notably in the eighteenth and nineteenth centuries, once tight-knit communities and personal relationships shifted to more professional and reserved interactions. This of course is part and parcel with all of the familiar dichotomies of the emergence of modern life – from rural to urban, from traditional to rational, from mechanical to organic solidarity, from feudalism to capitalism, and so forth.

Yet, in specific reference to death and dying, it was also a time in which the medical professions emerged in their modern form as agents associated with the process of death and dying. Hence, the irony that Michel Foucault, in *Birth of the Clinic* (1973), identified – the modern practice of medicine (and thus the institutional of the modern hospital) required a relaxation of moral prohibitions against the physician examining the body by palpating its surfaces and orifices. In this very act of modern diagnostic medicine, the professional at once became more intimate with the patient as the patient was inserted in the modern technologies of health and care for the body. As a result, insofar as care of body entailed attentions to its morbidity, awareness of death and dealing with it was bit by bit removed from everyday life. As the urban middle classes became increasingly privatized and sequestered from community involvement with the masses, so too did their attitudes toward death and dying. This gradually became an "individualist model of the Good Death" where the dying person assumes as much control as possible over her own death in order to please her individual desire (Kellehear 2007: 152). Kellehear concludes:

> Dying in hunter-gatherer societies was viewed as "unlucky", malevolent or perhaps "mercifully quick" deaths for their communities. And among settler societies dying was viewed as morally "good" or "bad" for both individual *and* communities. But among the urban middle classes all these moral prescriptions and judgments were transferred to themselves as individuals alone.

(ibid.: 152)

Kellehear may somewhat over state the case by his rather stark periodization of the major ages in the evolution of human understandings of death, but his scheme is a reliable enough representation of the uncertain role that mortality played in individual and collective self-identifications, and of how one might suspect that only in the Modern, Urban Age would death assume a clear place in identities and identifications. But, still again, an irony as the modern culture of individual self-identification emerged in association with the urban middle class, death actually slipped away to hide behind what Ernest Becker and others called the denial of death.

Major claims, developments and key contributions

Death as a source of identification work and the modern culture of denial

Elsewhere in this handbook, the reader can find a more explicit and detail presentation of the history of the identification concept (see Chapter 1). For now, the challenge before us is to account for the remarkable slippage between the emergence of modern concepts of self-identification and the ironic denial of what we call identification work as also the hard work of coming to terms with mortality.

From a bird's-eye view, this denial is a familiar story, first told in modern times by Max Weber whose famous *Protestant Ethic and the Spirit of Capitalism* is the *locus classicus* of the theory that modern capitalism required a spirit (or ethical disposition) of rational calculation which he labeled *this-worldly asceticism*. While Weber cleverly teased this widespread disposition out of earlier Calvinist doctrine, his highly influential theory entailed the assumption that the original religious effect would fade away, leaving his spirit of capitalism as a purely secular ethic. The genius of Weber's analysis is the insight that, in spite of its other-worldly purpose, the Protestant revolution in modern thought rooted in the ideal of a free individual able to reflect on his individual choices – in the seventeenth century on the choice to believe, in the twentieth century on the choice to engage in entrepreneurial activities that require free, rational calculations as to the costs and benefits of his actions. Quite in contrast to his contemporaries, Durkheim, the descendents of Marx, and even Freud, Weber's individual was, first, middle class, and second, an individual with, if not a clear self-identity, at least the mental equipment needed to reflect on the future consequences of his actions – hence, in effect, to formulate an ideal of where, so to speak, and who he wanted to be in the future. Yet, in keeping with the paradox that Becker and others later diagnosed, Weber himself (like most classical social theorists) could not account for the finality by which the meaning of actions would come to an end in death. This basic principle was of course a condensation of the already powerful (in Weber's day early in twentieth century) Enlightenment and Classical Economic theory that human economic progress implied growth without end – which, in turn, at the level of the individual identity, necessitated a denial of death and at the level of the modern ideology of human history required, in effect, that the nature of human history was that it would not end; or, that history itself would always make progress and, to be sure, never die. Hence the denial of death.

Yet, it hardly need be said that modern, urban and economic, culture still had to invent fundamental ways to deal with death – that is, is to anticipate or deny it. Either way, both attitudes generate the creative energy, which is culture building, but they also shape our identity in unconscious ways.

To overcome the bleakness and void that mortality threatens, even in the modern period (and this is another irony) human cultures sought shelter from what Kierkegaard calls the sickness unto death (or what be might be called the death anxiety). This is one reason that in spite of the general theory that the modern era was a profoundly secular age, in point of fact religion never really died away and instead, along with secular analogies (of which Marx's classless society is the most famous), contributed to the generation of a sense of life's meaning through creating unities and religious imagination. Thus, though in the modern age death was denied, it remains a powerful feature on the horizon of innovative solutions for the problem of human identity. In an odd sense the repression of death drove the engine to create bigger unions and make meaningful connections.

Needless to say, in a scientific age, the absence of evidence about a hereafter or an immortal soul makes it difficult for the modern and rationally trained mind to embrace the thought that life continues after the body dies. Near death experiences, for example, have been declared as hallucinations arising from chemical reactions in the brain. Scholars have split opinions regarding this issue. Looking back at history it is obvious that people not only frequently encountered death but also had customs to embed death in their daily life. However, in the nineteenth century things started to fundamentally change. Thus, to understand modern (or, if one wants, postmodern) attitudes toward death, it is important, as next we will do, to engage the key contributions to the dilemma of modernity's riddle – how can death be both a fact of life and source of meaning. We suggest that in general terms this involves dealing with the contradiction between the anticipation (or certain knowledge of) death and its denial.

From the tame death to shameful death – the erasure of identity

In premodern times, and what Aries called the tameness of death, people surrendered to the violation of their routine through plagues, wars, floods and the like. Before the Age of Reason, death was no secret nor was it an extraordinary event. Death was everywhere present, immutable, inescapable, and integrated in daily life. And, in this sense, identities where given in the sense that "everything was stuck to its place in the great chain of being and things ran their course by themselves" (Bauman 1992: 97). Zygmunt Bauman thus puts flesh on the bones of Aries's idea of the tame death – a taming brought about by brining death more or less consciously into the normal, if unsettled, core of human cultures.

Tame death or the anticipation of mortality is, therefore, the oldest death there is (Aries 1983: 29). The eighteenth century was the first time when death was "conceived as a major scandal of the whole human adventure" (Bauman 1992: 133). The effort of the Enlightenment was to change human fate and to turn the world into a better place controlled by reason. Thus, as we have said, began the process of radicalizing the tame death by denying its centrality – a move that was essential to the development of modern this-worldly moralities.

As Kellehear emphasizes in this historic development of the issue, in attitudes toward death that came with urbanization, increasing wealth, social power, education and secularization led to a questioning in the belief in an afterlife, was called into question. Death could no longer be a Good Death since it was senseless, savage, incomprehensible and thus seen as a threat. The decline of religious imagination meant that suffering had lost its meaning (Kübler-Ross 1976: 14) This in turn lead to a series of scientific attempts to explain, at least, the stages of dying, of which the most famous is the work of Elizabeth Kübler-Ross. Death had to be brought under human control, it was not longer tame, it had to be tamed and these attempts to account for the stages of dying allowed, at least, a methodical attitude toward the anticipation of death and, in turn, to the now wide-spread science of palliative care for the dying.

Still these developments were in the context of other developments, beginning late in the nineteenth century and contributed to the other pole of tension between anticipation and denial. Death became largely anonymous. Malignancies and chronic diseases had become more common even with the anticipation of a long life, supported by the facts through the twentieth century of a noted rise of life expectancy. Still, after what Foucault called the birth of the clinic, dying people came to be isolated from the rest of the society. They were, first in the middle classes but later more universally, removed from everyday experience and in effect absorbed into medical institutions such as hospitals and nursing homes (Aiken 2001: 16) and, in due course, hospices for the palliative care of dying. The key to the modern practice was the evolution of official institutions for the removal of death from ordinary life. The practice itself was, however, now new. In pre-industrial societies people removed themselves from contact with the dying individual *after* death. Bodies were kept of course in the home, or otherwise put on display, but they were quickly and routinely buried. In the Modern Age the community retreats and people retire before the individual dies, leaving his fate in the hands of medical personnel and specialized technologies (of which various homes for the aging are not well studied as part of the technologies of abandonment of the dying).

That which was once the domain of church has today become the domain of medicine and its many extension and apparatuses. Through this transition, so argues Elisabeth Kübler-Ross among others, death has lost its human dimension. Dealing with the chronic and terminally ill is mechanized, depersonalized, and dehumanized (Kübler Ross 1976: 12; Hunt 2005: 208). Yet, the transformation was not without other adjustments in the ancient doctrines. Even though the medicalization of dying came to be absorbed in a new institutional section, medical progress extended the life span and permitted another rather contradictory notion to enter the culture of death. The "good death" was thus to become the death of one who lived to old age – a death often considered good even as the elderly are abandoned to their own or institutional devices. The corollary thus became that the "bad death" was the death of the young. This of course had its culture corollaries (ones that went beyond the personal tragedy of the experience of the death of a child). A pre-mature death became in effect a threat to the natural life sequence, which itself had been medicalized through various psychologies of life's normal developmental ages, most of which portrayed death as the climax of old age and thus natural for those who enjoy longevity. Logically, death of a child or youth is perceived as particular dramatic (Howarth 1998: 673) precisely because in a culture where the meaning (or identity) of human life is an integral aspect of a general ideology of progress without limits, the "bad death" was one that, in youth, reminded all of the improbability of that general culture faith. In this ideology of denial one can see the traces of death's powerful grip on the human imagination. A culture may deny (which is to say: put out of sight) death but in the death of the very young (including those who die in war) the finitude of the self and thus of self-identification is omnipresent.

Death thus is a confounding puzzle to the very idea of modern self-understanding. Modernity is nothing if it is not a culture of mastery over everything – even those realities that do not fit into its paradigm of progress, growth, and security. Modernity in effect offered the promise of an erasure of the unpredictable, the unavoidable, the unexpected, and the unknown. And, to be certain, its remarkable scientific and technological innovations and advances lent plausible support to the promise. But death to be sure is another matter altogether. It cannot be over-powered or outrun. Jokes are made about this obvious fact: "There are only two things I must do: die and pay taxes." But since many do not actually pay taxes, somehow the joke implies the absurdity that death too need not extract its toll. As a joke, it is sad, as many jokes are – sad because the very wish to escape death reveals just how much it is deeply felt to be a betrayal to high, improbable promises of modernity. This explains the impossibility of the culture which individuals must face. The way we made a science of the stages of death's anticipation, and certainly to build institutions to remove the suffering of the dying from ordinary life, are noth-ing more than strategies for an emphatic denial death which was in and of itself the death of everything modernity stood for.

Thus, it happened that, amid all the wondrous courage of modern culture, death has lost its place in human life and become the silent enemy that humiliates those who cling fiercely to modernity's promises. Death, in our day, became indecent, dirty, and polluting and now is seen as nothing but waste in the production of life. As Zygmunt Bauman points out, the modern attempt to deconstruct mortality is a way of constituting the Other. We regurgitate our enemies because death is indigestible and coping with this constituted presence threatens us (Baumann 1992: 131). Death becomes a guilty secret, clandestine, and unmentionable. As we vomit in secret, so we die in secret.

Thus arose the secrecy that for a long while surrounded certain diseases such as cancer, AIDS, and Alzheimer's, among others. Although, as time passed, deadly and often long lasting diseases gradually were allowed into the public imagination. They began as stigmatizing afflictions and none more so that AIDS. Kellehear observes:

> The sheer numbers of people who now do not have "good deaths" or "well-managed deaths" because of age or AIDS are instead dying in shameful ways. The shame comes from the projected attitude and behaviour of younger and non-infected people on older and infected groups but also the internalised emotional and social responses of those victimised by these other people.
>
> *(Kellehear 2007: 210)*

Kellehear focuses primarily on Western societies' attitudes toward AIDS, where people die too young from a stigmatizing disease. Strikingly, in the decades since AIDS was first diagnosed in the 1980s even it has lost some of its public shame, but, and here Kellehear is particularly insightful, aging remains an object of revulsion. Alzheimer's and other forms of senile dementia are part of this revulsion, or better put, fear. But, again, popular sayings about the elderly such as "She is very, very old but her mind is clear as a bell" is as much a mark of the fear of losing one's mind in one's own old age as a special virtue of the elderly who, even at enormous cost, are still sheltered away in institutions, many of which are profit centers for large corporations. For the industry they are good, for the individuals they are often miserable. Kellehear thus emphasizes that dealing with the elderly who are taking "too long" to die are objects of economic and social rejection because they are unmanageable and unrecognizable. This is a way of saying that the terminal ill and elderly have in effect lost their identities. They are the dying who in taking too long to die are transferred to the realm of the shameful death.

The anticipation of death has been transformed into an act of judgment of the individual's lifestyle regarding a "good death," which in turn has become a convoluted concept, especially when it leads by logic if not overt wish to the expectation that the elderly would die well if theirs was a sudden, uncomplicated death. Needless to say this notion, often held in silence, bears on the deeper complications of the identity status of the very old and their ambiguous states in the system of modern values.

Grief and the recovery of identity

Just the same (and in spite of the code of silence covered bad deaths), it is possible to investigate other, less brutal cultural attitudes toward the unstable position death holds in modern culture. One of the most striking new areas of research and, we must add, practice is the study of and practice of grief in respect of both the anticipation and the denial of death. In the latter respect, grief could be said to be, like the medicalization of dying, a systematic field offering instruction for methods of grieving as a practice of "letting go" of the dead and as is often said "getting on with life." In this very personal realm, the death of the beloved Other always has a powerful impact on the individual's personal view of mortality, which in turn cannot help but affect the individual's sense of her identity.

If, as it is in modern culture, the meaningful life is achieved through the establishment of meaningful bonds of intimacy, creative living in community, and productive labor in the economic sphere, then in a culture where the death ends these connections, the self (or, as moderns still may say) is left in a lurch between life and death. While, needless to say, belief in the continuation of the life in the other world remains a widely held notion, death itself becomes a bond an individual has with other people. Oddly this is initially a status shared in the moment of death by the dead and their beloved survivors. Grieving, therefore, becomes a practical method (again, very often technically taught and learned) whereby the survivor redefines his relationship with the deceased. In this respect, grieving is part of the work in which the surviving individual transformations his or her identity – and transforms it in ways much deeper than being a member of a well-labeled social category such as an orphan, a widow or widower, a survivor of loved one's suicide, or mortal sacrifice in defense of the motherland at war. Those who outlive the dead undergo lifestyle changes as well as changes in the emotional and psychological landscape. Grief has come to be understood as the work of effecting those changes and, to be sure, those who attempt to hide their grief by putting on a good front of bravery experience changes whether they want them or not.

In the literature on the subject of grief, one finds this theme, as for example in Silverman and Klaas's edited work *Continuing Bonds – New Understandings of Grief*. One among a number of comments along these lines is:

> When we discuss the nature of the resolution of grief, we are at the core of the most basic questions about what it means to be human, for the meaning of the resolution of grief is tied to the meanings of bonds with significant people in our lives, the meaning of our

membership in family and community, and the meaning we ascribe in our individual lives in the face of absolute proof of our own mortality.

(Klaas and Silverman 1996: 22)

The twentieth-century model of grief supports the belief that successful mourning means disengagement with the deceased and the past. To continue to maintain a relationship with the dead is seen to be a pathological situation that hinders the individual's ability to make new attachments. In *Continuing Bonds* an alternative view is offered in which grief is adjusted to allow for a continuous attachment to the dead person. Studies and discussions in this book suggest that bonds with the deceased are maintained through memorializing and remembering, as well as a heightened awareness of the presence of the dead person that persists into the inner life as well as into outside interactions. To the skeptic, this line of thinking may seem vaguely mystical, even quasi religious in its way, but if we are to say (as we argue) that self-identity is as much (perhaps more so) social as well as personal, then the whole question of whether the death of a salient Other could or should erase the social status associations requires a great deal more thought and research than it has thus far received.

Though the studies collected in *Continuing Bonds* are a small sample, they are sociologically interesting and, we might say, a hopeful sign about future attitudes toward death and identity. Whereas the prevailing definition of death requires that grief serve as a taming of death and, thereby, a loss that needs to be rationalized and "worked through" in order to "get on with life," studies reported in *Continuing Bonds* give some good evidence that a significant loss can include adjustment both to the anticipated loss and to the final act of the death. Even in a secularized culture where belief in resurrections and eternal lives are less prevalent, what we find here is the idea (once again, a medical or mental health principle) that there is no need to cut the bonds of a former life. We would ask, if old lovers from the long ago still hover in our sense of our personal and social biographies, why not all the more that beloved dead of recent, adult life? Survivors will confirm that, if they embrace the facts of their own lives, one retains what has been lost and most especially in the form of the social identity that was gained by the lost one: once a mother, daughter, or wife, always such a one. At the least the experiences remembered remain alive so to speak in the continuing life – if, that is, the survivor allows them to live. And this, again, is the key issue in grief work in which many contributors to *Continuing Bonds* would seem to suggest that "working through" the loss need not be an erasure so much as a coming to terms with the absence of a continuing presence. To be sure, the death of a beloved requires a complex relation between continuation and change in personal identity. And against the background of a heightened awareness of one's own mortality death, continuing bonds with the deceased can be shaped just as much as transformed. There is much more to be understood on this subject, but even in a minimalist form we are able to note that, if what occurs is no more than only a sublimation or projected identification, the status of the continuing bonds between the living and the dead is a much under studied subject with a great deal of potential for identity studies and for an appreciation of the power of the denial of death in modern cultures.

Denial of death

Kellehear argues that, by nature, humans are not death denying and that historically humanity has evolved as a death-anticipating society through traditional customs and belief systems. Yet, if Kellehear and others come down on the optimistic side of this issue, there is another stream of thought that emphasizes the sheer terror that mortality poses and how humanity tries to overcome it. This alternative line of thought has, as you would expect, been informed by, and to an extent influenced by, the culture's death denial attitudes to which there are exceptions and even bold theories of the centrality of death to human nature and experience.

Of these exceptions none is more bold – and thereby more regularly ignored or in many cases scorned – than Sigmund Freud's dual drive theory, first announced in his 1920 paper "Beyond the pleasure principle." Here is where he enunciated the controversial idea that, in effect, life and death are the two most basic human drives. The one drive, Eros (mistaken as a merely sexual drive), is the drive (or instinct, an awkward translation of the German *Trieb*) of constructive energy that moves humans to build relationships and by inference engage in all manner of constructive social forms; the other drive, later labeled as Thanatos by Herbert Marcuse, is in effect the death drive by which Freud meant the instinct that moves humans to destroy relationships and social life itself. For Freud, one cannot speak of death without speaking of life. In an equally controversial work, *Civilization and Its Discontents* (1930), Freud extended his drive theory (itself in 1920 influenced by the atrocities and destruction of the First World War) into a weak but evident social theory of the deadliness of modern warfare and aggression. In the decade between 1920 when "Beyond of the pleasure principle" essentially renounced the earlier simpler ideas of pleasure, sexuality and libido in favor of the primacy of the life-preserving drive, he came to see (as few thoughtful Europeans could fail to see) that the drive toward death and destruction was no less powerful and, at certain times (notably those of that period of war and economic despair), violence and aggression actually dominated collective life. How much this insight was a historical one is hard to say (though some argue reasonably that it was), certainly Freud's clinical work led him to the dual drive theory in which the life and death instincts were locked in a seemingly irresolvable struggle not only in the human psyche, but also in human culture itself. By 1930, in *Civilization and Its Discontents,* Freud was examining the question of why war gave men unconscious satisfaction that could not be derived from the need to maximize pleasure and minimize pain (Bocock 1983: 72).

At the least Freud put death back on the table of, if not public discourse, a prominent sector of social and psychological thought. He was far from alone in the middle decades of the twentieth century in, as some might put it, bringing death back. The shock of the two world wars from 1914 through 1945, of the Holocaust and the Gulag, of economic despair led many, some not as acute on the subject as was Freud, to realize that in modern society death has many faces. Wars, threats from weapons of mass destruction, epidemics of various kinds and, in more recent times, AIDS, school shootings, and the ubiquity of terrorism (which in some ways had become by the end of first decade of the twenty-first century a vague, almost empty term, to describe the terrors of a world gone wild – gone, that is, violent). In the interim, the threat of global warming brought death back in still another more global way as representations of death and violence in mass media brought them into the most personal circles of modern culture. The entertainment industries that by the 1950s and 1960s were intruding in the home and personal life through the development of televisual and later personalizable entertainment media were not only broadcasting sounds and images never before see openly in public but were also, so to speak, getting inside the heads, or psyches, of post-war individuals.

These many and various aspects of a destructive force are symptomatic of the repressed flip-side of human desire. Again Freud and many of his followers put the theory of the two basic instincts to good use (if that is the word) in providing an important resource for the study of modern and late modern culture – a culture that could not, after Freud, be any longer simply characterized as one that promised life forever and better but gave, instead, unrelenting death and a new magnitude of large scale destruction.

While Freud's theory of the psychical apparatus, which he maintained to the very end of his life, falls far short of a satisfying general social theory of the relations between death and identity, it did take a giant step in the direction of making the connection even if by the perverse means of investing the individual's self-identifications with a feeble precipitate of pressures – both internal and external – that are largely beyond his individual control and certainly not when it comes to the acting out of the destructive drives.

Denial of death and the hero systems

Ernest Becker in *The Denial of Death* (1973) took up the ideal of human heroism as a reflex of the terror of death. The hero is an object of fascination, even in modern times, because heroic actions or lives encourage confidence in the possibility of immortality. Becker's explanation for the urge to heroism is narcissism. One of the main aspects of narcissism is the feeling that everyone is expendable except ourselves (Becker 1973: 2).

> In man a working level of narcissism is inseparable from self-esteem, from a basic sense of self-worth. . . . his sense of self-worth is constituted symbolically, his cherished narcissism feeds on symbols, on an abstract idea of his own worth, an idea compose of sounds, words, and images, in the air, in the mind, on paper. And this means, that man's natural yearning for organismic activity, the pleasures of incorporation and expansion, can be fed limitlessly in the domain of symbols and so into mortality.
>
> *(ibid.: 3)*

Again, we see in Becker, a bold attempt to account for the basic riddle that death is real, yet not real enough to escape denial. The Unconscious does not recognize either death or for that matter time. Thus in the hero the conscious individual is drawn to the warm spark of an inner feeling of immortality; reflexively, the terror of mortality moves the individual toward heroism:

> He must desperately justify himself as an object of primary value in the universe; he must stand out, be a hero, make the biggest possible contribution to world life, show that he counts more than anything or anyone else. . . . It is still a mythical hero system in which people serve in order to earn a feeling of primary value, of cosmic specialness, of ultimate usefulness to creation, of unshakable meaning.
>
> *(ibid.: 4–5)*

Becker further points out that "society has always been a symbolic action system, a structure of statuses and roles, customs and rules of behaviours, designed to serve as a vehicle for earthly heroism" and thereby "every society is a religion" (ibid.: 5). Thus heroism is an issue of self-esteem that seeks affirmation and recognition in the outside world. Furthermore, heroism is effectively an "ideology of justification" that allows people to face death and to go on with life because it, paradoxically, transforms human fear of death into the illusion of self-perpetuation (ibid.: 217). Through this, the human quality of self-preoccupation in the name of self-preservation demands much of a tight-knit structure of heroic outlets. By pursuing an identity in the name of heroism, an identity shows superiority in comparison with another individual; individuals have uplifted themselves toward immortality by giving their lives a meaning that might outlive death. This, as Becker recognizes, establishes an odd kind of moral competitive market for the status of a hero, thus for the possibility of attaining an enduring life. Or is it an identity that is sought after? Society, hence, is divided into winners and losers, which opens a deep gap on the sharp end of human interdependency and the work of self-sustaining and self-expression.

The fear of death is behind all our functions, which feeds the self-preservation drive, but this mechanism is also pushing us away from the intensity and depth – and hence greatness – that mortality bestows upon our lives. Humanity faces an existential paradox of having a dual nature, to be half animal and half symbolic. The individual is within and without nature through self-consciousness. And from this double nature arises the vital lie of the human character. So humankind does not only fear death, but we also shy away from life in contemplation of our individuation and compelling life experiences. Becker observes: "We might call this existential paradox the condition of *individuality within finitude*. Man has a symbolic identity that brings him sharply out of nature. He is a symbolic self, a creature with a name, a life history" (Becker 1973: 26). And further: "all our meanings are build into us from the outside, from dealings with others. This is what gives us a 'self' and a superego. . . . and we never feel we have authority to offer things on our own" (ibid.: 48). Thus the overwhelming terrors of this world not only challenge one to become a hero, but also, and ironically, it demands that individuals shy away from "the all consuming appetites of others" (ibid.: 53).

Becker, though drawing also on Freud, underscores an opening up of symbolic culture as a defining resource for the modern individual's deep confusion with death as a threat to personal identity. Surely repression is a protective response to this fear of death, and through repression and promises of immortality modernity has disconnected heroism and the nature of death (ibid.: 11–12). Still what remains is that to deny mortality, and by giving into illusions of security, modern man makes himself vulnerable. Human heroism is a blind "driveness that burns people out" (ibid.: 6) and thus may well be the weakest link in the chain of the modern search for a heroic life beyond the end. To nourish the hunger for self-esteem, the individual chooses to make life valid by creating greatness through sacrifices, degradation and destruction. In the end, this is a back door that brings death hauntingly back into life itself.

Strategies of immortality

Zygmunt Baumann in *Morality, Immortality, and Other Life Strategies* (1992) stresses that it is impossible to define death, which for all intents and practical purpose is in absolute contrast to being. If death is non-existence, it is an unimaginable "hovering beyond reach of communication," the end of all perception (Bauman 1992: 2). However, one can perceive the death of others and hence get an idea of one's own mortality. The reason why the death of others is shattering and painful is because it does not affect the continuity of one's own perception so much as create a void that remains after the demise of the other.

Modern societies, especially in its industrial and post-industrial phases, are forced, one might say, to deconstruct mortality for many of the reasons already mentioned – the failure of the liberal ideal of ever progressive life and growth, the spread of everyday and global violence, out of control environmental problems, scarcities of clean water and air, not to mention nourishment and global epidemics. Bauman offers his own list of the realities that threaten even the tenuous modern notions regarding death and its overcoming (ibid.: 9). Here Bauman is thinking along the lines of Norbert Elias who pointed out mankind's "longing for immortality constantly misleads them into to symbols of immutability" (Elias 1985: 81). The power of humans is limited and therefore the unavoidable nature of the human finitude means a threat to the social order. This is the reason why the dying need bystanders but this is also the reason why people avoid everything that reminds them of their mortality. People may attempt to die a tame death, noiseless and hygienic, leaving no trace of our connections of life and death (Keleman 1975: 63), when in larger perspective even the departure of one individual threatens for those in her presence the very fabric of social order.

As Bauman points out, the awareness of mortality is the ultimate condition of cultural creativity as such. Culture is a "never stopping factory of permanence" and thus enfolds as a suppression of mortality awareness. Culture itself, as well as the study of it, allured us into engaging in tasks and projects (making money, gathering of knowledge, etc.), which aim for a kind of fulfillment that will reach beyond our biological existence. Hence death is a threat to the social as it interrupts the creative yearnings induced by culture.

Human societies have always, we presume, encouraged and supported strategies for dealing with death – strategies that Bauman (and Elias) call strategies of immortality; which is to say, methods in ordinary life that promise to extend the meaning of an individual life beyond the individual himself. Immortality relates to surviving, to getting beyond death, denying it. Immortality strategies seek to take the sinister and horrifying significance off death. Immortality is something, especially in the modern age, that human individuals need to build in order to prevent them from getting caught up in the open loop of ontological bleakness: "immortality is not a mere absence of death; it is the defiance and denial of death" (Bauman 1992: 7). The very collective project of creating a death-defying culture has the effect of making the creators effectively God-like; hence the continuing appeal of various religious and spiritual practices in a reputedly secular age. Living, as it were, above the fact of human finitude creates meaning and purpose of a very special and very probably very basic kind. One thinks here of course of Emile Durkheim's classic idea that religion, or at least the transcending of social bond, lends to the individual the sense of community that allows the most basic (and to Durkheim only) identity the individual can have – that of belonging to something bigger than one's self. Yet, as Baumann notes, this kind of meaning cannot be generated or maintained without suppressing the awareness of death (ibid.: 8). Once again, even in the latest stage of the modern age, death haunts all strategies to identify one's self as an enduring individual. Of these, mass culture entertainment is the prominent example.

Death as entertainment that buttresses death-denying identities

It is well known that from the 1920s onward there has been a long tradition of criticism of the destructive elements in mass entertainment: Theodor Adorno's deep criticism of modern mass cultures and media, the writings of his friend Walter Benjamin on the commercial origins of public spaces, and culminating, some would say, in Herbert Marcuse's biting attack in *One Dimensional Man* (1964) on the depoliticizing effects of repressive desublimation, operating through the over-stimulating effects of televisual and other media. In this line of thought, taken in relation to the parallel, if more psychoanalytic, lines we have presented to this point, there is an obvious tension between the (public) absence and the (private) presence of death.

To look at death from another perspective, be it a death drive or a need to integrate mortality into daily life, is to look at common media and there to encounter again the death issue. Deaths are so common in news media, magazines, computer games, cinema, and televisual dramas that their shear number disappears behind an almost constant, numbing, exposure to death in media of all kinds.

Without now getting into the finer points of debate about capitalism's role in the phenomenon, death has suffused a virtually limitless range of public images and sounds. It has become for all intents and purposes a phantasmagoria accessible for consumption. Though hard to diagnose from surface evidence, the effects of capitalism on individuals and their concepts of love and death as well as sustaining as sense of socially accepted self-identity are a matter of serious importance. As the main character, advertiser Donald Draper, pointed out in the TV series *Mad Men* "Love is invented by men like me in order to sell nylons," not only the desire for love, but also human's natural curiosity about death is channeled for entertainment and capitalistic purposes.

However, death in the media is dramatized, glamorized and trivialized and reflects a misconception and misinterpretation of death. This kind of illusion does not mean it fulfills a possible desire to anticipate death. It barely touches us beyond media portrayals since this representation of death is lacking a connection with people's own experiences.

Fortunately, the evidence is slowly dawning through the study of and reflection up mass media. As Richard Kalish in *Death, Grief, and Caring Relationships* (1985) points out, intellectual knowledge that death could occur at any moment does not mean that death becomes an emotional reality (Kalish 1985: 89). The consumer always has the possibility to avoid death scenes if the pictures get too disturbing; yet few do it seems. Thus, even as she is bombarded by death images at every turn, the individual, some say, is tempted to "maintain the illusion of personal invulnerability and even exemption from the curse of mortality" (Akien 2001: 6). The interest in violence in popular consumer culture could very well be conceived as a manifestation of Thanatos in the culture itself. And we might add that until, or if, a better *general* concept – as distinct from the theory – comes along it might as well serve its purposes. However, better to begin, least, to understand, say, obsession with morbid themes – from countless images of Saddam Hussein's dead body in the news or entertainment such as violent TV shows and ego-shooter games. These, and much more, are sign (or, better put, symptoms) of the depth of infatuation with, and a presence of, the death theme in late modern social and cultural structures.

Whereas death in the context of entertainment seemingly has no emotional impact, the death of a celebrity such as Princess Diana or public personages such as Martin Luther King, Jr. or President Kennedy are evidently capable of precipitating mass mourning – a mourning that extends even to the annual recognition of these very public deaths. Here again Ernest Becker's ideas are apt. The fascination with an idol or a leading charismatic hero figure is a "reflex of the fatality of the human condition," the fear of life (Becker 1973: 145) behind which lurks the need for security or the "oceanic" feeling of embeddedness out from which the individual is seldom able to grow. This, obviously, is not a philosophical claim as to human nature itself, but a way of isolating, however indirectly, the historical and cultural factors in shaping, and reshaping, the ways in which humans societies try to understand themselves, individual and/or collectively, as mortal beings.

Whether or not it is sufficient to call the mechanism for this very human struggle a transference effect, it certainly seems that whether the object to which the fear of death is transferred is a sacred or heroic figure, the same process is at work. The individual gains some sense of immortality by aspiring to and identifying with the transcending object. Simply being close to this object of transference, the immortalized person or figure, terror of death is, again, tame by the displacement, which can have the psychological effect of creating the sense of gaining immortality. This is of course most explicit in religious objects, especially those of the Abrahamic religions of the West where monotheistic Gods – Allah, Yahweh, Christ – are, if not exactly heroes, certainly other-worldly objects. Surely, the this-worldly hero as transference object has less power over the identity of his or her followers. The bereavement of masses after the loss of such a heroic idol reminds the follower of his own mortality and of our transient state of existence (Becker 1973: 148), while, as Becker and others allow, also creating the sense of at least proximity to continuing of life or self after the time of one's death.

Criticism

We who dare to examine the relations between and among identities and morality bear an unusual burden, not faced, we suppose, by other students of identity. There simply is not a vast literature in social sciences on the subject. Those we have examined in this chapter serve the good purpose of, at least, introducing the classic theories about death and dying. But, as we have seen especially in the modern age, there is a very limited body of literature on the role of death in identity formation – and what there is, while very challenging and helpful, tends to bear a great relevance to the study of the cultures of death. We, as others have, honor Freud for his insights and thus enduring influence on ties between the death or destructive drives and the fate of the individual ego or psyche. Yet, there remains a serious gap in the study of the positive elements of self-identification. It is, we might suggest (even if the thought is a bit defeatist), that Bauman is right – that mortality is simply part of the unthought-of human life. Death is clearly a limit of some kind and, in an individual experience, it would *seem* (and no one can be sure of this) that the very modern concept of self-identity, nurtured as it was in modern, liberal cultures, simply cannot handle finitude. Here, however, more philosophical writers such as Emmanuel Levinas in books such as *Time and the Other* and even the later writings of Jacques Derrida might be useful guides for social theorists and scientists.

For the time being, until a new generation of social researchers decide, if they do, to take up the subject more directly, we must rest with the advances that have been made. Becker, for one notable example, while he alludes to it, finds fault with Freud's death drive theory. He is arguably right, though not entirely convincingly so, that Freud introduced the idea of the death drive in order to sustain his theories about humans as merely pleasure-seeking individuals. Yet, whatever the limits of his wider theories, Freud realized that identifying humans as mainly pleasure-seeking creatures failed to explain the destructive tendencies in the world. In this sense, death helped Freud to keep his theories about the pleasure-seeking individual intact while at the same time opening up, late in life, in *Civilization and Its Discontents*, the importance of a historical and cultural examination of destructive drives. Yet, Becker and others are right in setting the limit on Freud's foundational ideas. In Becker's words: "The fiction of death as an 'instinct' allowed Freud to keep the terror of death outside his formulations as a primary human problem of ego mastery. He did not have to say that death was *repressed* if the organism carried it naturally in its processes" (Becker 1973: 99). Certainly later writings that took Freud into account opened other avenues of research. But even they fell short of what we might call a positive theory of death – or better perhaps – of the dead in the life of the individual. Some of the more clinical works such as *Continuing Bonds* are a beginning of movement in this direction.

Kellehear, too, though his purpose is mostly to survey the history of the social concept of death, offers the prospect of new work and understanding. At the least, he emphasizes the failure of psychoanalysis to move beyond slim and hardly useful works such as Freud's *Moses and Monotheism* into a fully disciplined embrace of sociological, ethnographic or even biographical approaches and the data they might offer. Since the main psychoanalytic agenda is rational, materialistic-logical, it also fails to acknowledge society's religious and quasi-religious work to come to terms with human mortality (Kellehear 2007: 55). Whether it is fair for Kellehear to say, as he does, that followers of the psychoanalytic approach have little or no empirical support of their theories (ibid.: 57–8) is a point on which we would demur, if only because, on the one hand, clinical research is itself empirical and, on the other, there are countless preliminary studies from various psychological instances.

Still there are continuities as well as differences in more recent studies. As with Bauman's immortality strategies, Kellehear opposes the definition of death as radically opposed to life. Bauman is right, we think, to say that death is unthinkable, but this does not prevent him from denying its reality as a human experience. Historically speaking death has proven itself an experience capable of transforming life and lives, and this sense of supporting both the individual's and the culture's constructive strategies. Kellehear, for one, even doubts, that death poses such a threat to life that other thinkers believe it does. Kellehear did, after all, described the cultural programs early in human social history whereby death came to be anticipation and, thus, through religious and other mechanisms, able to exert a telling influence of a positive kind on the living. These surely were not traditions that spawned a mindset in which death could be taken into self-identity and, as we say, this may suggest a kind of limit.

In fact, though it is not the primary purpose of our chapter, one task that lies ahead may well be the complete rethinking of self-identity or, as some such as Erving Goffman in *Stigma: Notes on the Management of Spoiled Identity* (1963) have suggested of the very concept of ego-identity as arising from a stable interior faculty, in earlier times called the soul but in modern times the Self.

Future developments

Whatever becomes the fate in future social studies of identity and self-identification (which, we remind, is a related but separate issue from social identification), it is perfectly obvious that death and mortality are at the core of the human condition. Attitudes and ways of dealing with death change over times, but death itself remains and cannot be gotten around. As a consequence, it seems quite apparent that as death becomes more, not less, a fact of social life, and that the most urgent general future development required is at the least to advance the study of death itself in human societies and thereby to come to terms with a fact of life, to be sure, but also a fact that by its sheer persistence defies received ideas and beliefs as to meaning of this life.

Life expectancies have dramatically increased within the last century. According to the World Health Organization, in 1900 the global average lifespan at birth was just 31 years, and below 50 years in even the richest countries. By the mid-twentieth century, average life expectancy rose to 48 years and in 2005 to 65.6 years; the life expectancy even reached over 80 years in some countries such as Japan. By 2030, average life expectancy at birth for women in countries such as the USA will be 85 years. From this point of view it might be assumed that these numbers as they apply to the core and semi-peripheral areas of the global push the issue of death further away from the place it requires in modern thought.

But, there is another story globally, and that is the extreme numbers of earlier deaths among children in the peripheral zones of the modern world – especially Africa where AIDS and malnutrition are epidemic. But also, worldwide where the numbers of homeless peoples – either refugees or squatters – created zones of exclusion wherein millions are simply ruled out of whatever liberal state benefits provide citizenship. Immigrant workers in America and still parts of Europe are victims of sometimes cruel methods of exclusion, many urban conglomerates such as North Jakarta, Lagos, Sao Paulo, Mumbai include either at their centers or on their margins millions of displaced individuals seeking some chance for mere survival from civil strife, disease, or hunger and yet are for all intents and purposes dead to what civil societies may exist in those urban centers. Even the affluent and modernizing states, in the West and East, experience threat of war, famine or natural catastrophes. The terrorist attack on the World Trade Center has become a symbol of the vulnerability of even the core nations. Some such as Žižek in *Welcome to the Desert of the Real* (2002) have proposed that attacks from outside to the centers of wealth are basically reminders of the realities that most of the global population faces – that the global reality is effectively a desert: a desert of death. This kind of thinking is developed in different ways by Achille Mbembe in his famous essay, "Necropolitics" (2003) that begins to drawn together ideas from writes such as Arendt, Foucault, Agamben and others into a theory of these zones of exclusions as the elements of the politics of the late modern global society – a politics not of life but of death; hence necropolitics.

Even if radical proposal of the kind presented by Žižek and Mbembe among others are too strong to consider for the time being (and certainly they require much more empirical research), there is evidence close to home, so to speak, that are not far from the normal perceptions of ordinary life. However, despite medical progress, new diseases are cropping up. Obesity and diabetes, among other prominent examples, are threatening the progress made in increasing life expectancy. Before modern hygienic standards, people died from extrinsic causes, but namely diseases. Now over 70 percent of people in the Western world die from the new – and one might say self-induced – endemic problems, such as heart disease, cancer, and stroke. Then, too, though it would appear to be another extreme case, we would mention the case of natural catastrophes. Once floods, fires, as well as epidemics, were considered either acts of the gods or, in a more secular vein, as acts beyond human control. Yet, increasingly, it is apparent that floods are not immune to environmental causes and that many disasters could be anticipated, or, at least, those beyond anticipation could be responded to in a more timely way. It explains what can only be called the social incompetence in the now many oil spills and the tardiness of clean-up efforts, or of the floodings and earth quakes in New Orleans in 2005 or Haiti and Pakistan in 2010 to which the response of governmental and non-governmental agencies have been slow or even actively frustrated. Some positive thoughts can be assigned to the global threats of climate change that awareness of these global realities may stop the "erosion of awareness of dying" (Kellehear 2006: 210). They will certainly challenge the way we think of ourselves, and think of life as such.

One of the more sensational yet philosophical well ground advances is Peter Singer's pro- posal of new ethic approaches toward life and death in *Rethinking Life and Death* (1994). Quite in addition to the natural catastrophes approach, Singer argues that the border between the living and the death is blurred by a technical medical world which is able to freeze embryos in liquid nitrogen, transplants organs and allows brain dead women with no chance of recovery to carry a child to term. Many object mightily to some of the conclusions Singer seems to infer from this obvious fact of life, but he does frame for consideration the question of what is to be done about the over-ageing societies. When medical and biological technologies promise for some the prospect of a much longer old age, even in the face of pain and loss of quality life prospects, there will be a need to discuss the highly controversial issue of the right to commit assisted suicide. Singer observes that the traditional views about the sanctity of life need to be revised. Aging aside, cases of anencephalics, cortically dead infants, patients in a vegetative state, and those who are medically declared brain dead, show that a definition of death has no clear and set criteria anymore (Singer 1994: 191–2). In either case the question of when and how (in the case of assisted suicides) death may occur demands a profound revision in what we would call the ethics of self-identity. As tragic as the individual cases may be, Singer and others open up an important new aspect of ethical and scientific research as a field of opportunity for rethinking death as both a personal and a social issue. Indeed, much progress has been made among medical ethicists and that work needs to be taken more serious into account by social sciences.

In conclusion, if we were to single out one line of development that might be more fruit- ful than others, we would suggest the necessity of thinking about death *and* identity as global problems. To the same extent that globalization has forced a rethinking of personal identity as either, all too simple, a matter of ethnic or national associations, so to it opens the prospect of identity itself as a through and through global prospect. To be sure, self-identities will be shaped by family, groups, communities, and states. But in a world in which the included and excluded alike must think more deeply about their identities in references to the wide array of global dif- ferences – social, cultural, and economic – so too will this necessity bring individuals, as it has brought nations and corporations, face to face with the sometimes deadly zones of global life and global process. Whatever else terrorism stands for, it at least represents a prominent feature of destructiveness that arises from global exclusions of all kinds – exclusions that are localized mostly in the periphery, but also ones that presented themselves in the global cities where beggars and homeless people, and in some places the dead on the streets, present irrefutable evidence that as this world becomes more global so too must individuals rethink who they are and rethink in the face of an ever-increasing omnipresence of death.

References

Ariès, Phillipe (1974) *Western Attitudes Toward Death: From the Middle Ages to the Present*. Harmondsworth: Penguin Books.
Ariès, Phillipe (1983) *The Hour of our Death*. London: Johns Hopkins University Press.
Aiken, Lewis (2001) *Dying, Death, and Bereavement*, 4th edition. London: Lawrence Erlbaum Associates.
Bauman, Z. (1992) *Mortality, Immortality and Other Life Strategies*. Cambridge: Polity.
Becker, E. (1973) *The Denial of Death*. New York: The Free Press.
Bocock, R. (1983) *Sigmund Freud*. New York: Tavistock Publications.
Elias, N. (1985) "Ageing and dying: some sociological problems," in *The Loneliness of the Dying*. Oxford: Blackwell.
Howarth, G. (1998) "'Just live for today'. Living, caring, ageing and dying," *Ageing and Society*, 18: 673–89.
Hunt, Stephen (2005) *The Life Course: A Sociological Introduction*. New York: Palgrave Macmillan.
Kalish, Richard A. (1985) *Death, Grief, and Caring Relationships*. California: Brooks/Cole Publishing Company.
Keleman, S. (1975) *Living your Dying*. Berkeley: Random House.
Kellehear, A. (2007) *A Social History of Dying*. Cambridge: Cambridge University Press.
Kübler-Ross, E. (1976) *On Death and Dying*. New York: Macmillan Publishing.
Mbembe, Achille (2003) "Necropolitics," translated by Libby Meintjes, *Public Culture*, 15(1): 11–40.
Silverman, P.R. and Klass, D. (1996) "Introduction: What's the problem?" in Dennis Klass et al. (eds) *Continuing Bonds – New Understandings of Grief*. Washington, DC: Taylor & Francis.
Singer, P. (1994) *Rethinking Life and Death*. Melbourne: The Text Publishing Company.
Žižek, Slavoj (2002) *Welcome to the Desert of the Real*. New York: Verso.

Part 3
Identity-politics and its consequences

16

Sexual identity-politics

Activism from gay to queer and beyond

Mark Casey

Introduction

This chapter focuses on the complex entwinement of sexual identity-politics and sexuality struggles for freedoms that emerged in the latter part of the twentieth century to the ongoing challenges, political movements and identity claims that minority sexual groups continue to experience in the early twenty-first century. The chapter primarily draws upon the experiences of sexual minorities in the United States and Western Europe due to the initial emergence of documented sexual politics within these locals. However, through the chapter's approach it will become clear to the reader that claims around specific sexual identities, rights movements or historical events have to be understood through the specifity of geographical location, time, culture and the intersection of other identities present. This chapter will examine the important historical and intellectual developments which gay liberation and lesbian feminist movements gave birth to during the 1960s and 1970s. It will then move to discuss the advent of the HIV and AIDS crisis in the 1980s and the emergence of queer activism in the late 1980s and 1990s, in so doing the major claims and developments, and the contributions that queer political action provided in understandings of sexual identities, will be examined. The successes of the assimilationist agenda and normalising discourses in the late 1990s and early twenty-first century provide further analysis of current politicised claims and developments. Contributions made by the assimilationist agenda for understandings of 'sexual citizenship', particularly in the global north, will also be drawn upon. The main criticisms that can be framed around each of these key sexual minority movements will then be presented. In concluding, the chapter will offer an insight into future developments for sexual identities suggesting that citizenship rights struggles and gains in the global north, although potentially beneficial to many lesbians, gay men and heterosexuals, must not eclipse the material realities of those excluded from such 'gains' within the global north or the growing identity movements and right-wing backlash to lesbian and gay 'rights' and identities in the global south.

Within the United States and Western Europe, the late 1960s and early 1970s were a pivotal time for the claiming of sexual identities, particularly for the once despised homosexual, who during these years gained significant achievements. This historical period reflected a new identity beginning to emerge, distinctive from the past and rejecting previous medical-ised understandings offered of 'homosexual identity' by the sexologists several decades earlier. Non-heterosexuals were now beginning to produce their own sexual identities that had previ-ously been denied to them, through the medical and psychological regulation and naming of their '*homosexuality*', instead claiming and celebrating their identities as lesbian women and gay men. However, it is important to understand the emergence of this politicised action and gains through an acknowledgement of 'what went before'. This 'pre-Stonewall' era (Taylor et al., 2002) can be recognised as showcasing the importance of the growing spatial concentration of lesbians and homosexual men in large urban areas in the US, along with the emergence of 'first wave' assimilationist politics. During the late 1940s and early 1950s, lesbians and homosexual men were forming their own subcultures and communities in major US and Western European cities, formed around shared characteristics regarding sexual object choice and gender perform-ance (Chauncey 1994). The gradual emergence of these underground social movements can be attributed to a significant number of social and cultural developments post-SecondWorld War (see Adam, 1987 for a further discussion).

One of the first recorded 'rights groups' to be established for lesbians and homosexual men was 'The League' in 1948 in Denmark (Lutzen 1998: 235). In the US the first lasting social movement established by and for homosexual men was the 'Mattachine Society' in 1951, soon to be followed by the lesbian rights group 'Daughters of Bilitis'. In the UK the 'Homosex-ual Law Reform Society' and the London-based lesbian organisations 'Kenric' and 'Minori-ties Research Group' had existed throughout the course of the 1940s and 1950s. Although lacking access to political power and facing routine opposition from the state, these groups began to challenge the double binary which non-heterosexual's existed within, being at once invisible and yet highly visible through the stigmatised, penalised and criminalised position they held within most societies. The goals of the early homophile movements varied over the years. Some of the groups such as The League, the Mattachine Society and Daughters of Bilitis wanted assimilation for lesbians and homosexual men – making similar demands to those present within current claims to 'heteronormative' citizenship rights. These groups were recognised through their assimilationist aims, presenting lesbians and homosexual men through normative discourses, unthreatening to and as sharing similarities with heterosexuals. As D'Emilio (1989: 469) has shown, the US groups fostered a culture of middle-class (white) respectability, with members wearing gender-appropriate clothing and hairstyles. The identity they wished to foster was one of sameness, where the lesbian or homosexual body was not a threat to heterosexuals or wider 'normal society'.

Emerging lesbian and homosexual groups in the 1950s shared the common desire to edu-cate professionals about the realities of homosexuality, with the hope that, in turn, (medical) professionals would advocate changes in state policies on behalf of homosexuals. The role of medicine in stigmatising and problematising dysfunctional lesbian or homosexual male identi-ties had considerable weight and influence upon wider professional, public and governmental beliefs held against these groups. These homophile movements were often only known via word of mouth, with homosexuality still being illegal in countries such as the UK – they did not publicise their meetings for fear of exposing their members as homosexuals and the con-sequential punishment this could bring from the state. However, such groups really could not formulate a mass movement rally as the Gay Liberation Front (GLF) was soon to achieve. For all the groups' struggles, through their assimilationist beliefs and the desire for members to present gender specific identities, they failed to provide an affirmative and prideful collective identity for members.

Historical and intellectual development

The 1960s and 1970s was undoubtedly one of the most important periods in the history of sexual politics this century. This was a time which saw the revival of feminism and the emergence of lesbian and gay liberation movements, at the same time morality campaigners redoubled their efforts to resist social changes associated with 'sexual liberalism'.

(Richardson 2000: 35)

Both the young gays and the young lesbians dissociated themselves from what they perceived as the pathetic homophiles who wanted to be accepted. Who the hell they asked wants to be accepted by this patriarchal, capitalist, imperialist, compulsory heterosexual corrupt society.

(Lutzen 1998: 235)

The weak political clout of the early homophile movements was challenged with the emergence of the Gay Liberation Movement in the summer of 1969 in the US, with this soon spreading to other Western nations. A major concern for lesbian and gay liberation in the late 1960s and 1970s was to question and deconstruct assumptions around sexuality and gender. In particular they attacked the ability of science and medicine in defining dominant constructions of homosexuality and its worth, value and meaning. Previously unquestionable identity labels, based within essentialist notions, were now the focus of a new generation of politicised and angry sexual minorities.

The emergence of the gay liberation movement and the identities so associated, at least within the US, is often pinpointed to an exact date and time: 1.20 a.m. on Saturday 28 June 1969. On this day police officers raided a well-known gay bar, the Stonewall Inn on Christopher Street in Greenwich Village in New York. Although the police raid in itself was not an uncommon occurrence – with police persecution of homosexuals growing during the 1960s in several US states and cities, the reactions of the bar's patrons on the other hand was startlingly different. Rather than allowing themselves to be arrested or victimised, patrons within the bar resisted and fought back, turning the raid into two days and nights of riots (Engel 2002). This event is understood as being symbolically crucial because it signifies the emergence of new and more radical group action of a previously docile, invisible, victimised, regulated and seemingly powerless minority. The actions and the identities that were to grow from the emergence of gay liberation were mirrored in other movements and groups that embodied the New Left – such as the student movement, the anti-war movement, black power movement and the second-wave feminist movement. These movements utilised a new vocabulary to understand their situations, where instead of aiming for assimilation and equality with the white, heterosexual majority, their goal was focused upon liberation of identities and self-determination (ibid.: 386–7). The Stonewall riots and the political fallout marked a move away from the assimilationist agenda of groups such as the Mattachine Society (who in response to Stonewall pleaded for homosexuals not to fight with the police), and the claiming of new identities through the use of terms such as 'gay' instead of homosexual, reflecting a real shift in self-perception, group identity and belonging.

Soon after the riots, various organisations, including the GLF were created to mobilise gay men and lesbians into a viable political force. Activists in the early 1970s were denouncing the *invisibility* and *silence* that many felt characterised the homosexual lifestyle. However, leaders of organisations central to the liberation movement demonstrated uncanny ability to mobilise these supposedly silent and isolated masses, where by the middle of the 1970s over one thousand lesbian and gay organisations existed within the US alone. This quick organisation of thousands of lesbians, gay men and their friends belied the rhetoric of isolation and invisibility. Isolated men and women do not create, almost overnight, a mass movement premised upon a shared group identity. In other words, the gay and lesbian movement did not suddenly start at a given hour on a certain day, following a specific event – although the myth of the Stonewall riot would have us believe this. Rather it embodies a historical process marked by diverse opportunities, multiple organisational networks and instances, such as the Stonewalls riots, which ushered in a shift in the personal perspectives of lesbians and gay men themselves. Other factors that have been discussed earlier in this chapter, from the cultural and social developments post-Second World War, the establishment of homosexual organisations in the 1940s and 1950s (although different in their politics), to the growing concentration of lesbians and homosexual men within some metropolitan settings, tied in with continued regulation and resistance, all fed the development and birth of the gay liberation and its powerful politics at the end of the 1960s.

The gay liberation movement was not concerned with the goals of lesbians and gay men alone, but with overturning what it viewed as the white male hegemony that characterised modern capitalism. By asserting that all individuals were sexually androgynous, gay liberation attempted to obliterate the boundaries of the patriarchal gender dynamic that insist on masculine/feminine and homo/hetero division. The GLF was a group of revolutionary homosexual men and women formed with the realisation that complete sexual liberation for all people could not come about unless existing social institutions were abolished. The roots of oppression that gay people suffered were claimed to run deep in society, in particular the structure of family patterns of socialisation and Judeo-Christian culture. Legal reform and education against prejudice was wanted, but such reform was not understood as sufficient whilst existing social structures remained. The GLF, therefore, saw itself as part of the wider movement aiming to abolish all forms of social oppression, working to ally itself with other oppressed groups such as the women's liberation movement, black people and other national minorities and the working class. The GLF did not believe that any existing revolutionary theory had all the answers to the problems facing lesbians and gay men, but it found strength in its members and through challenging negative and constraining identities (Engel 2002).

As Stein (1997: 264) has shown, the GLF strongly rejected the notion that homosexuality represented a perversion in identity development, where instead lesbian and gay identities and the relationships they would allow were to be celebrated as more 'complete' than their non-sexual homosocial counterparts. GLF rejected the notion that it was simply about a minority group seeking rights and instead encouraged everyone to deepen their same-sex relationships, to move beyond the simple hetero/homo binary. For Engel (2002) and Weeks (2007), the struggle of the GLF to end oppression raised consciousness amongst a growing urban collective of lesbians and gay men. Their demands focused upon a number of key issues such as informing that all people who feel attracted to a member of their own sex should know that such feelings are good and natural, to stopping psychiatrists from treating homosexuality as though it were a problem or a sickness. The GLF wanted that police harassment should end, that employers should no longer be allowed to discriminate against anyone on account of their sexual preference and that the age of consent for homosexuals should be reduced to the same age as for heterosexuals. Through their highly visible organisation and growing political power, the GLF allowed women and men to share their experiences, discover commonalities and foster a collective identity. For Engel (2002: 388) 'radicals chose the word "gay" because it was how homosexuals referred to each other, the word symbolised self-definition and as such was a recognition of internal power'. The term 'homosexual' that had been imposed upon a sexual minority for so many decades by science and medicine, a term of illness, was rejected and overturned.

The act of coming out and the visible claiming of one's sexual identity became a significant group and political event during the 1970s. Where once claiming a homosexual identity or being diagnosed *as* homosexual could be characterised as a deeply personal experience, claiming a gay or lesbian identity was in part claiming to belong to a wider positive group identity. Part of the claims to name oneself as lesbian or gay, and the rejection of the medicalised naming of the 'homosexual', was the fundamental restructuring of the definition of 'coming out' by the GLF. Whereas the phrase had previously referred to an individual acknowledgement of homosexuality to oneself, gay liberationists transformed it into an extremely public and political act. Where coming out was to be symbolised as an act of the total rejection of the negative definitions that society inflicted on the homosexual, and substituted both acceptance and pride in one's gayness. As the work of Sala and De La Mata Benitz (2009: 835) has found, for lesbians in Spain during the late 1970s and early 1980s the act of coming out was the rejection of 'a historically stigmatised, silenced and forcibly invisible identity' that was a source of 'personal suffering'. In coming out, these women were able to deconstruct these stigmatised meanings, giving themselves a sense of self-satisfaction and personal empowerment. Coming out was the ultimate means to conflate the personal and political, in that it was combining the personal act of coming out with the political act of claiming a visibility and rejecting a medicalised 'homosexuality' in the naming of oneself as lesbian or gay. Through acknowledging oneself as lesbian or gay, a person exposed themselves to social injustice, hence such individuals had a personal tie to the success of gay liberation (D'Emilio 1983). Through the process of coming out, the victim status was discarded; homosexuality was transformed from a stigma to be hidden to a source of pride to be celebrated. Indeed by coming out, the homosexual became gay (Engel 2002: 388). Coming out as gay man or lesbian was the psychological and political break necessary to do what the homophile movement in the 1950s could never accomplish – attract a large following based around a positive concept of shared identity.

Over the course of the 1970s divisions began to mount between some lesbians and gay men within their political values and identity claims. The ideals of the GLF were increasingly understood as failing to answer or address successfully the needs of lesbians, where the politics of identity that had been so pivotal increasingly became a politics of difference. For many lesbians the claiming of a lesbian identity became associated with the claiming of a political identity, as a political alternative, rather than as a derivative of (failed) heterosexuality (see Lutzen 1998; Richardson 2000). The claiming of a lesbian identity as a politicised identity during the 1970s and early 1980s was reflected in the establishment of new lesbian identities, such as lesbian feminist, radicalesbians, political lesbian and woman–identified woman. This gradual claiming of 'lesbian' as a political identity moved the lesbian category away from an identity based exclusively on sexual practice alone. Any woman could now claim a political lesbian identity without ever having engaged in sexual acts or desire to do so with another woman. For those theorists such as Ken Plummer and Jeffrey Weeks, the 'Woman-identified woman' paper by the Radicalesbians and the Leeds Revolutionary Feminists 'Love thy enemy?' paper in 1970, acted as initial attempts in the association of a lesbian identity with a political agenda. This emergence of a new politicised group of women for Lutzen (1998: 236) is shown in the grouping of women who were 'feminists using their private life as a revolutionary force. They regarded heterosexuality as an oppressive institution that you could evade by becoming a lesbian.' These ideals and the challenging of heterosexual power and privilege, along with the value of a political lesbian identity were theoretically engaged with in Adrienne Rich's ground breaking paper 'Compulsory heterosexuality and lesbian existence'.

But we must acknowledge that not all lesbians were aligned with the increasing politicisation of lesbian identity. Some lesbians were concerned that lesbianism was becoming too associated with a critique and rejection of heterosexuality, rather than acting as a positive identity that could be claimed, and one in which sexual attraction to other women could be signalled. As the work of Nicol and Smith (2008: 679) has shown, some lesbians and gay men were still invested in the assimilationist politics that began a decade earlier. As they have documented, a minority of lesbians and gay men in the US spent the early 1970s trying to apply for marriage licences with legal challenges mounted in the province of Manitoba in the US.

For gay men during this time, *and* some lesbians, the claiming of a gay or lesbian identity was not as politicised as it was for most lesbian feminists, but was tied in with an increasing engagement in the consumption of commodities, services and spaces in the public visibility for this 'new' gay identity. The claiming of a gay identity through the act of coming out and an engagement within the commercialisation of 'gay lifestyles', particularly within the US, increasingly defined what it meant to be a gay man during the 1970s and early 1980s. For gay men who lacked their own institutions, political consciousness or historical roots, the importance in the claiming of an identity for empowerment and community growth became a central concern. Rights claims were no longer based upon a desire for tolerance towards their sexual identities within the spheres of the private, but increasingly were demands for equality and a new visibility in the public.

But, significant developments and shifts in movements of sexual politics were to occur through the emergence of the AIDS crisis of the 1980s and the consequential backlash against lesbians, but in particular gay men. In response to this crisis a new age of activism developed, with AIDS creating a new context in which people could talk about sex. Lesbians and gay men now had a legitimate focus to discuss safe(r) sex practices in public sites, from the park, to the café to daytime television chat shows – leaving the spaces of the private behind and claiming inclusion and lesbian and gay visibility within everyday public sites (see Plummer 2008).

Major claims, developments and key contributions

> The AIDS movement had distinct aims from the gay and lesbian movement, but perhaps more importantly, it achieved those aims through strategies never conceived as possible by the gay rights activists in the 1970s.
>
> *(Engel 2002: 390)*

The advent of HIV and AIDS in the early 1980s in the US and its quick globalised spread brought a new backlash from the conservative right against newly confident lesbians and gay men. Their confidence celebrated in the liberal sexual lifestyles of many in the 1970s was now facing a serious threat with the arrival of this unknown (terminal) illness. The lack of political will or desire to address the emerging AIDS crisis by both the Reagan and the Bush administrations in the US and the Thatcher government in the UK had the consequence that gay men and lesbians increasingly mobilised themselves to tackle the emerging crisis. Together with AIDS, the 1980s saw a backlash against lesbian and gay rights discourses, with the British government introducing 'Section 28' in 1988 to ban the 'promotion of homosexuality' within schools in the UK. Fuelled by the impact of HIV and AIDS on gay communities and the anti-homosexual feelings and responses that HIV and AIDS revitalised, especially among the 'moral right', a new perspective on sexuality and sexual politics emerged. Lesbian and gay political action groups that had functioned at the local level, in response to this crisis became nationally orientated (Engel 2002). And as Richardson (2000) argues, the emergence of AIDS and the growing power of the conservative right created a new shared political interest between lesbians and gay men. The fracture lines that had developed between the GLF and political lesbian movements decreased as both lesbians and gay men overcome their divisions to tackle both AIDS and continued homophobia within society and mainstream politics. The then political and social climate gave birth to new and powerful *queer* political movements in the form of 'AIDS Coalition to Unleash Power' (ACT UP) and 'Queer Nation' in the US, and the UK-based 'OutRage!' ACT UP was established in the US in March 1987, to promote media attention for the AIDS crisis in the hope of creating a universal awareness and gaining political leverage. For Joshua Gamson (1996) activists within ACT UP drew on the supposed abnormality and various expressions of gay identity to challenge the process by which stigmatised identities were defined.

The political events of ACT UP were most apparent in the US cities of New York and Washington DC, allowing them almost direct access to the powerful US media and government. The actions of ACT UP often evolved from the rejection of the stigmatised or (deserving) 'victim status' identity of those with HIV and AIDS, and the turning of grief into anger and active, politicised identities. Such activists were drawing on the labels given to lesbians and gay men living with HIV and AIDS and in turn using them to challenge ingrained processes by which such identities had been defined and stigmatised. By the end of 1993, it was estimated that around 200,000 gay men were infected with HIV in the US alone – with such large numbers contributing to the radicalisation of the lesbian and gay population. ACT UP's most famous slogan '*Silence = Death*' can be understood as a denouncement of the homophobic authorities and their ineffective response to the AIDS epidemic. Through ACT UP's demonstrations, civil disobedience and politicised protests, media attention was guaranteed.

At a meeting of ACT UP in New York in 1990 the political group Queer Nation was founded. Queer Nation developed in attempts to address and overcome racial and gender divisions within lesbian and gay communities, by uniting under the label 'queer'. Queer Nation wanted to challenge and bring to the political forefront concerns that AIDS had eclipsed. In particular Queer Nation had in its focus institutionalised homophobia, the dominance of heterosexuality and the desire to achieve full liberation and rights for all sexualities. Queer Nation, as with the GLF before it, emphasised visibility as a means to safe public existence, using 'in your face politics' to appropriate national icons of space. It was particularly famous for its 'queer Kiss-ins' at American malls, where masses of lesbians or gay men would gather and kiss, to fracture the heteronormativity of such sites. Queer Nation urged lesbians and gay men to leave the ghettos and queer the heteronormative street. Queer Nation sought to develop radical understandings of citizenship and to make the nation a safe place for queers, not just create spaces of limited tolerance.

Queer activism, in the form of groups such as ACT UP and Queer Nation, was part of a greater opposing logic directed towards the distinct identities and group logic of earlier gay liberation. Where for Weeks (1989) the shift from 'homosexual' to 'gay' two decades earlier was a shift of not just new labels for old realities, but it pointed to a changing reality – both in a way that a hostile society saw the homosexual and in the way those who had previously been stigmatised saw and presented themselves. Similarly, the project of queer in distinguishing itself from earlier identity labels (such as homosexual, lesbian and gay) that formed its history, reflects a changing reality for 'sexual others' during the late 1980s and 1990s. Queer Nation sought to unite its members under the umbrella term of 'queer' taking a once negative homophobic term and reclaiming it as a sign of power, pride and identity:

> queer means leading a different sort of life. It's not about the mainstream, profit margins, patriotism, patriarchy or being assimilated. It's not about . . . privilege and elitism. It's about being on the margins, defining ourselves.
>
> *(Blasius and Phelan 1997: 74, cited in Engel 2002: 395)*

Unlike gay liberation's eventual desire to name and make claims to identity positions, queer activism saw socially produced binaries such as gay/straight, man/woman, as the basis of oppression. These identities were then positioned as unstable experiences of the self, that only become fixed primarily in the service of social control. The key to true liberation was to disrupt these categories and refuse them, rather than embrace them. These 'deconstructionist politics' saw collective identities such as lesbian, gay and heterosexual as obstacles to true resistance and change, with queers urged to resist and refuse these. For Richardson (2000: 37) queer was used as a term to indicate an identity or political position that questions and rejects the very notion of sexual difference and deviance, where both difference and deviance are dependent for their meaning on an assumed (hetero)sexual norm. Warner (1993) presents queer politics as opposing society itself, protesting not only against normal behaviour of the social, but the very idea that 'normal behaviour' exists. However, for Gamson (1996), the ultimate challenge of queerness is not just the questioning of the content of collective identities but its concern with the questioning of the unity, stability, viability, and political utility of sexual identities even as they are used and assumed.

The value and political power of groups such as ACT UP, Queer Nation and OutRage! began to decline during the 1990s. In the US a new Democrat government took office developing responsive programmes to the HIV and AIDS crisis, whilst being lead by a 'gay friendly' President Bill Clinton. In the UK, Western Europe and Australasia new governments, along with the growing power wielded by the European Court of Human Rights, began to adopt markedly positive policies and laws concerned with the position of non-heterosexuals within their respective societies. These developments, tied with a wider acceptance of lesbians and gay men in the wider public and the media, made the actions of the queer movement appear dated and out of touch with a growing assimilationist agenda and clamouring claims to citizenship rights (see Richardson 2000; Grindstaff 2003; Bonthuys 2008).

> In the first six months after the first civil partnership in December 2005, over 6000 were contracted . . . What seemed unthinkable 30 yeas ago, impossible 20 years ago, improbable (at least in famously slow moving Britain) 10 years ago, is now up and running with only the rumblings of the evangelical religious and occasional jokes about who does the dishes and wears the trousers to remind us of an earlier time when *heterosexual* marriage was the only access to sanctioned sexuality and respectability, and when homosexuals were 'the most evil men in Britain'.
>
> *(Weeks 2007: 3)*

For Weeks (2007) in his key book *The World We Have Won*, the rapid changes witnessed within the UK, Western Europe, Australasia, Canada, Mexico, Argentina, South Africa and the US reflect a world in transition. These changes are part of wider claims to citizenship rights – from the claim to same-sex unions or marriage, adoption rights, pension rights, employment rights, discrimination laws and fertility rights – transforming the way in which we understand and theorise sexual identities and the way in which people live their intimate lives. Ken Plummer (2008), who like Jeffrey Weeks has experienced and documented the struggles of non-heterosexuals since the 1970s, recently reflected upon key events around sexualities since the beginning of this century, along with suggesting new areas of focus that are now arising. For Plummer, as for Weeks, the rise of new citizenship rights discourses are transforming the way that lesbians, gay men and heterosexuals live their personal lives, epitomised in the rise of assimilationist politics. What were once a 'rather straightforward' bundle of rights and responsibilities, that were primarily reserved for (some) heterosexuals, have developed into a complex and evolving series of rights and responsibilities accessible to heterosexuals, lesbians and gay men through a growing normative agenda.

The growth of assimilation politics and the normalising discourses around lesbian and gay intimate lives for those such as Nicol and Smith (2008) can be attributed to developing from the queer movement of the 1990s. However, as they acknowledge, some lesbians and gay men were making claims to marriage in the early 1990s at the height of queer activism. The filing of the same-sex marriage case in Hawaii by two lesbians for the right to marry reflects that not all lesbians and gay men bought into or valued the actions of groups such as Queer Nation or the queer identities they espoused. As critics of queer have shown, can it ever really engage with the material realities of everyday life for lesbians and gay men – from employment, pensions, housing and inheritance, and other such citizenship rights that marriage bestows? The rise and power of the assimilationist agenda in the US during the middle to latter part of the 1990s was responded to by the US Congress with the Defence of Marriage Act (DOMA) that prohibits the recognition of same-sex marriage within federal law. The passing of DOMA refused same-sex couples, who may marry within certain US states, access to rights and obligations of marriage under US federal law. By 2001, thirty-five US states had statues banning same-sex marriage in the US (Grindstaff 2003: 258). Although initially the passing of DOMA could be theorised as reflecting the power and dominance of heterosexual norms and the centrality of heterosexual identity and practice to meanings of citizenship, if we borrow from Weeks (2007) it can be argued that the mere fact of having to pass a law to 'protect' the institution of heterosexual marriage reflects significant changes in the position and identities of non-heterosexuals within US society. As lesbians and gay men have left the ghettos and claimed a previously unknown level of visibility, the power and privilege of heterosexuality in the domains of gender order, family and sexual reproduction has crumbled (Weeks 2007: 9).

The centrality of claims to marriage, parent status and family rights within contemporary lesbian and gay discourses cannot be attributed solely to shifts in lesbian, gay or queer identities. As Kelly (2007) reminds us, there have been significant shifts within and between gender identities. Where only a few decades ago (heterosexual) men and women had distinct roles in marriage – men were expected to be the primary wage earner and women were expected to be the primary caregiver – in contemporary societies these roles are changing significantly. The shift within gender norms and gendered expectations allows discourses to open around relationships and families that not only challenge traditional gender roles, but also offer a different format to the traditional nuclear family. As Weeks (2007: 15) reflects, marriage (in the UK) has become for the majority of the population, a matter of choice, carrying rights and responsibilities. The meaning of marriage has long ceased to be what it was, often being the only gateway to adulthood, respectability and financial security. The changes that occurred between the 1960s and 2000s for Weeks have severed the automatic unity between marriage, sex, reproduction and parenting. The lesbian or gay family, rather than challenging the heterosexual family unit can be understood as part of a wider diversity in 'ways of doing' family. As Turner (1999: 32) has claimed, 'the liberal regime of modern citizenship privileges parenthood, rather than heterosexuality as such, as the defining characteristic of the normal citizen and as a basis for social entitlement'.

For Richardson (2000) what has now been witnessed since the beginning of this century is the expansion of political campaigns and discourses concerned with issues of family and intimate relationships. Campaigns by gay and lesbian groups are increasingly focused upon securing various rights as citizens on the same basis as heterosexuals. For Richardson, the AIDS crisis, although giving rise to queer activism, also brought into sharp relief the lack of legal recognition for non-heterosexual relationships, with consequences for pensions, housing, inheritance and other rights. The assimilationist agenda that can be found within some of these campaigns echoes some of the desires of the early homophile movements in the 1950s and 1960s. Similar to these earlier movements, lesbian and gay identities are often presented as non-threatening and as distinct from the (hyper)sexualised lives stereotyped upon lesbians, gay men and queers. Where for Sala and De La Mata Benitez (2009) and others, the value of identity allows lesbians and gay men to make claims to citizenship rights *as* lesbians and gay men, although this is often packaged in discourses borrowed from the homophile movements around 'their similarity' to heterosexuals. This assimilationist agenda in its use of presenting lesbians and gay men through their similarity reflects the institutionalisation of heterosexuality within citizenship rights and discourses. To make equal claims to equal rights, lesbians and gay men must forego their difference and (hetero)normalise their values and intimate lives. For Richardson (2000: 11) good citizenship and the values and rights it bestows must be understood within a heterosexual context. However, for others, such as Turner (1999), the liberal regime of modern citizenship rights discourses privileges identities and institutions such as parenthood and marriage. Where as in the past the homosexual was condemned in his inability to present a lasting monogamous marriage or to reproduce, which in turn failed it in its support for citizenship, in those societies that now offer diverse 'citizenship rights' to lesbians and gay men, they are now tolerated and accepted through their legitimisation (and normalisation) within the institution of marriage/civil unions and active parenting through adoption and fostering.

Approaches to the inclusion of lesbians and gay men into the act of marriage or civil union can be theorised from two perspectives – those in support, and those against. Often those in support of gay marriage argue that irrespective of whether lesbians and gay men want to marry, they should have the ability to decide for themselves. In allowing non-heterosexuals to marry, legal rights that are denied to non-married couples can be accessed and obtained. Such access can improve the material everyday lives of lesbian and gay couples, allowing them next of kin status, inheritance rights, tax breaks and adoption rights (in some countries). In accessing certain citizenship rights through their legal union, lesbians and gay men can make claims to a visibility in citizenship markers as partners and parents. As Kelly (2007: 410) reflects, 'pro-gay marriage advocates argue that, since the right to marry is viewed as part of being a first-class citizen, denying this right to gays [and lesbians] consigns them to second class citizen status'. The previous exclusion of lesbians and gay men from marriage created a hierarchy of monogamous intimate partnerships – the married and the non-married, with worth and value given to married heterosexuals (Bonthuys 2008: 727). This 'de-heterosexualising' of marriage that is only at best partial and limited across the world (and contentious in the US) represents a shift in the value systems of Western societies (Weeks 2007: 15).

However, for those opposed to lesbian and gay marriage the 'de-heterosexualising of marriage' or the growing assimilation and normalisation of lesbians and gay men into heteronormative institutions are problematic. The religious right, especially in the US, but also to be found across Africa, Western Europe and Australasia, have been particularly vocal in their opposition to allowing lesbians and gay men to marry and claim other such similar citizenship rights. Richardson (2000: 79) reflects on President Mugabe of Zimbabwe and his outspoken attacks on lesbians and gay men, condemning homosexuality as 'Uun-African' and an imported 'foreign concept and practice'. Lesbians and gay men within Zimbabwe are not only denied rights as Zimbabweans but are denied identifying as African through their 'un-African' identities. Equally in the US, the most recent Bush administration was vocally opposed to growing politicised claims for the right to lesbian and gay marriage, the right to adopt or even the basic right to serve in the US army. For Bush, lesbians and gay men were the 'other', unequal and abhorrent to heterosexual values, identities and institutions. Within Europe the Vatican under a new and more conservative pontiff, Pope Benedict, has been an outspoken critic of granting once heterosexual privileges and rights to lesbians and gay men in many European nations. The granting of increased citizenship rights and the growing value placed upon lesbians and gay men, especially within Western Europe, has been positioned as a direct threat to the institution of marriage and heterosexuality itself by the Vatican.

Main criticisms

The 1960s and 1970s as we have seen, were a pivotal time for the naming and claiming of new sexual identities. The negative values and meanings that were held around the medicalised 'homosexual' – which for over half a century had placed the homosexual as the inferior 'other' to the heterosexual, were challenged and rejected. The act of coming out became central to political claims to visibility, rights and the desire to name oneself as lesbian or gay. However, the experience and meaning behind 'coming out' as celebrated in the 1970s in the US and other Western nations cannot be universalised to all those who claim a non-heterosexual identity. As the work of Ridge et al. (1999) has shown, 'coming out' and being openly gay may lack cultural relevance to some ethnic minority groups. For such groups, coming out will intersect with rejection and separation from their ethnic networks, wider societal racism and difficulties in attempts to assimilate into what was and continues to be a mainly white, able-bodied, middle-class gay male culture. The desires of the GLF and the centrality of 'coming out' were very much US and Western European specific, having limited or no relevance to the sexual lives of non-heterosexuals in South America, Asia, Africa and Eastern Europe during this historical moment. Coming out discourses challenged the medical authority of the earlier sexologists who named and classified the modern homosexual, who themselves were based within Western Europe and the US. The modern homosexual was a Western construct, and although exported to a number of non-Western countries (Weeks 1989), for many nations around the globe, meanings around homosexual or gay or lesbian held little relevance at this time. For theorists such as Mary McIntosh, Michel Foucault, Diane Richardson, Jeffrey Weeks, Ken Plummer and Stevi Jackson, involved in 'the historical investigation of sexual identities' during this historical period, they did not approach lesbian and gay identities as essentialist or universal in meaning. Such identities they have argued were never denied or waiting to be claimed. Instead they theorised these new identities as constructed within and by discursive fields, Western products of the late twentieth century. The identities that were now being celebrated by the GLF and other such similar political movements were not pre-existing and 'just hidden in history', but were historically and socially constructed and given specific meaning within limited geographical locations during the 1960s and 1970s.

Another critique that can be levelled at the gay liberation movement is that the gay male movement, and some lesbians, increasingly bought into their own commercialisation, targeted as new consumers within the increasingly visible 'gay ghettos'. The politics that had upheld the values of the gay liberation movement increasingly gave way to rampant commercialisation. As a number of observers have commented, lesbians and gay men did not envisage the extent to which the new gay culture of the 1970s would be heavily commercialised by capitalism seeking a new target market. As Jeffrey Weeks, Diane Richardson and Ken Plummer reflect, the earlier aspirations of the gay liberation movement for an alternative sexual–political culture and identities had been answered by the organisation of a *huge* gay market. Profits could now be made from the newly confident sexual minorities, in the provision of specialist clothing, sex toys, commercial cruising grounds and through the growing centrality of commercial lesbian and gay social spaces for urban lesbians and gay men. Coming out that had been so politicised during the

1970s, increasingly came to be understood as an end in itself, and not as a challenge to the het-eronormativity that continued to exist within society. Lesbians and gay men were increasingly targeted as consumers, an emerging market to be valued and desired by capitalism, which only several years earlier had been understood as central to the oppression of non-heterosexuals.

For writers such as Crimp (1993), as the 1980s progressed, identity-politics and the identities it nurtured were increasingly problematised through an essentialist position. Identity-politics had failed in its inability to form alliances with those movements which secured the identities of les-bians and gay men. The failure of gay liberation to truly grasp race, social class and gender within its own ranks and how these identities impacted and intersected with sexual identity caused the focus of newly politicised, AIDS-aware lesbians and gay men to shift. Crimp (1993) goes on to position that the AIDS crisis brought lesbians and gay men face to face with the consequences of their separatism and liberalism – with the emergence of queer asserting new political identities, as has been discussed earlier in this chapter. However, the queer political movement was and is not without its critics. In particular there have been significant differences between various generations of men and women in how useful or threatening the project of queer has been. The queer linguistic tactic that has attempted to reclaim and embrace a term of stigma had been rejected by many older lesbians and gay men or those who still craved assimilation and wider citizenship rights. In using letters from the San Francisco *Bay Times* in the early 1990s, Joshua Gamson (1996) strongly illustrates the generational divide in the usage or resistance to the term 'queer'. For one writer, they asserted that the age of thirty-five marks those accepting of the queer label from those rejecting it. Younger people, a number of readers claimed, could only reclaim the word 'queer' because they had not felt the strong sting, ostracism, police batons and baseball bats that accompanied the this word a generation earlier. Whereas for older generations, queer's oppressive meaning can never be lifted, can never be turned over from overpowering to empowering. For those who were still pushing an assimilationist agenda in the early 1990s, wanting in on heterosexual rights and norms, the use of queer and the associated political actions were seen as rocking an already fragile claim to 'normality'. Queers actions and the associated beliefs went against the grain of civil rights strategies, where the *appearance* of normality (if not a true 'hetero-normality' itself) was central to getting into the political room. The queer slogan of the 1990s 'we're here, we're queer, get used to it', was a highly unapologetic call for a queer confrontational and political visibility.

Queer political action and the embracing of a queer identity allowed non-normative sexual identities to claim a new public visibility within the heteronormative public sphere. Queer provided fertile ground for an accelerated community-based response to mainstream political inaction to the AIDS crisis. But the queer project was short lived, with the growing question-ing of queer as a 'catch all term' and vocal claims around the value of identities such as lesbian and gay. As Khayatt (2002: 498) argues, the term 'queer' presumes a middle-class, urban, white, euro-North American, where such labels cannot be transposed to other nations, cultures and ethnicities without calling into question who first made claims to these and consequently, the very category itself. As Ridge et al. (1999: 46) suggest, queer (as with the earlier GLF) had a cultural leaning towards an 'Atlantic-centric' view of the world, entangled within the cultures of the global north, engaging little with those of the global south. For Butler (1997), queer marked a predominantly white movement – ignoring the material realities of racism and ethnic difference. The movement in its desire to unite men and women created false unities between them. Butler asks, does queer engage with the material power inequalities and widespread social divisions or does it ignore these specifities of important material differences? In its challenge to and deconstruction of identity categories, queer ignores and erases the value of identity-politics. As Bannerji (1995, cited in Khayatt 2002: 495) points out, identities such as lesbian and gay have provided many individuals with a moment of naming themselves with identities of their choosing. Identity categories, although undoubtedly reinforcing a gay/straight binary, allow minority groups to claim a visibility, to challenge discrimination and to claim wider citizenship rights *as* lesbians and gay men. To remove labels (and the identities so associated) can remove opportunities to challenge very real material inequalities experienced by diverse sexual minority groups.

The broadening of access to marriage and civil unions for lesbians and gay men, as this chapter has shown, has been celebrated and welcomed by many. However, the advent of lesbian and gay marriage and unions has not been welcomed by all lesbians, gay men or heterosexuals. The strong assimilationist agenda of the early twenty-first century can be theorised as continuing to support the wider institution of marriage and heterosexuality, with sexual identities themselves continuing to exist unproblematically. Although there are many lesbians and gay men who wish to marry, some of the strongest critics of lesbian and gay marriage, and the identities it supports, have been other lesbians and gay men. The assimilation politics of the last ten to fifteen years and the growing normalisation of lesbian and gay identities and lifestyles are critiqued by those such as Richardson (2000), Grindstaff (2003) and Bonthuys (2008). For these authors and others, the changes in citizenship rights discourses strengthens the position of marriage, monogamy and parenting as the template and the ideal which heterosexual, lesbian and gay adults should strive for. At the same time as lesbian and gay marriage or unions allow some same-sex couples to access marriage-like status and rights, others are excluded from the benefits bestowed. The meaning behind such a union reinforces the notion of commitment, exclusive sexual relations with one partner and the value of the couple over the individual.

The (hetero)normalisation of lesbians and gay men is shifting the binary that once existed between 'good' heterosexuals and 'bad' homosexuals. Now that lesbians and gay men can claim identities and lifestyles that are supported as valid, worthwhile and positive by the state, those who oppose such normalising tendencies maintain their 'bad' gay and lesbian position. Such 'bad' lesbians and gay men are increasingly positioned against the normalised, monogamous and 'good' lesbian or gay man. As Grindstaff (2003: 260) suggests, the normative operations of power are often elided within marriage debates, where marriage discourses are both disciplinary and heteronormative. Equally as the work of Bonthuys (2008) and Bates (2010) have shown, the normative principles around lesbian and gay marriage often ignore the complexity of social class, ethnicity and gender that intersect with sexual identity in impacting who can make claims to a normative identity and a same-sex marriage. As with earlier groups such as the GLF, ACT UP and Queer Nation, the current assimilationist agenda is often represented through the young, attractive, white, non-threatening and commercially viable gay male body. For Ridge et al. (1999) and Bates (2010), the experiences of ethnic minority men and lesbians within the 'gay world' tend to destabilise the notion of a unified and inclusive community. The 'dominance of Anglo cultures over other ethnic cultures' in lesbian and gay life in the global north is institutionalised to the extent that white privileges go unspoken (Ridge et al. 1999: 45). The lesbian and gay press may now include multiple adverts for lesbian and gay unions, weddings, parenting and home buying, but the images are primarily of white, young, able-bodied, middle-class lesbians and gay men.

Conclusion and future developments

In concluding this chapter and thinking through future developments, it feels like we have almost come 'full circle' from the early assimilationist desires of the homophile movements to the assimilationist success stories of today. Struggles over identity for homosexuals, lesbians and gay men have marked every decade since the 1950s. The emergence of the homophile movements post-Second World War in the UK and US signalled a growing desire and confidence by increasing numbers of urban lesbians and homosexual men to access new visibility, rights and inclusions into the wider heteronormative world. Markedly different from what was to arrive in the 1960s through to the 1990s, they began the slow process of building what was to become a new era of identity-politics and claims for non-heterosexuals in both Western and non-Western nations. The ideals of the homophile movement must be recognised as brave and daring in a time when the homosexual was the central focus of anxieties and paranoia present during the 1950s. Although those supportive of the homophile movement wanted increased tolerance and acceptance, they did not have the political will or power to challenge identity labels themselves. However, their assimilationist ideals and portrayals of 'respectability' were soon to be challenged with the advent of identity-politics. The 1960s and 1970s, as we have seen, were a pivotal time for the naming and claiming of new sexual identities. Lesbians and gay men rejected the rhetoric of isolation, coming together in their thousands to challenge the white male heterosexual hegemony that modern capitalism characterised. Through organisations such as the Gay Liberation Front, lesbians and gay men claimed new, politicised sexual identities.

Coming out and the claiming of a gay or lesbian identity, the naming of oneself *as* gay, increasingly represented a political act. Through coming out, one was not only rejecting a heterosexual identity, but also the power of medicine to name the homosexual. In coming out the homosexual was now gay. For many lesbians the claiming of a lesbian identity focused on the claiming of a political identity, reflected in the establishment of numerous lesbian political groups during the 1970s. Women could now claim a lesbian identity beyond meanings of sexual relationships alone, challenging the oppressive institution of heterosexuality and traditional gender identities and roles. As the 1970s gave way to the arrival of the 1980s, a new era arrived that challenged the newfound confidence and visibility of lesbians and gay men. Through the advent of AIDS, the religious and political right had a new platform to challenge non-heterosexual identities and practice and assert the centrality of heterosexuality within culture and society. In response, a new era of political action and identities arrived in the form of queer.

The birth of groups such as ACT UP and Queer Nation and the queer identities they (and the academy) espoused reflected the arrival of a new, angry and potentially more inclusive politicised movement. For queer and those who adopted its deconstructionist politics, collective identities were seen as an obstacle to true change within society, where the naming of oneself as gay, lesbian and even heterosexual should be refused. In queer's attack on identity categories and the binaries that these are so often dependent upon (gay/straight, man/woman) the false truths of both gender and sexual identities were shown. However, as with the GLF, the queer movement increasingly came to be defined through a white, middle-class, young, urban and gay male identity position. As critics have shown (see Butler 1997; Ridge et al. 1999), queer created false unities between men and women, whilst ignoring wider societal racism and the intersection between sexuality, ethnicity, gender and social class. Ultimately, queer activism and the identities associated failed due to its inability to incorporate diverse social realities beyond the urban centres of the US or Western Europe and the arrival of a new wave of powerful assimilationist politics based upon lesbian and gay identities.

The last decade has witnessed a previously unthinkable growth of citizenship rights discourses and claims within many Western (and some non-Western) countries. What we are currently witnessing is the emergence of rights and identities not based on sexual identity alone, but 'intimate citizenship' (Richardson 2000; Weeks 2007). Citizenship rights and obligations such as marriage, parenting, adoption, taxation and so on, that were once simple markers of heterosexuality are being opened to and welcoming of lesbians and gay men. The hierarchy between heterosexuals and lesbians and gay men and their diverse access to markers of citizenship is increasingly blurred and fractured. The arrival of a political movement based around intimate citizenship is allowing lesbians and gay men to claim other identities that reflect value and inclusive citizenship. Lesbians and gay men are no longer only marked by their sexual identity, but they can claim a visibility and inclusion as monogamous partners, parents, tax payers, home owners and so on. But as we have seen, although these developments are welcomed by many, the rise of the assimilationist agenda and normative politics is problematised by others. In the desire to access citizenship rights and status, lesbians and gay men are having to 'play by the rules' as set out by the wider (hetero)normative state. In so doing it can be argued that the (hetero)normalisation of lesbians and gay men has created a new binary between 'good' lesbians and gays, and the less respectable, non-monogamous lesbian or gay man. However, through the opening of marriage to non-heterosexuals, states around the globe are also slightly queered, where heterosexual privilege and values can no longer exist unproblematically. The embracing of citizenship rights discourses, in particular in relation to sexuality by individual states, but more importantly by the European Court of Human Rights and the United Nations is having consequences for the ability of individual countries to maintain the heterosexual/homosexual binary within the citizenship rights and responsibilities they will bestow upon their populations. Such values and struggles over intimate citizenship are creating new claims around neo-colonialism and Westernisation of sexual values, identities and rights within the global south.

The current citizenship rights granted to non-heterosexuals and the growing worth given to lesbian and gay lives and relationships must not eclipse the growing global backlash against lesbians, gay men and those heterosexuals who support them. As many Europeans, North and South Americans and Australians celebrate the right to marry, adopt, raise children, gain inheritance, have employment protection and so on, many other lesbians and gay men are facing a new era of hate, ignorance and violence. From the recent hanging of gay men in Iran, to the murder of lesbian and gay activists in Jamaica, the imprisoning of gay men in Malawi and Zimbabwe, the murder of gay men in Iraq and Afghanistan, growing homophobic violence within a number of EU nations and the growing challenges by the religious right in the US, Australia and Europe to the newly secured rights of lesbians and gay men – the coming future of lesbian and gay rights and identities is uncertain. For Plummer, the growing globalisation of sexual identities is flagging 'important schisms over gender and sexualities between fundamentalist worlds (Christian, Muslim and others) and non-fundamentalist worlds' (2008: 10). The intersecting of sexuality with other identities such as ethnicity, gender and social class, along with religion and geographical location has very real material consequences for the sexual identity/ies people desire or want to claim. As lesbian and gay identities and the lifestyles so associated continue to be globalised and co-exist, mix or come into conflict with local cultures and ways of being, the earlier monolithic generalisations around sexual identity and the values of the movements that underpinned them in the global north may have little or no meaning in other localities. What is clear as we reflect on our gains and what the future may hold is that struggles over sexual identities have been central to the multiple political movements of the last fifty years and are continuing to be key to current citizenship right claims and conflicts within both the global north and the global south.

References

Adam, B.D. (1987) *The Rise of the Gay and Lesbian Movement*. Boston: Twayne Publishers.

Bates, D.D. (2010) 'Once married African American lesbians and bisexual women: identity development and the coming out process', *Journal of Homosexuality* 57: 197–225.

Bonthuys, E. (2008) 'Possibilities foreclosed: the civil union act and lesbian and gay identity in South Africa', *Sexualities* 11(6): 726–39.

Butler, J. (1997) 'Critically queer', in S. Phelan (ed) *Playing with Fire: Queer Politics, Queer Theories*. London: Routledge.

Chauncey, G. (1994) *Gay New York: Gender, Urban Culture and the Makings of the Gay Male World (1890–1940)*. New York: Basic Books.

Crimp, D. (1993) 'Right on girlfriend!' in M.Warner (ed.) *Fear of a Queer Planet: Queer Politics and Social Theory*, pp. 300–20. London: University of Minneapolis Press.

D'Emilio, J. (1983) *Sexual Politics, Sexual Communities: The Making of a Homosexual Minority in the United States, 1940–1970*. Chicago: University of Chicago Press.

D'Emilio, J. (1989) 'Gay politics and community in San Francisco since World War II', in M. Duberman, M. Vicinus and G. Chauncey (eds) *Hidden from History: Reclaiming Gay and Lesbian Past*, pp. 456–76. New York: New American Library.

Engel, S. (2002) 'Making a minority: understanding the formation of the gay and lesbian movement in the United States', in D. Richardson and S. Seidman (eds) *Handbook of Lesbian and Gay Studies*, pp. 377–402. London: Sage.

Gamson, J. (1996) 'Must identity movements self-destruct? A queer dilemma', in S. Seidman (ed.) *Queer Theory/Sociology*. Oxford: Blackwell.

Grindstaff, D. (2003) 'Queering marriage: an ideographic interrogation of heteronormative subjectivity', *Journal of Homosexuality* 45(2/3/4): 257–75.

Kelly, R. (2007) 'Gay marriage: why now? Why at all?' in S. Seidman, N. Fischer and C. Meeks (eds) *Introducing the New Sexuality Studies: Original Essays and Interviews*, pp. 405–11. London: Routledge.

Khayatt, D. (2002) 'Toward a queer identity', *Sexualities* 5(4): 487–501.

Lutzen, K. (1998) 'Gay and lesbian politics: assimilation or subversion: a Danish perspective', *Journal of Homosexuality* 35(3/4): 233–43.

Nicol, N. and Smith, M. (2008) 'Legal struggles and political resistance: same-sex marriage in Canada and the USA', *Sexualities* 11(6): 667–87.

Plummer, K. (2008) 'Studying sexualities for a better world? Ten years of sexualities', *Sexualities* 11(1/2): 7–22.

Richardson, D. (2000) *Rethinking Sexuality*. London: Sage.

Ridge, D., Hee, A. and Minichiello, V. (1999) '"Asian" men on the scene: challenges to "gay communities"', *Journal of Homosexuality* 36(4/5): 43–68.

Sala, A. and De La Mata Benitez, M. (2009) 'Developing lesbian identity: a sociological approach', *Journal of Homosexuality* 56: 819–38.

Stein, M. (1997) 'Birthplace of the nation', in B. Beemyn (ed.) *Creating a Place for Ourselves: Lesbian, Gay and Bisexual Community Histories*, pp. 253–88. London: Routledge.

Taylor, V., Kaminski, E. and Dugan, K. (2002) 'From the Bowery to the Castro: communities, identities and movements', in D. Richardson and S. Seidman (eds) *Handbook of Lesbian and Gay Studies*, pp. 99–115. London: Sage.

Turner, B. (1999) 'Cosmopolitan virtue: citzenship, reactive nationalism and masculinity'. Presented at the *Re-thinking Citizenship: Critical Perspectives for the 21st Century* conference. University of Leeds, 29–30 June, 1999.

Warner, M. (1993) *Fear of a Queer Planet: Queer Politics and Social Theory*. London: University of Minneapolis Press.

Weeks, J. (1989) *Sex, Politics and Society: The Regulation of Sexuality Since 1800*. London: Longman.

Weeks, J. (2007) *The World We Have Won*. London: Routledge.

17

Environmentalism and identity-politics

Eileen M. McGurty

Introduction: historical roots of environmentalism and identity

One of the most significant characteristics of the contemporary age is widespread, unrelenting threats to the earth's life systems. While the term "ecological crisis" can seem like ideological hyperbole, the possibility of a complete breakdown is not completely far-fetched. Consider the statement by Rajenda Pachauri, head of the Intergovernmental Panel on Climate Change: "We are risking the ability of the human race to survive." The recent attention to climate change can occlude the many other possible avenues for ecological collapse. Rampant destruction of habitat and biodiversity means ongoing loss of critical ecosystem services upon which all of life depends. Unrelenting and constant assault on ecosystems with synthetic chemicals does not allow for adaptation, resulting in irreparable changes to life support system. The rate of extraction and use of resources, especially clean water, hinders recharge and guarantees complete and rapid depletion. The global changes, moreover, are experienced in specific places by particular people. The climate refugees from the African Sahal, the resident of the US Midwest forced to flee their homes when the natural flood plain could no longer absorb the stress of major storms, residents of the Ukraine still living with the effects of radiation over twenty years after the debacle at Chernobyl, and the residents of northern Iraq unable to access enough clean water from the Tigris-Euphrates because of upstream development projects all know the reality of global ecological crisis in their daily lives.

Environmental destruction and ecological collapse are not new phenomena; many civilizations have crumbled when they neglected ecological limits. Nor are environmental issues a development of the twentieth century; in fact, externalities associated with industrial production have been at the heart of many critiques of capitalism. In contemporary complex society, however, environmental destruction has taken on more weighted meaning. Shaking up the "grand narrative" of modernity means a complete reassessment of the relationship between human and non-human nature. The whole modernist project, rooted in the separation of object/nature from subject/mind, is built on a premise that the human subject is superior to nature, which must be brought under control of the mind for the benefit and prosperity of humans. In a world of massive deforestation, global warming, depleted fisheries, expanding deserts, widespread extinction, and ubiquitous contamination, the idea that humans can control nature is highly questionable, as is the underlying notion of identity supporting the project of domination. In fact, the dualism upon which science, technology, industrialism and capitalism was built is turning out not to be our savior but the source of our destruction. The relationship between identity and environmentalism is, therefore, at the very heart of the reconceptualization of the subject leveled by the postmodern turn.

In this chapter, I outline the two most influential approaches to the reconceptualization of the subject in light of the current ecological crisis. First, the changing relationship of society to uncertainty and the implications for a transformed agency leads to a new location for "practices of the self" in consumption as a potential vehicle for producing sustainability. Risk and uncertainty in contemporary complex societies also offer a new lens on how global ecological destruction actually reinforces practices of domination in very local contexts. Environmental justice emphasizes that institutional responses to environmental risks exacerbates both environmental problems and oppressive regimes. A second approach to the ecological crisis of our contemporary moment is a toppling of the nature/culture dichotomy. This dethroning can either emphasize the subjectivity of nature or stress the role of culture in constituting nature.

Risk and agency

The "risk society" thesis, attributed to both Ulrich Beck and Anthony Giddens, is one approach to understanding subjectivity in the light of the ecological crisis. Giddens and Beck examine how the experience of environmental devastation transforms and produces identities. Although each scholar traces a different path for the manifestation of risk in contemporary society, both Giddens and Beck see the pervasiveness of risk in organizing society as a product of the modernization process.

In the industrial society of an earlier modernity, where environmental contamination was spatially constrained, the poor were more likely to be impacted. In other words, class and risk were highly interrelated. According to Beck, the risk society completely unravels the relationship between risk and class so that wealth and positions of power are no longer protected from the full assault of risks. His point was reinforced as media coverage of several incidences of contamination of homes in middle-class communities forever uncoupled the fear of environmental risk from class. The various "Love Canals" demonstrated that no one could escape. The idea that wealth no longer guaranteed safety from environmental harm also offered an explanation for the emergence of the contemporary environmental movement. In this analysis, the increased affluence of the post-war period sparked environmental concern because once basic survival needs are met, concern for so-called higher-order issues could be addressed (Hays 1989). Beck, however, takes the analysis of the rise of environmental concern further by arguing that basic survival is no longer a guarantee, no matter how much wealth one has accumulated or no matter what one's social location. In this view, affluence does not simply make room for "luxuries" such as environmental concerns. Instead, the transformed nature of risks means that environmental concerns are no longer luxuries but are basic to survival.

The contention that traditional class-based politics lose meaning in a risk society because the wealthy and powerful are no longer protected from the uncertainties wrought by modernization dovetails with a "new social movement" (NSM) explanation of the rise of environmentalism. NSM theory argues that social movements in the contemporary age are unlike the traditional capital/labor conflicts because in NSMs the middle class are politicized. The demographic profile of active members of the environmental movement (white, middle-class, well-educated) would seem to confirm environmentalism as a NSM. Also, the multiple ideas within environmentalism competing for legitimacy (e.g. green parties, deep ecology, eco-feminism) shift away from relations of production and toward quality of life.

While an apparent "newness" emerged in the proliferation of environmentalism that relegated class less meaningful, the environmental justice movement emerged to challenge the idea that environmental problems could be decoupled from domination and oppression. While labor, in the traditional sense, could no longer fully explain exposure and risk, some people still were at higher risk than others. It is true that no one could escape nuclear destruction and that exposure to chemical contamination was invisible and could impact virtually anybody, no matter their social position. However, the local impacts of environmental risks could still be discerned. It was not true that everyone had an equal exposure to environmental risks, but rather than a straightforward explanation for inequitable distribution of hazards based on class, the primary factor shaping the distribution of risk was harder to locate (Schlosberg 1999).

Nature as subject

One response to the ecological consequences of modernity is to flip the Cartesian subject on its head by imbuing nature with subjectivity and agency. In 1949, the scientist Aldo Leopold offered the simple proclamation: "A thing is right when it tends to preserve the integrity, stability and beauty of the biotic community. It is wrong when it tends otherwise." Environmental ethicists use this idea as a foundation for the intrinsic value of nature thesis.

The strongest position of nature as subject argues that not only is the concept of an individualized, all-powerful self incorrect, but it is also the primary cause of contemporary ecological crisis. Climate change, massive habitat destruction, species eradication, and the overall state of ecological destruction on the global scale require a complete reassessment of the assumption that the self has power over nature. In this view, when the false dichotomy of object (non-human nature) and subject (humans) is dissolved, non-human nature is imbued with inherent value. The hubris of humanity as the center of the universe, so-called "anthropocentrism," is challenged and replaced with an "ecocentric" perspective that makes humans one member among many of an expansive community. Dethroning of the self and elevating the subjectivity of non-human nature implies that ethical considerations must be extended to the entirety of the ecosphere, not only to the human part of the whole.

The ecocentric view is indebted to the Norwegian philosopher Arne Naess (1973), who coined the term "deep ecology" to refer to a more radical approach than environmental reform. His ideas are built on several others who had articulated similar sentiments. For Naess, the central point is to understand that "organisms [are] knots in the biospherical net or field of intrinsic relations" (1973: 16). Identity, therefore, does not point to a separate entity but the result of a set of relationships. These relationships are not limited to other humans but include the entirety of the non-human world as well. Naess claimed Rachel Carson as part of the shifting understanding toward an ecocentric approach. Her compelling narrative in *Silent Spring* (1962) about the consequences of unbridled pesticide use for non-human and human nature took the world by storm with its call for recognizing humans as part of nature and nature as part of humans. Ecocentrism is an attempt to systematically examine this concept and its implications.

It is possible to talk about both the ontological and the epistemological social construction of nature. First, nature in a very material way is shaped and reshaped by social processes. The physical construction of the non-human world by the actions of humans and their social institutions, moreover, is not a phenomenon of the contemporary age. Usually, the reconstitution of nature by different societies is intimately linked to the reinforcement of specific, dominant social interests. For example, for millennia, indigenous people regularly engaged in fire regimes to create landscapes that produced flora and fauna more useful to their societies than would otherwise be present. Environmental historians have shown how the pre-colonial landscapes of Africa, the Americas and Australia were anything but fixed, pristine, standing apart from complex social processes. Agriculture is the prime example of how social systems physically shape landscapes, selecting some species over others, manipulating soil, water and species into structures that in turn shape the society that built them. While pre-modern agriculture was significantly different from contemporary processes in its ability to manipulate natural processes because of the limitations of technology, agricultural landscapes have always been socially constructed nature.

If nature is inescapably social, it does not exist apart from our knowledge of it and is not a testing ground for independent truth claims. Even if a "real world" existed out there, our socially constructed preconceptions will thoroughly be infused into our observations of it. As a result, a social constructionist view of nature focuses on the difficulty in separating observations about the natural world from social processes, leading to only partial knowledge. Not only is this incomplete, but it is also an expression of the power dynamics that support dominant, elite interests. Truth claims, therefore, become deeply political and become instruments of power and domination.

David Harvey (1974) took this position in his critique of the emphasis of overpopulation as the root cause of global environmental problems. By stressing population growth in the Third World over increasing consumption in the industrialized world, environmental problems were not a product of the capitalist structures of alienation. As a result, cries for population control were not a solution to some objective analysis of environmental degradation but were deeply political manifestations of hegemony. The example illustrates how a singular knowing of nature is not possible; instead, only plural, socially embedded knowledges are available. Harvey's critique demonstrates that social constructionism can function as critique and is not necessarily a break with modernity.

Major claims and developments of the field and key contributions

Risk and agency

Beck (1992) argues that an increase in risk awareness emerges from the actual outcomes and unfulfilled promises of modernization. Modern science and technology were supposed to bring order to nature and to provide estimations of the risks from nature so that they could be managed. It seemed, however, that the myriad effects of science created their own set of threats that are different from those of industrial society of an earlier modernity. The environmental problems of industrial society were location specific; for example, the air or water or land adjacent to a factory became contaminated. To be sure, much of this contamination was severe and deadly, but it was spatially contained. Contemporary environmental issues are not spatially limited. The global reach of environmental contamination is now a reality: PCBs, for example, can be found in the tissue of Arctic animals. Neither are contemporary environmental risks temporally confined, reaching into future generations with possible cumulative and irreversible damage. Contemporary societies face risks that are catastrophic – nuclear annihilation, climate change, and irreversible effects of widespread chemical contamination. These risks are invisible, unknowable, and incalculable, despite the best efforts of science. The result is a deeply felt anxiety about the promise of modernization. Risks, not as probabilistic outcomes but as unknown future threats, define the way that people understand their world and themselves. The anxiety experienced deeply affects institutions in a risk society, which are caught in an irreconcilable conflict. On the one hand, in order to manage the anxiety and keep control of the situation, institutions must acknowledge that the potential for catastrophe is real. Denial would only add to the anxiety and ferment more uncertainty in the promise of modernity. On the other hand, these same institutions must also obscure the origins of the risks and avoid taking responsibility for them. In the end, institutions of the risk society walk a delicate line between assurances that risks can be managed while denying complicity in their formation and proliferation.

Uncertainty about the future is the determining factor in contemporary societies. The new world we find ourselves in is one of "reflexive modernization," a term that Beck uses to mean that modernity has become "a theme and a problem itself" (Beck 1997: 8). By reflexivity, Beck does not mean intentionality in which actors reflect on knowledge about the contemporary situation and then choose to act. Instead, he emphasizes the unintended ways that life changes are made as a reflex to modernization. In part Beck is trying to show how reflexive modernization is not necessarily a step further along the Enlightenment path.

Reflexive modernity also leads to a detraditionalization, which requires a more purposeful engagement in negotiating the contours of risk. The process of individuation leads to cultural innovations and is marked by fluid identities. There is nothing inherently progressive about individuation – Beck sees terrorism as part of this same process. Rather, the shift away from traditions and transformations to the social institutions that produced and supported those norms can take any number of trajectories. In the political arena, Beck argues that individuation and its accompanying move away from traditional institutions leads to subpolitics, the "decoupling of politics from government" (Beck 2009: 95). Subpolitics fragments the locations of politics so that the possible spaces for action continue to proliferate. For environmental politics, this means that decisions shift from traditional sites of power to multiple spaces – the supermarket, the protest, the boardroom, or the home. For example, when demonstrations against the location of an unwanted land use (i.e. – waste facility or chemical plant) lead a company to abandon its plans, the official political process is not part of the decision-making process.

Giddens also emphasizes the role of risk in reflexive modernity: "At a certain point – very recently in historical terms – we started worrying less about what nature can do to us and more about what we have done to nature" (2000: 44). Giddens stresses the idea that modernization, especially through scientization, has produced the ability to perceive the world differently. Scientific skepticism, increased fragmentation, and the compression of time and space have changed the social perception of threats (ibid.). He also emphasizes the positive relationship of risk to production. Risk is necessary for the capitalist project; it drives the whole system. Giddens contends that, while risk is necessary, it is not just the risks that have changed but our experience of risk. When risks become incalculable, like the possibility of nuclear annihilation or completely veiled chemical contamination, the entire enterprise changes. The concept of risk was constructed when scientific skepticism, a foundational element of modernization, was turned inward to critique science, modernization, and the very idea of progress (Lupton 1999). In this way, risks were not objective realities but were tied to values and in constant flux. Risks, along with the knowledge and institutions built around them, were never outside society and the construction of meaning. In Lupton's words, risks are "assemblages of meanings, logics, and beliefs cohering around material phenomena, giving these phenomena form and substance" (1999: 31).

In a risk society, scientific knowledge is never neutral but is constructed within a particular social and cultural milieu. The politics of risk, then, are deeply entwined with the politics of knowledge. For Beck (2009) a risk society is entrenched in the condition of "non-knowing," so that more and better knowledge does not necessarily correlate with the ability to decide and to act. While probabilities might be calculable for some risks, these statistics tell us nothing about what is a rational choice under such conditions or at what point a concern is reasonable caution or merely irrational fear. For Giddens, the role of knowledge is also central to the processes of contemporary societies. The plethora of information that enable reflexivity reveal not only the unintended consequences of actions but also the fluid nature of expert knowledge. The uncertainty of knowledge leads to an uncertain subject whose actions are constantly reevaluated. The self is continually created in response to the barrage of expert knowledge, which must be constantly evaluated for its trustworthiness. The dilemma for everyone in contemporary society is the ongoing question: How to act in an infinitely contingent world (Giddens 1991)?

If, as Giddens says, the reflexive project is the hallmark of the contemporary age, then consumption is the primary location of the work of the self. The proliferation of commodities in the era of globalized economy is undeniable; in contemporary society, consuming is the most common activity in public places. Globalization has, in effect, shifted the possibility for transformation away from the sphere of production and into the arena of consumption. For environmentalism, the question is whether the identity work of the marketplace is sufficient to undo the ecological damage that has been done and prevent future harm. Advocates of sustainable consumption argue that it is primarily changes in consumption that will enable the necessary transformations of institutions. Through consuming, an individual has the possibility of impacting the intricate web of social relations in a globalized world: "My decision to purchase a particular item of clothing, for example, or a specific type of foodstuff, has manifold implications . . . [an] extraordinary, and still accelerating, connectedness between everyday decisions and global outcomes" (Giddens 1994: 57–8).

Consumption requires "a habitual forgetfulness" (Billig, as quoted in Wright 2004). This is a necessity because commodities hide the violence against ecosystems and people that are part of production processes. Commodities conceal the domination so that consumers do not have to face their own complicity in the system that enables these destructive practices. The purpose of sustainable consumption is to unveil the multiple connections to the human and non-human world that each commodity contains so that consumers can choose commodities that will further an agenda of sustainability. The ability to substitute alternative consumption practices that are less damaging to the human and non-human world is at the heart of sustainable consumption.

Sustainable consumption exposes the product life cycle and commodity supply chains that heretofore had been hidden. Each action we take, even the simple act of buying a cup of coffee, has a direct affect on the entire earth and people far away from the place of our action. A close and careful look at a product life cycle demonstrates the global reach and timelessness of the very tangible ramifications of our daily decisions. In a globalized world, the expanding space between each stage in the product life cycle is supposed to hide consequences. Sustainable consumption, however, compresses space and enmeshes the consumer, the producer, and the ecosystems in the supply chain.

The goal of sustainable consumption is to require a full accounting of the entire product life cycle. This has ramifications for both the producer and the consumer. The producer is challenged to internalize the full costs of production, not relying on people and ecosystems to unwittingly pay costs. For the consumer, sustainable consumption can become a practice of the self where values are infused into everyday choices. The globalized system, seemingly impenetrable, actually has a crack in it, and small actions can have meaningful impacts (Fuller 1999: 5–6).

The reconstitution of identity from changing patterns of risk complicated the relationship of environmental quality and class, but power and domination did not disappear from the landscape. The legacy of racism and colonialism means that voting with your feet was not possible for everyone. In the United States, environmental racism became the primary way of thinking about the relationship between oppression and environmental degradation. First articulated in the wake of a protest against a chemical landfill in a rural, predominately African American community, environmental racism shaped much of the discussion in the nascent environmental justice movement (McGurty 2007). Robert Bullard (2000) argued that inequitable exposure of people of color to environmental burdens was a violation of civil rights. He also documents extensive efforts to improve the environmental quality in communities of color, thereby undermining the assumption that they did not have the luxury to be worry about environmental matters. A similar approach of human rights-based environmental activism emerged throughout the developing world. For example, Guha (1989) shows a similar development of peasants in the forests of Uttar Pradesh in India. They launched steady and successful campaigns against deforestation practices that infringed on their rights of use. While the rise of environmental justice activism challenged the idea that environmentalism should be considered either classless (à la Beck) or a phenomenon of the middle class (à la NSM), there was some evidence to support the claim that prior to the environmental justice movement, the poor and people of color were ambivalent toward environmentalism (McGurty 2007).

Identity in environmental justice is a complex matter. Activists do not easily embrace the term "environmentalist" because they associate this identity with a more traditional environmental focus on non-human nature and a disregard toward people burdened with multiple avenues of oppression and environmental assault. As a result, there is a redefinition in the environmental justice identity that understands environmental work as fundamental to emancipation. Under the transformed identity, environmental practice takes on new meanings. For example, effort to improve housing conditions for the urban poor is environmental work, and the effort to halt siting of a hazardous waste in the same neighborhood is work for human rights.

The critique by environmental justice that traditional environmental efforts put nature above people is too simplistic an understanding. Resource conservation and nature preservation are central to the mission of an environmental agenda, many who work on environmental issues are motivated by their connection to non-human nature, and many of the oldest environmental organizations have long histories of exclusion and racism (Merchant 2003). However, a massive regulatory infrastructure championed by traditional environmental organizations has improved the health and well-being of many throughout the industrialized world.

The deeper conflict with traditional environmentalism is not the focus on some abstract idea of nature over the well-being of people, but the assumption that what is good for the environment in general will always be equally beneficial for everyone. It is this assumption of universality, with its underlying and often inadvertent elitism, that is challenged by the environmental justice embrace of an environmental identity. Building the infrastructure to protect people and the environment from the worst ills that industrialism has to offer ignores the structures of inequalities that already exist and presumes that somehow environmental practices will not be impacted by that system. Unfortunately, not only is the assumption incorrect, the laws, regulations, and institutions set up to implement the new environmental practices became part of the problem, causing more risk to be borne by some people over others. By not considering the possibility that environmental burdens disproportionately impact the poor and people of color, the environmental establishment perpetuates these inequities with their solutions to the problems. The insistence of universality of risk and the refusal to include a distributive analysis in the assessment of the problem led to solutions that not only caused more burdens for the poor and marginalized, but also never really addressed the root of the problem. The regulatory structure moved risks around in such a way as to cause more inequity, and did nothing toward reducing risks (Hurley 1995).

Hazardous waste management provides an excellent illustration. The general approach by most governments is to require so-called "cradle to grave" oversight by generators of waste. The grave, in this case, is some type of treatment or disposal facility. In order to implement this management scheme, many new waste facilities around the world have been built. Prior to these mandates, hazardous wastes were more likely to be haphazardly strewn about the landscape, dumped into waterways or spewed into the air. Now, the toxins from all these media must be brought under control, shipped to a facility where they are treated, burned or buried. Control of wastes and accountability of the generators to ensure safe delivery of wastes to the "grave" was supported by many prominent environmental voices around the world. As a result of moving toxins around the graves are located in disenfranchised communities. In retrospect, no one is surprised but when solutions to hazardous waste problem were constructed, the environmental establishment – including environmental movement organizations – could not even conceive of such an outcome because the analysis of the problem took the universalist approach (McGurty 2007). The original solution not only perpetuated the system of oppression but also led to an expansion of the generation of hazardous waste. These unintended consequences of an approach that ignored systems of domination showed the limitations of traditional environmental ideas. The environmental justice lens that emphasized the local and differential over the universal forced an alternative approach to waste management. The reconceptualization focused on a transformation of production processes that would eliminate hazardous waste rather than the control of wastes.

Environmental justice also emphasizes that people who are affected by contamination have a particular, and meaningful, way of understanding their situation and its impact on their bodies, families, work, and lives. A full understanding of environmental risk, then, must incorporate these "situated knowledges," rather than construct approaches that are solely based on abstract theories about risk. Situated knowledge is, according to Haraway, "simultaneously an account of the historical contingency for all knowledge claims and knowing subjects . . . and a no-nonsense commitment to faithful accounts of the real world" (1991: 187). While incomplete and limited, situated knowledge stays meaningful by remaining deeply reflexive about the parameters of its partiality. For example, popular epidemiology is one way to document local knowledge into assessments of risks, impacts of contamination, and effectiveness of regulatory structures. In popular epidemiology, communities living with contamination construct and implement their own health study, based on their intimate knowledge of place.

Nature as subject

If it is true that identity is fully enmeshed with our relationship to the natural world, then to truly know ourselves, the great work of our time is to find a way to reaffirm this. Identification with nature, then, would be central to the process of "Self-realization." Building on Naess, Warwick Fox (1995) developed the idea with his notion of the "transpersonal ecology." To identify personally with nature implies a direct interaction with natural entities in specific locales. These can be individuals or more abstract entities, such as ecosystems or watersheds. A transpersonal identification "extends beyond (or that is *trans-*) one's egoic, biographical, or personal sense of self" (Fox 1995: 197). "Self-realization" through the process of transpersonal identification moves from the level of the cosmos and inward toward the particular individual. Naess takes the opposite trajectory, moving from the particular to the universal in his concept of "felt nearness." In his rendering, the realization of the self as expansive comes from the connections with friends and communities, leading to humanity and eventually the whole cosmos. One possible reading of self-realization as an approach to environmental ethics is that actions taken on behalf of non-human nature are also ways of honoring the one's self: saving nature becomes saving yourself. Naess (1999) offers a more nuanced approach that has the potential of avoiding eradication of others through forced assimilation. Rather than see the process as a simple expansion of the atomistic self that absorbs others, he starts with an understanding of the self as ontologically relational. The self does not act as an isolated ego relating to others in the realm of commodification. Further, self-realization does not postulate that one is lost into the unitary whole, but rather that positive relations with others enable one to find oneself (Naess 1999).

Self-realization as a process to solve the ecological crisis leads to the advocacy of *wildness* experiences. Wildness is not to be construed solely as a place, as in "wilderness designated area." Harkening back to Thoreau's famous pronouncement, "In Wildness is the preservation of the World," wildness is understood as free, self-willed and self-determining order. Returning to wildness radically affirms the freedom of the self, but not as autonomous separate individual selves transcendent to the natural world. The "ecological self" is free in wildness, a self that is fully embodied and embedded in biology (Sessions 2006). Defending themselves against the attack that they do not make room for people (Guha 1989), ecocentrics argue that "free nature" consists of places relatively untrammeled by human behavior, not necessarily completely devoid of humans.

Ecocentrism is not only an approach to environmental ethics developed by intellectuals. Advocates adopt individual and communal lifestyles that create more opportunities for identification with nature and self-realization. The applications to environmental policy are also many, advocacy for wilderness being among the most prominent. The controversial Earth First! movement in the United States claimed their philosophical foundation as deep ecology although many distanced themselves from the group that advocated violence to protect wilderness. Arne Naess remained active in Green politics in Norway until well into his eighties. Another engagement of the philosophy entails experiential workshops designed for participants to explore an expanded sense of self.

Merchant (1980) lays out the relationship between the development of the scientific world-view of nature and the subjugation of women. On the one hand, nature was seen as a machine – dead, inert, and made of easily interchangeable parts. This perspective served the needs of scientific investigation and experimentation quite well. Francis Bacon articulated a particularly strong view of this idea. Nature must be "bound into service" and made a "slave" and "molded" by technology. On the other hand, nature was gendered, and as a female, nature is not simply a machine but its life force, "nature's womb" must be penetrated to discover "her secrets." None other than Descartes argued that the very purpose of science was to "render ourselves the masters and possessors of nature." For Merchant and other feminists, the problem with the Cartesian subject is not only its false dichotomy but also that it establishes the structure for domination of nature and women as mutually reinforcing systems of oppression. She argued that the production of scientific information, started in the seventeenth century, was implicated in the domination both of nature and of women. It is the scientized and mechanized world-view that provided the foundation for modernity, and capitalism enabled the domination of a gendered nature as female and was the foundation for the intimate linkage between the subjugation of both women and nature. In the mechanized view of nature, as espoused by Descartes, matter consists of passive and interchangeable parts; nature behaved according to laws that could be discerned and predicted by science and technology; knowledge of nature did not depend on the context but could be abstracted from the specifics; problems could be divided into as many parts as needed to resolve mathematically; and information is received in discrete minute particles. In the seventeenth century, the application of these methods were linked to the study and control of the female body and to the torture of women suspected of "consorting with the devil."

Merchant further argued that it was necessary to "re-examine the formation of a world-view and a science that, by reconceptualizing reality as a machine rather than a living organism, sanctioned the domination of both nature and women" (1980: xxi). These assumptions about the nature of the world have been challenged by new development in sciences. For example, in ecology, "disturbance" is no longer viewed as an anomaly but the norm, since ecosystems are in relation to their surroundings and are constantly in process. The shift away from a mechanical view of nature that decouples our manipulation of nature and the domination of women starts with very different ontological and epistemological assumptions. In the new world-view, connections, not parts, are the important phenomena so that changes in one part will impact both other parts and the whole; synergism ("The whole is greater than the sum of the parts") is the dominant structure; knowledge is always context dependent; open systems with non-linearity are the norm so that small inputs can spontaneously produce large effects. These qualities mesh well with new developments in ecosystem ecology, which approaches the study of ecosystems with nested and overlapping organization, contingent boundaries and variable scales, related to function and process.

One arm of the feminist response to the association of nature with women, as expressed by ecofeminists, was to turn "being close to nature" on its head and use it as a source of power rather than as a rationale for the subjugation of women. By re-appropriating women's bodies and the role that women play in reproduction, ecofeminists wanted to reclaim power for women. The meta-narrative of science and technology as progressing linearly toward ultimate freedom was shattered. Ecofeminists claimed women's "nature to nurture" as the vehicle to free humans and non-human nature alike from the chains of the scientized world-view.

Ecofeminism has been strongly maligned by academics for these essentializing tendencies, but in reality, there are really very few scholars who embrace a simple re-appropriation of women as naturally closer to nature. A more subtle form of the problem is the call for "an ethic of care" as a feminist response to a masculine thinking that has gotten us into our environmental predicament. The idea is that women's experiences as nurturers or mothers should form the foundation of a new relationship with non-human nature. Salleh explains it this way: "women are organically and discursively implicated in life affirming activities, and they develop gender-specific knowledges grounded in that material base" (1997: 161). In the various approaches of ethics of care, harnessing "women's ways of knowing" offers a promise of transformation both for nature and for women. Much of the scholarship using gendered epistemology as a basis for caring ethics is grounded in evidence from women environmental activists. Many women involved in toxic waste activism, particularly, explain their efforts as emerging from their role as mothers and caretakers. The research that emphasizes these narratives from activists often neglects any discussion of how the political work of these women strains their traditional roles in the private sphere, creating conflicts with a more private understanding of what "mother" means. When the care ethic is approached as a type of celebration of the so-called "subsistence perspective," it ignores the fact that many women engaged in subsistence work do not have much choice about the conditions of their lives.

In fact, there are many approaches posited by feminists to avoid naturalizing women while also embracing the idea that environmental problems and emancipation of women must be considered in concert. These approaches, taken together, are attempts to articulate "ethically responsible, situated, relational subjects engaged in ecofeminist political actions" (Merchant 2006: 515). Val Plumwood (2006) rejects the atomic model of Descartes and posits a "relational self," one that is both interconnected with the other while also remaining separate. A relational self has an "ecological rationality," that does not minimize the other, or deny its creativity and agency. This ecologically rational self has a very different relationship with land from the Lockean ownership model, undermining the whole notion of private property, which is at the foundation of many environmental conflicts. In this way, land becomes an agent of change for humans who engage it with a sense of bonding to place over time (Plumwood 2006).

There are a variety of other approaches to move the discussion away from the notion of women being closer to nature than men. For example, Warren (2000) argues for a "strategic essentialism," which makes use of sound science and historical analysis to generalize about interconnections among the domination of women, other humans, and non-human nature. For Warren, ecofeminist ethics are based on values "that presuppose that our relationships to others are central to an understanding of who we are" (2000: 100). Merchant for her part, argues for a partnership ethic.

While ecocentrics posit "nature as subject," another approach to overturning the object/subject dichotomy is to emphasize the role of culture in creating both the self and nature. In the social constructionist view, nature as pure subject, à la ecocentrism is deeply problematic because the separation of nature and culture is impossible. Although the ecocentric perspectives wants to see nature as subject, the emphasis on "living in harmony with" undermines their intention. By assuming a clear separation between the social and natural, where the latter is understood to be unchanging at its foundation, ecocentrism posits a nature that is external with essential characteristics that can be studied and understood in a universal sense. The result is a fully objective nature, not the subject that ecocentrics hope for.

Any statements made about nature tell us more about who is making the claims and their interests than they say about nature. Physical descriptions and normative judgments about any particular piece of nature will vary depending on who is doing the talking and will express not only the attributes of the place but also the social processes the speakers are engaged in and how they use that piece of nature. The qualities of, say, the Arctic ice cap or a temperate rain forest, or African savanna, are not fixed. Their changing representation is dependent on the social practices and institutions of those doing the observation.

If our ideas about nature are fully social, then the notions we have about environmental protection are also imbued with social meanings. The prime example of this relates to the quintessential call of the ecocentrics: wilderness preservation. The holism of ecocentrism emphasizes an ideal landscape as one with vast areas of undisturbed nature. However, wilderness is, from a social construction vantage point, not nature at its fullest, but "quite profoundly a human creation – indeed, the creation of very particular human cultures at very particular moments in human history" (Cronon 1995: 69). Cronon documents how the idea of nature has shifted over the past several centuries from something fully alienating and hostile to an empowering place, embodying both the sublime and the primitive, embraced by ecocentrics as the model for self-realization. Further, whether understood as the place of savagery or refuge, wilderness always exists in a dualistic relationship with civilization. The romantic understanding of wilderness as the ideal place because of its absence of humanity could only be created by "people whose relationship to the land was already alienated" (ibid.: 80). The "trouble with wilderness," then, is that it creates a model of the only genuine nature as one where human presence is the central problem. A longing for a pure nature of the sort that is in opposition to civilization leaves us "little hope of discovering what an ethical, sustainable and *honorable* human place in nature might actually look like" (ibid.: 81).

Main criticisms

Risk and agency

Critics argue that Beck's insistence on this approach to reflexivity overemphasizes the importance of risk in defining the current in addition to limiting the possibility of agency and reflection (Elliott 2002, 2009). Critics also reject Beck's insistence that contemporary risks are unable to be calculated, arguing that he misunderstands science.

Despite support from a wide range of actors, many scholars argue that sustainable consumption is anything but a blueprint for a path out of our dilemma. The complexity of product life cycles and supply chains means that claims of increased sustainability from specific products are difficult to verify. However, even if there was an actual, measurable improvement from one product over another, the fundamental challenge to the sustainable consumption approach is a critique of the idea that shopping is the solution to our global crisis. Environmentalists have long argued that proliferating consumption is the actual root problem of the environmental crisis. If so, not only is consuming more, no matter how it is produced, ineffective, but it is also adding to the problem. Sustainable consumption is also seen as a reification of a rational atomistic self-working to maximize self-interest, even if part of the utility involves altruism. The model makes assumptions based on the traditional view of the market. It assumes that consumers have, or can reasonably access, information about the impacts along supply chains, and that the knowledge is sufficient to motivate a change in behavior. Sustainable consumption is predicated on the idea that consumers actually can make a more sustainable choice in the marketplace. Yet, how many can really choose transit over car use for daily mobility needs, even if they knew the environmental and social impacts of each option? Sustainable consumption as solution to environmental crisis assumes that producers will respond to market signals and transform their production practices based on those signals. However, the desired results are few and far between because the assumptions about consumer information and price signals are not a sufficient explanation for how production decisions are made (Seyfang 2009).

Sustainable consumption, as a practice of the individual, not a collective practice, challenges the idea that individuation can become progressive politics in the realm of the everyday sub-politics. Since sustainable consumption is a middle-class phenomenon, it can function as another reproduction of class position at the expense of others. The belief that knowledge can lead to changes in behavior can easily be dismantled in the face of evidence showing that knowledge of consequences and consumer choices are not directly linked.

Another critique of sustainable consumption shows how it can actually perpetuate the hidden relations in production by romanticizing and exotifying the natural systems that are supposed to be helped by the purchase of alternatively produced goods. The resulting fetish is not an avenue of emancipation but a reinforcement of the power dynamics. As a counter to the critique that sustainable consumption only serves to reinforce the status quo, Dobson (2003) argues for an alternative sustainable consumption, one based on local, decentralized, smaller-scale economics. In this approach, an "ecological citizen" can use consumer behavior as political action by only taking up an equitable amount of ecological space. By Dobson's accounting, not all sustainable consumption is the same: there is a qualitative difference between a sustainable consumption practice of community-supported agriculture and organic products sold at the supermarket. Also, there is a need to link shopping to more formal political practices in order to transform the individual actors of consumption into agents of collective change.

Nature as subject

There are three categories of critiques to the complete dissolution of nature/culture boundaries and emphasis of the subjectivity of non-human nature. The first challenge argues that the dissolution of nature/culture is unwarranted because human artifacts and natural entities can clearly be delineated. The second challenge affirms the false dichotomy between nature and culture as well. However, critics argue that the insistence on a unitary self denies differences and leads to a continuation of domination by either exclusion or assimilation. According to Plumwood (1991), the abstract and impersonal universal self advocated by the process of self-realization replicates the grand narratives of modernity that ignored particularities and created the basis for practices of domination. In the third challenge, holism of the type advocated by ecocentrists undermines attachments to particular landscapes. Ecocentric holism runs the added risk of mistaking one's own interests for the interest of the other with which one has identified. As women, people of color, and indigenous people around the world can attest, this is exactly the justification of their oppression. The same potential holds for the non-human world, so there is no guarantee that arriving at an expanded sense of self will lead to ecological salvation.

The critique that challenges universality of an expanded self has particular salience to feminists who understand the subjugation of women and nature are at the very foundation of modernity. King (1989) posits that the domination of women and non-human nature "are intimately connected and mutually reinforcing" because women are associated with being closer to nature. Industrial capitalism uses this presumed proximity to justify the continued subjugation of women and explain the apparent natural supremacy of men.

Ecofeminists were challenged on two fronts. First, tying the understanding of women to their biology, even if as a celebration rather than a diminution, reified an essential difference between women and men, as well as the cascade of opposing ideas that came from the subject/object supposition that provided the foundation for modernity. In this way, ecofeminism was actually propping up the very foundation that it was attempting to dismantle. Clearly, socially constructed gendered identities were easily unveiled as more fluid and mutable than the ecofeminist view allows. But the same could be said for sex – there are gradations in biology, so that the clear association of female bodies with a particular participation in reproduction is not applicable either. Second, positing a unitary view of women across time and space undermined the ability to see that women in different social locations – women of color, working-class women, women in the Third World – are subject to oppression, sometimes by other women where hierarchies intersect with class, nation, or race (Warren 2000). The so-called nurturing role of women is often thrust upon poor women and women of color as an exacting of their labor. Also, some women have been able to escape the worst of the assaults of environmental contamination, as documented in the environmental racism literature.

Another critique of the approach that embraces an association of women and nature can lead to a view that indigenous women and Third World women, usually more directly enmeshed in non-human nature through their work, are the original ecofeminists. The Indian feminist and environmentalist Vandana Shiva (1990) contributes to this view by arguing that the precolonial subcontinent was more ecological than the "maldevelopment" that the West brought because it had a unity of masculine and feminine principles. Without the female principle, men become separated from both nature and women, resulting in widespread ecological disaster in India. In Shiva's view, the infamous women tree huggers of the Chipko movement in northern India capture the feminine principle that is needed to ward off further ecological havoc – women tree huggers. For Sturgeon and other critics, Shiva's analysis of the Chipko movement illustrates how the celebration of "indigeneity" – either indigenous women, Third World women or premodern European women – intends to support difference but results in a reconstitution of white privilege.

Haraway is one of the most radical feminist critiques the ecofeminist approach: "There is nothing about being female that naturally binds women. There is not even such a state as 'being' female, itself a highly complex category constructed in contested sexual scientific discourses and other social practices" (1991: 155). Her "Cyborg Manifesto" offers a radical anti-dualistic view, arguing that building feminist politics on the image of a cyborg, rather than a nurturer, was more appropriate. Not only are the distinctions between humans and machines already blurred, but also the cyborg metaphor allowed a full dissolution of pre-determined categories. The cyborg emphasizes that even the human body does not fit neatly into one category over another. In this context, then, how can identity-based politics be meaningful? For feminists concerned with the fate of non-human nature, cyborgs complicate the vision of ecologically supportive practices.

The social constructionist approach to topple nature as object was a flash point for ecocentrists. Cronon was vilified for distracting much needed attention away from protection of the last remaining wild areas. For ecocentrics, the "trouble with Cronon" is that he apparently does not understand biology, and the necessity of large areas of land to support evolutionary processes. Moreover, "Cronon may be correct that ideas of nature don't exist outside of cultural understandings, but Nature in all its self-governing complexity most certainly does exist" (Willers, as quoted in Proctor 1998: 357). From the critics' viewpoint, embracing wilderness as an idea formed by a particular culture in a particular time leads to the conclusion that the world does not exist – it is all in our heads. Cronon flatly denies such an absurd position. The point at issue, rather, is if our ideas about wilderness say more about that something "out there" or more about the cultural meanings infused in the concept of wilderness. The challenge to environmentalism grounded in a constructionist perspective is the seeming impossibility of knowing we cannot really know what is out there as it really is, yet knowing that some practices will be more sustainable than others.

Critics argue that an insistence on a cultural analysis is a throwback to the anthropocentric hubris of modernity that thought nature could be constructed into anything humanity wills. Trying to create a non-human world to their liking, ecocentrics say, is the problem that needs to be overcome and constructionists are only reinforcing the wrongheaded thinking that led to the brink of disaster. Yet, the constructionist view does not necessarily lead down that path. The primary point is that numerous social and natural processes, at multiple geographic scales, are intimately woven into a complex fabric of hybridization. White (1996) shows how the Columbia River is an entity constantly in flux, shaped as much by natural process as the modification of societies through time. While the river is not the same as it was prior to European contact, it is not dead either. The river is an "organic machine," not unlike Haraway's cyborg, where the natural and the human are difficult to distinguish. The Columbia is but one example; hybridization is the norm, not the exception.

The continuing importance of perspectives environmental identities

In contemporary complex society, the challenge of living in a hybrid world brings the possibility that these transformations will lead to systems that no longer sustain basic life functions. For example, the current Columbia River supports species today that are different from those of the past thriving in the river. Is it possible that the river, or any ecosystem, could be so modified that it completely collapses? Some would argue that transformations of this sort have already occurred and are ubiquitous. In the face of the real potential of widespread ecological shifts, the very idea of our ability to control nature and harness it for our own benefit is doubtful. This uncertainty challenges the core understanding of human subjectivity upon which our contemporary world has been built. The possibility for a future that does not undermine its own ecological foundation is rooted in a complete reconceptualization of that identity. Several approaches have theorized a self that can support a new and sustainable relationship with the earth: practices of the self in the everyday, environmental identities that link global processes of change to local and differential impacts, and a toppling of the nature/culture dichotomy, either by infusing nature with subjectivity or emphasizing the role of culture in constituting nature. The trajectory that a reconceptualized self will take in relationship to sustainable practices is the great challenge of our age.

References

Beck, U. (1992) *Risk Society: Toward a New Modernity*. London: Sage.
Beck, U. (1997) *The Reinvention of Politics*. Cambridge: Polity.
Beck, U. (2009) *World at Risk*. Cambridge: Polity.
Bullard, R. (2000) *Dumping in Dixie: Race, Class and Environmental Quality*, 3rd edition. Boulder, CO: Westview Press.
Carson, R. (1962) *Silent Spring*. New York: Houghlin Mifflin.
Cronon, W. (1995) "The trouble with wilderness, or getting back to the wrong nature," in W. Cronon (ed.) *Uncommon Ground: Rethinking the Human Place in Nature*. New York: W.W. Norton.
Dobson, A. (2003) *Citizenship and the Environment*. Oxford: Oxford University Press.
Elliott, A. (2002) "Beck's sociology of risk: a critical assessment," *Sociology*, 36(2): 293–315.
Elliott, A. (2009) *Contemporary Social Theory: An Introduction*. London and New York: Routledge.
Fox, W. (1995) *Toward a Transpersonal Ecology: Developing New Foundations for Environmentalism*. Albany: SUNY Press.
Fuller, D. (1999) *Sustainable Marketing: Managerial-Ecological Issues*. Thousand Oaks, CA: Sage.
Giddens, A. (1991) *Modernity and Self-Identity: Self and Society in the Late Modern Age*. Stanford, CA: Stanford University Press.
Giddens, A. (1994) 'Living in a post-traditional society', in U. Beck, A. Giddens and S. Lash (eds) *Reflexive Modernization*. Cambridge: Polity.
Giddens, A. (2000) *Runaway World: How Globalization is Reshaping Our Lives*. London: Routledge.
Guha, R. (1989) *The Unquiet Woods: Ecological Change and Peasant Resistance in the Himalya*. Berkeley, CA: University of California Press.
Hays, S. (1989) *Beauty, Health, and Permanence: Environmental Politics in the United States, (1955)–(1985)*. New York: Cambridge University Press.
Haraway, D. (1991) *Simians, Cyborgs and Women: The Reinvention of Nature*. New York: Routledge.
Harvey, D. (1974) "Population, resources, and the ideology of science," *Economic Geography*, 50: 256–77.
Hurley, A. (1995) *Environmental Inequalities: Class Race and Industrial Pollution in Gary, Indiana, 1945–1980*. Chapel Hill, NC: University of North Carolina Press.
King, Y. (1989) "The feminism of ecology," in J. Platt (ed.) *Healing the Wounds: The Promise of Ecofeminism*. Philadelphia: New Society.
Leopold, A. (1949) *A Sand County Almanac and Sketches Here and There*. Oxford: Oxford University Press.
Lupton, D. (1999) *Risk*. London: Routledge.
Merchant, C. (1980) *The Death of Nature: Women, Ecology and the Scientific Revolution*. San Francisco: Harper & Row.
Merchant, C. (2003) "Shades of darkness: race and environmental history," *Environmental History*, 8(4): 380–94.
Merchant, C. (2006) "The scientific revolution and *The Death of Nature*," *Isis*, 97(3): 513–33.
McGurty, E. (2007) *Transforming Environmentalism: Warren County, PCBs, and the Origins of Environmental Justice*. New Brunswick, NJ: Rutgers University Press.
Naess, A. (1973) "The shallow and the deep, long range ecology movements: a summary," *Inquiry*, 16: 95–100.
Naess, A. (1999) "The ecofeminism versus deep ecology debate," in N. Witoszek and A. Brennan (eds) *Philosophical Dialogues: Arne Naess and the Progress of Ecophilosophy*. Lanham, MD: Rowman & Littlefield.
Plumwood, V. (1991) "Nature, self and gender: feminism, environmental philosophy and the critique of rationalism," *Hypatia*, 6(1): 3–27.
Plumwood, V. (2006) "The concept of a cultural landscape: nature, culture and agency in the land," *Ethics & the Environment*, 11(2): 115–50.
Proctor, J. (1998) "The social construction of nature: relativists accusations, pragmatists and critical realists responses," *Annals of the Association of American Geographers*, 88(3): 352–76.
Salleh, A. (1997) *Ecofeminism as Politics: Nature, Marx and the Postmodern*. New York: Zed Press.

Eileen M. McGurty

Schlosberg, D. (1999) *Environmental Justice and the New Pluralism: The Challenge of Difference for Environmentalism*. Oxford: Oxford University Press.

Sessions, G. (2006) "Wildness, cyborgs, and our ecological future: reassessing the deep ecology movement," *The Trumpeter*, 22(2): 121–82.

Seyfang, G. (2009) The *New Economics of Sustainable Consumption Seeds of Change*. London: Palgrave Macmillan.

Shiva, V. (1990) *Staying Alive: Women, Ecology and Survival in India*. New Delhi: Zed Press.

Warren, K. (2000) *Ecofeminist Philosophies*. Lanham, MD: Rowman & Littlefield.

White, R. (1996) *The Organic Machine: The Remaking of the Columbia River*. New York: Hill and Wang.

Wright, C. (2004) "Consuming lives, consuming landscapes: interpreting advertisements for Café Direct coffees," *Journal of International Development*, 16: 665–80.

18

Black freedom struggles and African American identity

David Stein

Intellectual development

> The more authentic question was not whether the slaves (and the ex-slaves and their descendents) were human. It was, rather, what *sort* of people they were . . . and could be. Slavery altered the conditions of their being, but it could not negate their being.
>
> *(Robinson 2000: 125)*

What we now can recognize as "Black freedom struggles" are as old as Blackness itself. Formed within and through – but also, beyond – the dialectic of capitalism and slavery, the "history of Blackness," as Fred Moten suggests, is "testament to the fact that objects can and do resist" (Moten 2003: 1). Moten opens his book with these lines to rupture the presumptions that equate personhood and subjectivity. Subjectivity, to Moten is "defined by the subject's possession of itself and its objects" (ibid.: 1). Accordingly, Moten must investigate how, historically, Blackness strains the commonly held assumptions separating subject and object. This also reveals how Blackness strains notions of the subject rooted in the political and philosophical discourses of liberalism buttressed by a Lockean understanding of natural liberty and property ownership. To understand Blackness, rather, Moten is more interested in resistance to the subjects' identifications. He investigates how humans who were defined and treated as property have resisted that assertion to be property, as well as the construction of desire to own property.

While the "social cauldron" of Black freedom struggles is Western civilization, it cannot be solely defined as a response to the slave trade and the advent of racial capitalism (Robinson 2000: 72–3). Cedric Robinson's writing is one of the most influential in making such an argument. He suggests that:

> Black radicalism is a negation of Western civilization, but not in a direct sense of a simple dialectical negation . . . Black radicalism . . . cannot be understood within the particular context of its genesis. It is not a variant of Western radicalism whose proponents happen to be Black. Rather, it is a specifically African response to an oppression emergent from

the immediate determinants of European development in the modern era and framed by orders of human exploitation woven into the interstices of European social life from the inception of Western civilization.

(ibid.: 72–3)

While in our current intellectual moment such comments about the specific African response may invoke troubling ideas about essential identities, this is not Robinson's argument. What he shows through his research is how, against all odds and oppositions, Blackness and Black community were formed. Robinson's thesis finds affinity with Moten's argument, and is rooted in the historical materialist methodology. Out of the many social systems, within the place now called Africa, that were irreparably ruptured as a result of colonialism and slavery, there were specific cultures that lived on. This is what Robinson investigates in his analysis of the conditions of possibility for Black radicalism. He argues that the transportation of "African labor to the mines and plantations of the Caribbean and subsequently to what would be known as the Americas meant also the transfer of African ontological and cosmological systems" (ibid.: 122). These systems of being and meaning formed the core of what he identifies as the Black radical tradition.

The great Martinician poet, theorist, and politician Aimé Césaire related a similar point about the histories of the societies destroyed by colonial regimes and enslavement. Césaire along with Léon Damas and Léopold Senghor inaugurated the Negritude arts movements in 1935. Damas (from French Guinea) and Senghor (from Senegal) met Césaire while studying at the Ecole Normale Supérieore, and all had a deep investment in overturning the regimes of violence that brought their homes and the colonial world into being. Césaire would argue that these sites "were societies that were not only ante-capitalist . . . but also anti-capitalist . . . I make a systematic defense of the societies destroyed by imperialism" (Césaire 2000: 44). Césaire wrote these words almost a decade after the fall of the Nazi regime, in the midst of anti-colonial nationalist movements throughout the world. In this text, *Discourse on Colonialism*, he also theorized the connection between colonialism and the rise of fascism suggesting that fascism within Europe was an outgrowth of colonial regimes.

While both Césaire and Robinson demand that one appreciate the rupture and the deliberate decimation of possibilities that colonialism instantiated, neither proposes "going back" to before colonialism as a viable response to the enormous violences. Césaire argues that "it is the indigenous peoples of Africa and Asia who are demanding schools and colonialist Europe that refuses them . . . it is the colonized man that wants to move forward, and the colonizer who holds things back" (ibid.: 46). Both are dialectical about the question of redress. They both understand how enslaved labor provided the engine of Marx's so-called primitive accumulation of capital in the Americas and Europe (what Robinson has also called "imperial accumulation"); so the demand for redress is a part of the historic mission to locate the wealth of the planet in the labor that created it.

Major developments

Capture and the slave ship

I am a reminder that twelve million crossed the Atlantic Ocean and the past is not yet over. I am the progeny of the captives. I am the vestige of the dead. And history is how the secular world attends to the dead.

(Hartman 2007: 18)

What was the experience of capture and enslavement? How can the historian or the theorist represent this reality? What types of texts and archives must the scholar use and subvert in order to investigate these questions? These are conundrums that have perplexed and frustrated scholars' attempts to write about the Middle Passage and slavery. The stories of history are dictated by the limits of archives. But archives are always places of knowledge production, not simply retrieval. It was not until the 1960s, for example, that historians began to be attentive to "what the slave felt, thought, or did" (Huggins 1990: xxiv). Accordingly, the archive of the slave trade requires one to scrape for sources of meaning to answer Cedric Robinson's question: what sort of people were they?

Saidiya Hartman is one of the most important and imaginative scholars writing about the history and present of enslavement. "Contrary to popular belief," Hartman explains, "Africans did not sell their brothers and sisters into slavery. They sold strangers: those outside the web of kin and clan relationships, nonmembers of the polity, foreigners and barbarians at the outskirts of their country, and lawbreakers expelled from society" (2007: 5). This point is crucial to understand the context of Robinson's arguments about the making of Blackness and the invention of race and racism. Racism and race have been fused together as historical experiences and have, in-turn, created new communities. Hartman agues against apologists for the slave trade who maintain innocence on the ground that "Africans sold Africans." "In order to betray your race, your first had to imagine yourself as one. The language of race developed in the modern period and in the context of the slave trade" (ibid.: 5). Hartman, here, is being historical and accounting for how the people involved in the slave trade imagined themselves in those moments. Additionally though, she points to the fact that slavery was not initially determined by what we now call race for "it was not until the sixteenth and seventeenth centuries that the line between the slave and the free separated Africans and Europeans and hardened into a color line" (ibid.: 5). Hartman's goal in her research is to illuminate the present by investigating the "lives undone and obliterated in the making of human commodities" (ibid.: 6). In order to do this, though, she must revise and write against many of the dominant conventions of historical writing.

Nathan Huggins argues that the rupture of one's community ties were essential to the attempted process of converting humans into commodities. Huggins and Hartman both, for example, discuss how the barracoons along the western coast of Africa became the "factory" for constructing the enslaved (Hartman 2007: 6; Huggins 1990: 36–7). In 1481 the Portuguese built Elmina Castle and while it was planned to be used to hold nonhuman goods, it would become a site of terror and loss – a prison to hold captured people before the forced passage – a school where death was the chief lesson (Hartman 2007: 111; Huggins 1990: 36). With this in mind, it its important to consider the fact that Elmina and the British-built Cape Coast Castle were called "factories," because these are the places that built the modern world. In fact, Hartman notes "factory" had "its first usage in the trading forts of West Africa" (Hartman 2007: 111). This note should clarify, as Eric Williams did in *Capitalism and Slavery* and as Sidney Mintz did in *Sweetness and Power*, the essential link between the slave trade and the industrial revolution.

Hartman argues, "the dungeon was the womb in which the slave was born" (ibid.: 111). But this was not the only thing made. Even the most awful forms of oppression built into them conditions for their negation. One of the many keys to elucidate the fact that freedom struggles of various sorts, scales, and success have always existed is the knowledge that these barracoons were necessary to prevent the would-be enslaved from "self-inflicted injury which would lower their value" (Huggins 1990: 36).

The prisons on Africa's west coast were one key site for the development of the slave trade. Another was the actual slave ships. Marcus Rediker describes the slave ship as "combination of war machine, mobile prison and factory . . . central to the making of modern capitalism"

David Stein

(Rediker 2007: 9–13). Like the barracoons, an entire industry would rise in response to the problem of how to restrain the enslaved people from harming themselves and to compel life in enslavement. Hartman describes the case of an enslaved girl who refused to eat and the lengths the captain went to compel her to do otherwise. She writes of the captain, "he had used the *speculum orbis* (to pry her teeth apart and shovel in some food), thumbscrews (to make her submit), coals pressed near the lips (to scare her), and four days of the whip (to break her stubbornness), all to no avail" (p. 145). What does it mean for the understanding of Black freedom struggles that such industries existed to manufacture such products used precisely to manufacture humans into slaves? As we know from the fact that such an industry existed, this case was not in isolation. So, neither the oppression nor the resistance should be imagined to be isolated either.

Rediker describes resistance to the tools of forced life. In a scene on the slave ship *Brooks* between 1783 and 1784, the speculum orbis could not be used upon an enslaved man who was attempting to commit suicide (p. 17). The enslaved man was refusing to eat and pulled apart his throat with his hands. The doctor on the ship stitched up the wound, and the slaveholders were unable to use the speculum orbis as a result. The subsequent day after the wound had been treated, the man "tore out the sutures and cut his throat on the other side" (p. 18). After more attempts to compel this man to become human capital, he died upon the slave ship approximately ten days after these incidents. As the doctor on the ship attempted to treat this wound the man said that "'he would never go with white men'" (p. 18). The doctor on the ship related this story in 1790 at a British parliamentary hearing on the slave trade. When asked if he thought this man was insane, the doctor replied, "'by no means insane'" (p. 18). Rediker writes, "the man's decision to use his own fingernails to rip open his own throat was an entirely rational response to landing on a slave ship" (pp. 18–19).

Not only were incidents such as these common place, but there were both voluntary and involuntary suicides that cannot be made sense of through contemporary medical science. Huggins writes of how many of the would-be enslaved died "from no disease and no apparent conscious act. Europeans were baffled for an explanation. Some claimed these captives had wanted death so badly that they held their breath, suffocating themselves . . . whether or not medical science had ever known such a phenomenon, the captains of the slave ships sought an answer to it" (1990: 51). As with the production of torture tools to compel life, captains employed all sorts of tactics to ensure their profit. Nets were mounted on the sides of ships to prevent some of the captives from jumping (Huggins 1990: 50). Attracted by the human waste thrown off the ships, sharks would follow along their routes and captains would use the threat and practice of throwing crew overboard in an attempt to maintain discipline amongst both the enslaved and the crew (Rediker 2007: 39–40).

The system of capture and forced passage to enslavement was the key factory for building the modern world. In addition to structuring modern capitalism, out of this experience of terror and against the attempted destruction of African pasts a sense of Blackness was created. Rediker (2007) argues that those captive in the slave ship were of "different classes, ethnicities, and genders" all together, but that "dispossessed Africans formed themselves into informal mutual-aid societies, in some cases even 'nations,' on the lower deck of a slave ship" (pp. 130–1). Through these renderings of the enslaved experience one can see how "the enslaved now appear as the first and primary abolitionists as they battle[d] the conditions of enslavement aboard the ships on a daily basis" (pp. 11–12). Robinson makes a similar point both about the identity-making apparatus and the resistance built within it: "The peoples of Africa and the African diaspora has endured an integrating experience that left them not only with a common task, but a shared vision" (p. 166). This shared vision of life and liberation against and through the most severe regimes of oppression is the hallmark of the Black freedom struggles and the identities formed therein.

Enslavement and the Haitian revolution

The contention that enslaved Africans and their descendents could not envision freedom – let alone formulate strategies for gaining and securing freedom – was based not so much on empirical evidence as on an ontology, a implicit organization of the world and its inhabitants.

(Trouillot 1995: 73)

Colonial America of the early seventeenth century was the space in which the opposing demands of freedom and enslavement were worked out. Initially the status of Black people in the English colonial settlements was ambiguous and vacillated between statuses of "slaves, indentured servants and freemen" (Robinson 1997: 2–3). However, this began to change toward the later part of the century. Virginia in the post-1660 era enacted many laws that in turn calcified a racial capitalist order that at that time was still in the making. Cedric Robinson reports:

In 1662, a law was passed preventing a child from inheriting the father's status if the mother was a "negro woman"; in 1667, another law prevented baptism from freeing "slaves by birth"; in 1680, a law was passed "for preventing Negroes Insurrections"; in 1692, another to aid "the more speedy prosecution of slaves committing Capitall Crimes" established special courts for slave trials . . . the incremental construction of slave law mirrored reality: "Englishe" men were sexually consorting with African women; Africans were acculturating to colonial society; and slave workers were turning toward resistance.

(ibid.: 2–3)

Laws are always crucial to understand how states are formed and changed; such laws need the actions of people to create their significance – laws always mediate bodies. The 1667 law that established the maternal status lineage for Black women was essential for bringing a particular type of gender difference into being for the enslaved. This law allowed for and encouraged the rape of enslaved women by the masters. Jennifer Morgan in *Laboring Women* has documented how laws such as these caused slave owners and traders to envision enslaved women's wombs as sites of speculation and venture capital in the form of future slaves. Laws and practices such as these would circumscribe a very limited sense of

representational possibilities for African Americans: 1) motherhood as female bloodrite is outraged, is denied at the *very same time* that it becomes the founding term of a human and the social enactment; 2) a dual fatherhood is set in motion, comprised of the African father's *banished name* and body and the captor father's mocking presence . . . only the female stands *in the flesh* both mother and mother-dispossessed.

(Spillers 1987: 80)

Spillers and Morgan show how laws such as these enabled specific forms of racial-gendered terror for the enslaved.

In the early colonial period, the relations of law, race, and power were not clean and clearcut in specific locals within colonial America, let alone across different places. Though Virginia, Carolina, and Georgia would all become dominated by slave economies, the "colonies' destiny

David Stein

of slave owning was barely discernible from their origins" (Robinson 1997: 3). Such knowledge is crucial to remember for it displays how racial regimes are constructed over time and everyday, but their results are not natural or inevitable.

While the early resistances by slave and bonded laborers took on many forms – "appeals to the courts, physical violence, flight, and rebelliousness" – by the beginning of the eighteenth century, legal rights for the enslaved had been eviscerated (pp. 8–9). Before this occurred there were examples of European servants and African slaves working together to plot revolts. The establishment of slave codes destroyed what could have been other alliances and social movement formations. For example, "with the enactment of the slave codes, both Black and Native American slaves were denied allies in the Euro-American poor" (p. 9). In the subsequent era, slave uprisings mounted. As Robinson notes after documenting the many and various forms that resistance took, "slavery gave the lie to its own conceit: one could not create a perfect system of oppression and exploitation" (p. 11).

Another form of resistance included escape and marronage. While it is no surprise that maroon communities of fugitive slaves have been difficult for historians to document, it is also a topic that many scholars have deliberately neglected. Maroon communities were not exclusively Black, though they were the most prominent group. These communities were made up of European poor servants, escaped slaves, and Native Americans (p. 13). Whole networks of abolitionists also aided these types of resistances and escapes. Most famously the Underground Railroad provided help and support for those escaping from enslavement and fleeing to Canada and is thought to have supported the escapes of 60,000 enslaved people (pp. 29–30). Of course, while the network was crucial, "it was the intelligence, desire, and courage of the fugitive slaves themselves that jolted the Underground Railroad into movement" (p. 31). Harriet Tubman, a formerly escaped slave herself, was a "general" along the routes helping to free some 300 slaves by assisting the navigation of treacherous terrain that had increased in danger after the passage of the 1850 Fugitive Slave Law (p. 30). Later, during the Civil War, Tubman would utilize her skill as a guide in this terrain to lead Union Army troops and also spent time organizing intelligence units amongst the enslaved (p. 31).

Starting in the nineteenth century, the Black freedom struggles expanded to fight against the entire enslavement regime. While most historians note the British Abolitionist movement against the slave trade (though not slavery), these struggles are best exemplified by such large-scale planned uprisings of the enslaved as Gabriel's rebellion in Richmond, the Pointe Coupee Conspiracy in Louisiana, and Nat Turner's rebellion in Virginia. Robinson clarifies what all of these modes of resistance meant for the construction of Black culture:

> For the slaves, acts of resistance and the lore that swelled around them . . . provided the integument of a Black culture, the materials for a historical consciousness and a sense of community, and a moral system for determining how the lord of the cosmos negotiated the existence of good and evil . . . in a social order obsessed with domination and policing of the spirit, resistance was the antithetical core, the soul of Black life. But the secret languages, the furtive acts, even the covert taxes on non-Blacks exacted through sarcasm, word-play, indirection, and humor were not sufficient to themselves.
>
> (p. 40)

Indeed, as Robison notes, these struggles were essential to the historic feat that is Black survival. But the historic mission – the common task and shared vision – was liberation.

The liberation struggles of this era received their most powerful inspiration from the Haitian Revolution. San Domingo, on the dawn of the revolution, "supplied two-thirds of the overseas trade of France and was the greatest individual Market for the European slave trade" and was the "most profitable colony the world had ever known" (James 1989: ix, 57). The great Trinidadian writer, theorist, and activist C.L.R James wrote one of the most comprehensive histories of this struggle and would argue that the seeds of the revolution were the context and contradictions of the experiences of the enslaved. "Men make their own history, and the Black Jacobins of San Domingo were to make history which would alter the fate of millions of men and shift the economic currents of three continents" (p. 25). The quotidian experiences of the enslaved formed the core of the Haitian Revolution, and, accordingly, the religious cosmology of Voodoo was a key factor: "Like revolutionary peasants everywhere, they aimed at the extermination of their oppressors . . . Voodoo was the medium of the conspiracy" (pp. 85–6). Like Robinson and Moten, James draws on songs in order to argue that the ontological totality of Blackness was not and could not be identified by that of oppression. James documents lyrics to songs with lines such as: "we swear to destroy the whites and all that they possess; let us die rather than fail to keep this vow" (p. 18). Such cultural forms exemplify the revolutionary tradition that circulated through Haiti. Knowing this, it should be no surprise that in 1803, as the Revolution entered its twelfth year, the US House of Representatives instituted "a ban on Haitian refugees because they posed a 'danger to the peace and security of the United States'" (Robinson 1997: 24).

As structures of oppression create the condition of their demise, James argues that it was the Black Jacobins of San Domingo that revised and reconceived the best of the French Revolution for their own ends. He writes, "the Blacks were taking their part in the destruction of European feudalism begun by the French Revolution, and liberty and equality, the slogans of the revolution, meant far more to them than any Frenchman" (James 1989: 198).

However, for all the revolutionary inspiration that the Haitian Revolution would inspire, it was also victim to a harsh counter-revolution. The revolt in Haiti shook not only the French economy to its core, it "challenge[d] the ontological and political assumptions of the most radical writers of the Enlightenment" (Trouillot 1995: 82). Following the revolution, Haiti was victim to international trade isolation. Peter Hallward notes:

> France only re-established the trade and diplomatic relations essential to the new country's survival after Haiti agreed, in 1825, to pay its old colonial master a "compensation" of some 150 million francs for the loss of its slaves – an amount roughly equal to the French annual budget at the time, or around ten years' worth of total revenue in Haiti – and to grant punishing commercial discounts. With its economy still shattered by the colonial wars, Haiti could only begin paying this debt by borrowing, at extortionate rates of interest, 24 million francs from private French banks.
>
> *(Hallward 2004: 26)*

In James's analysis though, he also takes to task the revolutionary leader, Toussaint L'Ouverture, for his failures. For all of L'Ouverture's revolutionary brilliance and military strategy, James is frustrated with his inability to envision what would come next. James writes that for L'Ouverture "the ultimate guarantee of freedom was the prosperity of agriculture" (James 1989: 242). But this was not enough for it created a shift from an old despotism to a new one (though he points out that this is not simply a substitution). In his appendix written twenty-five years after the original publication, James would write, "Toussaint could see no road for the Haitian economy but the sugar plantation" (ibid.: 393). As with the escaped slaves and the maroon communities, the Haitian revolution was a success, but not of the mass liberationist variety necessary to break apart the violences of slavery, capitalism, and patriarchy.

David Stein

The Civil War, reconstruction, and abolition democracy

> The true significance of slavery in the United States to the whole social development of American, lay in the ultimate relation of the slaves to democracy . . . if all labor, white as well as black, became free, were given schools, and the right to vote, what control could or should be set to the power and action of these laborers?
>
> *(Du Bois 1935/1992: 184)*

Michel-Rolph Trouillot has argued that the Haitian Revolution has been epistemologically erased by most scholarship in spite of, or perhaps as a result of, being the most fundamentally human of the modernity's revolutions; the French and American Revolutions, for example, were revolutions that served the interests of Man, as opposed to the entire human species. "The Haitian Revolution was unthinkable in the West not only because it challenged slavery and racism but because of the way it did so . . . [it] expressed itself mainly through its deeds, and it is through political practice that it challenged Western philosophy and colonialism" (Trouillot 1995: 87–9). As this great revolution has been erased, the greatest social movement victory in the US history is not remembered as such. This, of course, is the great general strike of the enslaved that abolished slavery within the US.

Contrary to the popular national mythology, the Civil War was not a referendum on slavery as a political and economic structure; rather, it was a struggle over power. The leading industrial capitalists of the North and the plantocrats of the South both "shared the same ambition – control of the surplus capital produced by slave labor" (Robinson 1997: 68). The Southern plantocrats wanted assurances they could retain "their rule over a thriving slave economy, the maintenance of a societal stratification based on slavery, and the defense of master/slave culture" while the Unionists of the North wanted to ensure the power of the industrial bourgeoisie within a national economy still reliant on slavery (ibid.: 67). The Unionists wanted to dominate the economy and the federal government with the help of "protective tariffs, a national banking system, labor regulation and federal corporate and stock supports" (ibid.: 67–8). As the great abolitionist and former slave Frederick Douglass said, the war was initiated, "in the interests of slavery on both sides. The South was fighting to take slavery out of the Union, and the North was fighting to keep it in the Union" (Du Bois 1935/1992: 61). Initially, most leaders on both sides thought that the struggle would end after a brief three-month conflict. Obviously, most miscalculated.

One the chief miscalculations is rooted in the same epistemological presumptions that Trouillot discussed – that the enslaved did not desire freedom. It was assumed by the racist planter-elite that the enslaved were simple, loyal, and dependent, and would continue that way without the harsh cudgels of plantation power. However, as we have seen, when given the opportunity, the enslaved did all they could to struggle for liberation whether in this world or the next. So, with the slaveholders occupied fighting another enemy, the enslaved used their advantage to rebel through defections and insurrections (Robinson 1997: 68). This would become the general strike that decimated the infrastructure of the South. The great African American scholar and activist W.E.B. Du Bois emphasized this point: "The Southern worker, black and white, held the key to the war; and of the two groups, the black worker raising food and raw materials held an even more strategic place than the white" (Du Bois 1935/1992: 63). Every battle that the North won, and space the Union Army moved into meant more fugitive slaves joining their ranks (ibid.: 62). While there were some 33,000 Black people from free states who fought, "the overwhelming majority of Blacks who served in the Union army (179,000) and navy (10,000) were slaves. For a time, the slaves transformed the Union military into an army of liberation and the conflict into a war for freedom" (Robinson 1997: 68, 76). The general strike involving about 500,000 people was not only "to stop work. It was a strike on a wide basis against the conditions of work . . . they wanted to stop the economy of the plantation system, and to do that they left the plantations" (Du Bois 1935/1992: 62). And they were successful. With the labor and infrastructure of the South devastated, the North won militarily and on January 1, 1865 the Thirteenth Amendment to the Constitution was passed outlawing enslavement or involuntary servitude except for those convicted of crimes. This was followed with the Fourteenth Amendment in 1868 that overturned the Dred Scott Decision (1857) and established citizenship rights for former slaves.

However, this abolition of slavery would be one of negative abolition. Slavery was abolished, but new institutions were not sustained to attempt to redress the violences of slavery, for its supporting structures – racism, patriarchy, and capitalism – all remained intact. There were efforts to create what Du Bois called abolition democracy – a positive abolition to join with the negative one that would work to abolish the vestiges of slavery. But such institutions as the Freedmen's Bureau – established to assist in acquisitions of land, food, housing, healthcare, education – were disestablished or eviscerated of their power after Andrew Johnson replaced Abraham Lincoln as president.

While the Fourteenth Amendment is the most high profile of the attempts for abolition democracy coming from Congress from 1865 to 1877 (the era of "radical reconstruction") – some of the most important were those of the majority Black legislature of South Carolina. Throughout the South during this era, "African Americans led the fight for free universal public education" (Kelley 2002: 130). In South Carolina, this movement for education for everyone was particularly strong: "Freed people contributed nearly thirteen-thousand dollars to keep twenty-three schools running, schools that had been established by the Freedman's Bureau . . . between 1866 and 1870, newly freed people contributed more than three-quarters of a million dollars in cash to sustain their own schools" (ibid.: 130).

Nevertheless, after the federal government removed its support for reconstruction, what Du Bois calls a "counter-revolution of property" was commenced whereby "an organized monarchy of finance . . . overthrew the attempt at a dictatorship of labor in the South" (Du Bois 1935/1992: 580). The construction of the railroads and roadways (a portion of which was done by former slaves who had been convicted of crimes and leased to private industry) provided the backbone of the shift to this "new American industrial empire" (ibid.: 580–6). The refusal of the white working classes across the US to align with Black labor was vital to this. "National industry could get its way easier by alliance with Southern landholders than by sustaining Southern workers. They did not know that when they let the dictatorship of labor be overthrown in the South they surrendered the hope of democracy in America for all men" (ibid.: 592). Horribly, this reveals what had been noted as the primary goal of the North for the Civil War – "to reappropriate the human, capital, and natural resources of the South . . . by 1870, 80 percent of the super rich would now be Northerners" (Robinson 1997: 82, 69).

The birth of Jim Crow and the anti-lynching movement

> There would be no lynching if it did not start in the schoolroom.
>
> *(Woodson 1977: 3)*

Freedom, as has been shown, came neither cheap nor easy for any involved in the Black freedom struggles. It was always a process, each and everyday to carve out space for survival and more. For example, as Black women entered the "free" workforce after slavery, they would steal time from their employers by attaching books to nearby fences so they could read and study while washing clothes (Hunter 1997: 42). Such practices brought meaning to the word freedom. For the formerly enslaved freedom was not simply of the liberal variety rooted in property ownership. It was far more. "Freedom meant the reestablishment of lost family connections, the achievement of literacy, the exercise of political rights, and the security of a decent livelihood without the sacrifice of human dignity or self-determination" (ibid.: 43). To this end, the struggle to take hold of one's laboring capacities remained essential to the long struggle for freedom both before and after slavery. The formerly enslaved refused to allow freedom to mean "free to sell one's labor."

The late 1870s and 1880s were a period of immense labor struggle amidst a capitalist crisis. This was the age of major strikes most notable of which were the Great Railroad Strike of 1877 and the 1886 fight for eight-hour work days via a general strike in Chicago, which eventually culminated in the Haymarket massacre. In a post-bellum urban city such as Atlanta, the struggles were not identical, but remained fierce and tumultuous. In Atlanta in early July of 1881 a group of Black women working as laundry washers met in a church to form the Washing Society so as to begin to organize for a uniform rate of pay, as well as respect at their jobs. The decision to meet in a church was no mere accident either. Historically, as Eddie Glaude has shown, the Black church had been a space for fashioning freedom dreams both adapted from and created anew through the exodus story. "During the violent, oppressive, and disheartening trial that was post-Civil War America, Black Christianity was at once the dominant moral philosophy, the centering source of collective and personal identity, and the conceptual marking device for the historical past and political destiny of Blacks" (Robinson 1997: 98). The church also provided some much-needed cover from the society of constant surveillance to which African Americans were subjected. Indeed, organizing meant even greater threats to one's safety. In order to mask their activities, "it is likely that all of the domestic workers' associations in Atlanta . . . adopted the institutional framework of secret societies" in order to manage this (Hunter 1997: 88). In addition to the church serving these purposes, it was a likely place for this group of women to meet because women represented the majority of the church members (p. 69).

The Washing Society called a strike on July 19. The protest was considered to be the "largest and most impressive among black Atlantans during the late nineteenth century" (p. 88). Their demands met their situation – a uniform rate of pay. There were frequent instances of non-payment of wages as well as payments in the form of clothes or food, or docking of wages, or promising one wage and paying another. Additionally, "laundry work was critical to the process of community building because it encouraged women to work together in community spaces within their neighborhoods, fostering informal networks of reciprocity that sustained them through health and sickness, love and heartaches, birth and death" (p. 62). Uneven wages for the same and similar work undermined the efficacy of these communities and the potential for unification – communities they had been building since reconstruction (p. 94); indeed, this struggle was not only about wages, but about the self-regulation of their work and finding those spaces of freedom within one's work even under conditions not of their own choosing. Of course, the communities that had been formed through struggle were vital to the success of the strike. In three weeks, the number of striking workers grew from twenty to three thousand (p. 91).

Such struggles were examples of the centrality of everyday networks and everyday acts of resistance to daily life in the post-slavery South: "The strike is also suggestive of the character of domination in the emergent New South. White employers certainly had the power to confine black women to domestic work, but not the unilateral power to determine how and under what conditions that labor would be organized" (p. 97). Like before, resistance often took other forms as well, of the less visible and high-profile variety. Just as women stole time as a mode of resistance, the theft of commodities also occurred, and the definition of what this was often depended on one's perspective: "While 'pan-toting' was regarded as theft by many employers, household workers believed they had the right to take home leftovers, excess food, and redundant or broken utensils for their use . . . theft at the workplace is also a strategy to recover unpaid wages and/or compensate for low wages and mistreatment" (Kelley 1994: 20).

However, it is successful organization such as the Washing Society as well as the everyday acts of resistance such as pan-toting that provided the backdrop for the increasing oppressive power that would arise as Jim Crow. Hunter elucidates this, "despite effective community mobilizations on many fronts – indeed, because of their effect – blacks were increasingly met with systematic encroachments on their civil and human rights . . . political disenfranchisement, vigilante violence, and de jure segregation intensified in the 1890s and began to tip the scales of justice decidedly in the favor of whites" (Hunter 1997: 98).

While such struggles occurred in the growing urban cities of the New South, Black people in rural areas also struggled to take hold of their labor capacities. Much of the farmland remained owned by White people and many Black farmers were tenants. Of course there was resistance to this – the formation of The Colored Farmers' National Alliance and Cooperative Union in 1888 boasted a membership of 40,000 members in South Carolina and 20,000 in Virgina by 1891 (Robinson 1997: 103–4). But the 1890s would prove to be the reaction to this, especially concerning the possibilities of biracial alliances: "In the 1890s the Southern white reformers and the Democratic party appropriated segregation as the basis of their new social order . . . thus ended Black mass participation in white agrarian radicalism" (ibid.: 105).

In addition to the institution of segregation policies, legally codified in the 1896 *Plessy v. Ferguson* decision, lynching became the most prominent practice attempting to roll back the racial, gendered, and capitalist order to an antebellum mode. "In the 1890s, Blacks confronted the most oppressive conditions since the ending of slavery" (ibid.: 105). While the most severe time period for lynching was 1892–1902, from 1882–1968 there were 4,743 recorded lynchings. But lynching also worked in concert with a whole range of terror-producing acts – "rape, beating, torture, mutilation, arson, threats" (ibid.: 105). However, like before, social movements arose to respond to this increase in oppression.

In 1892 in Memphis, Black shop owner Tom Moss and his business partner were killed by a White mob. This event was catalytic for Tom Moss's friend, former school teacher Ida B. Wells (Hill 2008: 121). Wells would become one of the most important voices in creating, theorizing, and organizing the anti-lynching movement. As a journalist, Wells began to document and write about the frequency of lynchings as part of the attempt to "break the big lie" that undergirded the racist rational for lynching: Black deviance, impropriety, and criminality (ibid.: 121). In order to do this, Wells needed not only to show the innocence of the lynching victims, but to reframe the conversation to center how these acts were premised on the relations between state violence and state-sanctioned violence. In turn, Wells's theorized the situation as that of a police-mob continuum that identified the White mob as part of the criminal legal system premised on maintaining the gendered racial capitalist order.

Wells utilized her pen and her voice to bring attention to the issue of lynching, practicing mass political education campaigns as part of her organizing strategies. With her writings being ignored by all but the Black press, in 1893 and 1894, she traveled to England for a speaking tour and inspired the formation of anti-lynching societies within Britain (Robinson 1997: 105). But Wells did not only demand the end of lynching: "She intended to agitate for an even more ambitious objective than the end of lynching: the launching of a civilizing mission that would bring the rule of law and economic rights for Blacks and women" (ibid.: 105).

As the twentieth century began, provoked by increased mob killings of African Americans, Wells and other Black activists and intellectuals such as Du Bois, William Monroe Trotter, and Mary Church Terrell would work along with some 300 others to form the National Association for the Advancement of Colored People (NAACP) in 1909. From the outset, the NAACP was a group that brought together political and ideological tensions between liberals and radicals. Though its leadership came largely from the White and Black middle class, "it was largely through the efforts of grassroots Black women that the NAACP grew into a national organization," swelling to have 42,000 dues-paying members and 155 chapters within the South alone within a decade (Robinson 1997: 110, 117). While Wells's work and the formation of the NAACP are highlights of the social movement to end lynching and legal and extra-legal terror, in many places they could not confront the violence of White supremacy. Racism was rising, exemplified with the formation of the Ku Klux Klan in 1915 in Georgia and President Woodrow Wilson's endorsement of the racist film *Birth of a Nation* (ibid.: 113). Resultantly, "the most eloquent and effective response to lynching was Black migration to the North" (ibid.: 110). From 1890 to 1910, over 200,000 Black Southerners went to the North, and 300,000–1,000,000 went over the subsequent years from 1910 to 1920 (ibid.: 111).

While, cities such as Detroit, Chicago, and New York, each of which tripled their Black populations from 1910 to 1930, would prove to have similar ideologies of racism (albeit sometimes different articulations), the Great Migration to the North represented the dream and demand to struggle to imbue freedom with a sense of meaning (ibid.: 110–11). The Great Migration provided the basis for the formation of a number of other groups and political philosophies to come together in the shadow of the First World War. Marcus Garvey, an immigrant from Jamaica organized the Universal Negro Improvement Association (UNIA) with a vision of international Black nationalism. A. Phillip Randolph, Chandler Owen, and Cyril Briggs and other key Black members of the Communist Party USA (CPUSA) formed the African Blood Brotherhood (ABB) as a secret organization (as the Washing Society was compelled to be) and "urged Blacks to form mass working class organizations" (Hill 2008: 154). "The ABB was as Black nationalist as UNIA, and . . . persuaded the Communist International in 1928 to consider the 'Negro Question' in America as one of Black self-determination" (Robinson 1997: 119). Indeed, such a strategy pushed the CPUSA during its radical "Third Period" (1928–1933) to incubate members of the Black left who saw communism and anti-racism as linked strategies for the goal of self-determination. At the onset of the Depression, communists:

> collaborated with the Black poor in the northern cities and Southern fields. Organizing tenant rent strikes, protest marches and demonstrations; the mobilization of an international campaign to save the Scottsboro boys; writers' clubs; and sharecropper and trade unions were understood as the necessary precursors of the proletarian solidarity required for the ultimate defeat of capitalism.
>
> *(ibid.: 121–2)*

All of these tactics and strategies and alliances became the planted seeds that would soon flower as freedom struggles grew in militancy and numbers after the Second World War.

Major developments: the Civil Rights and Black Power eras

In order for us as poor and oppressed people to become part of a society that is meaningful, the system under which we now exist has to be radically changed. This means that we are going to have to learn and to think in radical terms. I use the term radical in its original meaning – getting down to the root cause. It means facing a system that does not lend itself to your needs and devising means by which you change that system.

(Ella Baker in Ransby 2003: 1)

As the US entered the Second World War in 1941, previously unemployed people from the Great Depression entered the work force by serving in the military or getting jobs in war-related production. In addition to providing the ships, airplanes, guns, cannons, tanks, and munitions for US soldiers, the US became the production center for all the Allied powers. Though the African American share in the war economy was small, as a result of the increased capital investment in industries (Congress put in place a spending bill of $300 billion) there were jobs available for African Americans in automobile, shipbuilding, aircraft, tobacco, and textile industries. This enabled another large-scale migration for many African Americans. In the 1940s, two million African Americans left the South – often for jobs in California and Michigan and another one million moved within the South but to cities (Robinson 1997: 127). While many of the jobs were in manufacturing (a 135 percent increase between 1940 and 1946), this did not always mean good jobs (ibid.: 127). While Black workers saw their numbers within industrial trade unions grow during the flurry of Congress of Industrial Organizations (CIO) organizing during the war (growing from 150,000 unionized African American workers in 1935 to 1.25 million in 1945), about 80 percent of the Black working class was outside of unions (Kelley 1994: 164). Furthermore, "the upgrading of unionized black workers did not happen without a struggle; throughout the war white workers waged 'hate strikes' to protest the promotion of blacks, and black workers frequently retaliated with their own wildcat strikes to resist racism" (ibid.: 164).

For many African Americans, this era was one of optimism about potential for a "Double Victory": fascism abroad and racism at home. But while double victory and economic empowerment heartened some, it proceeded unevenly. While there were great economic gains in this era, regional and class divisions that had existed all along – between free Black people and the enslaved, for example – were intensified and increased.

As cities burgeoned with working people, often living in close quarters or doubling up as a result of housing shortages, the chasm between middle-class and skilled working class blacks, on the one hand, and the unemployed and working poor on other, began to widen. Intraracial class divisions were exacerbated by cultural conflicts between established urban residents and the newly arrived rural folk.

(Kelley 1994: 164–5)

Nevertheless, these shifts in labor, capital, and geography also provided the opportunity for many Black workers to continue with what would come to be called civil rights organizing, in addition to struggling on the job; from 1942 to 1946 the NAACP membership in Detroit increased from 100 to 1,991 (Robinson 1997: 127). However, as with earlier eras, a backlash came as well.

As the US came out the war, the increased Union organizing (specially from the leftist CIO) was one of the prime "concerns of large employers and political conservatives" (p. 135). Particularly threatening was the connection (for example, in a place such as Detroit) between organized labor and civil rights movements. Additionally the optimism of the double victory campaign was proving increasingly unstable: "Violent reception accorded returning Black veterans provided evidence that the war's challenge to the racial social order had inspired the fear of a loss of status among white workers" (p. 131). Likewise, the experience of war, the bombings of Dresden, Hiroshima, and Nagasaki exacerbated misgivings about the moral efficacy upon which the war was propagated and the contradictions arising from US racism. Indeed, all of these national and international tensions in the postwar period provided the context for the civil rights era: "The racewar of the postwar era proceeded not merely from determined attempts to preserve the organization of oppression of the prewar years. The Second World War had loosed resistance from the colored oppressed and a state of revulsion, loathing, and trepidation among those whites implicated by the race order" (p. 131). All of these trends and complications coalesced along with the Red Scare and in 1947 Congress passed the Taft–Hartley Act which curbed union power, forced union officials to disavow communist affiliations and purge more radical members and visionaries: "Such organizations as the UAW, the CIO, and the NAACP were turned over or returned to anti-communist 'moderate' leaders and more 'practical' reformers" (p. 131).

The NAACP agenda, starting in the 1930s, prioritized "middle-class interests, political sensibilities, and cultural values" (p. 135). This would eventually flower as the *Brown v. Board of Education* decision (1954), overturning the separate but equal doctrine of *Plessy v. Ferguson*. This case was a landmark in the project for equal rights under the law and the legal fight against segregation, but when combined with the communist purges, much of the more radical vision that was nurtured by the women organizers and the NAACP mass membership (in 1946, 450,00 members and 1,073 branches) was undermined. As a result, "the NAACP lost membership and its mass character (in the Los Angeles chapter, for example, membership fell from 14,000 in 1945 to 2,500 in 1950), but it regained its middle-class character" (p. 137). One of the most important lessons to take from the evolution of organizations within the context of the Black freedom struggles is the dialectical motion of the movements.

Accordingly, it is important to recognize that legal strategies such as *Brown v. Board* were utilized alongside and underneath broader social movement struggles – the legislation was part of the goal – but never the goal in itself. The great activist William Patterson of the Civil Rights Congress (CRC) in 1952 explained the need to think tactically about the role of legal struggles within movements arguing that "legal action alone can never go over to the offensive in the fight to preserve the people's interests" (Hill 2008: 248). For most of those affiliated with what is now called the "Civil Rights Movement," the law became a tactical place to organize, and could condition new organizing sites and strategies, rather than an end.

An important example of this came from Patterson and the CRC which would heed the advice of Ida B. Wells when she said, "we should be in a position to investigate every lynching and get the facts for ourselves. If there was no chance for a fair trial in these cases, we should have the facts to use in an appeal to public opinion" (ibid.: 119). Accordingly, the CRC would use the 1948 UN Convention on the Prevention and Punishment of the Crime of Genocide to highlight to an international audience the racism of the police–mob continuum and its practices of anti-Black state-sanctioned premature death. In their petition to the UN charging the United States with genocide, they elucidated the changing forms of racism: "Once the classic method of lynching was the rope. Now it is the policeman's bullet . . . the killing of Negroes has become police policy in the Unites States and that police policy is the most practical expressions of government policy" (Patterson 1970: 8–9). The question of course became how to change this and during the 1950s many activists went to the South – where the African American legacy of fighting the mob, police, and government were most durable.

Ella Baker, exemplified the dialectical motion of Black freedom movements throughout the twentieth century as she nurtured the growth of a number of the most important organizations. One of the most dynamic Civil Rights era organizers to come out of the NAACP, Baker "honed her skills as a rank-and-file organizer" as a field secretary and national director of branches from 1940 to 1946 (Ransby 2003: 106). For Baker, the "goal was not a single 'end' but rather an ongoing 'means,' that is, a process . . . [that] had to involve oppressed people, ordinary people, infusing new meanings into the concept of democracy and finding their own individual and collective power to determine their lives and shape the direction of their history" (ibid.: 1). The Montgomery Bus Boycott of 1955 to 1956 was not a spontaneous act of civil disobedience and Rosa Parks was not simply tired. Parks was a long-time organizer and activist – a decade before she refused to give up her seat, for example, she and another key Montgomery activist, E.D. Nixon (who worked with the Brotherhood of Sleeping Car Porters), attended a leadership workshop that Baker put on (ibid.: 142).

Following the bus boycott, Baker was vital to the development of the Southern Christian Leadership Conference (SCLC); along with her colleague Bayard Rustin she helped organize their founding meeting in 1957. While SCLC is most famous for bringing their high-profile spokesman, Martin Luther King Jr., to prominence, it was quotidian activism and organizing of everyday people that gave the Civil Rights Movement its force. Charles Payne explains:

> Finding Dr. King to take leadership of the movement was fortuitous, but the local activists had put themselves in a position to be so lucky through the lifetimes of purposeful planning and striving . . . whether in Mississippi or Montgomery, taking the high drama of the mid-fifties and early sixties out of the longer historical context implicitly overvalues those dramatic moments and undervalues the more mundane activities that helped make them possible – the network-building, the grooming of another generation of leadership, the sheer persistence

> *(Payne 1995: 417–18)*

This is a lesson that the prescient Baker understood as it was unfolding. After the student sit-in movement began in Greensboro in February of 1960, Baker took on a role mentoring and supporting the young activists. At what would become the founding meeting of the Student Nonviolent Coordinating Committee (SNCC) in Raleigh, she urged them to maintain "autonomy from established civil rights organizations . . . [and] offered the sit-in leaders a model of organizing and an approach to politics that they found consistent with their own experience and would find invaluable in the months and years to come" (Ransby 2003: 239–42). SNCC would go on to push and exacerbate many of the contradictions inherent in the US democratic form as they worked with an older generation of long-time local activists to pursue voting rights in Mississippi.

If Ella Baker acted as a link between the NAACP and SNCC, then the SNCC organizers can be thought of as a link with the Black Power movements of the late 1960s. While a useful conceptualization, such a rendering also obscures a bit of the more dynamic complications inherent in movement struggles. For example, the Revolutionary Action Movement (RAM) formed in Ohio 1962 and could be thought of as the "first black Maoist-influenced organization in history" (Kelley 2002: 72–3). RAM was inspired by the thinking of Robert Williams, a former Monroe, North Carolina NAACP president who had formed armed self-defense groups to combat the Klan in 1957 and at the time of RAM's founding was living in exile in Cuba while theorizing Black nationalism and Third World Solidarity (ibid.: 70–1). But for many, the shifts in analysis came from 1964 to 1966. Following the Mississippi Freedom Summer of 1964, where there was immense and violent racist backlash to the SNCC activists, there were the brief victories of the Civil Rights Act of 1964 followed by the Voting Rights Act of 1965. However, against the backdrop of Malcolm X's assassination, the Vietnam War, race uprisings in New York, New Jersey, Chicago, and Philadelphia in 1964, followed by Watts in 1965, the demands of the Black freedom struggles could not be contained by legislative acts alone (Robinson 1997: 150).

In the subsequent years, two of the social movements articulating these demands would emerge from Oakland and Detroit – places where in the 1940s African Americans from the South had moved. Following uprisings in 1966 in Cleveland, Milwaukee, San Francisco, Atlanta, Lansing, Wauhegan, and as Stokeley Carmichael became one of the leading figures within SNCC, "Black Power" became the vernacular to express the fact that a revolution was necessary to solve the problems of the political conjuncture.

In the summer of 1967, in Detroit, there was one of the most massive uprisings in the twentieth century US – 41 people were killed, 347 injured, "damage estimates reached $500 million" (Georgakas and Surkin 1998: 13). Out of such a place came the Revolutionary Union Movements and the League of Revolutionary Black Workers. The Black industrial working class membership of these movements formed out of a number of wildcat strikes, and arose against the racism and conservatism of the United Auto Workers (UAW) union: "the UAW would risk outright scandal rather than let blacks assume any power" (ibid.: 41). For these organizers, working in one of the country's most important manufacturing centers, they saw taking control over their jobs as the initial stages in "assuming state power," and envisioned "workers having all the pie . . . to produce goods only for social needs" (ibid.: 36). From 1967 to 1974 this movement flourished and provided a glimpse of the dynamic organizing strategy that was enabled when Black workers put forward a vision of liberation rooted in taking hold of their labor and putting it to life-affirming ends.

In 1967 at Oakland City College, two students, Bobby Seale (a former RAM member) and Huey Newton, created the Black Panther Party for Self-Defense (BPP): "It was in the context of the urban rebellions that several streams of black radicalism, including RAM, converged . . . there was a fundamental difference between the Panthers' ideology of socialism and class struggle and that of black nationalist groups, even on the Left" (Kelley 2002: 93). As such, BPP brought together a type of revolutionary nationalism that was built off the Marxist insights of the Cuban and Chinese revolutions and adapted new theories in the context of their situation (ibid.: 94). Their programs were innovative: for example, their free breakfast, educational, and healthcare programs challenged the deleterious effects of capitalism, patriarchy, and racism, while at the same time building a social movement vision of the world they wanted to see.

While much has also been written dividing BPP and cultural nationalist organizations such as Ron Karenga's US Organization, it is impossible to separate their sharp ideological differences from the fact that the FBI's counterintelligence program (COINTELPRO) exacerbated these differences in an attempt to undermine their movement-building strategies, even orchestrating the assassinations of UCLA students and Los Angeles BPP leaders John Huggins and Bunchy Carter. By 1969, COINTELPRO had "orchestrated the assassination of some twenty-nine Black Panthers (including Fred Hampton in Chicago) and the jailings of hundreds of others. But their repression had also forged revolutionaries of young Black men and women whose original intent, as civil rights activists and nationalists, was essentially reformist" (Robinson 1997: 152). As more of their members were faced with imprisonment and worse, BPP built upon the theories of earlier social movement formations such as the anti-lynching movement's analysis that viewed the law as white supremacist, and police repression as part of the police–mob continuum; for example, "W.E.B. Du Bois and William Patterson both defined the imprisonment of Black people as an ideological and economic problem, Du Bois referring to the 'national railroading to jails' of Black youth, and Patterson describing Black youth as political prisoners" (Hill 2008: 272–3). With this analysis, the BPP, where able to see the "accusation of criminality as fundamental to American racism" (ibid.: 69).

Criticism and future developments

> Racism is state-sanctioned and/or extra-legal production of group-differentiated vulnerability to premature death.
>
> *(Gilmore 2007: 247)*

African American identity formations and Black freedom struggles of the twenty-first century are vexed and contradictory. As Ruth Wilson Gilmore has suggested, there is one Black man in the White House, but one million imprisoned in the big house. AIDS and HIV rates for Black women are at an all-time high. African Americans and other peoples of color survive extremely high rates of diabetes and asthma – key indicators of the continued importance of environmental and food justice organizing. While much of the knowledge produced continues to suggest that the US is post-racial, the distribution of premature death remains decidedly racialized. As the most devastating military impulses of COINTELPRO moved from the shadows of government to its main public persona in the 1980s, the Keynesian capitalist welfare state was decimated with neoliberal policies. Despite this, Black freedom movements and the identities formed therein continue and will continue into the future to do what they have throughout – struggle for life and liberation against the deathly structures of racism, capitalism, and patriarchy that do not define their being, but are a condition of it. Those struggling to do this give meaning to Robin D.G. Kelley's words, "revolution is not a series of clever maneuvers and tactics but a process that can and must transform us" (Kelley 2002: xii).

References

Césaire, Aimé (1972/2000) *Discourse on Colonialism*. New York: Monthly Review Press.
Du Bois, W.E.B. (1935/1992) *Black Reconstruction in America 1860–1880*. New York: Atheneum.
Georgakas, Dan and Marvin Surkin (1998) *Detroit: I Do Mind Dying*. Cambridge: South End Press.
Gilmore, Ruth Wilson (2007) *Golden Gulag: Prisons, Surplus, Crisis, and Opposition in Globalizing California*. Berkeley: University of California Press.
Hallward, Peter (2004) "Option Zero in Haiti," *New Left Review*, 27 (May June).
Hartman, Saidiya (2007) *Lose Your Mother: A Journey Along the Atlantic Slave Route*. New York: Farrar, Straus, and Giroux.
Hill, Rebecca (2008) *Men, Mobs, and Law: Anti-Lynching and Labor Defense in U.S. Radical History*. Durham: Duke University Press.
Huggins, Nathan (1977/1990) *Black Odyssey: The African American Ordeal in Slavery*. New York: Vintage Books.
Hunter, Tera (1997) *To 'Joy My Freedom': Southern Black Women's Lives and Labors after the Civil War*. Cambridge, MA: Harvard University Press.
James, C.L.R. (1963/1989) *The Black Jacobins: Toussaint L'Ouverture and the San Domingo Revolution*. New York: Vintage Books.
Kelley, Robin D.G. (2002) *Freedom Dreams: The Black Radical Imagination*. Boston: Beacon Press.
Kelley, Robin D.G. (1994) *Race Rebels: Culture, Politics, and the Black Working Class*. New York: The Free Press.
Moten, Fred (2003) *In the Break: The Aesthetics of the Black radical Tradition*. Minneapolis: University of Minnesota Press.
Patterson, William (1970) *We Charge Genocide: The Crime of Government against the Negro People*. New York: International Publishers.
Payne, Charles (1995) *I've Got the Light of Freedom: The Organizing Tradition and the Mississippi Freedom Struggle*. Berkeley: University of California Press.
Ransby, Barbara (2003) *Ella Baker and the Black Freedom Movement: A Radical Democratic Vision*. Chapel Hill: University of North Carolina Press.
Rediker, Marcus (2007) *The Slave Ship: A Human History*. London: John Murray.
Robinson, Cedric (1997) *Black Movements in America*. New York: Routledge.

Robinson, Cedric (2000) *Black Marxism: The Making of the Black Radical Tradition*. Chapel Hill: University of North Carolina Press.

Spillers, H. (1987) "Mama's baby, papa's maybe: an American grammar book," *Diacritics*, 17: 64–81.

Trouillot, Michel-Rolph (1995) *Silencing the Past: Power and the Production of History*. Boston: Beacon Press.

Woodson, Carter Godwin (1977) *The Mis-Education of the Negro*. New York: AMS Press.

19

The politics of Islamic identities

Sundas Ali

Introduction

Excuse me, sir, but may I be of assistance? Ah, I see I have alarmed you. Do not be frightened by my beard: I am a lover of America.

(Changez)

The journey of Changez, the hero in Mohsin Hamid's novel *The Reluctant Fundamentalist* (2007), offers a powerful account of identity dilemmas faced by many young Muslims today. With a qualification from Princeton University under his belt, Changez is the most prominent new employee at a New York firm. Yet the events of September 11, 2001 make him question all the allegiances which he had hitherto held onto so strongly: to America, the beacon of his educational and professional success, and to Pakistan, the country of his birth and upbringing as well as his religion and culture. Caught in a web he struggles to reconcile the competing forces of his identity; the entanglement of being a Muslim, Pakistani, and American begins to feel burdensome. Then one day during a business lunch, an interesting class of warrior is described to him. He learns that the janissaries of the Ottoman Empire were captured Christian boys trained to be soldiers in a Muslim army, at that time the greatest army in the world. Ferocious and utterly loyal, they fought to eradicate their own civilisations, so they had nothing else to turn to. It is at this moment, when at the crossroads of his identity, Changez realises himself to have become a 'modern-day janissary', in his words, 'a servant of the American empire at a time when it [is] invading a country with a kinship to mine' (p. 173).

It is a story, on the one hand, of a graduate like any other, seeking recognition and stability in an uncertain world. On the other hand, it is the memoir of a young Muslim who in the twenty-first century feels perplexed in trying to confront the baggage of multiple identity labels. This quietly told and cleverly constructed fable of infatuation and disenchantment with the United States, set on the treacherous fault lines of current East–West relations, is a refreshing narration into the topic of identity for many Muslims worldwide, particularly in the West. Are they Muslim first or British, American, or French? Where does their loyalty lie? Why does there even have to be a contradiction?

The purpose of this chapter is to review the politics of Islamic identities in Western Europe, North America, Australia, the Middle East, and Asia. It first provides a brief overview of the historical developments that have taken place with respect to Muslims, and how their changed situation implicates their current position. Second, it examines the claim of a growing transnational Islamic identity by reviewing the evidence on religiosity for Muslim identities, along with a discussion of multiple forms of identification. An inquiry is also made into how religious identities are formed, factoring in the complex social phenomena at play. Third, it studies ways in which Islam can intertwine with identity, making a distinction between 'Islamic' and 'Islamist' identities and the consequences this has for political mobilisation or violence. Potential reasons for Islamist violence are also considered. Finally, it investigates whether the narrative surrounding Islamic identities trespasses limits of proportionality and reasonability.

Historical and intellectual development

The golden age: once upon a time

> To be a Muslim in a world like that of the Arab traveller Ibn Battuta, who spent years traversing a powerful and extensive Islamic world that covered the Middle East, Spain, parts of Africa, and large parts of Asia, while Europe was only beginning to emerge from its Dark Ages was very different from being a Muslim in the mid-20th century when a few European countries had gained political and economic control over most of the areas where Muslims lived.
>
> (Abu-Lughod 2004: 6)

The above passage tells an important story. It touches upon the memory of outstanding achievements during Islam's first six or so centuries, when Islam's culture was the most advanced and it inspired its followers to build civilisations that were envied and admired by their rivals in the Middle Ages. Muslims sponsored the most advanced scientific and technical research, deployed victorious armies and enjoyed the best health, lived the longest, and had the highest rates of literacy. These fruits of success were evident from the beginning: in AD 622 Prophet Muhammad sought exile in Medina to escape oppression from Mecca, but returned eight years later as its ruler. As early as the year 715, Muslim conquerors had mobilised an empire that extended from Spain in the West to India in the East. To be a Muslim brought with it the honour of belonging to a winning civilisation.

However, with a turn of events the power and influence of Muslims gradually began to diminish and not very long ago the fall of the Ottoman Empire in 1924 brought their united rule to an end. This decline spurred into a series of further troubling events for Muslims: the ongoing struggle of the Palestinians in the Israeli–Palestinian conflict (1948–present) and the defeat of Muslims in the Six-Day Arab–Israeli War (1967). The reasons which brought about the decline of the Muslim world, economically and politically, are beyond the scope and purpose of this chapter and will not be addressed here. However, it is important to note that the changed situation of Muslims, especially brought about by colonisation and foreign dominance, is bound to have had some bearing on the conscience and identity of Muslims in modern times (Diner 2009).

From its golden age to where it stands now, arguably in its dark ages, the trauma of Islam in modern times results from this sharp and unmistakable contrast between medieval successes and more recent tribulations. Some seventy-five years ago, Arslan in his book *Our Decline and Its Causes* (1944) took up this question: 'Why have muslims fallen behind, and why have others forged ahead?' His inquisition still holds today. If anything, this issue has amplified over time. A glance at majority Muslim countries shows us that many of them have not managed to catch up with the rate of developments taking place in Western and even non-Western countries, notably Far East Asia. As the Imam of a Mosque in Jerusalem put it not long ago, 'Before, we were masters of the world and now we're not even masters of our own mosques.' Their past achievements still echo in their social, cultural, and physical landscapes in the contemporary Muslim world. However, in current times the Islamic spirit finds expression not so much in rebuilding the past grandeur of these civilisations through the economic and technological advancement of Muslim societies, but through movements of resistance against Western hegemony and of Islamic reassertion (Hassan 2008).

The trigger was pulled on 9/11 when two hijacked planes crashed into the twin towers of the World Trade Centre. Almost immediately following the attacks, policy-makers and commentators declared a 'clash of civilisations', as hypothesised in Huntington's 1993 *Foreign Affairs* article. But what did Huntington want to say? Conflicts between civilisations, posited Huntington, will increase due to an increased interaction, and the most pronounced conflict will be between the West and Islam. A divide was constructed between the modern, progressive, enlightened, and democratic societies of the West and the backward, archaic, uncivilised, and autocratic societies of the Middle East. Researchers, policy-makers, and journalists have devoted increasing attention to relations between the Muslim world and the West. Conflicts in the greater Middle East, such as the war in Afghanistan (2001–present) and Iraq (2003–present), as well as heated controversies within Western countries, such as the 2006 debate over the publication of cartoons portraying the Prophet Muhammad in a Danish newspaper, and debates in France and elsewhere over the wearing of veils by Muslim women have ignited fierce arguments over the role of Islam in Western societies, multiculturalism, and the assimilation of Muslim minorities.

Despite being the fastest-growing religion in the world, claims Aslan (2006), Islam remains shrouded in ignorance and fear, mostly in the West. The Gallup World Religion Survey in 2009 found Americans to be more than twice as likely to express prejudice against Muslims than against Christians, Jews, or Buddhists. About a third of Americans believe that there is essentially no thing as a moderate Muslim, that Islam equals violence, fundamentalism, and terrorism. In their study of Western attitudes towards Muslims in Britain, France, Germany, Spain, and the US – where integration and assimilation of Muslim minorities, as well as broader tensions between Western and Muslim nations, have been major issues in recent years, Wike and Grim (2010) find 'threat perception' – defined as the perceptions of threat that one's political enemies pose – to be a major, and perhaps the single most important predictor of in-group attitudes towards out-groups; people who feel threatened by Muslims are more likely to associate negative characteristics with them.

They also found security threats and cultural threats to have different effects on public views. Consistently, across all five countries, perceived threats related to security were strongly and directly related to attitudes towards Muslims, while cultural threats concerning integration and the compatibility of Islam with life in the West were indirectly related. Nevertheless, concerns about cultural threats fed concerns about security, which in turn lead to negative attitudes. In other words, 'realistic' or 'existential' threats are the most significant determinant of Western public opinion regarding Muslims, as opposed to 'symbolic' threats. Consequently, in the eyes of some this fear warrants the need for protection against Islamic rogues and radicals who threaten the security and values of liberal democracy and global capitalism. At the core of such arguments, suggests Schwedler (2001), is the notion that the spread of Islam as a religion entails a growing transnational Islamic identity that can mobilise the Islamic world against a number of 'others': the West, secularism, liberal democracy and modernity in general. However, before discussing this claim of a growing transnational Islamic identity, we must review any such evidence of religiosity among Muslims.

Major claims and developments

Muslim identities in Western Europe

Academics have noted the prominence of religion as a marker of identity among young Muslims in Europe. For young Muslims, while their experiences differ from that of the first generation in a number of ways, these differences need to be understood in terms of the different phases in the process of identity formation among this generation. During the height of Islamophobia of the 1980s in Britain, characterised by events such as the 1989 'Rushdie Affair' which is identified in much of the literature as a key moment in the development of British Muslim identity-politics, young Muslims were under tremendous pressure to either reject Islam or to turn to Islam as a vehicle of socio-economic protest. Studies by Bochner (1982) and Hutnik (1985) indicated the importance of religion to the identity of young Pakistani and Bangladeshi Muslims in which Muslim identity was listed by 80 per cent of them as the strongest and most assertive identity item. While the climate changed in Britain during the 1990s, nonetheless, young Muslims were increasingly questioning the nature of Islam, in part as a reaction to inter-generational conflicts and in part as a consequence of heightened intra-Muslim youth interaction in educational institutions, youth forums, and cyber space. The 1994 Fourth National Survey of Ethnic Minorities in Britain confirmed earlier findings as 83 per cent of Pakistani Muslims mentioned religion to be an important self-defining attribute.

The 2001 Citizenship Survey in Britain asked participants to list the top ten things that would say something important about themselves. Muslims chose religion to be a more important marker of identity than ethnicity. The 2006 Pew Global Attitudes Poll found 72 per cent of Muslims in Britain to believe that Muslims have a very strong (28 per cent) or fairly strong (44 per cent) sense of Islamic identity and 77 per cent felt this sense of identity was increasing. Eighty-six per cent of Muslims felt this was a positive development. The 2007 Citizenship Survey asked some highly relevant questions, one was: What is the most important aspect of your identity? With family being first pick by Muslims, religion was the second most important aspect of their identity, chosen by over 31 per cent. Family for non-Muslims was also the most important aspect of their identity, but religion ranked lower in their list (chosen by 12.8 per cent of Jews, 11.1 per cent Sikhs, 8.5 per cent Buddhists, 5.5 per cent Christians, and 4 per cent Hindus). Furthermore, among Muslims there were age differences in attachment to religion. Younger Muslims aged 16 to 24 years were more likely than their counterparts over the age of 25 to choose religion as their most important identity (41 per cent and 28 per cent respectively). A similar age variation was observed for the general population, although the proportions were much smaller.

In their research on Muslim women studying at British universities, Tyrer and Ahmad (2006) found that Muslim women respondents rejected notions of an essential, authentic primordial ethnic identity which they should adhere to and instead stressed the dynamic, contingent, and fluctuating nature of their identities. Brubaker and Cooper (2000) capture this antithesis between positions that highlight fundamental or abiding sameness and stances that expressly reject notions of basic sameness. The former can be called 'strong' or 'hard' conceptions of identity, the latter 'weak' or 'soft' conceptions. While the Muslim women in Tyrer and Ahmad's study acknowledged their formal ethnicities, or the ethnic identity that was 'expected of them', they were also clear that parental or ancestral heritage did not determine who they were. Instead, they asserted their agency in defining their identities in their own terms and sub-sequently displaced these in favour of a notion of 'Muslim' identities, which were highly subjec-tive and felt to be more inclusive of other aspects to their identities. Almost without exception, respondents emphasised 'being Muslim' when discussing their identities in clear, coherent, and confident terms, while also highlighting the subtle racialised expectations they faced from others vis-à-vis their identities.

There is, however, mounting evidence to suggest that even if Muslims feel religion to be important to their self-identification, they do not all think it conflicts with also feeling British. In Ali's (forthcoming) analysis of Muslim British identity in the 2007 Citizenship Survey, responses to the question 'How strongly do you belong to Britain?' provide intriguing results (Table 19.1). When the two positive categories ('Fairly strongly' and 'Very strongly') are combined, Muslims rank higher than Christians and Jews in positive identification with British national identity, 88 per cent of Muslims are likely to belong to Britain, compared to 86 per cent of Christians and 81 per cent of Jews. Therefore, contrary to claims about Muslims being alienated from British mainstream society, they are almost as likely as Christians to feel they belong to Britain.

Clearly, then the importance of religion to the identity of Muslims is more convoluted than we may think; simply ticking the box 'Muslim' rather than 'British' does not suggest that the respondent is more religious and less nationalistic or is undergoing an 'identity crisis'. A govern-ment report, 'Attitudes, values and perceptions: Muslims and the general population in 2007–08', revealed that Muslims expressed strong feelings of belonging, both to their neighbourhoods and to Britain as a whole, and more than nine in ten Muslims agreed that they personally felt a part of British society. A Gallup Poll of the Muslim World in 2007 found that despite British Muslims' strong identification with their religion, a majority condemned terrorist attacks on civilians and did not want to live in segregated communities.

Research on Muslim identities in other Western European countries offers interesting results. Findings from Germany show that its settled immigrants from Turkey are substantially more religious than native Germans and other groups of former guest-workers. Qualitative studies suggest that within the Muslim immigrant group religion has a different meaning for the first and second generation. Supposedly, Turkish women who grew up in Germany draw a sharp line between religious and traditional norms and rules and consider the former as a source of identity and emancipation rather than of oppression. 'Neo-Muslimas', as they have been termed, tend to choose partners who follow the 'true Islam' signifying that religion has changed

Table 19.1 British identification by religion

Religion	How strongly do you belong to Britain? Row percentages				
	Very strongly	*Fairly strongly*	*Not very strongly*	*Not at all strongly*	*Base*
Christian	48	38	12	3	8,861
Buddhist	30	40	24	6	127
Hindu	47	42	9	2	743
Jewish	53	28	13	6	53
Muslim	46	42	10	2	1,756
Sikh	45	48	6	1	341
Other religion	45	35	16	4	382
No religion at all	37	42	17	5	1,662
Total %	44	39	13	4	13,925

Source: Citizenship Survey 2007

its meaning for the second-generation Muslims (Diehl et al. 2009). Klinkhammer (2003) provides a thought-provoking account of this modern construction of Islamic life taking place in Germany. Her impression is painted when she sees a Muslim couple walking through the streets of a German town:

> She was wearing a headscarf, not the traditional scarf, which does not completely cover the hair, but the long veil, which covers all but the face and goes down to the shoes. While the couple was walking hand in hand . . . they were sharing a can of coca cola. I must confess . . . I was very surprised at this sight because I associated Islamic clothes like the veil with a strict segregation of the sexes and . . . generally indicated a traditional and hierarchical relationship of the sexes. However, the fact that they were walking hand in hand seemed to me to be a public expression of a modern ethic of love, a nearness and solidarity of the sexes without ties to the traditional bonds of the family. And I associated the can of coca cola with Western consumer mentality and youth culture. The curiosity which this sight aroused in me, which I was now to see more and more often made me want to understand it better.

Here Klinkhammer highlights a theoretical point of interest about the approach usually taken towards second-generation Muslim religiosity. This above sight challenged her not only because of its anti-dogmatic message, but also because of the aspect of modernity within it. In the literature about Islam and modernity, no harmony between the two can be found. On the contrary, one finds discontinuity and disharmony. But clearly this does not always seem to be the case.

France has certainly witnessed increasing attention in the past few years over the role and rights of Muslims in French society, with heated debates surrounding the wearing of religious symbols in schools, the 'headscarf affair', and more recently the banning of the face-veil. Despite these turbulent issues, the majority of France's Muslims have retained their loyalty to the state and the country of their citizenship, with a minority giving priority to certain religious interpretations (Leveau and Hunter 2002). Taking place are efforts to develop new interpretations of Islam and new syntheses of Islamic and French values that would enable the new generation to live as French and Muslim. And although the second and subsequent generation of French Muslims have maintained relations with their parents' homelands, they are not, however, inclined to accept the cultural and political systems of the authorities of their countries of origin. Instead, they have been attempting to participate more actively in public debates. The *Forum citoyens des cultures musulmanes* launched by young Muslims is in many ways exemplary. Members come from a broad spectrum, including religious and secular backgrounds, but gather around shared French and Muslim identities. The 2007 Gallup Poll of the Muslim World showed that an overwhelming majority of Muslims in Germany and France said they were loyal to their country and saw no contradiction between being German or French and Muslim.

Research from Belgium shows that young Muslims born from immigrants of Muslim (Mediterranean) countries display a strong Belgian identity but a low insertion and concrete integration into Belgian culture (Saroglou and Mathijsen 2007). The authors, however, distinguish between these two realities. First, it is possible to declare myself a Belgian ('I belong to this country, I am a Belgian citizen, I have rights because of that') without translating this identity into an embracing of 'classically or native Belgian' elements of social life ('I'm a Belgian citizen, but of a different culture'). Second, it is likely that acculturation (concrete attitudes and activities that manifest an insertion into the 'Belgian way of life' measured by elements such as: language spoken, friendships, hobbies, customs, values and willingness to transmit the Belgian culture to the next generation) is less easy to access and is achieved later in the time process for Muslim immigrants than the mere claiming of a Belgian identity. Because of a certain socio-economic marginalisation of their community and because of a certain cultural and religious distance – be it real or perceived – between 'Oriental' Islam and 'Western' Christianity, young Muslims of Mediterranean origin may have more difficulty than other (in fact mostly Christian) immigrants in integrating into the Belgian way of life. Finally, it is not to be excluded that young Muslim immigrants of Arab and Turkish origin, compared with other young immigrants, accentuate their claim to be Belgians by reserving at the same time their right to live the reality of 'being Belgian in their own way'.

The European Social Survey in 2008 asked its respondents the question 'How religious are you?' on a ten-point scale with 0 being 'not at all religious' and 10 being 'very religious'. Findings in Table 19.2 make us rethink the common conception that all Muslims are religious, and the number of those that are religious is not significantly large. Across all the fifteen countries, the number of Muslims reporting to be 'very religious' on average is very modest (19 per cent). Looking closer at the countries, we observe that countries which have had a long-standing population of Muslims such as Bulgaria, Israel, and Russia have fewer Muslims choosing to be religious. Perhaps immersion and multiculturalism is thriving better in their communities, and their identity is not 'called into question'. When their culture and religion is more accustomed with that of the mainstream, they do not feel threatened or defensive, making them less likely to assert these agencies. But in countries where Muslims are recent arrivals going back only a few decades, discrimination against them has been prominent, accentuating the need for them to resort to their religious identity, mostly by the second- and third-generation Muslims. The results confirm this by showing Greece, Belgium, UK, Spain, and Germany as having the highest number of religious Muslims, where the very characteristic under scrutiny – their religion – can become a pertinent aspect of the threatened minority's self-identification or form a collective group identity.

Table 19.2 Muslim religiosity by country

Country	Not at all religious	1–3	4–6	7–9	Very religious	Base
	How religious are you? Row percentages					
Belgium	0	1.6	24.5	42.6	31.1	61
Bulgaria	2.3	17.8	41.3	28.6	9.8	346
Switzerland	0	22.6	32.2	30.6	14.5	62
Germany	2.2	13.3	26.7	35.5	22.2	45
Denmark	0	21.1	31.6	42.1	5.3	19
Spain	0	1.9	15.3	55.8	26.9	52
France	0	14.5	38.2	34.6	12.7	55
UK	1.7	5.1	30.6	35.6	27.1	59
Greece	3	9.1	21.2	21.2	45.5	33
Israel	8.7	8	36.8	33.8	12.6	310
Netherlands	0	2.3	27.3	54.6	15.9	44
Norway	5.6	11.2	66.7	5.6	11.1	18
Russia	1.6	7	25.1	46.1	20.3	128
Sweden	0	12	48	28	12	25
Turkey	0.9	2.5	32	46.2	18.4	2,289
Total %	1.7	10	33.2	36.1	19	3,546

Source: European Social Survey 2008

* Row percentages for levels 1–9 are presented in three aggregated groups: 1–3, 4–6, and 7–9.

Furthermore the size of the Muslim population in each country has a bearing on the level of religiosity reported. Countries with the larger Muslim groups, most notably Bulgaria, Israel, and Russia report low religiosity. Perhaps belonging to communities of a large size, with some visibility and characteristics, makes them more insulated to discrimination from the host community. On the other end, countries with smaller Muslim populations report greater religiosity. This is most likely accentuated by a greater pressure to conform, leading them to dampen or reject mainstream national identification and take up the identity they feel most at threat. Therefore a pattern is observed between the history and size of the Muslim group in its host community and their expression of religiosity.

Muslim identities in North America and Australia

Academics working on Muslim American identities argue that an underlying goal of such work is 'to unsettle the perception that there is only one Muslim identity and that it is essentially and always a religious one' (Leonard 2005: 473). Leonard identifies African Americans, Arab Americans, and South Asian Americans as three major Muslim groups in the US, with a strong emphasis that there is no single 'diasporic orientation' (ibid.: 474). Such diversity, combined with a frequent assumption by non-Muslims that for Muslims their religious identity is the most salient, encourages young Muslims to examine their religious identity in relation to other aspects of their being. Leonard concludes: '"Muslim American" might be thought of as an emerging pan-ethnic label among young Muslims' (ibid.: 476).

Studying young Arab Muslims in San Francisco, Naber (2005) provides a good example of such 'pan-ethnic' Islamic identity. The 'racialisation' of Islam in the US, she finds, has contributed to the emergence and adoption of the 'Muslim first' collective identity. Such identity can be strategically deployed by young Muslims to distance themselves from the undesirable 'Arab', 'Arab Muslim', or 'Middle Eastern' identity that is often associated with terrorism. At the same time, the 'Muslim first, Arab second' identity, which intimately intersects with race and gender, is also seen as empowering by young Muslim women in particular to negotiate with their families their choice of a partner across racial lines (ibid.: 479). Also an increase in the number of young Muslim women who choose to wear Hijab reveals new noticeable aspects of Muslim identity in the US, which is becoming salient.

Schmidt (2004: 33) offers an insightful account of a young Muslim woman attempting to reconcile her Islamic and American identities:

> After the 11 September 2001 terrorist attack, I attended a lecture . . . 'Islam – the source of universal peace'. What stands clearest to me – is the imagery of the woman sitting in front of me. Not because she was dressed 'traditionally' wearing the hijab, thereby testifying that she was a practicing Muslim woman. Rather, I remember her because her hijab took the form of the American flag, the Stars and Stripes, emphasized by the shining blue garment that she wore under it. This woman sent the signal of being Muslim and American at the same time. Perhaps it could be argued that her statement of identification was a defensive act, fighting the processes of exclusion that increased in the wake of the terrorist attacks. But it could also be argued that her choice was the result of a conscious evaluation of identity, a token of an Islamic identity integrated and woven into the fabric of American life and public space.

For Schmidt, this woman's simultaneous radiation of a religious and national identity was a striking combination of symbols linked to her appearance; 'a linkage that seemed difficult to separate'. The symbols were easily recognisable and their message was easy to interpret. Her attire skilfully united what would otherwise be 'imagined cultural contradictions'. If, however, her hijab depicting the Stars and Stripes was removed, the integrity of her identity would disintegrate.

Identity research in Australia indicates that young Muslims, more so than in the 1980s, are proudly asserting their Islamic identity through religious practices, partly as a consequence of participating in Islamic youth groups, and partly from the enthusiasm with which they have decided to stake their claim to full and uncompromised acceptance in multicultural Australia. Young Muslims, who are also publicly visible in their identification with Islam, said this in Marshallsay's (2007) study:

> Islamic identity is uppermost for me followed by Australian identity.
>
> For me religious identity comes first, then my ethnic/cultural identity, followed by Australian identity.
>
> I identify myself as an Australian citizen, although religion is also an important aspect of my identity.

Marshallsay also brings out a group of Muslims who are often missing from the discussion of Islamic identity, and these are the ones for whom religion is only one layer of their multiple identities. While not denying their Islamic heritage, they are still in the process of searching for the 'essence of religion'. One young woman feels that she has no right to call herself a Muslim as she does not practise the requirements of the faith except for attendance at the mosque on the occasion of the two Eid festivals. However, she does not reject Islam as she says:

> 'I'm secular in my outlook, and for me, my religious identification is more in terms of being a Hari Raya Muslim. I go to the mosque with my mum for these congregational prayers. At the moment, I'm still searching for what it means to be a Muslim. But I also do all the other things that young Australians do like partying etc'.

For this young woman, the cultural aspects of the religion are aspects that she follows as part of family traditions. In other aspects, she sees herself as no different from her peers from non-Muslim backgrounds. Some of the secular-oriented young men were more ardent in not having religion dictate their sense of identity. One young man believes in being a 'citizen of the world':

> I don't care for all this labelling, whether in religious or any other way, ethnic or cultural. We are all human beings.

Another two young men place greater priority on their ethnic identity:

> Religion is not a priority for me. Definitely my national/ethnic identity first. Religion is not that important for me. Being an Australian means more to me.

Thus, for some young Muslims Islam transcends other aspects of identity, whereas for others it is possible to identify with the cultural heritage of one's parents, as well as with the context in which one lives. On the whole, however, for young Muslims in Australia, Australian identity is important and they see this in conjunction with their own religious and ethnic or cultural identity.

Sundas Ali

Muslim identities in the Middle East and Asia

Some scholars view the Middle East as having been entrenched in powerful 'old and deep-rooted identities' until recently, when the West brought new ideologies that caused the region's peoples to conceptualise themselves differently (Lewis 1998). For Lewis, the identity of individuals in the Middle East is not formed by nationality, citizenship, or descent, but instead by religion. It is the membership of a religious community which forms the foundation of their identity. As we shall see, the 'determinants' of identity are considerably more complex than Lewis suggests.

For Abu-Lughod (2004) contemporary US media images, fuelled by the self-presentations of some vocal groups in the Middle East, encourage us to think of people in the Middle East primarily in terms of their identities as Muslims. But this she thinks is misleading, as not only is the Middle East composed of people following the three major world religions that originated there, but people in the region, like people everywhere, define themselves in multiple ways, often depending on the context. For people living in the predominantly Muslim Middle East, just as in the multicultural but predominantly Christian US, one's religious identity is only one aspect of who one is; it does not define whether or not you do actually worship, or do so regularly or fervently. Although many things go into forming any individual's personal identity, in the Middle East it is helpful to think about the intersections of five major factors: (1) religion, (2) nationalism, (3) ethnicity, (4) mode of livelihood, and (5) gender and family.

Of course, however, this plurality in identity is not to deny the importance of religion for many Muslims across Muslim majority countries. In fact, large percentages of Muslims say that they think of themselves first as a Muslim, rather than as a citizen of their particular country. A 17-Nation Pew Global Attitudes Survey (2005) found that large majorities in Pakistan (79 per cent), Morocco (70 per cent) and Jordan (63 per cent) say they self-identify first as Muslims, rather than as Pakistanis, Moroccans, or Jordanians. In Turkey, even with its more secular traditions, 43 per cent of Muslims identify primarily with their religion rather than their nationality. Indonesians are closely split with 39 per cent self-identifying as Muslims first, 35 per cent as Indonesians and 26 per cent saying both equally. In Lebanon, however, just 30 per cent of Muslims say they view themselves primarily in terms of their faith, rather than as Lebanese. A British Council report, 'Pakistan: the next generation' (2009), also found that about three-quarters of the Pakistani youth define themselves as being Muslims first and then Pakistani. The report also helpfully identified factors behind this religiosity. It found the despair among the young generation to be rooted in the condition of their lives. Only a fifth of those interviewed had permanent full-time jobs, half said they did not have sufficient skills to enter the workplace, and one in four could not read or write. While most do not trust their government, they attach their loyalty to religion.

A recent study shows that Turkish youth understand identity as a social construct. In the context of Turkey, explains Selcuk Sirin in his interview, 'Turkish youth have multiple identities', political parties or political groups only describe their own identity in opposition to others, making it very difficult to find people who have multiple identities. However, his research showed that young people in Turkey are not buying into this split idea of 'left vs. right' or 'Islamists vs. Secularists', instead they have multiple identities. They combine patterns of political identity such as religious identification, the degree to which one feels part of the Turkish nation and the feeling of belonging to what we call the 'secular movement' or 'Ataturkism'. In all three areas, he measured the participants' degree of identification, not by asking them 'either-or' questions, such as, 'Do you have a Muslim identity or are you a Kemalist?', because that is the kind of question that has created the current situation in Turkey: 'Are you this or that?' In

334

reality, people say, 'I like Ataturk and I also feel like a Muslim'. Young people in particular do not see identity as an 'either-or' question.

A 'new Islam'

Faced with dilemmas of identity, young Muslims have been found to respond in different ways. Some turn away from Islam as an unwanted and irrelevant vestige of the past that emphasises their 'otherness'. This leads them to embrace secularism, eliminate Islam from their lives, and integrate and even 'assimilate' culturally to become 'German, Dutch, French, or British'. Despite these efforts they still face racial and ethnic obstacles, and nor can they escape their 'Muslim background' because for many Westerners, when it comes to Islam, ethnicity and religion reinforce each other. Many Muslims resort to reaffirming their Muslimness, but practising Islam as a minority religion confronts them with the question of the relevance of traditional Islam, which their parents practice, to the new social setting. Given this, some choose to construct their own modern version of Islam and in doing so go as far as stripping away varying cultural traditions that first-generation migrants have held to be Islamic. This approach can often be misguided and does not always work well with the older Muslims. Kureishi in his short story, *My Son the Fanatic* (1994), depicts this process from the perspective of a father whose son has 'returned' to Islam. Exploring the nature of the intergenerational gap in the Muslim community, Lewis (2007) shows how normal tensions are exaggerated as children are educated in a language and culture different from that of their parents. He thinks patriarchal 'clan politics' and a breakdown in communication between young Muslims and traditional Muslim leaders dispossess Islamic youth, leading a small but significant minority to turn to radical groups for somewhere to belong and something to believe in.

This identity search can lead some young Muslims to join radical organisations, such as Hizb ut-Tahrir and Al-Muhajiroun in Britain, whose membership does not necessarily make one a 'better' Muslim, and can do more harm than good not just for community cohesion, but also for Muslim intergenerational dialogue. Protesting against the immorality and imperialism of the West, members of Hizb ut-Tahrir often frame themselves as 'fish living out of water' and advocate the restoration of the Islamic Caliphate, a return to, in their view, the 'true Islam'. Ed Husain, an ex-radical, capitulates his personal journey in his book *The Islamist* (2007). From a theatre-loving schoolboy to an Islamic fundamentalist, his story begins in primary school in the 1980s, where he plays with 'Jane, Lisa, Andrew, Mark, Alia, Zak' and learns about Islam from his family and a spiritual guide he called 'Grandpa'. His father, a devout Muslim opposed to Islamist views, ignores the advice of Ed's teachers not to send his son to Stepney Green, an all-boy, all-Muslim secondary school, a decision he later regrets. Soon, Ed identifies himself not as British or Asian, only 'Muslim'. Ed describes his journey towards fanaticism as gradual, first coming across Islamism in the school textbook *Islam: Beliefs and Teachings* (2006) by Ghulam Sarwar, which says: 'Religion and politics are one and the same in Islam'. Enticed by its teachings and encouraged by a close friend, Brother Falik, Ed becomes drawn towards Islamism and the formation of the caliphate, a transnational Islamic state with a central foreign policy of jihad. Ed turns to Hizb ut-Tahrir where successful and articulate professionals reinforce his nascent views. Defying the teachings of his grandpa and parents, he spends two years involved with a Hizb cell. Friends who disappear to training camps later become key figures in al-Qaeda.

The evidence in preceding sections demonstrates that religious identity construction is indeed manifold and complex. But does the importance of religion for Muslim identities suggest that a transnational Islamic identity is uniting Muslims across vast distances in a common struggle? Surely, all religions possess a mobilising capacity in their shared norms and practices,

but is religious identity per se behind the political mobilisation of Islamic groups in very different social and political contexts?

Understanding Islam and identity

According to Schwedler (2001), for those who fear the mobilising potential of Islam, as they
watch the number of Muslims increase daily, the concern is not 'Islamic' identity but 'Islamist' identity. 'Islam' is the religion, with 'Muslims' as its followers and the adjective 'Islamic' is
suitable to describe anything that is of or related to Islam, as in 'the Islamic faith'. 'Islamism', or
political Islam, refers to a wide variety of often competing political movements that treat Islam
as the central tenet of a political project. An 'Islamist' then is a Muslim who advocates a political agenda where the application of Shariah, or Islamic law, is central. All Islamists are Muslims, though all Muslims are not Islamists. In fact, only a tiny percentage of Muslims engage in
political projects that can properly be called Islamist. Far more identify with ideologies that are
distinctly nationalist, socialist, communist, or democratic. The Middle East alone is populated
with hundreds of political groups and parties that identify themselves as social democrats, Muslim communists, liberal democrats, and Muslim and Islamist democrats, to name just a few. A
voluminous literature illustrates not only that Islam and democracy are compatible, but also that
they may be complementary (Esposito and Voll 1996; Kramer 1995; Soroush 2000).

In a major research project of more than six thousand Muslim respondents from Southeast,
South, and Central Asia and the Middle East, Hassan (2008) reveals the heartening statistics that
87 per cent of Muslims, 86 per cent of Western Christians, and 83 per cent of all humanity
support democratic ideals (ibid.: 255). Reza Aslan speaking on FORA.tv's programme *Islamic
Identity in the US* argues that Muslims around the world, particularly in the Middle East and the
larger Arab world, are by no means isolated, they see the lives of American Muslims and they
want it, they make it very clear that political participation, political freedom and democracy are
issues they believe will work in their societies. Numerous polls have shown massive majorities who believe there is no fundamental clash between ideas of Islam and democracy. It is also
important to recognise that a third of the Muslim world is already democratic; the largest Muslim country in the world, Indonesia, is a democracy; the second largest, Pakistan, is a democracy; India, the third largest, even though Muslims are a small minority in it, is a democracy;
Bangladesh, Turkey, Malaysia, and Senegal are democracies. Thus let us retire this notion that
Islam and democracy cannot work.

In the larger sense of why some extremist groups in *certain* countries are becoming successful in elections, one must look beyond the surface. Their success is truly mixed; for instance,
in Indonesia's 2009 election, the so-called Islamists were soundly defeated. And as in Pakistan's
2008 election, the Islamist parties despite the fact that they banded together to create one almost
super party did very poorly, not getting over 5 per cent of the vote. Islamist political parties in
Jordan, Kuwait and Yemen have failed to mobilise supporters for their agendas in recent years
and have performed poorly in parliament, despite their efforts to mobilise Islamic identity. Along
with this, the states' manipulation of electoral systems to limit Islamists' gains is also a reason.
In Turkey, the success of Islamists at the polls in 1995 had more to do with state manipulation
– in an effort to exclude Kurds – of the electoral system than with the spread of Islamism. The
Kurds then pooled their votes with Islamist candidates from the Welfare Party. Such instances of
leftist-Islamist alliance illustrate that the political opportunities available to political groups often
play a greater role in mobilisation than identities (Schwedler 1998–99).

However, in countries such as Egypt, Palestine, and Lebanon, some groups despite having
no avenue for political participation whatsoever for half a century have done exceedingly well

when suddenly given an opportunity to participate in the political realm and to actually run for elections. Aslan says the fact that Hamas did well in the 2006 elections in Palestine should not be surprising for us, neither should the success of the Muslim Brotherhood which has been feeding and clothing poor people for half a century in Egypt, which has built schools and hospitals and has provided educational grants for Egyptians to go abroad and study. Who thought that when they were first allowed to run for office that they were not going to do well, questions Aslan, who thought this? This is nothing to do with what we would consider extremism; it has to do with the universal law for politics: 'he who cleans the streets gets the votes, the end'.

Therefore it would be fair to stipulate that there is certainly a transnational Islamic or Muslim identity entailing the shared basic values and norms of the Islamic faith, however differently they are interpreted. But to the extent that Islam represents a single collective identity, when identity is characterised by so many complexities and diversities, is perhaps not so useful analytically (Schwedler 2001). This is not to say that Islamic identity is a meaningless category; it can mean much to those who see themselves as part of a broader Muslim community. But Islamic identity is also the product of many different historical, political and social processes. To understand particular instances of Islamic identity, one must therefore look at discrete political, social and economic contexts through which particular Islamic identities have been forged.

Main criticisms

'Deep down inside'

Some scholars are of the view that despite the emerging literature on identities, there is still a fixation on conceptualising identity in narrow terms. Maalouf (2000b), a Lebanese author living in France, feels there is very often an obsession with singling out one aspect of an individual's identity, placing it over others in importance. But for him, there is no one aspect of his identity which is more important than the others, and nor does he possess multiple identities. Instead, he ardently professes that he only has a single identity which is made up of many aspects, coming together in harmony to form a single entity. He expresses his frustration at constantly having to reassure people of his 'real identity':

> How many times, since I left Lebanon in 1976 to live in France, have people asked me, with the best intentions in the world, whether I felt 'more French' or 'more Lebanese'? And I always give the same answer: 'Both!' I saw that not in the interests of fairness or balance, but because any other answer would be a lie. What makes me myself rather than anyone else is the very fact that I am poised between two countries, two or three languages and several cultural traditions. It is precisely this that defines my identity. Would I exist more authentically if I cut off a part of myself?
>
> To those who ask the question, I patiently explain that I was born in Lebanon and lived there until I was 27; that Arabic is my mother tongue; that it was in Arabic translation that I first read Dumas and Dickens and Gulliver's Travels; and that it was in my native village, the village of my ancestors, that I experienced the pleasures of childhood and heard some of the stories that were later to inspire my novels. How could I forget all that? How could I cast it aside? On the other hand, I have lived for 22 years on the soil of France; I drink her water and wine; every day my hands touch her ancient stones; I write my books in her language; never again will she be a foreign country to me.

So am I half French and half Lebanese? Of course not. Identity can't be compartmentalised. You can't divide it up into halves or thirds or any other separate segments. I haven't got several identities: I've got just one, made up of many components combined together in a mixture that is unique to every individual. Sometimes, after I've been giving a detailed account of exactly why I lay claim to all my affiliations, someone comes and pats me on the shoulder and says 'Of course, of course – but what do you really feel, deep down inside?'

(2000b: 1–2).

Such thinking, though it is widespread, exposes a view of humanity which Maalouf thinks is dangerous. The danger is twofold. First, a failure to recognise the complexity, the multi-dimensionality, of the 'Other' makes their dehumanisation easier. Second, imposing on the 'Other' a rigid, singular (and usually inferior) identity will provoke them, in anger and defiance, to pick up arms to 'assert their identity'. This, he says, is how ordinary men are 'transformed into butchers'. It presumes that 'deep down inside' everyone there is just one affiliation that really matters, a sort of 'fundamental truth' about each individual, an 'essence' determined once and for all at birth, never to change thereafter. As if all the rest, 'a person's whole journey through time as a free agent; the beliefs he acquires in the course of that journey; his own individual tastes, sensibilities and affinities; in short his life itself', counts for nothing. And when prompted to 'assert their identity', individuals are meant to seek within themselves that same alleged fundamental allegiance, which is often religious, national, racial or ethnic, and having located it they are supposed to 'flaunt it proudly in the face of others' (ibid.: 3).

Further, Maalouf illustrates that those who claim a more heterogeneous identity are marginalised. For example, a young man born in France of Algerian parents carries within him two different loyalties or 'belongings', and he ought to be allowed to use both (as well as the many other ingredients which make up his personality). Within him, French, European, and other Western influences blend with Arab, Berber, African, Muslim and other influences. If he is encouraged to accept his identity in all its diversity and is allowed to live it fully, then it should embody a basket of enriching and fertile experiences. But it can be agonising if whenever he claims to be French, other people look on him as a traitor or disloyal, and if every time he insists his ties with Algeria and its history, culture and religion he is seen to be mistrustful, and perhaps even presented with outright hostility. Although common sense supports him being able to claim both allegiances, neither the law nor people's attitudes allow him to accept his amalgamated identity peacefully (ibid.: 3). The common exercise of carving out a person's identity into sections, thinks Maalouf, does not do justice to the true nature of identity, which is able to function in a multi-dimensional way.

A reactive identity

There is mounting literature on the impact that unfair treatment can have in constructing a person's identity. Peek's (2005) model illustrates this point, by identifying how religious identity can develop in response to a crisis. Within hours of the events and aftermath of 9/11, an unprecedented number of xenophobic incidents began to take place. Thousands of Muslims and Arabs endured discrimination, harassment, racial and religious profiling, and verbal and physical assault. Most of the Muslim students in Peek's study, despite this reaction, persevered and publicly affirmed their religious identities, with many reporting that this difficult time actually strengthened their religious identity.

Noreen, born and raised in America but of Indian origin, describes how 9/11 affected her daily life:

For me, religion was always at the front part of my life. But now that Islam is on the forefront of everything, it seems there's the need to use that as my defining characteristic, a greater need to do that, now more than ever.

(Peek 2005: 231)

Peek reminds us that much of the discourse surrounding 9/11 involved dualities such as 'good and evil' and 'us and them'. Natasha, a second-generation immigrant of Egyptian descent, talked about this duality:

It was big . . . I was like, if they're not going to accept me as an American . . . if they're going to tell me I don't deserve to be here, when I am an American, if they're going to try to make me feel that way, then, hey, I'm going to be a Muslim. No one's going to ever tell me, 'You can't be a Muslim. You're not a Muslim. Go back to some other planet where there isn't Islam'. I felt like I had to choose then. I don't think I felt like I had to choose before then. But . . . it was like, well, fine. If I have to choose, I choose to be Muslim.

(ibid.: 234)

Just as the students were aware that they had been cast as the 'Other' immediately following 9/11, they also thought there was some expectation for them to choose between their American and Muslim identities (Peek 2005).

The cycle of discrimination, failed expectations, and non-assimilation has led many Muslim youth in Europe to reject European majority culture in favour of a minority identity that serves as a response to European rejection. In Germany, a Turkish street gang has appropriated the name Barbaren, a disparaging term long used to refer to foreigners, thereby co-opting and embracing the identity of otherness thrust upon them. Similarly, young French Muslim women have taken to wearing the hijab, or headscarf, in public places. Thus the impetus is less religiosity per se than the need for a mechanism to define the community in relation to increasingly hostile attacks and the pressure to abandon their own cultural practices and integrate into French society. Arguably, identity does not become an issue until it is threatened – for example, French speakers in an English-speaking society (Canada perhaps). Calming identity conflicts, writes Maalouf (2000a), 'will mean making people, especially minorities, feel included'.

Scholars in Britain suggest that there has been something of a shift from racism directed at British African Caribbean youth to racism directed at Asian youth since the 1990s and a rapid growth in anti-Muslim prejudice in Britain. This was noted in the Runnymede Trust's report, 'Islamophobia: a challenge for us all' (1997). The Parekh Report, 'The future of multi-ethnic Britain' (2000), commented that Muslims, because of their cultural difference, have become the principal target of racist resentment in recent times. Where a group suffers rejection by the majority, 'reactive ethnicity' or 'oppositional culture' may be the result (Fordham and Ogbu 1986) leading the group to dampen or reject mainstream national identification. Ali (forthcoming) found that while socio-economic outcomes are important determinants for Muslims' attachment to Britain, perceptions of discrimination are significantly more important contributors; the unfair nature of discrimination is more problematic than socio-economic difficulties alone. While the so-called 'melting pot' may occur where majority and minority engage in mutual acculturation, the opposite may emerge where there is mutual rejection, leading to a distinctive culture (Heath et al. 2010).

The 2008 European Social Survey asked its respondents: 'Would you describe yourself as being a member of a group that is discriminated against in this country?' With the average level of discrimination felt by Muslims across all countries being 12.2 per cent, we observe different levels for both large and small Muslim groups. Countries with large Muslim populations are found to have lower percentages of Muslims perceiving discrimination: 13.2 in Israel and 13.8 in Bulgaria. But a greater number of Muslims in countries with smaller Muslim populations seem to feel discriminated, as seen by the high levels in Denmark, the Netherlands, France, Germany and UK, all well above the average. Figure 19.1 shows this negative correlation between the size of the Muslim group and their perceptions of discrimination.

The survey also found that a significant number of Muslims in all these countries report 'Religion' to be cause of their discrimination. When asked the question 'On what grounds is your group discriminated against?', the percentage of those that chose 'Religion' to be the cause was 36.8 in Denmark, 33.9 in the UK, 29.5 in the Netherlands, 28 in Sweden, and 21.2 in Spain. As we noted in Table 19.2 Muslims in these countries also report high religioisity, supporting our hypothesis that when religion becomes the basis of apprehensive treatment, many Muslims become more, rather than less, religious as a result. Saroglou and Mathijsen (2007) also found that the high scores of religion among immigrants in Belgium reflected a deepening of association with Islam as a way of protesting against marginalisation or against Western values. These 'reactive' forms of identity formation may compensate for a lack of social approval and are most likely to emerge in hostile reception contexts marked by discrimination and a lack of upward mobility, which create the need for alternative sources of social status and identity. Since religion is an important foundation of ethnicity for many immigrant groups, this should also apply to religious acculturation processes. Thus a strong link can be made between religious discrimination and religious identity.

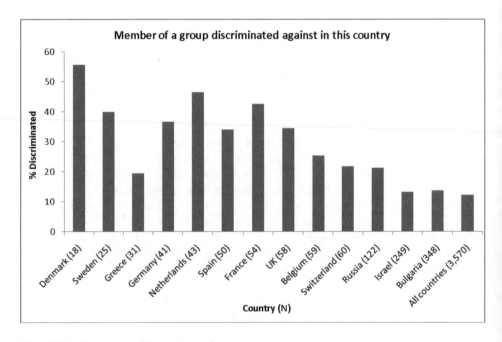

Figure 19.1 Perceptions of discrimination by country

Source: European Social Survey 2008

Islamists in search of humanity

We love death the way you love life.
(Shehzad Tanweer)

These words uttered by Tanweer, one of the 7/7 London suicide bombers, have proved more incomprehensible in the West than perhaps any other statement made by contemporary militants. Indeed, they are so alien to the Western outlook that they have been cited as proof that the attackers were nihilists at best, if not cultish death-worshippers. However, Devji (2009) invites us to think more carefully about them. He thinks remarkably little public consideration has been given to the often-extended jihadist arguments. The 'War on Terror' has been conducted with a resolute determination to refuse a hearing to the 'enemy', whose motives Western governments have more or less made up for themselves. But perhaps the enemy has something to say. Our fixation on the sanctity of human life, Devji reminds us, is relatively new, and represents an impoverishment of our cultural roots. By placing so much emphasis on love of life, he suggests, today's humanists have divorced their conception of humanity even further from Christianity than Islam. He uses the thinking of Mahatma Gandhi to make clear just how limited the Western conception of life has become.

The key to understanding the world-view of contemporary Islamist militants, in Devji's view, is the global reach of Islam as 'the natural religion of humanity'. While their optimal desire might be to convert the Western world to Islam, they would be happy if it returned to the principles of Christianity. Devji points out the centrality of charges of hypocrisy in Islamist critiques of Western – above all US-policy: 'It is no exaggeration to say that hypocrisy represents an obsession for militant rhetoric' (2009: 83). Men such as the London bombers do not fit the old stereotype of 'professional terrorists', they are 'self-conscious amateurs', and there is very little in the way of a 'conversion narrative' or a moment of decision to be found in their lives. Devji argues that new forms of militancy, such as the actions of al-Qaeda, are informed by the same desire for agency and equality that animates other humanitarian interventions, such as environmentalism and pacifism. To the militant, victimised Muslims are more than just symbols of ethnic and religious persecution – they represent humanity's centuries-long struggle for legitimacy and agency. Acts of terror, therefore, are fuelled by the militant's desire to become a historical actor on the global stage. Though they have yet to build concrete political institutions, militant movements have formed a kind of global society, and as Devji makes clear, this society pursues the same humanitarian objectives that drive more benevolent groups.

On a domestic level, factors such as the role of poverty and lack of democracy in Arab and Muslim nations can help to explain tendencies towards violence. Regional considerations such as the Palestinian–Israeli conflict, Hezbollah in Lebanon, Jemaah Islamiyah (JI) in Southeast Asia, and Hizb ut-Tahrir in Central Asia all work to accentuate the cause of militant Islamists. And on a global scale, external actors such as the US and Western Europe have inadvertently helped transnational Islamists through their invasions of Afghanistan and Iraq (Alaolmolki 2009). For Ramakrishna (2009), the rationale behind JI's terrorist acts in Indonesia is driven by their amplified existential anxiety over their identity. This condition develops when a person's identity and culture interacts with geopolitical factors, local historical forces, and ideology to create the fear of group extinction. In the case of JI members, Darul Islamism is particularly central as this ideology not only provides a shared belief system and cohesion amongst its adherents, but also creates a sense of historic victimisation which in turn develops into an 'us-versus-them' vision of the world.

In his research, Hassan (2008) was struck, especially in the Middle East, by the all-pervasive sense of humiliation that arose from the inability of the Arab countries to equal the military and economic superiority of Israel, and this sense of humiliation he thinks is a major underlying cause of Islamic militancy and terrorism. These feelings of humiliation are further reinforced by the economic power and absolute technological superiority of the West vis-à-vis Muslim countries and the privileged treatment accorded to Israel by the US in its foreign policy. The actions of Jihadis, notes Hassan, are not motivated simply by a 'blind bloody-mindedness' or by an 'overwhelming desire to book a comfortable place in the hereafter'. For them, their jihad is religion in practice and is fundamentally a political action through which they are pursuing the establishment of a just society. Jihad, in the view of Hassan, is agreeable to resolution through negotiation with all parties being accepted and treated as equal citizens of a globalising world.

But for this to happen, first 'jihad' needs to be re-understood. Literally, jihad is given the fearful phrase 'holy war' but most Islamic scholars agree that jihad is nothing but struggle. In one sense, this struggle is intended to make the self good as a foremost virtue. In another sense, it is a struggle waged against injustice and oppression, and other bad practices in the environment. Of these two, Muslim scholars favour the first – it is the greater jihad, a life-long activity among Muslims. Declaring war on others in defence of Islam is accepted, but on certain conditions: only when the Ummah, or the global Muslim community, is on the verge of life and death, and when livelihood and survival is at stake. The Quran even warns the faithful about exceeding the limits, or else he is likewise guilty and risks penalty during the Day of Judgement. The Quran reads, 'Fight in the cause of God those who fight you, but do not transgress limits, for God does not love transgressors' (Chapter 2, Verse 190).

Ali (2003) rejects the notion that 9/11 was a historical event of singular significance, arguing instead that it was a 'mere pinprick in the catalogue of atrocities humans have perpetrated against each other' – including atrocities perpetrated by the US – and that it would have eventually been targeted. The real significance of 9/11, he argues, is that nineteen Muslim hijackers felt strongly enough about the US to commit suicide in order to make the political statement of striking a blow at it, and that the US must address the question of why. Sardar (2008) reminds us of the anti-colonial slogan British socialists used in his youth: 'If you drop bombs on the heads of natives in their cities, the natives will drop bombs on yours.' But whatever our creed, argues Gambetta (2006: 299), 'most of us still want to succeed by living not by dying', and to this effect signs of hope are existent even in the Islamic world. For instance, the Hezbollah, the inventor of modern suicide missions, has become more rooted in political life as an ordinary party and discouraging the role of violence-based terror.

An exaggerated narrative?

There is evidence suggesting that perhaps the narratives surrounding Muslims are overrated or blown out of proportion. It seems reasonably clear, argue Wike and Grim (2010), that headlines from the last few years have influenced how non-Muslims in the West think about Islam and its followers. Here, Ali's (2007) analysis of the way Islamists were represented in certain Western media outlets after 9/11 is useful. Investigating news and entertainment media, she shows how, at the hands of influential commentators, Islamic fundamentalism has become 'a socially constructed concept'. Through various representational practices, as described in Hall's book, *Representation: Cultural Representations and Signifying Practices* (1997), media agents have played a significant role in giving 'meaning' to the culture of radical Islamists. The frequent association of terms such as 'extremist', 'radical', 'Islamist' (and very often of 'Muslims') to Islamic fundamentalists in her sample of newspaper articles transmits a negative discourse of a 'disillusioned' people seeking 'revenge' or 'virgins in heaven'. Any attempt to put rationalisation in the heads of the 'lost youthful Muslims' was followed by a statement which discredited any such truth.

With some exceptions, Islamic fundamentalism was portrayed as an ideologist cult. Associating Islam to 'terrorism' gave it some personality which the reader could understand and relate to. Coined under new terms, this 'threat' or 'cancerous tumour' we are facing in the twenty-first century was shown to be intangible, something we cannot pin point and fight. Such depictions may lead one to question whether the Western media has lost its investigative approach. One might feel brave enough to even suggest that Islam has not only been hijacked by the terrorists but also by the mass media and policy-makers. Words such as 'freedom' and 'democracy' were used continuously to enlighten an audience of the 'plural' Western culture, highlighting the 'difference' between the West and radical Islamists. The differences in articulation across various media outlets demonstrated the fluidity in the language – signs and symbols – used to represent radical Islamists, thus reaffirming their socially constructed identity.

Some argue that Western-preferred explanations for Islamist violence are intended to curtail debate and critical thought, rather than offer true explanations and in doing so have been fixated in their denial of rationality in Islamism (Crooke 2009). The argument goes that Islamist armed resistance against the West did not emerge in a vacuum and its emergence was neither irrational nor motivated by divinely inspired whimsy, but is capable of a clear and reasoned historical explanation. Instead, at the heart of it the dispute is between two opposing views on what constitutes the 'essence of man'. Underlying the conflict are differing religious insights – but this is not a straight confrontation between Christianity and Islam. The Anglo-Saxon tradition, which America embodies, emerged from the long-running struggle between Protestantism and Catholicism. Crooke observes that since the days of Oliver Cromwell, in the mid-seventeenth century, the mainly English-speaking world has come to regard its enemies as all those who hate liberty and God, and are immoral. These originally Protestant themes can now be observed in Western dialogue with Islam.

Conclusions and future developments

There has increasingly been the view that the true sense of threat in Western countries arises from radical Islamism, which is expanding dramatically and is portrayed as a new post-Cold War 'threat'. Several events, most notably 9/11, have drawn attention to security threats posed by small groups of violent Islamic extremists. We should be wary, however, of making hasty conclusions.

We do find evidence suggesting the importance of religion to the identity of many Muslims living in non-Muslim majority countries and to some extent for those in Muslim majority countries as well. In contrast to their parents, who display strong diasporic ties to their ethnic affiliation and the country of origin, for a number of young Muslims in the West their religious identity is the most salient. They tend to play down their ethnic affiliation to a degree where religious identification takes precedence over ethnic or national ties. Some young Muslims claim that their vision of Islam is less culturally adulterated and closer to the ideal and essence of Islam. Furthermore, there isn't a monolithic form and practice of Islam among Muslims, and even if religion is important to their self-identification, identity research suggests that shared identities usually mean different things to different people. There is agreement among academic scholars that the expression of religion by young Muslims is influenced by a myriad of complex social phenomena, be it the manoeuvring of their parents' customs or traditions, the engineering of feminist agendas, or distancing themselves from adverse racial connotations.

Importantly, it was found that intolerance of cultural difference and demand for total assimilation can lead to the opposite reaction: a 'reactive ethnicity', or the adoption of Islam, partly as a form of rebellion against an inhospitable social environment. There is a point beyond which discrimination and rejection by the majority society result not in Muslims' denial of their religion, but rather in its reaffirmation. Rejected and unwanted, they turn to that which sets them apart as a form of cultural self-assertion and a basis of identity. Thus Islam can become a form of self-defence and a source of solidarity against a hostile dominant culture. While the vast majority of young Muslims in the West stress the compatibility of Islam with Western culture, there do exist some radical tendencies. However, research has continually shown that in most Muslim communities only small minorities actually hold extremist views.

The vast majority of Muslim youth want what most youth want: to fit in, even if they wish to retain religious traditions. They feel most strongly tied to the countries in which they live rather than ancestral homelands and understand themselves to be stakeholders in Western societies. Participation, cooperation, and dialogue are the operative terms in their mind. Most Muslim youth do not stand out from their non-Muslim peers. Often, discussions about whether or not Muslim youth 'fit in' and 'identify as European or American' focus on small minorities within Muslim communities. For example, the controversy in France over whether headscarves should be allowed in public centred around only an estimated 1,500 Muslim youth and adults who wear headscarves, out of an approximate population of seven million Muslims in France. Young Muslims are hence constructing both new identities and new frameworks for the practice of Islamic politics in response to the conditions of life in contemporary society.

Alongside encouraging findings on constructive identity developments among Muslims, there is also evidence to support the existence of Islamist violence. Domestic, regional, and global factors can help to explain tendencies towards violence and can work to accentuate the cause of militant Islamists. Scholars suggest that humiliation can be a major underlying cause of Islamic militancy and terrorism. The key condition that makes it possible for some to humiliate others – which leads individuals to engage in violence – is a failure to understand the true nature of identity. Identity is neither monolithic nor static; it is built up and changes throughout a person's lifetime. A failure to recognise the fluidity, multiplicity, and malleability of identity is not only misguided but also dangerous. Furthermore, our obsession with security has seriously unbalanced our sense of civic values and increased our vulnerability to terrorism so that, in effect, terror increasingly determines our public agenda.

What can we conclude about the mobilising capacity of Islamic identity across diverse historical contexts? It would be fair to posit that because Islamic identities represent multifaceted narrative fields, they hold no more innate mobilising capacity than any other identity. To speak of an Islamic identity as a threat – in the same manner as speaking of Islamic civilisation as a threat – not only suggests a level of coordination among Islamic communities that does not exist, but also neglects diverse historical contexts, the mechanisms by which collective identities function politically, and the political opportunities (including state intervention) that shape mobilisation. The aim is not to deny the existence of Islamic identity but to focus on scrutinising the processes and mechanisms that contribute to identity formation.

Finally, in ending this chapter a scene from the movie *My Name is Khan* (2010) comes to mind. It is the story of an Indian Muslim immigrant, disabled by Asperger's syndrome, in the US who sets out on a mission to meet the president to say to him, 'My name is Khan and I am not a terrorist.' Due to his special kind of autism, Rizwan Khan thinks in black and white, right or wrong, and has little appreciation of social nuances. At one point, Rizwan enters into a mosque to pray in a new and unfamiliar city, where he overhears a man fomenting dissent among fellow worshippers and calling for violence. He calls the man 'Satan' for encouraging hatred and division rather than love and unity among the Muslim community, and throws a stone at him bringing to mind the ritual stoning of the devil during Hajj, the annual pilgrimage to Mecca. In ritually confronting and opposing extremism, Rizwan establishes himself as an ideal representation of true Islamic behaviour. His quiet merit and devotion to humanity eventually wins him supporters all over the country. Similarly for Ed, in the end it was exactly this suffocating school of thought among Muslims, as identified by Rizwan – Islamism's disregard for Islam itself – which had moved him to reject fundamentalism, in his words, 'true faith had not touched my heart in a decade'.

References

Abu-Lughod, L. (2004/1995) 'Thinking about identity', *Spotlight on the Muslim Middle East Issues of Identity*. The American Forum for Global Education.
Alaolmolki, N. (2009) *Militant Islamists: Terrorists without Frontiers*. Santa Barbara, CA: Praeger Security International.
Ali, S. (2007) 'Representation of Islamic fundamentalism: the Western media', unpublished thesis (MSc International Relations), Department of Politics, University of Bristol.
Ali, S. (forthcoming) 'Muslim identity and sense of belonging towards Britain: a case of reactive ethnicity?'
Ali, T. (2003) *The Clash of Fundamentalisms: Crusades, Jihads and Modernityi*. London: Verso Books.
Aslan, R. (2006) *No God But God: The Origins, Evolution and Future of Islam*. London: Arrow Books.
Bochner, S. (1982) 'The social psychology of cross-cultural relations', in S. Bochner (ed.) *Cultures in Contact: Studies in Cross-cultural Interaction*. Oxford: Pergamon.
Brubaker, R. and Cooper, F. (2000) 'Beyond "Identity"', *Theory and Society*, 29: 1–47.
Crooke, A. (2009) *Resistance: The Essence of the Islamist Revolution*. London and New York: Pluto Press.
Devji, F. (2009) *The Terrorist in Search of Humanity: Militant Islam and Global Politics*. London: C. Hurst & Co.
Diehl, C., Koenig, M. and Ruckdeschel, K. (2009) 'Religiosity and gender equality: comparing natives and Muslim migrants in Germany', *Ethnic and Racial Studies*, 32(2): 278–301.
Diner, D. (2009) *Lost in the Sacred: Why the Muslim World Stood Still*, trans. S. Rendall. Princeton and Oxford: Princeton University Press.
Esposito, J.L. and Voll, J.O. (1996) *Islam and Democracy*. New York: Oxford University Press.
Fordham, S. and Ogbu, J.U. (1986) 'Black students' school success: coping with the burden of "acting white"', *The Urban Review*, 18(3): 176–206.
Gambetta, D. (ed.) (2006) *Making Sense of Suicide Missions*. Oxford: Oxford University Press.
Hamid, M. (2007) *The Reluctant Fundamentalist*. London: Hamish Hamilton.
Hassan, R. (2008) *Inside Muslim Minds*. Melbourne: Melbourne University Press.
Heath, A., Rothon, C. and Ali, S. (2010) 'Identity and public opinion', in A. Bloch and J. Solomos (eds) *Race and Ethnicity in the 21ˢᵗ Century*. Baskingstoke: Palgrave Macmillan.
Hutnik, N. (1985) 'Aspects of identity in multi-ethnic society', *New Community*, 12(1): 298–309.
Klinkhammer, G. (2003) 'Modern constructions of Islamic identity: the case of second generation Muslim women in Germany', *Marburg Journal of Religion*, 8(1). Online: archiv.ub.uni-marburg.de/mjr/klinkhammer.html.
Kramer, G. (1995) 'Islam and pluralism', in R. Brynen et al. (eds) *Political Liberalization and Democratization in the Arab World, Volume I: Theoretical Perspectives*. Boulder, CO: Lynne Rienner Publishers.
Leveau, R. and Hunter, S.T. (2002) 'Islam in France', in S. Hunter (ed.) *Islam, Europe's Second Religion: The New Social, Cultures, and Political Landscape*. Santa Barbara, CA: Praeger Publishers.
Leonard, K.I. (2005) 'Young American Muslims: multiple identities', *The Muslim World*, 95(4): 473–7.
Lewis, B. (1998) *The Multiple Identities of the Middle East*. New York: Schocken Books.
Lewis, P. (2007) *Young, British and Muslim*. London: Continuum.
Maalouf, A. (2000a) *In the Name of Identity: Violence and the Need to Belong*. New York: Penguin Books.
Maalouf, A. (2000b) *On Identity*. London: The Harvill Press.
Marshallsay, Z. (2007) 'Overcoming minority standpoint – articulating multiple identities among Muslim youth in transnational contexts', refereed paper presented at the Australasian Political Studies Association Conference, Monash University.
Naber, N. (2005) 'Muslim first, Arab second: a strategic politics of race and gender', *The Muslim World*, 95(4): 479–5.
Peek, L. (2005) 'Becoming Muslim: the development of a religious identity', *Sociology of Religion*, 66 (3): 215–42.

Ramakrishna, K. (2009) *Radical Pathways: Understanding Muslim Radicalization in Indonesia.* Santa Barbara, CA: Praeger Security International.

Sardar, Z. (2008) *Balti Britain: A Journey through the British Asian Experience.* London: Granta Books.

Saroglou, V. and Mathijsen, F. (2007) 'Religion, multiple identities, and acculturation: a study of Muslim immigrants in Belgium', *Archiv fur Religionpsychologie* 29.

Schmidt, G. (2004) 'Islamic identity formation among young Muslims: the case of Denmark, Sweden, and the United States', *Journal of Muslim Affairs*, 24(1): 31–45.

Schwedler, J. (1998–99) 'A paradox of democracy? Islamist participation in democratic elections', *Middle East Report*, 209: 25–9.

Schwedler, J. (2001) 'Islamic identity: myth, menace, or mobilizer?' *SAIS Review*, XXI (2) Summer–Fall 2001.

Soroush, A. (2000) *Reason, Freedom, and Democracy in Islam.* New York: Oxford University Press.

Tyrer, D. and Ahmad, F. (2006) *Muslim Women and Higher Education: Identities, Experiences and Prospects.* Liverpool: Liverpool John Moores University and European Social Fund.

Wike, R. and Grim, B.J. (2010) 'Western views toward Muslims: evidence from a 2006 cross-national survey', *International Journal of Public Opinion Research*, published by Oxford University Press on behalf of The World Association for Public Opinion Research.

20

Indigenous identities

From colonialism to post-colonialism

Anthony Moran

Introduction: historical and intellectual development of indigeneity in the contexts of colonialism and post-colonialism

'Indigenous identity' is paradoxical. On the one hand, it refers to the ancient, distinctive, localised identities and ways of life of typically small, 'traditional', pre-industrial cultural groups closely tied to (or, rather, intertwined as identities with) lands occupied since 'time immemorial'. On the other hand, it also refers to a very modern, global political movement that has emerged through recent globalising phenomena including the development of international human rights fora, frameworks and discourses. Indigenous representatives claim that indigenous cultures are 'oral cultures' and that oral traditions are still central to their identities and forms of cultural organisation and transmission. And yet, since the 1990s indigenous groups have become a major presence on the Internet, which has become a textual, electronic vehicle for indigenous resurgence, for survival and revival of language and traditions (Niezen 2005). Indigenous people have also made extensive use of the research and writings of ethnographers and anthropologists to reconstruct and reinvent their traditions in the present.

Indigenous identity also has its roots in earlier forms of globalisation, namely imperialism and colonialism, without which the concept of indigeneity, and the commonality of culture and experience it implies, would not exist. For example, before Australia was colonised by the British in 1788, there were hundreds or thousands (depending how they are categorised) of small hunter–gatherer, nomadic named populations but there were no Aborigines, or indigenous peoples as such. This united category is inseparable from colonialism. Indigenous identity, therefore, draws its sustenance from notions of historical cultural continuity and survival against the odds, but is also modern; it is at once local and global, expressed in thousands of distinct peoples making up a homogenous category of 'indigenous peoples'.

The use of the term 'indigenous' to describe people and identities is historically recent, dating from the mid-twentieth century when the International Labour Organisation (ILO) sought to highlight and defend the labour and other rights of 'indigenous populations', most notably in the 1953 report *Indigenous Peoples: Living and Working Conditions of Aboriginal Populations in Independent Countries*, and in the 1957 *International Labour Organisation Convention (No. 107)*

Concerning the Protection and Integration of Indigenous and Other Tribal and Semi-Tribal Populations in Independent Countries. Prior to that, from the seventeenth century onward, 'indigenous' was more typically used as an adjective to describe the plants and livestock native to a particular place (Niezen 2005: 539). Beginning in the 1950s, and especially since the 1980s, it has become the widely accepted designation for a diverse set of peoples organised in a global political movement with a distinct form of identity claims.

Of course, discussions of the people now called 'indigenous' date back much further, including the accounts given by European explorers of the 'savages' or 'natives' they met in the 'uncivilised' regions of the world. Later, ethnographers and anthropologists wrote of such peoples under the categories of 'tribes', 'primitives', 'savages' or 'aborigines'. One of the most famous early European attempts to protect the interests of such peoples was the Aborigines' Protection Society, formed in 1837 by British humanitarians as an international society focused on protecting the rights of colonised 'natives'. The peoples now called 'indigenous' fought for their rights to land and resources in frontier struggles in earlier centuries long before they came to imagine themselves as 'indigenous'. Then, they named themselves by tribal or band names, which many groups still use up to the present day. In countries such as the US and Canada that came to treaty arrangements with some tribes, they were officially described as 'Domestic Dependent Nations' or 'First Nations' respectively.

Indigenous identities and claims are inextricably bound up with the long period of colonisation from the late fifteenth century 'discovery' of the Americas, through to the 1950s that saw the beginning of the period when decolonisation movements swept across the world. While decolonisation meant that formerly colonised peoples gained their independence and freedom from colonising powers, indigenous peoples were those left behind in states where they (with some exceptions) became minorities encompassed by surrounding societies and dominated by other more powerful ethnic groups and nations. This occurred also in newly decolonised, independent states such as India, Indonesia, Malaysia and Bangladesh where indigenous minorities would later make their own indigenous claims to land and resources, and for recognition of culture and identity against dominating nation-states. Indigenous peoples are now said to exist in most parts of the world, as more than four thousand distinct cultures making up over 300 million in population, according to much-quoted estimates (Niezen 2003: xii). They vary from tiny, only recently officially recognised populations such as the Ainu in Japan, to more politically visible but still proportionately small minority populations of Native Americans and Inuit and Cree in the US and Canada, Saami in Sweden, Norway, Finland and Russia, Aborigines and Torres Strait Islanders in Australia, and Maori in New Zealand, to large, sometimes majority, indigenous populations in some parts of Latin America, such as in Bolivia, Guatemala, Ecuador and Mexico, and majority indigenous populations in Fiji and Greenland.

Post-colonial, a political term characterising those nations that have thrown off the yoke of colonialism, is only tenuously applicable to indigenous peoples and their contemporary situations. At best, indigenous peoples experience degrees of de-colonisation. Often, they are struggling and surviving as dominated and economically depressed peoples in white settler societies. Indigenous peoples frequently reject the idea that they exist in a post-colonial state, arguing, rather, that they continue to experience the colonial conditions that have long threatened their identities, and their capacities to live decent and culturally 'authentic' lives (see Alfred and Corntassel 2005). Their battle against colonialism continues, even as some of them have successfully challenged regimes of assimilation, and gained some rights to land, cultural autonomy, self-government and self-determination. As indigenous writers Taiaiake Alfred and Jeff Corntassel (2005: 601) argue, colonialism is a continuing, developing regime of domination, that indigenous people must continue to resist:

we live in an era of postmodern imperialism and manipulations by shape-shifting colonial powers; the instruments of domination are evolving and inventing new methods to erase Indigenous histories and senses of place. Therefore, 'globalisation' in Indigenous eyes reflects a deepening, hastening and stretching of an already-existing empire. Living within such political and cultural contexts, it is remembering ceremony, returning to homelands and liberation from the myths of colonialism that are the decolonising imperatives.

Post-colonialism, a doctrine and movement that has its origins in the work of anti-colonial writers including Frantz Fanon, Aimé Césaire and later Edward Said, has developed as a doctrine and movement largely spearheaded in the West by intellectuals from the Indian subcontinent, such as Gayatri Spivak and Homi K. Bhabha. Some of its arguments, strategies and aims, in particular allowing the 'subaltern' to speak beyond colonialism, are of relevance to indigenous peoples, although they and their plights have perhaps been sidelined in postcolonial debates in favour of peoples belonging to former colonies, now independent postcolonial nations. Nevertheless, as I show later, Said's 'Orientalism' critique has been taken up and refashioned as a critique of 'Aboriginalism' by indigenous and non-indigenous intellectuals.

One way to think about the peculiarity of 'indigeneity' as an identity phenomenon is to compare it with usages of ethnicity and ethnic group. As Ronald Niezen points out, Serbs do not typically refer to themselves as 'ethnic' Serbs (and thus tying them to a more encompassing 'ethnic' category), while people from distinct indigenous cultures will often refer to themselves not just by their specific name (i.e. Cree, Inuit, Aranda, Maori, etc.) but also as 'indigenous', and wear the label with a sense of pride. Where 'ethnicity' is an abstract category, 'indigenous' is a concrete identity (Niezen 2003: 3). Niezen uses the term 'indigenism' to capture the global character of indigenous identity.

Niezen (2003) has also argued that what makes indigenous identity claims unique, distinguishing them for example from ethnonationalist claims, is their grounding in international networks. Indigenous peoples throughout the world make use of a global indigenous rights movement to make what are often very localised claims about identity, cultural rights and land and control of natural resources. Indeed, what is unique about the indigenous movement is the extent to which it is organised though and supported by a developing United Nations framework and set of rights instruments. The early role of the ILO has already been mentioned, and to this can be added the work of committees and forums including non-government organisations (NGOs) and those organised through the United Nations, including the Committee on the Elimination of Racial Discrimination (1962–), the United Nations Working Group on Indigenous Populations, formed in 1982 and later replaced by the United Nations Expert Mechanism on the Rights of Indigenous People (2008–), in addition to other important forums such as the United Nations Permanent Forum on Indigenous Issues (2000–), the United Nations Human Rights Council (2006–), and the Committee on Economic, Social and Cultural Rights (1987–).

On Thursday, 13 September 2007 the United Nations General Assembly adopted the 'United Nations Declaration on the Rights of Indigenous Peoples' by a majority of 144 states, with four voting against (Australia, Canada, New Zealand and the US) and eleven abstaining. Australia later reversed its position and accepted the declaration. This was the culmination of more than two decades of work by the United Nations Working Party on Indigenous Populations, and more than a decade after the release of the finalised draft in 1993. It promotes a comprehensive rights regime covering economic, cultural and language rights, and political rights including the right to self-governance and self-determination. The right of self-determination was one of its most controversial aspects and the major stumbling block for those countries that voted against it, who argued that it promoted separatism (despite the clear statement in Article 46 that none of the outlined rights imply the right to 'dismember or impair, totally or in part, the territorial integrity or political unity of sovereign and independent States').

Many scholars date the contemporary resurgence of indigenous identities and claims to the 1960s, when resource extraction and economic modernisation impinged dramatically on the ways of life of indigenous peoples who had, till then, managed to survive at the fringes of capitalist societies, and when social movements for change, including the Civil Rights and Black Power movements, inspired indigenous peoples to agitate in new ways and to rethink their identities. The 'Red Power Movement' in the US in the late 1960s, led by figures such as Lakota author, activist and director of the National Congress of American Indians Vine Deloria Jr. (1933–2005), emphasised pan-Indian identity, and was given momentum by the 1969 occupation by Native American activists of a disused federal prison on Alcatraz Island in San Francisco Bay. The attempt in the late 1960s by Prime Minister Pierre Trudeau to revoke Indian Status, along with infrastructure developments such as hydroelectric schemes and the damming of waterways traditionally used for fishing and hunting, are cited as causes of Canadian indigenous resurgence. In some parts of Latin America, it is argued, indigenous identity-politics emerged as late as the 1990s in the context of the collapse of communism (which fragmented socialist oppositions), the embrace of neoliberalism by governments and the collapse of traditional corporatist political pacts between peasants and the state (Jung 2003; Yashar 1998). In effect, peasants became indigenes as the category of peasant became politically redundant and as the category indigenous was gaining momentum at the level of international politics. After Mexico ratified ILO Convention 169 that called for the protection of indigenous cultural rights and rights to self-government in 1990, indigenous identity had a new salience in domestic Mexican politics as peoples reorganised as 'indigenous' could appeal to international forums over failures of the Mexican state to abide by the Convention's principles (Jung 2003).

This later phase of indigenous identity-politics might be best characterised as a reiteration in the contemporary period of much longer and continuous struggles. These include: the frontier wars of many countries dating back to the fifteenth century; the treaty arrangements in the US, Canada and New Zealand during the eighteenth and nineteenth centuries; struggles for Aboriginal rights (mainly equal citizenship, but with important specific claims over traditional lands) from the 1920s in Australia, including the failed effort of Yorta Yorta elder William Cooper to petition King George V on behalf of Australia's Aborigines for rights including Aboriginal representation in the federal parliament; and international lobbying such as the failed attempt by Levi General Deskaheh, representing groups of Canada's indigenous peoples, to get a hearing concerning a dispute with Canada over tribal self-government, at the League of Nations in the 1920s (Niezen 2003: 31–6).

Today indigenous identity is classified in official statements and by indigenous peoples themselves with remarkable uniformity across the world (for a useful discussion, see Corntassel 2003). It is often couched in defensive terms, and always with reference to historical processes of invasion and colonisation. It includes a claim of historical continuity with pre-contact peoples existing in particular places since 'time immemorial', an assertion of distinct culture and tradition and sometimes language that is still being passed down through the generations, claims about distinct economic and political existence, and usually some reference to self-identification. Some of this is captured by the attempt to define indigeneity for the United Nations by Jose R. Martinez Cobo, the Special Rapporteur for the Sub-committee to study the problem of discrimination against indigenous populations:

> Indigenous communities, peoples and nations are those which, having a historical continuity with pre-invasion and pre-colonial societies that developed on their territories, consider

themselves distinct from other sectors of the societies now prevailing in those territories, or parts of them. They form at present nondominant sectors of society and are determined to preserve, develop and transmit to future generations their ancestral territories and their ethnic identity, as the basis of their continued existence as peoples, in accordance with their own cultural patterns, social institutions and legal systems.

(Cobo 1987: 48)

All such definitions are, however, provisional and cannot capture all groups in the world that consider themselves to be indigenous (Kingsbury 1998). To point to just one example, indigenous Fijians, who slightly outnumber non-indigenous Fijians (such as those of Indian immigrant descent), are the politically and culturally dominant group in Fiji.

Major claims and developments of the field, and key contributions

As noted earlier, accounts of indigenous peoples appeared in the diaries, notes and memoirs written by European explorers, ethnographers and anthropologists. Indigenous peoples, as exemplars of particular ways of life, played an important role in the development of explanations of different types of society, and in particular played a role as the 'other' in understandings of what made Western civilisation distinct. Indigenous peoples like the so-called 'Hottentots' of southwestern Africa (now known as Khoikhoi) and the Aborigines of Australia played a role in the development of racial classifications, and in anthropological evolutionism in the nineteenth century. In these instances, indigenous people were typically seen as residing at the bottom of the racial scale, sometimes forming the link between humans and animals, or representing the 'backward', early stage of societal evolution.

Among sociologists, Emile Durkheim (1858–1917) famously made use of ethnographic and anthropological studies of indigenous peoples such as North American Indians (the Iroquois) and Australian Aborigines (Kamilaroi, Kurnai, Arunta, etc.) in both *The Division of Labour in Society* (1893) and *The Elementary Forms of the Religious Life* (1912). Durkheim used such accounts of tribal peoples to develop his concept of 'mechanical solidarity', involving solidary bonds based on sameness and minimal role differentiation and distinguished from modern, 'organic solidarity' based on the division of labour; and he returned to them to make major claims about the role of religion in society, especially through his use of the example of totemism (based on accounts of Australian Aborigines) to explain the distinction between the sacred and the profane. The anthropologist Robert Redfield (1897–1958) used his understanding of indigenous Mexican life and culture together with accounts of other indigenous peoples to construct his influential notion of the 'folk society', and to explain societal and cultural change along a 'Folk-Urban Continuum'. Redfield described folk society as small in scale, with intimate relations between all members and a characteristically intense sense of we-ness and group belonging. It was self-referential and isolated from other groups and their influences. These were primarily oral cultures, non-historical and regulated by tradition and ritual, with limited role-differentiation and a simple division of labour. Folk societies used primitive forms of technology, were self-sufficient, subsistence societies characterised by highly personalised rather than abstract relations. Folk society and the 'Rural-Urban Continuum' were highly influential concepts and ways of understanding change in the twentieth century, including among urban and rural sociologists, and in what became the sub-discipline of 'community studies'.

Anthropologists have played key historical and contemporary roles in the development of indigenous studies. Spencer and Gillen's *Native Tribes of Central Australia* (1899) reverberated among social scientists and philosophers in Europe's metropolitan centres, as did Bronislaw

Malinowski's studies of the Kula of the Trobriand Islands. In his hugely influential *Argonauts of the Western Pacific* (1922), based on his intensive method of participant observation to get at the meaning of action, ritual and custom through everyday life, Malinowski made his famous attempt to inhabit the 'native point of view'. Well-known contemporary anthropologists such as David Maybury-Lewis have highlighted the differential plight of indigenous peoples in different parts of the world. Robert Paine did pioneering anthropological studies of the Saami of northern Europe from the 1950s onward, wrote important studies of nomadic life in the world's northern regions, and critiqued 'welfare colonialism' in the 'White Arctic'. Anthropologists have also often been in the frontline as advocates for indigenous rights, articulating indigenous claims against dominating states and explaining and defending indigenous world-views to wider publics. And it is anthropologists, often collaborating with and supporting indigenous claimants, who governments and courts have often relied on for expert opinion about indigenous beliefs, traditions and traditional land connections when assessing indigenous rights to land and to the protection of sacred places and traditional heritage.

Important earlier works by historians, anthropologists and sociologists devoted to analysing the history and fate of indigenous people have challenged assumptions about the character of indigenous people; for example, emphasising that they were not 'timeless', unchanging peoples belonging to the pre-history of humanity or at an early stage of social evolution. These include anthropologist and historian Edward H. Spicer's pioneering book *Cycles of Conquest: The Impact of Spain, Mexico and the United States on the Indians of the South West, 1533–1960*, first published in 1962. Spicer set out in this major study to explain culture change among Native Americans as a result of colonial conquest, and in doing so showed the agency and adaptive responses of these peoples over 500 years. He described Native Americans as 'enduring peoples' with a particular sense of identity based on three characteristics – relationship to land, common spiritual bond, and language use – and his conception was later influential among indigenous scholars (Corntassel 2003: 91). Eric Wolf in *Europe and the People Without History* (1982) argued against the notion that ethnographers and anthropologists studying 'primitives' were studying 'historyless' people. Since the beginnings of European expansion from 1400 onward, all peoples across the globe were increasingly and thoroughly interconnected through complex webs of interaction forming a 'common world':

> These changes affected not only the peoples singled out as the carriers of 'real' history but also the populations anthropologists have called 'primitives' and have often studied as pristine survivals from a timeless past. The global processes set in motion by European expansion constitute *their* history as well. There are thus no 'contemporary ancestors', no people without history, no peoples – to use Lévi-Strauss's phrase – whose histories have remained 'cold'.
>
> *(Wolf 1982: 385)*

Wolf's extended discussion (ibid.: ch. 6) of the impact of the European-controlled fur trade, from the seventeenth century onward, on the economic, political and social relations of various North American Indians, including transformations of the operations and meanings of kinship relations, convincingly illustrates the point.

More recently, historian and critic of anthropology James Clifford in *The Predicament of Culture* (1988) has examined the complexity of indigenous identity through his study of the Aboriginal land claims of the Mashpee in Cape Cod, and used the example of indigenous people to reflect on the new uncertainties of post-colonial realities and complexities of all identities as everyone, including indigenous peoples, gets swept up in the movement of modernity, albeit in their own unique ways. Identity becomes always mixed, hybrid, a play of homogenising and differentiating elements. He rejects what he calls the Western regime of time-consciousness that relegates indigenous culture to a historical past:

> Throughout the world indigenous populations have had to reckon with the forces of 'progress' and 'national' unification. The results have been both destructive and inventive. Many traditions, languages, cosmologies, and values are lost, some literally murdered; but much has simultaneously been invented and revived in complex, oppositional contexts.
>
> *(Clifford 1988: 16)*

Clifford (ibid.: 284) points to the unsettling nature of contemporary indigenous identity and land claims for the colonising West, as powerful 'impure' natives upset the old images of powerless, forlorn, vanishing though 'authentic' Indian victims living in museum-like conditions, and assert their indigenous status to do 'non-traditional' things.

In recent decades anthropologists have been accused of paternalism in relation to the 'native' and 'tribal' people they have studied. In anti-colonial and post-colonial critiques (some from within the discipline of anthropology itself), anthropologists have been criticised for imposing their own Eurocentric views on others, and of speaking for 'natives' under the misguided presumption that they, as non-indigenous observers, could ever really inhabit, understand or articulate indigenous views and voices. In the last few decades some in the discipline have attempted to reorganise it in response to critiques of its being complicit with colonialism. Notable figures include Renato Rosaldo in *Culture and Truth* (1989) who stressed the entanglement of anthropologists with the colonial enterprise, and Johannes Fabian who in *Time and the Other* (1983) showed how anthropological writing operates through a structure and politics of time that obscures the 'coevalness' of anthropologists and their 'tribal' or 'primitive' informants. Vincent Crapanzano has championed the development of a 'dialogic' anthropology highlighting the role played by anthropologists in constructing ethnographic encounters, and emphasising the way that anthropologists themselves construct meaning through writing their ethnographies, rather than simply report on 'native' meaning systems as revealed to them, given expression in works such as *Tuhami: Portrait of a Moroccan* (1980).

Along with other non-indigenous writers, opinion-makers and government officials, anthropologists have sometimes been accused of participating in the construction of 'Aboriginalism', that at once distorts indigenous identities and renders them more amenable to domination by non-indigenous society. It is here that the discourse of post-colonialism has its most explicit influence in shaping the critique of both indigenous and non-indigenous scholars in relation to indigenous identity claims. The critique of Aboriginalism – which draws on Edward Said's notion of 'Orientalism' – involves the idea that settler states and their ideological workers (politicians, bureaucrats, religious officials and missionaries, intellectuals, social commentators, artists and writers, etc.) create and impose a compliant 'Aboriginal' identity that can be negotiated with and ruled (see for example Alfred and Corntassel 2005). The state decides who is and is not Aboriginal, and uses these categorisations to decide what rights will be granted and/or denied to indigenous people. Indigenous peoples are coerced in the process, sometimes collaborating with states and courts to deny the existence of other indigenous groups, or to deny the validity of certain indigenous beliefs, traditions and claims (Weaver 2001). More broadly, Aboriginalism includes coercive, often romanticised academic constructions of the indigenous other, historically and in the present, as well as popular understandings of indigenous peoples evident in everyday life (for example stereotypes, stories and images passed down as folklore, local history), films, television, fiction and art.

Aboriginalism is counterposed with the more authentic identities that can only be known and expressed by indigenous peoples themselves. For example, Hilary Weaver, an indigenous Lakota intellectual, in a paper reflecting on the nature of indigenous identity and various measures to assess it, finally asserts that 'most attempts to measure identity are of questionable adequacy and accuracy' and quotes approvingly another author, N.C. Peroff who states that:

> Indianness means different things to different people. And, of course, at the most elementary level, Indianness is something only experienced by people who are Indians. It is how Indians think about themselves and is internal, intangible, and metaphysical. From this perspective, studying Indianness is like trying to study the innermost mysteries of the human mind itself.
>
> (quoted in Weaver 2001: 249)

Indigenous people, she argues, must decolonise their own minds to rid themselves of the contaminating images and understanding of the indigene or the native imposed by colonialism.

Indigenous identity-politics thus frequently involves efforts to renegotiate understandings of identity, to resist colonialist imposition of identities, and to free indigenous peoples to recapture their authentic indigenous self-identities and world-views. In recent work from Australian indigenous scholars such as Aileen Moreton-Robinson, 'Aboriginalism' has been critiqued within a framework of whiteness studies. She has argued that 'whiteness' as an 'invisible norm' has contributed to the 'orientalisation' of Australian Aborigines, and she asserts the epistemological incommensurability between Aboriginal knowledge and a 'white' knowledge that assumes its universality (Moreton-Robinson 2004).

The growing role of indigenous intellectuals, leaders and activists in this critique has been another important development. Since the 1960s indigenous scholars, writers and activists themselves have made important contributions to an elaboration and defence of indigenous identity and culture as an act of resistance to colonialism and the claims of non-indigenous scholars about the backwardness of indigenous cultures. Pioneering works include N. Scott Momaday's Pulitzer prize-winning novel *House Made of Dawn* (1968) that chronicled modern Indian life on reservations, Vine Deloria Jr.'s *Custer Died for Your Sins* (1969) (discussed with his other work below), and *The Fourth World: An Indian Reality* (1974) co-authored by George Manuel (1921–89), Chief of the National Indian Brotherhood and Assembly of First Nations, a major work articulating and explaining a Canadian Indian, and indigenous, world-view. Manuel, of Canada's Shuswap people, launched the term 'Fourth World' to distinguish the situation and world-view of indigenous peoples across the world, from that of the American dominated First World, the Soviet dominated Second World and the underdeveloped Third World, a battleground for influence between the US and the Soviet Union and their allies. Manuel rejected the applicability to the Fourth World of the idea of underdevelopment and the need for 'modernisation' that dominated thinking about the Third World. Indigenous peoples had their own unique contributions to make in the contemporary world, and their cultures and identities were not backward or relics of the past. Fourth World peoples would find their own ways to self-determination, without necessarily modelling themselves on nation-states. *The Fourth World: An Indian Reality* also contained an important critique of the impact of colonialism in undermining the confidence of indigenous peoples in their capacity for, and right to, self-government. Apart from elaborating on the meaning of the Fourth World of indigenous peoples, George Manuel was also one of the founding members of the World Council of Indigenous Peoples in 1975, serving as its president till 1981 (Hall 2003: ch. 3).

'The Fourth World' became an important global movement, drawing in anthropologists and ethnographers including Robert Paine, and the geographer and promoter of indigenous rights across the world Bernard Q. Nietschmann. Nietschmann (1994) argued that 'The Fourth World' was made up of more than five thousand ancient, authentic (including indigenous) nations captured and dominated by 168 historically recent 'artificial' states that were the 'outgrowth of European kingdoms, overseas colonialism, and the division of large colonial empires into smaller and smaller neo-colonial pieces' (ibid.: 227), and that this situation was a major cause of 'ethnocide' and 'ecocide' throughout the world. The survival and diversity of nations, including indigenous nations, was essential to bio-diversity and the survival of the planet. 'Because most nation peoples depend upon local biological resources that occur within their historical, traditional territories', Nietschmann (ibid.: 231) argued, 'they have evolved lifeways generally adapted to sustaining environments and conserving biological diversity.' Giving greater self-determination to authentic nations, such as indigenous peoples who knew how to preserve their environments, as opposed to artificial states bent on environmental exploitation, was the only way to ensure environmental sustainability.

Within the developing field of indigenous scholarship several important characteristic themes and arguments have emerged. The anti-colonial critique is central, as is the emphasis on survival against the odds, and the assertion of the right to self-determination. The rootedness of indigenous identity in ancient law, tradition and land is frequently emphasised, though this does not mean that tradition cannot alter and change across time, or that indigenous people cannot adopt more 'modern' beliefs, lifestyles and practices. However, these negotiations between tradition and modernity, between indigenous belief systems or religion and 'Western' beliefs and religion can be fraught, with accusations by some indigenous people that others are not true indigenes because, for example, they have adopted Christianity (see Weaver 2001). Some assert the superiority of indigeneity as an environmentally sustainable form of culture, and as more spiritually rich than Western, industrialised culture – a source of the appeal of indigenous world-views to environmentalists and 'New-Age' thinkers and followers. It is articulated as a more holistic, authentic identity and culture, intertwined with nature and infused with a spirituality and wisdom lacking in the West. The 'Cartesian self' of the West, with its opposition between mind and matter, is contrasted with a more organic, spiritual indigenous self.

Vine Deloria Jr., mentioned earlier, was a historian and political activist who did much to articulate an indigenous world-view along the above lines. In his classic and popular first book, *Custer Died for Your Sins*, first published in 1969, Deloria Jr. excoriated white America for its treatment of American Indians, especially the abrogation of treaties by American governments, and also critiqued white civilisation more generally. He called for the teaching of Indian traditions to young Native Americans, the re-establishment of Indian religion, for forms of cultural separation from mainstream America, and for political separation of Indians from the American state. He encouraged the strengthening of reservation communities, tribalism, and a form of Indian nationalism among the majority of Indians who lived in urban areas. Already in this first major work, Deloria Jr. was arguing that Native Americans, as indigenous peoples, had a unique world-view and way of living that was in important ways superior to Western civilisation, and that in fact much of what went under the latter was destructive in the Americas. This book was important in asserting the survival of Native Americans in contemporary America, and for proclaiming that they would now speak for themselves rather than accept being spoken about by non-indigenous experts and government officials. The book also included a powerful – and typically sharp and witty – critique of Christian missionaries and anthropologists.

In *God is Red*, first published in 1972, Deloria Jr. set out to explain and defend the Native American world-view as a valid perspective incommensurable with much of Western science and Western religion, and as a far more deeply spiritual way of life more attuned with 'mother earth'. In the second edition of *God is Red*, published in 1992, Deloria Jr. created a dichotomy between so-called 'natural' peoples, such as Native Americans and indigenous people across the world, and those 'hybrid' peoples of the Islamic and Judeo-Christian civilisations who lived lives separated from nature. Deloria Jr. challenged the very metaphysical bases of Western thought, especially in works such as *The Metaphysics of Modern Existence* (1979), *Red Earth, White Lies* (1997) and the collection of his essays *Spirit and Reason* (1999). These works called for a deeper, truer multiculturalism through inhabiting indigenous ways of thinking. In *Red Earth, White Lies* (1997: 3) Deloria Jr. suggested that much of what the West had brought to the Americas should be rejected:

> Our present view of government, our avoidance of allegiance to high spiritual powers, and our exclusively scientific understanding of our world will continue to guide our thoughts and activities in the future and bring us to a complete collapse unless we achieve more mature understanding of our planet, its history, and the rest of the universe. Much of Western science must go, all of Western religion should go, and if we are in any way successful of ridding ourselves of these burdens, we will find that we can fundamentally change government so that it will function more sensibly and enable us to solve our problems.

Deloria Jr. asserted that Native American stories and explanations, including those about human and geological creation, were not simply symbolically or mythically true, but factually true in the way in which we believe scientific facts to be true. Western claims of scientific objectivity were spurious, and the refusal to accept the validity of other, non-Western knowledges unless they concurred with scientific arguments and claims was, according to Deloria Jr., inspired by colonialism and racism (Deloria Jr. 1997: ch. 2). Together with its critique and dismissal of much of Western science, including scientific claims about geological transformations providing a land bridge across the Bering Strait upon which indigenous peoples 'migrated' to America, the book had a trenchant critique of Christianity, seen as often the vehicle and guiding hand in the destruction of non-Western peoples, and operating on the destructive view that the earth was evil (Deloria Jr. 1997: 9).

Apart from the work of indigenous people themselves, there have also been important developments among non-indigenous intellectuals seeking to account for the nature of indigenous politics and identity claims through theories that combine a constructivist approach with notions of identity fluidity, political mobilisation and political opportunity. Some of the most innovative work along these lines has emerged in studies by anthropologists of Latin American indigenous struggles.

For example, the anthropologist Jan Hoffman French (2004) explains how in the 1970s a group of peasant sharecroppers in northeastern Brazil, of mixed Portuguese, indigenous, but mainly African descent 'without indigenous languages or cultural practices' (French 2004: 671), came to distinguish themselves from their neighbours and relatives as indigenous Xocó people, and adopted largely invented traditions and cultural practices to prove their indigenous status to the state, successfully in 1979. In northeastern Brazil racial and cultural mixing had been so intense that it had been believed previously that indigenous people no longer existed as a distinct category, replaced by a mestizo *sertanejo* culture and identity. After the enactment of a new law (the 'Indian Statute') in 1973 categorising Indian status with attendant 'rights to land, federal protection, medical care and benefits' (ibid.: 67), the peasants who became the Xocó were encouraged in their indigenous identity claims by Catholic supporters in the context of a political struggle with a land-owning family for whom they had worked for generations. French argues that what was evident in this identity assertion, that transformed some groups of peasants, but not others, into indigenous peoples assigned tribal names from the past, was a systematic downplaying of African heritage and of 'the richness of their sertanejo culture' (ibid.: 663–4) which they, nevertheless, carried on with in their everyday lives, alongside the newly adopted indigenous practices including a ritual dance (the 'toré') and the religious use of hallucinogenic drugs, adopted from other northeastern Brazilian tribes. The emergence of this identity revealed the dialogic nature of identity, the role of opportunity in particular local circumstances, and the role of the battle over resources in the construction of identities. French (ibid.: 664) argues that in this and similar cases:

> the upsurge of indigenous self-identification . . . is not just about (or not necessarily at all about) Indianness but is more fundamentally about political subjectivities forged in the struggle for land that, when tied to claims of indigenous identity, result in communities of likeness.

Where French emphasises the invention of identity in the context of political opportunity, Deborah Yashar (1999), surveying struggles more broadly across Latin America, gives a more nuanced explanation, suggesting a role for ethnic survival and renewal, especially in contexts where the reach of the state was weak (i.e. in the Amazon). She suggests that even in contexts where the state sought to incorporate indigenous people as peasants, indigenous identities survived alongside those political organisations of the rural poor such as peasant unions.

In her study of indigenous Mayan resistance and political struggle in Chiapas, Mexico, including the Zapatista rebellion of 1994, June Nash (1995) presents a subtle account of the interaction between an ideological context, involving a 500-year resistance to colonialism expressed as the continuation and reinvention of indigenous traditions and socialisation patterns, and political and economic contexts, that inspires the varying use of indigenous identity, traditions and claims. She argues for the superiority of these kinds of rich, contextual explanations when compared with more one-sided explanations that overemphasise the role of ethno-culture (including primordialism), rely on economic and class reductionism, or adopt abstract theoretical 'new social movements' arguments as if these can alone explain ethnic movements in Latin America. Notably, she shows how indigenous identity is organised differently, and has very different institutional relationships with political parties and governments in Highland areas and Lowland jungle areas of Chiapas, and that these different situations can produce more stratified and oppressive indigenous communal situations in one (the Highlands), and more egalitarian, collectivist indigenous situations in the other (Lowlands).

Marisol De La Cadena (2000), in her study of race, ethnicity and indigeneity in Peru, has argued for a complex process of de-Indianisation by which indigenous people through education and the acquiring of modern skills and cultural adaptation take up new kinds of identity but do not at the same time lose their indigenous identity. The indigenous participants in her anthropological study directly challenge more static conceptions of 'Indianness' including those organised through state classifications, rejecting the category 'Indian' which is deemed to represent backwardness and poverty, while continuing to honour indigenous histories, cultures and identities. De-indianisation is seen as a subaltern practice of resistance:

> de-Indianization is not the shedding of indigenous culture and subsequent 'integrating' . . . envisioned as the solution to violence in Peru. Neither does it mean 'assimilating,' and thus disappearing culturally, as some anthropologists have presented it . . . Rather, it is through active de-Indianization that subaltern cuzqueños have redefined essentialist notions of

culture. They accomplish this by replacing regional beliefs in fixed identities with infinite degrees of fluid Indianness or mestizoness.

(De La Cadena 2000: 6)

This refusal to be restricted by a category of 'pure', 'authentic' Aboriginality supposedly at odds with the modern world, while retaining a strong sense of indigenous culture and belonging, is an important indigenous contribution to the understanding of identity as a confluence of different influences and historical trajectories. One of Australia's leading indigenous intellectuals and political leaders, Noel Pearson, has argued for a complex notion of layered identity. Taking his cue from Amartya Sen's critique of multiculturalism, he argues that the mistake is to imagine that people inhabit 'singular identities' (Pearson 2009: 332–43). Neither group nor individual identities are singular. Reflecting on his own complex and multi-layered identity, he writes of his identifications with several different indigenous nations in Australia through his mixed heritage and deep connection with different lands both traditionally, based on tribal affiliation, and based on growing up on the Aboriginal mission of Hope Vale in Northern Queensland. Beyond these identifications, he also identifies with the region of Cape York Peninsula, the state of Queensland and, more ambivalently, with the Australian nation. He also identifies with Christianity and in particular Lutherans, and through them with other Aboriginal Lutherans from other missions, and even non-indigenous Lutherans of Scandinavian and German descent in Australia. Even more distant still, he feels a 'remnant connection with Neuendettelsau in Bavaria', the original source of the Lutheran missionaries who came to Australia, and which remains 'a spiritual wellspring for the people of my village' (ibid.: 335). He has argued that, like other peoples, Indigenous peoples can engage with the spirit of the Enlightenment while retaining their distinct indigenous identities. Pearson has suggested as a model Jewish people who have thoroughly engaged with the societies they live in, and have advanced economically, while at the same time retaining their distinct identities and sense of belonging to an ancient Jewish people. Pearson calls for a recognition within Australia of indigenous peoplehood, but argues that this does not have to involve separatism, but can co-exist with a process of integration.

Another important development has been the attempt to understand and defend indigenous rights within liberal and communitarian accounts of multiculturalism. Charles Taylor used the example of indigenous people in his famous essay 'The politics of recognition', defending a version of group rights that would allow them degrees of autonomy and state protection so that they could continue with their cultural traditions within larger states. Will Kymlicka in *Multicultural Citizenship* (1995) and elsewhere makes a famous distinction between the rights of immigrant ethnic minorities within nation-states where they have 'voluntarily' consented to enter a particular nation through the act of immigration, and therefore can expect little state protection of their distinct cultures; and those of indigenous peoples who were typically conquered and incorporated into nation-states against their will and without direct consent. The latter have rights to protection of their culture, including provisions to teach in their own languages, to be protected from intrusions from the external society, rights to land and special rights to hunt and so on. However, Kymlicka's liberalism means that he emphasises the right of individuals to 'exit' what they may experience as oppressive communal situations, and thus collective indigenous rights are limited by a broader 'Western' liberal framework, centred on individual liberty. This kind of limitation is not necessarily considered acceptable by indigenous peoples themselves, who see their rights as inherent and rooted in other, ancient indigenous traditions.

Main criticisms

Many of the criticisms of multiculturalism and the politics of identity extend to critiques of indigenous politics and the assertions of political rights and separatism based on cultural claims about the uniqueness of indigeneity. Political philosophers such as Brian Barry (2001) claim that the liberal state, 'difference-blind' and ignoring culture, has far more chance of achieving equality and social justice than any form of politics that bases claims for recognition, special privileges, and exemptions on the needs of culture and identity.

Some critics argue that within nation-states there has been so much genetic and cultural mixing of populations that indigenous peoples can no longer legitimately argue that they have a special claim on land and resources on the basis of being original occupants of lands and of having distinct, ancient cultures. Alternatively, it is argued that since indigenous status ultimately relies on some element of blood descent, that it involves a discredited concept of race to argue its case. In effect, such critics argue, requests for special conditions and protections based on claims to indigeneity, and their granting by states, are racist and discriminate against non-indigenous members of the same nation-states. The notion that within democratic states, one ethnic group is deemed to have a special place and a special relationship with the land, and special rights over decision-making on that land, clashes with notions of equality of all citizens within democracy.

Others argue against the authenticity of many indigenous identities, especially of those people living and working in industrial societies, sometimes university educated and living professional, middle-class lives. For some critics, much that passes itself off as indigenous identity and culture is fictive, a modern invention for political, monetary and other gains. This criticism, however, typically relies on the assumption that indigenous identity is static and that, where it changes or develops it inevitably disappears. The counter-claim is that this is a colonialist argument, conveniently consigning indigenous identities and communities to the vanquished past in order to ignore unpleasant and sometimes costly indigenous claims, and thus an ideology aimed to complete the colonial conquest.

Critics argue that recognition of indigenous identities and rights, including the right to live on ancestral lands partly separated from mainstream society and economy, and to continue on with activities and ways of life from a 'by-gone era', has had the disastrous consequence of creating and sustaining islands of welfare dependency and disadvantage. By rejecting assimilation policies, states have created artificial communities and non-sustainable lifestyles where children do not receive adequate schooling and education, including the acquisition of mainstream language, literacy and numeracy skills, and where people are allowed to sink into lives of poverty and substance abuse, where moral norms and discipline have broken down, and parental responsibility has been abandoned. These communities are artificially propped up by access to welfare benefits, and are riven by crime including sexual abuse of women and children. Though his argument does not accord with the claim that these problems are *caused* by the recognition of indigenous rights (including traditional land rights) and identities, Australian indigenous leader and intellectual Noel Pearson (mentioned previously) has spear-headed the campaign in Australia to reject 'passive welfare' in indigenous communities and to restore norms of responsibility in communities, especially responsibility for children's welfare (see Pearson 2009). Other indigenous leaders and intellectuals in Australia, including Marcia Langton and Mick Dodson, have been courageous critical voices against sexual and physical violence against women and children in Aboriginal communities.

Another area of criticism concerns the attempt to accommodate concepts of 'group' or 'collective' rights. Indigenous peoples often make claims for collective or group rights rather than simply individual rights, and some liberals such as Charles Taylor and Will Kymlicka lean in the direction of accommodating such concepts. Jurgen Habermas (1994), in his response to Taylor's essay 'The politics of recognition' makes a strong case that the concept of collective rights cannot be accommodated within liberal democratic theory, and that instead all claims to rights can only be based on the rights of individuals, including any claims to culture and respect. Within liberalism the freedom of the individual is sacrosanct, including the freedom to accept or reject cultural traditions, ways of life and collective identities. The democratic state should not get into the act of trying to preserve cultures; all that it should ensure is that there is no discrimination of individuals on the basis of culture, race, ethnicity, gender, sexuality and so on. Cultures and ways of life in modernity must be able to stand on their own merits; they must be able to convince their freely choosing individual members that they, or aspects of them, are worth preserving.

Indigenous peoples themselves dispute the conceptual distinction between individual and group underpinning debates about rights within liberalism and communitarianism. As individual, group, land and spirit are considered as forming an indivisible whole in a radically non-Western, incommensurable indigenous tradition and world-view, indigenous people see their claim to pursue indigenous group rights as unique and just (see Holder and Corntassel 2002; Niezen 2003: ch. 4). As Holder and Corntassel (2002: 128) point out, indigenous groups assert that the right to

> determine for themselves the terms on which members interact with outsiders and with one another is an essential part of protecting their right to self-determination and so represents a goal toward which any fight for group recognition must aim.

They argue that from an indigenous perspective there is no real contradiction between the pursuit of individual and group rights and goals, as 'the preserving of communal life can be important to individuals' well-being, in addition to the various spiritual and symbolic resources which such life may provide' (Holder and Corntassel 2002: 129).

Discussing the political ramifications of these issues when they are played out within nation-states, Guntrum Werther (1992) points out that successful indigenous claims to self-determination since the 1960s have involved a major concession from liberal democratic governments, resulting in a reformulation of the democratic state in which 'modern aboriginal polities exist based upon a non-liberal idea of political legitimacy (aboriginal status) and in which a dual construction of political rights is acknowledged' (Werther 1992: 85). Werther sees this as an ultimately unstable situation in which liberal assumptions about the nature of the democratic state are undermined, often in an unacknowledged way as part of historical, political compromises in the context of domestic and international pressures. Political backlashes from majority populations are an ever-present threat, especially as the reality of indigenous demands bites home, involving clashes over economic interests and control of resources. Also, there are competing nation-state policy aims such as modernisation and economic development, and Werther (ibid.: 42) believes that these will generally and ultimately predominate over claims associated with indigenous status.

Though there have been political compromises in already developed Western countries, countries in the process of economic development and industrialisation, as in some parts of Asia, have been less than enthusiastic about recognising traditional indigenous rights, and in some cases refuse to recognise indigenous identity at all, arguing that it is a Western and imposed concept, as was the case in China, India, Bangladesh, Myanmar and, in the main, Indonesia in noted political and legal controversies in the 1980s and 1990s (Kingsbury 1998).

Critics also raise the problem of oppression within indigenous communities and how this can be addressed if the surrounding state and society have made important concessions to self-government and cultural survival. Although himself a supporter of indigenous rights, anthropologist Ronald Niezen (2003: 99) provides examples from his own experiences of living on Aboriginal land in Canada. Cree women from neighbouring communities came to his home to discuss their problems as 'dissidents' of Aboriginal communities where they and others had been harassed and physically intimidated, lost their homes and possessions, were denied band membership and were denied access to public forums such as radio, because they disagreed with the policies of ruling factions. Experiences of corruption and rights abuses were widespread across indigenous communities, according to a grassroots national Aboriginal organisation, and the problem was that victims had no real avenue for redress, because of the provisions of the Indian Act and governments' reluctance to interfere with Aboriginal self-government.

Another sympathetic anthropologist, June Nash (1995), nevertheless explains how in the Highlands of Chiapas, Mexico, powerful, sometimes corrupt and violent indigenous factions developed through patron–clientelist relations with political parties and government. Asserting claims about indigenous tradition, they expelled thousands of indigenous Protestant converts from their communities, so that the latter became disenfranchised, dispossessed refugees. She also discusses forms of corruption where funds are diverted to the families of the powerful indigenous factions, and political violence when other indigenous people try to protest against corruption. Political parties and governments turn a blind eye as they rely upon the political support of the powerful indigenous factions.

As Niezen (2003: 219) explains, these examples of indigenous intra-communal oppression not only trouble indigenous victims, but also are deeply troubling to liberal human rights theorists. To what extent, they ask, does self-determination strengthen illiberal governments? In addition, if the principle of self-determination is accepted in a strong sense, what is to stop states from deciding that they are the true representatives of collectivities, and the true preservers of cultural integrity, and therefore to ride roughshod over the desires of diverse indigenous peoples and individuals?

The continuing importance of perspectives on indigenous identity and rights, and anticipated future developments

The development of indigenous rights in a global context represents an important and, in certain respects, unique set of political and identity claims based on the argument that the damage of colonisation can, at least partially, be undone. Indigenous peoples argue that in order for colonialism to be overcome, and for humanity to enter a true phase of post-colonialism, there must be radical acceptance of the survival and rights of identities and cultures that are radically different to Western identities and cultures. This is a politics of resistance, adaptation, accommodation and restoration. It also represents a continuing contribution to the discourse and practice of decolonisation across the globe.

Indigenous peoples' claims go beyond standard multicultural claims for equality and non-discrimination, to assert much more specific, indigenous rights and protections that are deemed to be inherent in their status as original peoples – rights that are not accorded to non-indigenous peoples. These claims will continue to challenge nation-states to make compromises and accommodations, to rethink their concepts of unitary citizenship, and perhaps to rethink the nature of their sovereignty and even their national identities. For this and related reasons, they will also continue to be controversial and inspire conflict.

According to Niezen, self-determination is at once the greatest challenge from indigenous peoples, and also a key unifying claim for the global indigenous movement. It is a challenge to the statist organisation of international relations (in its claim for indigenous rights that move beyond states) and a challenge to nation-states internally:

> There are thus two principle ways in which the indigenous peoples' movement challenges state sovereignty: One is at the international level, pressing for reforms within international law and eroding the statist orientation of the international system; the other is as a pluralistic force within states that presses for realization in practice of the notion, uncomfortable to many, of nations within nations, of peoples who have rights to self-determination nested within their rights as citizens of states.
>
> *(Niezen 2003: 148)*

As writers such as Deborah Yashar (1999) argue, the history of indigenous struggles for recognition and rights in Latin America tells an important new story about democratic developments that moves beyond simplistic theories of democratic consolidation. Rather, these struggles have contributed to a situation where everything is in flux, where democratic institution building remains fluid and indeterminate, and where states are called upon to reform themselves to better reflect and accommodate plural identities and administrative heterogeneity. States are continually debating issues of constitutional reform, decentralisation, recognising local territorial autonomy, legal pluralism and so on (Yashar 1999: 97). Indigenous peoples challenge democratic states to rethink citizenship beyond the notion of unitary citizenship, and to find new and innovative ways to enhance multicultural citizenship. The challenges from indigenous peoples have resulted in new forms of democratisation, and new ways of institutionalising participation and rights, combining commitments to 'universal claims to citizenship and differentiated claims to difference' (ibid.: 39). With calls for autonomy and respect for local forms of governance, indigenous peoples challenge assumptions about liberal democratic politics:

> Rather than delineate a single relationship between the state and its citizens, indigenous organizations demand multiple types of citizenship with boundaries that guarantee equal rights and representation at the national level and recognize corporate indigenous authority structures in the indigenous territory.
>
> *(ibid.: 39)*

The struggles of indigenous peoples have led to important developments in international norm setting, and are likely to continue to do so for the foreseeable future as the full implications of the adoption, by nearly all states, of the United Nations Declaration of the Rights of Indigenous Peoples is elaborated on the ground in myriad different contexts. Will Kymlicka (2007) points out that the pursuit of indigenous rights at the international level after the Second World War was the most significant contributor to the development of multicultural politics as we understand it today. It was through these arguments and claims that the modern reinvigoration of minority rights within states gathered momentum from the 1980s onwards.

Indigenous authors argue that indigenous people have made, and continue to make, an important contribution to the elaboration of rights discourse. Holder and Corntassel (2002) argue, for example, that the practical elaborations and claims about rights evident in many indigenous political struggles have major relevance for the theoretical arguments about individual and group rights, suggesting a pathway between arguments that suggest that the two types of rights are necessarily in conflict.

Finally, indigenous thinkers continue to challenge old dichotomies between tradition and modernity, Enlightenment and superstition or enchantment, mind and matter, cultural change and cultural continuity.

References

Alfred, T. and Corntassel, J.J. (2005) 'Being indigenous: resurgences against contemporary colonialism', *Government and Opposition* 40(2): 597–614.
Barry, B. (2001) *Culture and Equality*. Cambridge: Polity.
Clifford, J. (1988) *The Predicament of Culture: Twentieth Century Ethnography, Literature and Art*. Cambridge MA: Harvard University Press.
Cobo, J.R.M. (1987) 'Study of the problem of discrimination against indigenous populations', Vol V. U.N. doc E/CN.4/Sub.2/1986/7/Add.4
Corntassel, J.J. (2003) 'Who is indigenous? "Peoplehood" and ethnonationalist approaches to rearticulating indigenous identity', *Nationalism and Ethnic Politics* 9(1): 75–100.
De La Cadena, M. (2000) *Indigenous Mestizos: The Politics of Race and Culture in Cuzco, Peru, 1919–1991*. Durham and London: Duke University Press.
Deloria Jr., V. (1997) *Red Earth, White Lies: Native Americans and the Myth of Scientific Fact*. Colorado: Fulcrum Publishing.
French, J.H. (2004) '*Mestizaje* and law making in indigenous identity formation in northeastern Brazil: "After the conflict came the history"', *American Anthropologist* 106(4): 663–74.
Habermas, J. (1994) 'Struggles for recognition in the democratic constitutional state', in A. Gutmann (ed.) *Multiculturalism: Examining the Politics of Recognition*. Princeton, New Jersey: Princeton University Press, pp. 107–148.
Hall, A.J. (2003) *The American Empire and the Fourth World: The Bowl With One Spoon*. Montréal, Ithaca: McGill-Queen's University Press.
Holder, C.L. and Corntassel, J.J. (2002) 'Indigenous peoples and multicultural citizenship: bridging collective and individual rights', *Human Rights Quarterly* 24: 126–51.
Jung, C. (2003) 'The politics of indigenous identity: neoliberalism, cultural rights and the Mexican Zapatistas', *Social Research* 70(2): 433–62.
Kingsbury, B. (1998) '"Indigenous peoples" in international law: a constructivist approach to the Asian controversy', *The American Journal of International Law* 92(3): 414–57.
Kymlicka, W. (2007) *Multicultural Odysseys: Navigating the New International Politics of Diversity*. Oxford: Oxford University Press.
Moreton-Robinson, A. (2004) 'Whiteness, epistemology and indigenous representation', in A. Moreton-Robinson (ed.) *Whitening Race: Essays in Social and Cultural Criticism*. Canberra, ACT: Aboriginal Studies Press, 75–88.
Nash, J. (1995) 'The reassertion of indigenous identity: Mayan responses to state intervention in Chiapas', *Latin American Research Review* 30(3): 7–41.
Nietschmann, B. (1994) 'The Fourth World: nations versus states', in G.J. Demko and W.B. Wood (eds) *Reordering the World: Geopolitical Perspectives on the Twentieth Century*. Boulder, San Francisco and Oxford: Westview Press, 225–42.
Niezen, R. (2003) *The Origins of Indigenism: Human Rights and the Politics of Identity*. Berkeley: University of California Press.
Niezen, R. (2005) 'Digital identity: the construction of virtual selfhood in the indigenous peoples' movement', *Comparative Studies in Society and History* 47(3): 532–51.
Pearson, N. (2009) *Up From the Mission: Selected Writings*, Melbourne: Black Inc.
Weaver, H. (2001) 'Indigenous identity: what is it, and who *really* has it?', *American Indian Quarterly* 25(2): 240–55.
Werther, G.F.A. (1992) *Self-Determination in Western Democracies: Aboriginal Politics in a Comparative Perspective*. Westport, CN, and London: Greenwood Press.
Wolf, E.R. (1982) *Europe and the People Without History*. Berkeley: University of California Press.
Yashar, D.J. (1998) 'Contesting citizenship: indigenous movements and democracy in Latin America', *Comparative Politics* 31(1): 23–42.
Yashar, D.J. (1999) 'Democracy, indigenous movements, and the postliberal challenge in Latin America', *World Politics* 52 (October): 76–104.

21

(Anti-)globalization and resistance identities

Catherine Eschle

Introduction: historical/intellectual development of the literature on (anti-)globalization and resistance identities

'Globalisation' became an academic buzzword at the start of the 1990s and has since garnered enormous scholarly attention. Among many other topics, contributors to the literature on globalisation have explored the implications for the ways in which identities are formed and sustained. For scholars such as Anthony Giddens, Mike Featherstone and Manuel Castells, a world of global flows is seen as posing challenges to older certainties grounded in spatial fixity and clear boundaries between us and them and as conjuring new cultural hybridities, social ontologies, and defensive or reflexive selves. In this context, there has been much debate about 'resistance identities', of varying kinds and in many locations, and their relation to globalisation.

My focus in this chapter is, however, somewhat more specific. Since the 'Battle of Seattle' in 1999, when protestors against the World Trade Organisation succeeded in gaining global media attention and in disrupting business as usual among global elites, resistance against the violences and exclusions associated particularly with the economic dimensions of globalisation, or neo-liberalism, have captured political imaginations worldwide and given rise to a distinct body of literature. Moreover, for many commentators, apparently disparate phenomena such as the Seattle protest and other actions against international financial institutions, the Zapatista uprising in the Chiapas region of Mexico, and discussions of 'other possible worlds' at the World Social Forum in Porto Alegre, Brazil, are all interconnected: part of the most significant social movement to emerge on the world stage in recent years. Thus influential political philosophers Michael Hardt and Antonio Negri write about 'a great movement of the multitude' in their foreword to a collection of essays on the World Social Forum (Hardt and Negri 2003: xvi). Similarly, sociologists Donatella della Porta and Mario Diani (2006) invoke what they describe as 'the global justice movement' as a key exemplar throughout their textbook on social movements. It is this phenomenon, which I follow della Porta and Diani in calling the global justice movement,[1] and the body of work which it has produced and inspired, that I examine in what follows.

Literature on the global justice movement has grown exponentially since the turn of the century and is highly diverse, serving different purposes and speaking to different audiences

(Tormey 2004: 2–4). At least two broad categories can be distinguished. First, activist-oriented commentary writes about and on behalf of the movement, in a partisan, committed way and from an insider standpoint (e.g., Cockburn et al. 2000; Notes from Nowhere 2003). Work in this vein ranges from analyses of the operations of neoliberal globalisation to overviews of the global movement, and from advocacy of political visions and strategies to dispatches from the frontline of protest. Second, although academics have been rather late to the game, a growing scholarly literature now strives to analyse the movement in an ostensibly more objective fashion and from an outsider perspective. Here we have contributions from International Political Economy (e.g., Drainville 2004) and Geography (e.g., Routledge and Cumbers 2009), with perhaps the most sustained theoretical and empirical engagement being undertaken by scholars drawing on sociological social movement theory (e.g., della Porta 2007). Needless to say, the boundary between activist and academic commentary is unstable, with many authors making a conscious effort to bridge the divide (e.g., Reitan 2007; Maeckelbergh 2009). Moreover, it should be acknowledged that neither activist nor academic accounts simply describe the global justice movement, rather both actively participate in its construction (an argument developed at more length in Eschle 2004).

What do these writings have to tell us about identity? Intriguingly, they often position the global justice movement as *post*-identity, or, more specifically, as post-identity-politics. A preoccupation with identity is associated with the 'new social movements' of the 1960s and 1970s and the scholarly paradigm that arose to make sense of them and that emphasised the cultural and symbolic dimension of protest. More recently, it is associated with what is seen as the cooptation and internal fracturing of movements in the 1980s. As Amory Starr puts it:

> identity may no longer be the most important organizing principle for social movements as they embrace multiple oppressions, confront corporations on many fronts at once and recognize allies who cannot be contained by an identity-politics framework.
>
> *(2000: 166)*

More specifically, commentators claim that the global justice movement 'has transcended [the] identity politics' of the 1980s 'by seeking to forge a new internationalism' (Callinicos 2003: 113) and by returning to an emphasis on material struggles and class politics (Burgmann 2005),[2] thus moving beyond a narrow focus on cultural 'representation' (Klein 2000: 107–8). I will suggest later in the chapter that such a characterisation of past and present activism has unfortunate political effects, in terms of narrowing the parameters of our understanding of the global justice movement and sidelining some key voices within it. For now I want to emphasise that we are left with an analytical problem if we abandon the trope of identity altogether – if we conclude with Marianne Maeckelbergh that '[u]nderstanding the alterglobalisation movement no longer rests on the "new social movement" analytical category of "identity" and the exploration of how it is constructed' (2009: 21). I agree with the social movement scholars who argue rather that bringing identity into the picture enables the differentiation of movements from unconnected protest events by drawing our attention to a sense of shared political endeavour over time and space (della Porta and Diani 2006: 20–1). Focusing on identity also offers an alternative to the problems of a reductively rationalist, instrumental ontology which would see movements simply as a response to material incentives and an expression of the convergence of individual interests (Polletta and Jasper 2001: 283–4).

In this chapter, then, I aim to show how arguments about identity developed in social movement theory, in general, have been or could be used to help make sense of the global justice movement, in particular. The next section, entitled 'Identity and the global justice movement:

major claims and developments', begins with a brief review of social movement scholarship on the concept of 'collective identity', before turning to the ways in which this concept has been analysed in the context of struggles for global justice. It has been suggested that there is an intellectual puzzle here, given the extremely heterogeneous character of the movement. In response, I draw attention to arguments about the highly flexible and open-ended ways in which joint action is organised and collective identity developed across ideological difference amongst global justice movement activists, as well as to evidence of the fostering of cohesion through articulation of a common critique of 'the enemy' and confrontation with it. I also examine claims about the ways in which personal and social identities connect to the process of building collective identity within the movement. The subsequent section, entitled 'Criticisms of the global justice movement literature', points to problems with the arguments previously outlined. I sketch out my reservations with the ways in which personal, social and collective identity have been treated by the commentators on the movement. Ultimately, however, I seek to defend the concept of collective identity from its critics. The chapter concludes with a discussion of lines of enquiry for the future.

Identity and the global justice movement: major claims and developments

Collective identity and social movements

For social movement scholars, one of the most crucial concepts needed to make sense of their subject of study is that of *collective identity*. This term remains controversial (see McDonald 2002; Polletta and Jasper 2001), and it has been defined in a wide variety of ways: as 'the process by which social actors recognise themselves – and are recognised by other actors – as part of broader groupings, and develop emotional attachments to them' (della Porta and Diani 2006: 91), for example, or as 'constituted by a shared and interactive sense of "we-ness" and "collective agency"' (Snow 2001: 2). But there are some points of agreement. Notably, collective identity is increasingly approached in processual, interactional terms, with scholars highlighting 'identity work' and the mechanisms through which activists together negotiate and reconstruct a sense of themselves, or develop this sense through interaction with opponents, rather than focusing on identity as a property or thing, the apparently fixed and static claims about a movement presented to the world (Melucci 1996; Glass 2009; cf Snow 2001).[3]

Moreover, it seems to me that there is considerable convergence among analysts around three key features of collective identity formation. The first is a sense of *solidarity*, which I understand here broadly as a sense of affinity with and commitment to others in shared political struggle. In other words, collective identity involves the deliberate construction of a collectivity for political ends. The second key element has to do with *agency*, with much of the literature emphasising that collective identity may be a crucial ingredient enabling collective action – that shared grievances, for example, or access to social and economic capital are not in themselves sufficient – and, moreover, that the relationship may be reversed, that a sense of who we are is produced through acting together (e.g., della Porta and Diani 2006: 93). A third key element, at least for some scholars, is *emotion*, with collective identity conceived as a kind of 'emotional connection with a broader community' (Polletta and Jasper 2001: 285),[4] requiring emotional investment and helping to sustain activists emotionally (e.g., Melucci 1996: 71).

Collective identity understood in these terms is related to, but distinguishable from, other kinds of identity, as David Snow explains. Take *social identity*, for example, a term used widely in sociology to indicate those identities 'grounded typically in established social roles such as "teacher" and "mother" or in broader and more inclusive social categories such as gender categories or ethnic and national categories' (Snow 2001: 2).[5] Social identity is not politicised in all cases, often functioning simply to provide what Snow describes as 'orientational markers' in everyday life. However, it can also function as an important resource in the development of a sense of a collective self involved in social struggle, and it may become animated politically and emotionally in a way that effectively transforms it into the basis of social movement action. Or consider *personal identity*, consisting of 'the attributes and meanings attributed to oneself by the [individual] actor; they are self-designations and self-attributions regarded as personally distinctive' (ibid.: 2). Again, personal identities are not necessarily political in character. Nonetheless, collective identities may be adopted by individuals as 'a highly salient part of their personal identity and sense of self', and considerable analytical attention has been paid to the 'convergence' or 'correspondence' of personal and collective identification processes (ibid.: 3, 7–9). I have laboured the analytical distinctions and connections at work here in order to make it possible to disentangle analyses of personal and social identities in the global justice movement literature. I want first, however, to focus on the ways in which the concept of collective identity can help illuminate this movement.

Collective identity and the global justice movement

Analysts face a particular challenge when exploring the operations of collective identity in a movement that is not only transnational in scale but markedly diverse in its constituent parts. In general, they have emphasised what is seen as a characteristic heterogeneity and fluidity, rather than seeking to mask this in misleading assumptions of coherence.[6] It is notable, for example, that commentators mostly prefer to outline a range of context-specific aspirations, rather than proffering one unified global programme for change. In this vein, see Amory Starr's survey of manifestos (2005: part II), which include proposals for the abolition of national debt, assertions of the common ownership of the genetic building blocks of life, and calls for migrant rights and the abolition of national borders. 'It's astonishing that our diverse struggles, sustained by an array of cultures, buffeted by devastating assaults, have agreed on so much', Starr points out (2005: 45), but the overall effect of her representational strategy is to draw out specificity rather than commonality. Or writers may emphasise the diversity of actors and activities in different times and places, as in the vivid, kaleidoscopic overview provided by Notes from Nowhere (2003), ranging from the Sans Papiers in France to South African struggles against service privatisation, and from guerrilla gardening in the UK to the Argentinian Piqueteros. As Christina Flesher Fominaya sums up, 'the Global Justice Movement encompasses a multiplicity of identities, ideologies, issues, frames, collective action repertoires, and organizational forms' (2010: 377). In the context of this 'movement of movements', then, it seems legitimate to ask whether collective identity is politically feasible – or, indeed, to consider whether it is analytically useful or instead an outdated conceptual tool that should be abandoned (McDonald 2002).

Flesher Fominaya emphasises that the question of how collective identity is forged in the global justice movement is particularly pressing in the context of 'autonomous groups', which she defines in terms of 'their rejection of 'institutional ties to major parties and unions' and their organisation in terms of a 'horizontal network form' (2010: 378). Yet as the empirical research undertaken by Flesher Fominaya and others has shown, horizontal networks should not be seen as a barrier to collective identity but rather as a key element in its construction. I suggest we can analyse what is going on here in terms of a 'mode of action', or set of political practices underpinned by a coherent, normatively driven rationale (see Eschle and Maiguashca

2010: 185–6). Central to the 'identity work' of many within the global justice movement, the horizontal mode of action is built on the assumption of the inextricability of means and ends. In this it is influenced by anarchism, although not limited to self-described anarchists (Graeber 2002). Horizontal organising demands not only the flattening of hierarchies within groups in contradistinction to what are perceived as more 'vertical' structures, but also the fostering of open-ended, fluid and egalitarian relations between groups, in which decisions are made through discussion. Moreover, in sharp distinction to a majoritarian and representational politics, no one is entitled to speak for anyone else and each individual or group is free not to participate in actions they have refused to endorse or to organise their own initiatives. Marianne Maeckelbergh sums it up thus:

> The structural model being suggested in the democratic praxis of the alterglobalisation movement is not a liberal democratic model of representative democracy but rather a decentralised model based on collective and divisible agents who make decision through consensus . . . [This is] a form of democracy that rejects all formal and fixed representation . . . Through decentralisation and connectivity, decisions that affect an entire network of people can, in principle, be discussed at every node of that network and then decided through communication between nodes.
>
> *(2009: 225)*

As Flesher Fominaya shows in her ethnography of assemblies in Madrid, organising techniques in this vein are variably applied and can generate tension and the collapse of groups or inter-group projects as well as enabling agreement and joint action. Maeckelbergh agrees, acknowledging that 'this democratic model is far from perfect and is riddled with problems and inconsistencies at almost every turn' (2009: 225). It is certainly not uncontested within the movement, with many arguing for and practising more vertical and representational organising strategies. Nonetheless, from efforts to create 'open space' at the World Social Forum to the fluid organisation of different coloured 'blocs' at street protests, a preoccupation with organising according to principles of horizontality and autonomy is extensive. I am suggesting here that it constitutes one of the key ways in which a distinctive collective identity encompassing differences is constructed within the global justice movement.

Another way this is done is charted in the work of Donatella della Porta on 'tolerant' or 'flexible' identities in operation at the European Social Forum (2005: 186). If Flesher Fominaya and others direct us towards horizontal organising processes as one form of identity work predicated on openness and respecting diversity, della Porta's analysis indicates a similar principled flexibility with regard to the way in which ideological affinities and associational memberships are called into play. Specifically, she points to the high 'associational density' of the movement – the fact that participants are involved, and have often long been involved, in innumerable organisations from political traditions that opposed each other in the past. Activists navigate such complex movement terrain by valuing 'diversity' and 'inclusiveness'; showing a willingness to be 'contaminated' by the ideas and values of others; and focusing on 'limited identifications' around 'concrete initiatives' rather than expecting sustained collaboration around long term, abstract goals (della Porta 2005: 186–9). In this way, activists within the global justice movement seek to avoid what della Porta calls 'ideologism' (ibid.: 196), which I understand as a dogmatic attachment to specific ideological traditions (to a particular brand of Marxism, for example), functioning to narrow down group parameters and to build boundary walls between one group and another. The end result is a movement identity founded on the acknowledgement of difference:

At the cost of leaving margins of ambiguity as to the movement's proposals . . . the development of a collective identity that is 'open' and many-faceted makes it possible to hold together very different spirits, in part combining them, however gradually, and producing a high degree of identification among activists and sympathizers.

(ibid.: 200)

My own fieldwork with Bice Maiguashca on feminist organisations within the global justice movement strongly supports della Porta's arguments on this point. We found that feminist 'anti-globalisation' activists at the European and World Social Forums in Paris, Mumbai, London and Porto Alegre attach a normative value to the diversity of identities among activists – by being open to national variations in what it means to be feminist, for example, or by recognising and seeking to accommodate diverse ideological attachments amongst themselves. We also documented a marked drive amongst our activists to connect with others within and beyond feminist groups. Indeed, we were struck by the prevalence of the practice of networking, or articulation as our Brazilian interviewees called it, and by the extensiveness of the bonds between feminist 'anti-globalisation' groups and others, ranging from peace organisations to economic justice campaigns. In this context, like della Porta, we noted a certain flexibility in the mobilisation of ideological categories with activists declaring they would elaborate on the category of feminist in different ways depending on who they were talking to and even that they were wary of labelling themselves at all in case that proved a barrier in the effort to construct solidarity with others around shared goals (Eschle and Maiguashca 2010: ch. 8).

Taken together with the argument about a horizontal mode of action, these claims about the ways in which ideological and associational affinities are mobilised indicate the centrality of identity work in the global justice movement which acknowledges, navigates and even facilitates differences amongst those involved. It is ultimately, then, an error to puzzle over how collective identity is constructed in the global justice movement despite such extraordinary diversity among its constituent parts, when that diversity is consciously considered by participants to be at the heart of what gives the movement its distinctive character.

Having said that, diversity in the movement is not entirely unbounded, nor are identity construction processes without centripetal dynamics, and it is to the erection of boundaries and the building of bridges that I now turn. There are at least two identity construction processes of this kind visible in commentary on the global justice movement. The first can be seen in the clear convergence around the perception that movement activists share, in general terms, a critique of the current world order. As Paul Kingsnorth puts it (2003), this is a movement of 'one no, many yeses'. In this regard, it is notable that the literature on the movement does not simply function as a record of the views of activists, but, as a key site where critiques are elaborated and substantiated, contributes to the crystallisation and articulation of such views. In more concrete terms, by far the majority of commentators characterise 'the enemy' in terms of what William Ponniah and Thomas Fisher call 'corporate capitalism' or 'neoliberal globalisation':[7]

The perception is that corporate dominion has been organised across global space by the most powerful Northern states in the world, in collaboration with Southern economic and political elites. . . . Neoliberal globalization is not simply economic dominion of the world but also the imposition of a monolithic thought (*pensamiento unico*)[8] . . . the key instruments of contemporary globalization are the free trade agreements and policies propelled by the WTO, the North American Free Trade Agreement . . . and other regional trade agreements, and the privatisation policies of corporations, the G8 countries, the World Bank and the IMF.

(2003: 10–11)

Catherine Eschle

Along these lines, neoliberal globalisation is understood as a recently emergent system, one which has been consciously pursued by state and economic elites, and which has become both socially pervasive and global in scope (see, e.g., Starr 2000: ch. 1, 150–1). Accounts of the detrimental impacts of this system may then range from economic inequality and deprivation to political powerlessness and exclusion, and from ecological degradation to cultural imperialism and violence, but the point remains that these are not presented as a shopping list of disparate factors but rather as the effects of a coherent, structured process shaping the world today (see discussion in Eschle and Maiguashca 2010: ch. 5). It is this shared characterisation of 'the enemy', I suggest, that functions to draw ideological parameters around the global justice movement itself, shaping priorities for change and lending credence to della Porta's argument that the movement has a 'clearly left wing profile' (2005: 192).[9]

The second set of processes through which boundaries and affinities are constructed in the global justice movement is closely related, and has to do with the ways in which activists and commentators make sense of actual encounters with 'the enemy' on the ground. In this regard, it is pertinent to note the overwhelming emphasis in the literature on protest. Indeed it could be argued that 'disruptive' modes of protest, and large-scale protest 'events' – particularly those taking place in northern, urban centres and directed against the institutions most associated with neoliberal policies such as the World Trade Organisation and the G8 – are widely seen as synonymous with and defining of the movement (see, e.g., Starr 2005). Relatedly, an iconography and aesthetics of protest threads through the literature, most obviously in the form of photographs emphasising the vulnerability and courage of activists, and the creativity involved in their costumes and props, in the face of anonymous, brutal-looking, massed ranks of police (see, for example, Cockburn et al. 2000; Notes from Notes from Nowhere 2003). Other widespread elements of this iconography include the use made of the words and images of the Zapatistas (e.g., Kingsnorth 2003: ch. 1) and the transmogrification of victims of confrontation, such as Carlo Guiliani, shot dead by police in Genoa, into martyrs of the movement. As one writer puts it, 'We are all Carlo' (Collins 2004: 138). Social movement scholarship would lead us to expect that these elements in the representation of the global justice movement function not only to differentiate activists from their opponent/s, but also to bind the movement together, with a shared language, repetitious imagery and common cultural references providing the glue for a collective identity apparently forged in the white heat of confrontation. As we will see, there is a marked continuity here with arguments about the transformation of identity at the individual level.

Personal and social identities in the global justice movement

I explained above that social movement scholars have sought to differentiate collective identity from personal and social identity as conceptual categories, partly in order then to be able to study empirically the interrelationships between all three. Personal identity, and particularly the ways in which transformations in it bring an individual into collective action and help sustain that commitment over time, has been the particular focus of more social psychological approaches, and the literature on the global justice movement is no exception. In line with the emphasis on protest as defining of movement identity, research along these lines has examined pre-existing critical orientations to social hierarchy as predictors of involvement in different types of protest action (Cameron and Nickerson 2009). Subsequent linkages between the mobilisation of individuals in local protests and the processes by which they come to identify with a broader movement have also been analysed – on this, the impact of confrontation with authorities appears particularly key (e.g., Drury et al. 2003) – as have the reasons why individuals might feel personally empowered after a protest event and committed to further involvement (e.g., Barr and Drury 2009). On this last point, it seems that experienced activists are more likely to be able to (re)interpret the goals and impact of protest in a positive light and that collective discussion of an action in public space is very important to ensure the continued motivation of the less experienced (ibid.: 251–5).

I also want to mention here the very different work of Kevin McDonald (2002), which draws more on social theory to make sense of individual subjectivities within the movement. McDonald draws attention to the ways in which activists seek to find themselves and experience a kind of personal freedom through participation in the kind of loose affinity groups and non-representational politics described by Fominaya. This process should not be understood as a retreat to bourgeois individualism for McDonald, who emphasises that it is not explicable in terms of a rational actor model whereby the individual learns to articulate and pursue predefined interests. Nor is it reducible, in his view, to the process of identification with a collectivity. Rather, McDonald emphasises sensuous, embodied and interrelational ways of 'finding your place' (ibid.: 121) in the ephemeral protest contexts of the global justice movement, drawing particular attention to forms of action such as puppetry and music that transcend not only the discursive, but also intentional and representational modes of politics (ibid.: 123–4).

In comparison to personal identity, social identities in the global justice movement have received more limited attention. Della Porta touches on them with her discussion of the heterogeneous 'social bases' of collective action (2005). Arguing that participants in the global justice movement come from a surprisingly wide range of social backgrounds, della Porta draws attention to the high level of involvement of women and youth, the participation of 'new' middle classes as well as 'labour' more traditionally defined (as evidenced in the role of unions), and to those motivated by religion. While her analysis goes some way to confirming a resource mobilisation model by which individual access to economic and social capital is believed to be a key predicator of action, it more centrally stresses the role of prior mobilisation associated with these social groupings as a predictor of involvement in the movement (della Porta 2005: 180–6). Concluding with an emphasis on the relationship between pre-existing 'associational density' and the 'tolerant identities' constructed in the global justice movement, as explored previously, della Porta's discussion also hints at the prior and ongoing mobilisation of social identities in this context. This impression is reinforced by references in the wider literature, if rather fleeting, to nationalist identifications among activists and by more extensive discussions of indigenous identity, particularly with regard to the Zapatistas (e.g., Kingsnorth 2003: ch. 1). Nonetheless, analysis of social identity in the global justice movement remains limited overall, as will be discussed in the next section, along with connected problems in the analysis of personal and collective identity.

Criticisms of the global justice movement literature

My initial criticism of the global justice movement literature, then, has to do with the treatment of social identities within it. There is a lack of sustained attention to such identities in this movement context, along with a tendency to reduce them to the pre-political 'bases' of action, which are in my view problematic. My research with Bice Maiguashca has revealed that social identities such as 'woman', 'Black', 'lesbian' and 'Muslim', along with conjunctural combinations of these, are politicised before *and during* mobilisation in the global justice movement, serving both to precipitate and sustain individual involvement and to demarcate distinct collective actors in the form of autonomous organisations. For instance, gendered marginalisations and exclusions in groups and activities associated with the movement have precipitated a new wave of women-only spaces, in which younger women, in particular, are coming to a feminist analysis for the first time and which many of our interviewees robustly defended as a necessary element in the struggle for other possible worlds (Eschle and Maiguashca 2010: 73–4, see also 156–63).

Part of the reason why such groups organising around social identities have not been widely acknowledged or fully studied within the global justice movement literature, I suggest, is the tendency to position associated mobilisation as 'post-identity', and more particularly as 'post-identity-politics', as outlined at the outset of the chapter. When global justice movement commentators invoke the identity-politics of the 1980s, now transcended, they seek to juxtapose a past model of organising on the basis of social identities such as gender, race and sexuality, with what they see as the more inclusive and more materialist politics of the new wave of activism. But I would suggest that there are at least two problems with this move. First, it relies on stereotyped generalisations about the mobilisation of social identities in political contexts. As philosopher Linda Martín Alcoff has argued, leftist political commentary has long characterised identity politics as separatist in orientation, as reifying or fixing identities, and as partisan and solipsistic, incapable of speaking beyond a particular subject position. Moreover, identity-politics is seen as concerned with a politics of representation and symbols rather than with material interests of social justice.[10] Now, I do not doubt there are some instances where social identities have been mobilised in separatist, essentialist and solipsistic ways, detached from claims for social justice and seeking only to defend a particular subject position for its own sake. Such an 'identitarian' move echoes the 'ideologism' alluded to by della Porta in erecting boundaries between groups and preventing wider coalition-building. Yet this should not be regarded as inevitable in the mobilisation of social identities. Indeed, as Alcoff and others such as Iris Marion Young have argued forcefully, much of so-called identity-politics involves groups which face structural discrimination seeking to articulate and negotiate shifting and complex subject positions and to engage with others as equals in a broader politics of social justice.

My work with Maiguashca on feminist activism in the global justice movement reinforces this point. The many women-only groups we investigated during our research may mobilise social identities, but they rarely rely on fixed and unitary categories, as my discussion above already indicates. 'Women' as a category has in some cases been politicised during, rather than prior to, global justice movement struggles, and it has also been complicated and fractured by widespread efforts to investigate and accommodate conjunctural identities combining gender with class, race, religious and other identifiers. In addition, these women-only groups may organise separately, but they are not 'separatist'. Rather, they seek to develop durable, multiple connections with others in the global justice movement – which is why, of course, they were at the World Social Forum in the first place. In this way our interviewees avoid not only ideologism, but also the elements of the identitarian stance so feared by critics of identity-politics. Assumptions about how social identities are mobilised and to what political effect therefore need careful checking against specific empirical instances, including in global justice movement contexts.[11]

Second, the juxtaposition of the identity-politics of the past to the more inclusive and materialist politics of the present implies that the interlocking axes of oppression contested by members of women's groups, racialised and ethnic minorities, gays, lesbians and transsexuals continue to organise to contest have been transcended, at least within global justice movement circles. This can be seen, for example, in Maeckelbergh's thoughtful analysis of why what she calls the alterglobalisation movement is 'overcoming identity politics'. She argues that the movement in effect builds on the achievements of past identity-based organising while avoiding its pitfalls:

The respect shown between movement actors for each person '*as* different' is a necessary prerequisite for the functioning of the alterglobalisation movement . . . Without the fights waged around gender, race, ethnicity and sexuality over the past 30 years, the 'anti-oppression' principles of most alterglobalisation movement spaces would not exist. Today meetings between many different groups and actors are possible because structural discriminations *have been* recognised, and meeting structures are put in place to limit them, but it is no longer 'identity politics' because some shared identity is not the basis upon which . . . movement actors are demanding recognition. Rather than insisting the movement should focus on the WTO because it is the quickest means of achieving women's liberation, the fight against the WTO is carried out *while* incorporating an awareness of the power hierarchies that exclude women.

(2009: 20, emphasis in original)

Maeckelbergh is careful to indicate that patriarchal power hierarchies are still embedded within neoliberalism and should be challenged by the global justice movement. Yet she also characterises the movement as itself devoid of these hierarchies, as predicated upon their successful erasure among movement participants. Such a picture is likely to be contested by feminist 'anti-globalisation' activists. Our book presented considerable evidence that the global justice movement (like all social movements) is itself stratified by the multiple, complex relations of oppression it seeks to transform and that feminist groups active at the World Social Forum are fighting on many fronts: to counter the dominance of elite men and masculine styles in the organising processes of the Forum and in key events; to contest gender-blind characterisations of 'the enemy' and of social change; and to end incidences of sexual harassment. Organising as women and in women-only spaces has been a vital part of these efforts. Arguably, the overall point of all this is not to achieve women's representation in the World Social Forum for its own sake, but rather to ensure the integration of gender into the critiques and alternatives of the global justice movement. So Maeckelbergh may be onto something with her insistence that representational logics are not an end in themselves in this movement. Her overly sharp distinction between current activism and identity-politics, however, functions to obscure the ongoing struggles around diverse categories of oppression that are still to be found within contemporary mobilisation.

Turning to the treatment of personal identity in the global justice movement literature, it seems to me there is an issue about the overweening emphasis on protest, and particularly disruptive or law-breaking modes of protest. Such an emphasis reflects analytical tendencies within social movement theory more generally, as well as within dominant narratives of the global justice movement. As Maiguashca and I have argued, overall this has resulted in a lack of empirical attention to other types of activities present within the movement and consequently an analytical failure to get to grips with the range of political practices undertaken on the ground (Eschle and Maiguashca 2010: 184). Here I want to make the more specific point that focusing on protest narrows understanding of the processes by which individual activist subjectivities are mobilised, created and sustained. Notably, some versions of social movement theory, particularly that inspired by the work of Alberto Melucci, draw attention to the submerged networks that sustain activism in a more 'latent' or 'subterranean' form in between protest events (e.g., Polletta and Jasper 2001: 288; della Porta and Diani 2006: 95–6). Taking on board this dimension of global justice movement activity requires us to enquire into the ways in which personal identities are interwoven with collective identity mechanisms in interpersonal interactions, in cultural events, and in the ongoing maintenance of movement groups. Relatedly, we might investigate the connection between the 'hidden transcripts' of resistance to globalised neoliberalism in everyday life, charted by anthropologists such as James C. Scott and the mobilisation of individuals within the global justice movement. Or what about the more institutionalised forms of the movement, such as the international feminist non-governmental organisations and coordinating networks which were part of the picture in my study with Maiguashca? How do activist subjectivities shift within and between bureaucracies, and when moving between institutional and protest environments? Such questions barely register as yet on the radar of a movement literature which continues to see large-scale, disruptive protest events as defining of its subject matter.

With regard to collective identity, the focus on protest can be seen as problematic here too, limiting analysis of the ways and contexts in which a shared sense of a common political undertaking is constructed in the global justice movement. Flesher Fominaya, for one, insists on the need for further attention to the local assemblies which are the subject of her own research. These are political spaces in which a loose coalition of individuals and groups active on a particular issue get together at regular intervals to plan joint actions. Emphasising their participatory and deliberative character, Flesher Fominaya suggests these assemblies act as 'feedback loops' between 'latent arenas of social interaction' and more public, goal-oriented activities (2010: 397). And she reaches wider conclusions about the implications of this for the theorisation of collective identity in the global justice movement:

> the process of collective identity should not be confused with the 'collective identity product' or visible publicly projected identity of the movement. Visible mobilizations are only one arena in which collective identity formation takes place. Studying collective identity formation as process allows one to reveal the tensions, contradictions, and negotiations in the latent moments that generate the seeming 'unity' of movement in its visible moments of protest or confrontation.
>
> *(ibid.: 398)*

In sum, this is an argument for expanding our study of collective identity in the global justice movement beyond the protest events that have garnered so much attention from both participants and observers.

In contrast, McDonald argues for abandoning entirely this area of research, proposing instead that efforts to make sense of 'globalization conflicts' should focus on the 'public experience of self' (2002: 109–11, 114, 125). McDonald is concerned that structural shifts in a globalising world have transformed social relations and political responses in fundamental ways. Consequently 'it is the increasingly problematic status of individual experience . . . in network society, and not the mechanisms involved in mobilizing collective identity in relation to the political system, that needs to be at the centre of analysis' (ibid.: 114). As described above, his effort to produce such an analysis of global justice movement contexts (among others) is highly suggestive, particularly with regard to the sensual, embodied and interrelational character of individual subjectivities as experienced within the movement. Nonetheless, the claim that we should forsake the trope of collective identity altogether is, in my view, not convincing. McDonald's analysis is reliant largely on fleeting protest events – and indeed strongly emphasises the ephemeral or biodegradable aspects of affinity groups and collective projects in this context. Yet this is to ignore those groups and networks which have a more durable character, as well as the ongoing subterranean relationships that connect activists between protests. It is also to overstate the cohesion or the degree of solidarity assumed by proponents of the collective identity trope: as I have tried to demonstrate, plenty of research on the global justice movement seeks to put the diversity of participants at the heart of our understanding of the movement's shared identity rather than imposing a false unity or lamenting its absence. Finally, it seems to me that McDonald is arguing for a shift in our level of analysis of the global justice movement, from collective to personal identity. I propose, in contrast, that attention to both, and to their interplay, is still required. The global justice movement, after all, is more than the expression of multiple individual wills to freedom: it is a collective undertaking to change the very parameters within which individual freedom can be pursued.

Conclusion: future lines of enquiry

This chapter has taken a very particular cut into the question of '(anti-)globalization and resistance identities'. Drawing on social movement theorising about collective identity, I have focused on the processes through which such identities have been constructed in the global justice movement. On the one hand, literature on that movement emphasises that autonomous and horizontal principles of organising, along with tolerance of ideological difference, have contributed to an identity construction process which has diversity at its heart. On the other hand, the literature has developed analyses of a common enemy, and participated in the circulation of symbols and mythology about confrontation with that enemy in protest contexts, that together have helped to bind diverse groups in a common political project. I then discussed arguments in the field about the transformation of personal identities through protest and the mobilisation of pre-existing social identities, before exploring some of the limitations in the conceptualisation of each of these kinds of identities in the literature thus far. I closed the body of the chapter by defending from its critics the trope of collective identity as still of utility where the global justice movement is concerned.

I want in this conclusion to offer some speculations about future developments in analyses of this movement. For this, I return to the broad consensus around collective identity emerging in social movement theory and elaborated at the outset of the chapter. This consensus, I argued, has three conceptual pillars: solidarity, agency and emotion. I will now show that there is plenty of scope for further work on all three of these dimensions of collective identity in the context of the global justice movement.

To begin with, the relationship between solidarity and collective identity needs further empirical and conceptual unpacking. Such work has already begun. Peter Waterman (1998: 235–8) has long advocated the need to revise and complicate old understandings of solidarity in the light of the new movement context. This analysis has been echoed by Ruth Reitan in her more recent effort to construct a typology of solidarity in the movement based on how individuals become politicised (2007: 51–6). Both scholars distinguish several forms or mechanisms of solidarity at work, of which identity is only one (the others include altruism, reciprocity, substitution, complementarity, affinity and restitution). Yet there is a danger in these formulations of equating identity with a claim of sameness or 'exclusion of unalikes' (Waterman 1998: 235),[12] when we know this is not necessarily the case for the mobilisation of collective identity claims in the context of the global justice movement. In addition, further empirical study would reveal, I suspect, that boundaries between the different types of solidarity distinguished by these authors are porous and context-dependent. In sum, the effort to distinguish different solidarity dynamics is to be lauded, but there is scope for further work on this point. Moreover, the concept of *fluidarity*, invoked by McDonald as an alternative to what he sees as static and bureaucratic processes of solidarity-building (2002: 124), is deserving of further investigation. Indeed, the language of 'fluidifying' has been documented in some quarters of the movement, indicating an openness to others' viewpoints and a consequent slipperiness and instability in collective identity processes (della Porta 2005: 187). This language might perhaps offer a way forward for reframing the

375

relationship between identity and solidarity, one allowing for a fuller understanding of how both work in a particularly heterogeneous, fast-moving transnational movement context.

As for agency and collective identity, I have already implied that there is a need to expand our understanding of the kinds of agency found in the movement. As argued above, I see a pressing need to look 'beyond protest' in order to develop a more holistic, complex understanding of the relationship between the individual, the group and political practice. Here I want to point to the fact that, in addition, the sequential relationship between agency and identity need attention. It is too often emphasised in the literature on social movements that the formation of a collective identity is a necessary precursor to action, even as there are hints at the fact that action can produce identity. Taking the latter position seriously raises two sets of questions about the global justice movement. The first is suggested by Flesher Fominaya's argument that the *failure* of collective actions can contribute to the 'strengthening of movement collective identity through building up a shared history of having weathered difficulties together' (2010: 399). This analysis finds an intriguing echo in the social psychological literature in the preoccupation with how individuals maintain their commitment despite the fact that actions often do not achieve their tactical goals (Barr and Drury 2009). So how is it that even ostensibly unsuccessful movement outcomes can contribute to the successful construction of collective identities?

The second set of questions stems from my argument about the horizontal mode of action as a key way in which diverse identities are parlayed into a collective self-understanding in the global justice movement. Are there other modes of action which similarly shape collective identity formation? In this connection, the emphasis on surrealism and carnivalesque techniques of protest, widely found within the movement and its commentary, is highly suggestive. Ranging from parades of giant puppets, as described by McDonald, to parodical protests such as those by apparent business people aiming to save capitalism, to the slapstick activities of the Clandestine Insurgent Rebel Clown Army, this mode of action is based on a 'methodology' which refuses dichotomies between 'the personal and the political . . . activist and non-activist', and is oriented to 'transforming and sustaining the inner emotional life of . . . activists' (Klepto and Up Evil 2005: 244–5, 247). In what ways, then, does this mode of action help to forge a correspondence between personal and collective identities? In what ways does its humorous and subversive mediation of the relationship the movement and those with which it is in confrontation reforge activist understandings of self and other?

This brings me finally to the issue of the relationship between emotion and collective identity. On this point, there are widespread references in the literature to the importance of anger, rage and fury as passions driving involvement in, and presumably identification with, the global justice movement. However, as Maiguashca and I have argued, there is a need for a more nuanced understanding of the range of emotions involved in motivating global justice movement activists and of the ways in which emotional triggers are intertwined with and feed into cognitive processes (Eschle and Maiguashca 2010: 176). In relation to this, Flesher Fominaya has again blazed a trail in her analysis of the role of humour in collective identity construction (2007). She uncovers several facets to this role in the context of autonomous groups in Madrid, including the mobilisation of jokes to construct boundaries between insiders and outsides, their use to defuse tensions within groups, and the connection of wit to charismatic leadership. As Flesher Fominaya concludes, '[p]aying attention to humour and to emotions in general can help explain the emergence and trajectories of social movement groups', especially in the context of the global justice movement where the imposition of a unified ideological identity is refused (2007: 257). I would add that the prominence of a carnivalesque mode of action in the movement, as described above, encourages the view that further exploration of the implications of humour and play in this context could yield very rich results for our understanding of collective identity processes.

Notes

1 Many thanks to Christina Flesher Fominaya for sending me her articles and for her supportive and perceptive comments on the first draft of this chapter. I look forward to continuing our discussion. Thanks also to Bice Maiguashca for allowing me to draw on our joint book *Making Feminist Sense of the Global Justice Movement* and for sparking and contesting many of the ideas that I continue to develop here. The faults that remain are of course entirely my own responsibility.

   There is continuing disagreement about what the movement should be called. The 'anti-globalisation' label became widespread after the Seattle demonstration, apparently 'a coinage of the US media' (Graeber 2002: 63). The term has always been strongly contested by activists as overly negative and falsely implying an isolationist, parochial and protectionist orientation. Many activists prefer to describe the movement in which they participate as 'anti-neoliberal', 'anti-capitalist' or 'anti-economic globalisation', although the term 'anti-globalisation' still functions as a useful shorthand or codeword in much of the literature. Efforts to formulate a more accurate and more aspirational appellation include the 'global democracy movement', 'globalisation from below' and the 'global justice movement', with the latter becoming particularly widespread in Anglophone academic circles in recent years (e.g., della Porta 2007).

2 Verity Burgmann offers a slightly different take on this by claiming that the global justice movement 'could be interpreted as identity politics based upon class or at least upon socioeconomic disadvantage' (2005: 12). In other words, she is arguing that the movement expands our understanding of what 'counts' as identity politics rather than seeing it as abandoning the terrain of identity altogether. However, she also relies upon a distinction between identity-politics more narrowly understood and a more materialist and class-based politics to make her argument (see the comments by critics in the symposium that follows Burgmann's paper). Burgmann insists that, in expanding identity to encompass class, the movement in effect 'is an identity politics to end identity politics' (ibid.: 12).

3 This emphasis on identity as process problematises the distinction drawn by Marianne Maeckelbergh between what she characterises as an analysis of the *category* of identity, typical of new social movement theory, and a focus on '*process* – where process is a practice, a fluid action, an ongoing activity', which she thinks more suitable for research on the global justice movement (Maeckelbergh 2009: 21, emphasis in original).

4 Note that Polletta and Jasper are critical of the 'overextension' of the concept of collective identity, preferring a narrower definition in terms of 'an individual's cognitive, moral, and emotional connection with a broader community, category, practice, or institution' (2001: 285). They insist this is analytically separable from the concept of personal identity, but I find the shift to the level of the individual rather unhelpful in this regard. I also disagree with their effort to differentiate ideology from identity, as it seems to me that the ways in which ideology is mobilised in the identity claims of activists is a particularly interesting avenue of enquiry, particularly in global justice movement contexts.

5 There is a potential confusion on this point, with social psychological approaches to social movements using the term *social identity* in the same way as others use the term *collective identity*, or even invoking the two interchangeably (see, e.g., Cameron and Nickerson 2009).

6 Hence the popular moniker 'movement of movements'.

7 Note also that there is a significant strand of analysis among commentators and activists which prefers to characterise the problem in terms of continuities in the underlying system of capitalism (e.g., Callinicos 2003: 26; Tormey 2004). My research with Maiguashca on feminists in the movement also found this view, but a focus on the specific neoliberal formation of contemporary capitalism was substantially more prevalent (see Eschle and Maiguashca 2010: 86).

8 There seems to be no direct equivalent for this phrase in English. Perhaps the nearest we have is Margaret Thatcher's infamous TINA phrase 'There Is No Alternative'.

9 Although a handful of commentators have drawn attention to the existence of a right-wing, populist 'anti-globalisation' position (e.g., Starr 2000: 136–44), by far the bulk of the literature on the global justice movement does not include such elements in its characterisation of its subject matter.

10 See www.alcoff.com/content/afraidid.html. I should perhaps clarify that leftist anxiety around identity-politics gains much of its force from an implicit dichotomous juxtaposition of organising on the basis of social identities with class-based politics. This functions not only to obscure the economic

dimension of claims contesting discrimination on the basis of gender, race and sexuality but also to neglect the cultural and identity elements of class-based politics, see the symposium in *International Labor and Working Class History* following Burgmann 2005. This symposium also points to the very tangled and complicated class politics at work in the global justice movement, making it difficult to depict that movement straightforwardly in terms of a revival of a politics of class.

11 While accepting that social identities as a category may be overly neglected by analysts of the global justice movement, Flesher Fominaya suggests that activists in Western European movement contexts, particularly those associated with anti-capitalist and autonomous politics, see themselves not so much as post-identity as anti-identitarian, which she defines in terms of a rejection of shopping list, single-issue politics. As part of this, they are hostile to organising on the basis of discrete social identities. Such organising, Flesher Fominaya further suggests, may be more prevalent or important in global justice movement contexts beyond Western Europe (personal correspondence with author). The women's groups I describe above, however, were tracked by Maiguashca and myself in France and the UK as well as in Brazil and India. Moreover, I am arguing that these groups mobilise social identities but are non-identitarian in character. Nonetheless, I take the point that further investigation of social identities in the global justice movement will need to pay very close attention to the specificities of the highly diverse geopolitical and ideological terrains in which that movement operates.

12 Alcoff has indicated that this is a widespread usage of the concept of identity in scholarly literature but one which departs from both common-sense understandings and its mobilisation in social movements (see www.alcoff.com/content/afraidid.html).

References

Barr, Dermott and Drury, John (2009) 'Activist identity as a motivational resource: dynamics of (dis)empowerment at the G8 Direct Actions, Gleneagles, (2005)', *Social Movement Studies* 8(3): 243–60.

Burgmann, Verity (2005) 'From syndicalism to Seattle: class and the politics of identity', *International Labor and Working-Class History* 67: 1–21.

Callinicos, Alex (2003) *An Anti-Capitalist Manifesto*. Cambridge: Polity Press.

Cameron, James E. and Nickerson, Shannon L. (2009) 'Predictors of protest among anti-globalization demonstrators', *Journal of Applied Social Psychology* 39(3): 734–61.

Cockburn, Alexander, St Clair, Jeffrey and Sekula, Allan (2000) *Five Days that Shook the World: Seattle and Beyond*. London: Verso.

Collins, Thatcher (2004) 'A protestography', in Yuen, E., Burton-Rose, D. and Katsiaficas, G. (eds) *Confronting Capitalism: Dispatches from a Global Movement*, pp. xxxiv–vlviii. Brooklyn: Soft Skull Press.

Della Porta, Donatella (2005) 'Multiple belongings, tolerant identities and the construction of "another politics": between the European social forum and the local social fora', in Della Porta, D. and Tarrow, S. (eds) *Transnational Protest and Global Activism*, pp. 175–202. Lanham, MD: Rowman and Littlefield.

Della Porta, Donatella (ed.) (2007) *The Global Justice Movement: Cross National and Transnational Perspectives*. Boulder, CO: Paradigm.

Della Porta, Donatella and Diani, Mario (2006) *Social Movements: An Introduction*. Oxford: Blackwell.

Drainville, Andre (2004) *Contesting Globalization: Space and Place in the World Economy*. London: Routledge.

Drury, John, Reicher, Steve and Stott, Clifford (2003) 'Transforming the boundaries of collective identity: from the "local" anti-road campaign to "global" resistance', *Social Movement Studies* 2(2): 191–212.

Eschle, Catherine (2004) 'Constructing "the anti-globalisation movement"', *International Journal of Peace Studies* 9(1): 61–84.

Eschle, Catherine and Maiguashca, Bice (2010) *Making Feminist Sense of the Global Justice Movement*. Lanham, MD: Rowman and Littlefield.

Flesher Fominaya, Christina. (2007) 'The role of humour in the process of collective identity formation in autonomous social movement groups in contemporary Madrid', *International Review of Social History* 52 (Supplement S15): 243–58.

Flesher Fominaya, Christina (2010) 'Creating cohesion from diversity: the challenge of collective identity formation in the global justice movement', *Sociological Inquiry* 80(3): 377–404.

Glass, Pepper, G. (2009) 'Unmaking a movement: identity work and the outcomes of Zapatista Community Centers in Los Angeles', *Journal of Contemporary Ethnography* 38(5): 523–46.

Graeber, David (2002) 'The new anarchists', *New Left Review* 13: 61–73.

Hardt, Michael and Negri, Antonio (2003) 'Foreword', in Fisher, W.F. and Ponniah, T. (eds) *Another World is Possible: Popular Alternatives to Globalization at the World Social Forum.* Nova Scotia and London: Fernwood and Zed Books.

Kingsnorth, Paul (2003) *One No, Many Yeses: A Journey to the Heart of the Global Resistance Movement.* London: Free Press.

Klein, Naomi (2000) *No Logo.* London: Flamingo.

Klepto, Kolonel and Up Evil, Major (2005) 'The Clandestine Insurgent Rebel Clown Army goes to Scotland via a few other places', in Harvie, D., Milburn, K., Trott, B. and Watts, D. (eds) *Shut Them Down! The G8, Gleneagles 2005 and the Movement of Movements,* pp. 243–54. London: Dissent and Autonomedia.

Maeckelbergh, Marianne (2009) *The Will of the Many: How the Alterglobalisation Movement is Changing the Face of Democracy.* London: Pluto Press.

McDonald, Kevin (2002) 'From solidarity to fluidarity: social movements beyond "collective identity" – the case of globalization conflicts', *Social Movement Studies* 1(2): 109–28.

Melucci, Alberto (1996) *Challenging Codes: Collective Action in the Information Age.* Cambridge: Cambridge University Press.

Notes from Nowhere (2003) *We are Everywhere: The Irresistable Rise of Anti-Capitalism.* London: Verso.

Polletta, Francesca and Jasper, James M. (2001) 'Collective identity and social movements', *Annual Review of Sociology* (27): 283–305.

Ponniah, Thomas and Fisher, William F. (2003) 'Introduction: the World Social Forum and the reinvention of democracy', in Fisher, W.F. and Ponniah, T. (eds) *Another World is Possible: Popular Alternatives to Globalization at the World Social Forum,* pp. 1–20. London: Zed Books.

Reitan, Ruth (2007) *Global Activism.* London: Routledge.

Routledge, Paul and Cumbers, Andrew (2009) *Global Justice Networks: Geographies of Transnational Solidarity.* Manchester: Manchester University Press.

Snow, David (2001) 'Collective identity and expressive forms', *UC Irvine, Center for the Study of Democracy.* Online: www.escholarship.org/uc/item/2zn1t7bj (accessed 13 January 2010).

Starr, Amory (2000) *Naming the Enemy: Anti-Corporate Movements Confront Globalization.* London: Zed Books.

Starr, Amory (2005) *Global Revolt: A Guide to the Movements Against Globalisation.* London: Zed Books.

Tormey, Simon (2004) *Anti-Capitalism: A Beginners Guide.* Oxford: One World.

Waterman, Peter (1998) *Globalization, Social Movements and the New Internationalisms.* London and Washington: Mansell.

22

Identity-politics in the global age

Giorgio Shani

Our world, and our lives, are being shaped by the conflicting trends of globalization and identity.

(Castells 1997: 1)

Despite claims that, in the light of the twin events of September 2001 (hereafter 9/11) and 2008, 'the age of globalization is over' (Rosenberg 2005), globalization – whether illusory or real – remains one of the key buzzwords of the contemporary world. At its most basic, globalization refers to processes of increasing interconnectedness between peoples and societies such that events in one part of the world impact upon other peoples and societies far away. Expressing fundamental aspects of what Anthony Giddens terms 'time-space distanciation', it may be understood as 'a process (or set of processes) which embodies a transformation in the spatial organization of social relations and transactions-assessed in terms of their *extensity, intensity, velocity* and *impact*-generating transcontinental or interregional *flows* and *networks* of activity, interaction and the exercise of power' (Held et al. 1999: 16). Although no universally agreed definition exists, at the heart of the concept of globalization lies the idea of *change*. The world in which we live in is said to be in the midst of a profound economic, political and social transformation affecting every aspect of our lives, including our understanding of who we are: our *identity*. Globalization assumes that the world is becoming more *global*. Here global means connected with the natural habitat of humankind, our planet, Earth. It assumes that, until very recently, the concept of the *global*, as opposed to the international, national or even universal did not exist, or could not be *imagined*. In recent decades, however, as a result of advances in communications, it is possible to view images of the world from outer space. This has enabled us to visualize our common planet as a globe. Viewed from space, our planet has no natural borders or frontiers and human beings are merely one of the many different species of life living on it. The concept of globalization, therefore, assumes a progressive movement towards a *global consciousness* and ultimately a *global identity*. But is a global identity possible?

It will be argued in the course of this chapter that a global identity is, in fact, unlikely because identities are both relative and culturally constructed. Identities are relative because the 'self', one's understanding of whom one is, is always dependent upon the existence of an 'other', whom one is not. As psychoanalytical theory suggests, our understanding of whom we are comes from *outside* through a process of *identification*. Jacques Lacan (1977) argued that, since identity comes from 'outside', it is inherently a 'fictional' construct: all identities are 'imaginary' based on the fundamental misrecognition (*méconnaisance*) of the child with its *imago*. The subject and the social order in which the subject finds a place are both in a continuous process of becoming. Both are always in a process of formation.

However, there are clear cultural *limits* to the malleability and/or what Bauman terms 'liquidity' of contemporary identities which militate against the emergence of a global identity. Identities are *cultural* and social constructs. For Manuel Castells, identity is a process of construction of meaning on the basis of a cultural attribute, or related set of cultural attributes, that is/are given priority over other sources of *meaning*, defined as 'the symbolic identification by a social actor of the purpose of his/her action' (Castells 1997: 6). Most human beings find meaning through identification with a particular cultural community, defined in terms of language, religion, ethnicity and territory. Each cultural community has its own particular values, myths and memories which are, in turn, a product of that community's unique history. There is no global culture: there are no global languages, common values, myths, memories or interests – apart, perhaps, from a common interest in preserving our natural environment. It follows that, if globalization is about the creation of a global consciousness, then it must first *erase* the historical differences between particular communities. However, this has not been the case. In fact, globalization, or rather the contemporary intensification of the globalizing processes, does not resulted in the *erasure* of localized, cultural identities, but rather in their *transformation*. It is suggested that culture need not refer to a set of all-encompassing, biologically determined and territorially rooted 'primordial attachments' (Geertz 1963), as Castells appears to be close to suggesting, but to that which permits the individual to have a *bios*: to enjoy a life endowed with meaning and dignity; in contrast to the 'bare life' (Agamben 1998) depicted by much of modernist social science.

This chapter will focus on the impact of globalization on cultural identities. The first section will examine the contemporary globalization debate (see Held et al. 1999; Held and McGrew 2000; Scholte 2005). It will be argued that both the globalist, or hyperglobalist, and the sceptical positions may be seen as problematic because they assume a contradictory relationship between the *local* and the *global*. Hyperglobalists assume that globalization will inevitably result in the displacement of local, particular identities by a new global political or cultural identity. Sceptics, by casting doubt on the reality of globalization, tend to assume that local, *territorialized* identities remain immune to so-called 'global transformations'. The Transformationalist 'synthesis', however, sees the processes of globalization and localization as mutually interrelated (Robertson 2003). In the next section, the relationship between globalization, the nation-state and identity will be discussed. Four main claims concerning the emergence of a global civil society, the persistence of the nation-state, the clash of civilizations and the hybridization of identities will be advanced and then critically examined in the subsequent section on the grounds of homogeneity, ahistoricity, essentialism and malleability. Finally, in the concluding section on future developments it will be suggested that growth of the Internet in particular has facilitated and often enabled the formation of transnational networks among individuals and groups with a shared cultural background or interests. Reworking Benedict Anderson's conception of the nation as an imagined community, I will argue that globalization, through the Internet, has made the imagination of 'deterritorialized' *diasporic* identities possible on a global scale. This is not to claim that territorially based 'local' identities are no longer significant: the nation-state remains the basic unit of international political and socio-economic life and, as such, represents (and defines) 'home' for the overwhelming majority of the world's population. Rather, it is merely suggested that globalization has permitted the deterritorialization of localized identities and that these identities co-exist, and frequently clash with, other identities which have been similarly transformed by globalization. These range from concepts of the 'self' to that of 'humanity' and include gender, class, regional, racial and hybrid identities which have been discussed elsewhere (see Elliott 2007).

The globalization debate: historical and intellectual development

Three major approaches, or theses, have been established in the recent literature on the relationship between globalization and the nation-state: the hyperglobalist thesis, the sceptical thesis and the transformationalist thesis (Held and McGrew 2000; Held et al. 1999). It will be suggested that the transformationalist thesis, which developed in response to the sceptical criticisms of the hyperglobalist thesis, offers the most analytically useful account of contemporary globalization. These three approaches to the globalization debate will briefly be introduced before examining their differing perspectives on the impact of globalization upon collective identities.

The hyperglobalist thesis

For globalists or 'hyperglobalizers', globalization is seen as primarily an economic phenomenon. Economic globalization refers to the increasing and deepening enmeshment of national economies in global systems of production and exchange. A 'global' economy organized on the basis of market principles and production for profit has emerged following the collapse of state socialism and few states remain excluded from financial and economic markets. Manuel Castells has argued that a *global* economy is a historically new reality and is distinct from a *world* economy in that it has the capacity to work as a unit in real time and on a planetary scale. The dynamic driving globalization is capitalism; capital, to put it crudely, has been 'liberated' from national and territorial constraints, whilst markets have become globalized to the extent that the domestic economy has to adapt to global competitive conditions. The key beneficiaries of the globalization of the world economy have been multinational corporations (MNCs), which at the turn of the millennium accounted for 70 per cent of world trade (Held and McGrew 2000: 25); and, more perniciously, financial speculators who have profited from the removal of currency regulations, first in the UK in 1992, forcing the sterling to leave the European Exchange rate mechanism, and, with more far-reaching consequences, at the time of the East Asian Financial Crisis in 1997.

The de-nationalization of economies through networks of production, trade and finance has in turn helped revolutionize telecommunications. The Thatcher–Reagan economic reforms at the start of the 1980s in particular laid the groundwork for the 'technological revolution' by encouraging domestic and international competition in the telecommunications industry. The British Telecommunications Act of 1981 denationalized the telecommunications industry in the UK by privatising British Telecom (BT). This was mirrored in the US by the breaking up of AT&T's monopoly in 1984 with significant results. In return, AT&T was permitted to compete to provide value-added and enhanced information. The 1990s saw three 'revolutions' in information technology (IT) that have helped transform our lives: the World Wide Web, e-commerce and the wireless. Ironically, the Internet itself is an early product of this collaboration. The Internet began in the 1960s as a US Defence Department project to build a data network to connect its researchers (ARPANET) and has been transformed into a potentially universal, all-encompassing space as a result of technological innovation and corporate sponsorship. The invention of Hyper Text Markup Language (HTML) by a group of researchers at CERN in Geneva led by Tim Berners-Lee in 1991 paved the way for an image-driven, user-friendly World Wide Web easily accessible through corporate browsers such as Microsoft Internet Explorer and Netscape Navigator. The World Wide Web deterritorialized the Internet by organizing website content by information rather than by location. Each day the number of webpages increases nine times faster than the human population and the estimated online population at the turn of 2010 was 1.8 billion (www.internetworldstats.com/stats.htm).

Hyperglobalizers argue that the technological revolution has eroded the economic sovereignty of the nation-state generating a 'borderless economy' and ushering in a 'global age'. The nation-state, in the words of Kenichi Ohmae, 'has become an unnatural, even dysfunctional, unit for organizing human activity and managing economic endeavour in a borderless world' (Ohmae 1993: 79). Hyperglobalists point to the *constructed* nature of national or particular communities. The nation is seen, in Ernest Gellner's words, as 'invented' (Gellner 1983) to legitimize state power. Now that, under the impact of economic globalization, the nation is losing an important part of its old functions, that of constituting a territorially bounded 'national economy', nationalism is, particularly for many Marxist-inspired scholars no longer an important dynamic of historical development.

The sceptical anti-thesis

In contrast, sceptics would agree with Krasner that 'sovereignty is not being transformed fundamentally by globalization' (Krasner 1999: 34). The claim that globalization is undermining state sovereignty is at best 'exaggerated and historically myopic' (ibid.: 34) and at worst globalization is a self-serving myth (Hirst and Thompson 1996) propagated by neoliberal state elites to both 'naturalize' and 'internationalize' market orthodoxy. Furthermore, as the resurgence of ethno-national movements following the collapse of Soviet Union and the Federal Republic of Yugoslavia suggests, nationalism retains its emotive appeal and the nation-state provides the only realistic framework for the contemporary world order (Smith 2000).

For Hirst and Thompson, the hyperglobalist view is 'pernicious' for two reasons: first, because it is empirically weak; and second, because 'it demands policies that result in established entitlements being sacrificed in favour of market-based increases in growth that will prove illusory' (Hirst and Thompson 1996: xii). Drawing upon statistical evidence, Hirst and Thompson have concluded that contemporary levels of economic integration and interdependence are by no means unprecedented. Japan and the UK, for example, were less 'open' to foreign trade and investment in 1995 than they were in 1913. Indeed, the level of state autonomy under the Gold Standard or Pax Britannica in the period leading up to the First World War was much lower than it is today. The claim that we are entering a radically new phase in the internationalization of economic activity needs to be qualified by a comparison with other historical periods. Even that symbol of contemporary economic globalization, the Internet, is not historically unprecedented as by the turn of the century a system of international communications, the telegraph, had developed, linking parties together in much the same way as the Internet does today.

Rather than living in a globalized world, we are witnessing greater regionalization of international economic activity which has become increasingly concentrated in three major financial trading blocs: North America, the European Union and the Asia-Pacific. The South continues to be marginalized in the new 'global' economy with over two billion people still living on less than $2 a day. Nowhere is this more apparent than in the so-called 'digital divide'. Whereas a majority of people living in the developed world have access to the Internet, the overwhelming majority of Southern population do not! The global average penetration rate remains at 26.6 per cent with regional rates varying from 76.2 per cent in North America to 8.7 per cent in Africa (www.internetworldstats.com/stats.htm).

In many ways the world's underprivileged and poor have fewer possibilities for migration than they had in the past, particularly in the period between 1814 and 1914 when an estimated 60 million people left Europe for the 'new worlds' of the Americas and Oceania. Despite an increase in the total number of international migrants, statistics from the United Nations Human Development Program (2009) show that the global migration rate has remained remarkably consistent over the past half century at around 2 per cent of the human population. States remain sovereign in that 'while the state's claim to exclusive control of its territory has been reduced by international markets and new communications media, it still retains one central role that ensures a large measure of territorial control: the regulation of populations' (Hirst and Thompson 1996: 257). The case of the European Union illustrates the paradox of greater freedom of movement within major financial trading blocs with stricter immigration controls on those travelling from marginalized states (the South). Increasingly, the function of the state in the North has been to attract foreign direct investment whilst keeping unskilled foreigners out. A global market for labour does not exist in the same way as it does for capital as most labour markets continue to be nationally regulated and only marginally accessible to outsiders. State capacity, far from becoming irrelevant, has acquired new significance in the globalizing world economy for states alone possess the organizational ability necessary to overcome obstacles to change and, more importantly, to absorb and socialize risk. Indeed, some sceptics have claimed that the technological developments furthering economic globalization have actually helped increase the states capacity for regulation (Krasner 1999: 313).

The sceptical thesis, however, by focusing on the limitations, historical antecedents and the detrimental effects of the contemporary phase of globalization does not necessarily invalidate the globalist thesis. Globalization may not necessarily be *new* and the globalization of the world economy has been exaggerated by both the hyperglobalists and state elites but that does not alter their central premise that power has shifted away from the state and towards non-state actors such as MNCs, International Organizations (IGOs) and Non-Governmental Organizations (NGOs) in the post-Cold War period. Furthermore, the fact that globalization has led to the increasing marginalization of the poor in the 'new global economy' merely reinforces the globalist thesis that a global capitalist world economy is now in existence although it does challenge the neoliberal assumption that economic globalization leads to greater prosperity for everybody and, in the long run, to an equalization in incomes. In other words, if neoliberal economists are mistaken in their belief that everybody benefits from contemporary economic 'globalization' and if some sceptics can prove that 'globalization' has resulted in greater material inequality within societies and between societies, then 'globalization' must exist; it must be a 'reality'.

The transformationalist synthesis

Both the hyperglobalist thesis and the sceptical thesis may be seen as problematic. Hyperglobalists tend to overstate the effects of economic globalization on state sovereignty whilst sceptics tend to overstate the degree of autonomy that states enjoy in the international system. It is clear that sovereign states are not only actors within, but also products of, an international system which is undergoing transformation. The transformationalist synthesis may be seen as a qualified defence of the globalization thesis. Globalization, or rather the intensification of the globalizing processes, is seen to be *transforming* but not *eroding* state power. For transformationalists, the contemporary phase of globalization has its origins in the 'technological revolution'. The advent of 'techno-capitalism', developments in systems of communications initiated in the late 1960s has 'reconstituted and restructured' state power (Held et al. 1999: 8–9). Although the state remains the principal actor within the global political order, it is no longer the unique centre of authority and governance. Held argues that 'a "new sovereignty" regime is displacing traditional conceptions of statehood as an absolute, indivisible, territorially exclusive and zero-sum form of power' (Held et al. 1999: 9). Similarly, Sassen argues that although 'sovereignty remains a feature of the system . . . it is now located in a multiplicity of institutional arenas' and that this 'reconfiguration of space may signal a more fundamental transformation in the matter of sovereignty' (Sassen 1997: 29, 14).

Uncertainty lies at the heart of the tranformationalist synthesis. Uncertainty exists not only about the direction and meaning of change, and also about how change itself should be represented. Globalization is seen to have ushered in what Beck terms the 'risk society'. The globalization of capitalist modernity has greatly increased the hazards and insecurities that we face on a global scale: from terrorism, as exemplified by Al-Qaeda, to the risks posed to our natural environment by global warming, which have belatedly been recognized and institutionalized through the Kyoto Protocol. Similarly, financial integration, which has produced a convergence in exchange rates between currencies, has also brought with it a contagion effect in that economic crisis in one region may rapidly 'infect' other regions of the world economy as exemplified by the currency crises in East Asia in 1997–8 and the Eurozone in 2010. An even clearer illustration of the perils of untrammelled capitalist globalization can be found in the contemporary global financial crisis which had its 'local' roots in the sub-prime mortgage crisis and the collapse of Lehman Brothers in the US with 'global' consequences.

Transformationalists share with post-structural or postmodern accounts a rejection of the determinism of the Enlightenment 'meta-narratives' of liberalism and Marxism. Unlike the hyperglobalist thesis, proponents of the transformationalist synthesis are unable to make predictions about the future but agree that we are living through an age characterized by profound economic, political, social and cultural change encapsulated through the contradictory but mutually dependent processes of *globalization* and *localization*. Globalization is rendering boundaries and territorialized identities less salient, whereas localization is highlighting borders and intensifying the deep attachment to the land. The tension between globalization and localization may be seen in all realms of human activity, from the economic and political to the social and cultural. In the economic realm, the globalization of trade, production and investment refers to their expansion beyond state boundaries whilst localization refers to attempts to prevent the repatriation of profits by encouraging MNCs to reinvest in the local community. In the political realm, globalization facilitates the expansion of authority, policies and interests beyond state boundaries through supranational regional institutions such as the EU whereas localization refers to attempts to devolve power to the regions. Finally, in the social and cultural realms, the globalization of ideas and values refers to attempts to *imagine* a world beyond the nation-state, whilst localization implies attempts to preserve the traditions, values and identity of one's particular community.

However, as Robertson notes, these two seemingly opposed processes are not as contradictory as they appear. Our understanding of 'home', 'community' or 'identity' is not static but profoundly influenced by global processes of socio-economic and cultural transformation. Seen in this light, localization can be seen as an *aspect* of globalization rather than its polar opposite (Robertson 2003: 37). Robertson collectively subsumes these processes under the term 'glocalization'. Denoting a global outlook adapted to local conditions, the 'glocalization' entered the social sciences through Japanese marketing practice in the 1990s. However, it will be suggested that, following Robertson, 'glocalization' involves not only the *adaptation to* but also the (re)*construction of* localized identities.

Major claims and developments: globalization, the nation-state and identity

In this section, the impact of globalization upon collective identities will be examined. Four main claims, based on the three theses outlined above, will be advanced and critically examined in the next section. First, globalist assertions that the nation-state is gradually being eroded by the emergence of a *global civil society* based on the rights of the individual will be outlined. Next, the sceptical view that the nation-state continues to define the political identity of its citizens will be considered before turning to the Samuel Huntington's thesis that civilizational identity will gradually supplant that of the nation-state. Finally, the transformationalist view that globalization results not so much in a clash of civilizations but in the emergence of mixed, hybrid identities will be examined. This will be further elaborated upon in the section on future developments.

Global civil society

Globalization in a conventional sense refers to the globalization of liberal capitalist modernity. Following the collapse of Soviet-style Communism in the 1990s, it has been argued by neoliberals that liberal capitalist modernity remains the only viable mode of economic, social and political organization. For neoliberals, globalization is merely the belated *universalization* of freedom as represented by liberal democracy and the market economy. Since the collapse of the Soviet Union, liberal-democratic institutions have emerged in most states and even self-proclaimed 'socialist' states such as the PRC participate in a world economy organized on capitalist lines. Francis Fukuyama in *The End of History and the Last Man* (Penguin 1992) famously saw the fall of the Berlin Wall as the culmination of the Hegelian dialectic. For Fukuyama:

> There is a fundamental process at work that dictates a common evolutionary pattern for all human societies . . . something like a Universal History of mankind in the direction of liberal democracy.
>
> *(Fukuyama 1992: 48)*

The idea of a universal history of mankind was first suggested by Immanuel Kant in his *An Idea for a Universal History of Mankind*. Kant suggested that history would have an end point or a final purpose that was implied in man's current potentialities and which made the whole of history intelligible. For Kant, as for Hegel and Marx after him, this end point was the realization of human freedom, defined as the universalization of a just civic constitution. Only when all states accept such a constitution, adopting a republican form of government, and join a *Foedus Pacificum*, a pacific federation or union guaranteeing 'the Right of a foreigner not to be treated with hostility when he arrives on someone else's territory' would there be an end to conflict and, therefore, *perpetual* peace.

Although most *globalists* acknowledge that a global cosmopolitan ethic is at best embryonic, or presently limited to the developed North and the European Union in particular, they insist that globalization will inevitably lead to the dissemination of a global political cultural identity and the creation of a *global* civil society. The term 'civil' society emerged in Europe in the seventeenth and eighteenth century to denote a type of society distinct from the state of nature. For Thomas Hobbes, the state of nature was conceived of as a 'war, as if of every man, against every man' characterized by mutual fear, distrust and *anarchy*. Civil society, in contrast, was characterized by the rule of law, based on certain fundamental rights enforced by a political authority also subject to the rule of law. The origins of the term civil society lay in the *societas civilis* of classical antiquity: a zone of 'civility', entailing respect between members of a political community, based on security and trust.

Civil society received its first systematic consideration in John Locke's *Second Treatise on Civil Government*. For Locke, the term 'civil society' referred to a society of free men, equal under the rule of law, bound together by no common purpose but sharing a respect for each other's rights. A civil society was seen to have been constituted by a social contract whereby men exchanged their natural freedom in return for rights guaranteed by law. For Thomas Hobbes, the fundamental right had been a security which could only be provided by a *Leviathan* commanding absolute authority. However, for Locke, 'natural' rights included those of the preservation of life, liberty and property which was guaranteed by the sovereign.

Immanuel Kant's conception of a 'universal civil society' differed from that of Locke in that the individual's natural rights were balanced by a categorical imperative to treat other individuals as 'ends' in themselves. It was this categorical imperative which provided the basis for the realization of a 'community of ends'. As Mary Kaldor points out, this was attained through conflict between man's 'asocial sociability': man's ability to live in society as a social being and his tendency to think and act as an individual, 'to isolate himself, since he also encounters in himself the unsocial characteristic of wanting to direct everything in accordance with his own ideas' (Kaldor 2003: 25–6).

Contemporary neoKantians such as Kaldor, have seen in post-Cold War developments such as the spread of liberal democratic institutions, a renewed commitment by both intergovernmental and non-governmental organizations to humanitarian activism and intervention, and perhaps most importantly growing trends towards regional integration within the EU a realization of Kant's idea of 'a universal civil society'. For Kaldor:

> [T]he coming together of humanitarian and human rights law, the establishment of an international criminal court, the expansion of international peace-keeping, betoken an emerging framework of global governance, what Immanuel Kant described as universal civil society, in the sense of a cosmopolitan rule of law, guaranteed by a combination of treaties and institutions.
>
> *(Kaldor 2003: 7)*

Persistence of the nation-state

Sceptics on the other hand, are suspicious of claims of the emergence of a global civil society based on the universality of human rights or security. Human rights are seen as the weapon of strong states, their abuses used to justify coercive intervention in weak states such as in Yugoslavia, Afghanistan, Iraq and perhaps Libya. Whilst tribunals have been set up by the UN Security Council to deal with mass human rights violations in the Former Republic of Yugoslavia and Rwanda, powerful states, including the 'liberal' United States, have refused to ratify the Treaty of Rome that proposed the establishment of an International Criminal Court (ICC).

The persistence of the territorially defined sovereign state as the basic unit of international relations since the Peace of Westphalia in 1648 remains the central plank in the sceptic's argument against the existence of a global political culture. The Westphalian state, as Stephen Krasner has pointed out, is a system of political authority based on territory and autonomy (Krasner 1999). No external actor enjoys authority within the borders of the state. Since the French Revolution of 1789, the state's sovereignty over its territory has been increasingly legitimized by reference to the political community of the nation. The nation, for sceptics, continues to be territorially defined. Territory is 'home to the members of the community, the site of their history, a witness to their past struggles, triumphs and defeats' (Parekh 2003: 9). It demarcates members of a particular political community from others and forms an important part of their individual and collective identities. Whilst globalists consider the nation as 'invented', some sceptics follow A.D. Smith in viewing nations as having pre-modern 'ethnic cores'. The nation, Smith asserts, is built upon the myths and memories of a territorialized *ethnie*. The success of nationalist movements depends on the ability of elites to mobilize these myths and memories in the defence of a common national culture. A global culture, on the other hand, is essentially *memoryless* as there are no 'world memories' that can be used to unite humanity (Smith 2000: 241). Therefore, the task of the globalist project is futile:

> It is one thing to be able to pack imagery and diffuse it through world-wide telecommunications networks. It is quite another to ensure that such images retain their power to move and inspire populations, who have for so long been divided by particular histories and cultures, which have mirrored and crystallized the experiences of historically separated social groups.
>
> *(ibid.: 241)*

The 'global' images circulated through the mass media and 'information superhighway' are invariably those associated with a particular culture and historical period; namely that of the modern West. Those images and symbols whether from New York, Disneyland or Hollywood are read in different ways and in different languages by different *national* communities.

Clash of civilizations

In contrast with the sceptical position, Samuel Huntington's (in)famous 'clash of civilizations' thesis, first published as a riposte to the liberal triumphialism most closely associated with one of his pupils, Francis Fukuyama, in *Foreign Affairs* (1993) and subsequently in *The Clash of Civilizations and the Remaking of World Order* (1996), takes into account the transformative impact of globalization. The national community, Huntington contends, is under threat from increased international migration and a greater assertion of non-Western identities by migrant communities encouraged by mistaken policies of multiculturalism. Western societies should instead inculcate Judaeo-Christian values domestically and attempt to ward off a rising Islamic-Confucian challenge internationally to their hegemony.

The crux of Huntington's argument is that globalization has led to a re-awakening of civilizational identities both inside and outside the nation-state. Huntington accepts the impermanency of the nation-state and implicitly regards it as a modern construct to be contrasted with the primordiality of larger 'macro' identities based on culture, language and, particularly, religion. The world, according to Huntington, is divided up into seven or eight civilizations: Western, Slavic-Orthodox, Islamic, Confucian, Hindu, Japanese, Latin American and, possibly, African. The differences between these civilizations are seen as not only 'real', but also 'basic':

> The people of different civilizations have different views on the relations between God and man, the individual and the group, the citizen and the state, parents and children, husband and wife as well as differing views of the relative importance of rights and responsibilities, liberty and equality, equality and hierarchy. These differences are the products of centuries. They will not soon disappear.
>
> *(Huntington 1993: 25)*

Although Huntington acknowledges that civilizational differences do not necessarily give rise to violent conflict, he contends that the most important – and violent – future conflicts will occur along the 'cultural fault lines' which separate these civilizations from one another. At face value, this claim seems to have been borne out by the subsequent events of 9/11 and the ensuing 'war on terror'. Despite pretensions to the contrary the West, as led by the US and NATO, has indeed confronted a resurgent Islamic civilizational identity centred on the transnational *Umma* as violently espoused by Al Qaeda. Within the West, there has been a retreat from multiculturalism and a strengthening of economic, cultural and political ties most particularly within the European Union. These developments have arisen, Huntington argues, as a consequence of the greater interactions between different civilizations which result from the world becoming a 'smaller place'.

Hybridity

Finally, transformationalists and post-structuralists would question the very existence of fixed, civilizational identities grounded on language and religion, seeing them instead as hybrid, fluid and constantly changing. Identities, for transformationalists, are always plural. Globalization permits the construction of 'new' *syncretic* identities which co-exist with 'older' identities based on ethnicity, religion and language within the 'self' (Hall 1997). In contrast with the search for 'assimilation' or 'purity', transformationalists and post-structuralists in particular celebrate the 'fuzziness' of modern identities. Being 'between cultures' is seen as a source of strength rather than weakness as it opens up 'multiple worlds' in which to inhabit and multiple sources of political obligation: to the local, regional, national and global.

Chinese and Indian IT workers in the US, Vietnamese and Algerians in France, Bangladeshi in the UK, Turks in Germany and Moroccans in Italy, do not cease to be Chinese, Indian, Korean, Vietnamese, Algerian, Pakistani, Bangladeshi, Turkish or Moroccan but rather become both Chinese or Indian *and* American, Vietnamese *and* French, Bangladeshi *and* British, Turkish *and* German, Moroccan *and* Italian. In the process of acquiring more than one political home, the meaning of one's political identity changes. Being Chinese or Indian in the US is different from being Chinese or Indian in one's homeland – it refers to one's *place of origin* rather than one's *place of settlement*. One's place of origin becomes *deterritorialized* through the process of migration. The offspring of the Indian and Chinese IT workers may never see their 'homeland', or place of origin, India or China, but they will not cease to be Indian or Chinese within the context of their place of settlement, the United States, just as many of their fellow citizens continue to categorize themselves, and be categorized as Irish Americans, Italian Americans, and African Americans many generations after their 'arrival' in the US. The significance of being Indian or Chinese therefore changes in what may be termed a *diaspora* context .

Furthermore, they may also acquire a regional identity, or rather regional identities, which may reflect not only their place of settlement but also their ancestors' place of origin. Here Hawaii provides us with a good example of things to come. Okinawan migrants to Hawaii emigrated before their homeland was formally integrated into the Japanese mainland and kept their own culture, language and identity. Known as the *Uchinanchu*, Okinawan ethnicity was clearly distinguished from mainland '*naichi*' Japanese migrants. However, contemporary Hawaiians of Japanese and Okinawan descent are considered 'local': not only are they not mistaken for the hordes of Japanese tourists (some from Okinawa) who descend on Waikiki every year but also they are viewed as 'more' Hawaiian than *Haole* (i.e. Caucasian) migrants from the US mainland. A 'local' Hawaiian of Japanese and Okinawan descent, therefore, can lay claim to four socio-cultural identities: Okinawan, Japanese, 'local' and American. In

Hawaii, this is the rule and not the exception. Although '*haoles*' make up the largest single ethnic group, the vast majority of the Hawaiian population are of 'mixed' descent with indigenous Hawaiian blood intermingled with successive waves of migrants from East Asia: Chinese, Japanese, Korean and Filipino.

Globalization, with its roots in the colonial political economy, will lead to a similar 'creolization' of ethnic identities on a global scale. Nowhere is this better illustrated than in one of Hawaii's most famous sons: the forty-fourth president of the United States, Barack Hussein Obama. The son of a Muslim Kenyan father and a Caucasian mother from Kansas, Obama was born in Hawaii and raised in Indonesia (he has a half-Indonesian step-sister who is an academic at the University of Hawaii at Manoa) before returning to continue his education in the fiftieth state. Elected to serve in the Senate as representative for Illinois, Obama can lay claim to possibly seven different socio-cultural and regional identities: Hawaiian, Illinosian, Kenyan, Kansasan, Christian, Indonesian (possibly) and American! This no doubt goes someway to explaining the breadth of his appeal not only among Americans, who voted for him in 2008, but also global audiences as exemplified by the award of the 2009 Nobel Peace Prize.

Main criticisms

In this section, some of the main criticisms of the above claims will be briefly outlined. In the interests of clarity, these will be subsumed under four main headings: homogenization, ahistoricity, essentialism and malleability. Criticisms of global civil society will be addressed under the first of these headings, those concerning the persistence of nation-states as the only realistic framework for political action under the second, the clash of civilization thesis under the third and the final heading will address some of the criticisms with hybridization.

Homogenization

The first criticism sees in liberal conceptions of global civil society a blueprint for political, economic and cultural *homogenization* on a global scale. *Global* civil society, in a liberal sense, refers to the space of un-coerced human association embodying a *universal* cosmopolitan ethic, existing in opposition to the state and a states-system representing the interests of *particular* national communities. The liberal conception of global civil society assumes the existence of the 'unencumbered individual', that is, individuals unfettered by cultural or social norms and values. However, in reality, human beings are born and live within a particular political community, and are bound to their fellow citizens by special ties. These ties usually include a common interest in maintaining the stability and integrity of their community. Since human beings grow up within a particular community, they tend to feel a part of it and define their identity in terms of it. They, in the words of Bhikhu Parekh, 'see their community as theirs, feel a particular sense of responsibility for it, experience pride or shame when it does or does not live up to certain ideals, and take interest in its problems' (Parekh 2003: 8). Membership of a political community gives people what Aristotle termed a *bios*: a life endowed with meaning and dignity. This differed from *zoe*, which expresses the simple fact of living. For Giorgio Agamben, *zoe* was a 'bare life': one which could be 'killed but not yet sacrificed' (Agamben 1998). The distinction between *bios* and *zoe*, between 'inside' and 'outside' the political community, corresponds to the modern system of states but is not tied to a Westphalian imaginary. Other forms of political community can exist which are not tied to territory, culture, language or religion but there is always an 'outside': an 'other' or external threat against which to defend the community which demands the sacrifice of some of its members.

A universal, cosmopolitan 'global' civil society has no 'outside'. It demands that the 'other' become like the 'self': free, equal and bearers of inalienable rights to life, liberty and property. This gives rise to a contradiction: what if people choose not to join this new universal, 'rights-based' community but prefer the security afforded by their socially and culturally defined communities with their particular and sometimes exclusive traditions which may impinge upon the freedom and rights of others? Should they be forced to be free? Many advocates of a global civil society would agree and supported wars in Kosovo, Afghanistan and, some initially at least, Iraq which were justified on the grounds that tyrannical regimes systematically abused the rights of their citizens. Thus, the creation of an un-coerced human association embodying a cosmopolitan ethic paradoxically entails the legitimization of greater levels of coercion and violence against others.

This is best illustrated by the changing rationale for the West's longest contemporary war: Afghanistan. Whereas initially US intervention was legitimized on the grounds of national security and targeted Al-Qaeda for their alleged involvement in the 9/11 attacks, their Taliban 'protectors' quickly became the targets for the military campaign and the Taliban regime subsequently fell in the first few months. Thereafter, began a protracted guerrilla war waged by remnants of the Taliban regime against the Western-backed government of President Hamid Karzai which necessitated a prolonged occupation of the country by NATO troops. With the election of President Obama, it was hoped that the war would quickly end, given the new president's opposition and commitment to ending the war in Iraq. However, an additional 30,000 US troops and another 10,000 from NATO allies have been deployed in Afghanistan to counter the threat of a resurgent Taliban, not to the US but to its own people. It is, as yet, unclear how the dismissal of the main architect of the strategy, General McCrystal, will affect US policy in Afghanistan but it seems safe to conclude that, for the moment at least, the defeat of the Taliban and the achievement of a 'liberal peace', one which is dependent upon the creation of a democratically elected government, market economy and rule of (Western secular) law, remains a central Western objective. The people of Afghanistan, therefore, are being forcibly prevented from choosing to live in an Islamic theocracy with its own admittedly patriarchical customs and 'repressive' laws.

Ahistoricity

If the advocates of a global civil society are guilty of overstating the benign effects of globalization and turning a blind eye to the violence that the creation of a global civil society entails, then supporters of the contemporary world order based on the nation-state are equally guilty of a myopic and ahistorical tendency to equate what *is* for what *will be*. Simply put, the contemporary world order, based loosely on a set of general agreements first drawn up at the Peace of Westaphalia in 1648 in Europe and then forcibly exported to the rest of the world through colonization, is a historical product which is undergoing possibly unprecedented degrees of change. Far from being a permanent feature of the global political landscape, nations are 'imagined communities' which first came into existence in late modern Europe following the agricultural and industrial revolutions (Anderson 1991). 'Invented' by state elites through processes of linguistic and cultural homogenization (Gellner 1983), nations are neither 'natural' nor very old and were preceded by the establishment of territorialized states under dynastic monarchs. Once the king's head was 'cut off' by a guillotine in eighteenth-century France, sovereignty passed from the monarch to the people living inside the realm. Over the course of the next two centuries, the subjects of the political community became its citizens endowed with rights and obligations to one another.

However, the very nature of national citizenship and, in particular, the ties that bind members of political communities to one another, is being transformed by the profound economic and technological changes associated with globalization. Even for critics of ethical universalism, such as Bhikhu Parekh, the '"we" that constitutes and defines the political community is expanding to encompass those hitherto perceived as "they", and the moral gap between general duties and special duties, between those to human beings in general and to our fellow citizens, is beginning to narrow' (Parekh 2003: 11) as a result of increased interdependence between different political communities. Parekh argues that globalization has indeed transformed citizenship but not in the ways in which advocates of a global civil society envisage. Instead of global or cosmopolitan citizenship, globalization, or rather, the common risks and dangers which human beings in general face as a result of technological, economic and environmental change, has made *globally oriented citizenship* possible. Whilst a global citizen has no political home and is in a state of what Martha Nussbaum calls 'voluntary exile', a globally oriented citizen recognizes the reality and value of having a political home yet seeks to forge alliances with others. Parekh's globally oriented citizens call not for cosmopolitanism but for internationalism. Internationalism, for Parekh, 'respects the basic moral impulses lying at the heart of nationalism and cosmopolitanism whilst avoiding their pathologies'. Like nationalism, internationalism accepts the 'natural' division of the world into different communities and acknowledges the special ties that bind members of a political community together. However, unlike nationalism, internationalism accepts the general ties and common interests and concerns that bind human beings together. Globally oriented citizenship involves examining the policies of one's state, taking an active interest in the affairs of other countries and an active commitment in the creation of a just world order (Parekh 2003: 12–13). Such an order would include democratizing the structures of international institutions such as the United Nations Security Council, the IMF and World Bank and ensuring greater integration whilst respecting the sovereignty of member states over certain issues of national interest in the manner of the EU.

Parekh, however, assumes that globally oriented citizens have one 'political home' from which to discharge their obligations to others. This home, as we have seen, remains territorially defined. Increasingly, however, as a result of either the unevenness or the structural inequalities built into the processes of economic globalization, people seek opportunities to leave their territorially defined political homes in search of employment opportunities. Although states in the developed North have responded by introducing strict quotas on immigration as can be seen in the construction of a 'Fortress Europe' through the Schengen agreement, declining birth rates and ageing populations in general have led to labour shortages and greater incentives for migration from South to North. Consequently, many people have multiple 'political homes' as attested to by the rise of people with dual nationality and citizenship. Furthermore, even within states which deny the possibility of dual citizenship, there are multiple political loyalties which if not respected have the potential to threaten the integrity of the nation-state. Whereas most Europeans enjoy freedom of movement within the EU and are consequently allowed multiple 'homes' even if they hold citizenship of one member states, citizens of France, Belgium and several other European countries face restrictions in what they can wear. On 19 May 2010, the French cabinet approved a draft bill to ban face covering garments in public spaces, a ruling which has subsequently been ratified by parliament. This effectively disenfranchises many Muslim (and Sikh) French citizens who consider the headscarf or Turban (see Shani 2007) an integral part of their collective identities. While Parekh amongst others sees multiculturalism as a way to respect the cultural difference of ethno-religious minorities *within* the nation, it is clear that this is now a *transnational* rather than national issue. There are more Muslims living in the EU than Danes and Belgians and the 'veil issue' has the potential to radicalize Muslims throughout the Europe in the same way as the depictions of the Prophet Mohammed by a Danish cartoonist or even the wars in Iraq and Afghanistan.

Essentialism

It is the spectre of a resurgent, *transnational* Islamic civilization centred upon the *Umma* violently contesting the hegemony of 'Western' Judaeo-Christian values both domestically and internationally which animates Huntington's 'clash of civilizations' thesis. Undoubtedly, the events of 9/11, the London attacks of 7 July 2005 and earlier the Madrid train bombing of March 2003 has led to a greater receptivity towards Huntington's thesis and precipitated a move away from multiculturalism in Western societies, of which the ban on the veil is merely the latest manifestation (despite French claims that it does not target Islamic minorities and is in keeping with its secular values). However, even at the height of the 'war on terror' as the United States under a born-again Christian did battle on two fronts with two 'Muslim' enemies, the West and the Islamic world were far from united. Even if we choose to ignore the mass, popular protests against the war in Iraq and its growing unpopularity within the US itself, there remains the opposition of two powerful Western states: France and Germany. Turning to the Islamic world, we see support for the war in Iraq by many Sunni Gulf states yet some popular sympathy for the Taliban and Al-Qaeda as seen by the participation of foreign mercenaries in both Iraq and Afghanistan. The categorization of both the secular tyranny of Saddam Hussein and the Taliban theocracy of Mullah Omar furthermore obscures substantive social, political and cultural differences between the two regimes. Certainly Huntington's thesis cannot account for the Sunni-Shi'ia schism which divides the Islamic world and the internecine nature of civil war in Iraq which claimed far more lives that the actual invasion.

Indeed, it would be no exaggeration to claim that the animosities *within* civilizations have given rise to far bloodier conflicts than *between* civilizations. The tragic history of the first half of the twentieth century appears to bear this out as, with the exception of Japanese involvement, these were primarily Western civil wars acted out on a global stage. Huntington's insistence that the West shares a common Judaeo-Christian heritage not only obscures deep religious divisions between the two religious communities but also means that the Inquisition and the Holocaust must be seen not as a 'clash of civilizations' but as internal to the West, despite the fact that Jews were regarded as *racially* and culturally distinct from Europeans and forced to live apart for almost two thousand years. The Sunni-Shi'ia divide has its counterpart in the sectarianism which led to the Thirty Years' War in which entire populations belonging to different denominations were exterminated and which, three and a half centuries on from Westphalia, continues to divide Christian communities today, most particularly in Northern Ireland.

However, the historical accuracy of Huntington's thesis is not its principal defect; rather, its primary faults lie in the very categories he employs to divide humanity and, furthermore, in his crude and unsophisticated conception of culture. As Amartya Sen noted in an article for the *New York Times* published after the invasion of Afghanistan, the 'basic weakness of the theory lies in its program of categorizing people of the world according to a unique, allegedly commanding system of classification' (*New York Times*, 23 November 2001). Huntington *essentializes* culture seeing 'civilization' as an unchanging, territorialized, primordial attachment which defines an individual's identity. He ignores the multiplicity of individual identities based on nationality, language, region, ethnicity, gender, age, occupation, political affiliation, class and caste and ascribes to religion an all-encompassing and overarching framework which guides social life, personal morality and political action. Huntington downplays the common heritage of many of the world's 'civilizations', most notably those based on the monotheistic religions of Christianity and Islam, and ignores the interconnections between them. Islamic influences in Renaissance Europe and, through the Mughal Empire, in the evolution of a 'Hindu' civilization in India are therefore conveniently overlooked as Orientalist stereotypes of an intolerant, tyrannical Muslim 'Other', distinct from the modern, rational Western and traditional, spiritual Indian 'Self', are recycled and reproduced for contemporary audiences. It is no wonder that the late Edward Said, in an article for the *Nation* which appeared in the aftermath of 9/11, derided the 'clash of civilizations' as a 'clash of ignorance' (*The Nation* 22 October 2001)!

Furthermore, as both Said and Sen note, Huntington, despite protestations, implicitly sees *difference*, whether religious or civilizational, as engendering conflict. In a rapidly globalizing world, this is both impractical and pernicious. It is impractical in that Huntington's thesis does not seem to take into account the degree to which different civilizations are already intermingled and cannot be separated from one another. Muslims comprise almost 10 per cent of the population of France and are as *European* as their Judaeo-Christian and secular fellow citizens. As Sen points out, describing India as a 'Hindu civilization' misses the fact that India has more Muslims than any other country except Indonesia and Pakistan. It is pernicious in that the logical consequence of Huntington's argument would be to endorse a form of global *apartheid* and to legitimize 'ethnic cleansing' on the grounds that people from different civilizations cannot live together. This not only is patently untrue but also disregards the experiences of many people who inhabit 'multiple worlds' and negotiate civilizational differences on a daily basis.

Malleability

Although the claim that globalization is leading to a hybridization of identities appears to resonate with the experiences of the present generation, at least those living in multi-ethnic societies, there are clear limits to the degree to which 'thick' identities based on ethnicity, gender, language, nationality, religion and socio-economic status can be negotiated. Returning to our example of Barack Obama, we can see that although he may epitomize the very hybridity which transformationalists and post-structuralists argue is a central feature of globalization, his role as president of the United States reproduces the power of the (patriarchal) nation-state in international relations. Far from transforming world politics, his election appears to have reinvigorated the old 'imperial' order by breathing new life into the 'American Dream' and resuscitating the world capitalist economy.

The infinite flexibility of personal identities which is seen as a hallmark of our postmodern times is certainly belied by the resurgence of ethno-national and religious collective identities which has accompanied neoliberal globalization. Why, if identity is being *privatized* as Bauman suggests, should people feel the need to belong to *communities*, even if many recognize them as 'imagined'? Perhaps part of the reason may have something to do with the very insecurity engendered by the globalization of neoliberalism and its emphasis on informalization, dispensability and short-termism which Elliott and Lemert consider to be central to the 'new individualism'. In *The New Individualism: The Emotional Costs of Globalization* (2005), Elliott and Lemert argue that globalization brings with it a 'new individualism' centred on a fixation with 'instant change', whether of the body, selfhood or society, which people are not necessarily emotionally prepared to cope with. As Elliott notes, where people 'feel threatened or assaulted by social and technological upheavals, toleration of personal difference and cultural particularities sometimes diminishes' (Elliott 2007: 158). In such circumstances, people may find meaning through identification with other individuals with whom they share feelings of disposability and loss. This sense of insecurity has certainly been exacerbated by the financial crisis and global economic downturn. It remains to be seen, however, whether a new, transnational communal consciousness based on disposability will emerge in response to the economic crisis or whether any such 'global' coalition of the disposable will splinter along national, ethnic, religious or cultural lines, as suggested by the European response to the 'Greek' financial crisis.

Future developments: digital diasporas

One of the distinctive features of the contemporary age is that, in the words of James Clifford, 'the language of diaspora is increasingly invoked by displaced peoples who feel (maintain, revive, invent) a connection with a prior home . . . Many minority groups that have not previously identified this way are now reclaiming diasporic origins and affiliations' (Clifford 1994: 301). It is argued here that globalization, driven by a technological revolution which has made communication instantaneous over large distances, will facilitate this process by breaking down the barriers of territorial identity and by permitting the dissemination of what Paul Gilroy (1997) has termed a 'diaspora consciousness' through images of collective violence, flight and dispersion. Diaspora, like the nation before it, may be considered a form of 'imagined community'. For Anderson, the nation was imagined 'because the members of even the smallest nation will never know most of their fellow-members, meet them, or even hear of them, yet in the minds of each lives the image of their communion' (Anderson 1991: 6).

Whilst for Anderson, it was the development of what he termed 'print capitalism' that facilitated the imagination of the nation, it can be argued that 'digital capitalism' has made the imagination of new *deterritorialized* communities possible. By digital capitalism, I mean the global restructuring of capitalism around information technology. Information and Communication Technologies (ICTs) 'offer new resources and new disciplines for the construction of imagined selves and imagined worlds' (Appadurai 1996: 3). ICTs have provided the ability to communicate across the boundaries and transcend the limitations of the territorially defined national community, blurring the distinctions between inside and outside, the virtual (or 'imaginary') and the real. In the same way that nations in the New World nations imagined themselves as communities parallel and comparable to those in Europe, cyber-communities see themselves in a community parallel and comparable to the old communities of nation-states, but transcending the limitations of these communities with a new technology that seemingly makes time and space irrelevant.

ICTs not only deterritorialize existing linguistic or even national identities but also engender or strengthen alternative notions of community to that of the nation-state. Today, members of 'global' political movements divided by geography and ethnicity, ranging from the groups affiliated to the World Social Forum to Al-Qaeda can communicate with one another through global languages such as English, Spanish, Arabic or Chinese. In this sense, ICTs may be constitutive of an embryonic *transnational public sphere* operating alongside, and sometimes in opposition to, the Westphalian system of states.

Conclusion

In conclusion, the human 'family' is made up of many different cultural communities each with their own language, culture and history. These communities may all be *imagined* but as Anderson points out, the styles in which they are imagined differ and change over time. Globalization, and in particular the development of the Internet and related technologies, allows these cultural communities to be *imagined* in a different way. It allows people who identify with the same cultural community to communicate with each other across time and space and provides 'homelands' for diasporas and other deterritorialized migrant communities. Rather than facilitating the development of a global consciousness, it is argued that globalization and the Internet allows a *communal* consciousness to develop on a global scale. This is not to deny the existence of an embryonic global consumerist culture centred around Yahoo!, MTV and Starbucks but to suggest that this culture is experienced in different ways by people who identify with different ethno-national and religious groups. Yahoo! is a case in point: rather than reinforcing cultural homogenization it allows for, and indeed encourages, the celebration of difference through Yahoo groups. Tibet, Kurdistan and Khalistan may not exist on a map but online they represent *sovereign* communities. Globalization, in short, has severed the link between nation and state and facilitated the articulation of post-national, diasporic identities which co-exist with older territorialized and newer hybrid identities (Shani 2007) in the human 'family' of 'imagined communities'.

References

Agamben, G. (1998) *Homo Sacer: Sovereign Power and Bare Life*, trans. Daniel Heller-Roazen. Stanford: Stanford University Press.

Anderson, B. (1991) *Imagined Communities: Reflections on the Origin and Spread of Nationalism*, revised edition. London: Verso.

Appadurai, A. (1996) *Modernity at Large: The Cultural Dimensions of Globalization*. Minnesota: University of Minnesota Press.

Castells, M. (1997) *The Information Age,* vol. 2: *The Power of Identity*. Oxford: Blackwell.

Clifford, J. (1994) 'Diasporas,' *Cultural Anthropology* 9(3): 301–38; reprinted in R. Robertson and K.E. White (eds) (2003) *Globalization: Critical Concepts in Sociology*, vol. IV. London: Routledge.

Elliott, A. (2007) *Concepts of the Self*, 2nd edition. Cambridge: Polity.

Geertz, C. (1963) 'The integrative revolution: primordial sentiments and civil politics in new states,' in C. Geertz (ed.) *Old Societies and New States: The Quest for Modernity in Asia and Africa*. New York: Free Press, pp. 105–19.

Gellner, E. (1983) *Nations and Nationalism*. Oxford: Blackwell.

Gilroy, P. (1997) 'Diaspora and the detours of identity', in K. Woodward (ed.) *Identity and Difference*. London: Open University.

Hall, S. (1997) 'Old and new identities,' in A. King (ed.) *Culture, Globalization and the World-System*. London: Sage.

Held, D. and McGrew, A. (2000) 'The great globalization debate,' in D. Held and A. McGrew (eds) *The Global Transformations Reader*. Cambridge: Polity.

Held, D., McGrew, A., Goldblatt, D. and Peratton, J. (1999) 'Introduction,' in *Global Transformations*. Cambridge: Polity.

Hirst, P. and Thompson, S. (1996) *Globalization in Question*. Cambridge: Polity.

Huntington, S.P. (1993) 'The clash of civilizations?' *Foreign Affairs* Summer 72(3): 22–49.

Kaldor, M. (2003) *Global Civil Society: An Answer to War*. Cambridge: Polity.

Krasner, S. (1999) *Sovereignty: Organized Hypocrisy*. Princeton: Princeton University Press.

Lacan, J. (1977) *Écrits: A Selection*, trans. Alan Sheridan. London: Tavistock/Routledge.

Ohmae, K. (1993) 'The rise of the region state', *Foreign Affairs* 72(2): 78–88.

Parekh, B. (2003) 'Cosmopolitanism and global citizenship', *Review of International Studies* 29(1): 3–19.

Robertson, R. (2003) 'Globalisation or glocalisation?', in R. Robertson and K.E. White (eds) *Globalization: Critical Concepts in Sociology*. New York: Routledge.

Rosenberg, J. (2005) 'Globalization theory: a post-mortem,' *International Politics* 42: 2–74.

Sassen, S. (1997) *Losing Control: Sovereignty in an Age of Globalization*. New York: Columbia University Press.

Scholte, J.A. (2005). *Globalisation: A Critical Introduction*, 2nd edition. Basingstoke: Palgrave Macmillan.

Shani, G. (2007) *Sikh Nationalism and Identity in a Global Age*. London: Routledge.

Smith, A.D. (2000) 'Towards a global culture?' in D. Held and A. McGrew (eds), *The Global Transformations Reader*. Cambridge: Polity.

Index

abjection 190
Abu-Lughod, L. 326, 334
ACT UP 281, 282
acting 163–4
actor-network theory (ANT) 79, 97
Adkins, L. 194
Adler, A. 32
Adorno, T. 15–16, 205–6, 209, 215, 232, 266
Afghanistan 391, 393
African Blood Brotherhood (ABB) 318
Agamben, G. 151, 165, 381, 390
agency 46–7, 52, 161–2, 228, 292–3, 294–8,
    301–2, 366, 376
aggression 144–6, 241
Ahmad, F. 328
AIDS 260, 280–1, 282, 283, 286, 323
Aiken, L. 267
Alaolmolki, N. 341
Alcoff, L. M. 372, 378n12
Alexander, J. 108, 109
Alfred, T. 348–9
Ali, S. 329, 339, 342
Ali, T. 342
alienation 156–7, 175–6, 205, 210–11
Althusser, L. 69, 162
American Civil Rights Movement 21, 318–22, 350
Anderson, B. 381, 391, 395
anomie 154, 247
anonymity 223, 225–6, 231
anorexia nervosa 117, 242
anti-globalization and resistance identities *see*
    global justice movement
Anzaldúa, G. 25
Appadurai, A. 239, 395
Archer, M. 109, 110, 198
Ariès, P. 255–6, 258, 259
Aristotle 6, 390
Arnold, M. 15
Arsalan, A.R. 326–7
Artificial Intelligence (AI) 220, 222
Aslan, R. 327, 336, 337
assimilationist agenda 276, 280, 282–3, 284, 286,
    287

Augustine 7–8, 20
Austin, J.L. 188, 192
authentication 225–6
autobiography 116
autonomy 132–3, 137
avatars 226–7

Bacon, F. 299
Bakare-Yusuf, B. 193
Baker, E. 319, 320–1
Baker, S.A. 226
Baldwin, J. 178
Bales, K. 165, 166
Bannerji, H. 286–7
Baraitser, L. 59
Barker, M. 176–7
Barr, D. 371, 376
Barrett, M. 196
Barry, B. 359
Barth, F. 173–4
Barthes, R. 83, 86
Bartky, S.L. 43, 46
Bates, D.D. 287
Baudelaire, C. 225
Baudrillard, J. 83, 94–5, 96, 97, 212, 241
Bauman, Z. xii, 102–3, 107, 108, 112, 114–16,
    117–19, 121, 122, 123, 142, 151–2, 158–61,
    162, 165, 166, 247, 258–9, 260, 265, 266, 268,
    381, 394
Beasley, C. 197
Beauvoir, S. de 23, 34, 37, 42, 151
Beck-Gernsheim, E. 106, 112, 114–16, 119–20,
    121, 124–5, 194
Beck, U. xii, xx, 17, 103, 106–7, 109, 112,
    114–16, 119–20, 121, 122, 123, 124–5,
    158–60, 168, 194, 247, 292, 294–6, 301–2
Becker, E. 257, 264–5, 267, 268
Bell, D. 179, 241
Bellah, R. 95
Benedict, Pope 285
Benjamin, J. 37, 38, 39–41, 52, 56, 58–9
Benjamin, W. 203, 204–5, 209, 214, 225, 266
Bernard, J. 190